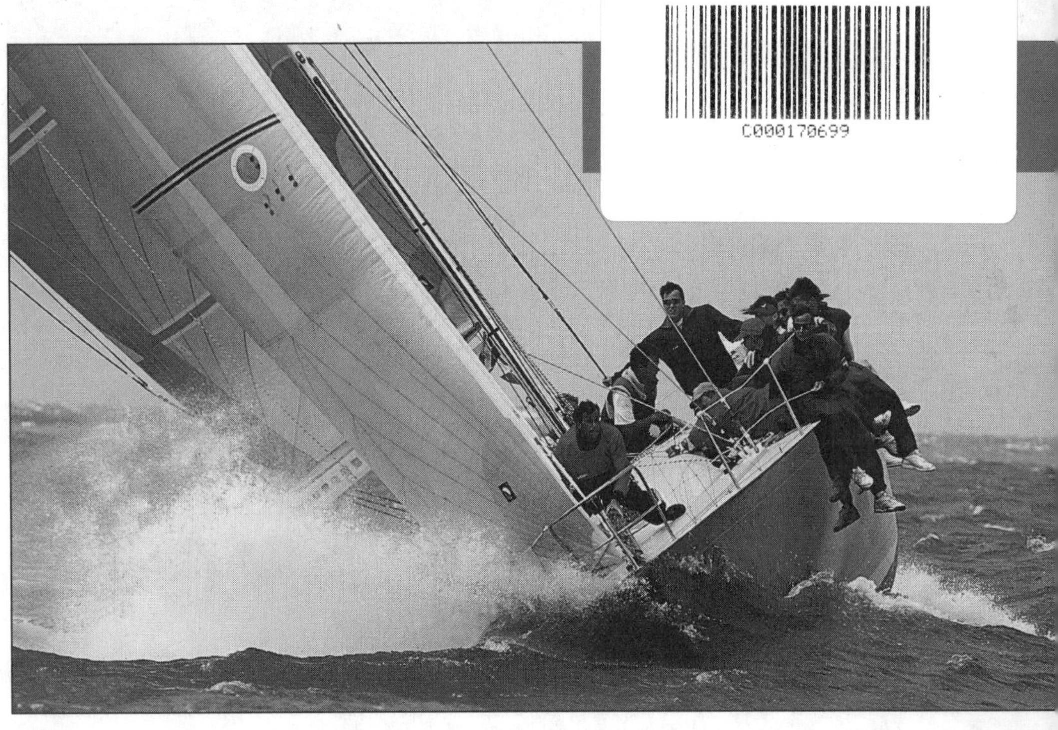

C000170699

Solaris™ 7 Administrator Certification

TRAINING GUIDE

Bill Calkins

Publisher	*David Dwyer*
Associate Publisher	*Al Valvano*
Managing Editor	*Gina Brown*
Product Marketing Manager	*Stephanie Layton*
Publicity Manager	*Susan Petro*
Acquisitions Editor	*Stacey Beheler*
Development Editor	*Shannon Leuma*
Project Editor	*Caroline Wise*
Copy Editor	*Gayle Johnson*
Technical Editors	*John Philcox*
	Grant Carstensen
Indexer	*Cheryl Lenser*
Manufacturing Coordinator	*Chris Moos*
Cover Designer	*Aren Howell*
Software Development Specialist	*Michael Hunter*
Proofreader	*Debra Neel*
Composition	*Ron Wise*

Copyright © 2001 by New Riders

FIRST EDITION: October

All rights reserved. No part of this book may be reproduced or transmitted in any form or by any means, electronic or mechanical, including photocopying, recording, or by any information storage and retrieval system, without written permission from the publisher, except for the inclusion of brief quotations in a review.

International Standard Book Number: 1-57870-249-6

Library of Congress Catalog Card Number: 00-101486

05 04 03 02 01 7 6 5 4 3 2 1

Interpretation of the printing code: The rightmost double-digit number is the year of the book's printing; the rightmost single-digit number is the number of the book's printing. For example, the printing code 00-1 shows that the first printing of the book occurred in 2001.

Composed in Times New Roman and MCPdigital by New Riders

Printed in the United States of America

Trademarks

All terms mentioned in this book that are known to be trademarks or service marks have been appropriately capitalized. New Riders cannot attest to the accuracy of this information. Use of a term in this book should not be regarded as affecting the validity of any trademark or service mark. Solaris is a trademark of Sun Microsystems, Inc.

Warning and Disclaimer

This book is designed to provide information about Solaris 7 Administrator Certification. Every effort has been made to make this book as complete and as accurate as possible, but no warranty or fitness is implied. The information is provided on an as-is basis. The authors and New Riders shall have neither liability nor responsibility to any person or entity with respect to any loss or damages arising from the information contained in this book or from the use of the discs or programs that may accompany it.

ABOUT THE AUTHOR

Bill Calkins is owner and president of Pyramid Consulting, a computer training and consulting firm located near Grand Rapids, Michigan, specializing in the implementation and administration of UNIX and Windows NT-based systems. He has more than 17 years of experience in UNIX system administration and consulting at more than 90 different companies. He has also worked as an instructor in both corporate and university settings, and he has helped hundreds of administrators get their certification. His experience covers all varieties of UNIX, including Solaris, HP-UX, AIX, IRIX, Linux, and SCO. When he's not working in the field, he conducts training and educational seminars on various system administration topics. He draws on his many years of experience in system administration and training to provide a unique approach to UNIX training.

ACKNOWLEDGMENTS

I would like to thank John Philcox and Grant Carstensen, who did a great job reviewing the technical content of this book from front to back. I met these guys through emails they sent with suggestions from the Solaris 2.6 series. They were so thorough that we thought they would make perfect technical editors on this follow-up book. Their combined experience provided valuable contributions throughout this book. John and Grant, I thank you for your dedication to this project.

Thank you also to Shannon Leuma, Laurie Petrycki, Stacey Beheler, and the rest of the team at New Riders for their assistance in getting this book to print.

ABOUT THE TECHNICAL REVIEWERS

These reviewers contributed their considerable hands-on expertise to the entire development process of this book. As this book was being written, these dedicated professionals reviewed all the material for technical content, organization, and flow. Their feedback was critical to ensuring that this book fits our readers' needs for the highest-quality technical information.

John Philcox is owner and director of Mobile Ventures Limited, a computer consultancy based in Cheltenham, Gloucestershire, in the United Kingdom, specializing in UNIX systems and networks. He has more than 20 years of experience in IT—14 of those with the SunOS and Solaris environments. He is a certified Solaris system administrator as well as a member of the Institution of Analysts and Programmers and the Institute of Management of Information Systems. He has worked in a number of large multivendor networks in both the public and private sectors. He was technical editor on *Solaris 2.6 Administrator Certification Training Guide, Part II* and is currently authoring his own book on Solaris system management with New Riders.

Grant Carstensen provided technical insight from an end-user's perspective for this project. He is a Senior Systems Administrator with Computer Sciences Corporation (CSC), a major provider of information technology services based in El Segundo, California. He has more than 15 years of experience in IT—seven of those with different flavors of UNIX. For the last four years he has focused on systems and network administration of predominantly SunOS and Solaris environments. His recent projects include being part of a team of administrators who rolled out Solaris 7 to more than 300 workstations. He subsequently assisted the team responsible for upgrading more than 4,000 systems to Solaris 8. He has a bachelor of science degree in Business Administration/Information Systems, and he has certifications in Microcomputer Repair and Computer Programming (COBOL).

DEDICATION

To my children, William, Nicole, Neal, and Dean. May you use your talents to pursue all your ambitions, whatever they may be.

CONTENTS AT A GLANCE

TABLE OF CONTENTS

TELL US WHAT YOU THINK!

As the reader of this book, you are the most important critic and commentator. We value your opinion, and we want to know what we're doing right, what we could do better, what areas you'd like to see us publish in, and any other words of wisdom you're willing to pass our way.

I welcome your comments. You can fax, email, or write me directly to let me know what you did or didn't like about this book—as well as what we can do to make our books stronger.

Please note that I cannot help you with technical problems related to the topic of this book, and that due to the high volume of mail I receive, I might not be able to reply to every message.

When you write, please be sure to include this book's title and author, as well as your name and phone or fax number. I will carefully review your comments and share them with the author and editors who worked on this book.

Fax: 317-581-4663

Email: nrfeedback@newriders.com

Mail: Al Valvano
New Riders
201 West 103rd Street
Indianapolis IN 46290 USA

Introduction

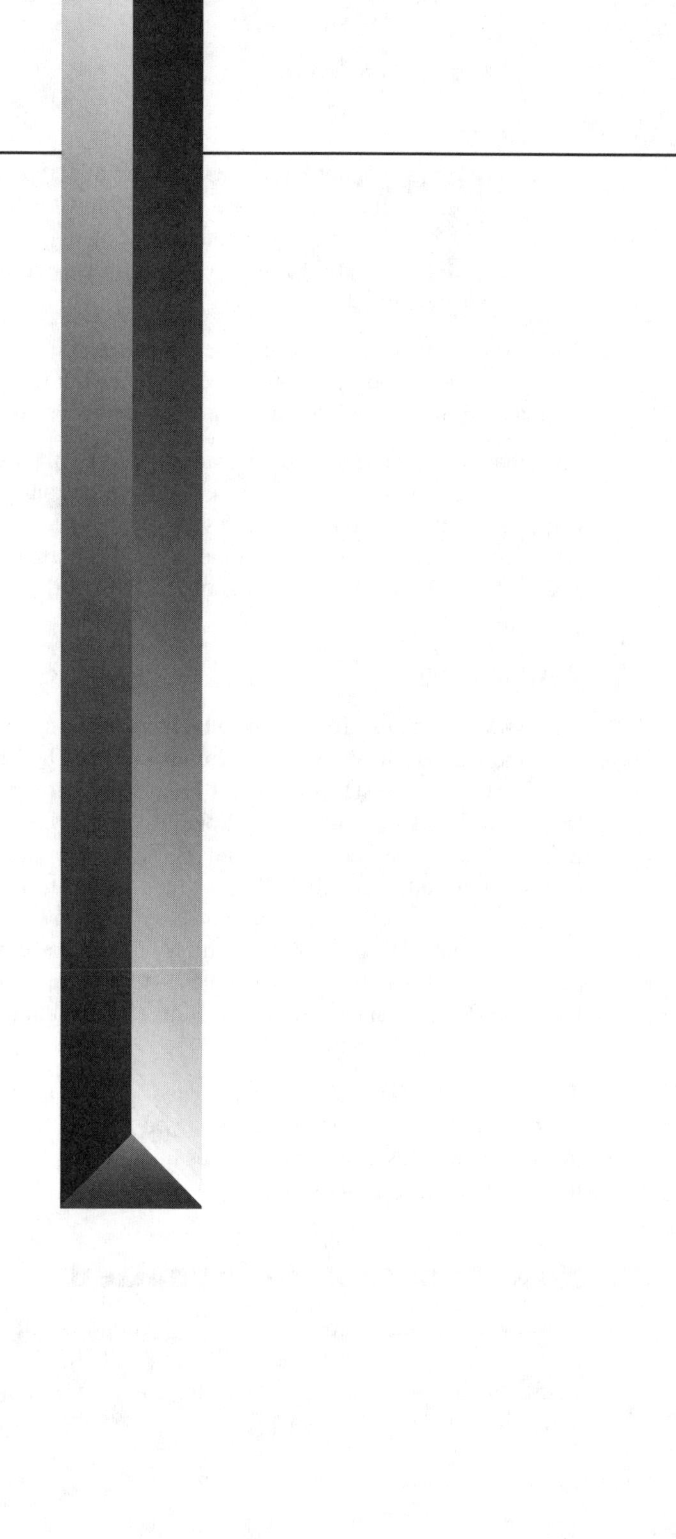

This book provides training materials and sample exams for anyone interested in becoming a Sun Certified System Administrator for Solaris 7. When used as a study guide, this book will save you a great deal of time and effort searching for information you will need to know when taking the exam.

This book covers the exam objectives in enough detail for the inexperienced reader to learn the objectives and apply the knowledge to real-life scenarios. Experienced readers will find the material in this book to be complete and concise, making it a valuable study guide.

This book is not a cheat sheet or cram session for the exam; it is a training manual. In other words, it does not merely give answers to the questions you will be asked on the exam. I have made certain that this book addresses the exam objectives in detail, from start to finish. If you are unsure about the objectives on the exam, this book will teach you what you need to know. After reading this book, test your knowledge using the sample questions on the CD-ROM.

Audience

This book is designed for anyone who has a basic understanding of UNIX and wants to learn more about Solaris system administration. Whether you plan to become certified or not, this book is the starting point to becoming a Solaris system administrator. It's the same training material that I use in my Solaris system administration classes; I have used it to train hundreds of system administrators. This book covers the basics as well as the advanced topics you need to know before you begin administering the Solaris operating system. My goal was to present the material in an easy-to-follow format, with text that is easy to read and understand. The only prerequisite is that you have used UNIX, you have attended a basic UNIX class for users, or you have studied equivalent material so that you understand basic UNIX commands and syntax. Before you begin administering Solaris, it's important that you've actually used UNIX.

This book is also intended for experienced system administrators who want to become certified. To pass the certification exams, you need to have a solid understanding of the fundamentals of administering Solaris. This book will help you review the fundamentals required to pass the certification exams.

How This Book Is Organized

This book is divided into two sections. Section I covers the objectives on exam 310-009, and Section II covers the objectives for exam 310-010. A complete description of both of these exams can be found on Sun's Web site at `http://suned.sun.com/USA/certification/solarismain.html`.

The third section contains the appendixes. They provide some additional reading that I will refer to throughout the book.

The test CD will prepare you for the questions you might see on the exam. It will thoroughly test your knowledge on all the exam objectives. If you're weak in any area, the sample questions will help you identify that area so that you can go back to the appropriate chapter and study the topic.

NOTE. *Visit my Web site,* `www.pdesigninc.com`*, to view the errata for this book.*

Conventions Used in This Book

- **Commands**—In the steps and examples, the commands you enter are displayed in a special monospaced font.
- **Arguments and options**—In command syntax, command options and arguments are enclosed in < >. (The words within the < > symbols stand for what you will actually type. You don't type the < >.)

  ```
  lp -d<printer name> <filename> <return>
  ```

- **Using the mouse**—When using menus and windows, you will select items with the mouse. Here is the default mapping for a three-button mouse:

Left button	Select
Middle button	Transfer/Adjust
Right button	Menu

  The Select button is used to select objects and activate controls. The middle mouse button is configured for either Transfer or Adjust. By default, it is set up for Transfer, which means this button is used to drag or drop list or text items. You use the left mouse button to highlight text, and then you use the middle button to move the text to another window or to reissue a command. The middle button can also be used to move windows around on the screen. The right mouse button, the Menu button, is used to display and choose options from pop-up menus.

- **Menu options**—The names of menus and the options that appear on them are separated by a comma. For example, "Select File, Open" means to pull down the File menu and choose the Open option.
- **Code continuation character**—When a line of code is too long to fit on one line of a page, it is broken and continued to the next line. The continuation is preceded by a code continuation character (➥).

What's New in Solaris 7

This section covers some of the features now available in Solaris 7 that were not available in Solaris 2.6. Although most changes are minor, it's important to note the differences.

This release of Solaris is called Solaris 7, not Solaris 2.7 as you might expect. As the Solaris product line continues to grow, this name change will make it easier for you to determine which products in the Solaris line you might want to use. In Solaris 7, the transition to the new name is in process. This means that you will still see references to Solaris 2.7, and even to Solaris 2.x in some of Sun's documentation. The name of the core operating system has not changed. In this release, it is SunOS 5.7.

Enhancements in this release include the following:

- **Solaris 64-bit operating environment**—Solaris 7 provides a 64-bit operating environment (SPARC only). The 64-bit Solaris operating environment is a complete 32-bit and 64-bit application and development environment supported by a 64-bit operating system. This permits maximum compatibility and interoperability for existing applications, both source and binary. At the same time, the 64-bit Solaris operating environment overcomes many of the limitations of the 32-bit system, most notably by supporting a 64-bit virtual address space as well as removing other existing 32-bit system limitations. The compatibility and interoperability in the 64-bit Solaris operating environment are so complete that there is no noticeable difference with existing applications, and `PATH` settings remain unchanged. The new `isainfo` program helps determine whether you are running on a 32-bit or 64-bit system. `isainfo` prints information about all the supported Instruction Set Architectures (ISA) of the running system. Finally, you can boot either the 32-bit or 64-bit Solaris operating environment on UltraSPARC machines.

NOTE. *Some sun4u systems need to be updated to a higher level of OpenBoot firmware in the flash PROM before they can run the 64-bit mode of the Solaris 7 11/99 operating environment. Only UltraSPARC processors can run in 64-bit mode. Systems that can run only the 32-bit mode are the sun4c, sun4d, and sun4m platform groups. These platforms do not require updated firmware to run Solaris 7 11/99 software. Currently, the only systems that may require this flash PROM update are Ultra 1, Ultra 2, Ultra 450, Sun Enterprise 450, and Sun Enterprise 3000, 4000, 5000, and 6000 systems.*

- **Web browser**—Solaris 7 includes the Netscape Communicator Web browser.
- **UFS logging**—UFS logging is the process of storing transactions (changes that make up a complete UFS operation) in a log before the transactions are applied to the UFS file system. After a transaction is stored, the transaction can be applied to the file system later. UFS logging provides two advantages. It prevents file systems from becoming inconsistent, thereby eliminating the need to run the `fsck` command. Also, because `fsck` can be bypassed, UFS logging reduces the time required to reboot a system if it crashes, or after an unclean halt. UFS logging is not enabled by default.

- **Dynamic reconfiguration**—Dynamic reconfiguration allows the service provider to add, or remove and replace, hot-pluggable system boards in a running system, eliminating the time lost in rebooting. This feature is available on certain SPARC systems only.
- **Network enhancements**—Solaris 7 includes enhancements in the areas of performance, security, sendmail, LDAP, RPC, NIS+, and BIND, to name a few. Also, the `traceroute` utility is included.
- **Answerbook**—Solaris 7 includes improvements to documentation and the ability for Answerbook to run on top of an existing Web server.
- **Graphics**—Solaris 7 includes improvements in graphics and imaging.
- **Common Desktop Environment (CDE)**—Solaris 7 includes improvements to the CDE and new tools to make it easy to find, manipulate, and manage address cards, applications, email addresses, files, folders, hosts, processes, and Web addresses.

For a complete list of enhancements, refer to the Solaris 7 Installation Library, found on the Solaris documentation CD.

NOTE. *The name of the Solaris Server Intranet Extensions CD has changed. The new version is called Solaris Easy Access Server (SEAS) 2.0.*

Taking the Exam

To take the exam, purchase an examination voucher from your local Sun Educational Services office by calling 1-800-USA-4SUN or by visiting their Web site. Go to `www.pdesigninc.com` for the latest link to the Sun certification Web site. Select the exam you want to purchase, and read the information on how to register for the exam. It will direct you to a phone number at Sun to order your voucher using one of the payment methods specified. Each voucher costs $150. After purchasing your voucher, you will receive a voucher number. You will be directed to call your local Sylvan testing center to schedule a date and time to take your exam. When you go to the testing center to take your exam, you can't bring any reference materials with you. At the end of the exam, you will receive your pass/fail grade, a score, and feedback on your performance. You can take the exams in any order you want, but you must pass both exams to become certified.

In addition, watch my Web site, `www.pdesigninc.com`. It contains the following:

- Late-breaking changes that Sun might make to the exam or the objectives. You can expect Sun to change the exams frequently. Make sure you check here before taking the exam.
- A FAQs page with frequently asked questions and errata regarding this book or the exams.
- Links to other informative Web sites.

You can also email me directly from this Web site with questions or comments about this book.

When you feel confident, take the real exams and become certified. Don't forget to drop me an email and let me know how you did (`wcalkins@pdesigninc.com`).

SECTION I

Part I

This section covers the following objectives for the Sun Certified System Administrator for Solaris 7 exam, Part I:

- System concepts
- The boot PROM
- Installing a standalone system
- Software package administration
- Maintaining patches
- The boot process
- Changing system states
- System security
- Adding users
- Administration of initialization files
- Advanced file permission
- Process control
- Disk configuration and naming
- Disk partitions and format
- Introduction to file systems
- Mounting file systems
- Backup and recovery
- LP print service
- Print commands

CHAPTER

1

System Startup

The following are the test objectives for this chapter:

- Booting the system
- Performing kernel initialization
- Using the run control scripts to stop or start services
- Performing a system shutdown

System startup requires an understanding of the hardware and the operating system functions required to bring the system up to a running state. This chapter discusses the operations that the system must perform from the time you power on the system until you receive a system logon prompt. After reading this chapter, you'll understand how to boot the system from the OpenBoot PROM, and what operations must take place to start up the kernel and UNIX system processes.

Booting the System

Bootstrapping is the process a computer follows to load and execute the bootable operating system. The name is coined from the phrase "pulling yourself up by your bootstraps." The instructions for the bootstrap procedure are stored in the boot PROM (Programmable Read-Only Memory).

The boot process goes through the following phases:

1. **Boot PROM phase.** After you turn on power to the system, the PROM displays system identification information and runs self-test diagnostics to verify the system's hardware and memory. It then loads the primary boot program, called `bootblk`.
2. **Boot program phase.** The `bootblk` program finds and executes the secondary boot program (called `ufsboot`) from the ufs file system and loads it into memory. After the `ufsboot` program is loaded, it loads the kernel.
3. **Kernel initialization phase.** The kernel initializes itself and begins loading modules, using `ufsboot` to read the files. When the kernel has loaded enough modules to mount the root file system, it unmaps the `ufsboot` program and continues, using its own resources. The kernel starts the UNIX operating system, mounts the necessary file systems, and runs `/sbin/init` to bring the system to the "initdefault" state specified in /etc/inittab.
4. **Init phase.** The kernel creates a user process and starts the `/sbin/init` process, which starts other processes by reading the /etc/inittab file.

   The /sbin/init process starts the run control (rc) scripts, which execute a series of other scripts. These scripts (/sbin/rc*) check and mount file systems, start various processes, and perform system maintenance tasks.

Power On

Before powering on the system, make sure that all your connections are secure. Check the SCSI cables that connect your external disk drives, tape drives, and CD-ROM to the system to make sure they are properly connected. Check your network connection. Also, make sure that the keyboard and monitor are connected properly. Loose cables can cause your system to fail the startup process.

CAUTION! *Always connect your cables* before *turning on the hardware, or you could damage your system.*

The correct sequence for powering on your equipment is to first turn on all your peripherals, such as external disk drives, tape drives, and CD-ROM; then turn on power to the monitor; and finally, turn on power to the system.

Boot PROM and Program Phases

The bootstrap process begins after power-up when information located in the hardware's PROM chip is accessed. Sun calls this the *OpenBoot* firmware, and it is executed immediately after you turn on the system. I cover OpenBoot in detail in the next chapter, but because it is part of the boot process, I'll also cover it briefly here.

The primary task of the OpenBoot firmware is to boot the operating system either from a mass storage device or from the network. OpenBoot contains a program called the monitor, which controls the operation of the system before the kernel is available. When a system is turned on, the monitor runs a quick self-test that checks such things as the hardware and memory on the system. If no errors are found, the automatic boot process begins. OpenBoot contains a set of instructions that locate and start up the system's boot program and eventually start up the UNIX operating system.

The boot program is stored in a predictable area on the system hard drive, CD-ROM, or other bootable device, and is referred to as the *bootblock*. The bootblock is responsible for loading the UNIX kernel into memory and passing control of the system to the kernel. The kernel (covered in detail later in this chapter) is the part of the operating system that remains running at all times until the system is shut down. The kernel is a file named /kernel/unix, or genunix (by default), and it is located on the bootable device.

Kernel Initialization Phase

The OpenBoot PROM automatically issues the `boot` command if the OpenBoot parameter `auto-boot` is set to true (default) and the OpenBoot PROM is not in fully secure mode. (See Chapter 2, "OpenBoot," for details on how this is set.) The system automatically starts the boot process after power has been turned on, and you do not see the `ok` prompt. To interrupt the auto-boot process, press Stop+A. The `ok` prompt appears. Table 1-1 lists the `boot` command options.

Table 1-1 *boot* Command Options

Option	Description
-a	An interactive boot
-r	A reconfiguration boot
-s	Boots into a single-user state
-v	Boots in verbose mode

`ok boot -v`, for example, boots the system in verbose mode, which displays a full listing of system messages during the boot phase. The `-v` option can be used with other boot options to get verbose output.

The boot program is responsible for loading the UNIX kernel into memory and passing control of the system to it. The `boot` command must access the OpenBoot parameter `boot-device`. The alias assigned to the boot device (disk or disk#) tells the boot device where to find the kernel and how to start it up. For example, the alias disk provides the boot path /sbus@1,f8000000/esp@0,40000/sd@3,0:a.

The *boot* Command

A noninteractive boot (`boot`) automatically boots the system using default values for the boot path. Initiate a noninteractive boot by typing the following command from the OpenBoot prompt:

```
ok boot
```

The system will boot without requiring any more interaction.

An interactive boot (`boot -a`) stops and asks for input during the boot process. The system provides a dialog box in which it displays the default boot values and gives you the option of changing them. You might want to boot interactively to make a temporary change to the system file or kernel. Booting interactively lets you test your changes and recover easily if you have any problems.

The following list provides details of the interactive boot process:

1. At the `ok` prompt, type `boot -a` and press Enter. The boot program prompts you interactively.
2. Press Enter to use the default kernel (/kernel/unix) as prompted, or type the name of the kernel to use for booting and press Enter.
3. Press Enter to use the default modules directory path as prompted, or type the path for the modules directory and press Enter.

4. Press Enter to use the default /etc/system file as prompted, or type the name of the system file and press Enter.
5. Press Enter to use the default root file system type as prompted (ufs for local disk booting, or nfs for diskless clients).
6. Press Enter to use the default physical name of the root device as prompted, or type the device name.

The following output shows an example of an interactive boot session:

```
ok boot -a
Resetting ...

Sun Ultra 5/10 UPA/PCI (UltraSPARC-IIi 270MHz), No Keyboard
OpenBoot 3.15, 128 MB memory installed, Serial #10642306.
Ethernet address 8:0:20:a2:63:82, Host ID: 80a26382
.
Rebooting with command: boot -a
Boot device: /pci@1f,0/pci@1,1/ide@3/disk@0,0:a  File and args: -a
Enter filename [kernel/sparcv9/unix]:
Enter default directory for modules [/platform/SUNW,Ultra-5_10/kernel /platform/sun4u/
➥kernel /kernel /usr/kernel]:
SunOS Release 5.7 Version Generic 64-bit [UNIX(R) System V Release 4.0]
Copyright (c) 1983-1998, Sun Microsystems, Inc.
Name of system file [etc/system]:
root filesystem type [ufs]:
Enter physical name of root device
[/pci@1f,0/pci@1,1/ide@3/disk@0,0:a]:
   configuring network interfaces: hme0.
Hostname: ultra5
The system is coming up.  Please wait.
checking ufs filesystems
/dev/rdsk/c0t0d0s5: is clean.
/dev/rdsk/c0t0d0s4: is clean.
/dev/rdsk/c0t0d0s7: is clean.
/dev/rdsk/c0t0d0s3: is clean.
starting routing daemon.
starting rpc services: rpcbindkeyserv: failed to generate host's netname when
➥ establishing root's key.
 keyserv done.
Setting default interface for multicast: add net 224.0.0.0: gateway ultra5
syslog service starting.
Print services started.
Apr 28 19:21:53 ultra5 sendmail[196]
volume management starting.
The system is ready.
ultra5 console login:
```

To view more detailed information during the boot process, use the -v option:

```
ok boot -v
```

The system responds with more detailed information:

```
Boot device: /pci@1f,0/pci@1,1/ide@3/disk@0,0:a  File and args: -v
Size: 314284+93248+121472 Bytes
cpu0: SUNW,UltraSPARC-IIi (upaid 0 impl 0x12 ver 0x13 clock 270 MHz)
SunOS Release 5.7 Version Generic 64-bit [UNIX(R) System V Release 4.0]
Copyright (c) 1983-1998, Sun Microsystems, Inc.
mem = 131072K (0x8000000)
avail mem = 122757120
Ethernet address = 8:0:20:a2:63:82
root nexus = Sun Ultra 5/10 UPA/PCI (UltraSPARC-IIi 270MHz)
pci0 at root: UPA 0x1f 0x0
pci0 is /pci@lf,0
PCI-device: pci@1,1, simba0
PCI-device: pci@1, simba1
PCI-device: ide@3, uata0
dad0 at pci1095,6460 target 0 lun 0
dad0 is /pci@1f,0/pci@1,1/ide@3/dad@0,0
         <ST34321A cyl 8892 alt 2 hd 15 sec 63>
root on /pci@1f,0/pci@1,1/ide@3/disk@0,0:a fstype ufs
PCI-device: ebus@1, ebus0
su0 at ebus0: offset 14,3083f8
su0 is /pci@1f,0/pci@1,1/ebus@1/su@14,3083f8
su1 at ebus0: offset 14,3062f8
su1 is /pci@1f,0/pci@1,1/ebus@1/su@14,3062f8
keyboard is </pci@1f,0/pci@1,1/ebus@1/su@14,3083f8> major <37> minor <0>
mouse is </pci@1f,0/pci@1,1/ebus@1/su@14,3062f8> major <37> minor <1>
se0 at ebus0: offset 14,400000
se0 is /pci@1f,0/pci@1,1/ebus@1/su@14,400000
stdin is </pci@1f,0/pci@1,1/ebus@1/se@14,400000:a> major <20> minor <0>
stdout is </pci@1f,0/pci@1,1/ebus@1/se@14,400000:a> major <20> minor <0>
  configuring network interfaces:SUNW,hme0: CheerIO 2.0 (Rev Id = c1) Found
PCI-device: network@1,1, hme0
hme0 is /pci@1f,0/pci@1,1/network@1,1
 hme0.
Hostname: ultra5
dump on /dev/dsk/c0t0d0s1 size 128 MB
SUNW,hme0: Using Internal Transceiver
SUNW,hme0: 10 Mbps half-duplex Link Up
The system is coming up.  Please wait.
checking ufs filesystems
/dev/rdsk/c0t0d0s5: is clean.
/dev/rdsk/c0t0d0s4: is clean.
/dev/rdsk/c0t0d0s7: is clean.
/dev/rdsk/c0t0d0s3: is clean.
starting routing daemon.
starting rpc services: rpcbindkeyserv: failed to generate host's netname when
➥ establishing root's key.
 keyserv done.
Setting default interface for multicast: add net 224.0.0.0: gateway ultra5
syslog service starting.
Print services started.
```

```
pseudo-device: pm0
pm0 is /pseudo/pm@0
PCI-device: SUNW,m64B@2, m640
m640 is /pci@1f,0/pci@1,1/SUNW,m64B@2
m64#0: 1152x900, 4M mappable, rev 4750.7c
pseudo-device: tod0
tod0 is /pseudo/tod@0
power0 at ebus0: offset 14,724000
power0 is /pci@1f,0/pci@1,1/ebus@1/power@14,724000
Apr 28 14:47:32 ultra5 sendmail[196]
volume management starting.
pseudo-device: vol0
vol0 is /pseudo/vol@0
sd2 at uata0: target 2 lun 0
sd2 is /pci@1f,0/pci@1,1/ide@3/sd@2,0
fd0 at ebus0: offset 14,3023f0
fd0 is /pci@1f,0/pci@1,1/ebus@1/fdthree@14,3023f0
The system is ready.
ultra5 console login:
```

If you are not at the system console to watch the boot information, you can use the UNIX `dmesg` command to redisplay information that was displayed during the boot process or view the information in the /var/adm/messages file.

To view messages displayed during the boot process, use one of the following methods:

- At a UNIX prompt, type `/usr/sbin/dmesg` and press Enter. The boot messages are displayed.

NOTE. *Several pages of information will be displayed, so I recommend that you pipe the* `dmesg` *command to more:* `/usr/sbin/dmesg|more`

- At a UNIX prompt, type `more /var/adm/messages` and press Enter.

System Run States

After the kernel is initiated by the `boot` command, it begins several phases of the startup process. The first task is for OpenBoot to load the kernel. As stated, by default, the kernel is named /kernel/unix and is located in the root (/) partition on the disk, with its path defined in an OpenBoot PROM alias named disk.

The kernel consists of a small static core and many dynamically loadable kernel modules. Many kernel modules are loaded automatically at boot time, but for efficiency, others—such as device drivers—are loaded from the disk as needed by the kernel. When the kernel loads, the system reads a file named /etc/system. Parameters in this file modify how the kernel gets loaded. Occasionally, kernel parameters in this file need to be adjusted.

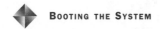

CAUTION! *Do not modify the /etc/system file unless you are certain of the results. A good practice is always to make a backup copy of any system file you modify in case the original needs to be restored. Incorrect entries could prevent your system from booting.*

After control of the system gets passed to the kernel, the system begins initialization and enters one of eight run states—also called init states—as described in Table 1-2. Because run state 4 is currently not used, there are only seven usable run states.

Table 1-2 The Eight System Run States

Run State	Description
0	Stops system services and daemons. Terminates all running processes. Unmounts all file systems.
S,s	Single-user (system administrator) state. Only root is allowed to log in at the console, and any users logged in are logged out when entering this run level. All file systems previously mounted remain mounted and accessible. All services except the most basic OS services are shut down in an orderly manner.
1	Single-user (system administrator) state. All file systems are still available, and any logged-in users can remain logged in. All services except the most basic OS services are shut down in an orderly manner.
2	Normal multiuser operation without NFS file systems shared. Sets the time zone variable. Mounts the /usr file system. Cleans up the /tmp and /var/tmp directories. Loads the network interfaces and starts processes. Starts the `cron` daemon. Cleans up the uucp tmp files. Starts the lp system. Starts the `sendmail` daemon.
3	Normal multiuser operation of a file server with NFS systems shared. Completes all the tasks in run level 2. Starts the NFS system daemons.
4	Alternative multiuser state (currently not used).
5	Power-down state. Shuts down the system so that it is safe to turn off power to the system. If possible, automatically turns off system power on systems that support this feature.
6	Reboots.

NOTE. *The difference between run level 1 and run level S,s is that in run level 1, users can still be logged in. If you issue an* `init s`, *user sessions get killed off. If you issue an* `init 1`, *users currently logged in will not be logged off. Run level 1 allows the system administrator to perform system maintenance while having users logged in. All services except the most basic OS services are stopped, however. Run level S allows system maintenance such as system backups, where all users must be off the system.*

The init state in which the system is running defines the services and resources available to users. When preparing to perform a system administration task, you need to determine which init state is appropriate for the task. Use Table 1-3 to determine what init state to use for a particular task. A system can run in only one init state at a time.

Table 1-3 The Eight System Run States Defined

Init State	When to Use It
0	To shut down the system so that it is safe to turn off the power (system administrator state).
S,s	Single-user (system administrator) state. Only root is allowed to log in at the console, and any users logged in are logged out when entering this run level. All file systems previously mounted remain mounted and accessible. All services except the most basic OS services are shut down in an orderly manner.
1	Single-user (system administrator) state. All file systems are still available, and any logged-in users can remain logged in. All services except the most basic OS services are shut down in an orderly manner.
2	For normal operations. Multiple users can access the system and the entire file system. All daemons are running except NFS server and syslog.
3	For normal operations, with NFS resource sharing available.
4	Alternative multiuser state (currently not used).
5	Power-down state. To shut down the operating system so that it is safe to turn off power to the system. All users are logged off the system, and the OS services are stopped in an orderly manner. When complete, it's safe to turn off power to the system and all peripherals. If supported by the system hardware, the power to the system is automatically turned off.
6	To shut down the system to run level 0 and then reboot to multiuser level (or whatever level is the default in the inittab file).

Swapper

The first task for the kernel is to start the *swapper* process. The swapper process is the part of the kernel that schedules all other processes. The swapper has a process ID of 0. Its first job is to start up the init process.

INIT Phase

The `/sbin/init` command generates processes to set up the system based on the directions in /etc/inittab. The init process is the parent of all other processes. It examines the contents of the /etc/inittab file to determine the order for starting up other processes and what to do when one of these processes ends. Each entry in the /etc/inittab file has the following fields:

```
id:runlevel:action:process
```

Table 1-4 provides a more-detailed description of each field.

Table 1-4 Fields in the inittab File

Field	Description
id	A unique identifier
runlevel	The run level
action	How the process is to be run
process	The name of the command to execute

The following example shows a default /etc/inittab file:

```
ap::sysinit:/sbin/autopush -f /etc/iu.ap
ap::sysinit:/sbin/soconfig -f /etc/sock2path
fs::sysinit:/sbin/rcS sysinit                    >/dev/console 2<>/dev/console
➥ </dev/console
is:3:initdefault:
p3:s1234:powerfail:/usr/sbin/shutdown -y -i5 -g0  >/dev/console 2<>/dev/console
sS:s:wait:/sbin/rcS                              >/dev/console 2<>/dev/console
➥ </dev/console
s0:0:wait:/sbin/rc0                              >/dev/console 2<>/dev/console
➥ </dev/console
s1:1:respawn:/sbin/rc1                           >/dev/console 2<>/dev/console
➥ </dev/console
s2:23:wait:/sbin/rc2                             >/dev/console 2<>/dev/console
➥ </dev/console
s3:3:wait:/sbin/rc3                              >/dev/console 2<>/dev/console
➥ </dev/console
s5:5:wait:/sbin/rc5                              >/dev/console 2<>/dev/console
➥ </dev/console
s6:6:wait:/sbin/rc6                              >/dev/console 2<>/dev/console
➥ </dev/console
fw:0:wait:/sbin/uadmin 2 0                       >/dev/console 2<>/dev/console
➥ </dev/console
of:5:wait:/sbin/uadmin 2 6                       >/dev/console 2<>/dev/console
➥ </dev/console
rb:6:wait:/sbin/uadmin 2 1                       >/dev/console 2<>/dev/console
➥ </dev/console
sc:234:respawn:/usr/lib/saf/sac -t 300
co:234:respawn:/usr/lib/saf/ttymon -g -h -p "`uname -n` console login: " -T sun -d
➥ /dev/console -l console -m ldterm,ttcompat
```

When the system is first booted, init starts all processes labeled sysinit in the inittab file. The initdefault entry in /etc/inittab identifies the default run level. In this example, the default is run level 3 (multiuser mode with network file sharing). The `init` daemon runs each process associated with this run level (that is, each entry that has a 3 in its run-level field). Each process is run using the entry from the action field. The action field can have one of the values listed in Table 1-5.

Table 1-5 inittab Action Fields

Field	Description
`powerfail`	The system has received a powerfail signal.
`wait`	Waits for the command to be completed.
`respawn`	Restarts the command.

rc Scripts

For each init state, there is a corresponding series of run control scripts, referred to as rc scripts, located in the /sbin directory, to control each init state. These rc scripts are as follows:

rc0

rc1

rc2

rc3

rc5

rc6

rcS

NOTE. *Many of the Solaris startup scripts can be identified by their "rc" prefix or suffix, which means "run control."*

For each rc script in the /sbin directory, a corresponding directory named /etc/rc<n>.d contains scripts to perform various actions for that run level. For example, /etc/rc2.d contains files used to start and stop processes for run level 2. At bootup, rc scripts are run in numerical order until the default run level is reached; for example, to get to run level 3, /sbin/rc1, /sbin/rc2, and /sbin/rc3 are run.

All run control scripts are also located in the /etc/init.d directory. These files are linked to corresponding run control scripts in the /etc/rc<n>.d directories.

NOTE. *On other UNIX systems, startup scripts are sometimes found in /sbin/rc<n>.d and in /etc/rc<n>.d directories. Links were put into Solaris so that users who are accustomed to other flavors of UNIX (HP-UX, SunOS, and so on) can locate the startup files easily. Also, any scripts they might have ported over that reference these startup files are compatible without modification.*

The following is a list of the scripts located in /etc/rc2.d:

```
ls /etc/rc2.d

K07dmi          S69inet              S74xntpd       S89bdconfig
K07snmpdx       S70uucp              S75cron        S92volmgt
K28nfs.server   S71rpc               S75savecore    S93cacheos.finish
README          S71sysid.sys         S76nscd        S96ab2mgr
S01MOUNTFSYS    S72autoinstall       S80PRESERVE    S99audit
S05RMTMPFILES   S72inetsvc           S80lp          S99dtlogin
S20sysetup      S73cachefs.daemon    S80spc
S21perf         S73nfs.client        S85power
S30sysid.net    S74autofs            S88sendmail
S47asppp        S74syslog            S88utmpd
```

The /etc/rc<n>.d scripts are always run in ASCII sort order. The number following the first letter (S or K) designates the order in which the scripts are run. The name following the number does not relate to the order in which they are run. The scripts have names of this form:

```
[K,S][0-9][0-9][A-Z]
```

Files beginning with K are run to terminate (kill) a system process. Files beginning with S are run to start a system process. The actions of each run-control-level script are summarized in the following lists.

The /sbin/rc0 script

- Stops system services and daemons
- Terminates all running processes
- Unmounts all file systems

The /sbin/rc1 script runs the /etc/rc1.d scripts and

- Stops system services and daemons except for the most basic OS services
- All file systems are still available, and any logged-in users can remain logged in
- Brings the system up in single-user mode

TIP. *Use the init S run level to perform system administration tasks when you want to ensure that other users cannot log in and access the system.*

The /sbin/rc2 script sets the TIMEZONE variable, runs the /etc/rc2.d scripts, and

- Mounts all file systems
- Enables disk quotas if at least one file system was mounted with the quota option
- Saves editor temporary files in /usr/preserve
- Removes any files in the /tmp directory
- Configures system accounting
- Configures the default router
- Sets the NIS domain
- Sets the `ifconfig` netmask
- Reboots the system from the installation media or a boot server if either /.PREINSTALL or /AUTOINSTALL exists
- Starts `inetd`, `rpcbind`, and `named`, if appropriate
- Starts the Kerberos client-side daemon (`kerbd`)
- Starts NIS daemons (`ypbind`) and NIS+ daemons (`rpc.nisd`), if appropriate
- Starts `keyserv`
- Starts `statd`, `lockd`, `xntpd`, `vold`, and `utmpd`
- Mounts all NFS entries
- Starts `automount`
- Starts `cron`
- Starts the `lp` daemons
- Starts the `sendmail` daemon

The /sbin/rc3 script runs the /etc/rc3.d scripts and

- Cleans up sharetab
- Starts `nfsd`
- Starts `mountd`
- If boot server, starts `rarpd`, `rpld`, and `rpc.bootparamd`

The /sbin/rc5 and /sbin/rc6 scripts run the /etc/rc0.d scripts and

- Kill all active processes
- Unmount all file systems

The /sbin/rcS script runs the /etc/rcS.d scripts to bring the system up to single-user mode and

- Establishes a minimal network
- Mounts /usr, if necessary
- Sets the system name
- Checks the / and /usr file systems
- Mounts pseudo file systems (/proc and /dev/fd)
- Rebuilds the device entries (for reconfiguration boots)
- Checks and mounts other file systems to be mounted in single-user mode

Run level init S is similar to run level 1, except that all file systems get mounted and are accessible.

Using the Run Control Scripts to Stop or Start Services

The advantage of having individual scripts for each run level is that you can run these scripts individually to turn off processes in Solaris without rebooting or changing init states.

For example, you can turn off NFS server functionality by typing `/etc/init.d/nfs.server stop` and pressing Enter. After you have changed the system configuration, you can restart the functionality by typing `/etc/init.d/nfs.server start` and pressing Enter.

Use the `pgrep` command to verify whether the service has been stopped or started:

```
pgrep -f <service>
```

The `pgrep` utility examines the active processes on the system and reports the process IDs of the processes. See Chapter 11, "Process Control," for details on this command.

Adding Scripts to the Run Control Directories

If you add a script, put the script in the /etc/init.d directory and create a link to the appropriate rc<n>.d directory. Assign appropriate numbers and names to the new scripts so that they will be run in the proper sequence.

The following steps illustrate how to add a run control script:

1. Become superuser.

2. Add the script to the /etc/init.d directory:

```
# cp <filename> /etc/init.d
# chmod 0744 /etc/init.d/<filename>
# chown root:sys /etc/init.d/<filename>
```

3. Create links to the appropriate rc<n>.d directory:

```
# cd /etc/init.d
# ln -s <filename> /etc/rc2.d/S<nnfilename>
# ln -s <filename> /etc/rc<n>.d/K<nnfilename>
```

4. Use the `ls` command to verify that the script has links in the specified directories:

```
# ls -l /etc/init.d/ /etc/rc2.d/ /etc/rc<n>.d/
```

The following example creates an rc script named "program" that will start up at run level 2 and stop at run level 0:

```
# cp program  /etc/init.d
 # cd /etc/init.d
 # ln -s /etc/init.d/program  /etc/rc2.d/S100program
 # ln -s /etc/init.d/program  /etc/rc0.d/K100program
 # ls -l /etc/init.d /etc/rc2.d /etc/rc0.d
```

The system will display the following:

```
/etc/init.d:
total 212
-rwxr—r—    3 root      sys            171 Sep  1  1998 ANNOUNCE
-rwxr—r—    3 root      sys            894 Sep  1  1998 MOUNTFSYS
-rwxr—r—    2 root      sys            256 Sep  1  1998 PRESERVE
-rw-r—r—    1 root      sys           2681 Sep  1  1998 README
-rwxr—r—    2 root      sys           2004 Sep  1  1998 RMTMPFILES
-rwxr—r—    1 root      sys           1955 Mar 24 21:26 ab2mgr
-rwxr—r—    1 root      sys            833 Sep  1  1998 acct
-rwxr—r—    1 root      sys            379 Sep  1  1998 mkdtab
...
...

-rwxr—r—    2 root      sys            989 Sep  1  1998 perf
-rwxr—r—    5 root      sys           1959 Sep  1  1998 power
-rw-r—r—    3 root      other          989 May 23 07:14 program
-rwxr—r—    2 root      sys           7768 Sep  1  1998 rootusr

/etc/rc0.d:
total 94
```

```
-rwxr—r—    3 root    sys        171 Sep  1  1998 K00ANNOUNCE
-rwxr—r—    6 root    sys        861 Sep  1  1998 K07dmi
-rwxr—r—    6 root    sys        404 Sep  1  1998 K07snmpdx
lrwxrwxrwx  1 root    other       19 May 23 07:21 S100program ->
➥ /etc/init.d/program
-rwxr—r—    5 root    sys       2804 Sep 12  1998 K10dtlogin
-rwxr—r—    6 root    sys       2307 Sep  1  1998 K28nfs.server
...
...
-rwxr—r—    5 root    sys       7317 Sep  1  1998 K43inet
-rwxr—r—    5 root    sys       1365 Sep  1  1998 K50asppp
-rwxr—r—    3 root    sys        399 Sep  1  1998 K78pcmcia

/etc/rc2.d:
total 134
-rwxr—r—    6 root    sys        861 Sep  1  1998 K07dmi
-rwxr—r—    6 root    sys        404 Sep  1  1998 K07snmpdx
-rwxr—r—    6 root    sys       2307 Sep  1  1998 K28nfs.server
-rw-r—r—    1 root    sys       1369 Sep  1  1998 README
-rwxr—r—    3 root    sys        894 Sep  1  1998 S01MOUNTFSYS
-rwxr—r—    2 root    sys       2004 Sep  1  1998 S05RMTMPFILES
lrwxrwxrwx  1 root    other       19 May 23 07:21 S100program ->
➥ /etc/init.d/program
-rwxr—r—    2 root    sys        624 Sep  1  1998 S20sysetup
-rwxr—r—    2 root    sys        989 Sep  1  1998 S21perf
-rwxr-xr-x  2 root    other     1644 Sep 10  1998 S30sysid.net
...
...
-rwxr—r—    5 root    sys        447 Sep  1  1998 S99audit
-rwxr—r—    5 root    sys       2804 Sep 12  1998 S99dtlogin
```

TIP. *If you do not want a particular script to run when entering a corresponding init state, change the uppercase prefix (S or K) to lowercase (s or k). Only files with an uppercase prefix are run. For example, change S99mount to s99mount to disable the script.*

System Shutdown

Solaris has been designed to run continuously, seven days a week, 24 hours a day. Occasionally, however, you need to shut down the system to carry out administrative tasks. At other times, an application might cause the system to go awry, and the operating system must be stopped to kill off runaway processes and then be restarted.

You can shut down the system in a number of ways, using various UNIX commands. With Solaris, taking down the operating system in an orderly fashion is important. When the system boots, several processes are started. These must be shut down before you power off the system. In addition, information has been cached in memory and has not yet been written to disk. The process of shutting down Solaris involves shutting down processes and flushing data from memory to the disk.

CAUTION! *Shutting down the system improperly can result in loss of data and the risk of corrupting the file systems.*

TIP. *To avoid having your system shut down improperly during a power failure, use a UPS (uninterruptible power supply) capable of shutting down the system cleanly before the power is shut off.*

Commands to Shut Down the System

When preparing to shut down a system, you need to determine which of the following commands is appropriate for the system and the task at hand:

`/usr/sbin/shutdown`

`/sbin/init`

`/usr/sbin/halt`

`/usr/sbin/reboot`

`/usr/sbin/poweroff`

Stop+A or L1+A (to be used as a last resort; see the following Caution)

CAUTION! *Using the Stop+A key sequence (or L1+A) abruptly breaks execution of the operating system and should be used only as a last resort to restart the system.*

The first three commands initiate shutdown procedures, kill all running processes, write data to disk, and shut down the system software to the appropriate run level. The `/usr/sbin/reboot` command does all of these tasks, but it then boots the system back to the state defined as initdefault in /etc/inittab. The `/usr/sbin/poweroff` command is equivalent to `init 5`. The last command, which is really a series of keystrokes, stops the system unconditionally.

/usr/sbin/shutdown

Use the `shutdown` command when shutting down a system that has multiple users. The `shutdown` command sends a warning message to all users who are logged in, waits for 60 seconds (the default), and then shuts down the system to single-user state. A command option (`-g`) lets you choose a different default wait time. The `-i` option lets you define the init state that the system will be shut down to. The default is run level s.

The `shutdown` command performs a clean system shutdown, which means that all system processes and services are terminated normally and file systems are synchronized. You need superuser privileges to use the `shutdown` command.

When the shutdown command is initiated, all logged-in users and all systems mounting resources receive a warning about the impending shutdown, and then they get a final message. For this reason, the shutdown command is recommended over the init command on a server.

TIP. *When using either* shutdown *or* init, *you might want to give users more advance notice by sending an email message about any scheduled system shutdown.*

The following are the recommended steps for shutting down the system:

1. As superuser, type the following to find out if users are logged in to the system:

   ```
   # who
   ```

2. A list of all logged-in users is displayed. You might want to send mail or broadcast a message to let users know the system is being shut down.
3. Shut down the system by using the shutdown command:

   ```
   # shutdown -i<init-state> -g<grace-period> -y
   ```

The following describes the options for the shutdown command:

-i<init-state>	Brings the system to an init state different from the default of S. The choices are 0, 1, 2, 5, and 6.
-g<grace-period>	Indicates a time (in seconds) before the system is shut down. The default is 60 seconds.
-y	Continues to shut down the system without intervention; otherwise, you are prompted to continue the shutdown process after 60 seconds. If you used the shutdown -y command, you are not prompted to continue; otherwise, you are asked, "Do you want to continue? (y or n)."

/sbin/init

Use the init command to shut down a single-user system or to change its run level. The syntax is

```
init <run level>
```

<run level> is any run level defined in Table 1-3. In addition, <run level> can be a, b, or c, which tells the system to process only /etc/inittab entries that have the a, b, or c run level set. These are pseudo-states, which may be defined to run certain commands, but which do not cause the current run level to change. <run level> can also be the keyword Q or q, which tells the system to re-examine the /etc/inittab file.

You can use `init` to place the system in power-down state (`init 0`) or in single-user state (`init 1`). For example, to bring the system down to run level 1 from the current run level, type

```
init 1
```

The system responds with this:

```
INIT: New run level: 1
Changing to state 1.
Unmounting remote filesystems: done.
System services are now being stopped.
Apr 29 09:39:10 ultra5 /usr/sbin/vold[1147]
Print services stopped.
syslogd: going down on signal 15
Killing user processes: done.
Change to state 1 has been completed.
Type Ctrl-d to proceed with normal startup,
(or give root password for system maintenance):
```

As another example, maybe you made a change to the /etc/inittab file and you want to have the system reread inittab and implement the change. Type

```
init q
```

No system messages will be displayed, and the inittab file will be re-examined.

NOTE. *The* `telinit` *command is available for compatibility. It is simply a link to the /usr/sbin/init command.*

/usr/sbin/halt

Use the `halt` command when the system must be stopped immediately and it is acceptable not to warn any current users. The `halt` command shuts down the system without any delay. It does not warn any other users on the system of the shutdown.

/usr/sbin/reboot

Use the `reboot` command to shut down a single-user system and bring it into multiuser state. `reboot` does not warn other users on the system of the shutdown.

The Solaris `reboot` and `halt` commands perform an unconditional shutdown of system processes. These commands shut down the system much more quickly than the `shutdown` command, but not as gracefully. No messages are sent to users. `reboot` and `halt` do not notify all logged-in users and systems mounting resources of the impending shutdown, but they do synchronize file systems.

/usr/sbin/poweroff

The `poweroff` command is equivalent to the `init 5` command.

NOTE. *`init` and `shutdown` are the most reliable ways to shut down a system because they use rc scripts to kill running processes and shut down the system with minimal data loss. The `halt` and `reboot` commands do not run the rc scripts properly and are not the preferred method of shutting down the system.*

Stopping the System for Recovery Purposes

Occasionally the system might not respond to the `init` commands specified earlier. A system that doesn't respond to anything, including `reboot` or `halt`, is called a "crashed" or "hung" system. If you try the commands just discussed but get no response, you can press Stop+A or L1+A to get back to the boot PROM (the specific Stop key sequence depends on your keyboard type). On terminals, press the Break key.

1. Use the abort key sequence for your system (Stop+A or L1+A).

   The monitor displays the `ok` PROM prompt.

2. Type the `sync` command to synchronize the disks:

   ```
   ok sync
   ```

3. When you see the `syncing file systems` message, press the abort key sequence for your system again.

4. Type the appropriate `reset` command to reset the hardware and start the boot process:

   ```
   ok reset
   ```

5. After you receive the `login:` message, log in and type the following to verify that the system is booted to the specified run level:

   ```
   # who -r
   ```

6. The system responds with

   ```
   .        run-level 3  Jun  9 09:19     3      0  S
   ```

Turning Off the Power

Only after shutting down the file systems should you turn off the power to the hardware. Turn off power to all devices after the system is shut down. If necessary, also unplug the power cables. When power can be restored, use the following steps to turn on the system and devices:

1. Plug in the power cables.
2. Turn on the monitor.
3. Turn on disk drives, tape drives, and printers.
4. Turn on the CPU.

Summary

This chapter reviewed the Solaris bootup and shutdown procedures. In the next chapter, I'll describe OpenBoot in more detail. In the upcoming chapters, you'll learn more about the Solaris operating environment and—just as important—the computer hardware. Thorough knowledge of these two system components is essential before you can adequately troubleshoot system startup problems.

CHAPTER

2

OpenBoot

The following test objectives are covered in this chapter:

- Understanding the OpenBoot environment, architecture, and interface
- Getting help in OpenBoot
- Using OpenBoot PROM commands to view system configuration information
- Understanding PROM full device names
- Understanding OpenBoot security
- Using OpenBoot PROM commands to perform basic hardware testing
- Using the `boot` command
- Loading the kernel

hapter 1, "System Startup," provided a general overview of the startup process, presented an introduction to OpenBoot, and gave specifics on /sbin/init, run levels, and run control scripts. This chapter provides more details on the OpenBoot firmware and kernel loading.

OpenBoot Environment

The hardware-level user interface that you see before the operating system starts is called the OpenBoot PROM (OBP). OpenBoot is based on an interactive command interpreter that gives you access to an extensive set of functions for hardware and software development, fault isolation, and debugging. The OBP firmware is stored in the socketed startup PROM (Programmable Read-Only Memory). The OpenBoot PROM consists of two chips on each system board: the startup PROM itself, which contains extensive firmware allowing access to user-written startup drivers and extended diagnostics, and an NVRAM (Non-volatile Random-Access Memory) chip.

The NVRAM chip has user-definable system parameters and writable areas for user-controlled diagnostics, macros, and device aliases. The NVRAM is where the system identification information is stored, such as the hostid. Many software packages use this hostid for licensing purposes; therefore, it is important that this chip be removed and placed into any replacement system board.

OpenBoot is currently at version 3, which is the version I describe in this chapter. Depending on the age of your system, you could have OpenBoot version 1, 2, or 3 installed. The OpenBoot firmware was first introduced on the Sun SPARCstation 1. Version 2 of the firmware first appeared on the SPARCstation 2 system, and OpenBoot version 3 is the version currently available on the Ultra series systems. Version 3 of the OpenBoot architecture provides a significant increase in functionality over the boot PROMs in earlier Sun systems. One notable feature of the OpenBoot firmware is a programmable user interface, based on the interactive programming language Forth. In Forth, sequences of user commands can be combined to form complete programs. This capability provides a powerful tool for debugging hardware and software.

Accessing the OpenBoot Environment

You can get to the OpenBoot environment in the following ways:

- By halting the operating system.
- By pressing the Stop and A keys simultaneously (Stop+A).

- When the system is initially powered on. If your system is not configured to start up automatically, it will stop at the user interface. If automatic startup is configured, you can make the system stop at the user interface by pressing the Stop and A keys after the display console banner is displayed but before the system begins starting the OS.
- If the system hardware detects an error from which it cannot recover (this is known as a Watchdog Reset).

CAUTION! *Using the Stop+A key sequence abruptly breaks execution of the operating system. It should be used only as a last effort to restart the system.*

OpenBoot Firmware Tasks

The primary tasks of the OpenBoot firmware are as follows:

- Test and initialize the system hardware.
- Determine the hardware configuration.
- Start the operating system from either a mass storage device or a network.
- Provide interactive debugging facilities for testing hardware and software.
- Allow modification and management of system startup configuration, such as NVRAM parameters.

Specifically, OpenBoot will perform the following tasks necessary to initialize the operating system kernel:

1. Display system identification information and then run self-test diagnostics to verify the system's hardware and memory. These checks are known as POST (Power-On Self-Test).
2. Load the primary startup program, `bootblk`, from the default startup device.
3. The `bootblk` program finds and executes the secondary startup program, `ufsboot`, and loads it into memory.
4. The ufsboot program loads the operating system kernel.

OpenBoot Architecture

The OpenBoot architecture provides an increase in functionality and portability compared to the proprietary systems of some other hardware vendors. Although this architecture was first implemented by Sun Microsystems as OpenBoot on SPARC (Scaleable Processor Architecture) systems, its design is processor-independent. Here are some notable features of OpenBoot firmware:

- **Plug-in device drivers**—A device driver that can be loaded from a plug-in device, such as an SBus card. This feature lets the input and output devices evolve without changing the system PROM.
- **FCode interpreter**—Plug-in drivers are written in a machine-independent interpreted language called FCode. Each OpenBoot system PROM contains an FCode interpreter. This allows the same device and driver to be used on machines with different CPU instruction sets.
- **Device tree**—Devices called nodes are attached to a host computer through a hierarchy of interconnected buses on the device tree. A node representing the host computer's main physical address bus forms the tree's root node. Both the user and the operating system can determine the system's hardware configuration by viewing the device tree.

  Nodes with children usually represent buses and their associated controllers, if any. Each such node defines a physical address space that distinguishes the devices connected to the node from one another. Each child of that node is assigned a physical address in the parent's address space. The physical address generally represents a physical characteristic unique to the device (such as the bus address or the slot number where the device is installed). The use of physical addresses to identify devices prevents device addresses from changing when other devices are installed or removed.
- **Programmable user interface**—The OpenBoot user interface is based on the interactive programming language Forth. Forth provides an interactive programming environment. It is a language that is used for direct communication between human beings and machines. It can be quickly expanded and adapted to special needs and different hardware systems. You'll see Forth used not only by Sun, but also by other hardware vendors, such as Hewlett-Packard.

NOTE. *Refer to ANSI X3.215-1994 (American National Standards Institute) if you're interested in more information on Forth.*

OpenBoot Interface

The OpenBoot firmware provides a command-line interface for the user at the system console. On older Sun systems such as the SPARCstation10 and SPARCstation20, this command-line interface has two modes: the Restricted Monitor and the Forth Monitor.

The Restricted Monitor

The *Restricted Monitor* provides a simple set of commands to initiate booting of the system, resume system execution, or enter the Forth Monitor. The Restricted Monitor is also used to implement system security.

The Restricted Monitor prompt is >. When you enter the Restricted Monitor, the following screen is displayed, showing the commands you can enter:

```
Type b (boot), c (continue), or n (new command mode) >
```

The Restricted Monitor commands are listed in Table 2-1.

Table 2-1 Restricted Monitor Commands

Command	Description
b	Boots the operating system.
c	Resumes the execution of a halted program.
n	Enters the Forth Monitor (commonly referred to as "new command mode").

The Forth Monitor

The *Forth Monitor,* the default mode in OpenBoot, is an interactive command interpreter that gives you access to an extensive set of functions for hardware and software diagnosis. These functions are available to anyone who has access to the system console.

The Forth Monitor prompt is `ok`. When you enter the Forth Monitor mode, the following screen is displayed:

```
Type help for more information ok
```

On older SPARCstations, if you want to leave the Forth Monitor mode and get into the Restricted Monitor mode, type

```
ok old-mode
```

NOTE. *When the system is halted, the PROM monitor prompt is displayed. The type of prompt depends on your system type. Older Sun systems, such as the Sun4/*nnn *series, use the greater-than sign (>) as the PROM prompt. Newer Sun systems use* `ok` *as the PROM prompt but support the* > *prompt. To switch from the* > *prompt to the* `ok` *prompt on newer Sun systems, type* `n` *at the* > *prompt.*

Old mode is not available on UltraSparc systems.

Getting Help in OpenBoot

At any time you can obtain help on the various Forth commands supported in OpenBoot by using the `help` command. The syntax for using help from the `ok` prompt is any of the choices listed in Table 2-2.

Table 2-2 OpenBoot Help

Command	Description
help	Displays instructions about using the help system and lists the available help categories.
help <category>	Shows help for all commands in the category. Use only the first word of the category description.
help <command>	Shows help for the individual command.

Because of the large number of commands, help is available only for commands that are used frequently.

The following example shows the `help` command with no arguments:

```
ok help
```

The system responds with the following:

```
Enter 'help command-name' or 'help category-name' for more help
(Use ONLY the first word of a category description)
Examples:  help select   -or-   help line
    Main categories are:
Repeated loops
Defining new commands
Numeric output
Radix (number base conversions)
Arithmetic
Memory access
Line editor
System and boot configuration parameters
Select I/O devices
Floppy eject
Power on reset
Diag (diagnostic routines)
Resume execution
File download and boot
nvramrc (making new commands permanent)
ok
```

If you want to see the help messages for all commands in the category `diag`, for example, type

```
ok help diag
```

The system responds with this:

```
test  <device-specifier>   Run selftest method for specified device
  Examples:
    test floppy          - test floppy disk drive
    test net             - test net
    test scsi            - test scsi
test-all          Execute test for all devices with selftest method
watch-clock       Show ticks of real-time clock
watch-net         Monitor network broadcast packets
watch-net-all     Monitor broadcast packets on all net interfaces
probe-scsi        Show attached SCSI devices
probe-scsi-all    Show attached SCSI devices for all host adapters
ok
```

If you want help for a specific command, type

```
ok help test
```

Help responds with the following:

```
test  <device-specifier>   Run selftest method for specified device
  Examples:
    test floppy          - test floppy disk drive
    test net             - test net
    test scsi            - test scsi
test-all          Execute test for all devices with selftest method
watch-clock       Show ticks of real-time clock
watch-net         Monitor network broadcast packets
watch-net-all     Monitor broadcast packets on all net interfaces
probe-scsi        Show attached SCSI devices
probe-scsi-all    Show attached SCSI devices for all host adapters
ok
```

PROM Full Device Names

OpenBoot deals directly with hardware devices in the system. Each device has a unique name representing both the type of device and the location of that device in the system addressing structure. The following example shows a full device pathname for a system with SBus architecture, such as a SPARCstation20:

```
/sbus@1f,0/esp@0,40000/sd@3,0:a
```

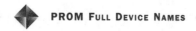

This example shows a full device pathname for a PCI bus system such as an Ultra5:

```
/pci@1f,0/pci@1,1/ide@3/disk
```

A full device pathname is a series of node names separated by slashes (/). The root of the tree is the machine node, which is not named explicitly but is indicated by a leading slash (/). Each device pathname has this form:

```
driver-name@unit-address:device-arguments
```

The components of the device pathname are described in Table 2-3.

Table 2-3 Device Pathname Parameters

Parameter	Description
driver-name	A human-readable string consisting of 1 to 31 letters, digits, and the following punctuation characters: , . _ + - Uppercase and lowercase characters are distinct. In some cases, the driver name includes the name of the device's manufacturer and the device's model name, separated by a comma. Typically, the manufacturer's uppercase, publicly listed stock symbol is used as the manufacturer's name (that is, SUNW,hme0). For built-in devices, the manufacturer's name is usually omitted (that is, sbus or pci). @ must precede the address parameter and serves as a separator between the driver name and unit address.
unit-address	A text string representing the physical address of the device in its parent's address space. The exact meaning of a particular address depends on the bus to which the device is attached. In this example: `/sbus@1f,0/esp@0,40000/sd@3,0:a` `1f,0` represents an address on the main system bus, because the SBus is directly attached to the main system bus in this example. `0,40000` is an SBus slot number. The example shows that the device is in SBus slot 0 and the offset is `40000`. `3,0` is a SCSI target and logical unit number. In the example, the disk device is attached to a SCSI bus at target 3, logical unit 0. See Appendix C, "Overview of SCSI Devices," for more information on SCSI host adapters, targets, and logical units.
device-arguments	A text string whose format depends on the particular device. It can be used to pass additional information to the device's software. In this example: `/sbus@1f,0/scsi@2,1/sd@3,0:a` The argument for the disk device is "a." The software driver for this device interprets its argument as a disk partition, so the device pathname refers to partition "a" on that disk.

The OpenBoot command show-devs is used to obtain information about devices and to display device pathnames. This command displays all the devices known to the system directly beneath a given device in the device hierarchy. show-devs used by itself shows the entire device tree. The syntax is

```
show-devs [device path]
```

Example:

```
ok show-devs
```

The system outputs the following information:

```
/TI,TMS390Z50@f,f8fffffc
/eccmemctl@f,0
/virtual-memory@0,0
/memory@0,0
/obio
/iommu@f,e0000000
/openprom
/aliases
/options
/packages
/obio/power@0,a01000
/obio/auxio@0,800000
/obio/SUNW,fdtwo@0,700000
/obio/interrupt@0,400000
/obio/counter@0,300000
/obio/eeprom@0,200000
/obio/zs@0,0
/obio/zs@0,100000
/iommu@f,e0000000/sbus@f,e0001000
/iommu@f,e0000000/sbus@f,e0001000/cgsix@2,0
/iommu@f,e0000000/sbus@f,e0001000/SUNW,DBRIe@f,8010000
/iommu@f,e0000000/sbus@f,e0001000/SUNW,bpp@f,4800000
/iommu@f,e0000000/sbus@f,e0001000/ledma@f,400010
/iommu@f,e0000000/sbus@f,e0001000/espdma@f,400000
/iommu@f,e0000000/sbus@f,e0001000/SUNW,DBRIe@f,8010000/mmcodec
/iommu@f,e0000000/sbus@f,e0001000/ledma@f,400010/le@f,c00000
/iommu@f,e0000000/sbus@f,e0001000/espdma@f,400000/esp@f,800000
/iommu@f,e0000000/sbus@f,e0001000/espdma@f,400000/esp@f,800000/st
/iommu@f,e0000000/sbus@f,e0001000/espdma@f,400000/esp@f,800000/sd
/packages/obp-tftp
/packages/deblocker
/packages/disk-label
```

Commands used to examine the device tree are listed in Table 2-4.

Table 2-4 Commands for Browsing the Device Tree

Command	Description
`.properties`	Displays the names and values of the current node's properties.
`dev device-path`	Chooses the specified device node, making it the current node.
`dev node-name`	Searches for a node with the specified name in the subtree below the current node and chooses the first such node found.
`dev ..`	Chooses the device node that is the parent of the current node.
`dev /`	Chooses the root machine node.
`device-end`	Leaves the device tree.
`"device-path" find-device`	Chooses the specified device node, similar to `dev`.
`ls`	Displays the names of the current node's children.
`pwd`	Displays the device pathname that names the current node.
`see wordname`	Decompiles the specified word.
`show-devs [device-path]`	Displays all the devices known to the system directly beneath a given device in the device hierarchy. `show-devs` used by itself shows the entire device tree.
`words`	Displays the names of the current node's methods.
`"device-path" select-dev`	Selects the specified device and makes it the active node.

OpenBoot Device Aliases

Device pathnames can be long and complex to enter. The concept of device aliases, like UNIX aliases, allows a short name to be substituted for a long name. An alias represents an entire device pathname, not a component of it. For example, the alias disk0 might represent the following device pathname:

```
/sbus@1,f8000000/esp@0,40000/sd@3,0:a
```

OpenBoot has the predefined device aliases listed in Table 2-5 for commonly used devices, so you rarely need to type a full device pathname.

Table 2-5 Predefined Device Aliases

Alias	Device Pathname
disk	/sbus@1,f8000000/esp@0,40000/sd@3,0:a
disk1	/sbus@1,f8000000/esp@0,40000/sd@1,0:a
disk2	/sbus@1,f8000000/esp@0,40000/sd@2,0:a
disk3	/sbus@1,f8000000/esp@0,40000/sd@3,0:a

If you add disk drives or change the target of the startup drive, you might need to modify these device aliases. Table 2-6 describes the `devalias` command, which is used to examine, create, and change OpenBoot aliases.

Table 2-6 *devalias*

Command	Description
devalias	Displays all current device aliases.
`devalias_alias`	Displays the device pathname corresponding to `alias`.
`devalias_alias device-path`	Defines an `alias` representing `device-path`.

NOTE. *If an alias with the same name already exists, the new value overwrites the old.*

The following example creates a device alias named disk3, which represents a SCSI disk with a target ID of 3 on a SPARCstation10 system:

```
devalias disk3 /iommu/sbus/espdma@f,400000/esp@f,800000/sd@3,0
```

To confirm the alias, type `devalias`, and the system will print all the aliases:

```
ok devalias
screen           /iommu@f,e0000000/sbus@f,e0001000/cgsix@2,0
disk5            /iommu/sbus/espdma@f,400000/esp@f,800000/sd@0,0
floppy           /obio/SUNW,fdtwo
scsi             /iommu/sbus/espdma@f,400000/esp@f,800000
net-aui          /iommu/sbus/ledma@f,400010:aui/le@f,c00000
net-tpe          /iommu/sbus/ledma@f,400010:tpe/le@f,c00000
net              /iommu/sbus/ledma@f,400010/le@f,c00000
disk             /iommu/sbus/espdma@f,400000/esp@f,800000/sd@3,0
cdrom            /iommu/sbus/espdma@f,400000/esp@f,800000/sd@6,0:d
tape             /iommu/sbus/espdma@f,400000/esp@f,800000/st@4,0
```

```
tape0          /iommu/sbus/espdma@f,400000/esp@f,800000/st@4,0
tape1          /iommu/sbus/espdma@f,400000/esp@f,800000/st@5,0
disk3          /iommu/sbus/espdma@f,400000/esp@f,800000/sd@3,0
disk2          /iommu/sbus/espdma@f,400000/esp@f,800000/sd@2,0
disk1          /iommu/sbus/espdma@f,400000/esp@f,800000/sd@1,0
disk0          /iommu/sbus/espdma@f,400000/esp@f,800000/sd@3,0
ttyb           /obio/zs@0,100000:b
ttya           /obio/zs@0,100000:a
keyboard!     /obio/zs@0,0:forcemode
keyboard      /obio/zs@0,0
```

User-defined aliases are lost after a system reset or power cycle unless you create a permanent alias. If you want to create permanent aliases, you can either manually store the `devalias` command in a portion of non-volatile RAM (NVRAM) called nvramrc or use the `nvalias` and `nvunalias` commands. The following section describes how to configure permanent settings in the NVRAM on a Sun system.

OpenBoot Non-Volatile RAM (NVRAM)

System configuration variables are stored in the system NVRAM. These OpenBoot variables determine the startup machine configuration and related communication characteristics. You can modify the values of the configuration variables, and any changes you make remain in effect, even after a power cycle. Configuration variables should be adjusted cautiously, however.

Table 2-7 describes OpenBoot's NVRAM configuration variables, their default values, and their functions.

Table 2-7 NVRAM Variables

Variable	Default	Description
`auto-boot?`	true	If true, start up automatically after power on or reset.
`boot-command`	boot	Command that is executed if `auto-boot?` is true.
`boot-device`	disk or net	Device from which to start up.
`boot-file`	Empty string	Arguments passed to the started program.
`diag-device`	net	Diagnostic startup source device.
`diag-file`	Empty string	Arguments passed to the startup program in diagnostic mode.
`diag-switch?`	false	If true, run in diagnostic mode.
`fcode-debug?`	false	If true, include name fields for plug-in device FCodes.
`input-device`	keyboard	Console input device (usually keyboard, ttya, or ttyb).

continues

Table 2-7 NVRAM Variables (continued)

Variable	Default	Description
nvramrc	Empty	Contents of NVRAMRC.
oem-banner	Empty string	Custom OEM banner (enabled by oem-banner? true).
oem-banner?	false	If true, use custom OEM banner.
oem-logo	No default	Byte array custom OEM logo (enabled by oem-logo? true). Displayed in hexadecimal.
oem-logo?	false	If true, use custom OEM logo (otherwise, use Sun logo).
output-device	screen	Console output device (usually screen, ttya, or ttyb).
sbus-probe-list	0123	Which SBus slots to probe and in what order.
screen-#columns	80	Number of on-screen columns (characters/line).
screen-#rows	34	Number of on-screen rows (lines).
security-#badlogins	No default	Number of incorrect security password attempts.
security-mode	none	Firmware security level (options: none, command, or full).
security-password	No default	Firmware security password (never displayed).
use-nvramrc?	false	If true, execute commands in NVRAMRC during system startup.

NOTE. *Older SPARC systems, because they use older versions of OpenBoot, might use different defaults and/or different configuration variables. As mentioned earlier, this text describes OpenBoot version 3.*

The NVRAM configuration variables can be viewed and changed using the commands listed in Table 2-8.

Table 2-8 Viewing or Modifying Configuration Variables

Command	Description
password	Sets the security password.
printenv	Displays the current value and the default value for each variable. To show the current value of a named variable, type printenv <parameter name>.
setenv variable value	Sets the variable to the given decimal or text value. Changes are permanent, but they often take effect only after a reset.

Table 2-8 Viewing or Modifying Configuration Variables (continued)

Command	Description
`set-default variable`	Resets the value of the variable to the factory default.
`set-defaults`	Resets variable values to the factory defaults.

The following examples illustrate the use of the commands described in Table 2-8.

All commands are entered at the `ok` OpenBoot prompt.

```
ok printenv
```

The system responds with this:

```
Parameter Name                  Value             Default Value

tpe-link-test?                  true              true
output-device                   screen            screen
input-device                    keyboard          keyboard
sbus-probe-list                 f0123             f0123
keyboard-click?                 false             false
keymap
ttyb-rts-dtr-off                false             false
ttyb-ignore-cd                  true              true
ttya-rts-dtr-off                false             false
ttya-ignore-cd                  true              true
ttyb-mode                       9600,8,n,1,-      9600,8,n,1,-
ttya-mode                       9600,8,n,1,-      9600,8,n,1,-
fcode-debug?                    false             false
diag-file
diag-device                     net               net
boot-file
boot-device                     disk5             disk
auto-boot?                      true              true
watchdog-reboot?                false             false
local-mac-address?              false             false
screen-#columns                 80                80
screen-#rows                    34                34
selftest-#megs                  1                 1
scsi-initiator-id               7                 7
use-nvramrc?                    true              false
nvramrc                         devalias          disk5 /iommu/sbus/espdma@f,400000/
➥esp@f,800000/sd@0,0
```

```
Parameter Name                    Value              Default Value

sunmon-compat?                    false              false
security-mode                     none               none
security-password
security-#badlogins               0                  <no default>
oem-logo                                             <no default>
oem-logo?                         false              false
oem-banner                                           <no default>
oem-banner?                       false              false
hardware-revision                                    <no default>
last-hardware-update                                 <no default>
testarea                          0                  0
mfg-switch?                       false              false
diag-switch?                      false              false
ok
```

To set the `auto-boot?` variable to false, type

```
ok setenv auto-boot? false
```

Verify the setting by typing

```
ok printenv auto-boot?
```

The system will respond with this:

```
auto-boot?     false     true
```

To reset the variable to its default setting, type

```
ok set-default auto-boot?
```

Verify the setting by typing

```
ok printenv auto-boot?
```

The system will respond with this:

```
auto-boot?     true     true
```

To reset all variables to their default settings, type

```
ok set-defaults
```

It's also possible to set these variables from the UNIX command line by issuing the `eeprom` command. You must be logged in as root to issue these commands. For example, to set the `auto-boot?` variable to true, type the following at the UNIX prompt:

```
eeprom auto-boot?=true
```

You can also view the OpenBoot configuration variables from a UNIX prompt by typing

```
/usr/sbin/eeprom
```

For example, to change the OpenBoot parameter `security-password` from the command line, use the following:

```
example# eeprom security-password=
Changing PROM password:
New password:
Retype new password:
```

CAUTION! *Setting the security mode and password can leave a system unable to boot if you forget the password. There is no way to break in without sending the CPU to Sun to have the PROM reset. OpenBoot security is discussed more in the next section.*

With no parameters, the `eeprom` command will display all the OpenBoot configuration settings, similar to the OpenBoot `printenv` command.

NOTE. *If you change an NVRAM setting on a SPARC system and the system will no longer start up, it is possible to reset the NVRAM variables to their default settings by holding down the Stop and N keys simultaneously while the machine is powering up. When issuing this command, hold down Stop+N immediately after turning on the power to the SPARC system; keep these keys pressed for a few seconds or until you see the banner (if the display is available). This is a good technique to force a system's NVRAM variables to a known condition.*

The NVRAM commands listed in Table 2-9 can be used to modify devaliases so that they remain permanent, even after a restart.

Table 2-9 NVRAM Commands

Command	Description
`nvalias alias device-path`	Stores the command devalias alias `device-path` in NVRAMRC. (The alias persists until the `nvunalias` or `set-defaults` commands are executed.) Turns on `use-nvramrc?`
`nvunalias alias`	Deletes the corresponding alias from NVRAMRC.

For example, to permanently create a devalias named disk3, which will represent a SCSI disk with a target ID of 3 on a SPARCstation10 system, type the following:

```
nvalias disk3 /iommu/sbus/espdma@f,400000/esp@f,800000/sd@3,0
```

OpenBoot Security

Anyone who has access to the computer keyboard can access OpenBoot and modify parameters unless you set up your security variables. These variables are listed in Table 2-10.

Table 2-10 OpenBoot Security Variables

Variable	Description
`security-mode`	Restricts the set of operations that users are allowed to perform at the OpenBoot prompt.
`security-password`	The firmware security password (it is never displayed). Do not set this variable directly. This variable is set using `password`.
`security-#badlogins`	The number of incorrect security password attempts.

CAUTION! *It is important to remember your security password and to set the security password before setting the security mode. If you forget this password, you cannot use your system; you must call your vendor's customer support service to make your machine bootable again.*

To set the security password, type the following at the `ok` prompt:

```
ok password
ok New password (only first 8 chars are used): <enter password>
ok Retype new password: <enter password>
```

To change the OpenBoot parameter `security-password` from the command line, use the following:

```
example# eeprom security-password=
Changing PROM password:
New password:
Retype new password:
```

CAUTION! *Setting the security mode and password can leave a system unable to boot if you forget the password. There is no way to break in without sending the CPU to Sun to have the PROM reset.*

The security password you assign must be between zero and eight characters. Any characters after the eighth are ignored. You do not have to reset the system; the security feature takes effect as soon as you type the command.

After assigning a password, you can set the security variables that best fit your environment.

`security-mode` is used to restrict the use of OpenBoot commands. When you assign one of the following three values, access to commands is protected by a password. The syntax for setting `security-mode` is

```
setenv security-mode <value>
```

The value that you enter for `security-mode` is one of the three values listed in Table 2-11.

Table 2-11 OpenBoot Security Values

Value	Description
`full`	All OpenBoot commands except `go` require a password. This security mode is the most restrictive.
`command`	All OpenBoot commands except `boot` and `go` require the password.
`none`	No password is required (default).

The following example sets the OpenBoot environment so that all commands except `boot` and `go` require a password:

```
setenv security-mode command
```

With `security-mode` set to `command`, a password is not required if you type the `boot` command by itself or the `go` command. Any other command will require a password, including the use of the `boot` command with an argument.

Here are examples of when a password might be required when `security-mode` is set to `command`:

`ok boot`	No password is required
`ok go`	No password is required
`ok boot vmunix`	A password is required

The system displays a password prompt as follows:

`Password:`	The password is not echoed as it is typed
`ok reset-all`	A password is required

The system displays a password prompt as follows:

`Password:`	The password is not echoed as it is typed

If you enter an incorrect security password, there will be a delay of about 10 seconds before the next startup prompt appears. The number of times that an incorrect security password can be typed is stored in the `security-#badlogins` variable. The syntax is as follows:

```
setenv security-#badlogins <variable>
```

For example, you can set the number of attempts to four with the following command:

```
setenv security-#badlogins 4
```

OpenBoot Diagnostics

Various hardware diagnostics can be run in OpenBoot. These can be used to troubleshoot hardware and network problems. These diagnostic commands are listed in Table 2-12.

Table 2-12 OpenBoot Diagnostics

Command	Description
`probe-scsi`	Identifies devices attached to a SCSI bus.
`test device-specifier`	Executes the specified device's self-test method. For example:
	`test floppy` tests the floppy drive (if installed).
	`test net` tests the network connection.
`test-all [device-specifier]`	Tests all devices that have a built-in self-test method below the specified device tree node. If `device-specifier` is absent, all devices beginning from the root node are tested.
`watch-clock`	Tests the clock function.
`watch-net`	Monitors the network connection.

The following examples use some of the diagnostic features of OpenBoot. The first example uses `probe-scsi` to identify all the SCSI devices attached to a particular SCSI bus. This command is useful for identifying SCSI target IDs that are already in use, or to check to make sure that all devices are connected and identified by the system.

```
ok probe-scsi
```

The system will respond with this:

```
Target 1
        Unit 0    Disk          SEAGATE ST1120N 833400093849
                                Copyright     1992 Seagate
                                All rights reserved 0000
Target 3
        Unit 0    Disk  MAXTOR LXT-213S SUN2074.20
```

TIP. *Use the* `probe-scsi` *command to obtain a free open SCSI target ID number before adding a tape unit, CD-ROM drive, disk drive, or any other SCSI peripheral. Only devices that are powered on will be located, so make sure that everything is turned on. Use this command after installing a SCSI device to ensure that it has been connected properly and that the system can see it. Also, use this command if you suspect a faulty cable or connection. If you have more than one SCSI bus, use the* `probe-scsi-all` *command.*

The next example tests the system video and performs various other tests:

```
ok test all
```

To test the diskette drive to determine whether it is functioning properly, put a formatted, high-density diskette into the drive and type

```
ok test floppy
```

The system should respond with this:

```
Testing floppy disk system. A formatted disk should be in the drive.
Test succeeded.
```

Type `eject-floppy` to remove the diskette.

Table 2-13 describes other OpenBoot commands that you can use to gather information about the system.

Table 2-13 System Information Commands

Command	Description
`banner`	Displays the power-on banner.
`show-sbus`	Displays a list of installed and probed SBus devices.
`.enet-addr`	Displays the current Ethernet address.
`.idprom`	Displays ID PROM contents, formatted.
`.traps`	Displays a list of SPARC trap types.
`.version`	Displays the version and date of the startup PROM.
`.speed`	Displays CPU and bus speeds.
`show-devs`	Displays all installed and probed devices.

The following example uses the `banner` command to display the CPU type, the installed RAM, the Ethernet address, the hostid, and the version and date of the startup PROM:

```
ok banner
```

The system responds with this:

```
SPARCstation 10 (1 X 390Z50), No Keyboard
ROM Rev. 2.10, 64 MB memory installed, Serial #3151780
Ethernet address 8:0:20:1a:c7:e3, Host ID: 723017a4
```

NOTE. *For Solaris 7 to work properly, your PROM release must be version 1.1 or higher. Use the* `banner` *command to find out the PROM release for your system.*

The next example uses the `.version` command to display the OpenBoot version and date of the startup PROM.

Type the following:

```
ok .version
```

The system responds with this:

```
Release 3.15 Version 2 created 1998/11/10 10:35
OBP 3.15.2 1998/11/10 10:35
POST 2.3.1 1998/08/07 16:33
```

The next example shows how to use the `.enet-addr` command to display the Ethernet address.

Type the following:

```
ok .enet-addr
```

The system responds with this:

```
8:0:20:1a:c7:e3
```

To display the CPU information, type

```
.speed
```

The system responds with this:

```
CPU  Speed : 270.00MHz
UPA  Speed : 090.00MHz
PCI  Bus A : 33Mhz
PCI  Bus B : 33Mhz
```

Input and Output Control

The *console* is used as the primary means of communication between OpenBoot and the user. The console consists of an input device used for receiving information supplied by the user and an output device used for sending information to the user. Typically, the console is either the combination of a text/graphics display device and a keyboard or an ASCII terminal connected to a serial port.

The configuration variables relating to the control of the console are listed in Table 2-14.

Table 2-14 Console Configuration Variables

Variable	Description
`input-device`	Console input device (usually keyboard, ttya, or ttyb).
`output-device`	Console output device (usually screen, ttya, or ttyb).
`screen-#columns`	Number of on-screen columns (the default is 80 characters per line).
`screen-#rows`	Number of on-screen rows (the default is 34 lines).

You can use these variables to assign the console's power-on defaults. These values do not take effect until after the next power cycle or system reset.

If you select `keyboard` for `input-device` and the device is not plugged in, input is accepted from the ttya port as a fallback device. If the system is powered on and the keyboard is not detected, the system will look to ttya—the serial port—for the system console.

The communication parameters on the serial port can be defined by setting the configuration variables for that port. These variables are shown in Table 2-15.

Table 2-15 Port Configuration Variables

Variable	Current Value	Default Value
`ttyb-rts-dtr-off`	false	false
`ttyb-ignore-cd`	true	true
`ttya-rts-dtr-off`	false	false
`ttya-ignore-cd`	true	true
`ttyb-mode`	9600,8,n,1,-	9600,8,n,1,-
`ttya-mode`	9600,8,n,1,-	9600,8,n,1,-

Here are the values for `ttya-mode` from left to right:

Baud rate: 110, 300, 1200, 4800, 9600, 19200

Data bits: 5, 6, 7, 8

Parity: n (none), e (even), o (odd), m (mark), s (space)

Stop bits: 1, 1.5, 2

Handshake: - (none), h (hardware: rts/cts), s (software: xon/xoff)

boot

The primary function of the OpenBoot firmware is to start up the system. Starting up is the process of loading and executing a stand-alone program. An example of a stand-alone program is the operating system or the diagnostic monitor. In this discussion, the stand-alone program is the operating system kernel. After the kernel is loaded, it starts the UNIX system, mounts the necessary file systems, and runs /sbin/init to bring the system to the "initdefault" state specified in /etc/inittab. This process was discussed in Chapter 1.

Starting up can be initiated either automatically or by typing a command at the user interface. It is commonly referred to as the bootstrap procedure. On most SPARC-based systems, the bootstrap procedure consists of the following basic phases:

1. The system hardware is powered on.
2. The system firmware (the PROM) executes a power-on self-test (POST). (The form and scope of these tests depends on the version of the firmware in your system.)
3. After the tests have been completed successfully, the firmware attempts to autoboot if the appropriate OpenBoot configuration variable (`auto-boot?`) has been set.

The OpenBoot startup process is shown here:

```
Boot device: disk:a  File and args:
SunOS Release 5.7 Version Generic 64-bit [UNIX(R) System V Release 4.0]
Copyright (c) 1983-1998, Sun Microsystems, Inc.
configuring network interfaces: hme0.
Hostname: ultra5
The system is coming up.  Please wait.
checking ufs filesystems
/dev/rdsk/c0t0d0s5: is clean.
/dev/rdsk/c0t0d0s4: is clean.
/dev/rdsk/c0t0d0s7: is clean.
/dev/rdsk/c0t0d0s3: is clean.
starting routing daemon.
starting rpc services:
keyserv done.
```

```
Setting default interface for multicast: add net 224.0.0.0: gateway ultra5
syslog service starting.
Print services started.
volume management starting.
Jun  1 06:33:05 ultra5
The system is ready.
ultra5 console login:
```

The startup process is controlled by a number of configuration variables. The ones that affect the startup process are described in Table 2-16.

Table 2-16 Boot Configuration Variables

Variable	Description
`auto-boot?`	Controls whether the system automatically starts up after a system reset or when the power is turned on. The default for this variable is true. When the system is powered on, the system automatically starts up to the default run level.
`boot-command`	Specifies the command to be executed when `auto-boot?` is true. The default value of `boot-command` is `boot` with no command-line arguments.
`diag-switch?`	If the value is true, run in the diagnostic mode. This variable is false by default.
`boot-device`	Contains the name of the default startup device that is used when OpenBoot is not in diagnostic mode.
`boot-file`	Contains the default startup arguments that are used when OpenBoot is not in diagnostic mode. The default is no arguments. (See Table 2-17 for details on when this variable is used.)
`diag-device`	Contains the name of the default diagnostic mode startup device. The default is `net`. (See Table 2-17 for details on when this variable is used.)
`diag-file`	Contains the default diagnostic mode startup arguments. The default is no arguments. (See Table 2-17 for details on when this variable is used.)

Typically, `auto-boot?` will be true, `boot-command` will be `boot`, and OpenBoot will not be in diagnostic mode. Consequently, the system will automatically load and execute the program and arguments described by `boot-file` from the device described by `boot-device` when the system is first turned on or following a system reset. The `boot` command and its options are described in Table 2-17.

`boot` has the following syntax:

```
boot [OBP name] [filename] [options] [flags]
```

`[OBP name]`, `[filename]`, `[options]`, and `[flags]` are optional.

Table 2-17 *boot* Command

Option	Description
OBP name	Specifies the OpenBoot PROM designations. For example, on Desktop SPARC-based systems, the designation /sbus/esp@0,800000/sd@3,0:a indicates a SCSI disk (sd) at target 3, lun0 on the SCSI bus, with the esp host adapter plugged into slot 0. This OBP name can be a devalias, such as disk0 (floppy 3 1/2-inch diskette drive), net (Ethernet), or tape (SCSI tape). If OBP name is not specified and diagnostic-mode? returns true, boot uses the device specified by the diag-device configuration variable.
filename	The name of the stand-alone program to be started up (for example, kernel/unix). The default is to start up /platform/platform-name/kernel/unix from the root partition. If specified, filename is relative to the root of the selected device and partition. If not, the boot program uses the value of the boot-file or diag-file based on the diag-switch? parameter.
options	-a The startup program interprets this flag to mean "Ask me," so it prompts for the name of the stand-alone program to load. -f When starting an Autoclient system, this option forces the boot program to bypass the client's local cache and read all files over the network from the client's file server. This option is ignored for all non-Autoclient systems. The -f option is then passed to the stand-alone program. -r Triggers device reconfiguration during startup. (This option is covered in Chapter 16, "Device Configuration and Naming.")
flags	The boot program passes all startup flags to filename. They are not interpreted by boot. (See the next section for information on the options available with the default stand-alone program, kernel/unix.)

If you want to start up the default program when auto-boot? is false, a few options are available for starting up the system from the ok prompt.

When you type

```
boot
```

the machine will start up from the default startup device using no startup arguments. This is set in the boot-device variable.

Type the following:

```
boot [OBP name]
```

When you specify an explicit OBP name, such as disk3, the machine will start up from the specified startup device using no startup arguments.

Here's an example:

```
boot disk3
```

The system will boot from the disk drive defined by the devalias named disk3. It will then load `kernel/unix` as the default stand-alone startup program.

Type

```
boot [options]
```

When you specify explicit options with the `boot` command, the machine will use the specified arguments to start up from the default startup device.

Here's an example:

```
boot -a
```

The system will then ask for the name of the stand-alone program to load. If you specify `kernel/unix`, which is the default, you will be prompted to enter the directory that contains the kernel modules. (See the next section for details on kernel modules.)

Type

```
boot [OBP name] [options]
```

When you specify the `boot` command with an explicit startup device and explicit arguments, the machine will start up from the specified device with the specified arguments.

Here's an example:

```
boot disk3 -a
```

This example will give the same prompts as the previous example, except that you are now specifying a different startup device. The system will start up the bootblock from the disk drive defined by the devalias named `disk3`.

During the startup process, OpenBoot performs the following tasks:

1. The firmware can reset the machine if a client program has been executed since the last reset. The client program is normally an operating system or an operating system's loader program, but `boot` can also be used to load and execute other kinds of programs, such as diagnostics. For example, if you have just issued the `test net` command, when you next type `boot`, the system will reset before starting up.

2. The boot program is loaded into memory using a protocol that depends on the type of the selected device. You can start up from disk, tape, floppy, or the network. A disk startup might read a fixed number of blocks from the beginning of the disk, whereas a tape startup might read a particular tape file.
3. The loaded boot program is executed. The behavior of the boot program can be further controlled by the `argument` string, if one was passed to the `boot` command on the command line.

The program loaded and executed by the startup process is a secondary boot program, the purpose of which is to load the stand-alone program. The second-level program is either `ufsboot`, when starting up from a disk, or `inetboot`, when starting up across the network.

If starting up from disk, the bootstrap process consists of two conceptually distinct phases: primary startup and secondary startup. The PROM assumes that the program for the primary startup (`bootblk`) is in the primary bootblock, which resides in blocks 1 to 15 of the startup device. The bootblock is created using the `installboot` command. The software installation process typically installs the bootblock for you, so you won't need to issue this command unless you're recovering a corrupted bootblock.

To install a bootblock on disk c0t3d0s0, type the following:

```
installboot /usr/platform/'uname -i'/lib/fs/ufs/bootblk /dev/rdsk/c0t3d0s0
```

You cannot see the bootblock. It resides in a protected area of the disk that cannot be viewed. The program in the bootblock area will load the secondary startup program, named `ufsboot`.

If when executing the `boot` command a filename was specified, this filename is the name of the stand-alone startup program to be loaded. If the pathname is relative (does not begin with a slash), `ufsboot` will look for the program in a platform-dependent search path. In other words, the relative path to the stand-alone program will be prefixed with */platform/platform-name*. *platform-name* will be specific to your hardware.

NOTE. *Use the* `uname -i` *command to determine your system's platform name. For example, on a SPARCstation10, the path will be /platform/SUNW,SPARCstation-10. Use the command* `uname -m` *to find the hardware-class-name of a system; for a SPARCstation10, the hardware-class-name will be sun4m. If you look in the /platform directory, you'll see that /platform/SUNW,SPARCstation-10 is merely a link to /platform/sun4m.*

On the other hand, if the path to *filename* is absolute, `boot` will use the specified path. The startup program then loads the stand-alone program and transfers control to it.

The following example shows how to specify the stand-alone startup program from the OpenBoot `ok` prompt:

```
ok boot disk5 kernel/unix -s
```

In the example, the PROM will look for the primary boot program (`bootblk`) on disk5 (/iommu/sbus/espdma@f,400000/esp@f,800000/sd@0,0). The primary startup program will then load `ufsboot`. This will load the stand-alone startup program named /platform/SUNW, SPARCstation-10/kernel/unix using the `-s` flag. Typical secondary startup programs, such as `kernel/unix`, accept arguments of the form `filename -flags` where `filename` is the path to the stand-alone program and `-flags` is a list of options to be passed to the stand-alone program. The example will start up the operating system kernel, which is described in the next section. The `-s` flag will instruct the kernel to start up in single-user mode.

Kernel

The secondary startup program, `ufsboot`, which was described in the preceding section, loads the operating system kernel. The platform-specific kernel used by `ufsboot` is named /platform/`uname -m`/kernel/unix.

The kernel initializes itself and begins loading modules, using `ufsboot` to read the files. After the kernel has loaded enough modules to mount the root file system, it unmaps the `ufsboot` program and continues, using its own resources. The kernel creates a user process and starts the `/sbin/init` process, which starts other processes by reading the /etc/inittab file. (The `/sbin/init` process is described in Chapter 1.)

The kernel is dynamically configured in Solaris 7. It consists of a small static core and many dynamically loadable kernel modules. A kernel module is a hardware or software component that is used to perform a specific task on the system. An example of a loadable kernel module is a device driver that is loaded when the device is accessed. Drivers, file systems, STREAMS modules, and other modules are loaded automatically as they are needed, either at startup or at runtime. After these modules are no longer in use, they can be unloaded. Modules are kept in memory until that memory is needed. The `modinfo` command provides information about the modules currently loaded on a system.

When the kernel is loading, it reads the /etc/system file where system configuration information is stored. This file modifies the kernel's treatment of loadable modules.

The following is an example of the default /etc/system file:

```
*ident    "@(#)system    1.18    97/06/27 SMI"   /* SVR4 1.5 */
*
* SYSTEM SPECIFICATION FILE
*
* moddir:
*
```

```
*Set the search path for modules. This has a format similar to the
*csh path variable. If the module isn't found in the first directory
*it tries the second and so on. The default is /kernel /usr/kernel
*
*Example:
*moddir: /kernel /usr/kernel /other/modules
* root device and root filesystem configuration:
*
*The following may be used to override the defaults provided by
*the boot program:
*
*rootfs:              Set the filesystem type of the root.
*
*rootdev:             Set the root device. This should be a fully
*                      expanded physical pathname. The default is the
*                      physical pathname of the device where the boot
*                      program resides. The physical pathname is
*                      highly platform and configuration dependent.
*
*Example:
*       rootfs:ufs
*       rootdev:/sbus@1,f8000000/esp@0,800000/sd@3,0:a
*
*(Swap device configuration should be specified in /etc/vfstab.)
* exclude:
*
*Modules appearing in the moddir path which are NOT to be loaded,
*even if referenced. Note that `exclude' accepts either a module name,
*or a filename which includes the directory.
*
*Examples:
*       exclude: win
*       exclude: sys/shmsys
* forceload:
*
*Cause these modules to be loaded at boot time, (just before mounting
*the root filesystem) rather than at first reference. Note that
*forceload expects a filename which includes the directory. Also
*note that loading a module does not necessarily imply that it will
*be installed.
*
*Example:
*      forceload: drv/foo
* set:
*
*Set an integer variable in the kernel or a module to a new value.
*This facility should be used with caution. See system(4).
*
*Examples:
*
```

```
*To set variables in 'unix':
*
*       set nautopush=32
* set maxusers=40
*
*To set a variable named 'debug' in the module named 'test_module'
*
*       set test_module:debug = 0x13
```

The /etc/system file contains commands of this form:

```
set parameter=value
```

For example, the setting for the kernel parameter MAXUSERS is set in the /etc/system file with the following line:

```
set maxusers = 40
```

Commands that affect loadable modules are of this form:

```
set module:variable=value
```

If a system administrator needs to change a tunable parameter in the /etc/system file, the `sysdef` command can be used to verify the change. `sysdef` lists all hardware devices, system devices, loadable modules, and the values of selected kernel-tunable parameters. The following is the output produced from the `sysdef` command:

```
*
* Hostid
*
  723017a4
*
* sun4m Configuration
*
*
* Devices
*
packages (driver not attached)
        disk-label (driver not attached)
        deblocker (driver not attached)
        obp-tftp (driver not attached)
options, instance #0
aliases (driver not attached)
openprom (driver not attached)
iommu, instance #0
                sbus, instance #0
                      espdma, instance #0
                               esp, instance #0
                                     sd (driver not attached)
                                     st (driver not attached)
                                     sd, instance #0
```

```
                                        sd, instance #1
                                        sd, instance #2 (driver not attached)
                                        sd, instance #3 (driver not attached)
                                        sd, instance #4 (driver not attached)
                                        sd, instance #5 (driver not attached)
                                        sd, instance #6 (driver not attached)
                      ledma, instance #0
                              le, instance #0
                      SUNW,bpp (driver not attached)
                      SUNW,DBRIe (driver not attached)
                               mmcodec (driver not attached)
                     cgsix, instance #0
    obio, instance #0
                    zs, instance #0
                    zs, instance #1
                    eeprom (driver not attached)
                    counter (driver not attached)
                    interrupt (driver not attached)
                    SUNW,fdtwo, instance #0
                    auxio (driver not attached)
                    power (driver not attached)
    memory (driver not attached)
    virtual-memory (driver not attached)
    eccmemctl (driver not attached)
    TI,TMS390Z50 (driver not attached)
    pseudo, instance #0
                    clone, instance #0
                    ip, instance #0
                    tcp, instance #0
                    udp, instance #0
                    icmp, instance #0
            arp, instance #0
            sad, instance #0
            consms, instance #0
            conskbd, instance #0
            wc, instance #0
            iwscn, instance #0
            ptsl, instance #0
            tl, instance #0
            cn, instance #0
            mm, instance #0
            md, instance #0
            openeepr, instance #0
            kstat, instance #0
            log, instance #0
            sy, instance #0
            pm, instance #0
            vol, instance #0
            llc1, instance #0
            ptm, instance #0
            pts, instance #0
            logindmux, instance #0
            ksyms, instance #0
```

```
*
* Loadable Objects
*
exec/aoutexec
exec/elfexec
exec/intpexec
fs/cachefs
fs/fifofs
fs/hsfs
fs/lofs
fs/nfs
                hard link: sys/nfs
fs/procfs
fs/sockfs
fs/specfs
fs/tmpfs
fs/ufs
fs/autofs
misc/consconfig
misc/des
misc/ipc
misc/klmmod
misc/klmops
misc/krtld
misc/nfs_dlboot
misc/nfssrv
misc/rpcsec
misc/rpcsec_gss
misc/scsi
misc/seg_drv
misc/seg_mapdev
misc/strplumb
misc/swapgeneric
misc/tlimod
misc/cis
misc/cs
misc/pcalloc
misc/pcmcia
misc/md_hotspares
misc/md_mirror
misc/md_notify
misc/md_raid
misc/md_stripe
misc/md_trans
sched/TS
sched/TS_DPTBL
strmod/bufmod
strmod/connld
strmod/dedump
strmod/ldterm
```

```
strmod/ms
strmod/pckt
strmod/pfmod
strmod/pipemod
strmod/ptem
strmod/redirmod
strmod/rpcmod
                hard link: sys/rpcmod
strmod/timod
strmod/tirdwr
strmod/ttcompat
strmod/hwc
strmod/bd
sys/c2audit
sys/doorfs
sys/inst_sync
sys/kaio
sys/msgsys
sys/pipe
sys/pset
sys/semsys
sys/shmsys
genunix
drv/arp
                hard link: strmod/arp
drv/arp
drv/be
drv/bpp
drv/clone
drv/clone
drv/cn
drv/cn
drv/conskbd
drv/conskbd
drv/consms
drv/consms
drv/esp
drv/icmp
drv/icmp
drv/ip
drv/ip
drv/isp
drv/iwscn
drv/iwscn
drv/le
drv/lebuffer
drv/llc1
drv/llc1
drv/log
drv/log
drv/mm
drv/mm
```

```
drv/openeepr
drv/openeepr
drv/options
drv/options
drv/pci_pci
drv/profile
drv/pseudo
drv/pseudo
drv/ptc
drv/ptc
drv/ptsl
drv/ptsl
drv/qe
drv/qec
drv/rts
drv/rts
drv/sad
drv/sad
drv/sd
drv/sd
drv/sp
drv/sp
drv/st
drv/st
drv/sy
drv/sy
drv/tcp
drv/tcp
drv/tl
drv/tl
drv/udp
drv/udp
drv/wc
drv/wc
drv/xbox
drv/fas
drv/hme
drv/socal
drv/pcic
drv/pcic
drv/pcs
drv/pem
drv/pem
drv/stp4020
drv/pcelx
drv/pcmem
drv/pcram
drv/pcram
drv/pcser
drv/pcata
drv/rtvc
drv/ses
```

```
drv/ses
drv/pln
drv/pln
drv/soc
drv/ssd
drv/ssd
drv/md
drv/md
*
* System Configuration
*
swap files
swapfile             dev  swaplo blocks   free
/dev/dsk/c0t0d0s3   32,3       8 205016 205016
*
* Tunable Parameters
*
 1298432               maximum memory allowed in buffer cache (bufhwm)
            986        maximum number of processes (v.v_proc)
             99        maximum global priority in sys class (MAXCLSYSPRI)
            981        maximum processes per user id (v.v_maxup)
             30        auto update time limit in seconds (NAUTOUP)
             25        page stealing low water mark (GPGSLO)
              5        fsflush run rate (FSFLUSHR)
             25        minimum resident memory for avoiding deadlock (MINARMEM)
             25        minimum swapable memory for avoiding deadlock (MINASMEM)
*
* Utsname Tunables
*
5.6  release (REL)
sparc4  node name (NODE)
SunOS  system name (SYS)
Generic_105181-03  version (VER)
*
* Process Resource Limit Tunables (Current:Maximum)
*
ffffffff:fffffffd          cpu time
ffffffff:fffffffd          file size
ffffffff:fffffffd          heap size
ffffffff:fffffffd          stack size
          0:7ffff000   core file size
ffffffff:fffffffd          file descriptors
          0:  800000   mapped memory
*
* Streams Tunables
*
          9   maximum number of pushes allowed (NSTRPUSH)
      65536   maximum stream message size (STRMSGSZ)
       1024   max size of ctl part of message (STRCTLSZ)
*
* IPC Messages
*
```

```
      0   entries in msg map (MSGMAP)
      0   max message size (MSGMAX)
      0   max bytes on queue (MSGMNB)
      0   message queue identifiers (MSGMNI)
      0   message segment size (MSGSSZ)
      0   system message headers (MSGTQL)
      0   message segments (MSGSEG)
*
* IPC Semaphores
*
     10   entries in semaphore map (SEMMAP)
     10   semaphore identifiers (SEMMNI)
     60   semaphores in system (SEMMNS)
     30   undo structures in system (SEMMNU)
     25   max semaphores per id (SEMMSL)
     10   max operations per semop call (SEMOPM)
     10   max undo entries per process (SEMUME)
  32767   semaphore maximum value (SEMVMX)
  16384   adjust on exit max value (SEMAEM)
*
* IPC Shared Memory
*
    1048576      max shared memory segment size (SHMMAX)
       1   min shared memory segment size (SHMMIN)
     100   shared memory identifiers (SHMMNI)
       6   max attached shm segments per process (SHMSEG)
*
* Time Sharing Scheduler Tunables
*
60      maximum time sharing user priority (TSMAXUPRI)
SYS     system class name (SYS_NAME)
```

The adb (absolute debugger) command can also be used to verify that a change was actually made after the system has been started up, but be careful using it.

CAUTION! adb *can change kernel parameters on a running system and could potentially crash your system if used improperly. Undertake the following procedures with caution. Improper entries in the /etc/system file or improper use of* adb *can result in a corrupted system, causing the system to crash or be unable to restart.*

If the kernel parameter you're looking for is not displayed with sysdef (for example, MAXUSERS), use adb. At the UNIX command prompt, when you're logged in as root, execute the following command:

```
adb -k /dev/ksyms  /dev/mem
```

/dev/ksyms is a special driver that provides an image of the kernel's symbol table. This can be used to examine the information in memory. `adb` will reply with the amount of physical memory (hex, in 4KB pages) as follows:

```
physmem 3dec
```

You will not receive a prompt after this, but `adb` is running and is ready for a command. To check a tunable parameter while in `adb`, use the following syntax:

`<parameter>/D`	Displays the integer parameter in decimal
`<parameter>/X`	Displays the integer parameter in hexadecimal

`<parameter>` is replaced with the kernel symbol being examined. For example:

```
maxusers/D
```

will display the MAXUSERS parameter in decimal notation as follows:

```
maxusers:      40
```

Type `shminfo_shmmax/D` to display the max shared memory segment size. The system responds with this:

```
shminfo_shmmax: 1048576
```

Exit `adb` by typing `$q` and pressing Enter.

Summary

Chapters 1 and 2 covered system startup, assuming that the OS was installed and configured. In the next chapter, I'll describe how to install the Solaris operating system from the OpenBoot PROM.

In this chapter I also discussed full device names. It's very important that you grasp how devices are named in Solaris. I'll revisit this topic in Chapter 16, where devices and device drivers are covered in depth.

CHAPTER

3

Installing the Solaris 7 Software

The following are the test objectives for this chapter:

- Preparing to install the Solaris 7 software
- Verifying the minimum Solaris 7 software system requirements
- Understanding Solaris software terminology
- Selecting a system configuration to install
- Understanding disk storage systems and partitions
- Understanding device drivers
- Understanding methods of installing the Solaris 7 software
- Installing Solaris 7

The Solaris installation process consists of three phases: system configuration, system installation, and post-installation tasks such as setting up printers, users, and networking. This chapter describes the various system configurations and the installation of the Solaris operating system on a workstation. Chapter 14, "Installing a Server," describes the installation process in more detail, especially on servers.

Requirements and Preparation for Installing the Solaris 7 Software

The first step in the installation is to determine whether your system type is supported under Solaris 7. Second, you'll need to decide which system configuration you want to install and whether you have enough disk space to support that configuration.

In preparation for installing Solaris 7 on a system, use Table 3-1 to check if your system type is supported. Also, make sure you have enough disk space for Solaris and all of the packages you plan to install. (The section on software terminology later in this chapter will help you estimate the amount of disk space required to hold the Solaris operating system.)

To determine your system type, use the `uname -m` command. The system will respond with the platform group and the platform name for your system. Compare the system response to the Platform Group column in Table 3-1. For example, to check for Sun platforms that support the Solaris 7 environment, use the command `uname -m`. On a Sun SPARCstation 10, the system returns `sun4m` as the platform name.

Table 3-1 Sun Platforms That Support the Solaris 7 Environment

System	Platform Name	Platform Group
x86-based	i86pc	i86pc
SPARCstation 1	SUNW, Sun_4_60	sun4c
SPARCstation 1+	SUNW, Sun_4_65	sun4c
SPARCstation SLC	SUNW, Sun_4_20	sun4c
SPARCstation ELC	SUNW, Sun_4_25	sun4c
SPARCstation IPC	SUNW, Sun_4_40	sun4c
SPARCstation IPX	SUNW, Sun_4_50	sun4c
SPARCstation 2	SUNW, Sun_4_75	sun4c

continues

Table 3-1 Sun Platforms That Support the Solaris 7 Environment (continued)

System	Platform Name	Platform Group
SPARCserver 1000	SUNW, SPARCserver-1000	sun4d
SPARCcenter 2000	SUNW, SPARCcenter-2000	sun4d
SPARCstation 5	SUNW, SPARCstation-5	sun4m
SPARCstation 10	SUNW, SPARCstation-10	sun4m
SPARCstation 10SX	SUNW, SPARCstation-10SX	sun4m
SPARCstation 20	SUNW, SPARCstation-20	sun4m
SPARCstation LX	SUNW, SPARCstation-LX	sun4m
SPARCstation LX+	SUNW, SPARCstation-LX+	sun4m
SPARCclassic	SUNW, SPARCclassic	sun4m
SPARCclassic X	SUNW, SPARCclassic-X	sun4m
SPARCstation Voyager	SUNW, S240	sun4m
SPARCstation 4	SUNW, SPARCstation-4	sun4m
Ultra 1 systems	SUNW, Ultra-1	sun4u
Ultra Enterprise 1 systems	SUNW, Ultra-1	sun4u
Ultra 30	SUNW, Ultra-30	sun4u
Ultra 2 systems	SUNW, Ultra-2	sun4u
Ultra Enterprise 2 systems	SUNW, Ultra-2	sun4u
Ultra Enterprise 150	SUNW, Ultra-1	sun4u
Ultra Enterprise 250	SUNW, Ultra-2	sun4u
Ultra 450	SUNW, Ultra-4	sun4u
Ultra Enterprise 450	SUNW, Ultra-4	sun4u
Ultra Enterprise 3000, 3500, 4000, 4500, 5000, 5500, 6000, 6500, 10000	SUNW, Ultra-Enterprise	sun4u
Ultra 5	SUNW, Ultra-5/10	sun4u

Table 3-1 Sun Platforms That Support the Solaris 7 Environment (continued)

System	Platform Name	Platform Group
Ultra 10	SUNW, Ultra-5/10	sun4u
Ultra 60	SUNW, Ultra-60	sun4u
Ultra 80	SUNW, Ultra-60	sun4u

NOTE. *Sun states that not all platforms and peripheral devices listed in this chapter are compatible. Contact your authorized Sun support provider for support information.*

Unsupported Frame Buffers

Frame buffers support the video on Sun systems much like a video card in a personal computer. The following frame buffers are not supported in the Solaris 7 release:

MG1 (bwtwo)

MG2 (bwtwo)

CG2 (cgtwo)

CG4 (cgfour)

TC (cgeight)

ZX (leo)

TZX (leo)

Unsupported Sun4c Architectures

The following sun4c architecture systems and servers based on these systems may no longer be supported in future releases of Solaris 7 beyond the 11/99 release:

SPARCstation SLC

SPARCstation ELC

SPARCstation IPC

SPARCstation IPX

SPARCstation 1

SPARCstation 1+

SPARCstation 2

SPARCstation Voyager

SPARC Xterminal 1

Check partition 2 by using the `format` command to determine whether your disk drive is large enough to load Solaris. As you might recall, partition 2 represents the entire disk. The `format` command is covered in detail in Chapter 4, "Introduction to File Systems."

Minimum System Requirements

The computer must meet the following requirements before you can install Solaris 7 using the interactive installation method:

- The system must have a minimum of 16MB of RAM; however, performance with minimum RAM will be poor. Sufficient memory requirements are determined by several factors, including the number of active users and applications you plan to run.
- The media is distributed on CD-ROM only, so a CD-ROM is required either locally or on the network.
- See the next section for Solaris disk space requirements. Also, add additional disk space to support your environment's swap space requirements.
- The Programmable Read-Only Memory (PROM) must be level 1.1 or later.

Software Terminology: Packages, Clusters, and Configuration Clusters

The Solaris operating system comes on a CD-ROM and is bundled in packages. Packages are grouped into clusters. The following sections describe the Solaris bundling scheme.

Software Package

A software package is a collection of files and directories in a defined format. It is a group of files and directories that describe a software application, such as manual pages and line printer support. Solaris 7 contains approximately 80 software packages that total approximately 900MB of disk space.

A Solaris software package is the standard way to deliver bundled and unbundled software. Packages are administered by using the package administration commands and are generally identified by a SUNW*xxx* naming convention.

Software Clusters and Configuration Clusters

Software packages are grouped into software clusters, which are logical collections of software packages. For example, the online manual pages cluster contains one package. Some clusters contain multiple packages, such as the JavaVM 1.0 cluster, which contains the Java JIT compiler, JavaVM demo programs, JavaVM developers package, JavaVM man pages, and JavaVM runtime environment.

Clusters are grouped into four configuration clusters to make the software installation process easier. During the installation process, you will be asked to install one of the four configuration clusters. These four configuration clusters are end-user support, developer system support, entire distribution, and entire distribution plus OEM system support.

- **End-user system support**—438MB (32-bit support) and 532MB (64-bit support). This configuration cluster contains the end-user software plus the following:
  - Windowing software
  - Common Desktop Environment (CDE)
  - OpenWindows
  - Motif runtime libraries
  - Energy-saving software (Power Management)
  - Basic networking support (`telnet`, `rlogin`, `ftp`)
  - Basic language and partial locale support
  - Removable media support (Volume Management)
  - Standard UNIX utilities (`sed`, `awk`, `nroff`, `troff`, `grep`, `pipes`, `ld`, `ldd`, `spell`)
  - Basic printer support (`lp`, `lpstat`, `lpr`)
  - System support for audio playback and recording
  - Java VM (the capability to run Java applications)
  - Patch utilities
  - Additional hardware support (PCMCIA)
- **Developer system support**—716MB (32-bit support) and 837MB (64-bit support). Contains the end-user software plus the following:
  - Development support
  - CDE/Motif Developer software, runtimes, and manuals
  - Java VM (the capability to develop Java applications)
  - OS demo code
  - Power Management GUI tools
  - Online manual pages
  - Solaris 1.x compatibility tools
  - Kernel probing support (TNF)

    - Extended language and partial locale support
    - Programming tools and libraries
    - Extended terminal support (`terminfo`)
    - Extended X support (XGL, XIL, XCU4)
    - Graphics header (for graphics application development)
    - ISO 8859 required fonts

- **Entire distribution**—787MB (32-bit support) and 895MB (64-bit support). Contains the end-user and developer software, plus the following:
    - AnswerBook2 (online documentation)
    - Full audio tools and demos
    - Enhanced security
    - UUCP networking (UNIX-to-UNIX copy)
    - DHCP server (Dynamic Host Configuration Protocol)
    - Additional language and partial locale support (Eastern European)
    - Additional hardware support (Leo, SX/CG14, SunVideo, SunButtons, SunDials, TCX)
    - Enhanced networking support (NIS server, point-to-point protocol)
    - Solstice Launcher
    - System recovery tools
    - Additional X features (complete fonts, PEX)
    - ISO 8559 optional fonts

- **Entire distribution plus OEM system support**—801MB (32-bit support) and 909MB (64-bit support). Contains the end-user, developer, and entire distribution software plus extended hardware support, which includes the following:
    - Voyager drivers and modules
    - sun4u (X server modules, VIS/XIL)
    - SunFastEthernet/FastWide SCSI adapter drivers
    - PCI drivers
    - M64 graphics accelerator
    - A-10 (PFU) and Fujitsu device drivers and system support

System Configuration to be Installed

Before installing the OS, you'll need to determine the system configuration to be installed. The configurations are defined by the way they access the root (/) and /usr file systems and the swap area. The system configurations are

- Server
- Clients, which include:
  - Diskless clients
  - JavaStation clients
  - Solstice AutoClients
  - Stand-alone systems

Server

A server system has the following file systems installed locally:

- The root (/) and /usr file systems, plus swap space
- The /export, /export/swap, and /export/home file systems, which support client systems and provide home directories for users
- The /opt directory or file system for storing application software

Servers can also contain the following software to support other systems:

- OS services for diskless clients and AutoClient systems
- Solaris CD image and boot software for networked systems to perform remote installations
- A JumpStart directory for networked systems to perform custom JumpStart installations

Client

A client is a system that uses remote services from a server. Some clients have limited disk storage capacity, or perhaps none at all, so they must rely on remote file systems from a server to function. Diskless clients, JavaStation clients, and Solstice AutoClients are examples of this type of client.

Other clients may use remote services (such as installation software) from a server, but they don't rely on a server to function. A stand-alone system, which has its own hard disk containing the root (/), /usr, and /export/home file systems and swap space, is a good example of this type of client.

Diskless Client

A diskless client is a system with no local disk. It is dependent on a server for all of its software and storage area. The OS is located on a server on the network. The diskless client boots from the server, remotely mounts its root (/), /usr, and /export/home file systems from a server, allocates swap space on the server, and gets all of its data from the server. Any files created are stored on the server.

A diskless client generates significant network traffic because of its need to continuously access the server for operating system functions and to access virtual memory space across the network. A diskless client cannot operate if it is detached from the network or if its server is not available.

JavaStation Client

The JavaStation is a client designed for zero administration. This client optimizes Java. The JavaStation client takes full advantage of the network to deliver everything from Java applications and services to complete, integrated system and network management. This type of client can create a lot of network traffic, so make sure your network has the needed capacity. The JavaStation has no local administration; booting, administration, and data storage are handled by servers via the network.

Solstice AutoClient

An AutoClient system is nearly identical to a diskless client, except that it caches all of its needed system software from a server. AutoClient systems use Solaris diskless and CacheFS technologies. CacheFS is a general-purpose file-system caching mechanism that improves performance and scalability by reducing server and network load. (See Chapter 18, "The NFS Environment," for a complete description of how CacheFS works.) An AutoClient system has the following characteristics:

- It requires a 100MB or larger local disk for swapping and caching. Its root (/) file system and the /usr file system are on a server somewhere on the network but are cached locally.
- It can be set up so that it can continue to access its cached root (/) and /usr file systems when the server is unavailable.
- It relies on servers to provide other file systems and software applications.
- It contains no permanent data, making it a field-replaceable unit (FRU).

An AutoClient system uses its local disk for swap space and to cache its individual root (/) file system and the /usr file system from a server's file systems. With the AutoClient configuration, administration is streamlined because the system administrator can maintain many AutoClient systems from a central location. Changes do not have to be made on individual systems. You must obtain a license for each AutoClient system you want to add to your network.

Table 3-2 gives a brief overview of each system configuration. It outlines which file systems are local and which are accessed over the network.

Table 3-2 System Configurations

System Type	Local File Systems	Local Swap	Remote File Systems
Server	root (/), /usr, /home, /opt/export, /export/home	Yes	Optional
JavaStation	None	No	/home
Diskless client	None	No	root (/), swap, /usr, /home
AutoClient	cached root (/), cached /usr	Yes	/var
Stand-alone	root (/), /usr, /export/home	Yes	Optional

Stand-Alone

On a stand-alone system, the OS is loaded on a local disk and the system is set to run independent of other systems for portions of the OS. It might be networked to other stand-alone systems. A networked stand-alone system can share information with other systems on the network, but it can function autonomously because it has its own hard disk with enough space to contain the root (/), /usr, and /home file systems and swap space. The stand-alone system has local access to operating system software, executables, virtual memory space, and user-created files. Sometimes the stand-alone will access the server for data or access a CD-ROM or tape drive from a server if one is not available locally.

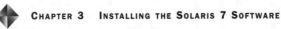

Performance of Clients Relative to a Stand-Alone System

A system administrator decides which system configuration to use based on available hardware and how much to streamline the administration of the network. For example, does the system have a large-enough local disk to hold all of the operating system? Also, would the features of the AutoClient, diskless, or JavaStation system configurations facilitate the administration of remote systems? For the most part, AutoClient configurations are used to ease system administration in a large network of systems. Because the OS is downloaded from a server at bootup, maintaining the workstation's OS from a centralized location is easy. Diskless clients, on the other hand, are used when disk space on the workstation is limited, but because swapping is done across the network, network bandwidth needs to be considered.

Looking at each system type from a performance and ease-of-management point of view, you see that the stand-alone system has the best performance but is the most difficult to administer. The diskless client is very easy to administer but has the poorest performance of the other client types.

The AutoClient system is also easy to administer and has better performance than the diskless client. With the cost of disk drives coming down and network bandwidth at a premium these days, this is usually a better alternative than the diskless client or even the JavaStation.

The JavaStation is the easiest to administer but requires more network bandwidth than the AutoClient. Also, the applications and services you plan to run must be Java-based.

Disk Storage Systems

Before you begin to install a system, you need to think about how you want data stored on your system's disks. With one disk, the decision is easy. When multiple disks are installed, you must decide which disks to use for the OS, the swap area, and the user data.

Solaris breaks disks into pieces called *partitions* or *slices*. A Solaris disk can be divided into a maximum of seven partitions.

Why would you want to divide the disk into multiple partitions? Some administrators don't; they use the entire disk with one partition. By using one partition, all of the space on the disk is available for anyone to use. When the system administrator creates a partition, the space in that partition is available only to the file system that is mounted on it. If another file system on the same disk runs out of space, it cannot borrow space from the other partition without repartitioning the disk. However, partitioning can provide some advantages. The following list describes some of the reasons why you might want to consider partitioning disks:

- Partitions allow finer control over such tasks as creating backups. UNIX commands, such as `ufsdump`, work on entire file systems. For backups, you might want to separate data and swap space from the application software so that backups are completed faster with a `ufsdump`. For example, you might want to back up only data on a daily basis. On the other hand, you'll need to take the system down to single-user mode to back up / and /usr, so separating the data will make your backup finish much faster and result in less downtime.

- If one file system gets corrupted, the others remain intact. If you need to perform a recovery operation, you can restore a smaller file system more quickly. Also, when data is separated from system software, you can modify file systems without shutting down the system or reloading operating system software.
- Partitions let you control the amount of disk storage allocated to an activity or type of use.
- If file systems are mounted remotely from other systems, you can share only the data that needs to be accessed, not the entire system disk.

The installation process gives you the option of creating partitions. Start with the default partition scheme supplied with the installation program. This scheme sets up the required partitions and provides you with the sizes required, based on the software cluster you select to install. The following is a typical partitioning scheme for a system with a single disk drive:

- **root (/) and /usr**—Solaris normally creates two partitions for itself: root (/) and /usr. The installation program determines how much space you need. Most of the files in these two partitions are static. Information in these file systems will not increase in size unless you add additional software packages later. If you plan to add third-party software after the installation of Solaris, make sure you increase this partition to accommodate the additional files you plan to load. If the root (/) file system fills up, the system will not operate properly.
- **swap**—This area on the disk doesn't have any files in it. In UNIX you're allowed to have more programs than will fit into memory. The pieces that aren't currently needed in memory are transferred into swap to free up physical memory for other active processes. Swapping into a dedicated partition is a good idea for two reasons: Swap partitions are isolated so that they don't get put on tape with the daily backups, and a swap partition can be laid out on a disk in an area to optimize performance.
- **/home**—On a single-disk system, everything not in root (/), /usr, or swap should go into a separate partition. /home is where you would put user-created files.
- **/var (optional)**—This area is used by Solaris for system log files, print spoolers, and email. The name /var is short for variable because this file system contains system files that are not static but are variable in size. One day the print spooler directory might be empty; another day it might contain several 1MB files. This separate file system is created to keep the root (/) and /usr file systems from filling up with these files. If the /var file system does not exist, make sure you make root (/) larger.

- **/opt (optional)**—By default, the Solaris installation program loads optional software packages here. Also, third-party applications are usually loaded into /opt. If this file system does not exist, the installation program puts the optional software in the root file system. If the /opt file system does not exist, make sure you make root (/) larger.

File systems provide a way to segregate data, but when a file system runs out of space, you can't increase it or "borrow" from a file system that has some unused space. Therefore, the best plan is to create a minimal number of file systems with adequate space for expansion. See Chapter 4 for additional information on planning and creating file systems.

Basic Considerations for Planning Partition Sizes

Planning disk and partition space depends on many factors: the number of users, application requirements, and the number and size of files and databases. Here are some basic considerations for determining your disk space requirements:

- Allocate additional disk space for each language selected (for example, Chinese, Japanese, Korean).
- If you need printing or mail support, create a partition for a separate /var file system and allocate additional disk space. You need to estimate the number and size of email messages and print files to size this partition properly.
- Allocate additional disk space on a server that will provide home file systems for users. Again, the number of users and the size of their files will dictate the size of this file system. By default, home directories are usually located in the /export file system.
- Allocate additional disk space on an OS server for diskless clients or Solstice AutoClient systems.
- Make sure you allocate enough swap space. Factors that dictate the amount of swap space are the number of users and application requirements. Consult with your application vendor for swap-space requirements. Usually vendors give you a formula for determining the amount of swap space you need for each application.
- Determine the software packages you will be installing, and calculate the total amount of disk space required. When planning disk space, remember that the Solaris Interactive Installation program lets you add or remove individual software packages from the software cluster you select.
- Create a minimum number of file systems. By default, the Solaris Interactive Installation program creates only root (/), /usr, and swap, although /export is also created when space is allocated for OS services. Creating a minimum number of file systems helps with future upgrades and file system expansion, because separate

file systems are limited by their slice boundaries. Be generous with the size of your file systems, especially root (/) and /usr. These file systems cannot be increased without completely reloading the operating system.

- Calculate additional disk space for copackaged or third-party software.

Partition Arrangements on Multiple Disks

Although a single large disk can hold all partitions and their corresponding file systems, two or more disks are often used to hold a system's partitions and file systems.

NOTE. *You cannot split a partition between two or more disks.*

For example, a single disk might hold the root (/) file system, a swap area, and the /usr file system, and a second disk might be used for the /export/home file system and other file systems containing user data. In a multiple-disk arrangement, the disk containing the root (/) and /usr file systems and swap space is referred to as the *system disk*. Disks other than the system disk are called *secondary disks* or *nonsystem disks*.

Locating a system's file systems on multiple disks lets you modify file systems and partitions on the secondary disks without shutting down the system or reloading the operating system software. Also, multiple disks let you distribute the workload as evenly as possible among different I/O systems and disk drives. They also let you distribute /home and swap directories evenly across disks.

Having more than one disk increases input/output (I/O) volume. By distributing the I/O load across multiple disks, you can avoid I/O bottlenecks.

NOTE. *A good way to improve system performance is to create more than one swap partition and assign each of them to separate disk drives. When the system needs to access swap, the disk I/O is spread across multiple drives.*

Device Drivers

A computer typically uses a wide range of peripheral and mass-storage devices, such as a SCSI disk drive, a keyboard, a mouse, and some kind of magnetic backup medium. Other commonly used devices include CD-ROM drives, printers, and plotters.

Solaris communicates with peripheral devices through *device files*. Before Solaris can communicate with a device, it must have a *device driver,* a low-level program that lets the kernel communicate with a specific piece of hardware. The driver serves as the operating system's "interpreter" for that piece of hardware.

When a system is booted for the first time, the kernel creates a device hierarchy to represent all devices connected to the system. Devices are described in three ways in the Solaris environment, using three distinct naming conventions: the physical device name, the instance name, and the logical device name. System administrators need to understand the device names when using commands to manage disks, file systems, and other devices.

Physical Device Name

A physical device name represents the full device pathname of the device. Physical device files are found in the /devices directory and have the following naming convention:

```
/devices/sbus@1,f8000000/esp@0,40000/sd@3,0:a
```

You can display physical device names by using one of the commands listed in Table 3-3.

Table 3-3 Displaying Physical Device Names

Command	Description
`prtconf`	Displays system configuration information, including the total amount of memory and the device configuration as described by the system's hierarchy. The output displayed by this command depends on the type of system.
`sysdef`	Displays device configuration information, including system hardware, pseudo devices, loadable modules, and selected kernel parameters.
`dmesg`	Displays system diagnostic messages and a list of devices attached to the system since the last reboot.

TIP. *Use the output of the* `prtconf` *and* `sysdef` *commands to identify which disk, tape, and CD-ROM devices are connected to the system. The output of these commands displays the* `driver not attached` *message next to the device instances. Because these devices are always being monitored by some system process, the* `driver not attached` *message is usually a good indication that there is physically no device at that device instance.*

If you need to remind yourself of the meanings of the fields of a physical device name, refer to Chapter 1, "System Startup," for a detailed discussion.

Instance Name

The instance name represents the kernel's abbreviated name for every possible device on the system. For example, `sd0` and `sd1` represent the instance names of two SCSI disk devices. Instance names are mapped in the /etc/path_to_inst file and are displayed by using the commands `dmesg`, `sysdef`, and `prtconf`.

Logical Device Name

Logical device names are used with most Solaris file system commands to refer to devices. Logical device files in the /dev directory are symbolically linked to physical device files in the /devices directory. Logical device names are used to access disk devices in the following circumstances:

- Adding a new disk to the system
- Moving a disk from one system to another
- Accessing (or mounting) a file system residing on a local disk
- Backing up a local file system
- Repairing a file system

Logical devices are organized in subdirectories under the /dev directory by their device types, as shown in Table 3-4.

Table 3-4 Device Locations

Directory	Device Type
/dev/dsk	Block interface to disk devices
/dev/rdsk	Raw or character interface to disk devices
/dev/rmt	Tape devices
/dev/term	Serial-line devices
/dev/cua	Dial-out modems
/dev/pts	Pseudo terminals
/dev/fbs	Frame buffers
/dev/sad	STREAMS administrative driver

Logical device files have major and minor numbers that indicate device drivers, hardware addresses, and other characteristics. Furthermore, a device filename must follow a specific naming convention. A logical device name for a disk drive has the following format:

```
/dev/[r]dsk/cxtxdxsx
```

The fields of the logical device name are described in Table 3-5.

Table 3-5 Disk Drive Logical Device Name

Field	Description
cx	Refers to the SCSI controller number
tx	Refers to the SCSI bus target number
dx	Refers to the disk number (always 0, except on storage arrays)
sx	Refers to the slice or partition number

Here are a few examples of logical device filenames for disk drives:

- `/dev/dsk/c0t3d0s0`—Refers to slice 0 on a SCSI disk drive with a target ID of 3 on SCSI controller 0. Buffered device.
- `/dev/rdsk/c0t3d0s0`—Refers to slice 0 on a SCSI disk drive with a target ID of 3 on SCSI controller 0. Raw device.

Block and Character Device Files

Some devices, such as disk drives, have an entry under both the /dev/dsk directory and the /dev/rdsk directory. The /dsk directory refers to the block or buffered device file, and the /rdsk directory refers to the character or raw device file. The "r" in rdsk stands for "raw." Disk and file administration commands require the use of either a raw device interface or a block device interface. The device file used specifies whether I/O is to be handled in block or character mode, commonly referred to as I/O type.

Block device files transfer data, using system buffers to speed up I/O transfer. Storage devices, such as tape drives, disk drives, and CD-ROMs, use block device files. Under most circumstances, Solaris accesses the disk via the block device. Data is buffered or cached in memory until the buffer is full, and then it is written to disk.

Character device interfaces transfer only small amounts of data, one character at a time. With a character device file, data is written directly to the disk, bypassing system I/O buffers. Buffering is controlled by the application program. Terminals, printers, plotters, and storage devices use character I/O.

Different commands require different device file interfaces. When a command requires the character device interface, specify the /dev/rdsk subdirectory. When a command requires the block device interface, specify the /dev/dsk subdirectory. When you're not sure whether a command requires the use of /dev/dsk or /dev/rdsk, check the online manual page for that command.

Methods of Installing the Solaris 7 Software

You can use one of four methods to install the Solaris software: Interactive, Custom JumpStart, Web Start, or installation over the network.

Interactive

The Solaris Interactive Installation program guides you step by step through installing the Solaris software. The Interactive program does not let you install all of the software (Solaris software and copackaged software) in your product box at once; it installs only the SunOS software. After you install the Solaris software, you have to install the other copackaged software by using the copackaged installation programs.

Custom JumpStart

This method, formerly called Auto-Install, allows you to automatically—and identically—install many systems with the same configuration without having to configure each of them individually. JumpStart requires up-front setup of configuration files before the systems can be installed, but it's the most cost-effective way to automatically install Solaris software for a large installation.

All new SPARC-based systems have the JumpStart software (a preinstalled boot image) preinstalled on their boot disk. JumpStart lets you install the Solaris software on a new SPARC-based system just by inserting the Solaris CD into the system and powering on the system. You can install the JumpStart software on existing systems by using the `re-preinstall` command.

NOTE. *On a new system shipped by Sun, the installation software is specified by a default profile that is based on the system's model and the size of its disks; you don't have a choice of the software that gets installed. Make sure this JumpStart configuration is suited to your environment. The system loads the end-user distribution group and sets up minimal swap space. Partitions and their sizes are set up by using default parameters that might not be suitable for the applications you plan to install.*

When might you want to use JumpStart? For example, suppose you need to install the Solaris software on 50 systems. Of these 50 systems to be installed, 25 are in engineering as stand-alone systems with the entire distribution configuration cluster, and 25 are in the IS group with the developer distribution configuration cluster. JumpStart lets you set up a configuration file for each department and install the OS identically on all the systems. The process facilitates the installation by automating it and ensures consistency between systems.

Web Start

Solaris Web Start is Sun's browser-based "virtual assistant" for installing software. Using Solaris Web Start and Sun's Web browser, you select either a default installation or a customize option to install only the software you want, including the Solaris configuration cluster, Solstice utilities, and other copackaged software. From Sun's Web browser, an installation profile is created that is used by Solaris JumpStart to install the Solaris software and the other selected software products with minimal intervention. Web Start simplifies the creation of the JumpStart configuration file.

Installing Over the Network

Because the Solaris software is distributed on a CD, a system has to have access to a CD-ROM drive to install it. However, if you don't have a local CD-ROM, you can set up the system to install from a remote CD or CD image on a remote disk drive. The remote Solaris CD image must be provided by an installation server that has either the Solaris CD copied to its hard disk or the Solaris CD mounted from its CD-ROM drive. Installing the OS across the network is handy when a local CD-ROM is not available.

The Solaris Installation Process

Solaris is installed by using the Solaris Install tool—a GUI that is friendly and easy to use. The installation brings up various menus and asks for your input. The tool lets you go back to previous screens if you make a mistake, and it doesn't actually do anything to your system until the installation program gets to the end and tells you it is about to start the loading process. During the installation, help is always available via the Help button.

CAUTION! *The following procedure reinstalls your operating system. This means it destroys all data on the target file systems.*

If you're upgrading or installing Solaris on a new system, use the following steps to shut down and then perform the installation:

1. Become root.
2. Issue the `shutdown` command. This command brings the system to a single-user state by halting the window system and leaving you with a single root prompt on the console. It takes about a minute.
3. Issue the `halt` command. This command puts you into the PROM. You'll know you're in the PROM when you receive either an `ok` or a `>` prompt.

4. Put the Solaris installation CD into the CD player and boot from the CD. The correct way to do this depends on your system type. If the screen displays the > prompt instead of the `ok` prompt, type `n` and press Enter.

5. At the `ok` prompt, type `boot cdrom`.

NOTE. *On Sun systems with older EEPROMs, the process of booting from CD is different. For your particular system, boot to the CD-ROM as follows:*
*For a Sun 4/1*nn, *4/2*nn, *4/3*nn, *or 4/4*nn *system, type* `b sd(0,30,1)`.
For a SPARCstation 1(4/60), 1+(4/65), SLC(4/20), or IPC(4/40) system, type `boot sd(0,6,2)`.

The system boots from the CD-ROM. The process is slow, but the flashing light on the CD player shows activity. Eventually the system starts the GUI and presents you with the Solaris Installation program. Follow the instructions on the screen to install the software on the system. Have the following information available, because the installation tool will ask for it:

- **Hostname**—The name for the system. Hostnames should be short, easy to spell, and lowercase, and they should have no more than 64 characters. If the system is on a network, the hostname should be unique.
- **IP address**—This information must come from your site IP coordinator. 192.9.200.1 is one example of an IP address. IP addresses must be unique for every system on your network. For a large site, or a site that has a presence on the Internet, you should apply for a unique IP address from the NIC to ensure that no other network shares your address.
- **NIS or NIS+**—You'll need to specify which your system will be using.

When the installation program is finished gathering information, it asks you if it's okay to begin the installation. When the installation is complete, you are asked to supply a root password. Make sure you complete this step and supply a secure password.

This completes the installation of the Solaris operating system.

Summary

This chapter described the fundamentals of installing a system. It addressed the topics and terms you'll need to know when taking the first Solaris certified system administrator exam. Other chapters in this book discuss the various installation procedures, such as JumpStart, Web Start, and installing a server, in more detail in order to prepare you for taking the second exam. Subsequent chapters also discuss post-installation procedures such as setting up print queues, adding users, and setting up a backup procedure.

CHAPTER

4

Introduction to File Systems

The following are the test objectives for this chapter:

- Defining and understanding the Solaris 7 file system types, structure, parameters, and utilities
- Understanding disk geometry
- Understanding disk slicing
- Comparing the Logical Volume Manager to standard Solaris file systems
- Managing and controlling disk space use
- Understanding custom file system parameters (identifying utilities used to create, check, mount, and display file systems)

This chapter introduces you to Solaris file systems and provides some of the fundamental concepts you'll need for the first exam. After reading this chapter, you'll understand the fundamentals of disk drives and their geometry. You'll also understand how Solaris uses a disk for file storage through its file systems. Finally, you'll understand how to manage Solaris file systems and control disk space usage. The next chapter provides more details on constructing and tuning Solaris file systems.

NOTE. *A few topics covered in this chapter are required for the second exam, but are more appropriate in this chapter. A notation will be made when a particular topic is an objective for the second exam.*

A File System Defined

A *file system* is a structure of directories used to organize and store files on disk. It is a collection of files and directories stored on disk in a standard UNIX file system format. All disk-based computer systems have a file system. In UNIX, file systems have two basic components: files and directories. A *file* is the actual information as it is stored on the disk, and a *directory* is a listing of the filenames. In addition to keeping track of filenames, the file system must also keep track of files' access dates and ownership. Managing the UNIX file systems is one of the system administrator's most important tasks. Administration of the file system involves the following:

- Ensuring that users have access to data. This means that systems are up and operational, file permissions are set up properly, and data is accessible.
- Protecting file systems against file corruption and hardware failures. This is accomplished by checking the file system regularly and maintaining proper system backups.
- Securing file systems against unauthorized access. Only authorized users should have access to them. The data must be protected from intruders.
- Providing users with adequate space for their files.
- Keeping the file system clean. In other words, data in the file system must be relevant and not wasteful of disk space. Procedures are needed to make sure that users follow proper naming conventions and that data is stored in an organized manner.

You'll see the term "file system" used in several ways. Usually, "file system" describes a particular type of file system (disk-based, network-based, or virtual file system). It might also describe the entire file tree from the root directory downward. In another context, the term "file system" might be used to describe the structure of a disk slice, described later in this chapter.

The Solaris system software uses the virtual file system (VFS) architecture, which provides a standard interface for different file system types. The VFS architecture lets the kernel handle basic operations, such as reading, writing, and listing files, without requiring the user or program to know about the underlying file system type. Furthermore, Solaris provides file system administrative commands that let you maintain file systems.

Defining a Disk's Geometry

Before creating a file system on a disk, you need to understand the basic geometry of a disk drive. Disks come in many shapes and sizes. The number of heads, tracks, and sectors and the disk capacity vary from one model to another.

A hard disk consists of several separate disk platters mounted on a common spindle. Data stored on each platter surface is written and read by disk heads. The circular path a disk head traces over a spinning disk platter is called a *track*.

Each track is made up of a number of *sectors* laid end to end. A sector consists of a header, a trailer, and 512 bytes of data. The header and trailer contain error-checking information to help ensure the accuracy of the data. Taken together, the set of tracks traced across all of the individual disk platter surfaces for a single position of the heads is called a *cylinder*.

Disk Controller

Associated with every disk is a controller, an intelligent device responsible for organizing data on the disk. Some disk controllers are located on a separate circuit board (such as SCSI) and some are embedded in the disk drive (such as IDE/EIDE).

Defect List

Disks might contain areas where data cannot be written and retrieved reliably. These areas are called *defects*. The controller uses the error-checking information in each disk block's trailer to determine whether a defect is present in that block. When a block is found to be defective, the controller can be instructed to add it to a defect list and avoid using that block in the future. The last two cylinders of a disk are set aside for diagnostic use and for storing the disk defect list.

Disk Label

A special area of every disk is set aside for storing information about the disk's controller, geometry, and slices. This information is called the disk's label or Volume Table of Contents (VTOC).

To label a disk means to write slice information onto the disk. You usually label a disk after defining its slices. If you fail to label a disk after creating slices, the slices will be unavailable because the operating system has no way of knowing about them.

Partition Table

An important part of the disk label is the partition table, which identifies a disk's slices, the slice boundaries (in cylinders), and the total size of the slices. A disk's partition table can be displayed by using the `format` utility.

Solaris File System Types

Solaris file systems can be put into three categories: disk-based, network-based, and virtual.

Disk-Based File Systems

Disk-based file systems reside on the system's local disk. Here are the three types of disk-based file systems:

- **UFS**—The UNIX file system, which is based on the BSD FAT Fast file system (the traditional UNIX file system). The UFS file system is the default disk-based file system used in Solaris.
- **HSFS**—The High Sierra and ISO 9660 file system. The HSFS file system is used on CD-ROMs and is a read-only file system.
- **PCFS**—The PC file system, which allows read/write access to data and programs on DOS-formatted disks written for DOS-based personal computers.

Network-Based File Systems

Network-based file systems are file systems accessed over the network. Typically, they reside on one system and are accessed by other systems across the network.

The Network File System (NFS) or remote file systems are file systems made available from remote systems. NFS is the only available network-based file system. (NFS is discussed in detail in Chapter 18, "The NFS Environment," and is covered on the second exam.)

Virtual File Systems

Virtual file systems are virtual or memory-based file systems that create duplicate paths to other disk-based file systems or provide access to special kernel information and facilities. Most virtual file systems do not use file system disk space, although a few exceptions exist. Cache file systems, for example, use a file system to contain the cache.

Some virtual file systems, such as the temporary file system, might use the swap space on a physical disk. The following is a list of some of the more common types of virtual file systems:

- **SWAPFS**—A file system used by the kernel for swapping. Swap space is used as a virtual memory storage area when the system does not have enough physical memory to handle current processes.
- **PROCFS**—The Process File System resides in memory. It contains a list of active processes, by process number, in the /proc directory. Information in the /proc directory is used by commands such as `ps`. Debuggers and other development tools can also access the processes' address space by using file system calls.
- **LOFS**—The Loopback File System lets you create a new virtual file system. You can access files by using an alternative path name. The entire file system hierarchy looks as though it is duplicated under /tmp/newroot, including any file systems mounted from NFS servers. All files are accessible with a pathname starting from either / or /tmp/newroot.
- **CacheFS**—The Cache File System lets you use disk drives on local workstations to store frequently used data from a remote file system or CD-ROM. The data stored on the local disk is the cache. (CacheFS is discussed in detail in Chapter 18, and is covered on the second exam.)
- **TMPFS**—The temporary file system uses local memory for file system reads and writes. Because TMPFS uses physical memory and not the disk, access to files in a TMPFS file system is typically much faster than to files in a UFS file system. Files in the temporary file system are not permanent; they are deleted when the file system is unmounted and when the system is shut down or rebooted. TMPFS is the default file system type for the /tmp directory in the SunOS system software. You can copy or move files into or out of the /tmp directory just as you would in a UFS /tmp file system. When memory is insufficient to hold everything in the temporary file system, the TMPFS file system uses swap space as a temporary backing store as long as adequate swap space is present.

Disk Slices

Disks are divided into regions called disk *slices* or disk *partitions*. A slice is composed of a single range of contiguous blocks. It is a physical subset of the disk (except for slice 2, which represents the entire disk). A UNIX file system is built within these disk slices. The boundaries of a disk slice are defined when a disk is formatted by using the Solaris `format` utility, and the slice information for a particular disk can be viewed by using the `prtvtoc` command. Each disk slice appears to the operating system (and to the system administrator) as though it were a separate disk drive.

NOTE: *Solaris device names use the term "slice" (and the letter 's' in the device name) to refer to the slice number. Slices were called "partitions" in SunOS 4.x. This book attempts to use the term "slice" whenever possible; however, certain interfaces, such as the* `format` *and* `prtvtoc` *commands, refer to slices as partitions.*

A physical disk consists of a stack of circular platters. Data is stored on these platters in a cylindrical pattern. Cylinders can be grouped and isolated from one another. A group of cylinders is referred to as a *slice*. A slice is defined with start and end points, defined from the center of the stack of platters, which is called the *spindle*.

To define a slice, the administrator provides a starting cylinder and an ending cylinder. A disk can have up to eight slices, named 0 to 7, but it is not a common practice to use partition 2 as a file system. (See Chapter 3, "Installing the Solaris 7 Software," for a discussion of disk-storage systems and sizing partitions.)

NOTE. *Sometimes a relational database uses an entire disk and requires one single raw partition. It's convenient in this circumstance to use slice 2, because it represents the entire disk.*

When setting up slices, remember these rules:

- Each disk slice holds only one file system.
- No file system can span multiple slices.
- After a file system is created, its size cannot be increased or decreased without repartitioning the entire disk and restoring all data from a backup.
- Slices cannot span multiple disks; however, multiple swap slices on separate disks are allowed.

When I discuss logical volumes in the next chapter, I'll describe how to get around some of these limitations in file systems.

Also follow these guidelines when planning the layout of file systems:

- Distribute the workload as evenly as possible among different I/O systems and disk drives. Distribute /home and swap directories evenly across disks. A single disk has limitations on how quickly data can be transferred. By spreading this load across more than one disk, you can improve performance exponentially.
- Keep projects or groups within the same file system. This allows you to keep better track of data for backups, recovery, and security reasons. Some disks might have better performance than others do.
- Use the faster drives for file systems that need quick access and the slower drives for data that might not need to be retrieved as quickly.

- Use as few file systems per disk as possible. On the system (or boot) disk, you usually have three slices: /, /usr, and a swap area. On other disks, create one or (at most) two slices. Fewer, roomier slices cause less file fragmentation than many small, overcrowded slices. Higher-capacity tape drives and the capability of `ufsdump` to handle multiple volumes facilitate backing up larger file systems.
- It is not important for most sites to be concerned about keeping similar types of user files in the same file system.
- Occasionally, you might have some users who consistently create very small or very large files. You might consider creating a separate file system with more inodes for users who consistently create very small files. (See the sections on inodes and changing the number of bytes per inode later in this chapter.)

Displaying Disk Configuration Information

As described earlier, disk configuration information is stored in the disk label. If you know the disk and slice number, you can display information for a disk by using the print volume table of contents (`prtvtoc`) command. You can specify the volume by specifying any nonzero-size slice defined on the disk (for example, /dev/rdsk/c0t3d0s2 for all of disk 3 or /dev/rdsk/c0t3d0s5 for just the sixth slice). If you know the target number of the disk but do not know how it is divided into slices, you can show information for the entire disk by specifying either slice 2 or slice 0. The following steps show how you can examine information stored on a disk's label by using the `prtvtoc` command:

1. Become superuser.
2. Type `prtvtoc /dev/rdsk/`*`cntndnsn`* and press Enter.

Information for the disk and slice you specify is displayed. In the following steps, information is displayed for all of disk 3:

1. Become superuser.
2. Type `prtvtoc /dev/rdsk/c0t3d0s2` and press Enter.

   The system responds with this:

```
* /dev/rdsk/c0t3d0s2 (volume "") partition map
*
* Dimensions:
*      512 bytes/sector
*       36 sectors/track
*        9 tracks/cylinder
*      324 sectors/cylinder
*     1272 cylinders
*     1254 accessible cylinders
*
```

```
* Flags:
*   1: unmountable
*  10: read-only
*
*                                 First    Sector   Last
* Partition  Tag      Flags      Sector   Count    Sector   Mount Directory
  2          5         01        0        406296   406295
  6          4         00        0        242352   242351
  7          0         00        242352   163944   406295   /files7
```

The `prtvtoc` command shows the number of cylinders and heads, as well as how the disk's slices are arranged.

Using the *format* Utility to Create Slices

Before you can create a file system on a disk, the disk must be formatted, and you must divide it into slices by using the Solaris `format` utility. Formatting involves two separate processes:

- Writing format information to the disk
- Completing a surface analysis, which compiles an up-to-date list of disk defects

When a disk is formatted, header and trailer information is superimposed on the disk. When the `format` utility runs a surface analysis, the controller scans the disk for defects. It should be noted that defects and formatting information reduce the total disk space available for data. This is why a new disk usually holds only 90 to 95 percent of its capacity after formatting. This percentage varies according to disk geometry and decreases as the disk ages and develops more defects.

The need to perform a surface analysis on a disk drive has dropped as more manufacturers ship their disk drives formatted and partitioned. You should not need to use the `format` utility when adding a disk drive to an existing system unless you think disk defects are causing problems. The only other reason you should need to use `format` is if you want to change the partitioning scheme.

CAUTION! *Formatting and creating slices is a destructive process, so make sure user data is backed up before you start.*

The `format` utility searches your system for all attached disk drives and reports the following information about the disk drives it finds:

- Target location
- Disk geometry

- Whether the disk is formatted
- Whether the disk has mounted partitions

In addition, the `format` utility is used in disk repair operations to do the following:

- Retrieve disk labels
- Repair defective sectors
- Format and analyze disks
- Partition disks
- Label disks (write the disk name and configuration information to the disk for future retrieval)

The Solaris installation program partitions and labels disk drives as part of installing the Solaris release. However, you might need to use the `format` utility when

- Displaying slice information
- Dividing a disk into slices
- Formatting a disk drive when you think disk defects are causing problems
- Repairing a disk drive

The main reason a system administrator uses the `format` utility is to divide a disk into disk slices. The process of creating slices is as follows:

1. Become superuser.
2. Type `format`.

   The system responds with this:

   ```
   AVAILABLE DISK SELECTIONS:
   0. c0t0d0 at scsibus0 slave 24
   sd0: <SUN0207 cyl 1254 alt 2 hd 9 sec 36>
    . c0t3d0 at scsibus0 slave 0: test
   sd3: <SUN0207 cyl 1254 alt 2 hd 9 sec 36>
   ```

3. Specify the disk (enter its number).

   The system responds with this:

   ```
   FORMAT MENU:
       disk - select a disk
       type - select (define) a disk type
       partition - select (define) a partition table
       current - describe the current disk
       format - format and analyze the disk
   ```

```
repair - repair a defective sector
label - write label to the disk
analyze - surface analysis
defect - defect list management
backup - search for backup labels
verify - read and display labels
save - save new disk/partition definitions
inquiry - show vendor, product and revision
volname - set 8-character volume name
!<cmd> - execute <cmd>, then return
quit
```

4. Type `partition` at the format prompt. The partition menu is displayed.

NOTE: *It is not necessary to type the entire command. After you type the first two characters of a command, the* `format` *utility will recognize the entire command.*

```
format> partition

PARTITION MENU:
    0 - change '0' partition
    1 - change '1' partition
    2 - change '2' partition
    3 - change '3' partition
    4 - change '4' partition
    5 - change '5' partition
    6 - change '6' partition
    7 - change '7' partition
    select - select a predefined table
    modify - modify a predefined partition table
    name - name the current table
    print - display the current table
    label - write partition map and label to the disk
    !<cmd> - execute <cmd>, then return
    quit
```

5. Type `print` to display the current partition map.

   The system responds with this:

```
partition> print
Current partition table (original):
Total disk cylinders available: 2733 + 2 (reserved cylinders)

Part  Tag         Flag   Cylinders    Size      Blocks
  0   root        wm     0 -  202     150.66MB  (203/0/0)   308560
  1   swap        wu     203 -  332   96.48MB   (130/0/0)   197600
  2   backup      wm     0 - 2732     1.98GB    (2733/0/0) 4154160
  3   unassigned  wm     333 -  390   43.05MB   (58/0/0)     88160
  4   unassigned  wm     391 -  443   39.34MB   (53/0/0)     80560
```

```
5    unassigned     wm       444 -  801    265.70MB   (358/0/0)    544160
6    usr             wm       802 - 2182    1.00GB     (1381/0/0) 2099120
7    home            wm       2183 - 2732  408.20MB   (550/0/0)    836000
```

6. After you partition the disk, you must label it by typing `label` at the partition prompt:

```
partition> label
```

7. After labeling the disk, type `quit` to exit the partition menu:

```
partition> quit
```

8. Type `quit` again to exit the format utility:

```
format> quit
```

Logical Volumes

On a large server with many disk drives, standard methods of disk slicing are inadequate and inefficient. Limitations imposed by standard disk slices include the slices' inability to be larger than the file system that holds them. Because file systems cannot span multiple disks, the size of the file system is limited to the size of the disk. Another problem with standard file systems is that they cannot be increased in size without destroying data on the file system.

Sun has addressed these issues with two unbundled Sun packages: Solstice DiskSuite and Sun Enterprise Volume Manager. Both packages allow file systems to span multiple disks and provide for improved I/O and reliability compared to the standard Solaris file system. We refer to these types of file systems as logical volumes (LVMs).

Solstice DiskSuite comes with the server version of Solaris. The Enterprise Volume Manager is purchased separately and is not part of the standard Solaris operating system distribution. Typically, DiskSuite is used on Sun's multipacks, and the Enterprise Volume Manager package is used on the SparcStorage arrays. (LVMs, DiskSuite, and Enterprise Volume Manager are discussed in detail in Chapter 16, "Device Configuration and Naming," and are covered on the second exam.)

Parts of a UFS File System

UFS is the default disk-based file system used in the Solaris system software. It provides the following features:

- **State flags**—Shows the state of the file system as clean, stable, active, or unknown. These flags eliminate unnecessary file system checks. If the file system is "clean" or "stable," `fsck` (file system check) is not run when the system boots.

- **Extended fundamental types (EFT)**—32-bit user ID (UID), group ID (GID), and device numbers.
- **Large file systems**—A UFS file system can be as large as 1 terabyte (1TB) and can have regular files up to 2 gigabytes (2GB). By default, the Solaris system software does not provide striping, which is required to make a logical slice large enough for a 1TB file system. Optional software packages, such as Solstice DiskSuite, provide this capability.

During the installation of the Solaris software, several UFS file systems are created on the system disk. These are Sun's default file systems. Their contents are described in Table 4-1.

Table 4-1 Solaris Default File Systems

Slice	File System	Description
0	root	Root (/) is the top of the hierarchical file tree. It holds files and directories that make up the operating system. The root directory contains the directories and files critical for system operation, such as the kernel, the device drivers, and the programs used to boot the system. It also contains the mount point directories, in which local and remote file systems can be attached to the file tree. The root (/) file system is always in slice 0.
1	swap	Provides virtual memory or swap space. Swap space is used when you're running programs too large to fit in the computer's memory. The Solaris operating environment then "swaps" programs from memory to the disk and back, as needed. Although it is not technically required, it is common for the swap slice to be located in slice 1 unless /var is set up as a file system. If /var is set up, it uses slice 1, and swap is usually put on slice 4. The /var file system is for files and directories likely to change or grow over the life of the local system. These include system logs, vi and ex backup files, printer spool files, and uucp files. On a server, a good idea is to have these files in a separate file system.
2	Entire Disk	Refers to the entire disk and is defined automatically by Sun's `format` utility and the Solaris installation programs. The size of this slice should not be changed.
3	/export	Holds alternative versions of the operating system. These alternative versions are required by client systems whose architectures differ from that of the server. Clients with the same architecture type as the server obtain executables from the /usr file system, usually slice 6. /export is also where user home directories or file systems are located that will be shared across the network. This is discussed in more detail in Chapter 18.
4	/export/swap	Provides virtual memory space for diskless client systems if the system is set up for client support.
5	/opt	Holds additional Sun software packages such as AdminSuite and optional third-party software that has been added to a system. If a slice is not allocated for this file system during installation, the /opt directory is put in slice 0.

continues

Table 4-1 Solaris Default File Systems (continued)

Slice	File System	Description
6	/usr	Holds operating system commands—also known as executables—designed to be run by users. This slice also holds documentation, system programs (`init` and `syslogd`, for example), and library routines. The /usr file system also includes system files and directories that can be shared with other users. Files that can be used on all types of systems (such as man pages) are in /usr/share.
7	/home	Holds files created by users (also named /export/home).

You need to create (or re-create) a UFS file system only when you

- Add or replace disks
- Change the slices of an existing disk
- Do a full restore on a file system
- Change the parameters of a file system, such as block size or free space

When you create a UFS file system, the disk slice is divided into cylinder groups. The slice is then divided into blocks to control and organize the structure of the files within the cylinder group. A UFS file system has the following four types of blocks. Each performs a specific function in the file system:

- **Boot block**—Stores information used when booting the system.
- **Superblock**—Stores much of the information about the file system.
- **Inode**—Stores all information about a file except its name.
- **Storage or data block**—Stores data for each file.

The Boot Block

The boot block stores the procedures used in booting the system. Without a boot block, the system does not boot. If a file system is not to be used for booting, the boot block is left blank. The boot block appears only in the first cylinder group (cylinder group 0) and is the first 8KB in a slice.

The Superblock

The superblock stores much of the information about the file system. Here are a few of the more important things contained in a superblock:

- Size and status of the file system

- Label (file system name and volume name)
- Size of the file system's logical block
- Date and time of the last update
- Cylinder group size
- Number of data blocks in a cylinder group
- Summary data block
- File system state (clean, stable, or active)
- Pathname of the last mount point

Without a superblock, the file system becomes unreadable. The superblock is located at the beginning of the disk slice and is replicated in each cylinder group. Because it contains critical data, multiple superblocks are made when the file system is created.

A copy of the superblock for each file system is kept up-to-date in memory. If the system gets halted before a disk copy of the superblock gets updated, the most recent changes are lost, and the file system becomes inconsistent. The `sync` command forces every superblock in memory to write its data to disk. The file system check program `fsck` can fix problems that occur when the `sync` command hasn't been used before a shutdown.

A summary information block is kept with the superblock. It is not replicated but is grouped with the first superblock, usually in cylinder group 0. The summary block records changes that take place as the file system is used, listing the number of inodes, directories, fragments, and storage blocks within the file system.

The Inode

An inode contains all of the information about a file except its name, which is kept in a directory. An inode is 128 bytes. The inode information is kept in the cylinder information block and contains the following:

- The type of the file (regular, directory, block special, character, link, and so on)
- The mode of the file (the set of read/write/execute permissions)
- The number of hard links to the file
- The user-id of the file's owner
- The group-id to which the file belongs
- The number of bytes in the file
- An array of 15 disk-block addresses

- The date and time the file was last accessed
- The date and time the file was last modified
- The date and time the file was created

The maximum number of files per UFS file system is determined by the number of inodes allocated for a file system. The number of inodes depends on how much disk space is allocated for each inode and the total size of the file system. By default, one inode is allocated for each 2KB of data space. You can change the default allocation by using the `-i` option of the `newfs` command. This is discussed in Chapter 5, "Solaris File Systems: Advanced Topics."

The Storage Block

The rest of the space allocated to the file system is occupied by storage blocks, also called *data blocks*. The size of these storage blocks is determined at the time a file system is created. Storage blocks are allocated, by default, in two sizes: an 8KB logical block size and a 1KB fragmentation size.

For a regular file, the storage blocks contain the contents of the file. For a directory, the storage blocks contain entries that give the inode number and the filename of the files in the directory.

Free Blocks

Blocks not currently being used as inodes, indirect address blocks, or storage blocks are marked as free in the cylinder group map. This map also keeps track of fragments to prevent fragmentation from degrading disk performance.

Creating a UFS File System

Use the `newfs` command to create UFS file systems. `newfs` is a convenient front end to the `mkfs` command, the program that creates the new file system on a disk slice. (Please note that `newfs` is a topic covered on the second exam.)

On Solaris 7 systems, information used to set some of the parameter defaults, such as number of tracks per cylinder and number of sectors per track, is read from the disk label. `newfs` determines the file system parameters to use, based on the options you specify and information provided in the disk label. Parameters are then passed to the `mkfs` (make file system) command, which builds the file system. Although you can use the `mkfs` command directly, it's more difficult to use, and you must supply many of the parameters manually. (The use of the `newfs` command is discussed more in the next section.)

The disk must be formatted and divided into slices before you can create UFS file systems on it. `newfs` removes any data on the disk slice and creates the skeleton of a directory structure, including a directory named `lost+found`. After you run `newfs` successfully, it's a good practice to run the `fsck` command to check the integrity of the file system. (The `fsck` command is described later in this chapter.) After you run `fsck`, the slice is ready to be mounted as a file system.

To create a UFS file system on a formatted disk that has already been divided into slices, you need to know the raw device filename of the slice that will contain the file system. If you are re-creating or modifying an existing UFS file system, back up and unmount the file system before performing these steps:

1. Become superuser.
2. Type `newfs /dev/rdsk/`*`device-name`* and press Enter. You are asked if you want to proceed. The `newfs` command requires the use of the raw device name and not the buffered device name.

CAUTION! *Be sure you have specified the correct device name for the slice before performing the next step. You will erase the contents of the slice when the new file system is created, and you don't want to erase the wrong slice.*

3. Type `y` to confirm.

The following example creates a file system on `/dev/rdsk/c0t3d0s7`:

1. Become superuser by typing `su`, and enter the root password.
2. Type `newfs /dev/rdsk/c0t3d0s7`.

   The system responds with this:

```
newfs: construct a new file system /dev/rdsk/c0t3d0s7 (y/n)? y
/dev/rdsk/c0t3d0s7:      163944 sectors in 506 cylinders of 9 tracks, 36 sectors
83.9MB in 32 cyl groups (16 c/g, 2.65MB/g, 1216 i/g)
super-block backups (for fsck -b #) at:
32, 5264, 10496, 15728, 20960, 26192, 31424, 36656, 41888,
47120, 52352, 57584, 62816, 68048, 73280, 78512, 82976, 88208,
93440, 98672, 103904, 109136, 114368, 119600, 124832, 130064, 135296,
140528, 145760, 150992, 156224, 161456,
```

The `newfs` command uses optimized default values to create the file system. Here are the default parameters used by the `newfs` command:

- The file system block size is 8,192.
- The file system fragment size (the smallest allocatable unit of disk space) is 1,024 bytes.

- The percentage of free space is now calculated as follows: ((64 MB/partition size) ×100), rounded down to the nearest integer and limited to between 1 percent and 10 percent, inclusive.
- The number of inodes or bytes per inode is 2,048. This controls how many inodes are created for the file system (one inode for each 2KB of disk space).

Understanding Custom File System Parameters

Before you choose to alter the default file system parameters assigned by the `newfs` command, you need to understand them. This section describes each of these parameters:

- Logical block size
- Fragment size
- Minimum free space
- Rotational delay (gap)
- Optimization type
- Number of inodes and bytes per inode

Logical Block Size

The logical block size is the size of the blocks that the UNIX kernel uses to read or write files. The logical block size is usually different from the physical block size (usually 512 bytes), which is the size of the smallest block that the disk controller can read or write.

You can specify the logical block size of the file system. After the file system is created, you cannot change this parameter without rebuilding the file system. You can have file systems with different logical block sizes on the same disk.

By default, the logical block size is 8192 bytes (8KB) for UFS file systems. The UFS file system supports block sizes of 4096 or 8192 bytes (4 or 8KB, with 8KB being the recommended logical block size).

To choose the best logical block size for your system, consider both the performance desired and the available space. For most UFS systems, an 8KB file system provides the best performance, offering a good balance between disk performance and use of space in primary memory and on disk.

As a general rule, a larger logical block size increases efficiency for file systems in which most of the files are very large. Use a smaller logical block size for file systems in which most of the files are very small. You can use the `quot -c` file system command on a file system to display a complete report on the distribution of files by block size.

Fragment Size

As files are created or expanded, they are allocated disk space in either full logical blocks or portions of logical blocks called *fragments*. When disk space is needed to hold data for a file, full blocks are allocated first, and then one or more fragments of a block are allocated for the remainder. For small files, allocation begins with fragments.

The ability to allocate fragments of blocks to files rather than whole blocks saves space by reducing the fragmentation of disk space that results from unused holes in blocks.

You define the fragment size when you create a UFS file system. The default fragment size is 1KB. Each block can be divided into one, two, four, or eight fragments, resulting in fragment sizes from 512 bytes to 8192 bytes (for 4KB file systems only). The lower boundary is actually tied to the disk sector size, typically 512 bytes.

NOTE. *The upper boundary might equal the full block size, in which case the fragment is not a fragment at all. This configuration might be optimal for file systems with very large files when you are more concerned with speed than with space.*

When choosing a fragment size, look at the trade-off between time and space: A small fragment size saves space but requires more time to allocate. As a general rule, a larger fragment size increases efficiency for file systems in which most of the files are large. Use a smaller fragment size for file systems in which most of the files are small.

Minimum Free Space

The minimum free space is the percentage of the total disk space held in reserve when you create the file system. Before Solaris 7, the default reserve was always 10 percent. In Solaris 7, the minimum free space is automatically determined. This new method of calculating free space results in less wasted disk space on large file systems.

Free space is important because file access becomes less and less efficient as a file system gets full. As long as there is an adequate amount of free space, UFS file systems operate efficiently. When a file system becomes full, using up the available user space, only `root` can access the reserved free space.

Commands such as `df` report the percentage of space available to users, excluding the percentage allocated as the minimum free space. When the command reports that more than 100 percent of the disk space in the file system is in use, some of the reserve has been used by `root`.

If you impose quotas on users, the amount of space available to the users does not include the free space reserve. You can change the value of the minimum free space for an existing file system by using the `tunefs` command.

Rotational Delay (Gap)

The rotational delay is the expected minimum time (in milliseconds) that it takes the CPU to complete a data transfer and initiate a new data transfer on the same disk cylinder. The default delay depends on the type of disk and is usually optimized for each disk type.

When writing a file, the UFS allocation routines try to position new blocks on the same disk cylinder as the previous block in the same file. The allocation routines also try to optimally position new blocks within tracks to minimize the disk rotation needed to access them.

To position file blocks so that they are "rotationally well-behaved," the allocation routines must know how fast the CPU can service transfers and how long it takes the disk to skip over a block. By using options to the `mkfs` command, you can indicate how fast the disk rotates and how many disk blocks (sectors) it has per track. The allocation routines use this information to figure out how many milliseconds the disk takes to skip a block. Then, by using the expected transfer time (rotational delay), the allocation routines can position or place blocks so that the next block is just coming under the disk head when the system is ready to read it.

NOTE. *It is not necessary to specify the rotational delay (the* `-d` *option to* `newfs`*) for some devices.*

Place blocks consecutively only if your system is fast enough to read them on the same disk rotation. If the system is too slow, the disk spins past the beginning of the next block in the file and must complete a full rotation before the block can be read, which takes a lot of time. You should try to specify an appropriate value for the gap so that the head is located over the appropriate block when the next disk request occurs.

You can change the value of this parameter for an existing file system by using the `tunefs` command. The change applies only to subsequent block allocation, not to blocks already allocated. (`tunefs` is described in detail in the next chapter.)

Optimization Type

The optimization type is either space or time. When you select space optimization, disk blocks are allocated to minimize fragmentation and optimize disk use. Space optimization is the default.

When you select time optimization, disk blocks are allocated as quickly as possible, with less emphasis on their placement. Time is the default when you set the minimum free space to 10 percent or greater. With enough free space, the disk blocks can be allocated effectively with minimal fragmentation.

You can change the value of the optimization type parameter for an existing file system by using the `tunefs` command.

Number of Inodes and Bytes Per Inode

The number of inodes determines the number of files you can have in the file system, because there is one inode for each file. The number of bytes per inode determines the total number of inodes created when the file system is made: the total size of the file system divided by the number of bytes per inode. After the inodes are allocated, you cannot change the number without re-creating the file system.

The default number of bytes per inode is 2048 (2KB), which assumes that the average size of each file is 2KB or greater. Most files are larger than 2KB. A file system with many symbolic links will have a lower average file size. If your file system will have many small files, you can give this parameter a lower value.

NOTE. *Having too many inodes is much better than running out of them. If you have too few inodes, you could reach the maximum number of files on a disk slice that is practically empty.*

File System Operations

This section describes the Solaris utilities used for creating, checking, repairing, and mounting file systems. Use these utilities to make file systems available to the user and to ensure their reliability.

Synchronizing a File System

The UFS file system relies on an internal set of tables to keep track of inodes as well as used and available blocks. When a user performs an operation that requires data to be written to the disk, the data to be written is first copied into a buffer in the kernel. Normally, the disk update is not handled until long after the write operation has returned. At any given time, the file system, as it resides on the disk, might lag behind the state of the file system represented by the buffers located in physical memory. The internal tables finally get updated when the buffer is required for another use or when the kernel automatically runs the `fsflush` daemon (at 30-second intervals).

If the system is halted without writing out the memory-resident information, the file system on the disk will be in an inconsistent state. If the internal tables are not properly synchronized with data on a disk, inconsistencies result, and file systems need repairing. File systems can be damaged or become inconsistent because of abrupt termination of the operating system in these ways:

- Power failure
- Accidental unplugging of the system

- Turning off the system without the proper shutdown procedure
- Performing a Stop+A (L1+A)
- A software error in the kernel

To prevent unclean halts, the current state of the file system must be written to disk (that is, *synchronized*) before you halt the CPU or take a disk offline.

Repairing File Systems

During normal operation, files are created, modified, and removed. Each time a file is modified, the operating system performs a series of file system updates. When a system is booted, a file system consistency check is automatically performed. Most of the time, this file system check repairs any problems it encounters. File systems are checked with the `fsck` (file system check) command.

The Solaris `fsck` command uses a state flag, which is stored in the superblock, to record the condition of the file system. This flag is used by the `fsck` command to determine whether a file system needs to be checked for consistency. The flag is used by the /etc/bcheckrc script during booting and by the `fsck` command when run from a command line using the `-m` option. Here are the possible state values:

- **FSCLEAN**—If the file system was unmounted properly, the state flag is set to FSCLEAN. Any file system with an FSCLEAN state flag is not checked when the system is booted.
- **FSSTABLE**—The file system is (or was) mounted but has not changed since the last check point—`sync` or `fsflush`—which normally occurs every 30 seconds. For example, the kernel periodically checks to see if a file system is idle and, if it is, flushes the information in the superblock back to the disk and marks it FSSTABLE. If the system crashes, the file system structure is stable, but users might lose a small amount of data. File systems marked as FSSTABLE can skip the checking before mounting.
- **FSACTIVE**—When a file system is mounted and then modified, the state flag is set to FSACTIVE, and the file system might contain inconsistencies. A file system is marked as FSACTIVE before any modified data is written to the disk. When a file system is unmounted gracefully, the state flag is set to FSCLEAN. A file system with the FSACTIVE flag must be checked by `fsck`, because it might be inconsistent. The system does not mount a file system for read/write unless its state is FSCLEAN or FSSTABLE.
- **FSBAD**—If the root file system is mounted when its state is not FSCLEAN or FSSTABLE, the state flag is set to FSBAD. The kernel does not change this file system state to FSCLEAN or FSSTABLE. A root file system flagged FSBAD as part of the boot process is mounted as read-only. You can run `fsck` on the raw root device and then remount the root file system as read/write.

- **FSLOG**—If the file system was mounted with UFS logging, the state flag is set to FSLOG. Any file system with an FSLOG state flag is not checked when the system is booted.

`fsck` is a multipass file system check program that performs successive passes over each file system, checking blocks and sizes, pathnames, connectivity, reference counts, and the map of free blocks (possibly rebuilding it). `fsck` also performs some cleanup. The phases (passes) performed by the UFS version of `fsck` are described in Table 4-2.

Table 4-2 *fsck* Phases

fsck Phase	Task Performed
Phase 1	Checks blocks and sizes.
Phase 2	Checks pathnames.
Phase 3	Checks connectivity.
Phase 4	Checks reference counts.
Phase 5	Checks cylinder groups.

Normally, `fsck` is run noninteractively at bootup to preen the file systems after an abrupt system halt in which the latest file system changes were not written to disk. Preening automatically fixes any basic file system inconsistencies and does not try to repair more serious errors. While preening a file system, `fsck` fixes the inconsistencies it expects from such an abrupt halt. For more serious conditions, the command reports the error and terminates. It then tells the operator to run `fsck` manually.

A common question is "Is it ever necessary to run `fsck` on a file system that has UFS logging enabled?" Normally there is no need to run `fsck` on a file system that has UFS logging enabled. The one exception to this is when the log is bad (such as when a media failure causes the log to become unusable). In this case, logging will put the file system in an "error state," and you will be unable to mount it and use it until `fsck` is run. The safest option is to always run `fsck`. It will terminate immediately if logging is there and the file system is not in an error state.

Determining Whether a File System Needs Checking

File systems must be checked periodically for inconsistencies to avoid unexpected loss of data. As stated earlier, checking the state of a file system is automatically done at bootup;

however, it is not necessary to reboot a system to check if the file systems are stable. The following procedure outlines a method for determining the current state of the file systems and whether they need to be fixed:

1. Become superuser.
2. Type `fsck -m /dev/rdsk/cntndnsn` and press Enter. The state flag in the superblock of the file system you specify is checked to see whether the file system is clean or requires checking. If you omit the device argument, all the UFS file systems listed in /etc/vfstab with a `fsck` pass value of greater than 0 are checked.

In the following example, the first file system needs checking, but the second file system does not:

```
fsck -m /dev/rdsk/c0t0d0s6

** /dev/rdsk/c0t0d0s6
ufs fsck: sanity check: /dev/rdsk/c0t0d0s6 needs checking
fsck -m /dev/rdsk/c0t0d0s7
** /dev/rdsk/c0t0d0s7
ufs fsck: sanity check: /dev/rdsk/c0t0d0s7 okay
```

Running *fsck* Manually

You might need to manually check file systems when they cannot be mounted or when you've determined that the state of a file system is unclean. Good indications that a file system might need to be checked are error messages displayed in the console window or system crashes that occur for no reason.

When you run `fsck` manually, it reports each inconsistency found and fixes innocuous errors. For more serious errors, the command reports the inconsistency and prompts you to choose a response. Sometimes corrective actions performed by `fsck` result in some loss of data. The amount and severity of data loss can be determined from the `fsck` diagnostic output.

To check all file systems manually, follow these steps:

1. Become superuser.
2. Unmount the file system.
3. Type `fsck` and press Enter.

   All file systems in the `/etc/vfstab` file with entries greater than 0 in the `fsck pass` field are checked. You can also specify the mount point directory or `/dev/rdsk/cntndnsn` as arguments to `fsck`. The `fsck` command requires the raw device filename.

Any inconsistency messages are displayed. The only way to successfully change the file system and correct the problem is to answer "yes" to these messages.

NOTE: *The* `fsck` *command has a* `-y` *option that automatically answers yes to every question. But be careful: If* `fsck` *asks to delete a file, it will answer yes, and you will have no control over it. If it doesn't delete the file, however, the file system remains unclean and cannot be mounted.*

4. If you corrected any errors, type `fsck` and press Enter. `fsck` might not be able to fix all errors in one execution. If you see the message `FILE SYSTEM STATE NOT SET TO OKAY`, run the command again and continue to run `fsck` until it runs clean with no errors.
5. Rename and move any files put in `lost+found`. Individual files put in the `lost+found` directory by `fsck` are renamed with their inode numbers, so figuring out what they were named originally can be difficult. If possible, rename the files and move them where they belong. You might be able to use the `grep` command to match phrases with individual files and use the `file` command to identify file types, ownership, and so on. When whole directories are dumped into `lost+found`, it is easier to figure out where they belong and move them back.

Mounting File Systems

After you create a file system, you need to make it available. You make file systems available by mounting them. Using the `mount` command, you attach a file system to the system directory tree at the specified mount point, and it becomes available to the system. The root file system is mounted at boot time and cannot be unmounted. Any other file system can be mounted or unmounted from the root file system at any time.

The various methods used to mount a file system are described in the next sections.

Creating an Entry in the /etc/vfstab File to Mount File Systems

The /etc/vfstab (virtual file system table) file contains a list of file systems to be automatically mounted when the system is booted to the multiuser state. The system administrator places entries in the file, specifying what file systems are to be mounted at bootup. The following is an example of the /etc/vfstab file:

```
#device              device               mount  FS     fsck   mount    mount
#to mount            to fsck              point  type   pass   at boot  options
/dev/dsk/c0t0d0s0    /dev/rdsk/c0t0d0s0   /      ufs    1      no       -
/proc                -                    /proc  proc          no       -
/dev/dsk/c0t0d0s1    -                    -      swap          no       -
swap                 -                    /tmp   tmpfs  -      yes      -
/dev/dsk/c0t0d0s6    /dev/rdsk/c0t0d0s6   /usr   ufs    2      no       -
/dev/dsk/c0t3d0s7    /dev/rdsk/c0t3d0s7   /data  ufs    2      no       -
```

Each column of information follows this format:

- `device to mount`—The buffered device that corresponds to the file system being mounted.
- `device to fsck`—The raw (character) special device that corresponds to the file system being mounted. This determines the raw interface used by `fsck`. Use a dash (-) when there is no applicable device, such as for swap, /proc, tmp, or a network-based file system.
- `mount point`—The default mount point directory.
- `FS type`—The type of file system.
- `fsck pass`—The pass number used by `fsck` to decide whether to check a file. When the field contains a dash (-), the file system is not checked. When the field contains a value of 1 or greater, the file system is checked sequentially. File systems are checked sequentially, in the order that they appear in the /etc/vfstab file. The value of the pass number does not have any effect on the sequence of file system checking.

NOTE: *A common misconception is that the* `fsck pass` *field specifies the order in which file systems are to be checked. In SunOS system software, the* `fsck pass` *field does not specify the order in which file systems are to be checked. During bootup, a preliminary check is run on each file system to be mounted from a hard disk, using the boot script* `/sbin/rcS`*, which checks the / and /usr file systems. The other rc shell scripts then use the* `fsck` *command to check each additional file system sequentially. They do not check file systems in parallel. File systems are checked sequentially during booting even if the* `fsck` *pass numbers are greater than 1. The values can be any number greater than 1.*

- `mount at boot`—Specifies whether the file system should be automatically mounted when the system is booted. The rc scripts located in the /etc directory specify which file system gets mounted at each run level.
- `mount options`—A list of comma-separated options (with no spaces) used when mounting the file system. Use a dash (-) to show no options.

Using the Command Line to Mount File Systems

File systems can be mounted from the command line by using the `mount` command. The commands in Table 4-3 are used from the command line to mount and unmount file systems.

Table 4-3 File System Commands

Command	Description
`mount`	Mounts specified file systems and remote resources.
`mountall`	Mounts all file systems specified in a file system table (vfstab).
`umount`	Unmounts specified file systems and remote resources.
`umountall`	Unmounts all file systems specified in a file system table.

CD-ROMs containing file systems should be automatically mounted when the CD-ROM is inserted if Volume Manager is running. Disks containing file systems that have not yet been automatically mounted can be manually mounted by running the `volcheck` command.

As a general rule, local disk slices should be included in the /etc/vfstab file so that they automatically mount at bootup.

Unmounting a file system removes it from the file system mount point. Some file system administration tasks cannot be performed on mounted file systems. You should unmount a file system when

- It is no longer needed
- You check and repair it by using the `fsck` command
- You are about to do a complete backup of it

NOTE. *File systems are automatically unmounted as part of the system shutdown procedure.*

Displaying Mounted File Systems

Whenever you mount or unmount a file system, the /etc/mnttab (mount table) file is modified to show the list of currently mounted file systems. You can display the contents of the mount table by using the `cat` or `more` commands, but you cannot edit them as you would the /etc/vfstab file. Here is an example of a mount table file:

```
/dev/dsk/c0t3d0s0                    ufs     rw,suid 693186371
/dev/dsk/c0t1d0s6           /usr     ufs     rw,suid 693186371
/proc                       /proc    proc    rw,suid 693186371
swap                        /tmp     tmpfs   rw,dev=0 693186373
```

You can also view a mounted file system by typing `/etc/mount` from the command line. The system displays the following:

```
/ on /dev/dsk/c0t3d0s0 read/write/setuid/largefiles on ...
/usr on /dev/dsk/c0t3d0s6 read/write/setuid/largefiles on ...
/proc on /proc read/write/setuid on Fri May 16 11:39:05 1997
/dev/fd on fd read/write/setuid on Fri May 16 11:39:05 1997
/export on /dev/dsk/c0t3d0s3 setuid/read/write/largefiles on ...
/export/home on /dev/dsk/c0t3d0s7 setuid/read/write/largefiles on ...
/export/swap on /dev/dsk/c0t3d0s4 setuid/read/write/largefiles on ...
/opt on /dev/dsk/c0t3d0s5 setuid/read/write/largefiles on ...
/tmp on swap read/write on Fri May 16 11:39:07 1997
```

Mounting a File System with Large Files

The `largefiles` mount option lets users mount a file system containing files larger than 2GB. The `largefiles` mount option is the default state for the Solaris 7 environment. The `largefiles` option means that a file system mounted with this option may contain one or more files larger than 2GB.

You must explicitly use the `nolargefiles` mount option to disable this behavior. The `nolargefiles` option provides total compatibility with previous file system behavior, enforcing the 2GB maximum file size limit.

Mounting a File System with UFS Logging Enabled

The new UFS logging feature eliminates file system inconsistency, which can significantly reduce the time of system reboots. Use the `-o logging` option in the /etc/vfstab file or as an option to the `mount` command to enable UFS logging on a file system.

UFS logging is the process of storing file system operations to a log before the transactions are applied to the file system. Because the file system can never become inconsistent, `fsck` can usually be bypassed, which reduces the time to reboot a system if it crashes, or after an unclean halt.

The UFS log is allocated from free blocks on the file system. It is sized at approximately 1MB per 1GB of file system, up to a maximum of 64MB. The default is `nologging`.

NOTE. *Is it ever necessary to run* `fsck` *on a file system that has UFS logging enabled? The answer is yes. There is normally no need to run* `fsck` *on a file system that has UFS logging enabled. The one exception to this is when the log is bad. An example of this is when a media failure causes the log to become unusable. In this case, logging will put the file system in an "error state," and you will be unable to mount it and use it until* `fsck` *is run. The safest option is to always run* `fsck`*. It will bail out immediately if logging is there and the file system is not in an error state.*

Displaying a File System's Disk Space Usage

Use the df command and its options to see the capacity of each file system mounted on a system, the amount of space available, and the percentage of space already in use. Use the du (directory usage) command to report the number of free disk blocks and files.

NOTE. *File systems at or above 90 percent of capacity should be cleared of unnecessary files. You can do this by moving them to a disk, or you can remove them after obtaining the user's permission.*

The following is an example of how to use the df command to display disk space information. The command syntax is

```
df -F fstype -g -k -t <directory>
```

Table 4-4 explains the df command and its options.

Table 4-4 The *df* Command

Command	Description
df	The df command with no options lists all mounted file systems and their device names. It also lists the total number of 512-byte blocks used and the number of files.
directory	The directory whose file system you want to check. The device name, blocks used, and number of files are displayed.
-F fstype	Displays a list of unmounted file systems, their device names, the number of 512-byte blocks used, and the number of files on file systems of type fstype.
-g	Displays the statvfs structure for all mounted file systems.
-k	Displays a list of file systems, kilobytes used, free kilobytes, percent capacity used, and mount points.
-t	Displays total blocks as well as blocks used for all mounted file systems.

The following example illustrates how to display disk space information with the df command. Type

```
df -k
```

The system responds with this:

```
Filesystem          kbytes    used      avail     capacity  Mounted on
/proc               0         0         0         0%        /proc
/dev/dsk/c0t3d0s0   144799    23880     106440    19%       /
/dev/dsk/c0t3d0s6   1016455   496362    459106    52%       /usr
fd                  0         0         0         0%        /dev/fd
```

```
/dev/dsk/c0t3d0s3    41151     11       37025     1%     /export
/dev/dsk/c0t3d0s7    392503    9        353244    1%     /export/home
/dev/dsk/c0t3d0s4    37351     9        33607     1%     /export/swap
/dev/dsk/c0t3d0s5    255319    187031   42757     82%    /opt
swap                 107584    272      107312    1%     /tmp
```

Displaying Directory Size Information

By using the df command, you display file system disk usage. You can use the du command to display the disk usage of a directory and all its subdirectories in 512-byte blocks.

The du command shows you the disk usage of each file in each subdirectory of a file system. To get a listing of the size of each subdirectory in a file system, type cd to the pathname associated with that file system and run the following pipeline:

```
du -s  * | sort -r -n
```

This pipeline, which uses the reverse and numeric options of the sort command, pinpoints large directories. Use ls -l to examine the size (in bytes) and modification times of files within each directory. Old files or text files over 100KB often warrant storage offline.

The following example illustrates how to display the amount of disk space being consumed by the /var/adm directory using the du command. The largest files are displayed first, and the -k option displays the file size in 1024 bytes. Type

```
du -k /var/adm|sort -r -n
```

The system responds with this:

```
92       /var/adm
4        /var/adm/acct
1        /var/adm/sa
1        /var/adm/passwd
1        /var/adm/log
1        /var/adm/acct/sum
1        /var/adm/acct/nite
1        /var/adm/acct/fiscal
```

Controlling User Disk Space Usage

Quotas let system administrators control the size of UFS file systems by limiting the amount of disk space that individual users can acquire. Quotas are especially useful on the file systems where user home directories reside. After the quotas are in place, they can be changed to adjust the amount of disk space or number of inodes users can consume. Additionally, quotas can be added or removed as system needs change. In addition, quota status can be monitored. Quota commands let administrators display information about quotas on a file system or search for users who have exceeded their quotas.

After you have set up and turned on disk and inode quotas, you can check for users who exceed their quotas. You can also check quota information for entire file systems by using the commands listed in Table 4-5.

Table 4-5 Commands to Check Quotas

Command	Description
`quota`	Displays the quotas and disk usage within a file system for individual users on which quotas have been activated.
`repquota`	Displays the quotas and disk usage for all users on one or more file systems.

You won't see quotas in use much today, because the cost of disk space continues to fall. In most cases, the system administrator simply watches disk space to identify users who might be using more than their fair share. As you saw in this section, you can easily do this by using the `du` command. On a large system with many users, however, disk quotas can be an effective way to control disk space usage.

Summary

This chapter described the fundamentals of disk file systems and how they are managed. Chapter 5 will introduce some advanced topics in file system management, including managing removable media, advanced topics in creating and tuning file systems, DiskSuite, and the Solstice Volume Manager. System administrators spend a great deal of time managing and fine-tuning file systems to improve system efficiency. Understanding these topics is therefore critical for system administrators.

CHAPTER

5

Solaris File Systems: Advanced Topics

The following test objectives are covered in this chapter:

- Constructing a file system
- Tuning a file system
- Using large file systems
- Using additional options when mounting and unmounting file systems
- Working with removable media and volume manager
- Getting information on file systems

In Chapter 4, "Introduction to File Systems," I described how to create, check, mount, and display file systems with Solaris 7. I explained file system structure, disk geometry, disk slices, and the `format` utility. In Chapter 16, "Device Configuration and Naming," disk devices and device names are covered in detail. (Although Chapter 16 covers objectives for the Part II exam, I recommend reading that chapter to answer questions you might have after reading this chapter. File systems and devices go hand in hand but are not covered on the same exam; therefore, device configuration and naming are covered in Section II of this book.

In this chapter, I continue the discussion of file systems. Specifically, I cover the objectives outlined at the beginning of this chapter.

NOTE. *This chapter covers objectives for exams Part I and Part II; however, the majority of the information relates to the first exam. (The second exam has limited questions related to file systems.) I'll make a notation when the material relates to the Part II exam.*

Constructing a File System

Constructing file systems is a topic covered on both exams. In Chapter 4, I described how `newfs` is the friendly front end to the `mkfs` command. The `newfs` command automatically determines all the necessary parameters to pass to `mkfs` to construct new file systems. `newfs` was added in Solaris to make the creation of new file systems easier. It's highly recommended that the `newfs` command be used to create file systems, but it's also important to see what is happening "behind the scenes" with the `mkfs` utility. The syntax for `mkfs` is

```
/usr/sbin/mkfs [options] <character device name>
```

Its options are described in Table 5-1.

Table 5-1 The *mkfs* Command

Option	Description
`-F`	Used to specify the file system type. If this option is omitted, the /etc/vfstab and /etc/default/fs files are checked to determine a file system type.
`-m`	Shows the command line that was used to create the specified file system. No changes are made to the file system.
`-v`	Verbose. Shows the command line, but does not execute anything.
`-o <specific options>`	A list of options specific to the type of file system. The list must have the following format: `-o` followed by a space, followed by a series of `keyword [=value]` pairs, separated by commas, with no intervening spaces.

continues

Table 5-1 The *mkfs* Command (continued)

Option	Description
apc=<n>	Reserved space for bad block replacement on SCSI devices. The default is 0.
N	Prints the file system parameters without actually creating the file system.
nsect=<n>	The number of sectors per track on the disk. The default is 32.
ntrack=<n>	The number of tracks per cylinder on the disk. The default is 16.
bsize=<n>	Logical block size, either 4096 (4KB) or 8192 (8KB). The default is 8192. The sun4u architecture does not support the 4096 block size.
fragsize=<bytes>	The smallest amount of disk space, in bytes, to allocate to a file. The value must be a power of 2 selected from the range 512 to the logical block size. If the logical block size is 4096, legal values are 512, 1024, 2048, and 4096. If the logical block size is 8192, 8192 is also a legal value. The default is 1024.
cgsize=<cyls>	The number of cylinders per cylinder group. The default is 16.
free=<n>	The minimum percentage of free space to maintain in the file system. This space is off-limits to normal users. After the file system is filled to this threshold, only the superuser can continue writing to the file system. This parameter can be subsequently changed using the `tunefs` command. The default is 10 percent.
rps=<rps>	The rotational speed of the disk, specified in revolutions per second. The default is 60.
nbpi=<value>	The `value` specified is the number of bytes per inode, which specifies the density of inodes in the file system. The number is divided into the total size of the file system to determine the fixed number of inodes to create. It should reflect the expected average size of files in the file system. If fewer inodes are desired, a larger number should be used. To create more inodes, a smaller number should be given. The default is 2048.
opt=<value>	Space or time optimization preference. The `value` can be `s` or `t`. Specify `s` to optimize for disk space. Specify `t` to optimize for speed (time). The default is `t`. Generally, you should optimize for time unless the file system is more than 90 percent full.
gap=<milliseconds>	Rotational delay, specified in milliseconds. Indicates the expected time (in milliseconds) required to service a transfer completion interrupt and to initiate a new transfer on the same disk. The `value` is used to decide how much rotational spacing to place between successive blocks in a file. The default is determined by the actual disk used.
nrpos=<n>	The number of different rotational positions into which to divide a cylinder group. The default is 8.
maxcontig=<blocks>	The maximum number of blocks, belonging to one file, that is allocated contiguously before inserting a rotational delay. For a 4KB file system, the default is 14; for an 8KB file system, it is 7. This parameter can subsequently be changed using the `tunefs` command.

mkfs constructs a file system on the character (or raw) device found in the /dev/rdsk directory. Again, it is highly recommended that you do not run the mkfs command directly, but instead use the friendlier newfs command, which automatically determines all the necessary parameters required by mkfs to construct the file system. In the following example, the -v option to the newfs command will output all the parameters passed to the mkfs utility. (If you need more information on newfs, it is described in detail in Chapter 4.) Type the following:

```
newfs -v /dev/rdsk/c0t0d0s0
```

The system outputs the following information and creates a new file system on /dev/rdsk/c0t0d0s0:

```
newfs: construct a new file system /dev/rdsk/c0t0d0s0: (y/n)? y
mkfs -F ufs /dev/rdsk/c0t0d0s0 2097576 117 9 8192 1024 32 6 90 4096 t 0 -1 8 15
/dev/rdsk/c0t0d0s0:      2097576 sectors in 1992 cylinders of 9 tracks, 117 sectors
1024.2MB in 63 cyl groups (32 c/g, 16.45MB/g, 4096 i/g)
super-block backups (for fsck -F ufs -o b=#) at:
32, 33856, 67680, 101504, 135328, 169152, 202976, 236800, 270624, 304448,
338272, 372096, 405920, 439744, 473568, 507392, 539168, 572992, 606816,
640640, 674464, 708288, 742112, 775936, 809760, 843584, 877408, 911232,
945056, 978880, 1012704, 1046528, 1078304, 1112128, 1145952, 1179776, 1213600,
1247424, 1281248, 1315072, 1348896, 1382720, 1416544, 1450368, 1484192,
1518016, 1551840, 1585664, 1617440, 1651264, 1685088, 1718912, 1752736,
1786560, 1820384, 1854208, 1888032, 1921856, 1955680, 1989504, 2023328,
2057152, 2090976,
```

The *labelit* Command

After you create the file system with newfs, you can use the labelit utility to write or display labels on unmounted disk file systems. The syntax for labelit is

```
labelit [-F ufs] [-V] <special> [ fsname volume ]
```

Labeling a file system is optional. It's required only if you're using a program such as volcopy, which is covered in a moment. The labelit command is described in Table 5-2.

Table 5-2 The *labelit* Command

Parameter	Description
special	This name should be the physical disk section (for example, /dev/dsk/c0t0d0s6).
fsname	Represents the mount point (for example, root (/), /home, and so on) of the file system.
volume	Can be used to represent the physical volume name.

continues

Table 5-2 The *labelit* Command (continued)

Parameter	Description
-F	Specifies the file system type on which to operate. The file system type should either be specified here or be determinable from the /etc/vfstab entry. If no matching entry is found, the default file system type specified in /etc/default/fs is used.
-V	Prints the command line but does not perform any action.

NOTE. *If* `fsname` *and* `volume` *are not specified,* `labelit` *prints the current values of these labels. Both* `fsname` *and* `volume` *are limited to six or fewer characters.*

The following is an example of how to label a disk partition using the `labelit` command. Type

```
labelit -F ufs /dev/rdsk/c0t0d0s6 disk1 vol1
```

The system responds with this:

```
fsname:  disk1volume:  vol1
```

The *volcopy* Command

The `volcopy` command can be used by the administrator (root) to make a copy of a labeled file system. This command works with ufs file systems, but the file system must be labeled with the `labelit` utility before the `volcopy` command is issued. To determine if a file system is a ufs file system, issue this command:

```
fstyp  /dev/rdsk/c0t0d0s6
```

The system responds with this:

```
ufs
```

The `volcopy` command can be used to copy a file system from one disk to another.

The syntax for `volcopy` is

```
volcopy [options] <fsname> <srcdevice> <volname1> <destdevice> <volname2>
```

`volcopy` is described in Table 5-3.

Table 5-3 The *volcopy* Command

Option	Description
-F	Specifies the file system type on which to operate. This should either be specified here or be determinable from the /etc/vfstab entry. If no matching entry is found, the default file system type specified in /etc/default/fs is used.
-V	Prints the command line but does not perform any action.
-a	Requires the operator to respond "yes" or "no." If the -a option is not specified, volcopy pauses 10 seconds before the copy is made.
-o <options>	A list of options specific to the type of file system. The list must have the following format: -o followed by a space, followed by a series of keyword [=value] pairs, separated by commas, with no intervening spaces.
<fsname>	Represents the mount point (for example, /, u1, and so on) of the file system being copied.
<srcdevice> / <destdevice>	The disk partition specified using the raw device (for example, /dev/rdsk/clt0d0s7, /dev/rdsk/clt0d1s7, and so on).
<srcdevice> / <volname1>	The device and physical volume from which the copy of the file system is being extracted.
<destdevice> / <volname2>	The target device and physical volume.

NOTE. *`fsname` and `volname` are limited to six or fewer characters and are recorded in the superblock. `volname` can be a dash (-) to use the existing volume name.*

The following example copies the contents of /home1 to /home2:

```
volcopy -F ufs disk1 /dev/rdsk/c0t0d0s6 vol1 /dev/rdsk/c0t1d0s6 vol2
```

Other commands can also be used to copy file systems—`ufsdump`, `cpio`, `tar`, and `dd`, to name a few. These commands are discussed in Chapter 12, "Backup and Recovery."

Tuning File Systems

A situation might arise in which you want to change some of the parameters that were set when you originally created the file system. Perhaps you want to change the `minfree` value to free up some additional disk space on a large disk drive. Using the `tunefs` command, you can modify the following file system parameters:

- `maxcontig`
- `rotdelay`

- `maxbpg`
- `minfree`
- `optimization`

See Table 5-1 for a description of these options.

CAUTION! `tunefs` *can destroy a file system in seconds. Always back up the entire file system before using* `tunefs`.

The syntax for `tunefs` is

```
tunefs [ -a <maxcontig> ] [ -d <rotdelay> ] [ -e <maxbpg> ] [ -m <minfree> ]
➥ [ -o [ <value> ] special/filesystem
```

The `tunefs` command is described in Table 5-4.

Table 5-4 The *tunefs* Command

Option	Description
`-a <maxcontig>`	Specifies the maximum number of contiguous blocks that are laid out before forcing a rotational delay (see the `-d` option). The default value is 1, because most device drivers require an interrupt per disk transfer. For device drivers that can chain several buffers together in a single transfer, set this to the maximum chain length.
`-d <rotdelay>`	Specifies the expected time (in milliseconds) to service a transfer completion interrupt and to initiate a new transfer on the same disk. It is used to decide how much rotational spacing to place between successive blocks in a file.
`-e <maxbpg>`	Sets the maximum number of blocks that any single file can allocate from a cylinder group before it is forced to begin allocating blocks from another cylinder group. Typically, this value is set to approximately one quarter of the total blocks in a cylinder group. The intent is to prevent any single file from using up all the blocks in a single cylinder group. The effect of this limit is to cause big files to do long seeks more frequently than if they were allowed to allocate all the blocks in a cylinder group before seeking elsewhere. For file systems with exclusively large files, this parameter should be set higher.
`-m <minfree>`	Specifies the percentage of space held back from normal users (the minimum free space threshold). The default value is 10 percent.
`-o <value>`	Changes the optimization strategy for the file system. The `value` is either `space` or `time`. Use `space` to conserve space; use `time` to attempt to organize file layout to minimize access time. Generally, optimize a file system for time unless it is over 90 percent full.
`<special>/<filesystem>`	Enter either the special device name (such as /dev/rdsk/c0t0d0s6) or the file system name (such as /home).

The file system must be unmounted before you use `tunefs`.

To change the minimum free space (`minfree`) on a file system from 10 percent to 5 percent, type the following:

```
tunefs -m5 /dev/rdsk/c0t0d0s6

minimum percentage of free space changes from 10% to 5%
```

The manual page of `tunefs` recommends that `minfree` be set at 10 percent, and that if you set the value under that, you lose performance. This means that 10 percent of the disk is unusable. This might not have been too bad in the days when disks were a couple hundred megabytes in size, but on a 9GB disk, you're losing 900MB of disk space. The mention of loss of performance in the manual page is misleading. With such large disk drives, you can afford to have `minfree` as low as 1 percent. This has been found to be a practical and affordable limit. In addition, performance does not become an issue here, because locating free blocks even within a 90MB area is efficient. A rule of thumb is to use the default 10 percent `minfree` value for file systems up to 1GB, and then adjust the `minfree` value so that your `minfree` area is no larger than 100MB. As for the performance, applications do not complain about the lower `minfree` value. The one exception would be the root (/) file system, in which the system administrator can use his or her judgment to allow more free space just to be conservative, in case root (/) ever becomes 100 percent full.

Later, if you want to see what parameters were used when creating a file system, issue the `mkfs` command:

```
mkfs -m /dev/rdsk/c0t0d0s6
```

The system responds with this:

```
mkfs -F ufs -o nsect=117,ntrack=9,bsize=8192,fragsize=1024,cgsize=16,free=5,rps=
➥90,nbpi=2062,opt=t,apc=0,gap=0,nrpos=8,maxcontig=15 /dev/rdsk/c0t0d0s6 205334
```

The *fstyp* Command

Another good command to use to view file system parameters is the `fstyp` command. Use the `-v` option to obtain a full listing of a file system's parameters:

```
fstyp -v /dev/rdsk/c0t0d0s6
```

The system responds with this:

```
ufs
magic           11954   format  dynamic   time      Sat Oct   2 10:11:06 1999
sblkno          16      cblkno  24        iblkno    32        dblkno    528
sbsize          3072    cgsize  2048      cgoffset  64        cgmask    0xfffffff0
ncg             13      size    102667    blocks    95994
bsize           8192    shift   13        mask      0xffffe000
```

```
fsize           1024   shift     10        mask      0xfffffc00
frag            8      shift     3         fsbtodb   1
minfree         5%     maxbpg    2048      optim     time
maxcontig 15    rotdelay         0ms       rps       90
csaddr          528    cssize    1024      shift     9         mask      0xfffffe00
ntrak           9      nsect     117       spc       1053      ncyl      195
cpg             16     bpg       1053      fpg       8424      ipg       3968
nindir          2048   inopb     64        nspf      2
nbfree          11995  ndir      2         nifree    51577     nffree    1
cgrotor         0      fmod      0         ronly     0
fs_reclaim is not set
file system state is valid, fsclean is 1
blocks available in each rotational position
cylinder number 0:
   position 0:   0    8   15   22   30   37   44   52   59
   position 1:   1    9   16   23   31   38   45   53   60
   position 2:   2   10   17   24   39   46   61
   position 3:   3   18   25   32   40   47   54   62
   position 4:   4   11   19   26   33   41   48   55   63
   position 5:   5   12   20   27   34   42   49   56
   position 6:   6   13   21   28   35   50   57   64
   position 7:   7   14   29   36   43   51   58   65
cylinder number 1:
   position 0:  66   74   81   88  103  110  117  125
   position 1:  67   82   89   96  104  111  118  126
   position 2:  68   75   83   90   97  105  112  119  127
   position 3:  69   76   84   91   98  106  113  120
   position 4:  70   77   85   92   99  114  121  128
   position 5:  71   78   93  100  107  115  122  129
   position 6:  72   79   86   94  101  108  116  123  130
   position 7:  73   80   87   95  102  109  124  131
...
...
```

NOTE. *It's always a good idea to print the* `mkfs` *options used on a file system along with information provided by the* `prtvtoc` *command. Put the printout in your system log. If you ever need to rebuild a file system because of a hard drive failure, you can re-create it exactly as it was before.*

Large Versus Small Files

On a 32-bit system, a large file is a regular file whose size is greater than or equal to 2.31GB. A small file is a regular file whose size is less than 2GB. Some utilities can handle large files, and others cannot. A utility is called *large-file-aware* if it can process large files in the same manner as it does small files. A large-file-aware utility can handle large files as input and can generate large files as output. The `newfs`, `mkfs`, `mount`, `umount`, `tunefs`, `labelit`, and `quota` utilities are all large-file-aware for `ufs` file systems.

On the other hand, a utility is called *large-file-safe* if it causes no data loss or corruption when it encounters a large file. A utility that is large-file-safe is unable to properly process a large file, so it returns an appropriate error. Some examples of utilities that are not large-file-aware but are large-file-safe include the vi editor and the mailx and lp commands.

Mounting a File System

In Chapter 4, I described the basics of how to mount file systems. (I purposely did not bring up all the many options available in the mount command to avoid confusion.) The syntax for mount is

```
mount -F <fstype> [generic_options] [ -o specific_options ] [ -O ]
```

Table 5-5 describes these options.

Table 5-5 The *mount* Command

Option	Description	
-F <fstype>	Used to specify the file system type (fstype) on which to operate. If fstype is not specified, it must be determined from the /etc/vfstab file or by consulting /etc/default/fs or /etc/dfs/fstypes.	
generic_options	Can be any of the following:	
	-m	Mounts the file system without making an entry in /etc/mnttab.
	-r	Mounts the file system as read-only.
	-O	Overlay mount. Allows the file system to be mounted over an existing mount point, making the underlying file system inaccessible. If a mount is attempted on a preexisting mount point without setting this flag, the mount fails, producing the error device busy.
	-p	Prints the list of mounted file systems in the /etc/vfstab format. This must be the only option specified.
	-v	Prints the list of mounted file systems in verbose format. This must be the only option specified.
	-V	Echoes the complete command line but does not execute the command. umount generates a command line by using the options and arguments provided by the user and adding to them information derived from /etc/mnttab. This option should be used to verify and validate the command line.
	-o	Specifies fstype-specific options. See the -o <specific options> described next.

continues

Table 5-5 The *mount* Command (continued)

Option	Description	
`-o <specific options>`	Options that can be specified with the `-o` option. If you specify multiple options, separate them with commas (no spaces)—for example, `-o ro,nosuid`.	
	`-rw|ro`	Specifies read/write or read-only. The default is read/write.
	`-nosuid`	Disallows `setuid` execution and prevents devices on the file system from being opened. The default is to enable `setuid` execution and to allow devices to be opened.
	`-remount`	With `rw`, remounts a file system with read/write access.
	`-f`	Fakes an entry in /etc/mnttab but doesn't really mount any file systems.
	`-n`	Mounts the file system without making an entry in /etc/mnttab.
	`-largefiles`	Specifies that a file system might contain one or more files larger than 2GB. It is not required that a file system mounted with this option contain files larger than 2GB, but this option allows such files within the file system.
	`-nolargefiles`	Provides total compatibility with previous file system behavior, enforcing the 2GB maximum file size limit.

The following examples illustrate the options described in Table 5-5.

A file system has been created on disk c0t0d0 on slice s0. The directory to be mounted on this disk slice is /home2. To mount the file system, first create the directory called /home2, and then type the following:

```
mount /dev/dsk/c0t0d0s0 /home2
```

If the file system has been mounted, you return to a command prompt. No other message is displayed.

In the next example, the `-v` option is used with the `mount` command to display a list of all mounted file systems:

```
mount -v
```

The system responds with this:

```
/dev/dsk/c0t3d0s0 on / type ufs read/write/setuid/largefiles on Fri Oct  1 13:04:06
➥ 1999
/dev/dsk/c0t3d0s6 on /usr type ufs read/write/setuid/largefiles on Fri Oct  1 13:04:06
➥ 1999
```

```
/proc on /proc type proc read/write/setuid on Fri Oct  1 13:04:06 1999
fd on /dev/fd type fd read/write/setuid on Fri Oct  1 13:04:06 1999
/dev/dsk/c0t3d0s1 on /var type ufs read/write/setuid/largefiles on Fri Oct  1 13:04:06
➥ 1999
/dev/dsk/c0t3d0s3 on /export type ufs setuid/read/write/largefiles on Fri Oct  1
➥ 13:04:08 1999
/dev/dsk/c0t3d0s5 on /opt type ufs setuid/read/write/largefiles on Fri Oct  1 13:04:08
➥ 1999
swap on /tmp type tmpfs read/write on Fri Oct  1 13:04:08 1999
sparc4:/usr on /net/sparc4/usr type nfs nosuid/remote on Fri Oct  1 13:39:00 1999
```

Type the `mount` command with the `-p` option to display a list of mounted file systems in /etc/vfstab format:

```
mount -p
```

The system responds with this:

```
/dev/dsk/c0t3d0s0 - / ufs - no rw,suid,largefiles
/dev/dsk/c0t3d0s6 - /usr ufs - no rw,suid,largefiles
/proc - /proc proc - no rw,suid
fd - /dev/fd fd - no rw,suid
/dev/dsk/c0t3d0s1 - /var ufs - no rw,suid,largefiles
/dev/dsk/c0t3d0s3 - /export ufs - no suid,rw,largefiles
/dev/dsk/c0t3d0s5 - /opt ufs - no suid,rw,largefiles
swap - /tmp tmpfs - no
sparc4:/usr - /net/sparc4/usr nfs - no nosuid
/dev/dsk/c0t0d0s0 - /home2 ufs - no suid,rw,largefiles
```

The `-p` option is useful to obtain the correct settings if you're making an entry in the /etc/vfstab file.

The following example mounts a file system as read-only:

```
mount -o ro /dev/dsk/c0t0d0s0 /home2
```

The next example uses the `mount` command to mount a directory to a file system as read/writeable, disallow `setuid` execution, and allow the creation of large files:

```
mount -o rw,nosuid,largefiles /dev/dsk/c0t0d0s0 /home2
```

Type `mount` with no options to verify that the file system has been mounted and to review the mount options that were used:

```
mount
```

The system responds with information about all mounted file systems, including /home2:

```
/home2 on /dev/dsk/c0t0d0s0 read/write/nosuid/largefiles on Tue Oct 5 06:56:33 1999
```

NOTE. *After you mount a file system with the default* `largefiles` *option and large files have been created, you cannot remount the file system with the* `nolargefiles` *option until you remove any large files and run* `fsck` *to reset the state to* `nolargefiles`.

/etc/mnttab

When a file system is mounted, an entry is maintained in the mounted file system table called /etc/mnttab. This file contains information about devices that are currently mounted. The `mount` command adds entries to this file, and `umount` removes entries from this file. Do not manually edit this file. Each entry is a line of fields separated by spaces in this form:

```
<special> <mount_point> <fstype>  <options>  <time>
```

Table 5-6 describes each field.

Table 5-6 /etc/mnttab Fields

Field	Description
<special>	The resource to be mounted (that is, /dev/dsk/c0t0d0s0).
<mount_point>	The pathname of the directory on which the file system is mounted.
<fstype>	The file system type.
<options>	The list of mount options used to mount the file system.
<time>	The time at which the file system was mounted.

Here is a sample /etc/mnttab file:

```
more /etc/mnttab
/dev/dsk/c0t3d0s0  /  ufs  rw,suid,dev=800018,largefiles   938797446
/dev/dsk/c0t3d0s6  /usr  ufs  rw,suid,dev=80001e,largefiles   938797446
/proc  /proc  proc  rw,suid,dev=2900000  938797446
fd   /dev/fd fd   rw,suid,dev=29c0000  938797446
/dev/dsk/c0t3d0s1   /var  ufs  rw,suid,dev=800019,largefiles  938797446
/dev/dsk/c0t3d0s3  /export ufs  suid,rw,largefiles,dev=80001b  938797448
/dev/dsk/c0t3d0s5  /opt  ufs  suid,rw,largefiles,dev=80001d  938797448
swap  /tmp  tmpfs  dev=1  938797448
-hosts  /net  autofs  ignore,indirect,nosuid,nobrowse,dev=2b40001  938799233
-xfn  /xfn  autofs  ignore,indirect,dev=2b40003  938799234
sparc48:vold(pid362)  /vol  nfs  ignore,noquota,dev=2b00001  938799248
-hosts  /net/sparc4/usr autofs  nosuid,nobrowse,ignore,nest,dev=2b40004 938799536
sparc4:/usr  /net/sparc4/usr nfs  nosuid,dev=2b00002   938799540
/dev/dsk/c0t0d0s0  /home2  ufs  rw,nosuid,largefiles,dev=800000 939120993
```

Unmounting a File System

To unmount a file system, use the `umount` command:

```
umount <mount-point>
```

`<mount-point>` is the name of the file system you want to unmount. This can be either the directory name in which the file system is mounted or the device name path of the file system. For example, to unmount the /home2 file system, type

```
umount /home2
```

Alternatively, you can specify the device name path for the file system:

```
umount /dev/dsk/c0t0d0s0
```

Unmounting a file system removes it from the file system mount point and deletes the entry from the /etc/mnttab file. Some file system administration tasks cannot be performed on mounted file systems, such as `labelit`, `fsck`, and `tunefs`. You should unmount a file system if

- It is no longer needed or has been replaced by a file system that contains software that is more current.
- You need to check and repair it using the `fsck` command.
- You plan to do a complete backup.

NOTE. *File systems are automatically unmounted as part of the system shutdown procedure.*

The *fuser* Command

Before you can unmount a file system, you must be logged in as the administrator (root), and the file system must not be busy. A file system is considered busy if a user is in a directory in the file system or if a program has a file open in that file system. You can make a file system available for unmounting by changing to a directory in a different file system or by logging out of the system. If something is causing the file system to be busy, you can use the `fuser` command, described in Table 5-7, to list all the processes accessing the file system and to stop them if necessary.

NOTE. *Always notify users before unmounting a file system.*

The syntax for `fuser` is

```
/usr/sbin/fuser [options] <file>|<filesystem>
```

Replace `<file>` with the filename you are checking, or replace `<filesystem>` with the name of the file system you are checking.

Table 5-7 The *fuser* Command

Option	Description
-c	Reports on files that are mount points for file systems and on any files within that mounted file system.
-f	Prints a report for the named file but not for files within a mounted file system.
-k	Sends the SIGKILL signal to each process. Because this option spawns kills for each process, the kill messages might not show up immediately.
-u	Displays the user login name in parentheses following the process ID.

The following example uses the `fuser` command to find out why /home2 is busy:

```
fuser -u /home2
```

The system displays each process and user login name that is using this file system:

```
/home2:      8448c(root)     8396c(root)
```

The following command stops all processes that are using the /home2 file system by sending a `SIGKILL` to each one. Don't use it without first warning the users.

```
fuser -c -k /home2
```

Volume Manager

Volume manager (not to be confused with Enterprise Volume Manager, described in Chapter 16), with the `vold` daemon, is the mechanism that manages removable media, such as the CD-ROM and disk drives. Mounting and unmounting a file system requires root privileges. So how do you let users insert, mount, and unmount CD-ROMs and disks without being the administrator (root)? After a file system has been mounted and then you remove the medium, what happens to the mount? Usually when you disconnect a disk drive while it is mounted, the system begins displaying errors and messages. The same thing happens if you remove a disk or CD-ROM while it is mounted.

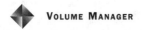

Volume manager, with its `vold` daemon, provides some assistance to overcome these problems. The `vold` daemon takes care of all the interfacing to the device, mounting and unmounting removable media and merging the media as transparently as possible within the normal Solaris file system. Volume manager provides three major benefits:

- By automatically mounting disks and CDs, it simplifies their use.
- It lets the user access disks and CDs without having to be logged in as root.
- It lets the administrator (root) give other systems on the network automatic access to any disks and CDs the users insert into your system.

To begin, let's look at the two devices the system administrator needs to manage: the disk drive and the CD-ROM. Volume manager provides access to both devices through the /vol/dev directory. In addition, volume manager creates links to the disk and CD-ROM devices through various directories, as shown in Table 5-8.

Table 5-8 Volume Manager Directories and Links

Link	Description
/vol/dev/diskette0	The directory providing block device access for the medium in floppy drive 0.
/vol/dev/rdiskette0	The directory providing character device access for the medium in floppy drive 0.
/vol/dev/aliases/floppy0	The symbolic link to the character device for the medium in floppy drive 0.
/dev/rdiskette	The directory providing character device access for the medium in the primary floppy drive, usually drive 0.
/vol/dev/aliases/cdrom0	The directory providing character device access for the medium in the primary CD-ROM drive.
/vol/dev/dsk/	The directory providing access to the CD-ROM buffered, or block, device.
/vol/dev/rdsk/	The directory providing access to the CD-ROM character, or raw, device.
/cdrom/cdrom0	The symbolic link to the buffered device for the medium in CD-ROM drive 0.
/floppy/floppy0	The symbolic link to the buffered device for the medium in floppy drive 0.

Volume manager automatically mounts CD and disk file systems when removable media containing recognizable file systems are inserted into the devices. The CD or disk file system is automatically mounted in the /vol/dev directories just described.

The `vold` daemon is the workhorse behind volume manager. It is automatically started at startup by the /etc/init.d/volmgt script. `vold` reads the /etc/vold.conf configuration file at startup. The vold.conf file contains the volume manager configuration information used by vold. This information includes the database to use, labels that are supported, devices to use, actions to take if certain media events occur, and the list of file systems that are unsafe to eject without unmounting. The vold.conf file looks like this:

```
# @(#)vold.conf 1.21     96/05/10 SMI
#
# Volume Daemon Configuration file
#

# Database to use (must be first)
db db_mem.so

# Labels supported
label dos label_dos.so floppy rmscsi pcmem
label cdrom label_cdrom.so cdrom
label sun label_sun.so floppy rmscsi pcmem

# Devices to use
use cdrom drive /dev/rdsk/c*s2 dev_cdrom.so cdrom%d
use floppy drive /dev/rdiskette[0-9] dev_floppy.so floppy%d
use pcmem drive /dev/rdsk/c*s2 dev_pcmem.so pcmem%d forceload=true
# use rmscsi drive /dev/rdsk/c*s2 dev_rmscsi.so rmscsi%d

# Actions
insert dev/diskette[0-9]/* user=root /usr/sbin/rmmount
insert dev/dsk/* user=root /usr/sbin/rmmount
eject dev/diskette[0-9]/* user=root /usr/sbin/rmmount
eject dev/dsk/* user=root /usr/sbin/rmmount
notify rdsk/* group=tty user=root /usr/lib/vold/volmissing -p

# List of file system types unsafe to eject
unsafe ufs hsfs pcfs
```

Each section in the vold.conf file is labeled as to its function. Of these sections, you can safely modify the devices to use, which are described in Table 5-9, and actions, which are described in Table 5-10.

The "Devices to use" section describes the devices to be managed by vold. It has the following syntax:

```
use <device> <type> <special> <shared_object> <symname> [ options ]
```

Table 5-9 vold.conf Devices to Use

Parameter Field	Description
device	The type of removable media device to be used. Legal values are cdrom and floppy.
type	The device's specific capabilities. The legal value is drive.

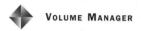

Table 5-9 vold.conf Devices to Use (continued)

Parameter Field	Description
special	Specifies the device or devices to be used. The path usually begins with /dev.
shared_object	The name of the program that manages this device. vold expects to find this program in /usr/lib/vold.
symname	The symbolic name that refers to this device. The symname is placed in the device directory.
options	The user, group, and mode permissions for the medium inserted (optional).

The special and symname parameters are related. If special contains any shell wildcard characters (that is, has one or more asterisks or question marks in it), symname must have a %d at its end. In this case, the devices that are found to match the regular expression are sorted and then numbered. The first device has a 0 filled in for the %d, the second device found has a 1, and so on.

If the special specification does not have any shell wildcard characters, the symname parameter must explicitly specify a number at its end.

The "Actions" section specifies which program should be called if a particular event (action) occurs. The syntax for the Actions field is as follows:

```
insert regex [ options ] <program> <program_args>
eject regex [ options ] <program> <program_args>
notify regex [ options ] <program> <program_args>
```

The different actions are listed in Table 5-10.

Table 5-10 *vold.conf* Actions

Parameter	Description
insert|eject|notify	The media action prompting the event.
regex	This Bourne shell regular expression is matched against each entry in the /vol file system that is being affected by this event.
[options]	Specifies which user or group name this event is to run (optional).
<program>	The full pathname of an executable program to be run if regex is matched.
program_args	Arguments to the program.

In the default vold.conf file, you see the following entries under the "Devices to use" and "Actions" sections:

```
# Devices to use
use cdrom drive /dev/rdsk/c*s2 dev_cdrom.so cdrom%d
use floppy drive /dev/rdiskette[0-9] dev_floppy.so floppy%d
use pcmem drive /dev/rdsk/c*s2 dev_pcmem.so pcmem%d forceload=true
# use rmscsi drive /dev/rdsk/c*s2 dev_rmscsi.so rmscsi%d

# Actions
insert dev/diskette[0-9]/* user=root /usr/sbin/rmmount
insert dev/dsk/* user=root /usr/sbin/rmmount
eject dev/diskette[0-9]/* user=root /usr/sbin/rmmount
eject dev/dsk/* user=root /usr/sbin/rmmount
notify rdsk/* group=tty user=root /usr/lib/vold/volmissing -p
```

When a CD is inserted into the CD-ROM named /dev/dsk/c0t6d0, the following happens:

1. `vold` detects that the CD has been inserted and runs the `/usr/sbin/rmmount` command. `rmmount` is the utility that automatically mounts a file system on a CD-ROM and floppy. It determines what type of file system, if any, is on the medium. If a file system is present, `rmmount` mounts the file system (for a CD-ROM, in /cdrom0).

   If the medium is read-only (either a CD-ROM or a floppy with the write-protect tab set), the file system is mounted as read-only. If a file system is not identified, `rmmount` does not mount a file system.

2. After the mount is complete, the `action` associated with the media type is executed. The `action` allows other programs to be notified that a new medium is available. For example, the default `action` for mounting a CD-ROM or a floppy is to start File Manager.

   These `actions` are described in the configuration file, /etc/rmmount.conf. Here's an example of the default /etc/rmmount.conf file:

   ```
   # @(#)rmmount.conf 1.3     96/05/10 SMI
   #
   # Removable Media Mounter configuration file.
   #
   # File system identification
   ident hsfs ident_hsfs.so cdrom
   ident ufs ident_ufs.so cdrom floppy rmscsi pcmem
   ident pcfs ident_pcfs.so floppy rmscsi pcmem

   # Actions
   action cdrom action_filemgr.so
   action floppy action_filemgr.so
   action rmscsi action_filemgr.so
   ```

3. If the user issues the `eject` command, `vold` sees the media event and executes the `action` associated with that event. In this case, it runs `/usr/sbin/rmmount`. `rmmount` unmounts mounted file systems and executes actions associated with the media type called out in the /etc/rmmount.conf file. If a file system is "busy" (that is, it contains the current working directory of a live process), the eject action fails.

The system administrator can modify vold.conf to specify which program should be called if media events happen, such as eject or insert. If the vold.conf configuration file is modified, `vold` must be told to reread the /etc/vold.conf file. Do this by stopping and starting `vold` as follows. Type

```
/etc/init.d/volmgt stop
```

Then type

```
/etc/init.d/volmgt start
```

Several other commands help you administer volume manager on your system. They are described in Table 5-11.

Table 5-11 Volume Manager Commands

Command	Description
`rmmount`	Removable media mounter. Used by `vold` to automatically mount /cdrom and /floppy if a CD or disk is installed.
`volcancel`	Cancels a user's request to access a particular CD-ROM or floppy file system. This command, issued by the system administrator, is useful if the removable medium containing the file system is not currently in the drive.
`volcheck`	The system administrator issues this command to check the drive for installed media. By default, it checks the drive pointed to by /dev/diskette.
`volmissing`	This action, which is specified in vold.conf, notifies the user if an attempt is made to access a CD or disk that is no longer in the drive.
`vold`	The volume manager daemon, controlled by /etc/vold.conf.

To some, volume management might seem more trouble than it's worth. To disable volume management, remove (or rename) the file named /etc/rc2.d/S92volmgt. Then issue the command `/etc/init.d/volmgt stop`. If you want to have volume management on the CD but not the floppy, comment out the entries in the "Devices to use" and "Actions" sections of the vold.conf file with a `#` as follows:

```
# Devices to use
use cdrom drive /dev/rdsk/c*s2 dev_cdrom.so cdrom%d
#use floppy drive /dev/rdiskette[0-9] dev_floppy.so floppy%d
```

```
use pcmem drive /dev/rdsk/c*s2 dev_pcmem.so pcmem%d forceload=true
# use rmscsi drive /dev/rdsk/c*s2 dev_rmscsi.so rmscsi%d

# Actions
#insert dev/diskette[0-9]/* user=root /usr/sbin/rmmount
insert dev/dsk/* user=root /usr/sbin/rmmount
#eject dev/diskette[0-9]/* user=root /usr/sbin/rmmount
eject dev/dsk/* user=root /usr/sbin/rmmount
notify rdsk/* group=tty user=root /usr/lib/vold/volmissing -p
```

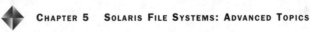

With the changes made to /etc/vold.conf, when the `vold` daemon starts up, it manages only the CD-ROM and not the floppy.

`vold` is picky. Knowing this is the key to not making `vold` crash or not work for some reason. With other computers, such as PCs, you can eject CD-ROMs with no problems. With Solaris, `vold` isn't that robust, so the system administrator needs to follow a few ground rules when using volume manager:

- Always use `vold` commands for everything to do with CD-ROMs and floppy disks. Use the commands listed in Table 5-11 to accomplish your task.
- Before pressing the button on the outside of the box to eject a CD-ROM disk, be sure to type `eject cdrom`. This is to ensure that you don't already have a CD in the reader.
- Never press the button to eject a CD when there is a CD already in the machine. This could cause `vold` to stop working. Again, use the `eject cdrom` command instead.
- Never kill the `vold` daemon. Instead, use the `/etc/init.d/volmgt stop` command. This is a good recommendation for all daemons that have scripts to stop and start them in the /etc/init.d directory. Killing the `vold` daemon often causes it to not restart or stop correctly.
- If you can't stop or start `vold` using the /etc/init.d/volmgt script, you need to restart the system to get `vold` working properly.

Troubleshooting Volume Manager

You might sometimes have problems with mounting a floppy or a CD-ROM. First, check to see if volume manager knows about the device. The best way to do this is to look in /vol/dev/rdiskette0 and see if there is something there. If not, the `volcheck` command has not been run or there is a hardware problem. If references to /vol lock up the system, it means that the daemon has died, and you need to restart the `vold` daemon as described earlier.

If `vold` is working properly, insert a formatted disk and type

```
ls -l /vol/dev/rdiskette0
```

The system responds with this:

```
total 0
crw-rw-rw-    1 nobody    nobody     91,   7 Oct 13 14:56 unlabeled
```

NOTE. *The volume is unlabeled; therefore, the file in /vol/dev/rdiskette0 is called unlabeled.*

Check to make sure that there is a link in /floppy to the character device in /vol/dev/rdiskette0. Type

```
ls -l /floppy0
```

The system responds with this:

```
total 18
lrwxrwxrwx    1 root      nobody          11 Oct 13 14:56 floppy0 -> ./unlabeled
```

If there's a name in /vol/dev/rdiskette0, as previously described, and nothing is mounted in /floppy/<name_of_media>, it's likely that data on the medium is an unrecognized file system. For example, maybe it's a `tar` archive, a `cpio` backup, or a Macintosh file system. Don't use volume manager to get to these file types. Instead, access them through the block or character devices found in /vol/dev/rdiskette0 or /vol/dev/diskette0, with user tools to interpret the data on them, such as `tar`, `dd`, or `cpio`. For example, if you're trying to access a `tar` archive on a disk, use this command:

```
tar tvf /vol/dev/rdiskette0/unlabeled
```

All `tar` files on the floppy disk will be listed.

To create a `tar` file on a floppy disk, the disk must contain a SunOS volume label. Use the `fdformat` command to format a disk and add a volume label. The syntax of the `fdformat` command is

```
fdformat [options] [<devname>]
```

This command is described in Table 5-12.

Table 5-12 The *fdformat* Command

Option	Description
`-b <label>`	Labels the medium with a volume label. A SunOS volume label is restricted to eight characters. A DOS volume label is restricted to all uppercase characters.
`-B <filename>`	Installs a special startup loader in `<filename>` on an MS-DOS disk. This option is meaningful only when the `-d` option (or `-t dos`) is also specified.

continues

Table 5-12 The *fdformat* Command (continued)

Option	Description
`-d`	Formats MS-DOS media.
`-D`	Formats a 720KB (3 1/2-inch) or 360KB (5 1/4-inch) double-density disk. This is the default for double-density-type drives. It is needed if the drive is a high or extended density type.
`-e`	Ejects the disk when done.
`-E`	Formats a 2.88MB (3 1/2-inch) extended-density disk. This is the default for extended-density-type drives.
`-f`	Force. Does not ask for confirmation before starting format.
`-H`	Formats a 1.44MB (3 1/2-inch) or 1.2MB (5 1/4-inch) high-density disk. This is the default for high-density-type drives; it is needed if the drive is the extended-density type.
`-l`	Formats a 720KB (3 1/2-inch) or 360KB (5 1/4-inch) double-density disk.
`-L`	Formats a 720KB (3 1/2-inch) or 360KB (5 1/4-inch) double-density disk.
`-m`	Formats a 1.2MB (3 1/2-inch) medium-density disk.
`-M`	Writes a 1.2MB (3 1/2-inch medium-density format on a high-density disk (use only with the `-t nec` option).
`-U`	Unmounts any file systems and then formats the disk.
`-q`	Quiet; does not print status messages.
`-v`	Verifies each block of the disk after the format.
`-x`	Skips the format, and only writes a SunOS label or an MS-DOS file system.
`-t dos`	Installs an MS-DOS file system and startup sector formatting. This is equivalent to the DOS `format` command or the `-d` option.
`-t nec`	Installs an NEC-DOS file system and startup sector on the disk after formatting. This should be used only with the `-M` option.

In Table 5-12, the device specified for `<devname>` depends on whether you're using volume manager or not. On systems using volume manager, replace `<devname>` with `floppy0`. If you're not using volume manager, replace `<devname>` with `rdiskette0`.

If `<devname>` is omitted, the default disk drive (/vol/dev/rdiskette0/unlabeled), if one exists, is used.

By default, `fdformat` uses the configured capacity of the drive to format the disk. For example, a 3 1/2-inch high-density drive uses disks with a formatted capacity of 1.44MB. After formatting and verifying, `fdformat` writes an operating-system label on block 0. Use the `-t dos` option (the same as the `-d` option) to put an MS-DOS file system on the disk after the format is done. Otherwise, `fdformat` writes a SunOS label in block 0.

To format the default disk device with a SunOS label so that it can be used to create a `tar` archive, insert the floppy disk and issue the following command:

```
fdformat <cr>
```

The system responds with this:

```
Formatting 1.44 MB in /vol/dev/rdiskette0/unlabeled
Press return to start formatting floppy
```

Press the Enter key. The system displays a series of dots, as follows, until formatting is complete:

```
....................................
```

You can then create a `tar` archive on the disk. Type

```
tar cvf /vol/dev/rdiskette0/unlabeled /etc/hosts
```

The /etc/hosts file is written to the disk in `tar` format.

If you're still having problems with volume manager, one way to gather debugging information is to run the `rmmount` command with the debug (`-D`) flag. To do this, edit /etc/vold.conf and change the lines that have `/usr/sbin/rmmount` to include the `-D` flag. For example:

```
insert /vol*/dev/diskette[0-9]/* user=root /usr/sbin/rmmount -D
```

This causes various debugging messages to appear on the console.

To see debugging messages from the volume manager daemon, run the daemon, `/usr/sbin/vold`, with the `-v -L 10` flags. It logs data to /var/adm/vold.log. This file might contain information that could be useful in troubleshooting.

You might also want to mount a CD-ROM on a different mount point using volume management. `vold`, by default, mounts the CD-ROM on the mount point /cdrom/cdrom0, but the user can mount it on a different mount point by following these instructions:

1. If volume manager is running, bring up File Manager and eject the CD-ROM by issuing the following command:

   ```
   eject cdrom
   ```

2. Stop the volume management daemon by typing

   ```
   /etc/init.d/volmgt stop
   ```

3. Create the directory called /test:

```
mkdir /test
```

4. Insert the CD-ROM into the CD drive and issue this command:

```
/usr/sbin/vold -d /test &
```

Now, instead of using the /vol directory, `vold` will use /test as the starting directory.

Information on File Systems

In Chapter 4, I described the `df` and `fsck` commands. The `df` command gives you capacity information on each mounted file system. The output of `df` and `fsck` is often misunderstood. This section goes into more detail on these two commands and describes their output so that you can better understand the information displayed. I begin with the `fsck` command. Remember, run `fsck` only on unmounted file systems, as shown in the following example. Type

```
umount /home2
fsck /dev/rdsk/c0t0d0s6
```

The system responds with this:

```
** /dev/rdsk/c0t0d0s0
** Last Mounted on /home2
** Phase 1 - Check Blocks and Sizes
** Phase 2 - Check Pathnames
** Phase 3 - Check Connectivity
** Phase 4 - Check Reference Counts
** Phase 5 - Check Cyl groups
5 files, 19 used, 95975 free (15 frags, 11995 blocks,  0.0% fragmentation)
```

`fsck` first reports some things related to usage, as shown in Table 5-13.

Table 5-13 *fsck* output

Field	Description
`files`	Number of files in the file system.
`used`	Number of data blocks used.
`free`	Number of data blocks free (fragments and whole blocks).

NOTE. *A fragment is one data block in size, and a block consists of a number of data blocks, typically eight.*

Then `fsck` reports more details of the free space, as shown in Table 5-14.

Table 5-14 *fsck* Output

Field	Description
`frags`	The number of free fragments (from fragmented blocks).
`blocks`	The number of free blocks (whole unfragmented blocks).
`% fragmentation`	Free fragments as a percentage of the whole disk size.

Fragmentation does not refer to fragmentation in the sense of a file's disk blocks being inefficiently scattered across the whole file system, as you see in a DOS file system.

In Solaris, a high percentage of fragmentation implies that much of the free space is tied up in fragments. In the previous example, fragmentation was 0 percent. High fragmentation affects creating new files—especially those larger than a few data blocks. Typically, high fragmentation would be caused by creating large numbers of small files. The solution is to either create a larger file system or decrease the block size (finer granularity).

For example, in a file system that creates predominantly 5KB files on an 8KB block size, many 3KB fragments are free and are never used. In the extreme case, this would result in a file system that is effectively full, despite only 5/8 of the file system being used. If the block size is decreased to 4KB, which is the smallest block size available in Solaris 7, there is some improvement. The solution can be summarized in Table 5-15.

Table 5-15 Block Sizes

Block Size	Typical Pattern
8KB blocks	Many 5KB fragment blocks and 3KB fragments are wasted.
4KB blocks	Many full blocks plus one full fragment block per four full blocks, which is much better.

Now, let's review the output from the `df` command:

```
mount /dev/dsk/c0t0d0s6 /home2
df  -k /home2
```

The system responds with this:

```
Filesystem            Kbytes    used    avail    capacity    Mounted on
/dev/dsk/c0t0d0s6     95994     19      91176    1%          /home2
```

The 95994 value in the output represents the file system size in KB. It includes the 5 percent `minfree` that you specified earlier with the `tunefs` command. The solution can be summarized in Table 5-16.

Table 5-16 Output from *df*

Field	Description
19KB used	The amount of space used in the file system.
91176KB available	Space available in the file system. This value is equal to the file system size less the `minfree%` less the space used (95994–5%–19).
1% capacity	Space used as a percentage, calculated as follows: kilobytes used/(kilobytes available – `minfree%`)

Summary

This concludes the discussion of local file systems. Chapter 16 discusses disk devices in detail. Although this topic is covered on the Part II exam, I recommend reviewing that chapter for a detailed description of the various device configurations that make up file systems. In Chapter 17, "Networking," and Chapter 18, "The NFS Environment," I discuss how to share file systems with other hosts on the network. The next chapter discusses system security and describes how to protect your systems and the data on them.

CHAPTER

6

System Security

The following are the test objectives for this chapter:

- Understanding physical security
- Controlling system access
- Controlling file access
- Understanding network security
- Securing superuser access
- Understanding the Automated Security Enhancement Tool (ASET)
- Employing common-sense security techniques

n addition, we will discuss auditing users. Although this topic appears on the second exam, I have included it in this chapter because the material fits well with the topics discussed and does not warrant a chapter of its own.

Keeping the system's information secure is one of the system administrator's primary tasks. System security involves protecting data against loss due to a disaster or system failure. In addition, it is the system administrator's responsibility to protect systems from the threat of an unauthorized intruder and to protect data on the system from unauthorized users. Some of the worst disasters I've seen have come from authorized personnel—even system administrators—destroying data unintentionally. Therefore, the system administrator is presented with two levels of security: protecting data from accidental loss, and securing the system against intrusion or unauthorized access.

The first scenario, protecting data from accidental loss, is easy to achieve with a full system backup scheme you run regularly. Regular backups provide protection in the event of a disaster. If a user accidentally destroys data, if the hardware malfunctions, or if a computer program simply corrupts data, the system administrator can restore files from the backup media. (Backup and recovery techniques are covered in Chapter 12, "Backup and Recovery.")

The second form of security, securing the system against intrusion or unauthorized access, is more complex. This book cannot cover every security hole or threat, but it does discuss UNIX security fundamentals. Protection against intruders involves the following:

- **Physical security**—Limiting physical access to the computer equipment.
- **Controlling system access**—Limiting user access via passwords and permissions.
- **Controlling file access**—Limiting access to data by assigning file access permissions.
- **Auditing users**—Monitoring user activities to detect a threat before damage occurs.
- **Network security**—Protecting against access through phone lines, serial lines, or the network.
- **Securing superuser access**—Reserving superuser access for system administration use only.

Physical Security

Physical security is simple: Lock the door. Limit who has physical access to the computer equipment to prevent theft or vandalism. In addition, limit access to the system console. Anyone who has access to the console ultimately has access to the data. If the computer contains sensitive data, keep it locked in a controlled environment with clean power and adequate protection against fire, lightning, flood, and other building disasters. Restrict access to protect against tampering with the system and its backups. Anyone with access to the backup media could steal it and access the data. Furthermore, if a system is logged in and left unattended, anyone who can use that system can gain access to the operating system and the network. Make sure your users log out or "lock" their screens before walking away. In sum, you need to be aware of your users' computer surroundings, and you need to physically protect them from unauthorized access.

Controlling System Access

Controlling access to systems involves using passwords and appropriate file permissions. To control access, all logins must have passwords, and the passwords must be changed frequently. Password aging is a system parameter set by the system administrator that requires users to change their passwords after a certain number of days. Password aging lets you force users to change their passwords periodically or prevent users from changing their passwords before a specified interval. Set an expiration date for a password to prevent an intruder from gaining undetected access to the system through an old and inactive account. For a high level of security, you should require users to change their passwords every six weeks. Once every three months is adequate for lower levels of security. Change system administration logins (such as root and sys) monthly, or whenever a person who knows the root password leaves the company or is reassigned.

Several files that control default system access are stored in the /etc/default directory. These files limit access to specific systems on a network. Table 6-1 summarizes the files in the /etc/default directory.

Table 6-1 Files in the /etc/default Directory

Filename	Description
/etc/default/login	Controls system login policies, including root access. The default is to limit root access to the console.
/etc/default/passwd	Controls default policy on password aging.
/etc/default/su	Specifies where attempts to su to root are logged and where these log files are located. The file also specifies whether attempts to su to root are displayed on a named device (such as a system console).

You can set default values in the /etc/default/passwd file to control user passwords. Table 6-2 lists the options that can be controlled through the /etc/default/passwd file.

Table 6-2 Flags in /etc/default/passwd

Flags	Description
MAXWEEKS	Maximum time period a password is valid.
MINWEEKS	Minimum time period before the password can be changed.
PASSLENGTH	Minimum length of the password, in characters.
WARNWEEKS	Time period warning of the password's ensuing expiration date.

The system administrator's job is to ensure that all users have secure passwords. Improper passwords can be broken by a system cracker and could put the entire system at risk. Enforce the following guidelines on passwords:

- Ensure that passwords contain a combination of six to eight letters, numbers, or special characters.
- A phrase such as "beammeup" works well as a password.
- Nonsense words made up of the first letter of every word in a phrase, such as "swotrb" for "Somewhere Over the Rainbow," work well for a password.
- Words with numbers or symbols substituted for letters, such as "sn00py" for "snoopy," also make good passwords.

On the other hand, here are some poor choices for passwords:

- Proper nouns, names, login names, and other passwords a person might guess just by knowing something about you (the user)
- Your name forward, backward, or jumbled
- Names of family members or pets
- Car license plate numbers
- Telephone numbers
- Social Security numbers
- Employee numbers
- Names related to a hobby or interest
- Seasonal themes, such as Santa in December
- Any word in the dictionary
- Simple keyboard patterns (asdfgh)
- Passwords you've used previously

Where User Account Information Is Stored

User account and group information is stored in files located in the /etc directory.

Most of the user account information is stored in the /etc/passwd file; however, password encryption and password aging details are stored in the /etc/shadow file. Group information is stored in the /etc/group file. Users are put together into groups based on their file access needs; for example, the "acctng" group might be users in the accounting department.

Each line in the /etc/passwd file contains several fields, separated by a colon (:), and is formatted as follows:

```
username:password:uid:gid:comment:home-directory:login-shell
```

Table 6-3 defines each field in the /etc/passwd file.

Table 6-3 Fields in the /etc/passwd File

Field Name	Description
username	Contains the information user or login name. User names should be unique and consist of one to eight letters (A through Z, a through z) and numerals (0 through 9) but no underscores or spaces. The first character must be a letter, and at least one character must be a lowercase letter.
password	Contains an x, which is a placeholder for the encrypted password that is stored in the /etc/shadow file.
uid	Contains a user identification (UID) number that identifies the user to the system. UID numbers for regular users should range from 100 to 60000, but they can go as high as 2147483647 (see the following Note). All UID numbers should be unique. UIDs less than 100 are reserved. To minimize security risks, avoid reusing UIDs from deleted accounts.
gid	Contains a group identification (GID) number that identifies the user's primary group. Each GID number must be a whole number between 0 and 60000 (60001 and 60002 are assigned to nobody and noaccess, respectively). GIDs can go as high as 2147483647 (see the following Note). GIF numbers under 100 are reserved for system default group accounts.
comment	Usually contains the user's full name.
home-directory	Contains the user's home directory pathname.
login-shell	Contains the user's default login shell.

NOTE. *Previous Solaris software releases used 32-bit data types to contain the UIDs and GIDs, but UIDs and GIDs were constrained to a maximum useful value of 60000. Starting with the Solaris 2.5.1 release and compatible versions, the limit on UID and GID values has been raised to the maximum value of a signed integer, or 2147483647. UIDs and GIDs over 60000 do not have full functionality and are incompatible with many Solaris features, so avoid using UIDs or GIDs over 60000.*

Each line in the /etc/shadow file contains several fields separated by colons (:). This line is formatted as follows:

```
username:password:lastchg:min:max:warn:inactive:expire
```

Table 6-4 defines each field in the /etc/shadow file.

Table 6-4 Fields in the /etc/shadow File

Field Name	Description
`username`	Contains the user or login name.
`password`	Might contain the following entries: a 13-character encrypted user password; the string *LK*, which indicates an inaccessible account; or the string NP, which indicates no password on the account.
`lastchg`	Indicates the number of days between January 1, 1970, and the last password modification date.
`min`	Contains the minimum number of days required between password changes.
`max`	Contains the maximum number of days the password is valid before the user is prompted to specify a new password.
`inactive`	Contains the number of days a user account can be inactive before being locked.
`expire`	Contains the absolute date when the user account expires. Past this date, the user cannot log into the system.

Each line in the /etc/group file contains several fields, separated by colons (:). This line is formatted as follows:

```
group-name:group-password:gid:user-list
```

Table 6-5 defines each field in the /etc/group file.

Table 6-5 Fields in the /etc/group File

Field Name	Description
`group-name`	Contains the name assigned to the group. For example, members of the accounting department might be called acct. Group names can have a maximum of nine characters.
`group-password`	Usually contains an asterisk or is empty. The `group-password` field is a relic of earlier versions of UNIX.
`gid`	Contains the group's GID number. It must be unique on the local system and should be unique across the entire organization. Each GID number must be a whole number between 0 and 60002, but it can go as high as 2147483647. Numbers under 100 are reserved for system default group accounts. User-defined groups can range from 100 to 60000 (60001 and 60002 are reserved and assigned to nobody and noaccess, respectively). See the previous Note regarding the use of UIDs and GIDs over 60000.
`user-list`	Contains a list of groups and a comma-separated list of user names, representing the user's secondary group memberships. Each user can belong to a maximum of 16 secondary groups.

By default, all Solaris 7 systems have the following groups already defined in the /etc/group file. Do not use the following groups for users. Also, some system processes and applications might rely on these groups, so do not change the GID or remove these groups from the /etc/group file unless you are absolutely sure of the effect on the system.

```
root::0:root
other::1:
bin::2:root,bin,daemon
sys::3:root,bin,sys,adm
adm::4:root,adm,daemon
uucp::5:root,uucp
mail::6:root
tty::7:root,tty,adm
lp::8:root,lp,adm
nuucp::9:root,nuucp
staff::10:
daemon::12:root,daemon
sysadmin::14:
nobody::60001:
noaccess::60002:
nogroup::65534:
```

NOTE. *Members of the* `sysadmin` *group (group 14) are allowed to use the Solstice AdminSuite software. A system administrator may assign this group to a backup system administrator or power user. Unless you are a member of the UNIX* `sysadmin` *group, you must become superuser on your system to use Admintool.*

Restricted Shells

System administrators can use restricted versions of the Korn shell (`rksh`) and Bourne shell (`rsh`) to limit the operations allowed for a particular user account. Restricted shells are especially useful for ensuring that time-sharing users, or users' guests on a system, have restricted permissions during login sessions. When an account is set up with a restricted shell, users may not do the following:

- Change directories
- Set the `$PATH` variable
- Specify path or command names beginning with /
- Redirect output

You can also provide the user with shell procedures that have access to the full power of the standard shell but impose a limited menu of commands.

NOTE. *Do not confuse the restricted shell /usr/lib/rsh with the remote shell /usr/bin/rsh. When specifying a restricted shell, you should not include the user's path—/bin, /sbin, or /usr/bin. Doing so allows the user to start another shell (a nonrestricted shell).*

Controlling File Access

After you have established login restrictions, you need to control access to the data on the system. Some users only need to look at files; others need the ability to change or delete files. You might have data that you do not want anyone else to see. You control data access by assigning permission levels to a file or directory.

Three levels of access permission are assigned to a UNIX file to control access by the owner, the group, and all others. Display permissions with the `ls -la` command. The following example shows the use of the `ls -la` command to display permissions on files in the /users directory:

```
ls -la    /users
```

The system responds with this:

```
drwxr-xr-x   2   bill    staff    512    Sep 23 07:02        .
drwxr-xr-x   3   root    other    512    Sep 23 07:02        ..
-rw-r—r—     1   bill    staff    124    Sep 23 07:02        .cshrc
-rw-r—r—     1   bill    staff    575    Sep 23 07:02        .login
```

The first column of information displays the type of file and its access permissions for the user, group, and others. The `r`, `w`, and `x` are described in Table 6-6. The third column displays the owner of the file—usually the user who created the file. The owner of a file (and superuser) can decide who has the right to read it, to write to it, or—if it is a command—to execute it. The fourth column displays the group to which this file belongs—normally the owner's primary group.

Table 6-6 File Access Permissions

Symbol	Permission	Means That Designated Users...
r	Read	Can open and read the contents of a file.
w	Write	Can write to the file (modify its contents), add to it, or delete it.
x	Execute	Can execute the file (if it is a program or shell script).
-	Denied	Cannot read, write to, or execute the file.

When listing the permissions on a directory, all columns of information are the same as for a file, with one exception. The `r`, `w`, and `x` found in the first column are treated slightly differently than for a file. They are described in Table 6-7.

Table 6-7 Directory Access Permissions

Symbol	Permission	Means That Designated Users...
r	Read	Can list files in the directory.
w	Write	Can add or remove files or links in the directory.
x	Execute	Can open or execute files in the directory. Also can make the directory and the directories beneath it current.
-	Denied	Do not have read, write, or execute privileges.

Use the commands listed in Table 6-8 to modify file access permissions and ownership, but remember that only the owner of the file or root can assign or modify these values.

Table 6-8 File Access Commands

Command	Description
chmod	Changes access permissions on a file. You can use either symbolic mode (letters and symbols) or absolute mode (octal numbers) to change permissions on a file.
chown	Changes the ownership of a file.
chgrp	Changes the group ownership of a file.

Default *umask*

When a user creates a file or directory, the default file permissions assigned to the file or directory are controlled by the user mask. The user mask should be set by the `umask` command in a user initialization file such as /etc/profile or .cshrc. You can display the current value of the user mask by typing `umask` and pressing Enter.

The user mask is set with a three-digit octal value such as 022. The first digit sets permissions for the user, the second sets permissions for the group, and the third sets permissions for others. To set the `umask` to 022, type

```
umask 022
```

By default, the system sets the permissions on a file to 666, granting read and write permission to the user, group, and others. The system sets the default permissions on a directory or executable file to 777, or `rwxrwxrwx`. The value assigned by `umask` is subtracted from the default. To determine the `umask` value you want to set, subtract the value of the permissions you want from 666 (for a file) or 777 (for a directory). The remainder is the value to use with the `umask` command. For example, suppose you want to change the default mode for files to 644 (`rw-r--r--`). The difference between 666 and 644 is 022, which is the value you would use as an argument to the `umask` command.

Setting the `umask` value has the effect of granting or denying permissions in the same way `chmod` grants them. For example, the command `chmod 022` grants write permission to group and others, and `umask 022` denies write permission to group and others.

Sticky Bit

The *sticky bit* is a permission bit that protects the files within a directory. If the directory has the sticky bit set, a file can be deleted by only the owner of the file, the owner of the directory, or root. This prevents a user from deleting other users' files from public directories. A `t` or `T` in the access permissions column of a file listing indicates that the sticky bit has been set:

```
drwxrwxrwt   2 uucp   uucp   512 Feb 12 07:32 /var/spool/uucppublic
```

Use the chmod command to set the sticky bit. The symbols for setting the sticky bit by using the chmod command in symbolic mode are listed in Table 6-9.

Table 6-9 Sticky Bit Modes

Symbol	Description
t	Sticky bit is on; execution bit for others is on.
T	Sticky bit is on; execution bit for others is off.

Access Control Lists (ACLs)

ACLs (pronounced "ackls") can provide greater control over file permissions when the traditional UNIX file protection in the Solaris operating system is not enough. The traditional UNIX file protection provides read, write, and execute permissions for the three user classes: owner, group, and other. An ACL provides better file security by allowing you to define file permissions for the owner, owner's group, others, specific users and groups, and default permissions for each of these categories.

For example, assume you have a file you want everyone in a group to be able to read. To give everyone access, you would give "group" read permissions on that file. Now, assume you want only one person in the group to be able to write to that file. Standard UNIX doesn't let you set that up; however, you can set up an ACL to give only one person in the group write permissions on the file. ACL entries are the way to define an ACL on a file, and they are set through the ACL commands. ACL entries consist of the following fields, separated by colons:

```
entry_type:uid|gid:perms
```

ACL entries are defined in Table 6-10.

Table 6-10 ACL Entries

ACL Field	Description
entry_type	The type of ACL entry on which to set file permissions. For example, entry_type can be user (the owner of a file) or mask (the ACL mask).
uid	The user name or identification number.
gid	The group name or identification number.
perms	Represents the permissions set on entry_type. Permissions are indicated by the symbolic characters rwx or an octal number as used with the chmod command.

The ACL mask entry indicates the maximum permissions allowed for users, other than the owner, and for groups. The mask is a quick way to change permissions on all users and groups. For example, the `mask:r--` mask entry indicates that users and groups cannot have more than read permissions, even though they might have write/execute permissions.

Setting ACL Entries

Set ACL entries on a file by using the `setfacl` command:

```
$ setfacl -s user::perms,group::perms,other:perms,mask:perms,acl_entry_list filename ...
```

The `-s` option replaces the entire ACL with the new ACL entries, if an ACL already exists on the file.

The following example sets the user permissions to read/write, group permissions to read-only, and other permissions to none on the txt1.doc file. In addition, the user bill is given read/write permissions on the file, and the ACL mask permissions are set to read/write, which means that no user or group can have execute permissions.

```
$ setfacl -s user::rw-,group::r--,other:---,mask:rw-, user:bill:rw- txt1.doc
```

Checking the New File Permissions

Check the new file permissions with the `ls -l` command. The plus sign (+) to the right of the mode field indicates that the file has an ACL:

```
$ ls -l
 total 210
 -rw-r-----+   1 mike  sysadmin  32100  Sep 11 13:11 txt1.doc
 -rw-r--r--    1 mike  sysadmin   1410   Sep 11 13:11 txt2.doc
 -rw-r--r--    1 mike  sysadmin   1700   Sep 11 13:11 labnotes
```

Verifying ACL Entries

To verify which ACL entries were set on the file, use the `getfacl` command:

```
$ getfacl txt1.doc
```

The system responds with this:

```
# file: txt1.doc
# owner: mike
# group: sysadmin
user::rw-
user:bill:rw-     #effective:rw-
group::r--          #effective:r--
mask:rw-
other:---
```

Copying a File's ACL to Another File

Copy a file's ACL to another file by redirecting the `getfacl` output as follows:

```
getfacl <filename1>: | setfacl  -f  -  <filename2>
```

In the following example, I copy the ACL from file1 to file2:

```
getacl file1 | setfacl -f - file2
```

Issuing the `getfacl` command, I can verify that the change has been made:

```
getfacl file*

# file: file1
# owner: root
# group: other
user::rw-
user:bcalkins:rw-                #effective:rw-
group::r--               #effective:r--
mask:rw-
other:---

# file: file2
# owner: root
# group: other
user::rw-
user:bcalkins:rw-                #effective:rw-
group::r--               #effective:r--
mask:rw-
other:---
```

Modifying ACL Entries on a File

Modify ACL entries on a file by using the `setfacl` command:

```
setfacl -m <acl_entry_list> <filename1> [filename2 ...]
```

The arguments for the `setfacl` command are described in Table 6-11.

Table 6-11 *setfacl* Arguments

Argument	Description
-m	Modifies the existing ACL entry.
<acl_entry_list>	Specifies the list of one or more ACL entries to modify on the file or directory. You can also modify default ACL entries on a directory. (See Table 6-12 for the list of ACL entries.)
<filename>	Specifies the file or directory.

The ACL entries that can be specified with the `setfacl` command are described in Table 6-12.

Table 6-12 ACL Entries for Files

ACL Entry	Description
`u[ser]::<perms>`	File owner permissions.
`g[roup]::<perms>`	File group permissions.
`o[ther]:<perms>`	Permissions for users other than the file owner or members of the file group.
`m[ask]:<perms>`	The ACL mask. The mask entry indicates the maximum permissions allowed for users (other than the owner) and for groups. The mask is a quick way to change permissions on all the users and groups. For example, the `mask:r-- mask` entry indicates that users and groups cannot have more than read permissions, even though they may have write/execute permissions.
`u[ser]:uid:<perms>`	Permissions for a specific user. For `uid`, you can specify either a user name or a numeric UID.
`g[roup]:gid:<perms>`	Permissions for a specific group. For `gid`, you can specify either a group name or a numeric GID.

Deleting ACL Entries from a File

To delete an ACL entry from a file, use the `setfacl -d <acl_entry_list>` command. The following example illustrates how to remove an ACL entry for user bcalkins on file1 and file2:

```
setfacl -d u:bcalkins file1 file2
```

Use the `getfacl` command, described earlier, to verify that the entries have been deleted.

In addition to the ACL entries for files, you can set default ACL entries on a directory that apply to files created within the directory.

Setting the Correct Path

Setting your path variable correctly is important; otherwise, you might accidentally run a program introduced by someone else that harms the data or your system. This kind of program, which creates a security hazard, is called a "Trojan horse." For example, a substitute `su` program could be placed in a public directory where you, as system administrator, might run it. Such a script would look just like the regular `su` command. The script would remove itself after execution, and you'd have trouble knowing that you actually ran a Trojan horse.

The path variable is automatically set at login time through the startup files .login, .profile, and .cshrc. Setting up the user search path so that the current directory (.) comes last prevents you or your users from running this type of Trojan horse. The path variable for superuser should not include the current directory (.) at all.

NOTE. *Solaris provides a utility called ASET (Automated Security Enhancement Tool) that examines the startup files to ensure that the path variable is set up correctly and does not contain a dot (.) entry for the current directory. ASET is discussed later in this chapter.*

The *setuid* and *setgid* Programs

When set-user identification (`setuid`) permission is set on an executable file, a process that runs this file is granted access based on the file's owner (usually root) rather than the user who created the process. This allows a user to access files and directories that normally are available only to the owner. For example, the `setuid` permission on the `passwd` command makes it possible for a user to edit the /etc/passwd file to change passwords. When a user executes the `passwd` command, that user assumes the permissions of the root ID, which is UID 0. The `setuid` permission can be identified by using the `ls -l` command. The `-s` in the permissions field of the following example indicates the use of `setuid`:

```
ls -l /etc/passwd
  -r-sr-sr-x   1 root     sys     10332 May  3 08:23 /usr/bin/passwd
```

Many executable programs have to be run as root (that is, as superuser) to work properly. These executables run with the user ID set to 0 (`setuid=0`). Anyone running these programs runs them with the root ID, which creates a potential security problem if the programs are not written with security in mind.

On the other hand, the use of `setuid` on an executable program presents a security risk. A determined user can usually find a way to maintain the permissions granted to him by the `setuid` process, even after the process has finished executing. For example, a particular command might grant root privileges through the `setuid`. If a user can break out of this command, he could still have the root privileges granted by the `setuid` on that file. Any intruder who accesses a system will look for any files that have the `setuid`.

Except for the executables shipped with Solaris that have their `setuid` to root, you should disallow the use of `setuid` programs—or at least restrict and keep them to a minimum.

TIP. *To find files that have* `setuid` *permissions, become superuser. Then use the* `find` *command to find files that have* `setuid` *permissions set:*

```
# find [directory] -user root -perm -4000 -exec ls -ldb {}\; >/tmp/filename
```

The set-group identification (`setgid`) permission is similar to `setuid`, except that the process's effective GID is changed to the group owner of the file, and a user is granted access based on permissions granted to that group. Using the `ls -l` command, you can see that the file /usr/bin/mail has `setgid` permissions:

```
-r-x--s--x   1 bin    mail    64376 Jul  16 1997   /usr/bin/mail
```

The following example illustrates how to set the UID on an executable file named myprog1:

```
chmod 4744  myprog1
```

Verify the change by typing

```
ls -l myprog1
```

The system responds with this:

```
-rwsr--r--    1    root    other    25    Mar    6    11:52    myprog
```

The following example illustrates how to set the GID on an executable file named myprog1:

```
chmod 2070 myprog1
```

Verify the change by typing

```
ls -l myprog1
```

The system responds with this:

```
----rws---    1    root    other    25    Mar    6    11:58    myprog
```

Any user can set the UID or GID permission for any file he owns.

Auditing Users

The next two sections describe a few of the commands used to view information about users who have logged into the system. (Please note that auditing is covered on the Part II exam.)

Monitoring Users and System Usage

As the system administrator, you'll need to monitor system resources and be on the lookout for unusual activity. Having a method to monitor the system is very useful when there is a suspected breach in security. For example, you might want to monitor the login status of a particular user. Use the `logins` command to monitor a particular user's activities as follows:

1. Become superuser.
2. Display a user's login status by using the `logins` command:

```
# logins -x -l username
```

For example, to monitor login status for the user calkins, type

```
# logins -x -l calkins
```

The system displays the following information:

```
calkins      200     staff          10    Bill S. Calkins
                    /export/home/calkins
                    /bin/sh
                    PS 030195 10 7 -1
```

Table 6-13 describes the information output of the `logins` command.

Table 6-13 Output from the *logins* Command

Field	Description
`calkins`	The login name.
`200`	The UID.
`staff`	The primary group.
`10`	The GID.
`Bill S. Calkins`	The comment field of the /etc/passwd file.
`/export/home/calkins`	The user's home directory.
`/bin/sh`	The user's default login shell.
`PS 030195 10 7 -1`	Specifies the password aging information: the last date the password was changed, the number of days required between changes, the number of days allowed before a change is required, and the warning period.

You'll want to monitor user logins to ensure that their passwords are secure. A potential security problem is to have users without passwords (in other words, users who use a carriage return for a password). Periodically check user logins by using the following method:

1. Become superuser.
2. Display users who have no passwords by using the `logins` command:

```
# logins -p
```

The system responds with a list of users who do not have passwords.

Another good idea is to watch anyone who has tried to access the system but failed. You can save failed login attempts by creating the /var/adm/loginlog file with read and write permission for root only. After you create the loginlog file, all failed login activity is written to this file automatically after five failed attempts.

The loginlog file contains one entry for each failed attempt. Each entry contains the user's login name, the tty device, and the time of the failed attempt. If a person makes fewer than five unsuccessful attempts, none of the attempts is logged.

The loginlog file might grow quickly. To use the information in this file and to prevent the file from getting too large, you must check it and clear its contents occasionally. If this file shows a lot of activity, someone might be attempting to break into the computer system.

Checking Who's Logged In

Use the Solaris `who` command to find out who's logged in to a system. To obtain this information, the `who` command examines the /var/adm/utmp file, which contains a history of all logins since the file was last created.

Without any arguments, the `who` command lists the login account name, terminal device, login date and time, and where the user logged in from. Here is an example:

```
# who
root        pts/3        May 11 14:47    (10.64.178.2)
root        pts/1        May 10 15:42    (sparc1.PDESIGNINC.COM)
root        pts/2        May 10 15:53    (sparc1.PDESIGNINC.COM)
root        pts/4        May 11 14:48    (pluto)
```

Here are some of the more common options used with the `who` command:

`-a` Processes /var/adm/utmp or the named file with `-b`, `-d`, `-l`, `-p`, `-r`, `-t`, `-T`, and `-u` options turned on. The following example shows the output you'll see with the `-a` option:

```
who -a
NAME        LINE          TIME          IDLE    PID  COMMENTS
   .        system boot   May 10 09:56
   .        run-level 3   May 10 09:56     3      0  S
rc2               .       May 10 09:56   old     70  id=   s2 term=0    exit=0
rc3               .       May 10 09:57   old    270  id=   s3 term=0    exit=0
sac               .       May 10 09:57   old    294  id=   sc
LOGIN       console       May 10 09:57  0:13    295
zsmon             .       May 10 09:57   old    297
LOGIN       console       May 10 09:57  0:13    299          (:0)
root      + pts/3         May 11 14:47          505          (10.64.178.2)
root      + pts/1         May 10 15:42  0:13    366          (ovserv.PDESIGNINC.COM)
root      + pts/2         May 10 15:53 22:02    378          (ovserv.PDESIGNINC.COM)
root      + pts/4         May 11 14:48  0:13    518          (holl300s)
```

`-b` Indicates the time and date of the last reboot, as shown in the following example:

```
who -b
.          system boot  May 10 09:56
```

`-m` Outputs only information about the current terminal:

```
who -m
root       pts/3        May 11 14:47     (10.64.178.2)
```

`-n <x>` Takes a numeric argument, <x>, which specifies the number of users to display per line. <x> must be at least 1. The `-n` option may only be used with the `-q` option (described next).

`-q` (Quick who) Displays only the names and the number of users currently logged on. When this option is used, all other options are ignored. Here's an example of the `-q` and `-n` options:

```
who -q -n2
root      root
root      root
# users=4
```

`-r` Indicates the current run level of the init process:

```
who -r
.          run-level 3  May 10 09:56      3      0  S
```

`-s` Lists only the name, line, and time fields. This is the default when no options are specified.

The *whodo* Command

The `whodo` command produces formatted and dated output from information in the /var/adm/utmp, /tmp/ps_data, and /proc/pid files. It displays each user logged in and the active processes owned by that user. The output shows the date, time, and machine name. For each user logged in, the system displays the device name, UID, and login time, followed by a list of active processes associated with the UID. The process list includes the device name, process-ID, CPU minutes and seconds used, and process name. The following is an example of the `whodo` command:

```
whodo

Thu May 11 15:16:56 EDT 2000
holl300s

pts/3          root       14:47
    pts/3              505     0:00 sh
    pts/3              536     0:00 whodo
```

```
pts/1          root       15:42
     pts/1           366     0:00 sh
     pts/1           514     0:00 rlogin
     pts/1           516     0:00 rlogin

pts/2          root       15:53
     pts/2           378     0:00 sh

pts/4          root       14:48
     pts/4           518     0:00 sh
```

Use the `-l` option with the `whodo` command to get a long listing:

```
whodo -l
  3:23pm  up 1 day(s), 5 hr(s), 27 min(s)  4 user(s)
User      tty             login@  idle    JCPU    PCPU  what
root      pts/3            2:47pm     6                 whodo -l
root      pts/1           Wed 3pm    35                 rlogin holl300s
root      pts/2           Wed 3pm 22:24                 -sh
root      pts/4            2:48pm    35                 -sh
```

The fields displayed are the user's login name; the name of the tty the user is on; the time of day the user logged in (in hours:minutes); the idle time, which is the time since the user last typed anything (in hours:minutes); the CPU time used by all processes and their children on that terminal (in minutes:seconds); the CPU time used by the currently active processes (in minutes:seconds); and the name and arguments of the current process.

The *last* command

The Solaris `last` command looks in the /var/adm/wtmpx file for information about users who have logged in to the system. The `last` command displays the sessions of the specified users and terminals in chronological order. For each user, `last` displays the time when the session began, the duration of the session, and the terminal where the session took place. The `last` command also indicates if the session is still active or if it was terminated by a reboot.

For example, the command `last root console` lists all of root's sessions, as well as all sessions on the console terminal:

```
# last root console |more
```

The system responds with this:

```
root    pts/2    10.64.178.2         Tue May 30 11:24    still logged in
root    pts/1    10.64.178.2         Fri May 26 14:26 - 15:47  (01:20)
root    pts/1    10.64.178.2         Fri May 26 11:07 - 13:37  (02:29)
root    pts/1    10.64.178.2         Fri May 26 10:12 - 10:23  (00:11)
root    pts/1    10.64.178.2         Fri May 26 09:40 - 09:42  (00:02)
```

```
root    console :0                   Wed May 24 16:36 - 16:38  (00:01)
root    console :0                   Wed May 24 16:20 - 16:36  (00:15)
root    pts/3   10.64.178.2          Wed May 24 13:52 - 14:22 (1+00:30)
root    pts/1   ultra5.PDESIGNINC    Mon May 22 15:14 - 15:15  (00:00)
root    pts/2   sparc21.PDESIGNINC   Wed May 10 15:53 - 15:47  (23:53)
```

Network Security

The most difficult system administration issue to address is network security. When you connect your computer to the rest of the world via a network such as the Internet, someone could find an opening.

Firewalls

A way to protect your network from unauthorized users accessing hosts on your network is to use a *firewall,* or a secure gateway system. A firewall is a dedicated system separating two networks, each of which approaches the other as not trusted—a secure host that acts as a barrier between your internal network and outside networks. The firewall has two primary functions: It acts as a gateway to pass data between the networks, and it acts as a barrier to block the passage of data to and from the network. In addition, the firewall system receives all incoming email and distributes it to the hosts on the internal network.

Solaris is a powerful operating system that executes many useful services. However, some of these services are unneeded and can pose a potential security risk, especially for a system connected to the Internet. The first place to start is /etc/inetd.conf. This file specifies which services the `/usr/sbin/inetd` daemon will listen for. `inetd` is the daemon that provides many of the Internet-related services. By default, /etc/inetd.conf is configured for 30 or more services, but you probably need only two: ftp and telnet. You eliminate the remaining unnecessary services by commenting them out. This is critical, because many of the services run by `inetd`, such as `rexd`, pose serious security threats. `rexd` is the daemon responsible for remote program execution. On a system connected to the rest of the world via the Internet, this could create a potential entry point for a hacker.

The next place to start disabling unneeded processes is in the /etc/rc2.d and /etc/rc3.d startup directories. As stated in Chapter 1, "System Startup," here you will find startup scripts launched by the init process. Again, some of these processes might not be needed. To keep a script from starting during the boot process, replace the capital S with a small s. Table 6-14 lists some of the startup scripts that might not be needed and could pose security threats to your system.

Table 6-14 Startup Scripts

Startup Script	Description
/etc/rc2.d/S73nfs.client	Used for NFS mounting a system. A firewall should never mount another file system.
/etc/rc2.d/S74autofs	Used for automounting. Again, a firewall should never mount another file system.
/etc/rc2.d/S80lp	Used for printing. (Your firewall should never need to print.)
/etc/rc2.d/S88sendmail	Listens for incoming email. Your system can still send mail (such as alerts) with this disabled.
/etc/rc2.d/S71rpc	Portmapper daemon. A highly insecure service. Required if you are running CDE.
/etc/rc2.d/S99dtlogin	The CDE daemon. Starts CDE by default.
/etc/rc3.d/S15nfs.server	Used to share file systems. (A bad idea for firewalls.)
/etc/rc3.d/S76snmpdx	The snmp daemon.

Firewalls are one of the fastest-growing technical tools in the field of information security. However, a firewall is only as secure as the operating system it resides on.

TCP Wrappers

Another issue is TCP Wrappers. TCP Wrappers is a tool commonly used on UNIX systems to monitor and filter connections to network services. Although it does not encrypt, TCP Wrappers does log and control who can access your system. It is a binary that wraps itself around inetd services, such as telnet or ftp. With TCP Wrappers, the system launches the wrapper for inetd connections, logs all attempts, and then verifies the attempt against an ACL. If the connection is permitted, TCP Wrappers hands the connection to the proper binary, such as telnet. If the connection is rejected by the access control list, the connection is dropped.

Why would a firewall need TCP Wrappers? Doesn't the firewall do all of that for you? First, in case the firewall is compromised or crashes, TCP Wrappers offers a second layer of defense. No firewall is 100 percent secure. Second, TCP Wrappers protects against firewall misconfigurations that could provide a point of entry for a hacker. Third, TCP Wrappers adds a second layer of logging, verifying other system logs.

NOTE. *Be sure to use a system other than the firewall to retrieve and compile TCP Wrappers. You should not have any compilers on the firewall.*

The /etc/default/login File

One last way to protect your system from unauthorized access—whether it's on the Internet or not—is via the /etc/default/login file. Make sure the following line is uncommented:

```
CONSOLE=/dev/console
```

With this entry, root is allowed to log in only from the secure system console and not via the network by using `telnet` or `rlogin`. However, this entry does not disallow a user from using the `su` command to switch to root after logging in as a regular user.

Modems

Modems are always a potential point of entry for intruders. Anyone who discovers the phone number can attempt to log in. Low-cost computers can be turned into automatic calling devices that search for modem lines and then try endlessly to guess passwords and break in. If you must use a modem, use it for outgoing calls only. An outgoing modem will not answer the phone. If you allow calling in, implement a callback system. The callback system guarantees that only authorized phone numbers can connect to the system. Another option is to have two modems that establish a security key between one and the other. This way, only modems with the security key can connect with the system modem and gain access to the computer.

The Trusted Host

Along with protecting the password, you need to protect your system from a root user coming in from across the network. For example, systemA is a *trusted host* from which a user can log in without being required to type a password. Be aware that a user who has root access on systemA could access the root login on systemB simply by logging in across the network if systemA is set up as a trusted host on systemB. When systemB attempts to authenticate root from systemA, it relies on information in its local files—specifically, /etc/hosts.equiv and /.rhosts.

The /etc/hosts.equiv File

The /etc/hosts.equiv file contains a list of trusted hosts for a remote system, one per line. A /etc/hosts.equiv file has the following structure:

```
system1
system2 user_a
```

If a user (root) attempts to log in remotely by using `rlogin` from one of the hosts listed in this file, and if the remote system can access the user's password entry, the remote system allows the user to log in without a password.

When an entry for a host is made in /etc/hosts.equiv, such as the sample entry for system1, this means that the host is trusted and so is any user at that machine. If the user name is also mentioned, as in the second entry in the same file, the host is trusted only if the specified user is attempting access. A single line of + in the /etc/hosts.equiv file indicates that every known host is trusted.

The /etc/hosts.equiv file presents a security risk. If you maintain an /etc/hosts.equiv file on your system, this file should include only trusted hosts in your network. The file should not include any host that belongs to a different network or any machines that are in public areas.

TIP. *Change the root login to something other than "root," and never put a system name into the /etc/hosts.equiv file without a name or several names after it.*

The .rhosts File

The .rhosts file is the user equivalent of the /etc/hosts.equiv file. It contains a list of hosts and users. If a host-user combination is listed in this file, the specified user is granted permission to log in remotely from the specified host without having to supply a password. Note that an .rhosts file must reside at the top level of a user's home directory, because .rhosts files located in subdirectories are not consulted. Users can create .rhosts files in their home directories—another way to allow trusted access between their own accounts on different systems without using the /etc/hosts.equiv file.

The .rhosts file presents a major security problem. Although the /etc/hosts.equiv file is under the system administrator's control and can be managed effectively, any user can create an .rhosts file granting access to whomever the user chooses—without the system administrator's knowledge.

When all of the users' home directories are on a single server, and only certain people have superuser access on that server, a good way to prevent a user from using a .rhosts file is to create (as superuser) an empty .rhosts file in the user's home directory. Then, change the permissions in this file to 000 so that changing it would be difficult, even as superuser. This would effectively prevent a user from risking system security by using a .rhosts file irresponsibly.

The only secure way to manage .rhosts files is to completely disallow them. One possible exception to this policy is the root account, which might need to have a .rhosts file to perform network backups and other remote services.

Securing Superuser Access

The UNIX superuser identity is immune from restrictions placed on other users of the system. Any UNIX account with a UID of zero (0) is the superuser. All UNIX systems have a default superuser login named root. The user of this account can access any file and run any command.

This login is valuable, because any user who might have gotten himself into trouble by removing access permissions or forgetting his password, or who simply needs a file from an area to which he doesn't have access, can be helped by root.

However, root access can be very dangerous. Root can delete anything, including the operating system (most system administrators have deleted the entire root file system at one time or another). The root login is both dangerous and necessary. System administrators must not give this password to anyone and should use it themselves only when required.

Restricting Root Access

Root access needs to be safeguarded against unauthorized use. Assume that any intruder is looking for root access. You can protect the superuser account on a system by restricting access to a specific device through the /etc/default/login file. For example, if superuser access is restricted to the console, the superuser can log in only at the console, which should be in a locked room. Anybody who remotely logs in to the system to perform an administrative function must first log in with his or her user login and then use the `su` command to become superuser.

Do the following to restrict superuser (root) from logging in to the system console from a remote system:

1. Become superuser.
2. Edit the /etc/default/login file.
3. Uncomment the following line:

```
CONSOLE=/dev/console
```

Monitoring Superuser Access

Solaris provides a utility for monitoring all attempts to become superuser. These logs are very useful when you're trying to track down unauthorized activity. Whenever someone issues the `su` command to switch from user and become root, this activity is logged in a file called /var/adm/sulog. The sulog file lists all uses of the `su` command, not only those used to switch user to superuser. The entries show the date and time the command was entered, whether it was successful, the port from which the command was issued, and the name of the user and the switched identity.

To monitor who is using the `su` command, you must first turn on this logging utility. To turn on logging of the `su` command, follow these steps:

1. Become superuser.
2. Edit the /etc/default/su file.

3. Uncomment the following line.

```
SULOG=/var/adm/sulog
```

Through the /etc/default/su file, you can also set up the system to display a message on the console each time an attempt is made to use the su command to gain superuser access from a remote system. This is a good way to immediately detect someone trying to gain superuser access to the system on which you are working.

Do the following to display superuser (root) access attempts to the console:

1. Become superuser.
2. Edit the /etc/default/su file.
3. Uncomment the following line:

```
CONSOLE=/dev/console
```

4. Use the su command to become root, and verify that a message is printed on the system console.

SUDO

SUDO, an acronym for "superuser do," is a public-domain software package that allows a system administrator to give certain users (or groups of users) the ability to run some (or all) commands as root, or as another user while logging the commands and arguments to a log file for auditing. SUDO allows the system administrator to give access to and track specific root commands without actually giving out the root password. To give a user access to a command that requires root privileges, the system administrator configures the access list or sudoers file. Here is a sample sudoers file:

```
# sample sudoers file.
# This file MUST be edited with the 'visudo' command as root.
# See the man page for the details on how to write a sudoers file.

# Host alias specification

# User alias specification
User_Alias       DBA=oracle
User_Alias       APPLMGR=applmgr
User_Alias       SA=tej1,wbc4,wck2,wbp9
User_Alias       OPER=tbw1,tdk1,tss1,wcs6,wjsh,yhq1,yjsd,ylb7

# Cmnd alias specification
Cmnd_Alias       MOUNT=/sbin/mount,/sbin/umount
Cmnd_Alias       BACKUP=/usr/sbin/ufsdump
Cmnd_Alias       RESTORE=/usr/sbin/ufsrestore
Cmnd_Alias       SHUTDOWN=/sbin/shutdown
```

```
Cmnd_Alias      KILL=/usr/bin/kill
Cmnd_Alias      CRONTAB=/usr/bin/crontab
# User privilege specification
root     ALL=(ALL) ALL
DBA      ALL=MOUNT,KILL,BACKUP
APPLMGR ALL=MOUNT,KILL
OPER     ALL=SHUTDOWN
```

To run a command, simply add `sudo` to your command as follows:

```
sudo shutdown
```

You'll be prompted for your personal password, not root's password. SUDO confirms that you are allowed to execute the command and logs what you did to the SUDO log file.

NOTE. *SUDO will cache your password so that you don't need to keep entering it for successive* `sudo` *commands. The default is 5 minutes for the caching of the password.*

The following are the advantages of SUDO:

- You don't have to give out the root password to everyone. It's a handy way to give users controlled access for commands they need to get their work done.
- It's a good tool to get beginning system administrators started without giving them full access.
- The audit logs are quite handy to track root activities. If something changes, you can go to the log to see when it happened and who did it.
- It works well and is a simple but effective point solution.

SUDO is not part of the Solaris 7 OS but is distributed freely on the Internet. Visit my Web site, `www.pdesigninc.com`, for an up-to-date site from which to download this program.

Automated Security Enhancement Tool (ASET)

The Solaris 7 system software includes the Automated Security Enhancement Tool (ASET), which helps you monitor and control system security by automatically performing tasks you would otherwise do manually. ASET performs the following seven tasks, each making specific checks and adjustments to system files and permissions to ensure system security:

- Verifies appropriate system file permissions
- Verifies system file contents
- Checks the consistency and integrity of /etc/passwd and /etc/group entries
- Checks on the contents of system configuration files

- Checks environment files (.profile, .login, .cshrc)
- Verifies appropriate eeprom settings
- Builds a firewall on a router

The ASET security package provides automated administration tools that let you control and monitor your system's security. You specify a low, medium, or high security level at which ASET will run. At each higher level, ASET's file-control functions increase to reduce file access and tighten your system security.

ASET tasks are disk-intensive and can interfere with regular activities. To minimize the impact on system performance, schedule ASET to run when the system activity level is lowest—for example, once every 24 or 48 hours at midnight.

The syntax for the aset command is

```
/usr/aset/aset -l <level> -d <pathname>
```

Options to the aset command are described in Table 6-15.

Table 6-15 *aset* Command Options

Option	Description	
<level>	Specifies the level of security. Valid values are low, medium, and high.	
	Low security	This level ensures that attributes of system files are set to standard release values. ASET performs several checks and reports potential security weaknesses. At this level, ASET takes no action and does not affect system services.
	Medium security	This level provides adequate security control for most environments. ASET modifies some of the settings of system files and parameters, restricting system access to reduce the risks from security attacks. ASET reports security weaknesses and any modifications it makes to restrict access. At this level, ASET does not affect system services.
	High security	This level renders a highly secure system. ASET adjusts many system files and parameter settings to minimum access permissions. Most system applications and commands continue to function normally, but at this level, security considerations take precedence over other system behavior.
<pathname>	Specifies the working directory for ASET. The default is /usr/aset.	

The following example runs ASET at low security using the default working directory /usr/aset:

```
# /usr/aset/aset -l low
======= ASET Execution Log =======
ASET running at security level low
Machine = holl300s; Current time = 0530_14:03
aset: Using /usr/aset as working directory
Executing task list ...
        firewall
        env
        sysconf
        usrgrp
        tune
        cklist
        eeprom
All tasks executed. Some background tasks may still be running.
Run /usr/aset/util/taskstat to check their status:
     /usr/aset/util/taskstat     [aset_dir]
where aset_dir is ASET's operating directory,currently=/usr/aset.
When the tasks complete, the reports can be found in:
     /usr/aset/reports/latest/*.rpt
You can view them by:
     more /usr/aset/reports/latest/*.rpt
#
```

Common-Sense Security Techniques

A system administrator can have the best system security measures in place, but without the users' cooperation, system security will be compromised. The system administrator must teach common-sense rules regarding system security, such as the following:

- Use proper passwords. Countless sites use passwords such as "admin" or "supervisor" for their root accounts.
- Don't give your password out to anyone, no matter who he says he is. One of the best system crackers of our time said that he would simply pose as a system support person, ask a user for his password, and get free reign to the system.
- If you walk away from the system, log out or lock the screen. Think of the damage if someone walked up to your station and sent a scathing email to the president of your company—with your name attached!
- Don't connect modems to your system without approval from the system administrator.

Summary

This chapter discussed fundamental concepts in system security. Although system crackers seem to always find new ways to break into systems, the concepts described in this chapter provide a strong defense against an attack. Chapter 7, "Setting Up User Accounts," will put these concepts to practical use as you set up and manage user accounts.

CHAPTER

7

Setting Up User Accounts

The following are the test objectives for this chapter:

- Using Admintool to add, delete, and modify user accounts
- Setting up, customizing, and administering initialization files
- Administering user home directories
- Understanding name services

Access to a system is allowed only through user login accounts set up by the system administrator. A user account includes information that a user needs to log in and use a system—a user login name, a password, the user's home directory, and login initialization files. User accounts can range from occasional guests needing read-only access to a few files, to regular users who need to share information between several departments.

Table 7-1 lists the methods and tools available in Solaris for adding new user accounts to the system.

Table 7-1 Adding New User Accounts

Environment	Recommended Tool	Availability
On remote and/or local systems in a networked name service (NIS, NIS+)	User and Group Manager (graphical user interface) from the Solstice AdminSuite	Available as a separate product. (Solstice AdminSuite is described in Chapter 20, "Solstice AdminSuite.")
Local system	Admintool (graphical user interface)	Provided with Solaris 7.
Command-line	Terminal window (CDE environment) or shell tool or command tool (OpenWindows environment)	Provided with Solaris 7.

One way to add user accounts is from the command line. Solaris supplies the user administration commands described in Table 7-2 for setting up user accounts.

Table 7-2 Account Administration Commands

Command	Description
`useradd`	Adds a new user account.
`userdel`	Deletes a user account.
`usermod`	Modifies a user account.

continues

Table 7-2 Account Administration Commands (continued)

Command	Description
groupadd	Adds a new group.
groupmod	Modifies a group (for example, changes the group ID or name).
groupdel	Deletes a group.

As with many UNIX commands, the command-line method of adding user accounts is cumbersome and confusing. For this reason, Sun has added user account administration to the Solaris Admintool. Admintool is a graphical user interface designed to ease several routine system administration tasks. When using Admintool, the system administrator is presented with a menu-like interface that is much easier to use than the ASCII interface supplied at the command prompt. Admintool does not change name service maps or tables when NIS or NIS+ is being used; this task is accomplished by an unbundled product called Solstice AdminSuite. For instructions on using AdminSuite, refer to Chapter 20. This chapter describes how to use the Solaris Admintool to administer user accounts on the system.

Adding a User Account with Admintool

To perform administrative tasks such as adding user accounts, the administrator must be logged in as superuser or be a member of GID 14 (sysadmin).

NOTE. *When you're adding or modifying user accounts, Admintool edits the files /etc/passwd, /etc/shadow, and /etc/group. As root, you could edit these files directly, but this is not recommended. Errors in any of the files could cause adverse effects on the system.*

The first step in setting up a new user account is to have the user provide the information you will need to administer this account. You'll also need to set up proper permissions so that the user can share information with other members of his or her department. To start, you'll need to know the user's full name, department, and any groups with which the user will be working. I like to sit down with the user and fill out an information sheet like the one shown in Table 7-3 so that I have all the information I'll need when I set up the account.

Table 7-3 User Information Data Sheet

Item	Description
User Name:	
UID:	
Primary Group:	
Secondary Groups:	
Comment:	
Default Shell:	
Password Status and Aging:	
Home Directory Server Name:	
Home Directory Path Name:	
Mail Server:	
Department Name:	
Department Administrator:	
Manager:	
Employee Name:	
Employee Title:	
Employee Status:	
Employee Number:	
Start Date:	
Desktop System Name:	

To add a new user login account, follow this procedure:

1. Start up Admintool as a member of the sysadmin group by typing `admintool` at the command prompt.

   The Users main menu appears, as shown in Figure 7-1.

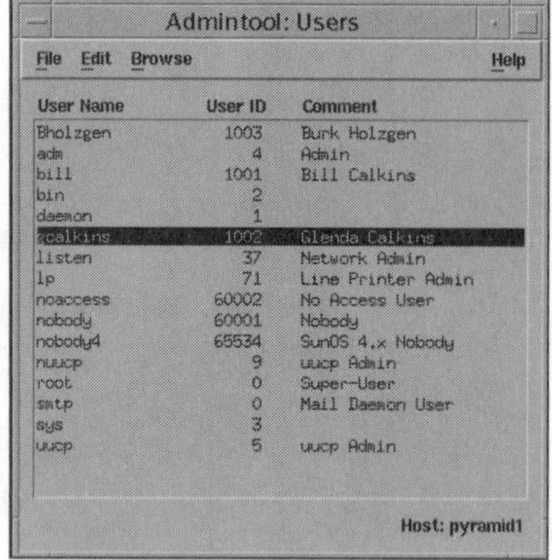

Figure 7-1
The Users main menu.

2. Choose Edit, Add to display the Add User window, shown in Figure 7-2.

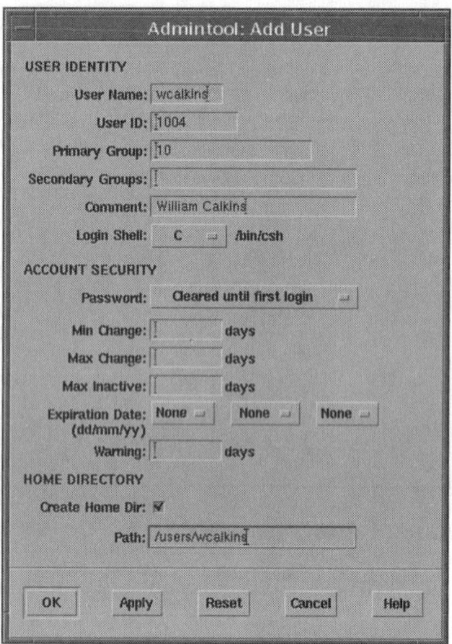

Figure 7-2
The Add User window.

3. Fill in the text boxes in the Add User window. Table 7-4 describes the information needed. If you aren't sure how to complete a field, click the Help button to see field definitions for this window.

4. After entering the information, click OK. The current list of user accounts is displayed in the Users main window.

Table 7-4 Add User Fields

Item	Description
User Name	Enter a unique login name that will be entered at the Solaris login prompt. Choose a name unique to your organization. The name can contain one to eight uppercase characters (A to Z) or lowercase characters (a to z) or digits (0 to 9), but no underscores. The first character must be a letter, and at least one character must be a lowercase letter.
User ID	Enter the unique user ID (discussed in Chapter 6, "System Security"). Admintool automatically assigns the next available UID; however, in a networked environment, make sure that this number is not duplicated by another user on another system. All UIDs must be consistent across the network. The UID is typically a number between 100 and 60002, but it can go as high as 2147483647. See the note in the description for "Primary Group" regarding UIDs over 60000.
Primary Group	Enter the primary group name or GID (group ID) number for the group to which the user will belong. This is the group the operating system will assign to files created by the user. Group 10 (staff) is a predefined group that is usually sufficient for most users. GIDs can range from 0 to 60002, but they can go as high as 2147483647. Note: Previous Solaris software releases used 32-bit data types to contain the user IDs (UIDs) and group IDs (GIDs), but UIDs and GIDs were constrained to a maximum useful value of 60000. Starting with the Solaris 2.5.1 release and compatible versions, the limit on UID and GID values has been raised to the maximum value of a signed integer, or 2147483647. UIDs and GIDs over 60000 do not have full functionality and are incompatible with many Solaris features, so avoid using UIDs or GIDs over 60000.
Secondary Groups	(Optional) Enter the names or GIDs, separated by spaces, of any additional groups to which the user belongs. A user can belong to as many as 16 secondary groups.
Comment	(Optional) Enter any comments, such as the full user name or phone number.
Login Shell	Click this button to select the shell the user will use, such as /bin/csh. If nothing is selected, the default shell is the Bourne shell (/bin/sh).
Password	Click this button to specify the password status. Selectable options are as follows: Cleared until first login. This is the default. The account does not have a password assigned. The user is prompted for a password on first login, unless `passreq=no` is set in /etc/default/login. Account is locked. The account is disabled with an invalid password and can be unlocked by assigning a new password. This type of account allows a user to own files but not to log in. No password; `setuid` only.

continues

Table 7-4 Add User Fields (continued)

Item	Description
	The account cannot be logged into directly. This allows programs such as `lp` and `uucp` to run under an account without allowing a user to log in.
	Normal password.
	The account will have a password that you set in the pop-up window that appears.
Min Change	(Optional) Enter the minimum number of days allowed between password changes. This is intended to prevent a user from changing the password and then changing it back a few seconds later, which would defeat the concept of password aging. The default is 0.
Max Change	(Optional) Enter the maximum number of days the password is valid before it must be changed; otherwise, the account is locked. Leaving the field blank means the password never has to be changed.
Max Inactive	(Optional) Enter the maximum number of days an account may go without being accessed before it is automatically locked. A blank field means the account remains active no matter how long it goes unused.
Expiration Date	(Optional) Enter the date when the user account expires. `None` means no expiration.
Warning	(Optional) Enter the number of days to begin warning the user before the password expires. A blank means no warning is given.
Create Home Dir Check Box	Check this box to have the user's home directory automatically created.
Path	Use the Path field to point to an existing directory or to specify a new directory to create.

NOTE. *Users can type the UNIX command* `passwd` *at the command prompt to change their passwords. Refer to Chapter 6 for additional information on setting passwords.*

Deleting a User Account with Admintool

Use Admintool to delete an existing user account. The procedure to delete a user account is as follows:

1. Start Admintool, if it's not already running, and choose Browse, Users.
2. In the Users window, select the user account entry you want to remove.
3. Choose Edit, Delete.
4. A message is displayed to confirm the removal of the user account (see Figure 7-3).

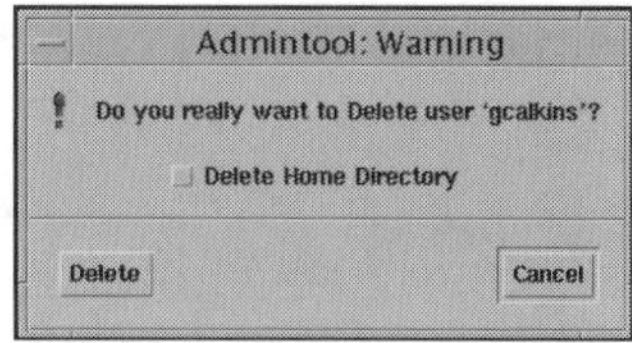

Figure 7-3
Confirmation that you want to delete the user account.

5. (Optional) Click the Delete Home Directory check box to delete the user's home directory and its contents. If you don't check the box, the user account will be deleted, but the contents of the user's home directory will remain.
6. Click OK when you are ready to delete the user account. The user account entry is deleted from the Users main window.

Modifying a User Account with Admintool

If a login needs to be modified—to change a password or disable an account, for example—use Admintool to modify these user account settings. The process is as follows:

1. Start Admintool, if it's not already running, and choose Browse, Users.
2. Select the user account entry to be modified.
3. Choose Edit, Modify.
4. The Modify User window is displayed, containing the selected user account entry (see Figure 7-4).

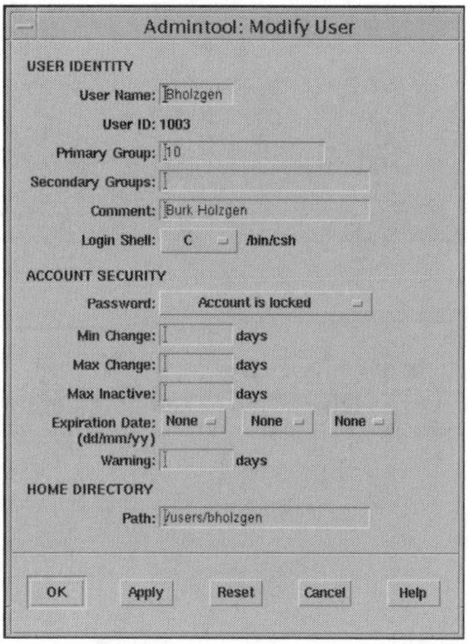

Figure 7-4
The Modify User window.

5. The following are descriptions of some of the modifications allowed:
   - Locking a login

     Choose Password: Account is locked.
   - Changing a user's password

     Enable a user account by changing the password status to Normal password or Cleared until first login.
6. Click OK, and the modification is made.

Adding a Group with Admintool

You might need to add a group that does not already exist on the system. Perhaps a new group of users called "engrg" (from the engineering department) needs to be added. The following steps describe how to add the new "engrg" group.

1. Start Admintool, if it's not already running, and choose Browse, Groups.
2. The Groups window is displayed, as shown in Figure 7-5.

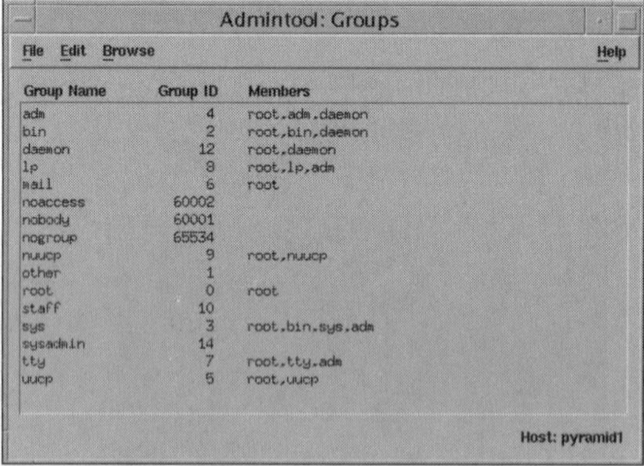

Figure 7-5
The Groups window.

3. Choose Edit, Add.
4. The Add Group window is displayed, as shown in Figure 7-6. If you're not sure how to complete a field, click the Help button to see field definitions for this window.

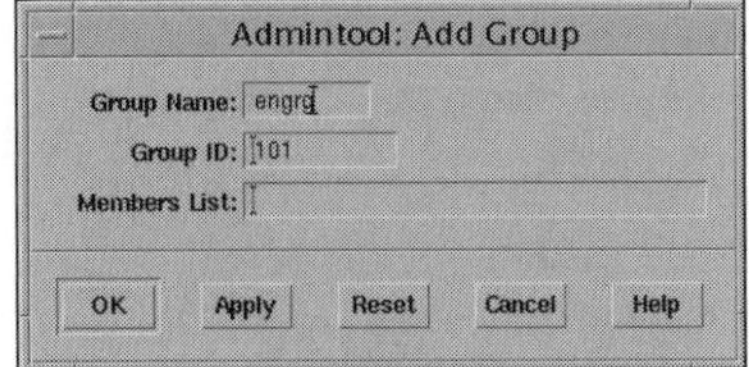

Figure 7-6
The Add Group window.

5. Type the name of the new group in the Group Name text box.
6. Type the group ID number for the new group in the Group ID text box. This should be a unique number.
7. (Optional) Type user names in the Members List text box. These are the users who belong to the new group. User names must be separated by commas. The list of users will be added to the group.
8. Click OK. The list of groups displayed in the Groups window is updated to include the new group.

Setting Up User Initialization Files

Part of setting up a user's home directory is providing *user initialization files* for the user's login shell. A user initialization file is a shell script that sets up a work environment for a user after the user logs in to a system. You can perform any task in a user initialization file that you can perform in a shell script, but its primary job is to define the characteristics of the user's work environment, such as search path, environment variables, and windowing environment. Each login shell has its own user initialization file (or files) located in the user's home directory. These files are run automatically when the user logs in.

Default user initialization files, such as .cshrc, .profile, and .login, are created automatically in the user's home directory when a new user account is added. The system administrator can predefine the contents of these files or can choose to use the system default files. The Solaris 7 system software provides default user initialization files for each shell in the /etc/skel directory on each system. These files are listed in Table 7-5.

Table 7-5 Default Initialization Files

Name	Description
local.cshrc	The default .cshrc file for the C shell.
local.login	The default .login file for the C shell.
local.profile	The default .profile file for the Bourne and Korn shells.

You can use these initialization files as a starting point and modify them to create a standard set of files that will provide a work environment common to all users. You can also modify them to provide the working environment for different types of users.

Customizing User Initialization Files

When a user logs into a system, the work environment is determined by the shell initialization files. The shell startup scripts can be modified to set environment variables and directory paths needed by a specific user. These startup scripts are located in the user's home directory.

When you are setting up user initialization files, it might be important to allow the users to customize their own initialization files. This can be accomplished with centrally located and globally distributed user initialization files called *site initialization files*. These files let you continually introduce new functionality to all of the user work environments by editing one initialization file. The local initialization file, located in the user's home directory, allows user-specific configuration.

A local initialization file lets users further customize their own work environment. Site initialization files are located in the /etc directory and can be edited only by root. They are designed to distribute site-wide changes to all user work environments. Individual user initialization files are located in each user's home directory and can be customized by the owner of that directory. When a user logs in, the site initialization file is run first, and then the initialization file located in the user's home directory is run.

NOTE. *Do not use system initialization files located in the /etc directory (/etc/profile, /etc/.login) to manage an individual user's work environment. These are site initialization files, considered to be global files, meant to be generic and used to set work environments for all users. The system will run this startup file first and will then run the user's startup file located in the home directory.*

The most common customizations to shell startup scripts are environment variables. Table 7-6 describes environment and shell variables you might want to customize in a user initialization file.

Table 7-6 Shell and Environment Variable Descriptions

Variable	Description
ARCH	Sets the user's system architecture (for example, sun4, i386). This variable can be set with `ARCH = `uname -p`` (in Bourne or Korn shells) or `setenv ARCH `uname -p`` (in the C shell). The shell has no built-in behavior that depends on this variable; it's just a useful variable for branching within shell scripts.

Table 7-6 Shell and Environment Variable Descriptions (continued)

Variable	Description
`history`	Sets the history for the C shell.
`HOME`	Sets the path to the user's home directory.
`LPDEST`	Sets the user's default printer.
`PATH` (or `path` in the C shell)	Lists, in order, the directories the shell searches to find the program to run when the user types a command. If the directory is not in the search path, users must type the complete pathname of a command. The default `PATH` is automatically defined in .profile (Bourne or Korn shell) or .cshrc (C shell) as part of the login process. The order of the search path is important. When identical commands exist in different locations, the first command found with that name is used. For example, suppose PATH is defined (in Bourne and Korn shell syntax) as `PATH=/bin:/usr/bin:/usr/sbin:$HOME/bin` and a file named "sample" resides in both /usr/bin and /home/glenda/bin. If the user types the command `sample` without specifying its full pathname, the version found in /usr/bin is used.
`prompt`	Defines the shell prompt for the C shell.
`TERM` (or `term` in the C shell)	Defines the terminal. This variable should be reset in /etc/profile or /etc/.login. When the user invokes an editor, the system looks for a file with the same name as the definition of this environment variable. The system searches the directory /usr/share/lib/terminfo to determine the terminal characteristics.
`MAIL`	Sets the path to the user's mailbox.
`MANPATH`	Sets the search path for system manual pages.
`umask`	Sets the default user mask.

The following example illustrates how to verify a user's environment settings and how to change them:

1. Log in as the user. This step lets you see the user's environment as the user will see it.
2. Edit the user's initialization files. The following steps suggest some changes and show the shell-specific syntax to use.
3. Set the user's default path to include the home directory and directories or mount points for the user's windowing environment and applications. To change the path setting, add or modify the line for `PATH` as follows:

   For the Bourne or Korn shell, the syntax is

   ```
   PATH=/dirname1:/dirname2:/dirname3:.; export PATH
   ```

For example, enter the following line in the user's $HOME/.profile file:

```
PATH=$PATH:/usr/bin:/$HOME/bin:/net/glrr/files1/bin:.;export PATH
```

For the C shell, the syntax is

```
set path =(/dirname1 /dirname2 /dirname3 .)
```

For example, enter the following line in the user's $HOME/.cshrc file:

```
set path=($path /usr/bin $HOME/bin /net/glrr/files1/bin .)
```

NOTE. *Prefixing* `$PATH` *(K shell) or* `$path` *(C shell) appends changes to the user's path settings already set by the site initialization file. When you set the* `PATH` *variable with this procedure, initial path settings are not overwritten and lost. Also note the "dot" (.) at the end of the list to denote the current working directory. The dot should always be at the end of the path, as discussed in Chapter 6.*

4. Check that the environment variables are set to the correct directories for the user's windowing environments and third-party applications. Type `env` and press Enter:

```
$ env

HOME=/home/ncalkins
HZ=100
LOGNAME=ncalkins
MAIL=/var/mail/ncalkins
MANSECTS=\1:1m:1c:1f:1s:1b:2:\3:3c:3i:3n:3m:3k:3g:3e:3x11:3
xt:3w:3b:9:4:5:7:8
PATH=/usr/bin
SHELL=/bin/sh
TERM=sun
TZ=EST5EDT
$
```

5. Add or change the settings of environment variables by entering either of the following lines.

For the Bourne or Korn shell, the syntax is

```
VARIABLE=value;export VARIABLE
```

The following example sets the user's default mail directory:

```
MAIL=/var/mail/ncalkins;export MAIL
```

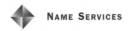

For the C shell, the syntax is

```
setenv VARIABLE value
```

The following example sets the history to record the last 100 commands:

```
setenv HISTORY 100
```

The Home Directory

The home directory is the portion of a file system allocated to a user for storing private files. The amount of space you allocate for home directories depends on the kinds of files the user creates and the type of work performed. An entire file system is usually allocated specifically for home directories, and the users all share this space. The system administrator needs to monitor user home directories so that one user does not use more than his fair share of space. Disk quotas are used to control the amount of disk space a user can occupy. They are discussed in Chapter 4, "Introduction to File Systems."

A home directory can be located on either the user's local system or on a remote file server. Although any directory name can be used, the home directory in either case is, by convention, /export/home/username. When you put the home directory in /export/home, it is available across the network in case the user logs in from several different stations. For a large site, you should store home directories on a server.

Regardless of where their home directory is located, users usually access it through a mount point named /home/username. When Autofs is used to mount home directories, you are not permitted to create any directories under the /home mount point on any system. The system recognizes the special status of /home when Autofs is active. For more information about Autofs and automounting home directories, refer to Chapter 18, "The NFS Environment."

To access the home directory anywhere on the network, you should always refer to it as `$HOME`, not as /export/home/username. The latter is machine-specific and should be discouraged. In addition, any symbolic links created in a user's home directory should use relative paths (for example, ../../../x/y/x) so that the links will be valid no matter where the home directory is mounted. The location of user home directories might change. By not using machine-specific names, you maintain consistency and reduce system administration.

Name Services

If you are managing user accounts for a large site, you might want to consider using a name service such as NIS or NIS+. A name service lets you store user account information in a centralized manner instead of storing it in every system's /etc files. When using a name service for user accounts, users can move from system to system using the same user account without having site-wide user account information duplicated in every system's /etc files. Using a name service also promotes centralized and consistent user account information. NIS and NIS+ are discussed in Chapter 19, "Name Services."

Summary

This concludes the discussion of how to add user login accounts to the system. By default, when users first log in, they are given the option of selecting the windowing environment they want to use—CDE or OpenWindows. OpenWindows is being phased out of Solaris and has been replaced with the Common Desktop Environment (CDE). Setup and customization of the CDE are described in Chapter 21, "Administration and Configuration of the CDE."

The next chapter switches gears a bit and describes the administration of Solaris 7 system software packages.

CHAPTER

8

Software Package Administration

The following are the test objectives for this chapter:

- Understanding the tools for managing the Solaris software
- Adding and removing software packages
- Listing and verifying installed software packages
- Installing and removing software patches

The system administrator is responsible for managing all software installed on a system. Installing and removing software is a routine task that is performed frequently. Chapter 3, "Installing the Solaris 7 Software," described the installation of the Solaris operating system. This chapter explains how to add and remove additional applications after the operating system has already been installed.

Sun and its third-party vendors deliver software products in a form called a software *package*. The term "package" refers to a method of distributing and installing software to systems where the products will be used. A package is a collection of files and directories in a defined format that conforms to the Application Binary Interface (ABI), a supplement to the System V Interface Definition. The Solaris operating environment provides a set of utilities that interpret the ABI format and provides the means to install or remove a package or to verify its installation.

Tools for Managing Software

Solaris provides two tools for adding and removing software from a system. Both are described in Table 8-1.

Table 8-1 Tools for Managing Software

Command	Description
Managing Software from the Command Line	
pkgadd	Adds software packages to the system.
pkgrm	Removes software packages from the system.
pkgchk	Checks the accuracy of a software package installation.
pkginfo	Displays software package information.
pkgask	Stores answers in a response file so that they can be supplied automatically during an installation.
pkgparam	Displays package parameter values.
Managing Software from the Graphical User Interface	
admintool	A GUI that is invoked from within CDE or OpenWindows.

Use the `pkgadd` or `pkgrm` commands directly from the command line to load or remove software packages. The `pkgadd` and `pkgrm` commands can be incorporated into scripts to automate the software installation process. Many third-party vendors use `pkgadd` in scripts as a means to install their software.

Admintool, on the other hand, provides an easy-to-use interface for installing and removing software packages. It is simply a graphical user interface to the pkgadd and pkgrm commands. Using the Admintool graphical interface is a convenient way to view software already installed on a system or to view the software that resides on the installation media. If you're unfamiliar with software-package naming conventions or are uncomfortable using command-line options, or if you're managing software on only one system at a time, you'll find Admintool an easy way to add and remove software packages.

Adding and Removing Software Packages

When you add a software package, the pkgadd command uncompresses and copies files from the installation media, such as the CD-ROM, to a local system's disk. When you use packages, files are delivered in package format and are unusable as they are delivered. The pkgadd command interprets the software package's control files and then uncompresses the product files and installs them on the system's local disk.

Here are a few things you should know before installing additional application software:

- Sun packages always begin with the prefix SUNW, as in SUNWvolr, SUNWadmap, and SUNWab2m. Third-party packages usually begin with a prefix that corresponds to the company's stock symbol.
- You can use the pkginfo command or Admintool to view software already installed on a system.
- Clients might have software that resides partially on a server and partially on the client. If this is the case, adding software for the client requires adding packages to both the server and the client.
- You need to know where the software will be installed, and you need to make sure you have a file system that has enough disk space to store the application software. Use the pkgparam command to determine where the package will be loaded. For example, type

  ```
  pkgparam -d /cdrom/cdrom0/s0/Solaris_2.7/Product SUNWvolr  SUNW_PKGTYPE
  ```

  SUNW_PKGTYPE is a special parameter that reports where a Solaris software package will be installed. If the package does not have the SUNW_PKGTYPE parameter set, the pkgparam command returns an empty string. For Sun packages, this usually means that the package will be installed in /opt.

  The system responds with the location where the application will be stored:

```
root
```

CAUTION! *When you remove a package, the* `pkgrm` *command deletes all the files associated with that package unless those files are also shared with other packages. Be sure you do not delete application software without using* `pkgrm`*. For example, some system administrators delete an application simply by removing the directory containing the application software. With this method, files belonging to the application that might reside in other directories are missed. With* `pkgrm`*, you'll be assured of removing all files associated with the application.*

Although the `pkgadd` and `pkgrm` commands do not log their output to a standard location, they do keep track of the product installed or removed. The `pkgadd` and `pkgrm` commands store information in a software product database about a package that has been installed or removed. By updating this database, the `pkgadd` and `pkgrm` commands keep a record of all software products installed on the system.

Adding Software Packages

The procedure for installing additional application software with Admintool is as follows:

1. Start Admintool as the user root by typing `admintool` at the command prompt.
2. The Users m

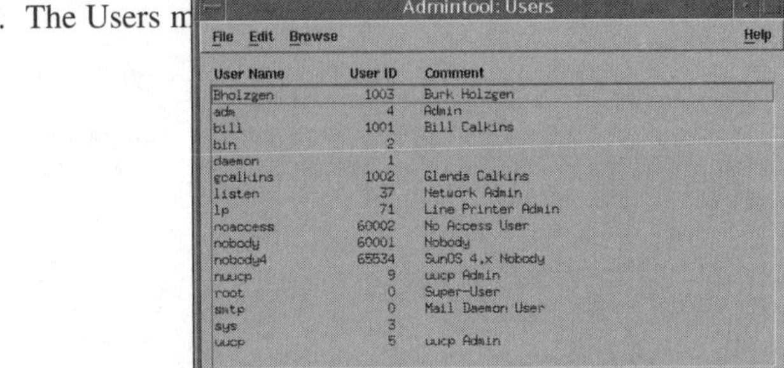

Figure 8-1
The Users main menu.

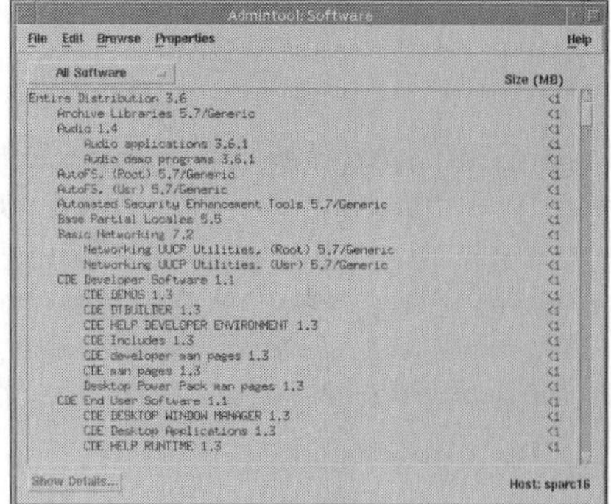

3. Choose Browse, Software. The Software window appears, as shown in Figure 8-2.

Figure 8-2
The Software window.

4. Choose Edit, Add. The Set Source Media window appears, as shown in Figure 8-3.

Figure 8-3
The Set Source Media window.

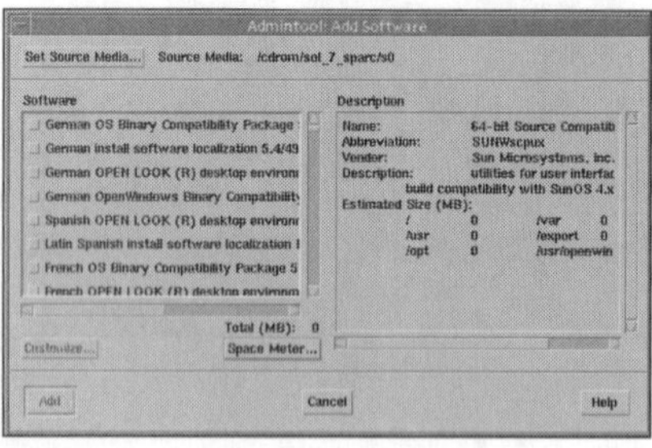

5. Specify the path to the installation medium. The default path from which to install the application is the mounted SPARC Solaris CD. Click OK to display the Add Software window, shown in Figure 8-4.

Figure 8-4
The Add Software window.

6. In the Software portion of the window, click the check boxes corresponding to the software you want to install. When you have selected all the packages, click the Add button.

A command tool window appears for each package being installed, displaying the installation output. When the installation is complete, the Software window refreshes to display the packages just added.

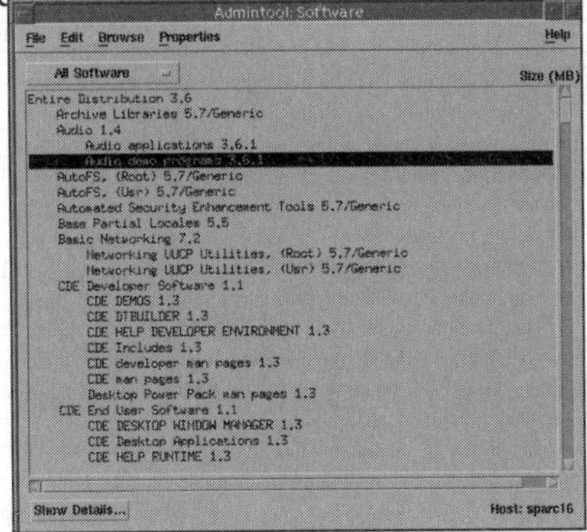

Figure 8-5
The Software window.

Removing Software Packages

The procedure for removing application software is as follows:

1. Start Admintool, if it's not already running, and choose Browse, Software. The Software wi[illegible]gure 8-5.

2. Select the software package you want to remove, and choose Edit, Delete. A message appears, asking you to confirm that you want to remove the software (see Figure 8-6).

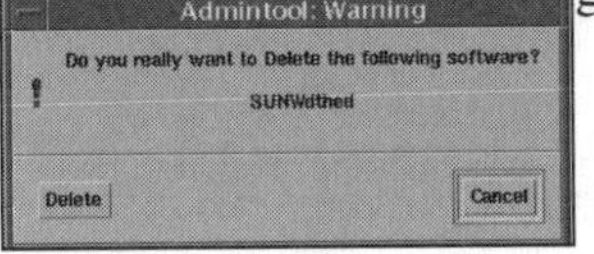

Figure 8-6
Confirm the software removal.

For each package … is displayed, asking for confirmation before deletin… hoose to delete the software, the

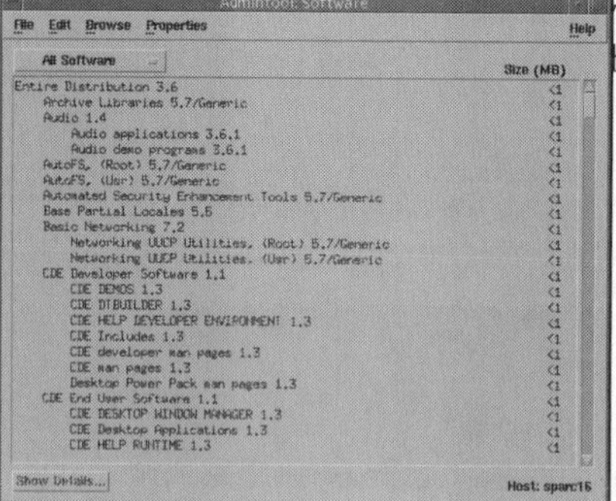

output from the removal process is displayed in the command tool window.

Listing and Verifying Installed Packages

At any time, you can use Admintool or issue the `pkginfo` command from the command line to get a complete listing of the software installed on a system. The Software window in Admintool display… oftware (see

```
Terminal
Window  Edit  Options                                              Help
# pkginfo |more
application HPNP          JetAdmin for Unix
system      SUNWab2m      Solaris Documentation Server Lookup
system      SUNWab2r      Solaris Documentation Server
system      SUNWab2s      Solaris Documentation Server
system      SUNWab2u      Solaris Documentation Server
system      SUNWaccr      System Accounting, (Root)
system      SUNWaccu      System Accounting, (Usr)
system      SUNWadmap     System administration applications
system      SUNWadmc      System administration core libraries
system      SUNWadmfw     System & Network Administration Framework
system      SUNWadmr      System & Network Administration Root
system      SUNWapppr     PPP/IP Asynchronous PPP daemon configuration fil
es
system      SUNWapppu     PPP/IP Asynchronous PPP daemon and PPP login ser
vice
system      SUNWarc       Archive Libraries
system      SUNWast       Automated Security Enhancement Tools
system      SUNWatfsr     AutoFS, (Root)
system      SUNWatfsu     AutoFS, (Usr)
system      SUNWaudio     Audio applications
system      SUNWaudmo     Audio demo programs
system      SUNWbcp       SunOS 4.x Binary Compatibility
system      SUNWbnur      Networking UUCP Utilities, (Root)
--More--
```

Figure 8-7).

Figure 8-7
The Software window.

You can obtain more information about individual software packages by double-clicking any of the listed software packages in Admintool.

Figure 8-8 illustrates the `pkginfo` command used from the command line, with `more` used to show the display of information one page at a time.

Figure 8-8
The pkginfo *output.*

Software Patches

Another system administration task is managing system software patches. A *patch* is a fix to a reported software problem. Sun will ship several software patches to customers so that problems can be resolved before the next release of software. The existing software is derived from a specified package format that conforms to the ABI.

Patches are identified by unique alphanumeric strings. The patch base code comes first, and then a hyphen, and then a number that represents the patch revision number. For example, patch 108721-01 is a Solaris 7 patch to correct an Admintool problem.

You might want to know more about patches that have previously been installed. Table 8-2 shows commands that provide useful information about patches already installed on a system.

Table 8-2 Helpful Commands for Patch Administration

Command	Function
`showrev -p`	Shows all patches applied to a system.
`pkgparam pkgid PATCHLIST`	Shows all patches applied to the package identified by `pkgid`.
`pkgparam pkgid PATCH_ \INFO patch-number`	Shows the installation date and name of the host from which the patch was applied. pkgid is the name of the package (for example, SUNWadmap).
`patchadd -R client_root_ \path -p`	Shows all patches applied to a client, from the server's console.
`patchadd -p`	Shows all patches applied to a system.
`patchrm patchname`	Removes a specified patch.

Installing a Patch

All Sun customers can access security patches and other recommended patches via the World Wide Web or anonymous FTP. Sun customers who have purchased a service contract can access an extended set of patches and a complete database of patch information. (This information is also available via the World Wide Web or anonymous FTP, and it is regularly distributed on CD-ROM. See Appendix D, "On the Web," for a listing of useful Web sites and where to access patches via the Web.)

Detailed information about how to install and remove a patch is provided in the Install.info file included with each patch. Each patch also contains a README file that contains specific information about the patch.

The `patchadd` command is used to install directory-format patches to a Solaris 7 system. It must be run as root. The syntax is

```
patchadd [ -d ] [ -u ] [ -B backout_dir ]
```

The `patchadd` command is described in Table 8-3.

Table 8-3 *patchadd* Command Options

Common Option	Description
-d	Does not create a backup of the files to be patched. The patch cannot be removed when this option has been used to install the patch. By default, `patchadd` saves a copy of all files being updated so that the patch can be removed if necessary. Do not use the -d option unless you're positive the patch has been tested.
-p	Displays a list of the patches currently applied.
-u	Installs the patch unconditionally, with file validation turned off. The patch is installed even if some of the files to be patched have been modified since their original installation.
-B backout_dir	Saves backout data to a directory other than the package database. Specify `backout_dir` as an absolute pathname.

NOTE. *Additional options to the* `patchadd` *command security can be found online in the Solaris system manual pages.*

The following example installs a patch to a stand-alone machine:

```
patchadd /var/spool/patch/104945-02
```

The following example installs multiple patches. The patchlist file specifies a file containing a list of patches to install:

```
patchadd -M /var/spool/patch patchlist
```

The following example displays the patches installed on a system:

```
patchadd -R /export/root/client1 -p
```

When you're installing a patch, the `patchadd` command copies files from the patch directory to the local system's disk. More specifically, `patchadd` does two things:

- It determines the Solaris version number of the managing host and the target host.
- It updates the patch package's pkginfo file with information about patches made obsolete by the patch being installed, other patches required by this patch, and patches incompatible with this patch.

The `patchadd` command will not install a patch under the following conditions:

- If the package is not fully installed on the host.
- If the patch architecture differs from the system architecture.
- If the patch version does not match the installed package version.
- If there is already an installed patch with the same base code and a higher version number.
- If the patch is incompatible with another, already installed patch. (Each installed patch keeps this information in its pkginfo file.)
- If the patch being installed requires another patch that is not installed.

Removing a Patch

Sometimes a patch does not work as planned and needs to be removed from the system. The utility used to remove, or "back out of," a patch is the `patchrm` command, described in Table 8-4. Its syntax is

```
patchrm [ -f ] [ -B backout_dir ]
```

Table 8-4 ***patchrm* Command Options**

Common Options	Description
`-f`	Forces the patch removal regardless of whether the patch was superseded by another patch.

`-B backout_dir`	Removes a patch whose backout data has been saved to a directory other than the package database. This option is needed only if the original backout directory, supplied to the `patchadd` command at installation time, has been moved. Specify `backout_dir` as an absolute pathname.

The following example removes a patch from a stand-alone system:

```
patchrm 104945-02
```

The `patchrm` command removes a Solaris 7 patch package and restores previously saved files, restoring the file system to its state before a patch was applied, *unless*

- The patch was installed with `patchadd -d`. (The `-d` option instructs `patchadd` not to save copies of files being updated or replaced.)
- The patch has been made obsolete by a later patch.
- The patch is required by another patch already installed on the system.
- The `patchrm` command calls `pkgadd` to restore packages saved from the initial patch installation.

General Guidelines

Some software packages do not conform to the ABI and therefore cannot be installed by using Admintool or the `pkgadd` command. For installation of products that do not conform to the ABI, follow the vendor's specific installation instructions. Here are a few additional guidelines to follow when installing new software on a system:

- Always be cautious with third-party or public-domain software. Make sure that the software has been tested and is free of viruses before installing it on a production system.
- Make sure the software package is supported under Solaris 7.
- Always read the vendor's release notes for special loading instructions. They might contain kernel parameters that need to be modified or suggest software patches that need to be applied.
- Do not install patches unless directed by Sun or one of your software providers. Some patches have not been tested thoroughly, especially when used in conjunction with

other software patches. Adverse system performance problems could result.

Adding and removing software packages is one of the simpler tasks you will encounter in system administration. As with all computer software, you should first load new software packages on a nonproduction system for test purposes. Only after the software has been thoroughly tested should you install it on a production system.

Summary

This chapter described Software Package Administration. Chapter 12, "Backup and Recovery," describes how to create a tape backup of everything you've installed. A good backup can save you time in the event of a hardware malfunction. With a good backup, you won't need to retrace the steps of installing software packages or patches and setting up users.

In some of the subsequent chapters I'll be describing how to configure some of the software packages you've installed such as the LP Print Service (Chapter 10, "The LP Print Service"), NFS (Chapter 18, "The NFS Environment"), NIS (Chapter 19, "Name Services"), AdminSuite (Chapter 20, "Solstice AdminSuite"), and the Common Desktop Environment (Chapter 21 "Administration and Configuration of the CDE").

CHAPTER

9

Writing Shell Scripts and Programs

The following are the test objectives for this chapter:

- Selecting a shell to use
- Setting shell variables
- Understanding shell built-ins
- Understanding shell conditionals
- Using repeat action statements
- Understanding shell functions

A thorough understanding of shell programming is a must for any system administrator. System administrators must be able to read and write shell programs, because many tasks can and should be automated by using them. An advantage of using a script or shell program to perform a particular task is that doing so ensures consistency—in other words, the task is performed the same way each time. Also, many software products come with installation scripts that have to be modified for your system before they will work. This chapter first introduces some shell basics, and then it describes some fundamentals of creating a shell script.

Shell Script Basics

A *UNIX script* is a sequence of UNIX commands, either in a file or typed at the command line, that perform multiple operations. Such files are also known as *batch files* in some systems. Another term for a script that might be familiar to you is *macro*. Usually *script* or *macro* refers to a simple command sequence, but *shell program* identifies a file containing a more complicated arrangement of commands. Shell programs use the shell's control and conditional commands, called built-ins, which are discussed later in this chapter.

To run a file as a script, the file's execution bit must be set. This means that the file looks like this when you list it:

```
% ls -l
-rwxr-xr-x  1 bcalkins       425  Jul 10 11:10      program.1
```

If the execution bit is set, what happens next depends on the first line of the file. If the first two characters on the first line are anything other than `#!`, the file is interpreted as a Bourne shell script. If the characters `#!` are followed by an explicit program location, such as /bin/csh, that program is run as an interpreter on the contents of the file. In other words, the program is run in the shell that is specified after the `#!` characters.

To create a C shell script, for example, type the following on the first line of the file:

```
#!/bin/csh
```

NOTE. *It's a good idea to put scripts and shell programs into their own directory to separate them from standard UNIX programs. They are commonly put into a directory named /usr/local/bin. It's also a good practice to suffix the program names with .sh, .csh, or .ksh so that they are readily identified as shell scripts.*

Selecting a Shell to Use

The login shell is the command interpreter that runs when you log in. The Solaris 7 operating environment offers three shells:

- The Bourne shell, which is the default shell (/sbin/sh)
- The C shell (/bin/csh)
- The Korn shell (/bin/ksh)

When writing scripts, you can use any of these three shells. The basic features of each shell are described in Table 9-1.

NOTE. *In addition to the three standard shells, the Common Desktop Environment (CDE), described in Chapter 21, "Administration and Configuration of the CDE," provides the Desktop Korn shell (`dtksh`). This shell gives Korn shell scripts a way to easily access most of the existing Xt and Motif functions used in the CDE graphical interface. To successfully use `dtksh`, you should have experience with Xlib, the Xt Intrinsics, the Motif widgets, and Korn Shell programming. It is also helpful to know the C programming language.*

Table 9-1 Basic Features of the Bourne, C, and Korn Shells

Feature	Bourne	C	Korn
Syntax compatible with sh	Yes	No	Yes
Job control	Yes	Yes	Yes
History list	No	Yes	Yes
Command-line editing	No	Yes	Yes
Aliases	No	Yes	Yes
Single-character abbreviation for login directory	No	Yes	Yes
Protect files from overwriting (noclobber)	No	Yes	Yes
Ignore Ctrl+D (ignoreeof)	No	Yes	Yes
Enhanced cd	No	Yes	Yes
Initialization file separate from .profile	No	Yes	Yes
Logout file	No	Yes	No

Other shells, such as `bash` and `tcsh`, are also available. Selecting a particular shell to use is personal preference. I find that most BSD UNIX users use the C shell because of its roots at Berkeley. Many of us old SunOS users still prefer to use the C shell because we've used it for so many years. On the other hand, I find that SystemV users prefer the Korn shell. These preferences stem from the early development days of UNIX. They are discussed in Appendix A, "The History of UNIX."

For system administration, the Bourne shell is best for writing scripts. It is the default shell in Solaris and is the only shell found on all UNIX systems. In addition, because it's located in /sbin, it's the only shell available when /usr is not mounted (that is, in single-user mode). The Bourne shell was designed from the beginning for use as a programming language, which explains its breadth of programming features. An additional reason for using the Bourne shell is that its conditionals and controls are compatible with all other shells, including the `dtksh` shell used in the CDE environment. `dtksh` is discussed in Chapter 21.

All examples in this chapter use the Bourne shell.

Bourne Shell Variables

A *variable* is a name that refers to a temporary storage area in memory. A value such as a text string or number is assigned to a variable and can be changed at any time. The Bourne shell uses two types of variables to store values: local and environmental. Each is described in this chapter.

A variable is either set to some particular value or is said to be "unset," which means that it does not exist as a variable. Shell variables are an integral part of shell programming. The shell variable provides the capability to store and manipulate information within a shell program. The variables you use are completely under your control, and you can set or unset any number of variables as needed to perform a particular task.

A variable name must begin with a letter and may contain letters, digits, and underscores, but no special characters. In the Bourne shell, environment variables are set with an assignment of `NAME=value`. In the following example, the `ME` and `BC` variables are set by entering the following at a command prompt:

```
ME=bill
BC="bill calkins"
```

Be sure not to have any white space before or after the equals sign (`=`). Double quotes, as used in the second example, are used when white space is present in the text string you are assigning to the variable. Whenever the shell sees a $variable, such as `$ME`, it substitutes into the command line the value stored for that variable.

Quoting

Unfortunately, many of the special characters used by the shell are also used by other programs—there simply are not enough characters to go around. When the special characters shown in Table 9-2 are used in the shell, they must be quoted. Quoting is used when an assigned value contains a special character, spaces, tabs, or newlines. Without the quotes, the special symbols will be interpreted as shell metacharacters instead of being passed as arguments to programs. The three methods of quoting used in the Bourne shell are described in Table 9-2.

Table 9-2 Quoting

Character	Description	Functionality
\	Backslash	Quotes the next character (also known as "escaping").
'	Single quote marks	No interpretation occurs.
"	Double quotes	All characters enclosed in double quotation marks are quoted, except backslash, accent grave, double quote, and the currency symbol.

Commands are read from the string between two back ticks (` `). The standard output from these commands may be used to set a variable.

NOTE. *Don't confuse the back tick with the single-quote character. A back tick is the symbol that appears on the same keyboard key as the ~ (tilde). The single-quote character appears on the same key as the " (double quote) character.*

With the back tick, no interpretation is done on the string before the string is read, except to remove backslashes (\) used to escape other characters. Escaping back ticks allows nested command substitutions like this one:

```
font=`grep font \`cat filelist\``
```

The backslashes inside the embedded command (`\`cat filelist\``) protect the back ticks from immediate interpretation by the shell. With the back slash (\), the back tick just before `cat` fails to match the initial one before `grep`. The two "escaped" back ticks will be interpreted on the second pass, and the command will execute correctly.

In other words, because this example has two sets of back ticks, we need to show the shell which back tick pairs up with the other. We do this using the back slash (\). The shell will look at the command string twice—once to pair up the back ticks, and a second time to run the command.

Delimiters

Some characters naturally act as delimiters in the Bourne shell. When encountered, such characters have the effect of separating one logical word from the next. The characters outlined in Table 9-3 have a special meaning to the shell and cause termination unless quoted.

Table 9-3 Delimiters

Character	Description
;	Command delimiter. Acts as a `<return>` and executes the commands sequentially.
&	Runs commands asynchronously.
( )	Groups commands into a single logical word.
Newline	Separates records (the default).
Spaces, tabs	Separates fields (the default).

Shell Variables

To display the value of a variable, enter the following at the command prompt (the dollar sign informs the shell that the following name refers to a variable):

```
echo $BC
```

The following is displayed:

```
bill calkins
```

Variables you set are local to the current shell unless you mark them for export. Variables marked for export are called *environment variables* and will be made available to any commands the shell creates. The following command marks the variable `BC` for export:

```
export BC
```

You can list local variables by typing the `set` command. You can list variables that have been marked for export by typing the `env` command. The Bourne shell has several predefined variables, some of which are described in Table 9-4. These variables get assigned automatically when a user logs in and are defined by the login program, the system initialization file, and the user's initialization files.

Table 9-4 Default Bourne Shell Variables

Variable	Description
ARCH	Sets the user's system architecture (for example, sun4, sun4c, sun4u).
CDPATH	Sets the search path for the cd command.
HOME	Sets the value of the user's home directory.
LANG	Sets the locale.
LOGNAME	Defines the name of the user currently logged in. The default value of LOGNAME is automatically set by the login program to the user name specified in the /etc/passwd file. You should only need to reference (not reset) this variable.
LPDEST	Sets the user's default printer.
MAIL	If this parameter is set to the name of a mail file and the MAILPATH parameter is not set, the shell informs the user of the arrival of mail in the specified file.
MAILCHECK	Specifies how often (in seconds) the shell will check for the arrival of mail in the files specified by the MAILPATH or MAIL parameters. The default value is 600 seconds (10 minutes). If set to 0, the shell will check after each prompt.
MAILPATH	Sets the mail path by defining a colon-separated list of filenames. If this parameter is set, the shell informs the user of the arrival of mail in any of the specified files. Each filename can be followed by % and a message that will be printed when the modification time changes. The default message is You have mail.
MANPATH	Sets the hierarchies of available man pages.
OPENWINHOME	Sets the path to the OpenWindows subsystem.
PATH	Lists, in order, the directories that the shell searches to find the program to run when the user types a command. If the directory is not in the search path, users must type the complete pathname of a command. The default PATH is automatically defined and set as specified in .profile (Bourne or Korn shell) or .cshrc (C shell) as part of the login process. Note: The order of the search path is important. When identical commands exist in different locations, the first command found with that name is used. For example, suppose that PATH is defined for user jean (in Bourne and Korn shell syntax) as PATH=/bin:/usr/bin:/usr/sbin:$HOME/bin and a file named "sample" resides in both /usr/bin and /home/jean/bin. If the user types the command sample without specifying its full pathname, the version found in /usr/bin is used.
PS1	Sets the primary prompt string, by default "$ ".
PS2	Sets the secondary prompt string, by default "> ".
SHELL	Sets the default shell used by make, vi, and other tools. When the shell is invoked, it scans the environment for this name.

Table 9-4 Default Bourne Shell Variables (continued)

Variable	Description
`TERM`	Defines the terminal. This variable should be reset in /etc/profile or /etc/.login. When the user invokes an editor, the system looks for a file with the same name as the definition of this environment variable. The system searches the directory referenced by `TERMINFO` to determine the terminal characteristics.
`TERMINFO`	Specifies the pathname for an unsupported terminal that has been added to the terminfo database. Use the `TERMINFO` variable in `$HOME/.profile` or `/$HOME/.login`. When the `TERMINFO` environment variable is set, the system first checks the `TERMINFO` path defined by the user. If it does not find a definition for a terminal in the `TERMINFO` directory defined by the user, it searches the default directory, /usr/share/lib/terminfo, for a definition. If it does not find a definition in either location, the terminal is identified as "dumb."
`TZ`	Sets the time zone used to display dates (for example, in the `ls -l` command). If `TZ` is not set in the user's environment, the system setting is used; otherwise, Greenwich Mean Time is used.

Built-Ins

Built-ins are used in shell programs to make decisions and to add intelligence to the task to be performed. Built-ins for the Bourne shell are listed in Tables 9-5 and 9-6. More information on the built-ins described in Table 9-5 is available in the Solaris online manual pages. The shell conditionals listed in Table 9-6 are described in this chapter. Each shell has its own set of built-ins, with the Bourne shell having the fewest. For this reason, it is the smallest and fastest of the three shells.

Table 9-5 Bourne Shell Built-Ins

Built-In	Description
`break`	Exits a `for` or `while` loop.
`continue`	Continues the next iteration of a `for` or `while` loop.
`echo`	Writes arguments on standard output.
`eval`	Evaluates and executes arguments.
`exec`	Executes a program. Executes in place of the current process so that `exec` does not create a new process.
`exit`	Exits the shell program.
`export`	Creates a global variable.

continues

Table 9-5 Bourne Shell Built-Ins (continued)

Built-In	Description
`priv`	Sets or displays privileges.
`read`	Reads a line from standard input.
`readonly`	Changes a variable to read-only.
`set`	Sets shell options.
`test`	Evaluates conditional expressions.
`times`	Displays execution times.
`trap`	Manages execution signals.
`umask`	Sets default security for files and directories.
`unset`	Unsets a local variable.
`wait`	Waits for a background process to complete.

Table 9-6 Bourne Shell Conditionals

Conditional	Description
`if-then-else-fi`	Tests a condition and selects an action based on the results of the test.
`case-esac`	Selects an action based on the value of the variable.
`for-do-done`	Repeats a sequence of commands until a predetermined condition is met.
`while-do-done`	Repeats a sequence of commands until a test condition is no longer true.
`until-do-done`	Repeats a sequence of commands until a test condition results in a successful status.

Shell Conditionals

In addition to the built-ins listed in Tables 9-5 and 9-6, the Bourne shell also contains some simple conditionals. A conditional command makes a choice depending on the outcome of a condition. Examples of simple conditionals are `&&` and `||`, which I will discuss along with the `if` and `case` conditionals in this section.

&& and ||

The simplest conditional in the Bourne shell is the double ampersand (`&&`). When two commands are separated by a double ampersand, the second command executes only if the first command returns a zero exit status (an indication of successful completion).

Here's an example:

```
ls -ld /usr/bin > /dev/null && echo "Directory Found"
```

If the directory /usr/bin exists, the message `Directory Found` is displayed.

The opposite of `&&` is the double bar (`||`). When two commands are separated by `||`, the second command executes only if the first command returns a nonzero exit status (indicating failure).

Here's an example:

```
ls -d  /usr/foo || echo "No directory found"
```

If the directory does not exist, the following message is displayed:

```
/usr/foo: No such file or directory
No directory found
```

True and False Programs

The Bourne shell contains the special programs `true` and `false`. The only function of the `true` program is to return a true (zero) exit status. Similarly, the function of the `false` program is to return a false (nonzero) exit status.

Here's an example:

```
True && echo True
```

The system responds with `True`.

Here's another example:

```
False || echo False
```

The system responds with `False`.

True and false tests will be discussed later, when we discuss `if` and `while` conditionals.

NOTE. *`&&` and `||` are useful conditionals for creating very simple scripts, but additional functionality is sometimes required. Therefore, the Bourne shell offers the `if` and `case` conditionals.*

if

One of the more important built-ins of the Bourne shell is the `if` conditional. The syntax of the `if` conditional is

```
if condition-list
       then list
     elif condition-list
       then list
    else list
    fi
```

The list following `if` is executed. If it returns a zero exit status, the list following the first `then` is executed. Otherwise, the list following `elif` is executed. If its value is zero, the list following the next `then` is executed. Failing that, the `else` list is executed. If no list is executed, the `if` command returns a zero exit status.

The next example illustrates the use of an `if` conditional statement:

```
if  [ -f  /tmp/errlog ]
    then
        rm /tmp/errlog
        echo "Error log has been removed"
    else
        echo "No errorlog  has been found"
fi
```

In this example, the program checks for a file named /tmp/errlog. If the file is present and is a regular file, the program removes it. If the file is not present, the file prints a message.

The Test Program

The previous example used the `if` test `-f` to evaluate a conditional expression. At the heart of each control structure is a conditional test. The `test` command is commonly used in shell programs to perform various tests and to determine whether certain files and directories exist. The test program performs three types of tests:

- It can test files for certain characteristics, such as file type and permissions.
- It can perform string comparisons.
- It can make numeric comparisons.

`test` indicates the success or failure of its testing by its exit status. `test` evaluates an expression and, if its value is true, sets a zero (true) exit status. Otherwise, a nonzero (false) exit status is set. All shell commands return a true (0) value when they complete successfully or a false (1) value when they fail. You can display the exit status of the last shell command by looking at the `$?` variable with the `echo` command. Table 9-7 lists some of the common conditions that can be evaluated.

Table 9-7 Built-In Test Functions

Test Condition	Description
`-r <filename>`	True if the filename exists and is readable.
`-w <filename>`	True if the filename exists and is writable.
`-x <filename>`	True if the filename exists and is executable.
`-f <filename>`	True if the filename exists and is a regular file.
`-d <filename>`	True if the filename exists and is a directory.
`-h <filename>`	True if the filename exists and is a symbolic link. With all other primitives (except `-L filename`), the symbolic links are followed by default.
`-c <filename>`	True if the filename exists and is a character special file.
`-b <filename>`	True if the filename exists and is a block special file.
`-u <filename>`	True if the filename exists and its set-user-ID bit is set.
`-g <filename>`	True if the filename exists and its set-group-ID bit is set.
`-k <filename>`	True if the filename exists and its sticky bit is set.
`-s <filename>`	True if the filename exists and has a size greater than zero.
`<s1> = <s2>`	True if strings `s1` and `s2` are identical.
`<s1> != <s2>`	True if strings `s1` and `s2` are not identical.
`<n1> -eq <n2>`	True if the integers `n1` and `n2` are algebraically equal. Any of the comparisons `-ne`, `-gt`, `-ge`, `-lt`, and `-le` may be used in place of `-eq`.
`-L <filename>`	True if the filename exists and is a symbolic link. With all other primitives (except `-h <filename>`), the symbolic links are followed by default.
These Test Functions May Be Combined with the Following Operators	
`!`	Unary negation operator.
`-a`	Binary and operator.
`-o`	Binary or operator (`-a` has higher precedence than `-o`).
`(expression)`	Parentheses for grouping. Notice also that parentheses are meaningful to the shell and, therefore, must be quoted.

Following is an example of where you might use a unary operator:

```
if  [ ! -f  /tmp/errlog ]
    then
        echo "No error log has been found"
fi
```

In this example, the statement `[ ! -f /tmp/errlog ]` tests whether the file `/tmp/errlog` does not exist.

case

Many programs are menu-driven; that is, they offer the user a menu of choices from which to select. The `case` statement makes it easy to set up a menu of choices. The general syntax for a `case` statement is as follows:

```
case value in
choice1) commands;;
choice2) commands;;
...
esac
```

A `case` command executes the list associated with the first pattern that matches the choice. Here's an example to describe how a `case` statement works:

```
echo Please enter the letter next to the command that you want to select:
echo 'a  date'
echo 'b  ls'
echo 'c  who'
read choice
case $choice in
a) date;;
b) ls;;
c) who;;
*)    echo Invalid choice - Bye.
esac
```

The list of choices is scanned to find the one that matches the value input by the user. The choice `*)` matches any value, so it's usually added as a last option—a catch-all.

Repeated-Action Commands

The Bourne shell provides three repeated-action commands, each of which corresponds to constructs you might have seen before in other programming languages:

- `for`
- `while`
- `until`

These commands cause a program to loop or repeat. They are described next.

The *for* Loop

A useful shell command is the `for` loop, which is the simplest way to set up repetition in a shell script. The syntax of a `for` loop is as follows:

```
for name [ in word . . . ]
do list
done
```

Each time a `for` command is executed, `name` is set to the next word taken from the `in word` list. If `in word . . .` is omitted, the `for` command executes the `do list` once for each positional parameter that is set. Execution ends when there are no more words in the list. The following example illustrates a simple `for` loop:

```
for i in eat run jump play
do
    echo See spot $i
done
```

When the program is executed, the system responds with this:

```
See spot eat
See spot run
See spot jump
See spot play
```

If you want to enter data interactively, you can add the shell special command `read`:

```
echo Hello- What\'s your name\?
read name
for i in $name
do
    echo $i
done
```

When executing the program, the user is asked to enter the word `list`. Notice the use of the backslash (`\`) so that the `'` and the `?` are taken literally and are not used as special characters.

The *while* Loop

A `while` loop repeats a set of commands continuously until a condition is met. The syntax for a `while` loop is

```
while condition-list
do commands
done
```

First, the `condition-list` is executed. If it returns a true exit status, the `do` list is executed, and the operation restarts from the beginning. If the `condition-list` returns a false exit status, the conditional structure is complete.

The following illustrates the `while` loop. The program checks to see if the file /tmp/errlog is present. If the file is not present, the program exits the loop. If the file is present, the program prints a message and runs again every 5 seconds until the file is removed.

```
while [ -f /tmp/errlog ]
    do echo The file is still there ; sleep 5
done
```

NOTE. *The special command* `sleep 5` *instructs the system to wait 5 seconds before running again.*

The *until* Loop

The `until` loop is a variant of the `while` statement. Just as the `while` statement repeats as long as the `condition-list` returns a true value, the `until` statement repeats until the `condition-list` returns a false value. The following example continues to display a message every 5 seconds until the file is created:

```
until [ -f  /tmp/errlog ]
    do echo the file is missing; sleep 5
done
```

Conditional structures such as `while` and `until` are executed by the shell as if they were a single command. The entire structure is scanned by the shell before any part of it is executed.

Shell Functions

Any good programming language provides support for functions. A *function* is a bundle of statements that is executed as a group. The bundles are executed just like a "regular" command and are used to carry out often-required tasks. An advantage of a function is that it is held in the computer's main memory, so execution is much quicker than with a script, which must be retrieved from disk. The current version of the Bourne shell supports shell functions; older versions of the Bourne shell did not. The syntax for shell functions is as follows:

```
name()
{
command-list
}
```

This command syntax defines a function named `name`. The body of the function is the `command-list` between `{` and `}`. This list is executed whenever `name` is specified as the name of a command. As an example, at the command prompt, type

```
hello()
{
echo hello there
}
```

The function is named `hello` and can be executed by typing `hello`. The output of the function is `hello there`. The exit status of a function is the exit status of the last command executed in the body.

Summary

Constructing your own commands with scripts and shell programs is a powerful and flexible tool to assist you in system administration. Routine tasks can be simplified and automated to free up your time and allow you to attend to more demanding tasks. Shell programming is a skill that all UNIX system administrators must have and is one of the keys to becoming a sophisticated UNIX user.

The next chapter describes configuring and administering the LP Print Service.

CHAPTER

10

The LP Print Service

The following are the test objectives for this chapter:

- Understanding the Solaris LP print service
- Setting up printer hardware and software
- Administering printers

Printers are a standard peripheral for any computer system. One of the first devices added to any new system is a printer. The multiuser nature of the Solaris operating environment means that the Solaris printer software is more complex than that of a single-user operating system. This means that adding a printer to a Solaris system requires more than just plugging it in.

This chapter describes how to set up local printers, set up access to remote printers, and perform some printer administration tasks by using the Admintool GUI or the command line. Most of the system administrator's needs for setting up printing services, adding printers to servers, or adding access from print clients to remote printers on print servers should be met by Admintool. Setting up a printer from the command line can be a very complex task. This chapter examines the hardware issues involved in connecting a printer to a Solaris system before moving on to examine the more complex part of the process—configuring the software.

The Solaris Print Service

The Solaris print service is a default cluster that is installed when the OS is initially installed. To verify that the package is installed, look for the following software packages:

SUNWClp: Line printer support

SUNWlpmsg: LP alerts

SUNWpsf: PostScript filters

SUNWpcr: SunSoft print client (root)

SUNWpcu: SunSoft print client (usr)

SUNWpsr: SunSoft print LP server (root)

SUNWpsu: SunSoft print LP server (usr)

NOTE. *Information on software packages can be obtained using the* `pkginfo` *command described in Chapter 8, "Software Package Administration."*

Setting up a Solaris printer involves setting up the spooler, the print daemon, and the hardware (the printer and the printer port). The system administrator needs to verify that there is at least 8MB of disk space available for /var/spool/lp. Print files will be sent to this location to prepare them for printing. Other configuration files are created, but Solaris takes care of that part for you. When setting up a printer, it makes the appropriate changes in the system's /etc/printers.conf file and the /etc/lp directory as required.

The Print Spooler

Spool stands for simultaneous peripheral operations online. The spooler is also referred to as the *queue*. Users execute the print spooler `lp` program when they want to print something. The print spooler then takes what the user wants to print and places it in the predefined /var/spool/lp print spooling directory.

Spooling space is the amount of disk space used to store and process requests in the print queue. The size of the /var directory depends on the size of the disk and how the disk is partitioned. If /var is not created as a separate partition, the /var directory uses some root partition space, which is likely to be quite small. A large spool directory could consume 600MB of disk space. Look at the size and partitioning of the disks available on systems that could be designated as print servers.

When connecting printers, first carefully evaluate the users' printing needs and usage patterns. If users typically print only short ASCII files without sophisticated formatting requirements, a print server with 20 to 25MB of disk space allocated to /var is probably sufficient. However, if many users are printing lengthy PostScript files, they will probably fill up the spooling space quite frequently. When /var fills up and users cannot queue their jobs for printing, workflow is interrupted. The size of /var is set when the operating system is loaded and disks are partitioned.

For SunOS users, the SVR4 `lp` program is equivalent to the BSD `lpr` print program. In SunOS, the print spooler is located in /usr/spool. When Sun switched from SunOS 4.x (which was based on BSD UNIX) to SunOS 5.x (which is based on SVR4 UNIX), print systems between BSD and SVR4 were quite different. Throughout this chapter, I'll make reference to the BSD print system for system administrators who might be familiar with it. The BSD printing protocol is an industry standard. It is widely used and provides compatibility between different types of systems from various manufacturers. For sites that have a mix of BSD and SVR4 UNIX, Sun has provided compatibility for both print systems in Solaris.

The Print Daemon

The `lp` process is the UNIX utility responsible for printing in SVR4 UNIX. The `lp` print daemon is started by `lpsched` and is the UNIX process responsible for taking output from the spooling directory and sending it to the correct printer. Again, for SunOS users, `lp` is equivalent to `lpd` in BSD UNIX.

Many methods can be used to define a printer on a Solaris system. Table 10-1 describes the tools Solaris provides for adding printers.

Table 10-1 Solaris Printer Utilities

Utility	Description
SunSoft Print Client Software	An interface that was previously available only with the Solstice AdminSuite set of administration tools. It is now available as part of the standard Solaris distribution software and is used to set up print clients.
Admintool	A graphical user interface used to create, modify, and delete printers on a local system. This is the recommended way for novice users to add printers.
Solstice AdminSuite	A graphical user Print Manager interface used to manage printers in a name service environment. Available only with the Solaris 7 server software distribution.
LP Print Service Commands	The command-line utilities used to set up and manage printers. These commands provide complete functionality; Admintool and the AdminSuite packages are somewhat limited for advanced tasks.

Setting Up the Hardware

Connecting printers to a UNIX system is no one's favorite activity, because it can quickly become a time-consuming task. Many printers are on the market, each with a slightly different interface. When connecting a printer locally to a Sun system, you have one of three options:

- An ethernet connection
- A parallel connection
- A serial connection

The type of connection depends on the connectivity options available on the printer itself. If the printer supports the option, an ethernet connection will be the best. If ethernet connectivity is not an option, a parallel connection is the preferred method. Most, if not all, printers have a parallel port. If no parallel option exists, the final choice is a serial connection.

Ethernet Connection

Many new printers come as standard with an ethernet interface. A printer with its own ethernet connection is referred to as a *network printer*. A network printer is a hardware device that provides printing services to print clients without being directly cabled to a print server. It is a print server with its own system name and IP address and is connected directly to the network. The ethernet interface may be internal or external to the printer. Using an ethernet interface to install a printer is recommended because of its speed.

Parallel Connection

Most printers, with a few rare exceptions, have a parallel interface. A parallel interface can have a tremendous advantage over a serial interface, especially if it uses a Centronics interface. The Centronics interface completely defines all wires used in the parallel connection between the printer and the computer. Simply connect the printer to the back of the Sun system by using a Centronics parallel cable. Some Sun systems do not have a DB25 parallel connector and require a special cable from Sun. Other older Sun systems do not have a parallel interface, so you must add one by purchasing an SBUS parallel interface from Sun.

Serial Connection

Some printers support both parallel and serial connections. Sometimes a printer is connected via the serial interface because the Sun station does not have an available parallel interface. Connecting a device using a serial interface requires a thorough understanding of serial transmission. This method of connecting a printer is the most difficult because of the complexity in establishing the proper "handshake," or means of communication, between the computer and the printer.

Setting Up the Software

For network printers, use the vendor's software to configure the operating system. After you have completed the vendor software installation, no further software configuration is required. You must obtain software from the printer manufacturer to install the printer on your system. Most are very easy to configure. The HP Jetdirect print server is the most popular, but it is by no means the only print server available.

The first step is to connect the print server to the network and set the IP address. This process varies on print servers, so follow the manufacturer's guidelines on how to do this. Next, install the print server software and follow the manufacturer's guidelines for configuring the printer. The vendor's software configures everything; no additional software configuration is required.

For printers that have a parallel or serial connection, you must use the Solaris tools to configure the operating system to recognize the printer.

BSD Versus SVR4 Printing Software

The software that drives the UNIX printing process is an area in which the two UNIX versions, BSD and SVR4, are similar and yet very different. The two print systems are similar in that both are based on the concept of spooling. Both SVR4 and BSD print services support the concept of an interface program, which acts as a filter through which all output sent to the printer is passed. Here are some sample uses of an interface program:

- **Adding a banner page**—Most UNIX systems automatically add a banner page to the front of a print job. The purpose of the page is to identify the owner of the printer output.

- **Adding or removing a line-feed character**—UNIX uses just the line-feed character to separate lines. The first problem you might encounter when testing a printer is that the text comes out in a stair-step manner. Most printers have a carriage return/line feed and auto line-feed dip switch that controls what the printer will use. The stair-step problem can be fixed by modifying the interface program that performs the necessary translation on all output going to the printer or by setting the printer's dip switch to the setting recommended by the hardware manufacturer.

The differences between BSD and SVR4 are in the configuration files and the spooling directories, which are configured automatically by the Solaris operating environment. There are also differences in the way that the `lpsched` daemon handles print jobs as compared to the `lpd` daemon in BSD.

BSD Print Service

Each printer connected to a BSD system must have its own spooling directory that is serviced by one `lpd` daemon. The spool directories are located in the /var/spool/lpd directory. Each printer has its own `lpd` daemon. In BSD, `lpd` accesses the file /etc/printcap for any information it requires concerning the printer. The printcap file is the system's printer database file and stores all of the necessary information about all printers connected to the system. To use a printer, that printer must have an entry in the /etc/printcap file. The `lpr` function is BSD's equivalent to `lp` under SVR4. If users want to print something, they use the `lpr` command, which sends the necessary information to a specified spooling directory.

SVR4 Print Service

In SVR4, one `lpsched` daemon services all printers. The `lpsched` daemon is continually running and provides the "power" for the print service. Only one instance of `lpsched` should be running at any one time.

The LP print service performs the following functions:

- Administers files and schedules local print requests
- Receives and schedules network requests
- Filters files (if necessary) so that they print properly
- Starts programs that interface with the printers
- Tracks the status of jobs
- Tracks forms mounted on the printer
- Tracks print wheels currently mounted
- Delivers alerts to mount new forms or different print wheels
- Delivers alerts about printing problems

Most of the LP configuration files are located in the /var/spool/lp directory, except for the interface files, which are located in the /etc/lp/interfaces directory. There should be a SCHEDLOCK file in /var/spool/lp that is responsible for ensuring that only one instance runs. You use the `lpadmin` command to add, configure, and delete printers from the system.

Information about printers can be found in the /etc/printers.conf and /etc/lp files. Solaris Admintool provides a graphical interface to many of the `lp` commands listed in Table 10-2.

Table 10-2 Solaris *lp* Commands

Command	Description
`accept/reject`	Enables or disables any further requests for a printer or class entering the spooling area.
`cancel`	Lets the user stop the printing of information.
`enable/disable`	Enables or disables any more output from the spooler to the printer.
`lp`	The user's print command. Places information to be printed into the spooler.
`lpadmin`	Allows the configuration of the print service.
`lpmove`	Moves print requests between destinations.
`lpsched`	Starts the print service.
`lpshut`	Stops the print service.
`lpstat`	Displays the status of the print service.

Although Solaris uses the SVR4 print model, it still supports BSD-style printing to provide interoperability. The widely used BSD printing protocol provides compatibility between different types of systems from various manufacturers.

Print Server Versus Print Client

The *print server* is a system that has a local printer connected to it and makes the printer available to other systems on the network. The *print client* is a remote system that can send print requests to a print server. A system becomes a print client when you install the print client software and enable access to remote printers on the system. Table 10-3 lists the Solaris software packages that need to be installed to support a print-server and print-client installation. If you've worked with an earlier version of Solaris, note that the Solaris 7 print software has been redesigned to provide more centralized print administration. If you are installing an earlier version of Solaris, the print package configuration is different.

Table 10-3 Solaris 7 Print Packages

Package Instance	Package Name
SUNWpcr	SunSoft Print - Client
SUNWpcu	SunSoft Print - Client
SUNWpsr	SunSoft Print - LP server
SUNWpsu	SunSoft Print - LP server
SUNWpsf	PostScript filters
SUNWscplp	SunSoft Print - Source compatibility
Solaris 2.5 Packages No Longer Found in the Software Distribution	
SUNWlpr	LP print service
SUNWlpu	LP print service: Client
SUNWlps	LP print service: Server

The print client issues print commands that let it initiate print requests. The `print` command locates a printer and printer configuration information.

When a print job is sent from the print client, the user issues either the SVR4-style `lp` command or the BSD-style `lpr` command. Any one of the styles shown in Table 10-4 can be used.

Table 10-4 Valid Print Styles

Style	Description
Atomic	The `print` command and option followed by the printer name or class. For example: `lp -d neptune filename`
POSIX	The `print` command and option followed by server:printer. For example: `lpr -P galaxy:neptune filename`
Context	Defined in the Federated Naming Service Programming Guide. For example: lpr -d thisdept/service/printer/printer-name filename

If the user doesn't specify a printer name or class in a valid style, the command checks the user's `PRINTER` or `LPDEST` environment variable for a default printer name. These variables can be set in the user's startup file to specify a default printer to use. If neither environment variable for the default printer is defined, the command checks the .printers file in the user's home directory for the default printer alias. If the command does not find a default printer alias in the .printers file, it then checks the print client's /etc/printers.conf file for configuration information. If the printer is not found in the /etc/printers.conf file, the command checks the name service (NIS or NIS+), if any.

Configuring Software for a Solaris Printer

The print client software and the Printer Manager application in Solstice AdminSuite offer a graphical solution for setting up and managing printers on a network. The advantage of the print client software is that it supports a name service (NIS or NIS+) that lets you centralize print administration for a network. You can also use the `lpadmin` command on the command line to configure printers on individual systems. Admintool provides an alternative method for installing printers in the Solaris environment. It provides a graphical interface to the `lp` commands listed in Table 10-2. This section describes how to use Admintool to set up the printer software.

You must run Admintool on the system to which you have attached the printer because it doesn't let you make changes to a remote system. When setting up a printer, Admintool makes the appropriate changes in the system's /etc/printers.conf file and /etc/lp directory.

NOTE. *If you're sitting at systemA and you want to connect a printer to systemB, you don't need to get into your car and drive to that location to run Admintool on systemB. From systemA, simply rlogin to systemB and type*

```
admintool -display local_systemA:0.0
```

SystemB's Admintool should now be displayed on systemA just as if you were sitting at systemB.

Follow these steps to configure a printer by using Admintool:

1. Type `admintool` to bring up the Admintool menu. The Admintool window appears.
2. Select Browse, Printers, as shown in Figure 10-1.

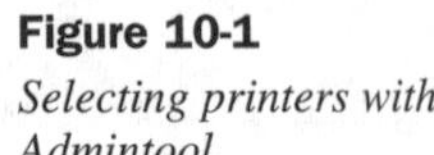

Figure 10-1
Selecting printers with Admintool.

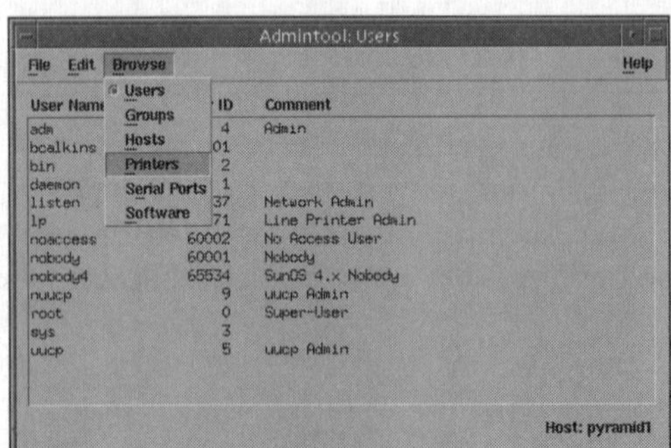

The Printers configuration window, shown in Figure 10-2, appears. Existing printers are displayed.

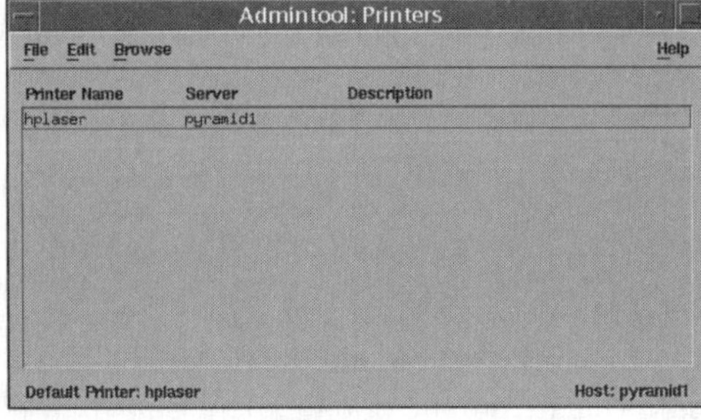

Figure 10-2
The Printers configuration window.

3. Choose Edit, Add.
4. If you're configuring a print client and the print server is located across the network, physically connected to another system, select Access to Printer from the pop-up menu, as shown in Figure 10-3.

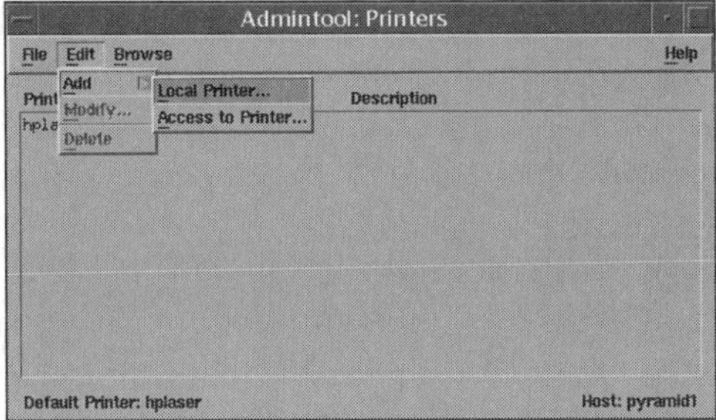

Figure 10-3
Printers window pop-up menu.

The Add Access To Printer window appears, as shown in Figure 10-4.

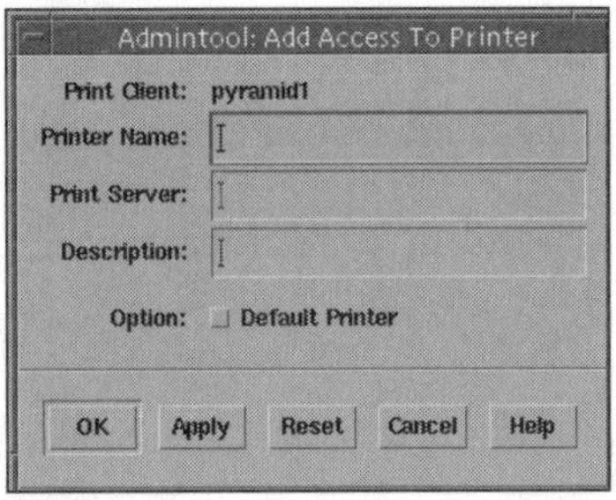

Figure 10-4
The Add Access To Printer window.

5. Fill in the information in the window as follows:
   - **Printer Name**—Enter the name of the printer on the remote system you want to access.
   - **Print Server**—Enter the name of the system to which the printer is connected.
   - **Description**—If you want to, enter a brief description of the printer.
   - **Option**—Check this option if you want to make this the system default printer.
6. Click the OK button. The window closes, and the information is added to the appropriate LP print system files.
7. If you're configuring a print server and the printer will be connected to the local system, select Local Printer from the pop-up menu shown in Figure 10-3. The window shown in Figure 10-5 is displayed.

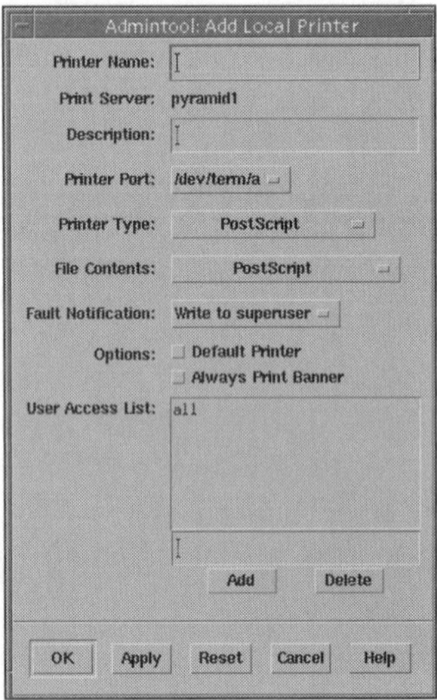

Figure 10-5
The Add Local Printer window.

8. Fill in the fields as follows:
   - **Printer Name**—Enter the name you want to call this printer.
   - **Description**—If you want to, enter a brief description of the printer.

- **Printer Port**—Click the button and select the port to which the printer is connected:

  /dev/term/a is serial port A.

  /dev/term/b is serial port B.

  /dev/bpp0 is the parallel port.

  Select Other if you've connected an SBUS card with another device name.

- **Printer Type**—Click the button to select the printer type that matches your printer. The printer types here correspond to printers listed in the /usr/share/lib/terminfo directory. The printer type you select must correspond to an entry in the terminfo database. UNIX works best with PostScript printers, because page formatting of text and graphics from within CDE is for a PostScript printer. If you want to select a PostScript printer, your printer must be able to support PostScript. If you're using an HP LaserJet printer, choose hplaserjet as the print type unless your LaserJet printer supports PostScript.
- **File Contents**—Click the button to select the format of the files that will be sent to the printer.
- **Fault Notification**—Click the button to select how to notify the superuser in case of a printer error.
- **Options**—Choose to print a banner or make this the default printer.

NOTE. *One printer can be identified as the default printer for the system. If a user does not specify a printer when printing, the job will go to the default printer.*

- **User Access List**—If you want to, enter the names of the systems allowed to print to this printer. If none are entered, all clients are allowed access.

9. After filling in all the fields, click the OK button. The window closes, and the new printer name appears in the Printers window, shown in Figure 10-2.

Using a Printer Not Listed on the Printer Types Menu

Printer types listed in the Print Manager window correspond to printers listed in the /usr/share/lib/terminfo directory. If a printer type is not available for the type of printer you are adding, you might need to add an entry in the /usr/share/lib/terminfo database. Each printer is identified in the terminfo database by a short name; for example, an HP LaserJet printer is listed under the /usr/share/lib/terminfo/h directory as hplaserjet. The entries for PostScript printers are in /usr/share/lib/terminfo/P. The name found in the directory is the printer type you specify when setting up a printer.

If you cannot find a terminfo entry for your printer, you can try selecting a similar type of printer; however, you might have trouble keeping the printer set in the correct modes for each print request. If there is no terminfo entry for your type of printer and you want to keep the printer set in the correct modes, you can either customize the interface program used with the printer or add an entry to the terminfo database. You'll find the printer interface program located under the /etc/lp/interfaces directory. Editing an interface file or adding an entry to the terminfo database is beyond the scope of this training guide. A printer entry in the terminfo database contains and defines hundreds of items. Refer to the *Solaris 7 System Administration Guide, Volume II* in the Answerbook2 online manuals for information on performing this task.

Administering Printers

Managing the print system involves monitoring the `lp` system and uncovering reasons why it might not be working properly. Other routine tasks involve canceling print jobs and enabling or disabling a printer while it's being serviced. This section provides instructions for the daily tasks you will perform to manage printers and the print scheduler. All of the following commands require superuser access.

Deleting Printers and Managing Printer Access

Use the Admintool to delete a printer from the system. In the Print Manager window of Admintool, highlight the printer you want to delete and select Edit, Delete, as shown in Figure 10-6. The printer queue will be deleted from the system.

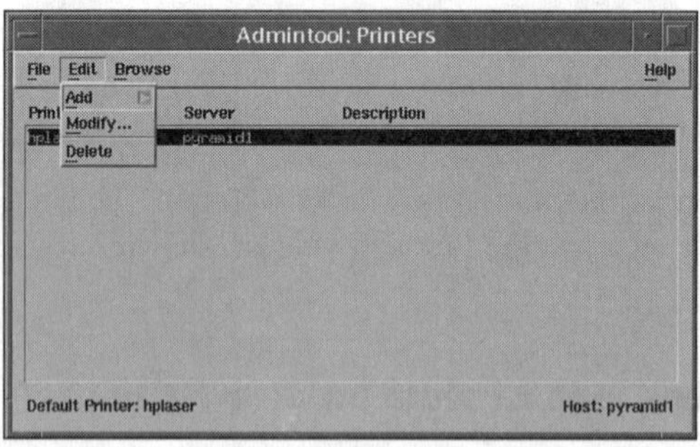

Figure 10-6
Deleting a printer.

To delete a printer at the command line, issue the following command on the system where the printer is connected:

```
lpadmin -x <printer-name>
```

The printer is deleted from the system.

Maybe you do not want to remove the printer from the print server but you want to keep a particular system from printing to the print server. Issue the following command on the print client from which you want to delete the printer:

```
lpsystem -r <print-server>
```

The print server is deleted from the print client's /etc/lp/Systems file.

Perhaps a printer will be going offline for repairs. To stop accepting print requests on a particular printer, type the following command on the system where the printer is physically connected:

```
reject <printer-name>
```

This step prevents any new requests from entering the printer's queue while you are in the process of removing the printer.

To allow a printer to keep taking requests but to stop the printer from printing the requests, type the following command on the system where the printer is physically connected:

```
disable <printer-name>
```

When stopping or disabling a printer, you might need to move existing jobs that have been queued to that printer. To move print jobs from one printer to another, use the `lpmove` command as follows:

```
lpmove <printer1> < printer2>
```

The arguments for the `lpmove` command are described in Table 10-5.

Table 10-5 *lpmove* Arguments

Argument	Description
`<printer1>`	The name of the printer from which all print requests will be moved.
`<printer2>`	The name of the printer to which all print requests will be moved.

If you move all the print requests to another printer, the `lpmove` command automatically stops accepting print requests for printer1. This next step is necessary if you want to begin accepting new print requests for the printer:

```
accept printer1
```

In the following example, the `lpmove` command moves print requests from the printer eps1 to the printer eps2, and the `accept` command tells the original printer, eps1, to resume accepting print requests:

```
lpmove eps1 eps2
accept eps1
```

Creating Printer Classes

You can put several locally attached printers into a group called a printer class. This might be helpful if you have several printers sitting next to each other, and it doesn't matter which printer your job goes to. When you have set up a printer class, users can then specify the class (rather than individual printers) as the destination for a print request. The first printer in the class that is free to print is used. The result is faster turnaround, because all printers get utilized. You create printer classes with the `lpadmin` command as follows:

```
lpadmin -c
```

No default printer classes are known to the print service; printer classes exist only if you define them. Here are some ways you can define printer classes:

- By printer type (for example, PostScript)
- By location (for example, 5th floor)
- By work group or department (for example, Accounting)

Alternatively, a class might contain several printers that are used in a particular order. The LP print service always checks for an available printer in the order in which printers were added to a class. Therefore, if you want a high-speed printer to be accessed first, you would add it to the class before you add a low-speed printer. As a result, the high-speed printer would handle as many print requests as possible. The low-speed printer would be reserved as a backup printer when the high-speed printer is in use.

Printer class names must be unique and may contain a maximum of 14 alphanumeric characters and underscores. You are not obligated to define printer classes. You should add them only if you determine that using printer classes would benefit the users on the network.

To define a printer class, follow these steps:

1. Log in as superuser or lp on the print server.

2. Define a class of printers by using the `lpadmin` command:

```
lpadmin -p <printer-name> -c <printer-class>
```

The arguments for `lpadmin` are described in Table 10-6.

Table 10-6 ***lpadmin*** **Arguments**

Argument	Description
-p <printer-name>	The name of the printer you are adding to a class of printers.
-c <printer-class>	The name of a class of printers.

The specified printer is added to the end of the list in the class in the print server's /etc/lp/classes/printer-class file. If the printer class does not exist, it is created. Verify the printers in a printer class by using the `lpstat` command:

```
lpstat -c printer-class
```

In the following example, the command adds the printer luna to the class roughdrafts:

```
lpadmin -p luna -c roughdrafts
```

Checking Printer Status

The `lpstat` command is used to verify the status of a printer. You can use this command to determine which printers are available for use or to examine the characteristics of a particular printer. The `lpstat` command syntax is

```
lpstat [-d] [-p <printer-name> [-D] [-l]] [-t]
```

The `lpstat` command options are described in Table 10-7.

Table 10-7 ***lpstat*** **Command Syntax and Options**

Option	Description
-d	Shows the system's default printer.
-p <printer-name>	Shows whether a printer is active or idle, when it was enabled or disabled, and whether it is accepting print requests. You can specify multiple printer names with this command. Use a space or a comma to separate printer names. If you use spaces, enclose the list of printer names in quotes. If you don't specify the printer name, the status of all printers is displayed.

continues

Table 10-7 *lpstat* Command Syntax and Options (continued)

Option	Description
-D	Shows the description of the specified printer.
-l	Shows the characteristics of the specified printer.
-t	Shows status information about the LP print service, including the status of all printers—whether they are active and whether they are accepting print requests.

Here are a few examples of the `lpstat` command:

```
lpstat -p hplaser
```

The system responds with this:

```
printer hplaser is idle. enabled since Jun 16 10:09 1998. available.
```

In the following example, the command requests a description of the printers hplaser1 and hplaser2:

```
lpstat -p "hplaser1 hplaser2" -D
printer hplaser1 faulted. enabled since Jun 16 10:09 1998. available.
unable to print: paper misfeed jam

Description: Printer by finance.
printer hplaser2 is idle. enabled since Jun 16 10:09 1998. available.
Description: Printer in computer room.
```

In the following example, the command requests the characteristics of the printer hplaser:

```
lpstat -p hplaser -l
 printer hplaser is idle. enabled since Jun 16 10:11 1998.
 available.
  Content types: any
  Printer types: unknown
  Description: Printer by computer room.
  Users allowed:
   (all)
  Forms allowed:
   (none)
  Banner not required
  Character sets:
   (none)
  Default is  pitch:
  Default page size:
```

Managing Printer Queues

Part of the routine task of managing printers is managing their queues. Occasionally large jobs get submitted that are not needed and can be aborted. Other times you might want to put a high-priority job ahead of other jobs that are waiting to be printed. The following outlines some of the routine tasks you might want to perform on the printer queues.

Deleting a Print Job

To remove someone else's print job from the print queue, you first need to become root. Then, determine the request ID of the print request to cancel by using the `lpstat` command as follows:

```
lpstat -u bcalkins
eps1-1    bcalkins     1261    Mar 16 17:34
```

In this example, user bcalkins has one request in the queue. The request ID is eps1-1.

Canceling a Print Request

Cancel a print request by using the `cancel` command. The command syntax is as follows:

```
cancel <request-id> | <printer-name>
```

The arguments for the `cancel` command are described in Table 10-8.

Table 10-8 *cancel* Arguments

Argument	Description
`<request-id>`	The request ID of a print request to be canceled. You can specify multiple request IDs. Use a space or a comma to separate request IDs. If you use spaces, enclose the list of request IDs in quotes.
`<printer-name>`	Specifies the printer for which you want to cancel the currently printing print request. You can specify multiple printer names with this command. Use a space or a comma to separate printer names. If you use spaces, enclose the list of printer names in quotes.

In the following example, the command cancels the eps1-3 and eps1-4 print requests:

```
cancel eps1-3 eps1-4
 request "eps1-3" cancelled
 request "eps1-4" cancelled
```

In the next example, the command cancels the print request that is currently printing on the printer eps1:

```
cancel eps1
 request "eps1-9" cancelled
```

Sending a Print Job at a Higher Priority

The `lp` command with the `-q` option assigns the print request a priority in the print queue. Specify the priority level as an integer from 0 to 39. Use 0 to indicate the highest priority and 39 to indicate the lowest. If no priority is specified, the default priority for a print service is assigned by the LP administrator.

The following example illustrates how to send a print job to printer eps1 with the highest priority:

```
lp -deps1 -q0 file1
```

Limiting User Access to a Printer

Allow or deny users access to a printer by using the `lpadmin` command. The command syntax is as follows:

```
lpadmin -p <printer-name> -u allow:<user-list> [ deny:<user-list>]
```

The arguments for the `lpadmin` command are described in Table 10-9.

Table 10-9 ***lpadmin*** **Arguments**

Argument	Description
`-p <printer-name>`	The name of the printer to which the allow or deny user access list applies.
`-u allow:<user-list>`	User names to be added to the allow user access list. You can specify multiple user names with this command. Use a space or a comma to separate names. If you use spaces, enclose the list of names in quotes. Table 10-10 provides the valid values for `user-list`.
`-u deny:<user-list>`	User names to be added to the deny user access list. You can specify multiple user names with this command. Use a space or a comma to separate names. If you use spaces, enclose the list of names in quotes. Table 10-10 provides the valid values for `user-list`.

The specified users are added to the allow or deny user access list for the printer in one of the following files on the print server:

/etc/lp/printers/printer-name/users.allow

/etc/lp/printers/printer-name/users.deny

Table 10-10 Values for Allow and Deny Lists

Value for *user-list*	Description
`user`	A user on any system.
`all`	All users on all systems.
`none`	No user on any system.
`system!user`	A user on the specified system only.
`!user`	A user on the local system only.
`all!user`	A user on any system.
`all!all`	All users on all systems.
`system!all`	All users on the system.
`!all`	All users on the local system.

NOTE. *If you specify* `none` *as the value for* `user-list` *in the allow user access list, the following files are not created for the print server:*

/etc/lp/printers/printer-name/alert.sh
/etc/lp/printers/printer-name/alert.var
/etc/lp/printers/printer-name/users.allow
/etc/lp/printers/printer-name/users.deny

In the following example, the command allows only the users bcalkins and bholzgen access to the printer eps1:

```
lpadmin -p eps1 -u allow:bcalkins,bholzgen
```

In the next example, the command denies the users bcalkins and bholzgen access to the printer eps2:

```
lpadmin -p eps2 -u deny:"bcalkins bholzgen"
```

Use the `lpstat` command to view access information about a particular printer. The following command displays access information for the printer named eps1:

```
lpstat -p eps1 -l
```

The system responds with this:

```
printer eps1 is idle. enabled since Mon Mar 20 14:39:48 EST 2000. available.

          Form mounted:
          Content types: postscript
          Printer types: PS
          Description: epson
          Connection: direct
          Interface: /usr/lib/lp/model/standard
          On fault: write to root once
          After fault: continue
          Users allowed:
          bcalkins
          bholzgen
          Forms allowed:
                 (none)
          Banner not required
          Character sets:

          Default pitch:
          Default page size: 80 wide 66 long
          Default port settings:
```

Accepting or Rejecting Print Requests for a Printer

As root, you can stop accepting print requests for the printer by using the `reject` command. The command syntax is as follows:

```
reject [-r "reason"] <printer-name>
```

The arguments for the `reject` command are described in Table 10-11.

Table 10-11 *reject* Arguments

Argument	Description
`-r "reason"`	Tells the users why the printer is rejecting print requests. The reason is stored and displayed whenever a user checks on the status of the printer using `lpstat -p`.
`<printer-name>`	The name of the printer that will stop accepting print requests.

The following example stops the printer eps1 from accepting print requests:

```
reject -r "eps1 is down for repairs" eps1
destination "eps1" will no longer accept requests
```

Any queued requests will continue printing as long as the printer is enabled. In the following example, the command sets the printer eps1 to accept print requests again:

```
accept eps1
destination "eps1" now accepting requests
```

Canceling a Print Request from a Specific User

Change to the root or lp user if you want to cancel print requests of other users. Cancel a print request from a specific user with the `cancel` command. The command syntax is as follows:

```
cancel -u <user-list> <printer-name>
```

The arguments for the `cancel` command are described in Table 10-12.

Table 10-12 *cancel* Arguments

Argument	Description
`-u <user-list>`	Cancels the print request for a specified user. `<user-list>` can be one or more user names. Use a space or a comma to separate user names. If you use spaces, enclose the list of names in quotes.
`<printer-name>`	Specifies the printer for which you want to cancel the specified user's print requests. `<printer-name>` can be one or more printer names. Use a space or a comma to separate printer names. If you use spaces, enclose the list of printer names in quotes. If you don't specify `<printer-name>`, the user's print requests will be canceled on all printers.

In the following example, the command cancels all the print requests submitted by the user bcalkins on the printer eps1:

```
cancel -u bcalkins  luna
request "luna-23" cancelled
```

In the following example, the command cancels all the print requests submitted by the user bcalkins on all printers:

```
cancel -u bcalkins
request "asteroid-3" cancelled
request "luna-8" cancelled
```

Changing the Priority of a Print Request

Change the priority of a print request by using the following `lp` command:

```
lp -i <request-id> -H <change-priority>
```

The options for the lp command are described in Table 10-13.

Table 10-13 *lp* Options

Option	Description	
-i <request-id>	The request ID of a print request you want to change. You can specify multiple request IDs with this command. Use a space or a comma to separate request IDs. If you use spaces, enclose the list of request IDs in quotes.	
-H <change-priority>	One of the three ways to change the priority of a print request: hold, resume, or immediate:	
	hold	Places the print request on hold until you cancel it or instruct the LP print service to resume printing the request.
	resume	Places a print request that has been on hold back in the queue. It will be printed according to its priority and placement in the queue. If you put a hold on a print job that is already printing, resume puts the print request at the head of the queue so that it becomes the next request printed.
	immediate	Places a print request at the head of the queue. If a request is already printing, you can put that request on hold to allow the next request to print immediately.
-q < priority-level >	Assigns the print request a priority in the print queue. Specify <priority-level> as an integer from 0 to 39. Use 0 to indicate the highest priority and 39 to indicate the lowest priority.	

In the following example, the command changes a print request with the request ID eps1-29 to priority level 1:

```
lp -i eps1-29 -q 1
```

Restarting the Print Scheduler

The print scheduler, lpsched, handles print requests on print servers. If printouts are not coming out of the printer, you might need to restart the print scheduler. To restart the print scheduler, you use the lpsched command. If a print request was printing when the print scheduler stopped running, that request will be printed in its entirety when you restart the print scheduler.

First, stop the scheduler by typing

```
/usr/lib/lp/lpshut
```

To restart the scheduler, type

```
/usr/lib/lp/lpsched
```

The lp system is started by the /etc/init.d script named lp. There is a link from this file to the /etc/rc2.d directory so that the lp service starts automatically every time the system is booted. The same script can be used to reset the entire lp service by issuing the following command:

```
/etc/init.d/lp stop
```

The lp service will be stopped. You can restart the lp service with the following command:

```
/etc/init.d/lp start
```

NOTE. *Be aware that the /etc/init.d/lp script starts and stops the entire print service and not just the scheduler. Use* `lpshut` *and* `lpsched` *to stop and restart the scheduler only.*

Setting a User's Default Printer

When you added the printer, you were given the option of selecting that printer as the default printer for that particular system. You might want to set the default printer at the user level so that, on a particular system, users can specify their own default printer. If users don't provide a printer name when sending a print job, the `print` command searches for the default printer in the following order:

1. `LPDEST` variable
2. `PRINTER` variable
3. System's default printer

These variables can be set in the user's .profile file.

Modifying the Printer with Admintool

The Solaris Admintool can be used to modify a printer after it has been added to the system. Modifications that can be made to a printer via Admintool include the following:

- Giving the printer description
- Indicating the printer port
- Listing file contents
- Providing fault notification
- Selecting a default printer

- Printing a banner
- Accepting and processing print requests
- Providing a user access list

To modify a printer via the Admintool, select Edit, Modify from the Printers window, as shown in Figure 10-7.

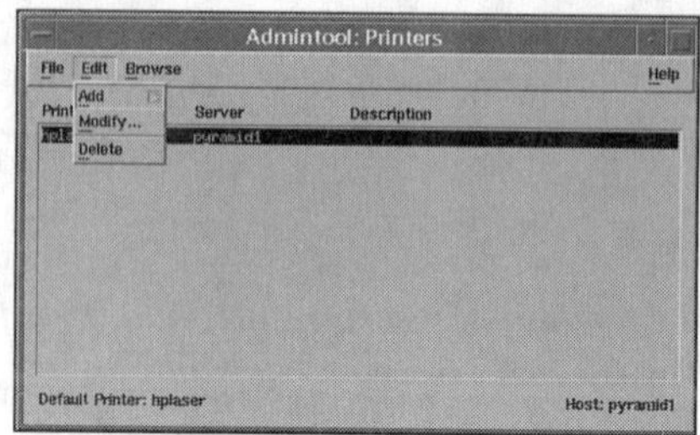

Figure 10-7
The Printers window.

The Modify Printer window appears, as shown in Figure 10-8.

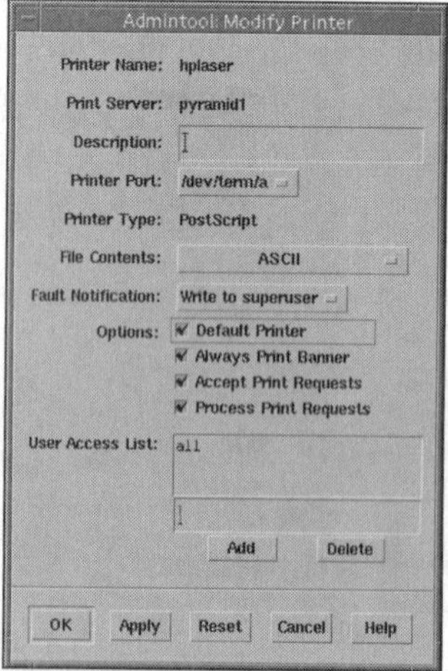

Figure 10-8
The Modify Printer window.

Modify the selected printer by selecting or filling in the appropriate fields in the Modify Printer window.

Summary

The majority of system problems I respond to are printer-related. You should also become familiar with your third-party applications and how they prepare print jobs to be sent to the spooler. Many of the problems I encounter are not with the Solaris print service, but in the way that the application formats the print job. This chapter introduced you to the Solaris print system and the `lpsched` daemon. Printers can also be administered in a networked environment using Solstice AdminSuite, described in Chapter 20, "Solstice AdminSuite." Chapter 11, "Process Control," explores all the Solaris processes. For a more detailed discussion of the `lpsched` daemon, refer to the *Solaris 7 System Administration Guide, Volume II* in the Answerbook2 online manuals.

CHAPTER

11

Process Control

The following are the test objectives for this chapter:

- Viewing a Solaris process
- Understanding how processes react to signals
- Understanding how Solaris schedules processes
- Using the Solaris batch-processing facilities

n addition to the test objectives on the previous page, I've included a section on syslog. Although syslog is an objective that's covered on the Part II exam, it fits well with the material in this chapter and did not warrant a chapter of its own.

Viewing a Process

Solaris is a multitasking environment in which a number of programs run at the same time. Each Solaris program is called a *process*. A process is a single program running in its own address space. A process under Solaris consists of an address space and a set of data structures in the kernel to keep track of that process. The address space is a section of memory that contains the code to execute a task. The kernel must keep track of the following data for each process on the system:

- Address space
- Current status of the process
- Execution priority of the process
- Resource usage of the process
- Current signal mask
- Ownership of the process

A process is distinct from a job or command, which may be composed of many processes working together to perform a specific task. Each process has a process ID associated with it and is referred to as a *pid*. You can look at processes that are currently executing by using the `ps` command. A process has certain attributes that directly affect execution. These are listed in Table 11-1.

Table 11-1 Process Attributes

Attribute	Description
`PID`	The process identification (a unique number that defines the process within the kernel).
`PPID`	The parent `PID` (the creator of the process).
`UID`	The user ID number of the user who owns the process.
`EUID`	The effective user ID of the process.
`GID`	The group ID of the user who owns the process.
`EGID`	The effective group ID that owns the process.
`Priority`	The priority at which the process runs.

Use the ps command to view processes currently running on the system. Adding the -l option to the ps command displays a variety of other information about the processes currently running, including the state of each process (listed under S). The codes used to show the various process states are listed in Table 11-2.

Table 11-2 Process States

Code	Process Status	Description
O	Running	The process is running on a processor.
S	Sleeping	The process is waiting for an event to complete.
R	Runnable	The process is on run queue.
I	Idle	The process is being created.
Z	Zombie state	The process was terminated and the parent is not waiting.
T	Traced	The process was stopped by a signal because the parent is tracing it.
X	Waiting	The process is waiting for memory to become available.

To see all the processes that are running on a system, type

```
ps -el
```

The system responds with the following output:

```
 F S UID PID PPID C PRI NI ADDR     SZ  WCHAN    TTY     TIME CMD
19 T 0   0   0    0 0   SY f0274e38 0   ?                0:01 sched
 8 S 0   1   0    0 41  20 f5af4888 162 f5af4a80 ?       0:01 init
19 S 0   2   0    0 0   SY f5af41c8 0   f02886a4 ?       0:00 pageout
19 S 0   3   0    1 0   SY f5af3b08 0   f028aeb4 ?       9:57 fsflush
 8 S 0   299 1    0 65  20 f5af26c8 368 f597e0ce console 0:00 ttymon
 8 S 0   101 1    0 41  20 f5af3448 340 f5d5bfae ?       0:00 in.route
 8 S 0   298 1    0 41  20 f5af2d88 350 f5982c78 ?       0:00 sac
 8 S 0   111 1    0 41  20 f5af2008 455 f5d5bf5e ?       0:01 rpcbind
 8 S 0   164 1    0 41  20 f5d5e890 691 f5d5ef38 ?       0:01 syslogd
 8 S 0   138 1    0 41  20 f5d5e1d0 450 f5d5be96 ?       0:00 inetd
 8 S 0   113 1    0 79  20 f5d5db10 462 f5d5bee6 ?       0:00 keyserv
 8 S 0   160 1    0 41  20 f5d5d450 650 f5d5bcb6 ?       0:00 automoun
 8 S 0   143 1    0 74  20 f5d5cd90 502 f5d5bebe ?       0:00 statd
 8 S 0   145 1    0 77  20 f5d5c6d0 409 f5d5be1e ?       0:00 lockd
 8 S 0   242 1    0 41  20 f5d5c010 514 f5d5b8a6 ?       0:01 vold
 8 S 0   184 1    0 46  20 f5e4a898 480 f5e4aa90 ?       0:01 nscd
 8 S 0   178 1    0 51  20 f5e4a1d8 360 f5982eb8 ?       0:01 cron
```

The manual page for the ps command describes all the fields displayed with the ps command as well as all the command options. Table 11-3 lists some important fields.

Table 11-3 Process Fields

Field	Description
F	Flags associated with the process.
S	The state of the process. The two most common values are S for sleeping and R for running. An important value to look for is X, which means that the process is waiting for memory to become available. When you frequently see this on your system, you are out of memory. Refer to Table 11-2 for a complete list of the process states.
UID	The user ID of the process owner. For many processes, this is 0, because they run setuid.
PID	The process ID of each process. This value should be unique. Generally, PIDs are allocated lowest to highest but wrap at some point. This value is necessary for you to send a signal, such as the `kill` signal, to a process.
PPID	The parent process ID. This identifies the parent process that started the process. Using the PPID allows you to trace the sequence of process creation that took place.
PRI	The priority of the process. Without the `-c` option, higher numbers mean lower priority. With the `-c` option, higher numbers mean higher priority.
NI	The `nice` value, used in priority computation. This is not printed when the `-c` option is used. The process's nice number contributes to its scheduling priority. Making a process nicer means lowering its priority.
ADDR	The memory address of the process.
SZ	The SIZE field. This is the total number of pages in the process. Each page is 4096 bytes.
WCHAN	The address of an event for which the process is sleeping (if it's -, the process is running).
STIME	The starting time of the process (in hours, minutes, and seconds).
TTY	The terminal assigned to your process.
TIME	The cumulative CPU time used by the process in minutes and seconds.
CMD	The command that generated the process.

You often want to look at all processes. You can do this using the command `ps -el`. A number of options available with the `ps` command control what information gets printed. A few of them are listed in Table 11-4.

Table 11-4 *ps* Command Options

Option	Description
-A	Lists information for all processes. Identical to `-e`.

continues

Table 11-4 *ps* Command Options (continues)

Option	Description
-a	Lists information about all processes most frequently requested. Processes not associated with a terminal will not be listed.
-f	Generates a full listing.
-P	Prints the number of the processor to which the process is bound, if any, under an additional column header PSR. This is a useful option on systems that have multiple processors.
-u <username>	Lists only process data for a particular user. In the listing, the numerical user ID will be printed unless you give the -f option, which prints the login name.

For a complete list of options to the `ps` command, refer to the Solaris online manual pages.

NOTE. *The UNIX* `sort` *command is useful when you're looking at system processes. Use the* `sort` *command as the pipe output to sort by size or* `PID`. *For example, to sort by* `SZ` *field, use the command* `ps -el | sort +9` *(remember,* `sort` *starts numbering fields with 0).*

The Solaris 7 release provides the `pgrep` command, which replaces the combination of the `ps`, `grep`, `egrep`, and `awk` commands that were used to manage processes in previous Solaris releases. The `pgrep` command examines the active processes on the system and reports the process IDs of the processes whose attributes match the criteria you specify on the command line. The command syntax for the `pgrep` command is

```
pgrep <options> <pattern>
```

`pgrep` options are described in Table 11-5.

Table 11-5 *pgrep* options

Option	Description
`-d <delim>`	Specifies the output delimiter string to be printed between each matching process ID. If no `-d` option is specified, the default is a newline character.
`-f`	The regular expression pattern should be matched against the full process argument string. If no `-f` option is specified, the expression is matched only against the name of the executable file.
`-g <pgrplist>`	Matches only processes whose process group ID is in the given list.
`-G <gidlist>`	Matches only processes whose real group ID is in the given list. Each group ID may be specified as either a group name or a numerical group ID.

Table 11-5 *pgrep* options (continues)

Option	Description
-l	Long output format. Prints the process name along with the process ID of each matching process.
-n	Matches only the newest (most recently created) process that meets all other specified matching criteria.
-P <ppidlist>	Matches only processes whose parent process ID is in the given list.
-s <sidlist>	Matches only processes whose process session ID is in the given list.
-t <termlist>	Matches only processes that are associated with a terminal in the given list. Each terminal is specified as the suffix following /dev/ of the terminal's device path name in /dev (for example, term/a or pts/0).
-u <euidlist>	Matches only processes whose effective user ID is in the given list. Each user ID may be specified as either a login name or a numerical user ID.
-U <uidlist>	Matches only processes whose real user ID is in the given list. Each user ID may be specified as either a login name or a numerical user ID.
-v	Matches all processes except those that meet the specified matching criteria.
-x	Considers only processes whose argument string or executable filename exactly matches the specified pattern.
<pattern>	A pattern to match against either the executable filename or full process argument string.

For example, the following pgrep example finds all processes that have "dt" in the process argument string:

```
pgrep -l -f "dt"
```

The system responds with this:

```
258 /usr/openwin/bin/Xsun :0 -nobanner -auth /var/dt/A:0-3YaaGa
256 /usr/dt/bin/dtlogin -daemon
280 /bin/ksh /usr/dt/bin/Xsession
259 /usr/dt/bin/dtlogin -daemon
327 /usr/dt/bin/dsdm
342 /usr/dt/bin/dtsession
3067 /usr/dt/bin/dtterm -C -ls -name Console
325 /usr/dt/bin/sdt_shell -c      unset DT;      DISPLAY=:0;      /usr/dt/bin/dt
328 -sh -c      unset DT;      DISPLAY=:0;      /usr/dt/bin/dtsession_res -merge
341 /usr/dt/bin/ttsession
349 dtwm
351 /usr/dt/bin/sdtperfmeter -f -H -t cpu -t disk -s 1 -name fpperfmeter
353 /bin/ksh /usr/dt/bin/sdtvolcheck -d -z 5 cdrom
```

```
730 /usr/dt/bin/dtterm -C -ls -name Console
1312 /bin/sh -c dtfile -noview
1313 dtfile -noview
1316 dtfile -noview
6886 /usr/dt/bin/dtscreen -mode blank
```

To find the process ID for the `lpsched` process, issue this command:

```
pgrep -l lpsched
```

The system responds with this:

```
6899 lpsched
```

Using Signals

Solaris supports the concept of sending software signals to a process. These signals are ways for other processes to interact with a running process outside the context of the hardware. The `kill` command is used to send a signal to a process. System administrators most often use the signals SIGHUP, SIGKILL, and SIGSTOP. The SIGHUP signal is used by some utilities as a way to notify the process to do something, such as reread its configuration file. The SIGHUP signal is also sent to a process if the telephone connection is lost or hangs up. The SIGKILL signal is used to abort a process, and the SIGSTOP signal is used to pause a process. Table 11-6 describes the many signals used.

Table 11-6 Signals Available Under Solaris

Signal	Number	Description
SIGHUP	1	Hangup. Usually means that the controlling terminal has been disconnected.
SIGINT	2	Interrupt. The user can generate this signal by pressing Ctrl+C or Delete.
SIGQUIT	3	Quits the process and produces a core dump.
SIGILL	4	Illegal instruction.
SIGTRAP	5	Trace or breakpoint trap.
SIGABRT	6	Abort.
SIGEMT	7	Emulation trap.
SIGFPE	8	Arithmetic exception. Informs a process of a floating-point error.
SIGKILL	9	Killed. Forces the process to terminate. This is a sure kill.
SIGBUS	10	Bus error.

Table 11-6 Signals Available Under Solaris (continues)

Signal	Number	Description
SIGSEGV	11	Segmentation fault.
SIGSYS	12	Bad system call.
SIGPIPE	13	Broken pipe.
SIGALRM	14	Alarm clock.
SIGTERM	15	Terminated. A gentle kill that gives processes a chance to clean up.
SIGUSR1	16	User signal 1.
SIGUSR2	17	User signal 2.
SIGCHLD	18	Child status changed.
SIGPWR	19	Power fail or restart.
SIGWINCH	20	Window size change.
SIGURG	21	Urgent socket condition.
SIGPOLL	22	Pollable event.
SIGSTOP	23	Stopped (signal). Pauses a process.
SIGTSTP	24	Stopped (user).
SIGCONT	25	Continued.
SIGTTIN	26	Stopped (tty input).
SIGTTOU	27	Stopped (tty output).
SIGVTALRM	28	Virtual timer expired.
SIGPROF	29	Profiling timer expired.
SIGXCPU	30	CPU time limit exceeded.
SIGXFSZ	31	File size limit exceeded.
SIGWAITING	32	Concurrency signal reserved by threads library.
SIGLWP	33	Inter-LWP signal reserved by threads library.
SIGFREEZE	34	Checkpoint freeze.
SIGTHAW	35	Checkpoint thaw.
SIGCANCEL	36	Cancellation signal reserved by threads library.

In addition, you can write a signal handler in a program to respond to a signal being sent. For example, many system administration utilities, such as the name server, respond to the SIGHUP signal by rereading their configuration files. This signal can then be used to update the process while running, without having to terminate and restart the process. For many signals, however, nothing can be done other than printing an appropriate error message and terminating the process.

Using the *kill* Command

The `kill` command sends a terminate signal (signal 15) to the process, and the process is terminated. Signal 15, which is the default when no options are used with the `kill` command, is a gentle kill that allows a process to perform cleanup work before terminating. Signal 9, on the other hand, is called a sure, unconditional kill because it cannot be caught or ignored by a process. If the process is still around after a `kill -9`, it is either hung up in the UNIX kernel, waiting for an event such as disk I/O to complete, or you are not the owner of the process.

The `kill` command is routinely used to send signals to a process. You can kill any process you own, and superuser can kill all processes in the system except those that have process IDs 0, 1, 2, 3, and 4. The `kill` command is poorly named, because not every signal sent by it is used to kill a process. This command gets its name from its most common use—terminating a process with the `kill -15` signal.

NOTE. *A common problem occurs when a process continually starts up new copies of itself—referred to as* forking *or* spawning. *Users have a limit on the number of new processes they can fork. This limit is set in the kernel with the* MAXUP *(maximum number of user processes) value. Sometimes, through user error, a process keeps forking new copies of itself until the user hits the* MAXUP *limit. As a user reaches this limit, the system appears to be waiting. If you kill some of the user's processes, the system resumes creating new processes on behalf of the user. It can be a no-win situation. The best way to handle these runaway processes is to send the STOP signal to suspend all processes and then send a KILL signal to terminate the processes. Because the processes were first suspended, they can't create new ones as you kill them off.*

You can send a signal to a process you own with the `kill` command. Many signals are available, but you need to worry about only two right now: 9 and 15. To send a signal to a process, first use the `ps` command to find the process ID (PID) number. For example, type `ps -ef` to list all processes and find the PID of the process you want to terminate:

```
ps -ef

UID     PID  PPID  C   STIME   TTY     TIME  CMD
root      0     0  0  Nov 27   ?       0:01  sched
root      1     0  0  Nov 27   ?       0:01  /etc/init -
root      2     0  0  Nov 27   ?       0:00  pageout
```

```
root      3     0  0   Nov 27  ?        12:52  fsflush
root    101     1  0   Nov 27  ?         0:00  /usr/sbin/in.routed -q
root    298     1  0   Nov 27  ?         0:00  /usr/lib/saf/sac -t 300
root    111     1  0   Nov 27  ?         0:02  /usr/sbin/rpcbind
root    164     1  0   Nov 27  ?         0:01  /usr/sbin/syslogd -n -z 12
root    138     1  0   Nov 27  ?         0:00  /usr/sbin/inetd -s
root    113     1  0   Nov 27  ?         0:00  /usr/sbin/keyserv
root    160     1  0   Nov 27  ?         0:01  /usr/lib/autofs/automountd
.
.
.
root    439   424  0   Nov 27  ?        0:00  /bin/cat /tmp/.removable/notify0
root   5497   433  1 09:58:02  pts/4    0:00  script psef
```

To kill the process with a PID number of 5497, type

```
kill -15 5497
```

Another way to kill a process is to use the `pkill` command. `pkill` functions identically to `pgrep`, which was described earlier, except instead of displaying information about each process, the process is terminated. A signal name or number may be specified as the first command-line option to `pkill`. The value for the signal can be any value described in Table 11-6. For example, to kill a process named `test`, issue the following command:

```
pkill -9  test
```

If no signal is specified, SIGTERM (15) is sent by default.

Scheduling Processes

Processes compete for execution time. Scheduling, one of the key elements in a time-sharing system, decides which of the processes will execute next. Although hundreds of processes might be present on the system, only one actually uses the CPU at any given time. Time-sharing on a CPU involves suspending a process and then restarting it later. Because the suspension and resumption of active processes occur several times each second, it appears to the user that the system is performing many tasks simultaneously.

UNIX attempts to manage the priorities of processes by giving a higher priority to those that have used the least amount of the CPU. In addition, processes that are sleeping on an event, such as a keyboard press, get higher priority than processes that are purely CPU-driven.

On any large system with a number of competing user groups, the task of managing resources falls on the system administrator. This task is both technical and political. As a system administrator, you must understand your company goals in order to manage this task successfully. When you understand the political implications of who should get priority, you are ready to manage the technical details. As root, you can change the priority of any process on the system by using the `nice` or `priocntl` commands. Before you do this, you must understand how priorities work.

Scheduling Priorities

All processes have an execution priority assigned to them—an integer value that is dynamically computed and updated on the basis of several different factors. Whenever the CPU is free, the scheduler selects the most favored process to resume executing. The process selected is the one with the lowest-priority number, because lower numbers are defined as more favored than higher ones. Multiple processes at the same priority level are placed in the run queue for that priority level. Whenever the CPU is free, the scheduler starts the processes at the head of the lowest-numbered non-empty run queue. When the process at the top of a run queue stops executing, it goes to the end of the line, and the next process moves up to the front. After a process begins to run, it continues to execute until it needs to wait for an I/O operation to complete, receives an interrupt signal, or exhausts the maximum execution time slice defined on that system. A typical time slice is 10 milliseconds.

A UNIX process has two priority numbers associated with it. One of the priority numbers is its requested execution priority with respect to other processes. This value (its nice number) is set by the process's owner and by root; it appears in the `NI` column in a `ps -l` listing. The other priority assigned to a process is the execution priority. This priority is computed and updated dynamically by the operating system, taking into account such factors as the process's nice number, how much CPU time it has had recently, and what other processes are running and their priorities. The execution priority value appears in the `PRI` column on a `ps -l` listing.

Although the CPU is the most-watched resource on a system, it is not the only one. Memory use, disk use, I/O activity, and the number of processes all tie together in determining the computer's throughput. For example, suppose you have two groups, A and B. Both groups require large amounts of memory—more than is available when both are running simultaneously. Raising the priority of Group A over Group B might not help if Group B does not fully relinquish the memory it is using. Although the paging system will do this over time, the process of swapping a process out to disk can be intensive and can greatly reduce performance. A better alternative might be to completely stop Group B with a signal and then continue it later, when Group A has finished.

Changing the Priority of a Time-Sharing Process with *nice*

The `nice` command is supported only for backward compatibility with previous Solaris releases. The `priocntl` command provides more flexibility in managing processes. The priority of a process is determined by the policies of its scheduling class and by its nice number. Each time-sharing process has a global priority that is calculated by adding the user-supplied priority, which can be influenced by the `nice` or `priocntl` commands and the system-calculated priority.

The execution priority number of a process is assigned by the operating system and is determined by several factors, including its schedule class, how much CPU time it has used, and its nice number. Each time-sharing process starts with a default nice number, which it inherits from its parent process. The nice number is shown in the `NI` column of the `ps` report.

A user can lower the priority of a process by increasing its user-supplied priority number. Only the superuser can increase the priority of a process by lowering its nice value. This prevents users from increasing the priorities of their own processes, thereby monopolizing a greater share of the CPU.

In UNIX, nice numbers range from 0 to +19. The highest priority is 0. Two versions of the command are available: the standard version, `/usr/bin/nice`, and a version that is part of the C shell.

Use the `nice` command as described in Table 11-7 when submitting a program or command.

Table 11-7 Setting Priorities with *nice*

Command	Description
Lowering the Priority of a Process	
`nice <command_name>`	Increases the nice number by four units (the default).
`nice +4 <command_name>`	Increases the nice number by four units.
`nice +10 <command_name>`	Increases the nice number by 10 units.
Increasing the Priority of a Process	
`nice -10 <command_name>`	Raises the priority of the command by lowering the nice number.
`nice - -10 <command_name>`	Raises the priority of the command by lowering the nice number. The two minus signs are required. The first is the option sign, and the second indicates a negative number.

As system administrator, you can use the `renice` command to change the priority of a process after it has been submitted. The `renice` command has the following form:

```
renice priority -n <value> -p <pid>
```

Use the `ps -el` command to find the PID of the process for which you want to change the priority. The process you want to change in the following example is named "largejob":

```
F S   UID   PID  PPID  C PRI NI       ADDR      SZ    WCHAN TTY      TIME  CMD
9 S     0  8200 4100  0  84 20  f0274e38     193            ?      0:00  largejob
```

Issue the following command to increase the priority of PID 8200:

```
renice -n -4 -p 8200
```

Issuing the `ps -el` command again shows the process with a higher priority:

```
F S   UID   PID  PPID  C PRI NI      ADDR      SZ    WCHAN TTY        TIME CMD
9 S     0  8200  4100  0  60 12 f0274e38     193            ?         0:00 largejob
```

Changing the Scheduling Priority of Processes with *priocntl*

The standard priority scheme has been improved under Solaris as part of its support for real-time processes. Real-time processes are designed to work in applications areas in which nearly immediate response to events is required. These processes are given nearly complete access to all system resources when they are running. Solaris uses time-sharing priority numbers ranging from –20 to 20. Solaris uses the `priocntl` command, intended as an improvement over the `nice` command, to modify process priorities. To use `priocntl` to change a priority on a process, type

```
priocntl -s -p <new-priority>  -i pid <process-id>
```

where `new-priority` is the new priority for the process and `process-id` is the PID of the process you want to change.

The following example sets the priority level for process 8200 to –5:

```
priocntl -s -p -5 -i pid 8200
```

The following example is used to set the priority (`nice` value) for every process created by a given parent process:

```
priocntl -s -p -5 -I ppid 8200
```

As a result of this command, all processes forked from process 8200 will have a priority of –5.

Consult the online manual pages for more information about the `priocntl` command.

Using the Solaris Batch-Processing Facility

A way to divide processes on a busy system is to schedule jobs so that they run at different times. A large job, for example, could be scheduled to run at 2 a.m., when the system would normally be idle. Solaris supports two methods of batch processing: the `crontab` and `at` commands. The `crontab` command schedules multiple system events at regular intervals, and the `at` command schedules a single system event.

Configuring Crontab

The `cron` daemon schedules system events according to commands found in each crontab file. A crontab file consists of commands, one per line, that will be executed at regular intervals. The beginning of each line contains five date and time fields that tell the `cron` daemon when to execute the command. The sixth field is the full pathname of the program you want to run. These fields, described in Table 11-8, are separated by spaces.

Table 11-8 The Crontab File

Field	Description	Values
1	Minute	0 to 59. An * in this field means every minute.
2	Hour	0 to 23. An * in this field means every hour.
3	Day of month	1 to 31. An * in this field means every day of the month.
4	Month	1 to 12. An * in this field means every month.
5	Day of week	0 to 6 (0 = Sunday). An * in this field means every day of the week.
6	Command	Enter the command to be run.

Follow these guidelines when making entries in the crontab file:

- Use a space to separate fields.
- Use a comma to separate multiple values in any of the date or time fields.
- Use a hyphen to designate a range of values in any of the date or time fields.
- Use an asterisk as a wildcard to include all possible values in any of the date or time fields. For example, an asterisk (*) can be used in the time field to mean all legal values.
- Use a comment mark (#) at the beginning of a line to indicate a comment or a blank line.
- Each command within a crontab file must consist of one line, even if it is very long, because crontab does not recognize extra carriage returns.

The following sample `crontab` command entry displays a reminder in the user's console window at 5 p.m. on the 1st and 15th of every month:

```
0 17 1,15 * * echo Hand in Timesheet > /dev/console
```

Crontab files are found in the /var/spool/cron/crontabs directory. Several crontab files besides root are provided during the SunOS software installation process; they are also located in this directory. Other crontab files are named after the user accounts for which they are created, such as bill, glenda, miguel, or nicole. They also are located in the /var/spool/cron/crontabs directory. For example, a crontab file named root is supplied during software installation. Its contents include these command lines:

```
10  3  *  *  0,4 /etc/cron.d/logchecker
10  3  *  *  0    /usr/lib/newsyslog
15  3  *  *  0 /usr/lib/fs/nfs/nfsfind
1   2  *  *  * [ -x /usr/sbin/rtc ] && /usr/sbin/rtc -c > /dev/null 2>&1
```

The first command line instructs the system to run `logchecker` at 3:10 a.m. on Sunday and Thursday. The second command line schedules the system to run `newsyslog` at 3:10 a.m. every Sunday. The third command line orders the system to execute `nfsfind` on Sunday at 3:15 a.m. The fourth command line instructs the system to check for daylight savings time and make corrections if necessary. If there is no RTC time zone or no /etc/rtc_config file, this entry will do nothing.

The `cron` daemon handles the automatic scheduling of crontab commands. Its function is to check the /var/spool/cron/crontab directory every 15 minutes for the presence of crontab files. It checks for new crontab files or changes to existing ones, reads the execution times listed within the files, and submits the commands for execution at the proper times.

Creating and Editing a Crontab File

Creating an entry in the crontab file is as easy as editing a text file using your favorite editor. The procedure is as follows:

1. (Optional) To create or edit a crontab file belonging to root or another user, become superuser.
2. Create a new crontab file, or edit an existing one, by typing

   ```
   crontab -e
   ```

3. Add command lines to the file, following the syntax described in Table 11-8.
4. Save the changes and exit the file. The crontab file is placed in /var/spool/cron/crontabs.
5. Verify the crontab file by typing

   ```
   crontab -l
   ```

   The system responds by listing the contents of the crontab file.

Controlling Access to Crontab

You can control access to crontab by modifying two files in the /etc/cron.d directory: cron.deny and cron.allow. These files permit only specified users to perform crontab tasks such as creating, editing, displaying, and removing their own crontab files. The cron.deny and cron.allow files consist of a list of usernames, one per line. These access control files work together in the following manner:

- If cron.allow exists, only the users listed in this file can create, edit, display, and remove crontab files.
- If cron.allow doesn't exist, all users may submit crontab files, except for users listed in cron.deny.

- If neither cron.allow nor cron.deny exists, superuser privileges are required to run crontab.

Superuser privileges are required to edit or create cron.deny and cron.allow.

During the Solaris software installation process, a default /etc/cron.d/cron.deny file is provided. It contains the following entries:

- daemon
- bin
- smtp
- nuucp
- listen
- nobody
- noaccess

None of the users listed in the cron.deny file can access crontab commands. The system administrator can edit this file to add other users who will be denied access to the crontab command. No default cron.allow file is supplied. This means that, after the Solaris software installation, all users (except the ones listed in the default cron.deny file) can access crontab. If you create a cron.allow file, only those users can access crontab commands.

Scheduling a Single System Event (*at*)

The `at` command is used to schedule jobs for execution at a later time. Unlike `crontab`, which schedules a job to happen at regular intervals, a job submitted with `at` executes once, at the designated time.

To submit an `at` job, type `at`. Then specify an execution time and a program to run, as shown in the following example:

```
at 07:45am today
at> who > /tmp/log
at> <Press Control-d>
job 912687240.a at Thu Jun 1 07:14:00 2000
```

When you submit an `at` job, it is assigned a job identification number, which becomes its filename along with the .a extension. The file is stored in the /var/spool/cron/atjobs directory. In much the same way as it schedules crontab jobs, the `cron` daemon controls the scheduling of `at` files.

The command syntax for `at` is

```
at -m <time> <date>
```

The at command is described in Table 11-9.

Table 11-9 *at* Command Syntax

Option	Description
-m	Sends you mail after the job is completed.
<time>	The hour when you want to schedule the job. Add am or pm if you do not specify the hours according to a 24-hour clock. midnight, noon, and now are acceptable keywords. Minutes are optional.
<date>	The first three or more letters of a month, a day of the week, or the keywords today or tomorrow.

You can set up a file to control access to the at command, permitting only specified users to create, remove, or display queue information about their at jobs. The file that controls access to at is /etc/cron.d/at.deny. It consists of a list of user names, one per line. The users listed in this file cannot access at commands. The default at.deny file, created during the SunOS software installation, contains the following usernames:

- daemon
- bin
- smtp
- nuucp
- listen
- nobody
- noaccess

With superuser privileges, you can edit this file to add other user names whose at access you want to restrict.

Checking Jobs in Queue (*atq* and *at-l*)

To check your jobs that are waiting in the at queue, use the atq command. This command displays status information about the at jobs you created. Use the atq command to verify that you have created an at job. The atq command confirms that at jobs have been submitted to the queue, as shown in the following example:

```
atq
Rank  Execution Date      Owner   Job            Queue   Job Name
1st   Jun  1, 2000 08:00  root    912690000.a    a       stdin
2nd   Jun  1, 2000 08:05  root    912690300.a    a       stdin
```

Another way to check an at job is by issuing the `at -l` command. This command shows the status information on all jobs submitted by a user, as shown in this example:

```
at -l
user = root    912690000.a    Thu Jun  1 08:00:00 2000
user = root    912690300.a    Thu Jun  1 08:05:00 2000
```

Removing and Verifying Removal of *at* Jobs

To remove the at job from the queue before it is executed, type

```
at -r [job-id]
```

where job-id is the identification number of the job you want to remove.

Verify that the at job is removed by using the `at -l` (or atq) command to display the jobs remaining in the at queue. The job whose identification number you specified should not appear. In the following example, we'll remove an at job that was scheduled to execute at 08:00 a.m. on December 3. First, check the at queue to locate the job identification number:

```
at -l
user = root    912690000.a    Thu Jun  1 08:00:00 2000
user = root    912690300.a    Thu Jun  1 08:05:00 2000
```

Next, remove the job from the at queue:

```
at -r 912690000.a
```

Finally, verify that this job has been removed from the queue:

```
at -l
user = root    912690300.a    Thu Jun  1 08:05:00 2000
```

Syslog

A critical part of the system administrator's job is monitoring the system. Solaris uses the syslog message facility to do this. syslogd is the daemon responsible for capturing system messages. The messages can be warnings, alerts, or simply informational messages. As the system administrator, you'll customize syslog to specify where and how system messages are to be saved.

NOTE. *Syslog is covered on the Part II exam.*

The syslogd daemon receives messages from applications on the local host or from remote hosts and directs messages to a specified log file. To each message that syslog captures, it adds a timestamp, the message type keyword at the beginning of the message, and a newline at the end of the message. For example, the following message was logged in the /var/adm/messages file:

```
May 12 06:50:36 ultra5 unix: NOTICE: alloc: /opt: file system full
```

Syslog allows you to capture messages by facility (the part of the system that generated the message) and by level of importance. Facility is considered to be the service area generating the message or error (such as printing, email, or network), whereas the level can be considered the level of severity (such as notice, warning, error, or emergency). Syslog also allows you to forward messages to another machine so that all your messages can be logged in one location. The syslogd daemon reads and logs messages into a set of files described by the configuration file /etc/syslog.conf. An entry in the /etc/syslog.conf file is composed of two fields:

```
selector     action
```

The selector field contains a semicolon-separated list of priority specifications of this form:

```
facility.level [ ; facility.level ]
```

The action field indicates where to forward the message.

There are many defined facilities; they are described in Table 11-10.

Table 11-10 Recognized Values for *facility*

Value	Description
user	Messages generated by user processes. This is the default priority for messages from programs or facilities not listed in this file.
kern	Messages generated by the kernel.
mail	The mail system.
daemon	System daemons, such as in.ftpd.
auth	The authorization system, such as login, su, getty, and others.
lpr	The line printer spooling system, such as lpr, lpc, and others.
news	Reserved for the USENET network news system.
uucp	Reserved for the UUCP system. It does not currently use the syslog mechanism.
cron	The cron/at facility, such as crontab, at, cron, and others.

Table 11-10 Recognized Values for *facility* (continued)

Value	Description
local0-7	Reserved for local use.
mark	For timestamp messages produced internally by syslogd.
*	An asterisk indicates all facilities except the mark facility.

Table 11-11 lists recognized values for the syslog `level` field. They are listed in descending order of severity.

Table 11-11 Recognized Values for *level*

Value	Description
emerg	For panic conditions that would normally be broadcast to all users.
alert	For conditions that should be corrected immediately, such as a corrupted system database.
crit	For warnings about critical conditions, such as hard device errors.
err	For other errors.
warning	For warning messages.
notice	For conditions that are not error conditions but may require special handling.
info	Informational messages.
debug	For messages that are normally used only when debugging a program.
none	Does not send messages from the indicated facility to the selected file. For example, the entry `*.debug;mail.none` in /etc/syslog.conf will send all messages except mail messages to the selected file.

Values for the `action` field can have one of four forms:

- A filename, beginning with a leading slash. This indicates that messages specified by the selector are to be written to the specified file. The file will be opened in append mode.
- The name of a remote host, prefixed with an @. An example is @server, which indicates that messages specified by the selector are to be forwarded to the `syslogd` on the named host. The hostname "loghost" is the hostname given to the machine that will log `syslogd` messages. Every machine is "loghost" by default. This is specified in the

local /etc/hosts file. It is also possible to specify one machine on a network to be "loghost" by making the appropriate host table entries. If the local machine is designated as "loghost," `syslogd` messages are written to the appropriate files. Otherwise, they are sent to the machine "loghost" on the network.

- A comma-separated list of usernames, which indicates that messages specified by the selector are to be written to the named users if they are logged in.
- An asterisk, which indicates that messages specified by the selector are to be written to all logged-in users.

Blank lines are ignored. Lines in which the first non-whitespace character is a # are treated as comments.

All of this becomes much clearer when you look at sample entries from an /etc/syslog.conf file:

```
*.err     /dev/console
*.err;daemon,auth.notice;mail.crit     /var/adm/messages
mail.debug     /var/spool/mqueue/syslog
*.alert     root
*.emerg     *
kern.err     @server
*.alert;auth.warning     /var/log/auth
```

In this example, the first line prints all errors and notices from the authentication system on the console. Whenever someone issues the `su` command, syslog writes a message to the console.

The second line sends all errors, daemon and authentication system notices, and all critical errors from the mail system to the file /var/adm/messages.

The third line sends mail system debug messages to /var/spool/mqueue/syslog.

The fourth line sends all alert messages to user root.

The fifth line sends all emergency messages to all users.

The sixth line forwards kernel messages of err (error) severity or higher to the machine named server.

The last line logs all messages from the authorization system of warning level or higher in the file /var/log/auth.

The level `none` may be used to disable a facility. This is usually done in the context of eliminating messages. For example:

```
*.debug;mail.none /var/adm/messages
```

selects debug messages from all facilities except those from mail. In other words, mail messages are disabled. The mail system, sendmail, logs a large number of messages. This information can be extremely large, so some system administrators disable mail messages or send them to another file that they clean out frequently. Before disabling mail messages, however, remember that sendmail messages come in very handy when you're diagnosing mail problems or tracking mail forgeries.

`syslogd` is started in the early stages of multiuser bootup from the /etc/rc2.d directory with a script called S74syslog. To restart the syslog facility, issue this:

```
/etc/rc2.d/S74syslog stop
/etc/rc2.d/S74syslog start
```

The syslog facility reads its configuration information from /etc/syslog.conf whenever it receives the HUP signal (such as `kill -HUP`). The first message is always logged by the `syslog` daemon itself when it places a timestamp on when the daemon was started.

Other Important Files Where Information Is Logged

Solaris has many files that hold logging information. Most of these files are stored in the /var/adm directory. The following list of these log files briefly describes the information they contain:

- **/var/adm/messages**—The messages file holds information that prints to the console. These might include root logins and `su` attempts.
- **/var/adm/lastlog**—This file holds the most recent login time for each user in the system.
- **/var/adm/utmp and /var/adm/utmpx**—The utmp database file contains user access and accounting information for commands such as `who`, `write`, and `login`. The utmp file is where information such as the terminal line and login time are stored for access by the `who` command.
- **/var/adm/wtmp and /var/adm/wtmpx**—The wtmp file contains the history of user access and accounting information for the utmp database. The wtmp file keeps track of logins and logouts since reboot. The `last` command, described in Chapter 6, "System Security," reads that file and processes the information.
- **/var/adm/acct**—This is the system accounting file. If enabled, the accounting file records a record for every process listing the following information: the name of the user who ran the command, the name of the command, the CPU time used, the completion timestamp of the process, and a flag indicating completion status. Accounting information can be very useful in monitoring who is doing what on your system.

- **/var/adm/sulog**—The sulog file holds records for everyone who has used the `su` command on the system. Here is a sample:

```
SU 04/29 09:39 + console root-daemon
SU 04/29 15:29 + console root-daemon
SU 05/02 05:38 + console root-daemon
SU 05/12 06:20 + console root-daemon
SU 05/12 07:59 + pts/1 root-bcalkins
```

- **/var/cron/log**—Keeps a record of all cron activity.

Good system administration requires that you look over your system logs frequently and keep their size in check. Some of these files can grow extremely large and fill up a file system quickly.

Summary

The system administrator needs to be aware of the processes that belong to each application. As users report problems, the system administrator can quickly locate the processes being used and look for irregularities. By keeping a close watch on system messages and processes, you'll become familiar with what is normal and what is abnormal. Don't wait for problems to happen—watch system messages and processes daily. Create shell scripts to watch processes for you and to look for irregularities in the system log files. By taking a proactive approach to system administration, you'll find problems before they affect the users.

Chapter 12, "Backup and Recovery," moves from system setup and processes to look at the system administrator's most important preventive maintenance task—system backups.

CHAPTER

12

Backup and Recovery

The following are the test objectives for this chapter:

- Using the Solaris utilities `tar`, `dd`, `cpio`, and `pax` to copy data
- Using `ufsdump` and `ufsrestore` to back up and restore data

Backing up a system involves copying data from the system's hard disks onto removable media that can be safeguarded in a secure area. Backups are used to restore data if files get corrupted or if data gets destroyed by system failure or a building disaster. Having a fault-tolerant disk array is not enough. Disk mirroring and RAID 5 protect your data in case of a hardware failure, but they do not protect against file corruption, natural disaster, or accidental deletion of a file. Backing up system data—the most important task you will perform—must be done on a regular basis. Although even a comprehensive backup scheme can't guarantee against loss of information, you can make sure the loss will be minimal.

This chapter describes methods available to perform a backup, types of backups, development of a solid backup strategy, and restoring data if you encounter a loss. First you'll find an explanation of the `tar`, `dd`, `cpio`, and `pax` commands, which are used to copy data from disk to disk or from disk to tape. Then the `ufsdump` and `ufsrestore` utilities are described as the preferred method of backing up data from a Solaris system to tape on a regular basis.

Solaris Backup and Restoration Utilities

Solaris provides the utilities listed in Table 12-1. They can be used to copy data from disk to removable media and restore it.

Table 12-1 Backup Utilities

Utility	Description
`tar`	Archives data to another directory, system, or medium.
`dd`	Copies data quickly.
`cpio`	Copies data from one location to another.
`pax`	Copies files and directory subtrees to a single tape. This command provides better portability than `tar` or `cpio`, so it can be used to transport files to other types of UNIX systems.
`ufsdump`	Backs up all files in a file system.
`ufsrestore`	Restores some or all of the files archived with the `ufsdump` command.

tar

The primary use of the `tar` (tape archiver) command is to copy file systems or individual files from a hard disk to a tape or from a tape to a hard disk. You can also use it to create a tar archive on a hard disk or floppy and to extract files from a tar archive on a hard disk or floppy. The `tar` command is popular because it's available on most UNIX systems; however, it is limited to a single tape. If the data you are backing up requires more than one tape, use the `cpio`, `pax`, or `ufsdump` commands, which I will describe later.

The `tar` command has the following syntax:

```
tar <options> <tar filename> <file list>
```

where `options` is the list of command options listed in Table 12-2.

Table 12-2 Command Options for *tar*

Option	Description
c	Creates a tar file.
t	Table of contents. Lists the names of the specified files each time they occur in the tar filename. If no file argument is given, the names of all files in the tar filename are listed. When used with the `v` function modifier, it displays additional information for the specified files.
x	Extracts or restores files from a tar filename.
v	Verbose. Outputs information to the screen as tar reads or writes the archive.
f	Uses the `tar filename` argument as the name of the tar archive. If `f` is omitted, `tar` uses the device indicated by the `TAPE` environment variable (if it is set). If the `TAPE` variable is not set, `tar` uses the default values defined in /etc/default/tar. If the name of the tar file is -, `tar` writes to the standard output.

For a more complete listing of command options, refer to the Solaris online manual pages.

The `<tar filename>` is used with the `f` option and can be any name you want. The filename can also be the name of a device, such as /dev/rmt/0 or /dev/rfd0. The `<file list>` is a list of files you want to include in the archive.

tar Examples

The following examples illustrate the use of the `tar` command.

To create a tape archive of everything in the /home/bcalkins directory on tape device /dev/rmt/0, type the following:

```
tar cvf /dev/rmt/0 /home/bcalkins
```

To list the files in the archive, type

```
tar tvf /dev/rmt/0
```

To restore the file /home/bcalkins/.profile from the archive, type

```
tar xvf /dev/rmt/0 /home/bcalkins/.profile
```

Use `tar` to create an archive file on disk instead of tape. The tar filename will be files.tar:

```
tar cvf files.tar /home/bcalkins
```

To extract files that were created using the preceding example, type

```
tar xvf files.tar
```

Notice the use of the full pathname. Using the full pathname to create the archive ensures that the files will be restored to their original location in the directory hierarchy. You will not be able to restore them elsewhere.

If you want to be able to restore files with a relative pathname in the preceding example, you could change to the /home/bcalkins directory and specify files to be archived as `./*`. This would put the files into the archive using a pathname relative to the current working directory rather than an absolute pathname (one beginning with a forward slash). Files can then be restored into any directory.

dd

The main advantage of the `dd` command is that it quickly converts and copies files with different data formats, such as differences in block size or record length.

The most common use of this command is to transfer a complete file system or partition from your hard disk to a tape. You can also use it to copy files from one hard disk to another. When you're copying data, the `dd` command makes an image copy (an exact byte-for-byte copy) of any medium, which can be either tape or disk. The syntax for the `dd` command is as follows; the command arguments are described in Table 12-3.

```
dd if=<input-file> of=<output-file> <option=value>
```

Table 12-3 *dd* Command Arguments

Argument	Description
`if`	Used to designate an input file. The input file can be a filename or a device name, such as /dev/rmt/0. If no input file is specified, input for dd is taken from the UNIX standard input.
`of`	Used to designate an output file. The output file can be a filename or a device name, such as /dev/rmt/0. If no output file is specified, output from dd is sent to the UNIX standard output.

Several other options can follow on the command line to specify buffer sizes, block sizes, and data conversions. See the Solaris online manual pages for a list of these options.

dd Examples

The next few examples illustrate the use of the dd command to copy data. The first example shows how the dd command is used to duplicate tapes. This procedure requires two tape drives—a source tape and a destination tape:

```
dd if=/dev/rmt/0 of=/dev/rmt/1
```

The next example uses dd to copy one entire hard disk to another hard disk. In the example, you need two disks, and both must have the same geometry:

```
dd if=/dev/rdsk/c0t1d0s2 of=/dev/rdsk/c0t4d0s2 bs=128
```

In this example, the option bs=128 specifies a block size. A large block size, such as 128KB or 256KB, will decrease the time to copy by buffering large amounts of data. Notice also that the raw device is specified. For this technique to work properly, you must use the raw (character) device to avoid the buffered (block) I/O system.

The dd command can be used with tar to create an archive on a remote tape drive. In the next example, tar is used to create an archive on a remote system by piping the output to a tape drive called /dev/rmt/0 on a remote system named xena:

```
tar cvf - <files> | rsh xena dd of=/dev/rmt/0 obs=128
```

Another example would be to read tar data coming from another UNIX system, such as Silicon Graphics. Silicon Graphics swaps every pair of bytes, making a tar tape unreadable on a Solaris system. To read a tar tape from an SGI system, type

```
dd if=/dev/nrst0 conv=swab | tar xvf -
```

In a similar way, a Solaris system can create a tar tape that can be read by an SGI system:

```
tar cvf - <files> | dd of=/dev/nrst0 conv=swab
```

cpio

The cpio command is used to copy data from one place to another. cpio stands for "copy input to output." When copying files with cpio, you present a list of files to its standard input and write the file archive to its standard output. The principal advantage of cpio is its flexible syntax. The command acts as a filter program, taking input information from the standard input file and delivering its output to the standard output file. The input and output can be manipulated by using the shell to specify redirection and pipelines. Here are the advantages of cpio over other UNIX utilities:

- cpio can back up and restore individual files, not just whole file systems. (tar and pax also have this capability.)

- Backups made by `cpio` are smaller than those created with `tar`, because the header is smaller.
- `cpio` can span multiple tapes; `tar` is limited to a single tape.

Because of its flexibility, `cpio` has more options and is perceived as a more complex command than `tar`.

The `cpio` program operates in one of three modes: copy-out (`cpio -o`), copy-in (`cpio -i`), or pass (`cpio -p`). Use copy-out when creating a backup tape and copy-in when restoring or listing files from a tape. The pass mode is generally used to copy files from one location to another on disk. You must always specify one of these three modes. The command syntax for the `cpio` command is

```
cpio <mode> <option>
```

where `mode` is `-i`, `-o`, or `-p` and `option` is an option from Table 12-4.

Table 12-4 Command Options for *cpio*

Option	Description
-c	Writes header information in ASCII format for portability.
-d	Creates as many directories as needed.
-B	Specifies that the input has a blocking factor of 5120 bytes to the record instead of the default 512-byte records. You must use the same blocking factor when you retrieve or copy files from the tape to the hard disk as you did when you copied files from the hard disk to the tape. You must use this option whenever you copy files or file systems to and from a tape drive.
-v	Verbose. Reports the names of the files as they are processed.
-u	Copies unconditionally. Without this option, an older file will not replace a newer file that has the same name.
-m	Retains the previous file modification time. This option is ineffective on directories that are being copied.

cpio Examples

The following example shows how to copy the directory /work and its subdirectories to a tape drive with the device name /dev/rmt/0. The `-o` option specifies copy-out mode, `-c` will output the header information in ASCII format, and I'm using the `-B` option to increase the blocking factor to 5120 bytes to improve the speed.

```
cd /work
ls -R | cpio -ocB > /dev/rmt/0
```

The next example shows how to copy the files located on a tape back into the directory named /work on a hard disk:

```
cd /work
cpio -icvdB < /dev/rmt/0
```

The `-i` option specifies copy-in mode, `-d` will create directories as needed to restore the data to the original location, and `-v` will display all the output.

Backing Up Files with Copy-Out Mode

To use copy-out mode to make backups, you send a list of files to the `cpio` command via the standard input of `cpio`. In practice, you'll use the UNIX `find` command to generate the list of files to be backed up. Copy-out mode is specified by using the `-o` option on the `cpio` command line. In the next example, a file named "list" contains a short list of files to be backed up to tape:

```
cpio -ovB list > /dev/rmt/1
```

Normally, as indicated in Table 12-4, `cpio` writes files to the standard output in 512-byte records. By specifying the `-B` option, you increase the record size to 5120 bytes to significantly speed up the transfer rate, as shown in the previous example. You can use UNIX commands to generate a list of files to be backed up by `cpio` in a number of other ways, as shown in the following examples.

Files can be backed up by entering filenames via the keyboard. Press Ctrl+D when you have finished typing filenames. Type

```
cpio -o > /dev/rmt/1
File1.txt
File2.txt
```

The `ls` command can be used to generate the list of files to be backed up by `cpio`. Type

```
cd /home/bcalkins
ls * | cpio -o >/dev/rmt/1
```

Use the `find` command to generate a list of files created by the user bcalkins and modified in the last five days. This is the list of files to be backed up:

```
find . -user bcalkins -mtime -5  -print | cpio -o > /dev/rmt/1
```

If the current tape fills up, the `cpio` program prompts you for another tape. You see a message that says

```
If you want to go on, type device/file name when ready
```

You should then change the tape and enter the name of the backup device (for example, /dev/rmt/1).

Restoring Files with Copy-In Mode

Use the copy-in mode of `cpio` to restore files from tape to disk. The following examples describe methods used to restore files from a `cpio` archive.

This first example restores all files and directories from tape to disk. The `cpio` options specified will restore files unconditionally (`-u`) to the /users directory and will retain previous file modification times (`-m`). Type

```
cd /users
cpio -icvumB < /dev/rmt/1
```

The next example selectively restores files that begin with "database." The `-d` option will create directories as needed. Type

```
cpio -icvdumB 'database*' < /dev/rmt/1
```

NOTE. *Single quotes must be used to pass the wildcard argument (`*`) to* `cpio`.

To get a list of files that are on tape, follow the next example:

```
cpio -ictB < /dev/rmt/1
```

The list of files on /dev/rmt/1 will appear on-screen.

Pass Mode

Pass mode generally is not used for backups. The destination must be a directory on a mounted file system, which means that pass mode cannot be used to transfer files to tape. However, you can use pass mode within `cpio` to copy files from one directory to another. The advantage of using `cpio` over `cp` is that original modification times and ownership are preserved. Specify pass mode by using the `-p` option in `cpio`. The following example copies all files from /users to /bkup:

```
cd /users
mkdir /bkup
ls * | cpio -pdumv bkup
```

Files will be listed to the screen as they are copied.

pax

New since Solaris 2.5 is the `pax` command, a POSIX-conformant archive utility that can read and write `tar` and `cpio` archives. It is available on most UNIX systems that are POSIX-compliant.

`pax` can read, write, and list the members of an archive file and copy directory hierarchies. The `pax` utility supports a wide variety of archive formats, including `tar` and `cpio`.

Here's a nice feature: If pax finds an archive that is damaged or corrupted while processing, pax attempts to recover from media defects. It searches through the archive to locate and process the largest possible number of archive members.

The action to be taken depends on the presence of the -r and -w options, which are referred to as the four modes of operation: list, read, write, and copy (described in Table 12-5). The syntax for the pax command is

```
pax <mode> <options>
```

Table 12-5 *pax*'s Four Modes of Operation

Option	Operation Mode	Description
-r	Read mode	(When -r is specified but -w is not.) pax extracts the filenames and directories found in the archive file. The archive file is read from disk or tape. If an extracted file is a directory, the file hierarchy is extracted as well. The extracted files are created relative to the current file hierarchy.
None	List mode	(When neither -r nor -w is specified.) pax displays the filenames or directories found in the archive file. The archive file is read from disk, tape, or the standard input. The list is written to the standard output.
-w	Write mode	(When -w is specified but -r is not.) pax writes the contents of the file to the standard output in an archive format. If no files are specified, a list of files to copy (one per line) is read from the standard input. A directory includes all the files in the file hierarchy rooted at the file.
-rw	Copy mode	(When both -r and -w are specified.) pax copies the specified files to the destination directory.

In addition to selecting a mode of operation, you can select one or more options from Table 12-6.

Table 12-6 Command Options for *pax*

Option	Description
-r	Reads an archive file from standard input and extracts the specified files. If any intermediate directories are needed to extract an archive member, these directories are created.
-w	Writes files to the standard output in the specified archive format. When no file operands are specified, standard input is read for a list of pathnames—one per line, without any leading or trailing blanks.
-a	Appends files to the end of an archive that was previously written.

Table 12-6 Command Options for *pax* (continues)

Option	Description
-b	Block size. The block size must be a multiple of 512 bytes, with a maximum of 32256 bytes. A block size can end with k or b to specify multiplication by 1024 (1K) or 512, respectively.
-c	Matches all file or archive members except those specified by the pattern and file operands.
-f <archive>	Specifies <archive> as the pathname of the input or output archive. A single archive may span multiple files and different archive devices. When required, pax prompts for the pathname of the file or device of the next volume in the archive.
-i	Interactively renames files or archive members. For each archive member matching a pattern operand or file matching a file operand, a prompt will be written to the terminal.
-n	Selects the first archive member that matches each pattern operand. No more than one archive member is matched for each pattern.
-p <string>	Specifies one or more file characteristic options (privileges). The string option-argument is a string specifying file characteristics to be retained or discarded on extraction. The string consists of the specification characters a, e, m, o, and p. Multiple characteristics can be concatenated within the same string, and multiple -p options can be specified. The meanings of the specification characters are as follows:
	a — Does not preserve file access times.
	e — Preserves everything: user ID, group ID, file mode bits, file access times, and file modification times.
	m — Does not preserve file modification times.
	o — Preserves the user ID and group ID.
	p — Preserves the file mode bits.
	-v — Verbose mode.
-x <format>	Specifies the output archive format, with the default format being ustar. pax currently supports cpio, tar, bcpio, ustar, sv4crc, and sv4cpio.

For additional options to the pax command, see the Solaris online manual pages.

When using pax, you can also specify file operands along with the options from Table 12-6. The operand specifies a destination directory or file pathname. If you specify a directory operand that does not exist, that cannot be written by the user, or that is not of type directory, pax exits with a nonzero exit status.

The file operand specifies the pathname of a file to be copied or archived. When a file operand does not select at least one archive member, pax writes these file operand pathnames in a diagnostic message to standard error and then exits with a nonzero exit status.

Another operand is the pattern operand, which is used to select one or more pathnames of archive members. Archive members are selected by using the filename pattern-matching notation described by fnmatch. Here are examples of pattern operands:

?	A question mark matches any character.
*	An asterisk matches multiple characters.
[	The open bracket introduces a pattern bracket expression.

When a pattern operand is not supplied, all members of the archive are selected. When a pattern matches a directory, the entire file hierarchy rooted at that directory is selected. When a pattern operand does not select at least one archive member, pax writes these pattern operands in a diagnostic message to standard error and then exits with a nonzero exit status.

pax Examples

The following examples illustrate the use of the pax command. For example, to copy files to tape, issue this pax command, using -w to copy the current directory contents to tape and -f to specify the tape device:

```
pax -w -f /dev/rmt/0
```

To list a verbose table of contents for an archive stored on tape device /dev/rmt/0, issue the following command:

```
pax -v -f /dev/rmt/0
```

The tape device in these two examples could have been a filename to specify an archive on disk.

The following command can be used to interactively select the files to copy from the current directory to the destination directory:

```
pax -rw -i . <dest_dir>
```

As you become more familiar with the pax utility, you'll begin to use it in place of tar and cpio because of its portability to other UNIX systems, its capability to recover damaged archives, and its capability to span multiple volumes.

ufsdump

Although the other Solaris utilities discussed in this chapter can be used to copy files from disk to tape, `ufsdump` is designed specifically for backups and is the recommended method for backing up your Solaris file systems. The `ufsdump` command copies files, directories, or entire file systems from a hard disk to a tape. The only drawback of using `ufsdump` is that the file systems must be inactive before you can conduct a full backup. If the file system is still active, anything in the memory buffers is not copied to tape.

You should back up any file systems critical to users, including file systems that change frequently. See Table 12-7 for suggestions on the file systems to back up and how often.

Table 12-7 File Systems to Back Up

File System	Frequency
root (/)	If you frequently add and remove clients and hardware on the network, or you have to change important files in root (/), this file system should be backed up. You should do a full backup of the root (/) file system between once a week and once a month. If /var is in the root (/) file system and your site keeps user mail in the /var/mail directory on a mail server, you might want to back up root (/) daily.
/usr	The contents of this file system are fairly static and need to be backed up only from once a week to once a month.
/export/home	The /export/home file system contains the home directories and subdirectories of all users on the system; its files are volatile and should be backed up daily.
Data	All data directories should be backed up daily.

The `ufsdump` command has many built-in features that the other archive utilities don't have:

- The `ufsdump` command can be used to back up individual file systems to local or remote tape devices or disk drives. The device can be on any system in the network. This command works quickly because it is aware of the structure of the UFS file system, and it works directly through the raw device file.
- `ufsdump` has built-in options to create incremental backups that will back up only those files that were changed since a previous backup, saving tape space and time.
- `ufsdump` has the capability to back up groups of systems over the network from a single system. You can run `ufsdump` on each remote system through a remote shell or remote login, directing the output to the system on which the drive is located.
- The system administrator can restrict user access to backup tables.
- The `ufsdump` command has a built-in option to verify data on tape against the source file system.

Backing up a file system with `ufsdump` is referred to as "dumping" a file system. When a file system is dumped, a level between 0 and 9 is specified. A level 0 dump is a full backup and contains everything on the file system. Level 1 through 9 dumps are incremental backups and contain only files that have changed since a previous dump at a lower level.

A good backup schedule involves a recommended three-level dump strategy: a level 0 dump at the start of the month (manually), automated weekly level 5 dumps, and automated daily level 9 dumps. The automated dumps are performed at 4:30 a.m., a time when most systems are typically idle. Automated daily dumps are performed Sunday through Friday mornings. Automated weekly dumps are performed on Saturday mornings. Backups are automated by creating a shell script and using `cron` to execute the script on a regular basis.

Table 12-8 shows the dump level performed on each day of a typical month. Note that the level 0 dump at the start of the month is performed manually, because the entire system must be idle before you can back up the root file system. One way to ensure that the system is not being used is to put the system in single-user mode. The level 9 and 5 dumps are automated with `cron` but also must be conducted when the file systems are not being used.

NOTE. *See Chapter 11, "Process Control," for more information on* `cron`.

Table 12-8 File System Dump Schedule

Floating	Monday	Tuesday	Wednesday	Thursday	Friday
1st of month	0				
Week 1	9	9	9	9	5
Week 2	9	9	9	9	5
Week 3	9	9	9	9	5
Week 4	9	9	9	9	5

The backup schedule in Table 12-8 accomplishes the following:

- Each weekday tape accumulates all files changed since the end of the previous week or the initial level 0 for the first week. All files that have changed since the lower-level backup at the end of the previous week are saved each day.
- Each Friday's tape contains all files changed since the last level 0.

This dump schedule requires at least four sets of five tapes—one set for each week and one tape for the level 0 dump. Each set will be rotated each month. The level 0 tapes should not be overwritten and should be saved for at least one year.

Be aware that even with the backup schedule outlined in Table 12-8, data can still be lost. If a hard disk fails at 3 p.m., all modifications since the 4:30 a.m. backup will be lost. Also, files that were deleted midweek will not appear on the level 5 tapes. Sometimes a user accidentally deletes a file and does not realize it for several weeks. When the user wants to use the file, it is not there. If he asks you to restore it from backup, the only tape it appears on is the level 0, and it could be too far out of date to be useful. If you don't overwrite the daily level 9 tapes frequently, you can minimize this problem.

The syntax for the `ufsdump` command is

```
/usr/sbin/ufsdump  <options>  <arguments>  <files to dump>
```

The options to the `ufsdump` command are described in Table 12-9.

Table 12-9 *ufsdump* options

Option	Description
`<options>`	A single string of one-letter option names.
`<arguments>`	Identifies option arguments and may be multiple strings. The option letters and the arguments that go with them must be in the same order.
`<files to dump>`	Identifies the files to back up. This argument must always come last. It specifies the source or contents of the backup. It usually identifies a file system, but it can also identify individual files or directories. For a file system, specify the name of the file system or the raw device file for the disk slice where the file system is located.

Table 12-10 describes the options and arguments for the `ufsdump` command.

Table 12-10 Options for the *ufsdump* Command

Option	Description
0 to 9	Backup level. Specify level 0 for a full backup of the whole file system. Levels 1 through 9 are for incremental backups of files that have changed since the last lower-level backup.
`a <archive-file>`	Instructs `ufsdump` to create an archive file. Stores a backup table of the tape contents in a specified file on the disk. The file can be understood only by `ufsrestore`, which uses the table to determine whether a file to be restored is present in a backup file and, if so, on which volume of the medium it resides.
`b <factor>`	Blocking factor. Specifies the number of 512-byte blocks to write to tape per operation.
`c`	Instructs `ufsdump` to back up to cartridge tape. When end-of-media detection applies, this option sets the block size to 126.

continues

Table 12-10 Options for the *ufsdump* Command (continued)

Option	Description
d <bpi>	Tape density. Use this option only when `ufsdump` cannot detect the end of the medium.
D	Diskette. Backs up to floppy disk.
f <dump-file>	Dump file. Specifies the destination of the backup. The `dump-file` argument can be one of the following: A local tape drive or disk drive A remote tape drive or disk drive Standard output Use this argument when the destination is not the default local tape drive /dev/rmt/0. If you use the `f` option, you must specify a value for `dump-file`.
l	Autoload. Use this option if you have an autoloading (stackloader) tape drive. When the end of a tape is reached, this option takes the drive offline and waits up to 2 minutes for the tape drive to be ready again. If the drive is ready within 2 minutes, it continues. If the drive is not ready after 2 minutes, autoload prompts the operator to load another tape.
n	Notify. When intervention is needed, this option sends a message to all terminals of all users in the `sys` group.
o	Offline. When `ufsdump` is finished with a tape or disk, it takes the drive offline, rewinds it (if it's a tape), and removes the medium if possible (for example, it ejects a disk or removes an 8mm autoloaded tape).
s <size>	Size. Specifies the length of tape in feet or the size of disk in a number of 1024-byte blocks. You need to use this option only when `ufsdump` cannot detect the end of the medium.
S	Estimates the size of the backup. Determines the amount of space needed to perform the backup (without actually doing it) and outputs a single number indicating the estimated size of the backup in bytes.
t <tracks>	Tracks. Specifies the number of tracks for 1/4-inch cartridge tape. You need to use this option only when `ufsdump` cannot detect the end of the medium.
u	Updates the dump record. For a completed backup of a file system, adds an entry to the file /etc/dumpdates. The entry indicates the device name for the file system's disk slice, the backup level (0 to 9), and the date. No record is written when you do not use the `u` option or when you back up individual files or directories. If a record already exists for a backup at the same level, it is replaced.
v	Verify. After each tape or disk is written, verifies the contents of the medium against the source file system. If any discrepancies occur, prompts the operator to mount a new medium and then repeats the process. Use this option on an unmounted file system only, because any activity in the file system causes it to report discrepancies.

Table 12-10 Options for the *ufsdump* Command (continued)

Option	Description
w	Warning. Lists the file systems appearing in /etc/dumpdates that have not been backed up within a day. When you use this option, all other options are ignored.
W	Warning with highlight. Shows all file systems that appear in /etc/dumpdates and highlights file systems that have not been backed up within a day. When you use this option, all other options are ignored.

The dump command uses these options by default:

```
ufsdump 9uf /dev/rmt/0 files-to-back-up
```

ufsdump Examples

The following examples illustrate the use of the ufsdump command. The following is an example of a full backup of the /users file system:

```
ufsdump 0ucf /dev/rmt/0 /users
  DUMP: Writing 63 Kilobyte records
  DUMP: Date of this level 0 dump: Sat Dec 12 13:13:22 1998
  DUMP: Date of last level 0 dump: the epoch
  DUMP: Dumping /dev/rdsk/c0t1d0s0 (pyramid1:/) to /dev/rmt/0.
  DUMP: Mapping (Pass I) [regular files]
  DUMP: Mapping (Pass II) [directories]
  DUMP: Estimated 10168 blocks (4.96MB).
  DUMP: Dumping (Pass III) [directories]
  DUMP: Dumping (Pass IV) [regular files]
  DUMP: Tape rewinding
  DUMP: 10078 blocks (4.92MB) on 1 volume at 107 KB/sec
  DUMP: DUMP IS DONE
```

In the following example, the local /export/home file system on a Solaris 7 system is backed up to a tape device on a remote Solaris 7 system called sparc1:

```
ufsdump 0ucf sparc1:/dev/rmt/0 /export/home
DUMP: Date of this level 0 dump: Sat Dec 12 11:50:1 3 1998
DUMP: Date of last level 0 dump: the epoch
DUMP: Dumping /dev/rdsk/c0t3d0s7 (/export/home) to /dev/rmt/0  on host sparc1
DUMP: mapping (Pass I) [regular files]
DUMP: mapping (Pass II) [directories]
DUMP: estimated 19574 blocks (9.56MB)
DUMP: Writing 63 Kilobyte records
DUMP: dumping (Pass III) [directories]
DUMP: dumping (Pass IV) [regular files]
DUMP: level 0 dump on Tue Oct 25 10:30:53 1994
DUMP: Tape rewinding
DUMP: 19574 blocks (9.56MB) on 1 volume
DUMP: DUMP IS DONE
```

ufsrestore

The `ufsrestore` command copies files from backups created using the `ufsdump` command. You can use `ufsrestore` to reload an entire file system from a level 0 dump and incremental dumps that follow it or to restore one or more single files from any dump tape. If `ufsrestore` is run by root, files are restored with their original owner, last modification time, and mode (permissions).

The syntax for the `ufsrestore` command is

```
ufsrestore  <options>  <arguments> < filename(s)>
```

The options for the `ufsrestore` command are described in Table 12-11.

Table 12-11 ***ufsrestore* Options**

Option	Description
`<options>`	You must choose one and only one of these options: `i`, `r`, `R`, `t`, or `x`.
`<arguments>`	Follows the `options` string with the arguments that match the options.
`<filename(s)>`	Specifies files to be restored as arguments to the `x` or `t` options and must always come last.

Table 12-12 describes some of the more common options and arguments for the `ufsrestore` command.

Table 12-12 **Command Options for *ufsrestore***

Option	Description
`i`	Interactive. Runs `ufsrestore` in interactive mode. In this mode, you can use a limited set of shell commands to browse the contents of the medium and select individual files or directories to restore. See Table 12-13 for a list of available commands.
`r`	Recursive. Restores the entire contents of the medium into the current working directory, which should be the top level of the file system. Information used to restore incremental dumps on top of the full dump is also included. To completely restore a file system, use this option to restore the full (level 0) dump and then each incremental dump. This is intended for a new file system that was just created with the `newfs` command.
`x <filename(s)>`	Extract. Selectively restores the files you specify using the `filename(s)` argument. `filename(s)` can be a list of files and directories. All files under a specified directory are restored unless you also use the `h` option. If you omit `filename(s)` or enter `.` for the root directory, all files on all volumes of the medium (or from standard input) are restored. Existing files are overwritten, and warnings are displayed.

Table 12-12 Command Options for *ufsrestore* (continued)

Option	Description
t <filename(s)>	Table of contents. Checks the files specified in the <filename(s)> argument against the medium. For each file, the full filename and the inode number (if the file is found) are listed. If the filename is not found, ufsrestore indicates that the file is not on the "volume," meaning any volume in a multivolume dump. If you do not enter the <filename(s)> argument, all files on all volumes of the medium are listed without distinguishing on which volume the files are located. When you use the h option, only the directory files specified in <filename(s)>—not their contents—are checked and listed. The table of contents is read from the first volume of the medium or (if you use the a option) from the specified archive file. This option is mutually exclusive with the x and r options.
b <factor>	Blocking factor. Specifies the number of 512-byte blocks to read from tape per operation. By default, ufsrestore tries to figure out the block size used in writing the tape.
m	Restores specified files into the current directory on the disk, regardless of where they are located in the backup hierarchy, and renames them with their inode number. For example, if the current working directory is /files, a file in the backup named ./database/test with inode number 156 is restored as /files/156. This option is useful when you are extracting only a few files.
s<n>	Skips to the *n*th backup file on the medium. This option is useful when you put more than one backup on a single tape.
v	Verbose. Displays the name and inode number of each file as it is restored.

For a full listing, refer to the Solaris online manual pages.

Table 12-13 lists the commands that can be used with ufsrestore when using interactive mode (ufsrestore -i).

Table 12-13 Commands for an Interactive Restoration

Command	Description
ls <directory-name>	Lists the contents of either the current directory or the specified directory. Directories are suffixed with a /. Entries in the current list to be restored (extracted) are marked by an * prefix. If the verbose option is in effect, inode numbers are also listed.
cd <directory-name>	Changes to the specified directory in the backup hierarchy.
add <filename>	Adds the current directory or the specified file or directory to the list of files to extract (restore). If you do not use the h option, all files in a specified directory and its subdirectories are added to the list. Note that it's possible that not all the files you want to restore to a directory will be on a single backup tape or disk. You might need to restore from multiple backups at different levels to get all the files.

continues

Table 12-13 Commands for an Interactive Restoration (continues)

Command	Description
`delete <filename>`	Deletes the current directory or the specified file or directory from the list of files to extract (restore). If you do not use the `h` option, all files in the specified directory and its subdirectories are deleted from the list. Note that the files and directories are deleted only from the extract list you are building. They are not deleted from the medium.
`extract`	Extracts the files in the list and restores them to the current working directory on the disk. Specify 1 when asked for a volume number. If you are doing a multitape or multidisk restoration and you are restoring a small number of files, start with the last tape or disk.
`help`	Displays a list of the commands you can use in interactive mode.
`pwd`	Displays the pathname of the current working directory in the backup hierarchy.
`q`	Quits interactive mode without restoring any additional files.
`verbose`	Turns the `verbose` option on or off. Verbose mode can also be entered as `v` on the command line outside interactive mode. When verbose is on, the interactive `ls` command lists inode numbers, and the `ufsrestore` command displays information on each file as it is extracted.

ufsrestore Examples

The following examples illustrate how to restore data from a tape by using `ufsrestore`.

Use the `ufsrestore` command to display the contents of the tape:

```
ufsrestore tf /dev/rmt/0
    2       .
 4249       ./users
12400       ./users/bill
12401       ./users/bill/.login
12402       ./users/bill/.cshrc
12458       ./users/bill/admin
12459       ./users/bill/junk
```

Use this command to restore a file from a backup that was created using `ufsdump`:

```
ufsrestore f /dev/rmt/0 filename
```

You can restore entire directories from a remote drive located on the system called sparc1 by adding `remote-host:` to the front of the tape device name, as illustrated in the next example:

```
ufsrestore rf sparc1:/dev/rmt/0 filename
```

Occasionally a file system becomes so damaged that you must completely restore it from a backup. If you have faithfully backed up file systems, you can restore them to the state of the last backup. The first step in recovering a file system is to delete everything in the damaged file system and re-create the file system using the `newfs` command. To recover a damaged file system, follow the following steps.

NOTE. *To restore the root or /usr file systems, see the next section.*

1. Unmount the file system as follows:

```
umount  /filesystem
```

   where `filesystem` is the name of the corrupted file system.

2. After unmounting the file system, issue the `newfs` command to create a new file system as follows:

```
newfs /dev/rdsk/<disk-partition-name>
```

   where `<disk-partition-name>` is the name of the raw disk partition containing the corrupted file system.

3. Mount the file system to be restored, and change to that directory:

```
mount /dev/dsk/c?t?d?s? <directory>
cd /<directory>
```

4. Load the tape, and issue the following command:

```
ufsrestore rf /dev/rmt/0
```

   The entire contents of the tape will be restored to the file system. All permissions, ownerships, and dates will remain as they were when the last incremental tape was created.

The next two steps are optional.

5. Remove the restoresymtable file created by the `ufsrestore` command. This is a temporary file and is not required after the file system has been successfully restored.

6. It's also a good idea to unmount the file system and run `fsck` to check the repaired file system.

Recovering the Root or /usr File System

Sometimes a careless administrator with root access accidentally deletes part or all of the root (/) or /usr file system. Other times the file system can become unusable because of a faulty disk drive or a corrupted file system. Follow this procedure if you ever need to recover the root (/) or /usr file system:

1. Replace and partition the disk if it has failed.
2. Re-create the file system by issuing the `newfs` command as follows:

   ```
   newfs /dev/rdsk/<disk-partition-name>
   ```

   where `<disk-partition-name>` is the name of the raw disk partition containing the corrupted file system.
3. Mount the new file system on a temporary mount point:

   ```
   mount /dev/dsk/<disk-partition-name> /mnt
   ```

4. Change to the /mnt directory:

   ```
   cd /mnt
   ```

5. Write-protect the tapes so that you don't accidentally overwrite them.
6. Load the tape and issue the following command:

   ```
   ufsrestore rf /dev/rmt/0
   ```

   The entire contents of the tape will be restored to the file system. All permissions, ownerships, and dates will remain as they were when the last incremental tape was created.
7. Verify that the file system is restored:

   ```
   ls
   ```

8. Remove the restoresymtable file that is created and used by `ufsrestore` to checkpoint the restoration:

   ```
   rm restoresymtable
   ```

9. Change to the root (/) directory:

   ```
   cd /
   ```

10. Unmount the newly created file system:

    ```
    umount /mnt
    ```

11. Check the new file system with `fsck`:

    ```
    fsck /dev/rdsk/< disk-partition-name>
    ```

    The restored file system is checked for consistency.

12. If you are recovering the root (/) file system, create the boot blocks on the root partition by using the `installboot` command:

    ```
    installboot  /usr/platform/`uname-i`/lib/fs/ufs/bootblk /dev/rdsk/
    ➥< disk-partition-name>
    ```

    The `installboot` command installs the boot blocks onto the boot disk. Without the boot blocks, the disk cannot boot. (`installboot` is covered again in Section II of this book.)

13. Insert a new tape into the tape drive and back up the new file system:

    ```
    ufsdump 0uf /dev/rmt/n /dev/rdsk/device-name
    ```

    A level 0 backup is performed. Always do an immediate backup of a newly created file system, because `ufsrestore` repositions the files and changes the inode allocation.

14. Reboot the system:

    ```
    init 6
    ```

    The system is rebooted.

The following example is an actual session that restores the root (/) file system from tape device /dev/rmt/0 to SCSI disk target 3 slice 0 on controller 0:

```
# mount /dev/dsk/c0t3d0s0 /mnt
# cd /mnt
# tapes
# ufsrestore rf /dev/rmt/0
```

NOTE. *The* `tapes` *command creates the /dev entries for the tape drive. It creates links in /dev/rmt to the actual tape device special files. The* `tapes` *command is covered in Chapter 16, "Device Configuration and Naming."*

Files get restored from tape:

```
# rm restoresymtable
# cd /
# umount /mnt
# fsck /dev/rdsk/c0t3d0s0
```

The system displays the fsck passes as the file system is checked:

```
# installboot /usr/platform/sun4m/lib/fs/ufs/bootblk/dev/rdsk/c0t3d0s0
# ufsdump 0uf /dev/rmt/0 /dev/rdsk/c0t3d0s0
# init 6
```

The system is rebooted.

Additional Notes About Restoring Files

When you restore files in a directory other than the root directory of the file system, ufsrestore re-creates the file hierarchy in the current directory. For example, if you restore files to /home that were backed up from /users/bcalkins/files, the files are restored in the directory /home/users/bcalkins/files.

When restoring individual files and directories, it's a good idea to restore them to a temporary directory such as /var/tmp. After you verify the files, you can move them to their proper locations. You can restore individual files and directories to their original locations; however, if you do so, be sure you are not overwriting newer files with older versions from the backup tape.

Don't forget to make regular backups of your operating system. With all the customization you've done, such as adding user accounts, setting up printers, and installing application software, losing this information would be disastrous. Whenever you make modifications that affect the root (/), /usr, /opt, or other operating system directories, bring the system down into single-user mode and do a level 0 dump.

Summary

This chapter described the standard copy and backup utilities available in Solaris. Although these utilities do a good job of backing up your data, if your company has several servers and large storage pools, you might want to investigate some of the more robust backup packages available from third parties. Most of these packages provide a comprehensive suite of utilities for conducting and managing backups in a complex computing environment. In most cases, they allow single-point backups—not only for Solaris, but for other operating systems as well.

This concludes Section I and the material that is covered on the Part I exam. The next section covers topics you'll need to know for the second exam. In many cases, Section II provides more details on topics that were introduced in this section but weren't objectives for the first exam.

SECTION II

Part II

This section covers the following objectives for the Sun Certified System Administrator for Solaris 7 exam, Part II:

- The Solaris network environment
- Installing a server
- Solaris syslog and auditing utilities
- Device administration
- The Service Access Facility (SAF)
- Adding terminals and modems
- Disk management and file system types
- Networks
- Configuring the NFS environment
- CacheFS file systems
- WebNFS
- Using Automount
- Naming Services
- NIS
- Solstice AdminSuite
- Adding network clients
- JumpStart automatic installation
- Administration and configuration of CDE

CHAPTER

13

Device Administration

The following are the test objectives for this chapter:

- Understanding Solaris port monitors, the Service Access Facility (SAF), and related configuration files
- Understanding how to use Admintool and the SAF commands to manage serial ports
- Adding terminals and modems to a system and using SAF and Admintool

This chapter describes the administration of terminals and modems within Solaris. In that context, we'll explore terminals, modems, port monitors, and services.

Terminals and modems provide access to local and remote system resources; therefore, setting up terminals and modem access is an important responsibility for a system administrator. Most experienced administrators agree that managing the terminals and modems in UNIX is one of their more complex tasks. Solaris provides support for nearly all models of alphanumeric terminals and modems, but with this flexibility comes complexity. Because of this complexity, Sun has added these tasks to Admintool to make them easier to perform. As with most Admintool functions, however, they do not provide the complete functionality you get at the command line. Occasionally, you'll encounter tasks that can be performed only from the command line. For this reason, this chapter covers not only the Admintool, but also the specific SAF commands as well. I'll begin by describing hardware and software terminology before describing how to manage them.

Hardware Terminology

This section briefly describes the hardware components involved—ports, terminals, modems, and cabling.

Ports

A *port* is a channel through which a device communicates with the operating system. A port is a "receptacle" into which a terminal or modem cable may be plugged. The port is controlled by software in the operating system called a *device driver*. Common types of ports include serial, parallel, small computer systems interface (SCSI), and Ethernet. The serial port software must be set up to provide a particular "service" for the device attached to the port. For example, you can set up a serial port to provide bidirectional service for a modem.

A serial port, using a standard communications protocol, transmits a byte of information bit by bit over a single line. Devices that have been designed according to RS-232-C or RS-423 standards—such as modems, alphanumeric terminals, plotters, and some printers—can be plugged into serial ports. Most systems have one or two serial ports. When many serial port devices must be connected to a single computer, you sometimes need to add an adapter board to the system. The adapter board, with its driver software, provides additional serial ports for connecting more devices than could otherwise be accommodated.

Terminals

Solaris supports two types of displays: the alphanumeric display and the bitmapped graphics display. The *alphanumeric display* and keyboard, referred to as a tty device, connects to a serial port and only displays text. Because the alphanumeric display is connected via a serial port, a system can support as many character display terminals as it has serial ports. If you run out of ports, you can add more. The disadvantage of the alphanumeric display is that it doesn't display windows or graphics and does not support a mouse.

The *bitmapped graphics display* is connected to the system via a graphics adapter of some kind. You simply need to plug the monitor in to the system to make it operational. On a bitmapped graphics display, you don't have to perform any special steps to administer it. The drawback, however, is that most computers support only one graphics display.

Modems

Modems are also connected to a system through a serial port and are used for remote access over telephone lines. Modems can be set up in three basic configurations:

- Dial-out
- Dial-in
- Bidirectional

A modem connected to the local computer might be set up to provide dial-out service, meaning that you can access other computers, but nobody outside can gain access to this computer. Dial-in service is just the opposite. It allows users to access a system from remote sites, but it does not permit calls to the outside world. Bidirectional access provides both dial-in and dial-out capabilities.

Cabling

Finally, a few words about *cabling*. The RS-232 standard defines two types of equipment: Data Terminal Equipment (DTE) and Data Communications Equipment (DCE). Most computers are DTE; modems are always DCE. DTE uses pin 2 to transmit data and pin 3 to receive data; DCE does the reverse. To connect a computer to a modem or printer (DTE to DCE), you make the cable connection straight through. To make a connection between two computers (DTE to DTE) or between a computer and a terminal, you need a cable with pins 2 and 3 crossed. This is often called a null-modem or modem-eliminator cable. To save yourself a great deal of frustration, make sure you've configured your cables properly before you configure the port monitor and services.

Software Terminology

Now that I've described the hardware pieces, I will briefly describe the components of the operating system that add functionality to the ports, terminals, and modems.

Service Access Controller (SAC)

The *Service Access Controller (SAC)* oversees the entire Service Access Facility (SAF). The SAC daemon is started at bootup in /etc/inittab by an entry like this one:

```
sc:234:respawn:/usr/lib/saf/sac -t 300
```

The `-t` option specifies how often the SAC daemon polls the port monitors.

The SAC daemon starts and controls various port monitors. SAC starts all the port monitors listed in its configuration file, /etc/saf/_sactab.

Port Monitors

The mechanism for gaining access to a service is through a *port monitor*. A port monitor is a program that continuously monitors a port for requests to log in or requests to access printers or files.

When a port monitor detects a request, it sets whatever parameters are required to establish communication between the operating system and the device requesting the service. Then the port monitor transfers control to other processes that provide the services needed.

A port can be an address on a network, a hard-wired terminal line, or an incoming phone line. The definition of what constitutes a port is strictly a function of the port monitor itself. Port monitors have two main functions: managing ports and monitoring ports for indications of activity.

The first function of a port monitor is to manage a port. The person who defines the port monitor defines how a port is managed. A port monitor is not restricted to handling a single port; it can handle multiple ports simultaneously. An example of port management is setting the line speed on incoming phone connections, reinitializing the port when the service terminates, and outputting a login prompt.

The second function of a port monitor is to watch the port for indications of activity. Two types of activity might be detected. The first tells the port monitor to take a specific port monitor action. For example, pressing the Break key indicates that the line speed should be cycled. Not all port monitors need to recognize and respond to the same indications; the person who defines the port monitor defines the indication used to attract the attention of the port monitor. The second activity a port monitor detects is an incoming service request. When a service request is received, a port monitor must be able to determine which service is being requested from the port. Note that the same service might be available on more than one port.

Solaris has two types of port monitors: ttymon and listen. ttymon connects incoming requests on serial lines to the login service and login program and would be the port monitor to handle modems and terminals. listen connects incoming print jobs to the lp facility and listens for network service requests.

NOTE. *You might be familiar with an older port monitor called getty. In Solaris, getty has been replaced by ttymon. These two programs serve the same function, but a single ttymon can replace multiple occurrences of getty.*

ttymon

Whenever you attempt to log in via a directly connected modem or alphanumeric terminal, the TTY Port Monitor (ttymon) goes to work. ttymon provides the Solaris user with the same services that getty did under previous versions of SunOS 4.1 software. When someone attempts to log in via an alphanumeric terminal or a modem, the serial port driver passes the operation to the operating system. The ttymon port monitor acknowledges the serial port activity and attempts to establish a communications link. ttymon determines what data transfer rate, line discipline, and handshaking protocol are required to communicate with the device connected to the serial port. Having established the proper handshaking with the modem or terminal, ttymon passes these parameters to the login program.

When SAC invokes an instance of ttymon, ttymon starts to monitor its ports. Each instance of ttymon can monitor multiple ports, which are specified in the port monitor's administrative file. The values used to initialize the port are taken from the appropriate entry in the /etc/ttydefs file. This information in /etc/ttydefs is used to initialize the baud rate and terminal settings for each port. The ttymon port monitor then writes the prompt and waits for user input. When valid input is received from the user, ttymon interprets the configuration entry in /etc/ttydefs for the port and creates an entry in /etc/utmp. The /etc/utmp file holds accounting information about the user for commands such as `who`. ttymon then establishes the service environment and invokes the service associated with the port.

After the service terminates, ttymon cleans up the /etc/utmp entry and returns the port to its initial state.

listen

The network listener service, listen, is a port monitor that runs under SAC. It monitors the network for service requests, accepts requests when they arrive, and invokes servers in response to those service requests.

Administering Terminals, Modems, and Ports

Three tools are available for administering terminals and modems: Admintool, the Service Access Facility (SAF) commands, and Solstice AdminSuite's Serial Port Manager. The next section describes how to add a modem to a system using Admintool—the preferred method. Second is a description of how to add a modem from the command line. Please note that Solstice AdminSuite's Serial Port Manager is not covered in this book. AdminSuite is much like Admintool but is used to configure systems in a networked name-service environment.

Adding a Modem Using Admintool

Setting up a serial port for a modem is much easier when using Admintool. This is the recommended method, because it eliminates the possibility of a typographical error. Here are the steps used to set up the serial port using Admintool:

1. Start Admintool if it's not already running.
2. Select Browse, Serial Ports, as shown in Figure 13-1.

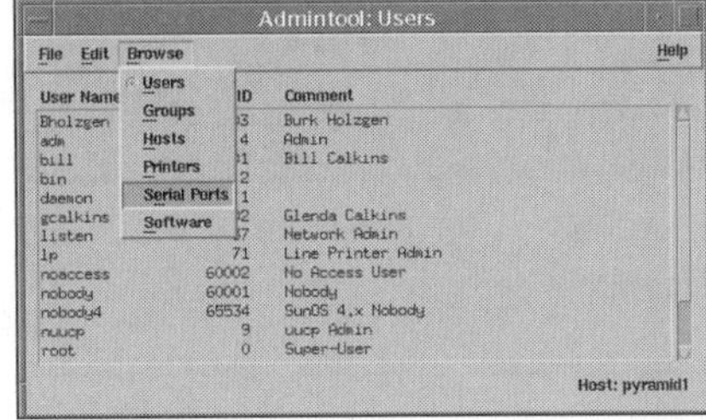

Figure 13-1
The Admintool Browse Menu.

3. In the Serial Ports window, shown in Figure 13-2, select the port that will be used with a modem.

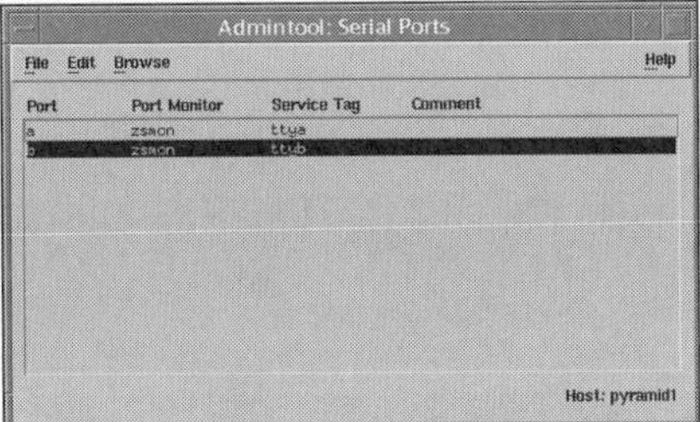

Figure 13-2
The Serial Ports window.

4. Choose Edit, Modify, as shown in Figure 13-3. The Modify Serial Port window appears.

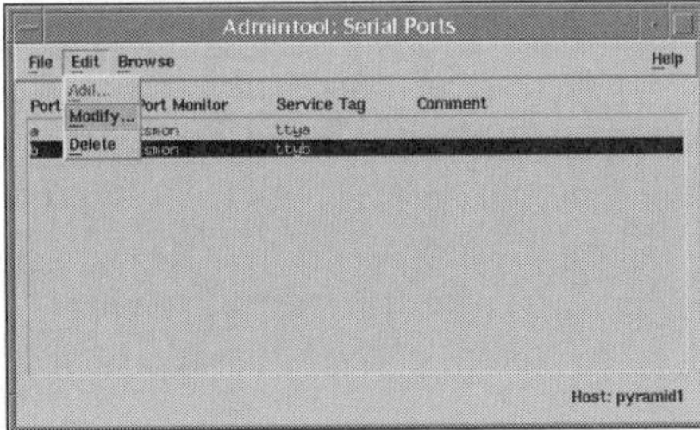

Figure 13-3
The Serial Ports Edit menu.

The Modify Serial Port window appears in Basic Detail mode. To enter additional details, select More or Expert Detail mode.

5. From the drop-down Template list, choose the modem configuration template that meets—or most closely matches—your modem service (see Figure 13-4).

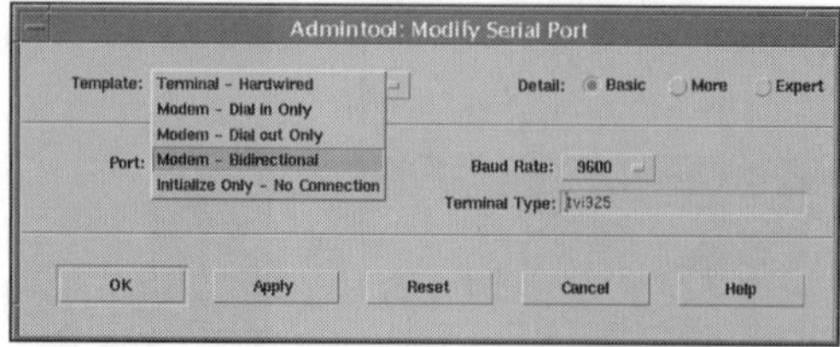

Figure 13-4
The Modify Serial Port Template list.

A description of each modem selection can be found in Table 13-1.

Table 13-1 The Modem Template

Modem Configuration	Description
Dial in Only	Users can dial in to the modem but cannot dial out.
Dial out Only	Users can dial out from the modem but cannot dial in.
Bidirectional	Users can dial either in or out from the modem.

6. Select the correct baud rate from the Baud Rate drop-down list, as shown in Figure 13-5.

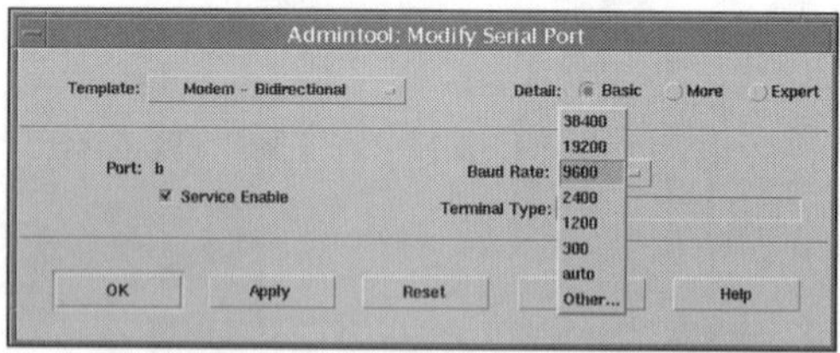

Figure 13-5
The Baud Rate drop-down list.

Figure 13-6 shows a completed Modify Serial Port window. The Expert Detail mode was selected to show all the options that can be configured.

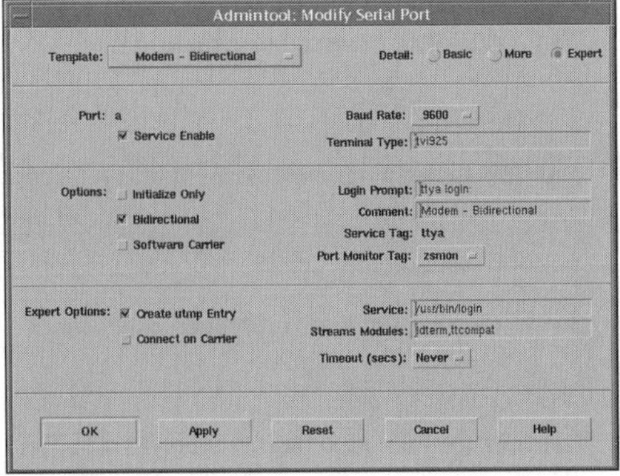

Figure 13-6
The Completed Modify Serial Port window.

Table 13-2 describes each configurable option shown in Figure 13-6.

Table 13-2 Modify Serial Port Window Items

Item	Description
Port	Lists the port or ports you selected from the Serial Ports main window.
Service	Specifies that the service for the port is turned on (enabled).
Baud Rate	Specifies the line speed used to communicate with the terminal. The line speed represents an entry in the /etc/ttydefs file.
Terminal Type	Shows the abbreviation for the type of terminal, such as ansi or vt100. Similar abbreviations are found in /etc/termcap. This value is set in the `$TERM` environment variable.
Option: Initialize Only	Specifies that the port software is initialized but not configured.
Option: Bidirectional	Specifies that the port line is used in both directions.
Option: Software Carrier	Specifies that the software carrier detection feature is used. If this option is not checked, the hardware carrier detection signal is used.
Login Prompt	Shows the prompt displayed to the user after a connection is made.
Comment	Shows the comment field for the service.
Service Tag	Lists the service tag associated with this port—typically an entry in the /dev/term directory.
Port Monitor Tag	Specifies the name of the port monitor to be used for this port. The default monitor is typically correct.

continues

Table 13-2 Modify Serial Port Window Items (continued)

Item	Description
Create utmp Entry	Specifies that a utmp entry is created in the accounting files upon login.
Connect on Carrier	Specifies that a port's associated service is invoked immediately when a connect indication is received.
Service	Shows the program that is run upon connection.
Streams Modules	Shows the streams modules that are pushed before the service is invoked.
Timeout (secs)	Specifies the number of seconds before a port is closed if the open process on the port succeeds and no input data is received.

7. Click OK to configure the port.
8. Use the `pmadm` command to verify that the modem service has been configured for use:

```
pmadm -l -s ttya
```

The serial port is now configured and ready for use.

Adding a Terminal Using Admintool

This section describes how to add a terminal by using the Solaris Admintool. Using the Admintool is the easiest way to add a terminal to your system. The steps are as follows:

1. Follow steps 1 through 4 in the preceding section. When the Modify Serial Port window appears, as shown in Figure 13-7, select Terminal - Hardwired from the Template menu.

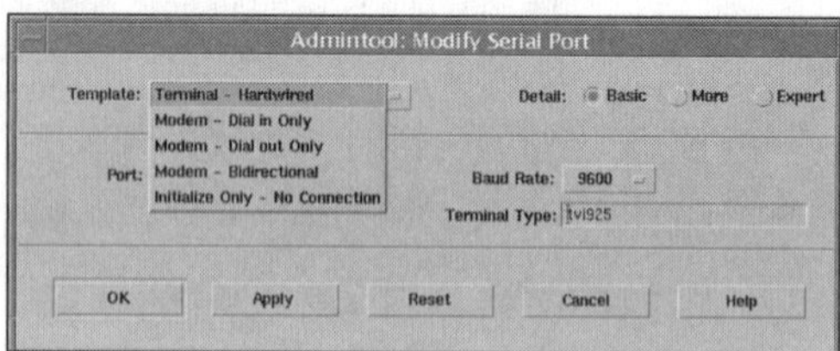

Figure 13-7
The Modify Serial Port window.

2. Change the values of template entries if desired. The template entries are described in Table 13-1.
3. Click OK to configure the port, and type `pmadm -l -s ttya` to verify that the service has been added.

Using the Service Access Facility (SAF)

The SAF is the tool used to administer terminals, modems, and other network devices. The SAF is an open-systems solution that controls access to system and network resources through tty devices and local-area networks (LANs). SAF is not a program; it is a hierarchy of background processes and administrative commands, including `sacadm`, `pmadm`, `ttyadm`, `sttydefs`, and `nlsadmin`. Table 13-3 describes these commands.

Table 13-3 SAF Commands

Command	Description
`sacadm`	Used to add, delete, enable, disable, start, and stop port monitors.
`pmadm`	Configures port monitor services and the associated processes for individual ports.
`ttyadm`	Formats input to `pmadm` for serial ports.
`sttydefs`	Creates and modifies entries in the /etc/ttydefs file to describe terminal line characteristics.
`nlsadmin`	Formats input to `pmadm` for remote printing.

In particular, SAF lets you do the following:

- Set up ttymon and listen port monitors (using the `sacadm` command)
- Set up ttymon port monitor services (using the `pmadm` and `ttyadm` commands)
- Set up listen port monitor services (using the `pmadm` and `nlsadmin` commands)
- Troubleshoot tty devices
- Troubleshoot incoming network requests for printing service
- Troubleshoot the SAC (using the `sacadm` command)

The configuration files associated with SAF are described in Table 13-4.

Table 13-4 Files Associated with SAF

File	Description
/etc/saf/_sysconfig	The per-system configuration script.
/etc/saf/_sactab	SAC's administrative file. Contains configuration data for the port monitors that the SAC controls.
/etc/saf/pmtag	The home directory for port monitor pmtag.
/etc/saf/pmtag/_config	The per-port monitor configuration script for port monitor pmtag (if it exists).
/etc/saf/pmtag/_pmtab	Port monitor pmtag's administrative file. Contains port monitor-specific configuration data for the services pmtag provides.
/etc/saf/pmtag/svctag	The per-service configuration script for service svctag.
/var/saf/log	SAC's log file.
/var/saf/pmtag	The directory for files created by pmtag, such as log files.

The SAF commands `sacadm`, `pmadm`, `ttyadm`, and `nlsadmin` are described in the next sections.

sacadm

Use the `sacadm` command to add, list, remove, kill, start, enable, or disable a ttymon or listen port monitor. You must be logged in as superuser to use this command. For example, the command syntax used to add a ttymon port monitor is

```
sacadm -a -p mbmon -t ttymon -c /usr/lib/saf/ttymon -v `ttyadm  -V` -y "TTY Ports a & b"
```

Notice the use of the `ttyadm` command.

To view the newly added port monitor, type

```
sacadm -l -p mbmon
```

The system responds with this:

```
PMTAG    PMTYPE    FLGS    RCNT    STATUS    COMMAND
mbmon    ttymon    -       0       STARTING  /usr/lib/saf/ttymon #TTY Ports a & b
```

The `sacadm` command options used for adding and viewing port monitors are listed in Table 13-5.

Table 13-5 *sacadm* Command Options

Command Option	Description
`-a`	Adds a port monitor.
`-c`	Defines the command string used to start the port monitor.
`-d`	Disables the port monitor.
`-e`	Enables the port monitor.
`-k`	Kills a port monitor.
`-l`	Lists the port monitor status.
`-p`	Specifies the pmtag `mbmon` as the port monitor tag.
`-r`	Removes a port monitor.
`-s`	Starts a port monitor.
`-t`	Specifies the port monitor type as ttymon.
`-v`	Specifies the version number of the port monitor.
`-y`	Defines a comment to describe this instance of the port monitor.

For more options to the `sacadm` command, view the online manual pages.

To kill a ttymon port monitor, type

```
sacadm -k -p mbmon
```

To restart a port monitor that has been killed, type

```
sacadm -s -p mbmon
```

To remove a port monitor, type

```
sacadm -r -p mbmon
```

pmadm

The Port Monitor Service Administrator (`pmadm`) command lets you administer port monitors' services. Use `pmadm` to add services, list the services of one or more ports associated with a port monitor, and enable or disable a service. An example would be a terminal service. You can also install or replace per-service configuration scripts or print information about a service.

Each instance of a service must be uniquely identified by a port monitor and a port. When you use the pmadm command to administer a service, you specify a particular port monitor via the pmtag argument and a particular port via the svctag argument.

pmtag and svctag are described in the next section. For each port monitor type, the SAF requires a specialized command to format port monitor-specific configuration data. This data is used by the pmadm command.

To add a standard terminal service to the mbmon port monitor, type

```
pmadm -a -p mbmon -s a -i root -v `ttyadm -V` -m "`ttyadm -i 'Terminal disabled' -l \
➥ contty -m ldterm,ttcompat -S y -d /dev/term/a -s /usr/bin/login`"
```

Options used in the pmadm command are described in Table 13-6. Note that the preceding pmadm command contains an embedded ttyadm command.

Table 13-6 *pmadm* Command Options

Command Option	Description
-a	Adds a port monitor.
-d	Disables the port monitor service.
-e	Enables the port monitor service.
-l	Lists the port monitor service information.
-p	Specifies the pmtag mbmon as the port monitor tag.
-s	Specifies the svctag a as the port monitor service tag.
-i	Specifies the identity to be assigned to svctag when it runs.
-v	Specifies the version number of the port monitor.
-m	Specifies the ttymon-specific configuration data formatted by ttyadm.

The next example uses the pmadm command to list the status of a TTY port, or all the ports associated with a port monitor. Type

```
pmadm -l -p mbmon
```

The system outputs the following information:

```
PMTAG     PMTYPE    SVCTAG    FLAGS    ID      <PMSPECIFIC>
mbmon     ttymon    a         -        root     /dev/term/a - - /usr/bin/login \
➥ - contty ldterm,ttcompat login: Terminal disabled - y  #Comment
```

The information reported is described in Table 13-7.

Table 13-7 Port Monitor Information

Service	Description
mbmon	The port monitor name, mbmon.
ttymon	The port monitor type, ttymon.
a	The service tag value.
-	Flags following are set using the pmadm -f command.
root	The ID assigned to the service when it's started.
<PMSPECIFIC> ***Information***	
/dev/term/a	The TTY port pathname.
/usr/bin/login	The full pathname of the service to be invoked when a connection is received.
contty	The TTY label in the /etc/ttydefs file.
ldterm,ttcompat	The streams modules to be pushed.
login: Terminal disabled	An inactive message to be displayed when the port is disabled.
y	The software carrier value. n indicates software carrier off, and y indicates software carrier on. Software carrier is turned on in the example.
#	Any comment. There is no comment in this example.

To disable a port monitor service, type

```
pmadm -d -p mbmon -s a
```

To enable a disabled port monitor service, type

```
pmadm -e -p mbmon -s a
```

Port Monitor Tag (pmtag)

The Port Monitor Tag (pmtag) is the name assigned to an instance of a port monitor. The pmtag is used to define groups of one or more actual port monitor processes. You can name port monitors anything you want, provided that the name is unique and is no longer than 14 characters. By default, Solaris assigns names such as zsmon for serial ports. Unless you have a good reason to do otherwise, the system-defined names are the best to use. It makes it much easier for other system administrators who might need to work on your system.

Service Tag (svctag)

Each port assigned to a port monitor has its own service tag. The name used for the service tag is tty followed by the name of the port created in the /dev/term directory. For example, the svctag for /dev/term/a would be ttya.

ttyadm

The `ttyadm` command is an administrative command that formats ttymon information and writes it to standard output. `ttyadm` provides a means of presenting formatted port monitor-specific (ttymon-specific) data to the `sacadm` and `pmadm` commands, which are described next in this chapter. `ttyadm` can be used, for example, to inform users that a port is disabled. You would do so by typing this:

```
ttyadm -i
```

The `-i` option specifies the inactive (disabled) response message to be sent to a terminal or modem when a user attempts to log in to a disabled port.

To keep the modem connection when a user logs off from a host, type

```
ttyadm -h
```

The system will not hang up on a modem before setting or resetting to the default or specified value. If `ttyadm -h` is not used, the host will hang up the modem when the user logs out.

Use the `-r` option with `ttyadm` to require the user to type a character before the system displays a prompt:

```
ttyadm -r
```

The `-r` option specifies that ttymon should require the user to type a character or press Enter a specified number of times before the login prompt appears. This option prevents a terminal server from issuing a welcome message that the Solaris host might misinterpret as a user trying to log in. Without the `-r` option, the host and terminal server might begin looping and printing prompts to each other.

Options to the `ttyadm` command are described in Table 13-8.

Table 13-8 *ttyadm* Command Options

Command Option	Description
-b	The bidirectional port flag. When this flag is set, the line can be used in both directions.
-d	Specifies the full pathname to the device to use for the TTY port.

Table 13-8 *ttyadm* Command Options (continued)

Command Option	Description
`-h`	Sets the hangup flag for the port.
`-i`	Specifies the inactive (disabled) response message.
`-l`	Specifies which TTY label in /etc/ttydefs to use.
`-m`	Specifies the streams modules to push before invoking this service.
`-p`	Specifies the prompt message, such as `login:`.
`-r count`	When the `-r` option is invoked, `ttymon` waits until it receives data from the port before it displays a prompt.
`-s`	Specifies the full pathname of the service to invoke when a connection request is received. If arguments are required, enclose the command and its arguments in quotation marks (").
`-T`	Sets the terminal type.

nlsadmin

Just as `ttyadm` works for ttymon, so the `nlsadmin` command works for listen. The listen port monitor's administrative file is updated by `sacadm` and `pmadm`, as well as by the `nlsadmin` command. The `nlsadmin` command formats listen-specific information and writes it to the standard output, providing a means of presenting formatted listen-specific data to the `sacadm` and `pmadm` commands. `nlsadmin` does not administer listen directly; rather, it complements the generic administrative commands `sacadm` and `pmadm`.

Each network can have at least one instance of the network listener process associated with it, but each network is configured separately. The `nlsadmin` command controls the operational states of listen port monitors. The `nlsadmin` command can establish a listen port monitor for a given network, configure the specific attributes of that port monitor, and start and kill the monitor. The `nlsadmin` command can also report on the listen port monitors on a machine.

Setting Up Modems and Terminals by Using SAF

Now that you've learned about `sacadm` and `pmadm`, here's how you put them together to add modems and terminals. To set up a bidirectional modem service from the command line, follow these steps:

1. Check to see if a zsmon process is running under SAC. To do so, type the following command:

```
sacadm -l
```

The system responds with this:

```
PMTAG    PMTYPE    FLGS    RCNT    STATUS     COMMAND
tcp      listen    -       0       ENABLED    /usr/lib/saf/listen tcp #
zsmon    ttymon    -       0       ENABLED    /usr/lib/saf/ttymon #
```

2. If you do not see a zsmon entry under PMTAG, execute the following command:

```
sacadm -a -p zsmon -t ttymon -c /usr/lib/saf/ttymon -v `ttyadm -V`
```

Check again to see if the zsmon entry is present. (The status will be STARTING. This is normal.)

3. Check to see if a zsmon port monitor is present. To do so, type the following command:

```
pmadm -p zsmon -l
```

The system responds with this:

```
PMTAG     PMTYPE     SVCTAG     FLGS    ID       <PMSPECIFIC>
zsmon     ttymon     ttyb       u       root     /dev/term/b b - /usr/bin/login \-
➥ 9600m ldterm,ttcompat login:  - - n  #Modem - Bidirectional
```

4. If a port monitor for zsmon is present, remove it by executing the following command:

```
pmadm -r -p zsmon -s <svctag>
```

where the value of `<svctag>` is found by using the output of the preceding command. In the example, this value is ttyb.

5. Now configure your port monitor. To do so, type

```
pmadm -a -p zsmon  -s ttyb -i root -fu -v `ttyadm -V` -m "`ttyadm -Sn  -d\
➥  /dev/term/b -b -m ldterm,ttcompat -l 9600m -s /usr/bin/login`" -y\
➥ "Modem -Bidirectional"
```

ttyb and /dev/term/b specify serial port B; 9600m specifies 9600 baud. Either of these can be modified to reflect a different serial port or baud rate setting.

6. Verify that the port monitor is present by typing

```
pmadm -p zsmon -l
```

The system should respond with output that looks like the following, but the baud rate and service tag might be different:

```
PMTAG      PMTYPE      SVCTAG   FLGS   ID         <PMSPECIFIC>
zsmon      ttymon      ttyb     u       root      /dev/term/b b -
/usr/bin/login    -      9600m      ldterm,ttcompat login:      -      - n   #Modem\
➥ -Bidirectional
```

Serial port B is now configured for a 9600 baud bidirectional modem. The steps are complex, so you need to be careful not to mistype a command string. Because of the complexity of adding a modem from the command line, Sun has added this task to Admintool.

The *tip* Command

Before I get into the steps involved in using a modem, I'll describe the `tip` command, which is used to connect to a remote system through an RS-232 connection. The `tip` command establishes a terminal connection to a remote host. Once the connection is established, a remote session using `tip` behaves like an interactive session on a local terminal. The syntax is as follows:

```
tip <-speed-entry> <hostname>|<phone number>|<device>
```

The /etc/remote file contains entries describing remote systems and line speeds used by `tip`. Entries include which serial port to use, modem settings, control strings, baud rate, and phone number. Here's a sample of an /etc/remote file:

```
#
pc0:\
        :dv=/dev/cua/pc0:br#38400:el=^C^S^Q^U^D:ie=%$:oe=^D:nt:hf:
pc1:\
        :dv=/dev/cua/pc1:br#38400:el=^C^S^Q^U^D:ie=%$:oe=^D:nt:hf:
pc2:\
        :dv=/dev/cua/pc2:br#38400:el=^C^S^Q^U^D:ie=%$:oe=^D:nt:hf:
pc3:\
        :dv=/dev/cua/pc3:br#38400:el=^C^S^Q^U^D:ie=%$:oe=^D:nt:hf:
pc4:\
        :dv=/dev/cua/pc4:br#38400:el=^C^S^Q^U^D:ie=%$:oe=^D:nt:hf:
pc5:\
        :dv=/dev/cua/pc5:br#38400:el=^C^S^Q^U^D:ie=%$:oe=^D:nt:hf:
pc6:\
        :dv=/dev/cua/pc6:br#38400:el=^C^S^Q^U^D:ie=%$:oe=^D:nt:hf:
pc7:\
        :dv=/dev/cua/pc7:br#38400:el=^C^S^Q^U^D:ie=%$:oe=^D:nt:hf:
cuab:dv=/dev/cua/b:br#2400
dialup1|Dial-up system:\
        :pn=2015551212:tc=UNIX-2400:
hardwire:\
        :dv=/dev/term/b:br#9600:el=^C^S^Q^U^D:ie=%$:oe=^D:
```

```
tip300:tc=UNIX-300:
tip1200:tc=UNIX-1200:
tip0|tip2400:tc=UNIX-2400:
tip9600:tc=UNIX-9600:
tip19200:tc=UNIX-19200:
UNIX-300:\
      :el=^D^U^C^S^Q^O@:du:at=hayes:ie=#$%:oe=^D:br#300:tc=dialers:
UNIX-1200:\
      :el=^D^U^C^S^Q^O@:du:at=hayes:ie=#$%:oe=^D:br#1200:tc=dialers:
UNIX-2400:\
      :el=^D^U^C^S^Q^O@:du:at=hayes:ie=#$%:oe=^D:br#2400:tc=dialers:
UNIX-9600:\
      :el=^D^U^C^S^Q^O@:du:at=hayes:ie=#$%:oe=^D:br#9600:tc=dialers:
UNIX-19200:\
      :el=^D^U^C^S^Q^O@:du:at=hayes:ie=#$%:oe=^D:br#19200:tc=dialers:
VMS-300|TOPS20-300:\
      :el=^Z^U^C^S^Q^O:du:at=hayes:ie=$@:oe=^Z:br#300:tc=dialers:
VMS-1200|TOPS20-1200:\
      :el=^Z^U^C^S^Q^O:du:at=hayes:ie=$@:oe=^Z:br#1200:tc=dialers:
dialers:\
      :dv=/dev/cua/b:
```

Each host has a default baud rate for the connection. Alternatively, you can specify a speed within the `tip` command-line argument as follows:

```
tip -9600 sparc1
```

When `phone-number` is specified, `tip` looks for an entry in the /etc/remote file of this form:

```
tip <-speed-entry>
```

When `tip` finds such an entry, it sets the connection speed accordingly. If it finds no such entry, `tip` interprets `<-speed-entry>` as if it were a system name, resulting in an error message. If you omit `<-speed-entry>`, `tip` uses the `tip0` entry from /etc/remote to set a speed for the connection.

When a device is specified, `tip` attempts to open that device, but it will do so using the user's access privileges rather than `tip`'s usual access privileges (setuid uucp). The user must have read/write access to the device. The `tip` command interprets any character string beginning with the slash character (/) as a device name.

If the phone number field in the `tip` command is an "at" symbol (@), the `tip` command searches the /etc/phones file. The /etc/phones file describing phone numbers is maintained by the user. The phone number file contains lines of this form:

```
<system-name> <phone-number>
```

Each phone number found for a system is tried until either a connection is established or an end-of-file is reached. Phone numbers are constructed from `0123456789-=*`, where the `=` and `*` are used to indicate that a second dial tone should be waited for.

Using the Modem

The following steps outline the process you need to follow to connect and use a modem on a Solaris system:

1. Connect the modem to the correct serial port on the Sun system by plugging the RS-232 cable into either ttya or ttyb. Make sure that the RS-232 cable is a "straight through" cable with pins 1 through 8 and pin 20 provided. Do not use a null modem (crossover) cable or a null-modem gender-adapter cable.

2. Check for the following entry in the /etc/remote file. If it is not there, add it after the `hardwire:\` entry. The following example adds the entry for the ttyb port:

   ```
   hardwire:\
                  :dv=/dev/term/b:br#9600:el=^C^S^Q^U^D:ie=%$:oe=^D:
   modem1:\
                  :dv=/dev/cua/b:br#9600:
   ```

   Make sure that the baud rate matches the baud rate you selected when setting up the serial port.

3. Check the permissions and owner of the modem port. The file /dev/cua/b should be rw-rw-rw- and the owner should be uucp. If not, use the `chmod` command to change the permission and the `chown` command to change the owner.

4. After modifying the /etc/remote file and checking the permission of the port, issue the following command:

   ```
   tip modem1
   ```

   You should get a `connected` message. If you get anything else—such as `all ports busy`—check the /etc/remote device entry as described in step 2.

5. Verify that the modem is responding to commands. Do so by typing

   ```
   at <cr>
   ```

   You should see an `OK` displayed.

6. Check the modem register and initialization string. Refer to Table 13-9 for common modem initialization strings and see if the modem type is referenced. If so, follow the manufacturer's instructions for using that string to initialize the modem. For example, the US Robotics Courier Modem string is

   ```
   AT&F1&B1&C1&D2X0S0=1&W
   ```

   If you do not know the initialization string, refer to the manuals supplied with your modem. If you still cannot figure out the initialization string, contact the modem manufacturer's technical support.

7. After setting up the modem, exit the "tip" utility by typing the following sequence:

   `<cr>~.`

   This is a carriage return followed by a ~ character and a . character.

Table 13-9 shows the strings used to initialize particular modems for use as dial-in and dial-out on Sun Solaris systems.

Table 13-9 Modem Initialization Strings

Modem	Initialization String
US Robotics modems	AT&F1&B1&C1&D2X0S0=1&W
Black Box Corporation	ATN0S37=0S0=1Q1&C1&D2&K3&W
All other modems	AT&FN0Q2X0&C1&D2S0=1&W

Summary

Setting up terminals and modems has always been a complicated task in UNIX. When you encounter problems, pinpointing the cause can be difficult. For example, not being able to access the modem could indicate an incorrect serial port setting, a cable configuration problem, or an incorrect initialization string on the modem. This is an area in which experience and practice can make all the difference in the world. In the early years of UNIX, nearly all peripherals were connected to the serial port. Now, many devices—such as printers and terminals—are connected via the network. Chapter 17, "Networking," describes how to set up your network and introduces you to some networking fundamentals.

CHAPTER

14

Installing a Server

The following test objectives are covered in this chapter:

- Understanding the server environment
- Installing software using the interactive installation program
- Understanding Solstice AdminSuite
- Installing Solstice AdminSuite
- Understanding the client/server relationship

Chapter 3, "Installing the Solaris 7 Software," discussed setting up a single stand-alone system. In this chapter, the emphasis is on installing and configuring a server. I begin by describing a server, its role, and its relationship to other systems on the network. Then, I describe how to install the operating system and some of the additional software packages that differentiate a server from a stand-alone system.

The Server

A *server* is a system that provides services and/or file systems, such as home directories or mail files, to other systems on the network. An *operating system (OS) server* is a server that provides the Solaris software to other systems on the network. For diskless clients, OS servers provide /usr, root (/), and swap file systems. For AutoClient systems, an OS server provides all system software required to set up the individual root (/) and /usr file systems required for local swapping and caching. There are file servers, startup servers, database servers, license servers, print servers, installation servers, and even servers for particular applications.

Systems that rely on servers are called *clients*. In other words, a client is a system that uses remote services from a server. Some clients have limited disk storage capacity, or perhaps none at all; these clients must rely on remote file systems from a server to function. Diskless and AutoClient clients are examples of this type of client. Other clients might use remote services, such as installation software, from a server. These clients don't rely on a server to function and are referred to as *stand-alone systems*.

System types are defined by how they access the root (/) and /usr file systems, including the swap area. Stand-alone and server systems mount these file systems from a local disk, whereas diskless and AutoClient clients mount the file systems remotely, relying on servers to provide these services. A stand-alone system has all its Solaris software on its local disk and does not require services from an OS server. Both networked and non-networked systems can be stand-alone systems in the Solaris operating environment.

The following is a brief description of the various clients you'll find in the Solaris 7 environment:

- **Diskless client**—A client that has no local disk or file systems. The diskless client boots from the server; remotely mounts its root (/), /usr, and /export/home file systems from a server; allocates swap space on the server; and gets all its data from the server. Any files created are stored on the server.

- **JavaStation**—A client that has no local file system and whose /home is accessed from a server across the network. The JavaStation runs only applications that are 100 percent pure Java. All data, applications, and configuration information reside on a centralized server that is running Netra J software, a Solaris operating environment. Java applications are downloaded on demand and are executed locally.
- **AutoClient**—A client system type that caches (locally stores copies of data as it is referenced) all its needed system software from a server. The AutoClient system has a local disk, but the root (/) and /usr file systems are accessed across the network from a server and are loaded in a local disk cache. Files in the / and /usr file systems are copied to the cache disk as they are referenced. If a Solstice AutoClient client accesses an application that is not already in its disk cache, that application is downloaded. If the application already resides in the client's disk cache, the application is accessed locally. AutoClient replaced the dataless client in Solaris 2.6.

Prerequisites for the Server

The server must meet a few minimum requirements before Solaris 7 can be installed:

- The Solaris 7 release supports all sun4c, sun4d, sun4u, and sun4m platforms. Some sun4c systems might not be supported in future releases of Solaris 7 beyond the 11/99 release. Check with your hardware vendor if you have a sun4c system to make sure it is supported before proceeding.
- To run a graphical user interface (GUI) installation, the system must have a minimum of 32MB of RAM. As a server, however, it is typical to have 256MB of RAM or more.
- The disk needs to be large enough to hold the Solaris OS, swap space, and the additional software, such as Solstice AdminSuite and AutoClient. You'll also need to allocate additional disk space on an OS server in the /export file system for diskless clients or Solstice AutoClient systems. Plan on a minimum of 1GB of disk space, but realistically you should have 2GB or more.

Installing Solaris 7 on the Server

Before beginning the installation, let's go over a preinstallation checklist.

First, gather the system identification information about your server. If the system is running, you can gather all this information by using the commands listed in Table 14-1.

Table 14-1 System Identification Information

Information Required	Command(s) Used to Gather the Information
System name	`/usr/bin/uname -u`
Primary network interface	`ifconfig -a`

IP address	`ypmatch <system_name> <host>`
	`nismatch <system_name>`
	`more /etc/inet/hosts`

Domain name	`/usr/bin/domainname`
Whether part of a subnet	`more /etc/netmasks`
What name service is used	`more /etc/nsswitch.conf`

Next, verify that you have enough disk space for Solaris 7 and all the copackaged and third-party software you plan to add. (Refer to Chapter 3 to find the total size of each software configuration cluster.) Normally, a server would have several gigabytes of disk space available for the operating system, so you'll be installing the full distribution cluster. Also, you need to check with your software vendor regarding space requirements for any third-party software packages as well as swap space requirements.

In addition, make sure you have enough disk space if you plan to run the following software:

- AnswerBook2
- Desktop Power Pack
- Internet Mail Service
- ODBC Driver Manager
- OpenGL
- Solstice AdminSuite
- Solstice AutoClient
- Solstice Backup
- Solstice DiskSuite
- Solaris 7 documentation
- Sun Hardware AnswerBook
- Sun MediaCenter One
- Sun WebServer

These packages occasionally change in size as they are updated, so contact Sun to obtain current disk space requirements for each of these packages.

TIP. *Software can be installed from a local CD or from a CD-ROM located on a system connected to the network. However, for speed, I recommend loading the software from a local CD-ROM drive.*

Installing Software Using the Interactive Installation Program

You are now ready to install your software. I recommend one of two methods to install the operating system: interactive or Web Start. The interactive installation process is described in this chapter. This option offers you the most flexibility when installing the OS. Web Start, described in Appendix E, "Web Start," does not let you set up additional disks, only the system disk. Use the Web Start option if you don't have a bitmapped system console attached to your system but you do have access to a Web browser attached to the same network.

The following steps provide an overview of the interactive software installation procedure:

1. Insert the Solaris 7 software CD in the CD-ROM drive.
2. At the OpenBoot `ok` prompt, type

   ```
   boot cdrom
   ```

   The system starts from the CD-ROM. After a few minutes, you'll enter the system identification section of the installation. Follow the system prompts, entering the information as it is presented. You are asked to select a language and locale. You'll also need to enter your system's hostname, IP address, and network information, so have this information available.
3. After the system identification section, you'll see the following dialog:

   ```
   Solaris Interactive Installation:

   This system is upgradeable, so you have two options for installing Solaris
   software.

   The upgrade option updates the Solaris software on the system to the new
   release, saving as many modifications as possible that you've made to the
   previous version of Solaris software. You should back up the system before
   using the upgrade option.
   ```

```
The initial option overwrites the system's disks with the new version of
Solaris software. Backing up any modifications that you've made to the previous
version of Solaris software is recommended before starting the initial option.
This option also lets you preserve any existing file systems.

After selecting an option and completing the tasks that follow, a summary of
your selections will be displayed.

F2_Upgrade     F4_Initial     F5_Exit     F6_Help
```

CAUTION! *All data on the OS partitions will be lost. These partitions include / (root), /usr, /opt, and /var.*

4. Press F4 to select a complete reinstallation of the software. You'll see the following dialog:

```
You'll be using the initial option for installing Solaris software on the
system. The initial option overwrites the system's disks when the new Solaris
software is installed.

On the following screens, you can accept the defaults or you can customize how
Solaris software will be installed by:

    - Allocating space for diskless clients or AutoClient systems
    - Selecting the type of Solaris software to install
    - Selecting disks to hold software you've selected
    - Specifying how file systems are laid out on the disks

After completing these tasks, a summary of your selections (called a profile)
will be displayed.
```

NOTE. *Because you want a complete reinstallation of the software, you'll select F4. The upgrade option is available if you are currently running Solaris 2.6 and you want to upgrade to Solaris 7. With the upgrade option, all customizations you made in Solaris 2.6 will be saved.*

5. Press F2 to continue. You'll see the following dialog:

```
Allocate Client Services?

Do you want to allocate space for diskless clients and/or AutoClient systems?

F2_Continue    F3_Go Back    F4_Allocate    F5_Exit    F6_Help
```

Press F2. Setting up client services is discussed in the later section "Adding AutoClient Support."

6. Select the additional languages from the following list that you want to use to display the user interface after Solaris software is installed. English is automatically installed by default.

```
[ ]  French
[ ]  German
[ ]  Italian
[ ]  Spanish
[ ]  Swedish

F2_Continue   F3_Go Back   F4_Allocate   F5_Exit   F6_Help
```

If you want to select a language other than English, select it here and then press F2 to continue.

7. If your system is an UltraSparc (sun4u) system and it supports the 64-bit architecture, select this option to install the Solaris 64-bit packages on this system:

```
[ ]  Select To Include Solaris 64-bit Support

F2_Continue    F3_Go Back    F5_Exit
```

If your system supports 64-bit, select this option and then press F2 to continue.

8. You'll see the following dialog:

```
Select Software:

Select the Solaris software to install on the system.

NOTE: After selecting a software group, you can add or remove software by
customizing it. However, this requires understanding of software dependencies
and how Solaris software is packaged.

 [ ]  Entire Distribution plus OEM support ..      656MB
 [X]  Entire Distribution ..................      637MB (F4 to Customize)
 [ ]  Developer System Support .............      572MB
 [ ]  End User System Support ..............      313MB
 [ ]  Core System Support ..................      117MB


F2_Continue   F3_Go Back   F4_Customize   F5_Exit   F6_Help
```

NOTE. *The End User System Support cluster is selected by default. In the preceding example, I selected the Entire Distribution cluster, which is common for servers. After you select the software cluster you want to install, if you press F4, you see an interactive menu that allows you to select and deselect software packages within a particular cluster.*

9. Select the software cluster you want to install, and press F2. For a server, I recommend selecting the Entire Distribution cluster so that everything gets loaded.

NOTE. *I always select the entire distribution on a server because it's frustrating to have to go back and install another package later, especially on a server supporting many users. Sometimes the Entire Distribution cluster is not installed because of the lack of disk space. With disk space as inexpensive as it is today, add a larger disk and install the entire distribution.*

After pressing F2, you'll see the following dialog:

```
Select Disks:
On this screen you must select the disks for installing Solaris software.
Start by looking at the Suggested Minimum field; this value is the approximate
space needed to install the software you've selected. Keep selecting disks until
the Total Selected value exceeds the Suggested Minimum value.

     Disk Device (Size)        Available Space
     =============================================
       [ ] c0t2d0    (1002 MB)                 1002 MB
       [X] c0t3d0    (1009 MB) boot disk       1009 MB

                                Total Selected:  1009 MB
                             Suggested Minimum:   591 MB


F2_Continue    F3_Go Back    F4_Edit    F5_Exit    F6_Help
```

10. Select your disks, and press F2. You'll see the following dialog:

```
Preserve Data?
Do you want to preserve existing data? At least one of the disks you've selected
for installing Solaris software has file systems or unnamed slices that you may
want to save.


F2_Continue   F3_Go Back   F4_Preserve   F5_Exit   F6_Help
```

11. Press F2, and the data on all file systems is erased. You'll see the following dialog:

```
Automatically Layout File Systems?

Do you want to use auto-layout to automatically layout file systems? Manually
laying out file systems requires advanced system administration skills.


F2_Auto Layout  F3_Go Back  F4_Manual Layout  F5_Exit  F6_Help
```

12. Press F2. The system automatically lays out the file systems. Sizes are determined by the software packages you selected. If you plan to add additional software, you can modify the file system sizes later. You'll see the following dialog:

```
Automatically Layout File Systems

On this screen you must select all the file systems you want auto-layout to
create, or accept the default file systems shown.

NOTE: For small disks, it may be necessary for auto-layout to break up some of
the file systems you request into smaller file systems to fit the available disk
space. So, after auto-layout completes, you may find file systems in the layout
that you did not select from the list below.

                File Systems for Auto-layout
                ========================================
                [X]  /
                [X]  /opt
                [X]  /usr
                [ ]  /usr/openwin
                [X]  /var
                [X]  swap


F2_Continue    F5_Cancel    F6_Help
```

13. Make your selection(s) and press F2.

NOTE. *I recommend adding /var and /opt as separate file systems if you expect to have large spool files and to add additional software products.*

For this example, I selected these additional file systems. You'll see the following dialog:

```
File System and Disk Layout

The summary below is your current file system and disk layout, based on the
information you've supplied.

NOTE: If you choose to customize, you should understand file systems, their
intended purpose on the disk, and how changing them may affect the operation
of the system.

File system/Mount point              Disk/Slice               Size
==============================================================
      /                                c0t3d0s0                 55 MB
      /var                             c0t3d0s1                 42 MB
      overlap                          c0t3d0s2               1009 MB
```

```
swap                                        c0t3d0s3            94 MB
/opt                                        c0t3d0s5            45 MB
/usr                                        c0t3d0s6           772 MB



F2_Continue   F3_Go Back   F4_Customize   F5_Exit   F6_Help
```

14. Press F2 to continue. You'll see the following dialog:

```
Mount Remote File Systems?

Do you want to mount software from a remote file server? This may be necessary
if you had to remove software because of disk space problems.



F2_Continue  F3_Go Back  F4_Remote Mounts  F5_Exit  F6_Help
```

15. Press F2 to continue, unless you want to set up remote mounts.

NOTE. *I usually wait until after the initial software installation to set up these mounts. Many times the system is not connected to a production network at this point, so the mount points are unavailable. It's also a personal preference to save this task for the post-installation phase, when I set up users, printers, and so on. I have a checklist of all the things I need to do after software installation, and setting up mount points is one of them.*

You'll see the following dialog:

```
Profile
The information shown below is your profile for installing Solaris software.
It reflects the choices you've made on previous screens.
  ===============================================================

        Installation Option: Initial
                Boot Device: c0t3d0s0
            Client Services: None
                   Software: Solaris 2.7, Entire Distribution

      File System and Disk Layout: /                     c0t3d0s0    55 MB
                                   /var                  c0t3d0s1    42 MB
                                   swap                  c0t3d0s3    94 MB
                                   /opt                  c0t3d0s5    45 MB
                                   /usr                  c0t3d0s6   772 MB


F2_Continue    F4_Change    F5_Exit    F6_Help
```

16. Verify the information, and press F2 if you agree.

NOTE. *Partition sizes and disk space requirements were discussed in Chapter 3. Review that chapter if you are unsure of the partitions and sizes that have been set up by the installation program.*

You'll see the following dialog:

```
Reboot After Installation?

After Solaris software is installed, the system must be rebooted. You can choose
to have the system automatically reboot, or you can choose to manually reboot
the system if you want to run scripts or do other customizations before the
reboot. You can manually reboot a system by using the reboot(1M) command.


             [X] Auto Reboot
             [ ] Manual Reboot


F2_Begin Installation    F5_Cancel
```

17. Make your selection, and press F2 to begin the installation. This completes the interactive installation. You'll see the following dialog as the software is being installed:

```
Preparing system for Solaris install
Configuring disk (c0t3d0)
- Creating Solaris disk label (VTOC)
Creating and checking UFS file systems
- Creating / (c0t3d0s0)
- Creating /var (c0t3d0s1)
- Creating /opt (c0t3d0s5)
- Creating /usr (c0t3d0s6)
Beginning Solaris software installation
     Solaris Initial Install
MBytes Installed:      0.00
MBytes Remaining:    493.77
                     89 07
```

A meter will appear at the bottom of the screen, showing the progress of the installation. When it reaches 100 percent, the system will reboot. When the interactive installation completes, you can install the Solstice AdminSuite package.

Solstice AdminSuite

By now, you should be familiar with AdminTool. I have described it several times as an easy-to-use graphical interface for user, printer, and serial device administration. Solstice AdminSuite is copackaged with the Solaris Operating Environment Application and Enterprise servers. It is similar to AdminTool in that it provides an easy-to-use GUI to facilitate routine server administration tasks. AdminSuite provides a unified suite of tools for administering your Solaris systems and for managing such functions as user accounts, hosts, groups, administrative data, printers, file systems, disks, and serial ports.

To start AdminSuite, type `solstice` at the command prompt and press Enter. The Solstice Launcher window appears, as shown in Figure 14-1.

Figure 14-1
The Solstice Launcher window.

AdminTool is used to manage a stand-alone system, whereas AdminSuite addresses your needs for reducing the cost and complexity of managing distributed systems. AdminSuite can assist you in administering your network in the following ways:

- It offers local administration of Solaris workgroups by using network services, such as Network Information Service (NIS). This centralizes desktop administration and makes remote management painless.
- It automates routine administrative tasks, such as host setup, printer setup, and user setup.
- It provides easy-to-use system administration tools consisting of an extensive GUI to facilitate centralized setup and maintenance of the network environment. Administration is done without requiring root privileges, making centralized administration a reality.

The next few sections cover the facilities provided by Solstice AdminSuite.

Host Management

Host Manager lets you manage information about clients on the network without manually creating or editing files. It is used to connect client systems to the network as well as to modify and delete them. Host Manager also allows you to add and delete OS services and to set up remote installation services. You can also use Host Manager on a local server to manage support for clients that need remote file resources and disk storage space. Supported client types include stand-alone, diskless, and AutoClient. Host Manager is discussed again in the "Adding AutoClient Support" section of this chapter.

User Management

User Manager allows easy setup and maintenance of user accounts. This includes adding new users, removing users, and updating user information. Some of the defaults that can be set include login shell, password policy, and identifying the user's mail server.

Group Management

Group Manager adds, displays, modifies, and deletes groups in the NIS name service environment, on a local system, or on a remote system (/etc files) in the same way that AdminTool manages local groups. Group Manager can also be used to add and change group passwords.

Administrative Data Management

Database Manager is used to manage system files, such as /etc/passwd and /etc/hosts, on the local system, on a remote system, or in the NIS database if you have appropriate access privileges.

Printer Management

Printer Manager is a GUI that lets you install, modify, and delete printers on an LP print server. Furthermore, if your site uses NIS, Printer Manager can provide centralized print administration.

Centralized print administration means that you don't have to individually configure remote printers for each print client on the network. If you use Printer Manager to install a printer, the printer is added to the name service and becomes available to all SunSoft print clients in the name service. Printer Manager and printers are discussed in Chapter 20, "Solstice AdminSuite."

Serial Port Management

Serial Port Manager is used to add and maintain port services for terminals and modems. Using Serial Port Manager to configure serial ports allows you to set up terminals and modems without having to create and edit the necessary files manually. It can display serial port information and facilitate port setup, modification, or deletion. It also provides templates for common terminal and modem configurations.

You can use Serial Port Manager to manage serial port information on the local system or on a remote system if you have the appropriate access privileges.

Storage Management

Storage Manager consists of two components: File System Manager and Disk Manager. These components help you manage the file systems and disk configurations for the systems on your network.

File System Manager enables the file system management of a server or a group of clients on a server. Disk Manager enables the management of disk slices and fdisk partitions on a single disk or a group of equivalent disks. Storage Manager also supports the management of High Sierra file system CD-ROMs.

With File System Manager, you can perform the following tasks:

- Create new file systems
- Modify file system options in the /etc/vfstab file
- Manage /etc/vfstab files on a single client, a group of diskless clients, or on an AutoClient system
- Mount or unmount file systems
- Share or unshare directories
- Include a file system in existing automounter maps
- Convert a directory into a mount point

With Disk Manager, you can perform the following tasks:

- Assign a name to a disk
- View and change fdisk partitions on x86 platforms
- Show and set the active fdisk partitions on x86 platforms
- View and change slice geometry on SPARC and x86 platforms
- Copy a disk's characteristics to one or more disks of the same type
- Edit disks of the same type simultaneously (or in batches)

All of these features of AdminSuite are discussed in more detail in Chapter 20.

After installing the AdminSuite package, install any additional Solaris software packages using AdminTool or `pkgadd`. This procedure is discussed in Chapter 8, "Software Package Administration."

Installing AdminSuite

AdminSuite comes with only the Server edition of the Solaris software distribution, and it only runs on Solaris version 2.4 or higher. The software is on the CD-ROM labeled "Solaris Server Intranet Extension" and is described in Chapter 20.

Preinstallation Checklist

To perform a full installation of AdminSuite, you need 35MB of free disk space for the spooled software area and an additional 15MB of disk space for each client architecture you plan to support.

The following software packages already need to be installed on your system: SUNWadmc, SUNWadmfw, SUNWsadml, and SUNWmfrun. If these packages are not already installed, go back to the Solaris CD-ROM and install them.

Before installing the AdminSuite software, you must remove any old versions of AdminSuite. Check to see if AdminSuite is already installed using the `pkginfo` command as follows:

```
pkginfo|grep -i adminsuite
```

The system responds with the following output if AdminSuite already exists:

```
system      SUNWadmsm      Solstice AdminSuite Storage Manager Application
system      SUNWsadma      Solstice AdminSuite Applications
system      SUNWsadmb      Solstice AdminSuite CLI
system      SUNWsadmc      Solstice AdminSuite Core Methods
system      SUNWsadmm      Solstice AdminSuite man pages
system      SUNWsadmo      Solstice AdminSuite Object Libraries
system      SUNWsadmp      Solstice AdminSuite Data Files
system      SUNWspapp      Solstice AdminSuite print application
```

If a previous version of AdminSuite exists, remove it as follows:

1. Log in as root.
2. Change directories to the /cdrom/cdrom0 directory.
3. Type

   ```
   ./rm_admin -v 2.2 -d /opt
   ```

Options to the `rm_admin` command are described in Table 14-2.

Table 14-2 ***rm_admin*** **Options**

Option	Description
-v	Represents the version of AdminSuite you want to remove. (In the preceding example, Version 2.2 is being removed.)
-d	Represents the directory in which the AdminSuite software is installed.
-f	Forces the removal of software with no confirmation prompt (optional, but recommended).

To install the AdminSuite software, you must be a member of the sysadmin group for each host you specify during installation. The following procedure describes how to become a member of the sysadmin group:

1. Log in as root to the system.
2. Edit the /etc/group file, adding the users you want to be authorized to install AdminSuite. A sample entry is as follows:

   ```
   sysadmin::14:bcalkins, bholzgen, sburge
   ```

   In this example, bcalkins, bholzgen, and sburge represent the users you are adding to the sysadmin group. You must be a member of the sysadmin group to install AdminSuite.
3. Verify that the user is a member of the sysadmin group by entering the following commands:

   ```
   su - sburge
   groups
      staff sysadmin
   exit
   ```

   Perform this step for each user you add to the system.

You are now ready to proceed with the installation of Solstice AdminSuite 2.3.

Insert the CD-ROM labeled "Solaris Server Intranet Extension." If your system is not running Volume Manager, you must mount the CD with the following commands before accessing it:

```
mkdir /cdrom
mount -F hsfs -o ro /dev/dsk/<c?t?d0s0> /cdrom
```

where `c?t?d0s0` represents the CD-ROM device on your system. Usually, it is set to `c0t6d0s0`.

The AdminSuite software is installed using the admin_install script found in the /AdminSuite directory on the CD-ROM. You can use the installation script to install the software on systems on the network as well as stand-alone systems. Help is available when you run the script, and the script dialog makes it easy for you to install the product.

The Installation Process

The following section describes the options presented by the script during the installation process. To install AdminSuite, follow these steps:

1. Change to the directory on the CD-ROM that contains the admin_install script. On a system running volume manager, the mount point is /cdrom/solaris_srvr_intranet_ext_1_0/AdminSuite_2.3+AutoClient_2.1.

2. Type

   ```
   ./admin_install
   ```

   The system responds with this:

   ```
   Welcome to the Solstice Installation Program ...
   To exit the installation process at any time, type 0
   and press the Return key.
          1. Install AdminSuite 2.3 and AutoClient 2.1
          2. Install SunSoft Print Client (Solaris 2.3 - 2.5.1 only)
          3. Install Software Usage Monitoring Toolkit
          4. Set up systems to use AdminSuite and AutoClient
          5. Installation Help
   Enter the number for one or more choices, separated by a space and
   then press the Return key.
   [default: 1]>>>
   ```

3. Enter option 1, Install AdminSuite 2.3 and AutoClient 2.1, and press Enter.

   The AdminSuite Software Location information appears, as follows:

   ```
   AdminSuite Software Location
   1. /opt
   Choose this option if you intend to support only one architecture of the
   software.

   2. /export/opt
   Choose this option if you need to support multiple architectures and if you will
   set up other systems that will NFS mount AdminSuite.

   3. Specify location
   Choose this option if you intend to set up other systems to NFS mount AdminSuite
   but you do not want to install the software in /export/opt.
   ```

```
4. Installation Help
Type 1, 2, 3, or 4 and press the Return key.
[default: 1]>>>
```

4. Choose option 1, /opt, which installs the software in the appropriate directory.

   This installation directory is the recommended directory. With this option, only one architecture can be used with the software. After you choose this option, the following installation summary appears:

   ```
   After confirming that the directory and host are correct, enter 1 to continue
   with the installation. You will see a scrolling list of the log activities. If
   the installation is successful, the following message will display in your
   installation window:
   Successfully installed product: AdminSuite/AutoClient

   ==== Installation Summary ====
   Product(s):      AdminSuite/AutoClient
   Install Directory:          /opt
   Host(s):          your_host_name
   Start Installation
   -----------------

   Do you want to start the installation?
   1. Start installation
   2. Cancel installation

   >>>
   ```

5. Verify the information provided in the Installation Summary. Type 1 and press Enter to continue with the installation.

   You will see a scrolling list of log activities. If the installation is successful, the following message appears:

   ```
   Successfully installed product: AdminSuite/AutoClient
   ```

   You'll be notified of any problems that might have occurred if the installation was unsuccessful.

6. Update your shell search path to include the location of the AdminSuite commands.

   If you use either the Bourne or the Korn shell, type

   ```
   PATH = $PATH:/opt/SUNWadm/bin
   MANPATH = $MANPATH:/opt/SUNWadm/man
   ```

   Enter these changes into your .profile startup file to make them permanent.

7. Start the Solstice Launcher with the following command:

```
/usr/bin/solstice &
```

The launcher should now contain the Solstice AdminSuite applications.

The Client/Server Relationship

Stand-alone systems and clients access the server for various reasons. A stand-alone system accesses the server for data, whereas a client accesses the server to obtain its operating system as well as data. The following sections describe each of these scenarios.

Adding AutoClient Support

After AdminSuite has been installed as described in the preceding section, Solstice AutoClient support software is also installed on the server. AutoClient software reduces the cost of desktop management and is a key component of centralized administration by providing the following benefits:

- **Hands-off installation**—System administrators no longer need to visit each desktop to install software. They can configure the Solstice AutoClient client on the server, and after an initial `boot net`, the operating system is automatically cached to the desktop. AutoClient provides an alternative to the traditional push method of software, eliminating the need to explicitly install software on the desktop.
- **Field-replaceable units**—Solstice AutoClient clients hold only cached data; the server holds all original data, where it can be securely managed. In the event of an AutoClient desktop hardware failure, the machine can be replaced and started up via the network. The user's downtime is significantly reduced.
- **Enhanced server scalability**—In contrast to the dataless client, Solstice AutoClient reduces NFS reads and network traffic, improving NFS server scalability. The client/server ratio of AutoClient workgroups is much higher than diskless or dataless workgroups.
- **Disconnectable option**—This option allows an AutoClient to continue operating if the server is unavailable, providing a higher level of availability for the client.
- **Command-Line Interface**—Allows administrators to choose between the graphical user interface (GUI) and the Command-Line Interface (CLI) to perform operations.
- **Efficient system-wide restart**—Clients restart directly from cache, reducing network traffic during a system-wide restart.

- **Centralized client patching**—Patching of Solstice AutoClients is centralized. All patches are applied once on the server. For example, if you add a software patch to an AutoClient system, you don't actually install the patch on the client, because its local disk space is reserved for caching. Instead, you add the patch to the server or to the client's root file system (which resides on the server) or to both. (This process is discussed later in this section.)
- **Remote halting and remote starting of clients**—Solstice AutoClient allows the system administrator to remotely halt clients and start them, providing administrative control from a management console.
- **Operation logging**—Creates a log entry for each major operation completed with the host manager, providing a record of past transactions for diagnostic purposes.

Solstice AutoClient turns the desktop's disk into a cache for the operating system, applications, and user data. If an AutoClient client accesses an application that is not already in its disk cache, the application is downloaded. If the application already resides in the client's disk cache, the application is accessed locally. Following the initial read of data into the desktop's disk cache, network traffic and CPU load are reduced, allowing a higher client/server ratio than diskless or dataless client types.

Table 14-3 lists the disk space requirements for AutoClient servers and AutoClient systems.

Table 14-3 Disk Space Requirements for AutoClient Servers and AutoClient Systems

File System	Minimum Disk Space Requirements
Servers of AutoClient Systems	
root (/)	1MB
/usr	4MB
/var	7.5MB
/export	17MB per OS service 20MB for each AutoClient system (typically in /export)
AutoClient Systems	
Cache for root (/) and /usr	70MB minimum

NOTE. *If you add an AutoClient system to a server, the /export/root directory is specified on the server by default to store the 20MB for each AutoClient system. However, you can specify any directory that has available disk space. Make sure the server has enough space for this directory.*

Unlike diskless clients, AutoClient systems do not require their swap space to be allocated on the server.

After the Solstice AutoClient software is installed on the server, AutoClient systems are installed, configured, and maintained with the command-line interface or with Host Manager. Host Manager, described earlier, is part of the AdminSuite package. It is a graphical user interface that allows for greater efficiency and ease of use in administering your AutoClient systems in a network environment. Using AdminSuite's Host Manager to administer your AutoClients is the method described in this chapter. Host Manager lets system administrators perform the following tasks:

- Add, modify, display, or remove AutoClient system support on a server
- Convert existing generic, stand-alone, and dataless systems to the AutoClient system type
- Change information about multiple AutoClient systems in one operation

The system files that may be modified by Host Manager when adding and maintaining AutoClient systems are listed in Table 14-4.

Table 14-4 Files Managed by Host Manager

System File	Where Modified	Description
bootparams	/etc files, NIS, or NIS+	A database listing the servers that provide the paths to a client's boot and installation software and a client's root and swap areas.
/etc/dfs/dfstab	Server providing the file services	A file containing a series of share commands that make file resources available to the client system.
ethers	/etc files, NIS, or NIS+	A database containing the client's Ethernet address.
hosts	/etc files, NIS, or NIS+	A database containing the client's host name and associated IP address.
timezone	/etc files, NIS, or NIS+	A database containing the client's time zone.
/export/root	Server providing the file services	A default directory that contains root files for a diskless client or AutoClient system.
/export/swap	Server providing the file services	A default directory that contains the swap file for a diskless client.
/tftpboot	Server providing the boot services	A directory containing SPARC client booting information.

Table 14-4 Files Managed by Host Manager (continued)

System File	Where Modified	Description
/rplboot	Server providing the boot services	A directory containing i386 client booting information.
/etc/inetd.conf	Server providing the boot services	A system file that starts the `tftp` and `rpl` boot daemons.
cred.org_dir	NIS+	An NIS+ table used to store the host's DES and LOCAL credentials.
/var/sadm/softinfo and /var/sadm/ ➥system/admin/ ➥services	Solaris 2.3 and 2.4 servers	Directories containing a list of OS services available on Solaris 2.3 and 2.4 servers.

If an X Window System is not available to run Host Manager, Table 14-5 describes command-line equivalents of Host Manager that can be used to manage AutoClient systems.

Table 14-5 Command-Line Equivalents of Host Manager

Command	Description
`admhostadd`	Adds support for a new system or OS server.
`admhostmod`	Modifies an existing system or OS server. You can also add OS services to an existing OS server.
`admhostdel`	Deletes an existing system or OS server.
`admhostls`	Lists one or more system entries in the selected name service.
`admhostls -h`	Lists hardware information of one or more system entries in the selected name service.

How an AutoClient System Works

The CacheFS technology is an important component of AutoClient systems. A *cache* is a local storage area for data. A *cached file system* is a local file system that stores files in the cache as they are referenced. Subsequent references to the same files are satisfied from the cache rather than retrieving them across the network from the server again. This functionality reduces the load on the network and the server, and it results in faster access for the AutoClient system. If the cache becomes full, space is reclaimed on a least recently used (LRU) basis. Files that have not been referenced for the longest time are discarded from the cache to create free space for the files that are currently being referenced.

An AutoClient system uses its local disk for swap space and to cache its individual root (/) and /usr file systems from the server's back file system. The back file system is the AutoClient's file system located back on the server and is usually located in /export/root/<hostname>. An AutoClient system uses consistency checking to keep a cached file system synchronized with its back file system.

By default, files that are updated in the server's back file systems are updated on the AutoClient system's cached file systems within 24 hours. However, if the update needs to occur sooner, you can use the `autosync` command. This command initiates consistency checking that synchronizes an AutoClient system's cached file systems with its server's back file systems. In addition, each time an AutoClient system is started, its cached file systems are checked for consistency and updated with its server's back file systems.

Using `autosync`, you can update individual AutoClient systems or all local AutoClient systems in your network to match their corresponding back file systems. You should do this update if you add a new package in the shared /usr directory or in one or more system / (root) directories, or if you add a patch. The procedures listed in Table 14-6, issued from the server, illustrate the use of the `autosync` command.

Table 14-6 *autosync* Examples

Example	Description
`autosync`	Updates all AutoClient systems.
`autosync -h <hostname>`	Use the -h option to specify a specific AutoClient system to update.
`autosync -h <hostname> /usr`	Updates only the cached file system /usr on a specific AutoClient system.

The system responds with the names of any systems that failed to be updated. No system response means that the updates were all successful. If the update fails, you will receive a message similar to this:

```
sparc4:: failed:
```

Consistency checking for an AutoClient system is different from a system running CacheFS. AutoClient files (/ and /usr) are not likely to change often, so consistency checking does not need to occur as frequently on an AutoClient system as it does on a system running CacheFS. This reduces traffic on your AutoClient network. Also, if you add new files to an AutoClient system, its server's back file systems are updated immediately, because an AutoClient system uses a write-through cache. A write-through cache is one that immediately updates its back file system as data is changed or added to the cache.

Setting Up the AutoClient Server

In the section "Installing AdminSuite," you installed Solstice AutoClient. After installing AutoClient, you must follow the next setup procedure to set up the server as an OS server for the AutoClient systems:

1. On the AutoClient server, type the following command to start the Solstice Launcher:

   ```
   /usr/bin/solstice &
   ```

   The Solstice Launcher window opens.

2. Click the Host Manager icon in the Solstice Launcher window.

   The Host Manager: Select Naming Service window is displayed, as shown in Figure 14-2. If you are using a naming service, it shows the server's domain name. If you are using local files, the system name is displayed.

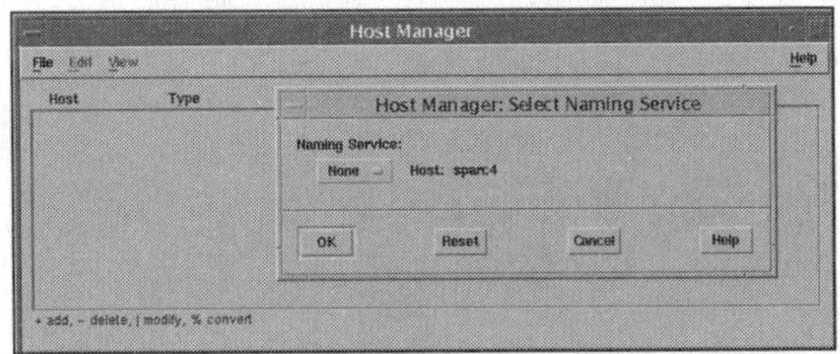

Figure 14-2
The Host Manager: Select Naming Service window.

3. Choose a Naming Service and click OK. (In the example, I'm not running a naming service, so I chose None.)

   The Host Manager window is displayed, as shown in Figure 14-3.

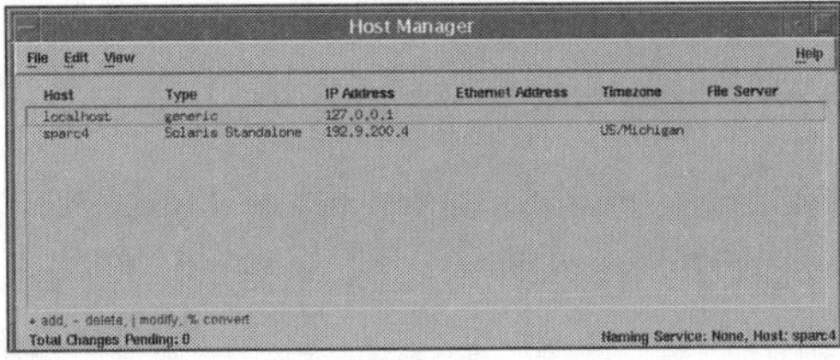

Figure 14-3
The Host Manager window.

4. Select the system that you want to convert to an OS server from the Host Manager main window. Select Edit, Convert, and then select "to OS server" from the pop-up menu, as shown in Figure 14-4.

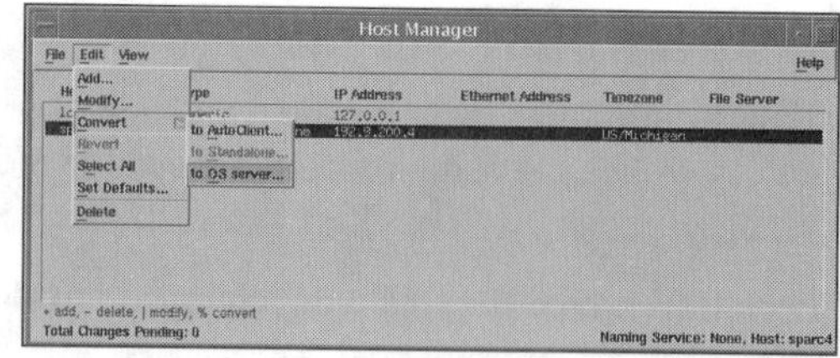

Figure 14-4
The Host Manager Edit window.

NOTE. *As shown in Figure 14-4, when the pop-up menu appears, "to AutoClient" is automatically selected, so you have to scroll down and select "to OS server." In the example, I chose sparc4 as the OS server that supports the AutoClient systems.*

The Host Manager: Convert window is displayed, as shown in Figure 14-5.

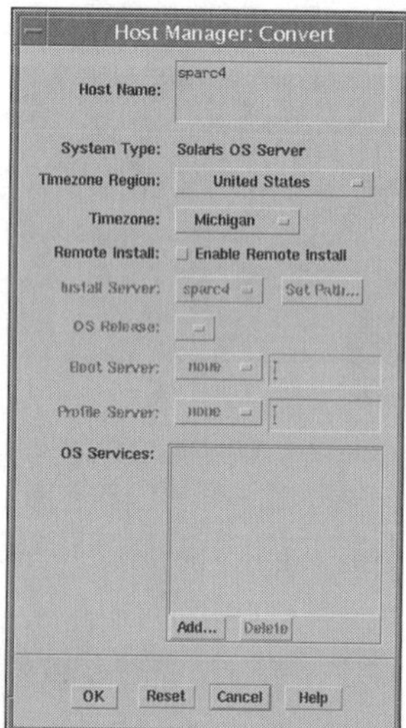

Figure 14-5
The Host Manager: Convert window.

5. In the Host Manager: Convert window, below the OS Services box, click Add. The Set Media Path window is displayed, as shown in Figure 14-6.

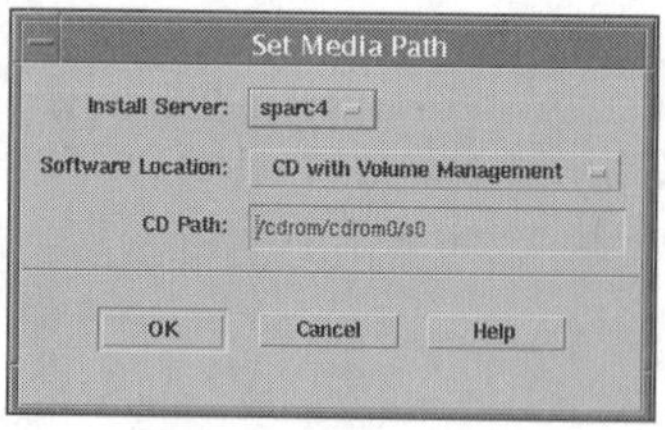

Figure 14-6
The Set Media Path window.

Fill in the Set Media Path window, following these guidelines:

- If you are using the Solaris CD-ROM as the Solaris CD-ROM image, and the CD-ROM is managed by Volume Manager, enter the path `/cdrom/cdrom0/s0`.
- If you mounted the CD-ROM manually, enter the path `<mount point to the CD>`.
- If you are using a copy of the Solaris CD-ROM image on the installation server's hard disk, enter the path `<directory where the image is loaded>`.

Click OK after you've finished filling in the options.

The Add OS Services window appears, as shown in Figure 14-7.

Figure 14-7
The Add OS Services window.

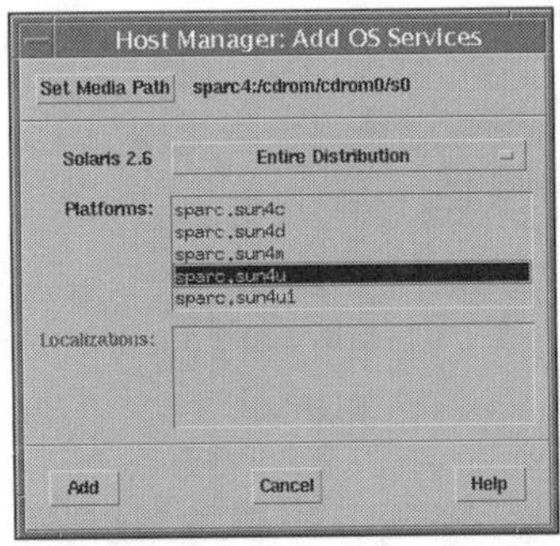

6. In the Add OS Services window, choose the distribution type. The default distribution type is Entire Distribution. Select the platform of the AutoClient system that you plan to support, and click Add. The Add OS Services window closes. If you want to add more services for other platforms, repeat this step.

NOTE. *To support clients of a different platform group, you must add an OS service for that platform. For example, if a server with Sun4m kernel architecture needs to support an AutoClient system with Sun4c kernel architecture, client support for the Sun4c kernel architecture must be added to the server. In addition, for clients that require a different Solaris release from the OS server, you must have the appropriate Solaris CD-ROM image to add this OS service. For example, if you have an OS server running Solaris 7 and you want it to support AutoClients running Solaris 2.5, you must add the Solaris 2.5 OS services to the OS server.*

7. The Host Manager: Convert window reopens. Figure 14-8 shows an example of a completed Add OS Services window. Click OK.

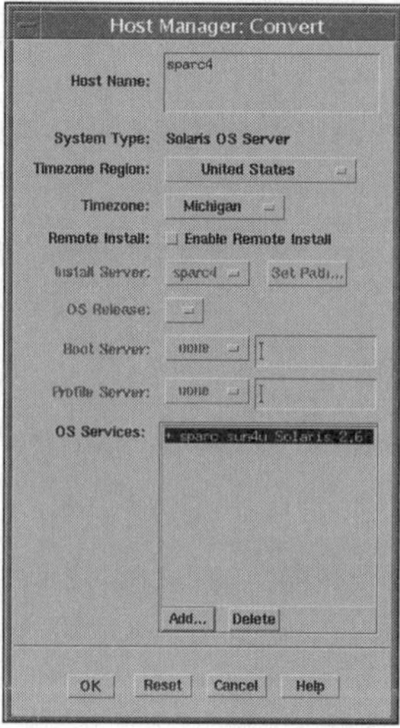

Figure 14-8
The Host Manager: Convert window.

The Host Manager window opens, as shown in Figure 14-9. The bottom of the window says Total Changes Pending: 1.

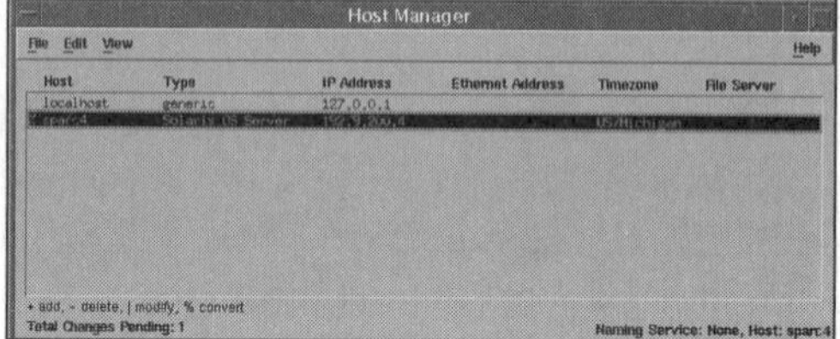

Figure 14-9
The Host Manager window.

8. Select File, Save Changes.

   To verify that all the OS services have been added, make sure that the status line at the bottom of the main window says All changes successful.

Adding AutoClients to the Server

After you add AutoClient OS services to the OS server, you need to add each AutoClient system. If an AutoClient is not listed in Host Manager, it cannot start from the OS server. You'll use Solstice Host Manager to do this. The steps are as follows:

1. In the Host Manager main window, select Edit, Add, as shown in Figure 14-10.

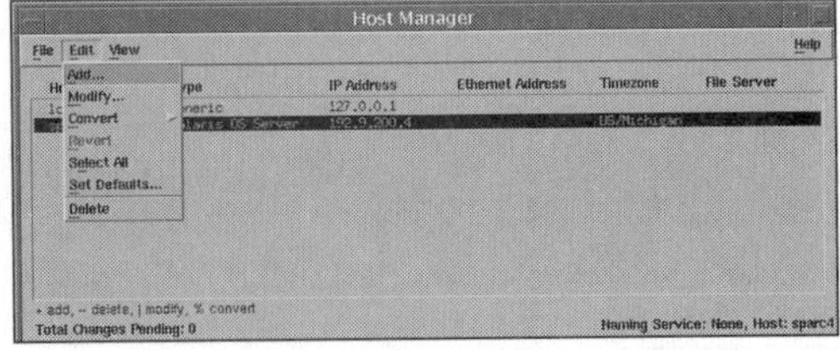

Figure 14-10
The Host Manager main window.

The Host Manager: Add window opens, as shown in Figure 14-11.

Figure 14-11
The Host Manager: Add window.

2. Fill in the system information for the AutoClient system. The System Type is set to Solaris Standalone. Change the System Type to Solstice AutoClient, as shown in Figure 14-12.

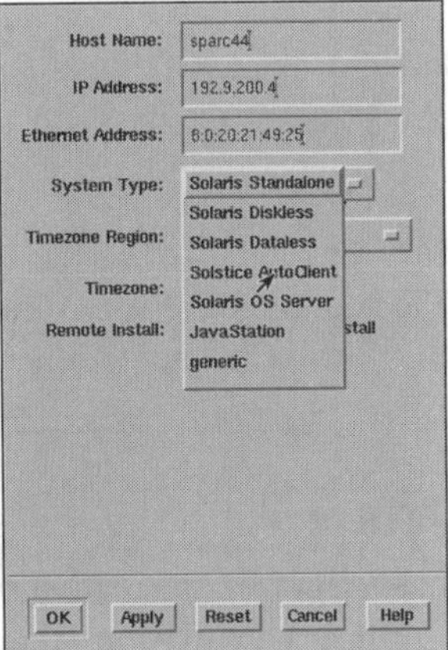

Figure 14-12
Select the System Type.

The Host M es to look like Figure 14-13.

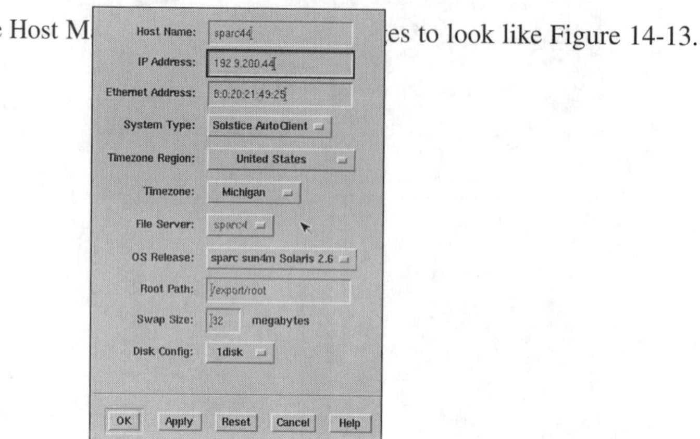

Figure 14-13
The Host Manager: Add window.

After enteri

You'll retur in Figure 14-14.

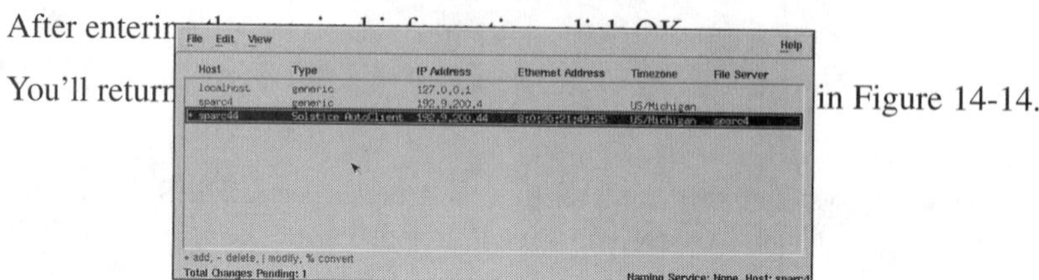

Figure 14-14
The Host Manager main window.

Repeat steps 1 and 2 to add subsequent AutoClient systems.

3. When you are ready to confirm the addition of all the AutoClient systems listed in the Host Manager window, choose File, Save Changes.

Starting an AutoClient System

On an AutoClient system, the operating system and application software are installed on the workstation by performing a `boot net` at the `ok` OpenBoot prompt on the workstation. The following command is used to start the AutoClient system for the first time:

```
ok boot net <cr>
```

The first time the AutoClient system is started, you are prompted to provide system configuration information for the AutoClient system. You're also prompted to create a root password.

Similar to the Solaris JumpStart product that is described in Chapter 15, "JumpStart," the client's disk and software are automatically set up and installed, but now, instead of requiring the ongoing administration of each client as a stand-alone, all the files used by the desktop are preserved on a network server.

After it is up and running, any changes made on the client are also written back to the server. Should the desktop system experience a component failure, a similarly configured system can be put in its place and brought back up in a matter of minutes. The net effect is that the desktop is a field-replaceable unit (FRU), and both backups and hardware maintenance have a reduced impact on the system administrator's time.

Patching an AutoClient System

As stated earlier in this book, a software patch is a collection of files and directories that replaces or updates existing files and directories that are preventing proper execution of the software. On diskless clients and AutoClient systems, all software resides on the server. If you add a software patch to an AutoClient system, you don't actually install the patch on the client, because its local disk space is reserved for caching. Instead, you add the patch to the server, to the client's root file system (which resides on the server), or to both. An AutoClient system's root file system is typically in /export/root/<hostname> on the server.

Applying patches to clients is typically complicated, because the patch might place software partially on the client's root file system and partially on the OS service used by that client. To reduce the complexity of installing patches on diskless clients and AutoClient systems, the Solstice AutoClient product includes the `admclientpatch` command. The options and uses of the `admclientpatch` command are listed and described in Table 14-7.

Table 14-7 ***admclientpatch*** **Options**

Option	Description
`-a <patch_dir/patch_id>`	Adds a patch to a spool directory on the server. `<patch_dir>` is the source directory where patches reside on a patch server. `<patch_id>` is a specific patch ID number, as in 102209-01.
`-c`	Lists all diskless clients, AutoClient systems, and OS services, along with patches installed on each that are served by this server.
`-p`	Lists all currently spooled patches.
`-r <patch_id>`	Removes the specified `<patch_id>` from the spool directory.

-s	Synchronizes all AutoClients so that the patches they are running match the patches in the spool directory.

admclientpatch provides a way to manage patches on all AutoClient systems. You can use it to initially establish a patch spool directory on the OS server. The spool directory is /opt/SUNWadmd/2.3/Patches. Then, by using admclientpatch with the -s option, you can synchronize patches running on the clients (and their associated services in /usr) so that they match the revisions of the patches in the spool directory.

The general procedure for maintaining patches on AutoClient systems is as follows:

Use admclientpatch -a or -r to create or update a spool directory of all appropriate patches on the local machine as follows:

```
admclientpatch -a /tmp/106828-01 <cr>
```

The system responds with this:

```
Copying the following patch into spool area: 106828-01 . done
```

If the patch being added to the spool directory makes any existing patches obsolete, admclientpatch archives the old patches in case they need to be restored.

On any client server, use admclientpatch -s to synchronize patches installed on clients with patches in the spool directory as follows. The -v option reports whether admclientpatch is adding new patches or backing out unwanted patches.

```
admclientpatch -s -v
Synchronizing service: Solaris_2.6
     Removing patches installed but not spooled.
     To find currently spooled patches, run 'admclientpatch -p'
         105654-03          .
     Installing patches spooled but not installed
         106828-01          ....................................
Synchronizing client: sparc44
     Installing patches spooled but not installed
         106828-01          .........

All done synchronizing patches to existing clients and OS services.
Note: The following machines were affected by these patches
and should be rebooted: sparc44
```

The admclientpatch command is a front end to the standard patch utilities, installpatch and backoutpatch. Using these utilities, installing and backing out a patch are distinct tasks. However, by using admclientpatch -s, you do not need to be concerned about whether you are installing or backing out a patch. The -s option ensures that admclientpatch takes the appropriate actions. It either installs the patch on the server and in the client's own file systems on the server, or it backs out the patch from the client and server and reinstalls the previous version of that patch. This is what is meant by synchronizing patches installed on the clients with patches in the patch spool directory.

If you use Host Manager to add new diskless clients and AutoClient systems to a network's configuration files, it automatically sets up those new clients with the patches in the patch spool directory. Host Manager might detect that the installation of a patch in an OS service area might have made all other clients of that service out of sync with the patch spool directory. If so, Host Manager issues a warning for you to run `admclientpatch -s` to synchronize the patches that are installed on existing diskless clients or on AutoClients with the patches in the patch spool directory.

Use the following command to verify that the patch has been added to the default patch spool directory:

```
admclientpatch -p
```

The system responds with a list of patches installed:

```
Solaris 2.4 sparc
102755-01     SunOS 5.4_x86: rpld fixes
101945-13     SunOS 5.4: jumbo patch for kernel
102039-04     SunOS 5.4: jumbo patch for package installation utilities
102066-02     SunOS 5.4: sendmail bug fixes

106828-01     SunOS:5.6: /usr/bin/date patch


Solaris 2.5 i386
102939-06     AutoClient 1.1: allow disconnected CacheFS mounts
Solaris 2.5 sparc
102906-06     AutoClient 1.1: allow disconnected CacheFS mounts
Solaris 2.5.1 i386
103007-06     AutoClient 1.1: allow disconnected CacheFS mounts
Solaris 2.5.1 ppc
102940-06     AutoClient 1.1: allow disconnected CacheFS mounts
Solaris 2.5.1 sparc
103006-06     AutoClient 1.1: allow disconnected CacheFS mounts
Solaris 2.5.1_ppc ppc
102940-06     AutoClient 1.1: allow disconnected CacheFS mounts
Solaris 2.6 sparc
106828-01     SunOS 5.6: /usr/bin/date patch
```

To verify that the patches in the Solstice AutoClient patch spool directory are running on diskless clients and AutoClient systems, use the `admclientpatch` command with the `-c` option:

```
admclientpatch -c
```

The system responds with this:

```
Clients currently installed are:
     sparc44     Solaris, 2.6, sparc
                 Patches installed :
OS Services available are:
     Solaris_2.6
                 Patches installed :  106828-01
```

This general procedure for maintaining patches assumes that the OS server (that is, the server providing OS services to clients) is the same system with the patch spool directory. However, if your site has several OS servers for your AutoClient systems, you might want to use a single file server for the patch spool directory and then mount that directory on the OS servers using NFS.

CAUTION! *Do not manually add or remove patches from the spool directory. Instead, use the* `admclientpatch` *command for all your patch administration tasks.*

Whenever you use AdminSuite Host Manager to add new clients, Host Manager consults the patch spool directory and automatically installs any relevant patches on those new clients.

Summary

This chapter discussed setting up the server. Many additional tasks take place after the OS is installed, such as setting up the NIS and the network environment. These topics are covered in Chapter 17, "Networking," and in Chapter 18, "The NFS Environment." Also, don't forget to back up your partitions (see Chapter 12, "Backup and Recovery") after you're done setting up the server.

Next we will take a look at setting up the server to support stand-alone installations using the JumpStart utility. Using JumpStart, clients on the network will look to the server for the installation of their OS.

CHAPTER

15

JumpStart

The following test objectives are covered in this chapter:

- Understanding when to use JumpStart
- Creating and testing a rules file
- Creating and testing a profile file
- Setting up JumpStart clients

There are four ways to install the Solaris software on a system: interactive installation (described in Chapter 3, "Installing the Solaris 7 Software"), custom JumpStart (described in this chapter), Web Start (described in Appendix E, "Web Start"), and installation over the network (described in Chapter 3). To install the operating system (OS) on a server, you'll use the interactive method described in Chapter 14, "Installing a Server." This chapter describes how to install the Solaris OS on clients using the custom JumpStart method.

Overview

There are two versions of JumpStart: JumpStart and custom JumpStart. JumpStart lets you automatically install the Solaris software on a SPARC-based system just by inserting the Solaris CD and powering on the system. You do not need to specify the `boot` command at the `ok` prompt. The software that is installed is specified by a default profile that is chosen based on the system's model and the size of its disks; you can't choose the software that is installed. For new SPARC systems shipped from Sun, this is the default method of installing the OS when you first power on the system.

The custom JumpStart method of installing the OS provides a way to install groups of similar systems automatically and identically. If you use the interactive method to install the OS, you must carry on a dialog with the installation program by answering various questions. At a large site with several systems that are to be configured exactly the same, this task can be monotonous and time-consuming. In addition, there is no guarantee that each system will be set up the same. Custom JumpStart solves this problem by providing a method to create sets of configuration files beforehand so that the installation process can use them to configure each system.

Custom JumpStart requires up-front work, creating custom configuration files before the systems can be installed, but it's the most efficient way to centralize and automate the OS installation at large enterprise sites. Custom JumpStart can be set up to be completely "hands off."

The custom configuration files that need to be created for JumpStart are the rules and profile files. Both of these files consist of several keywords and values and are described in this chapter.

Table 15-1 lists the various commands that are introduced in this chapter.

Table 15-1 JumpStart Commands

Command	Description
Solstice Host Manager	A GUI used to set up restart services for the clients.
setup_install_server	Sets up an install server to provide the OS to the client during a JumpStart installation.
add_install_client	Sets up a remote workstation to install Solaris from the install server.
check	Validates the information in the rules file.
pfinstall	Performs a "dry run" installation to test the profile.

Preparing for a Custom JumpStart Installation

The first step in preparing a custom JumpStart installation is to decide how you want the systems at your site to be installed. Here are some questions that need to be answered before you begin:

- Will the installation be an initial installation or an upgrade?
- What applications will the system support?
- Who will use the system?
- How much swap space is required?

These questions will help you group the systems when you create the profile and rules files later in this chapter.

Additional concerns to be addressed include what software packages need to be installed and what size to make the disk partitions. After you answer these questions, group systems according to their configuration (as shown in the example of a custom JumpStart near the end of this chapter).

The next step in preparing a custom JumpStart installation is to create the configuration files that will be used during the installation: the rules.ok file (a validated rules file) and a profile file for each group of systems. The rules.ok file is a text file that should contain a rule for each group of systems you want to install. Each rule distinguishes a group of systems based on one or more system attributes. The rule links each group to a profile, which is a text file that defines how the Solaris software is to be installed on each system in the group. Both the rules.ok file and the profiles must be located in a JumpStart directory that you define.

The custom JumpStart configuration files that you need to set up can be located on either a diskette (called a profile diskette) or a server (called a profile server). Use a profile diskette when you want to perform custom JumpStart installations on non-networked stand-alone systems. Use a profile server when you want to perform custom JumpStart installations on networked systems that have access to the server. This chapter covers both procedures.

What Happens During a Custom JumpStart Installation

This section provides a quick overview of what takes place during a custom JumpStart installation. Each step is described in detail in this chapter.

To prepare for the installation, you create a set of JumpStart configuration files, the rules and profile files, on a server that is located on the same network as the client you are installing. Next, you set up the server to provide a startup kernel that is passed to the client across the network. This is called the *startup server* (sometimes it is referred to as the *boot server*).

After the client starts up, the startup server directs the client to the JumpStart directory, which is usually located on the startup server. The configuration files in the JumpStart directory direct and automate the entire Solaris installation on the client.

To be able to start up and install the OS on a client, you need to set up three servers: a startup server, an install server, and a profile server. These can be three separate servers; however, in most cases, one server provides all these services.

Startup Server

The startup server is where the client systems access the startup files. This server must be on the local subnet (not across routers). When a client is first turned on, it does not have an OS installed or an IP address assigned; therefore, when the client is first started up, the startup server provides this information. The startup server supplies an IP address to the client by answering reverse ARP (Address Resolution Protocol), or RARP, requests from clients. RARP is a method by which a client is assigned an IP address based on a lookup of its Ethernet address. After supplying an IP address, the startup server transmits a "miniroot" kernel to the client via trivial file transfer program (tftp). The client uses this "miniroot" to start up.

Setting Up the Startup Server

The startup server is set up to answer RARP requests from clients using either the add_install_client command or the Host Manager. Before a client can start up from a startup server, the setup_install_server command is used to set up the startup server. Follow these steps to set up the startup server:

1. On the system that is the startup server, log in as root.
2. Insert and mount the Solaris 7 Hardware/Software CD into the CD-ROM drive. Change the directory to the mounted CD. Here's an example:

   ```
   cd /cdrom/sol_7_sparc/s0/Solaris_2.7/Tools
   ```

3. Use the setup_install_server command to set up the startup server. The -b option copies just the startup software from the Solaris CD to the local disk. Enter this command:

   ```
   ./setup_install_server -b <boot_dir_path>
   ```

   where -b specifies that the system is set up as a startup server and <boot_dir_path> specifies the directory where the kernel architecture is copied. (You can substitute any directory path.)

   For example, the following command copies the kernel architecture information necessary for starting up SPARC systems to be installed over the network:

   ```
   ./setup_install_server -b /export/install
   ```

   The system responds with this:

   ```
   Verifying target directory...
   Calculating space required for the installation boot image
   Copying Solaris_2.7 Tools hierarchy...
   Install Server setup complete
   ```

NOTE. *The following error indicates that there is not enough room in the directory to install the necessary files:*

```
ERROR: Insufficient space to copy Install Boot image 152691 necessary -
➥ 69372 available.
```

You'll need to either clean up files in that file system to make more room or choose a different file system.

The installation program will create a subdirectory named Solaris_2.7 in the /export/install directory.

Now that you've installed the client's startup files, you're ready to use Host Manager to set up the startup server to handle RARP requests from the clients. Host Manager is an easy-to-use GUI; it is the easiest method available. If Host Manager is not available, I suggest adding it to your server by installing Solstice AdminSuite. The installation is described in Chapter 14.

You start Host Manager by starting Solstice AdminSuite using the following command:

```
/usr/bin/solstice &
```

When the Solstice Launcher window opens, follow these steps to set up the startup server:

1. Click the Host Manager icon, shown in Figure 15-1.

Figure 15-1
The Solstice Launcher window.

The Host Manager window opens, asking you to select a naming service, as shown in Figure 15-2. (For this example, I selected None and then clicked OK.)

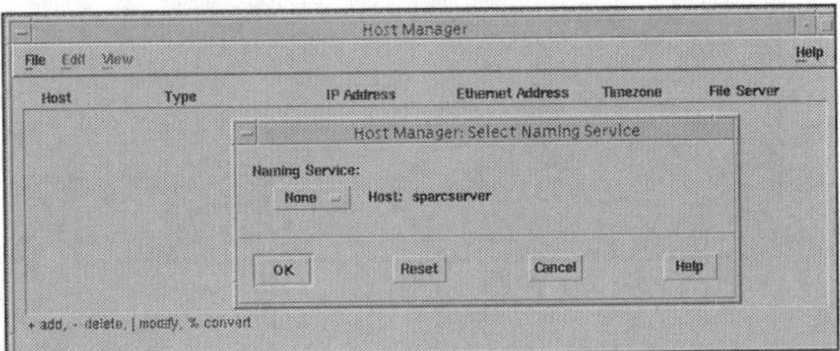

Figure 15-2
Select a naming service.

2. The Host Manager window opens, as shown in Figure 15-3.

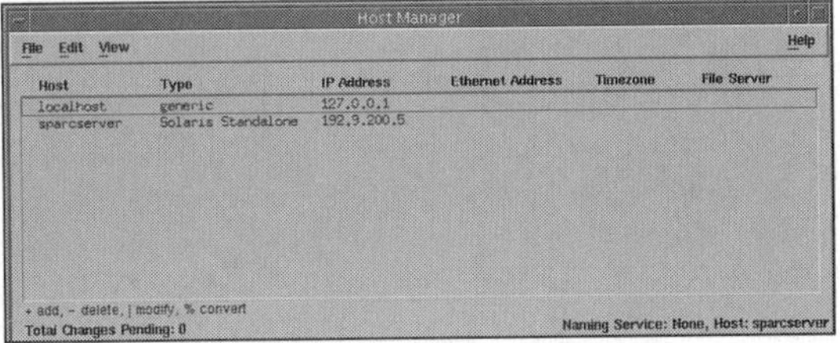

Figure 15-3
The Host Manager window.

3. Now you need to add information for the client. Select Edit, Add from the Host Manager window, as shown in Figure 15-4.

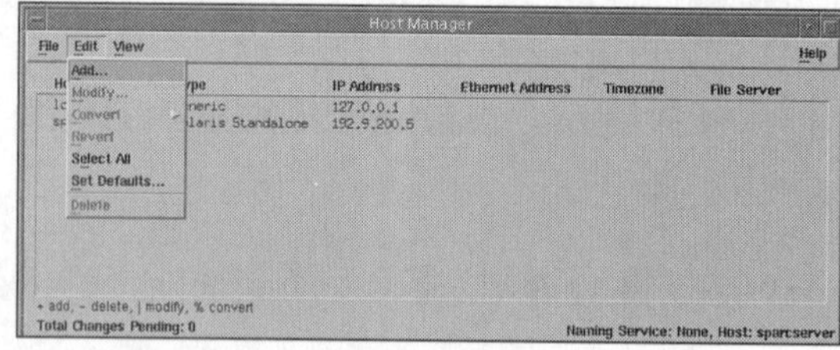

Figure 15-4
The Host Manager Edit menu.

4. The Host Manager: Add window opens, as shown in Figure 15-5.

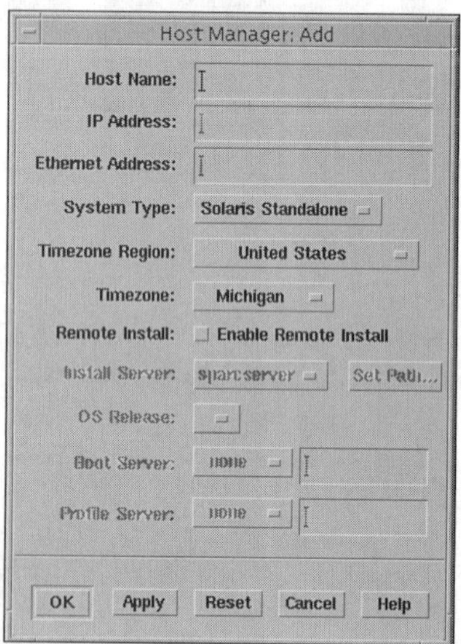

Figure 15-5
The Host Manager: Add window.

5. Table 15-2 describes all the fields in the Host Manager: Add window. Enter the hostname, IP address, and Ethernet address of the host you would like to add, and then click OK.

Table 15-2 Host Manager: Add Window Fields

Field	Description
Host Name	Specifies the host name of the client to be installed over the network. This is not the host name of the install server.
IP Address	Specifies the IP address to be assigned to the client (such as 192.9.200.5).
Ethernet Address	Specifies the client's hexadecimal Ethernet address (such as 8:0:20:1a:c7:e3).
System Type	Specifies whether the client is a stand-alone or server.
Timezone Region	Enters your time zone.
Remote Install	Enables Remote Install. This allows the client to start up from the specified install server.
Install Server	Specifies the install server and path to where the software resides. The default is the current server and the CD-ROM.
OS Release	Specifies the client architecture and Solaris release.
Boot Server	Specifies the startup server if you aren't using the current server.
Profile Server	Specifies the profile server and path to the installation configuration information.

The startup server is set up and ready to provide startup services to a client.

Install Server

The install server, sometimes called a media server, supplies the OS during a JumpStart installation. An install server can use either the Solaris CD image in its CD-ROM drive or a copy of the Solaris CD, which you can copy to the install server's hard disk. Network installations that use a Solaris CD image copied on an install server's hard disk are faster than installations from a CD-ROM drive.

Setting Up the Install Server

Creating an install server involves these steps:

1. Choose a system with a CD-ROM drive to be the install server.
2. Mount the Solaris CD as follows:

   Using the `setup_install_server` command, copy the Solaris CD to the install server's local disk. (This is an optional step, but if you load the CD image to the server's hard disk, the client installation will be much quicker.) To load the Solaris CD onto a local disk, follow these steps:

a. On the system that will be the install server, log in as root.

b. Insert and mount the Solaris CD into the CD-ROM drive.

c. Change to the following directory on the mounted CD:

```
cd /cdrom/sol_7 sparc/s0/Solaris_2.7/Tools
```

d. Use the `setup_install_server` command to copy the contents of the Solaris CD to the install server's local disk:

```
./setup_install_server <path>
```

`<path>` specifies the local directory where the Solaris CD image is copied on the install server. You can specify any directory path. For example, the following command copies the CD image from the Solaris CD to the /export/install directory on the local disk:

```
./setup_install_server /export/install
```

A subdirectory named Solaris 2.7 will be created in the /export/install directory.

NOTE. *The* `setup_install_server` *command tells you if you do not have enough disk space to copy the CD image from the Solaris CD.*

3. After copying the Solaris CD, you can use the `patchadd -c` command to patch the Solaris CD image on the install server's hard disk so that every client does not need to be patched after the installation.

Profile Server

If you are setting up custom JumpStart installations for systems on the network, you have to create a directory on a server called a JumpStart directory. This directory contains all the essential custom JumpStart configuration files, such as the rules file, the rules.ok file, and the profile.

The server that contains a JumpStart directory is called a profile server. It is usually the same system as the install or startup server, although it can be a completely different server. The JumpStart directory on the profile server should be owned by root and should have permissions set to 755.

Setting Up the Profile Server

To set up a profile server, follow these steps:

1. Choose the system that acts as the server, and log in as root.
2. Create the JumpStart directory anywhere on the server (such as mkdir/jumpstart).

3. To be certain that this directory is shared across the network, edit the /etc/dfs/dfstab file and add the following entry:

   ```
   share -F nfs -o ro,anon=0 /jumpstart
   ```

4. Type `shareall` and press Enter.
5. Place the JumpStart files (that is, rules, rules.ok, and profiles) in the /jumpstart directory.

When you create a profile server, you must make sure that systems can access it during a custom JumpStart installation. Every time you add a system for network installation, you need to either use the `-c` option of the `add_install_client` command or specify the profile server in Host Manager. The section "A Sample JumpStart Installation" near the end of this chapter describes how to specify the profile server in Host Manager to set up your clients for a network installation.

Setting Up a Profile Diskette

An alternative to setting up a profile server is to create a profile diskette (provided that the system to be installed has a diskette drive). If you use a diskette for custom JumpStart installations, the essential custom JumpStart files (the rules file, the rules.ok file, and the profiles) must reside in the root directory on the diskette. The diskette that contains JumpStart files is called a profile diskette. The custom JumpStart files on the diskette should be owned by root and should have permissions equal to 755. Here are the steps to create a profile diskette:

1. Format the diskette by typing

   ```
   fdformat -U
   ```

2. Create a UFS file system on the diskette. If your system uses Volume Manager, insert the diskette, and it will be mounted automatically.
3. Create a file system on the diskette by issuing the `newfs` command:

   ```
   newfs /vol/dev/aliases/floppy0
   ```

   (The `newfs` command is covered in Chapter 4, "Introduction to File Systems.")
4. Eject the diskette by typing

   ```
   eject floppy
   ```

5. Insert the formatted diskette back into the diskette drive.

You have completed the creation of a profile diskette. Now you can create the rules file and create profiles on the profile diskette to perform custom JumpStart installations.

The Rules File

The rules file is a text file that should contain a rule for each group of systems you want to install automatically. Each rule distinguishes a group of systems based on one or more system attributes and links each group to a profile, which is a text file that defines how the Solaris software is installed on each system in the group.

After deciding how you want each group of systems at your site to be installed, you need to create a rules file for each specific group of systems to be installed. The rules.ok file is a generated version of the rules file that the Solaris installation program uses to perform a custom JumpStart installation.

After you create the rules file, validate it with the check script by changing to the /jumpstart directory and issuing the `check` command. If the check script runs successfully, it creates the rules.ok file. During a custom JumpStart installation, the Solaris installation program reads the rules.ok file and tries to find the first rule that has a system attribute matching the system being installed. If a match occurs, the installation program uses the profile specified in the rule to install the system.

A sample rules file for a Sparcstation LX is shown next. Notice that all the lines in the file are commented out. These are simply instructions and sample entries to help the system administrator make the correct entry. The last, uncommented line is the rule I added for the example. I'll describe the syntax later. Each line in the code table has a rule keyword and a valid value for that keyword. The Solaris installation program scans the rules file from top to bottom. If the program matches an uncommented rule keyword and value with a known system, it installs the Solaris software specified by the profile listed in the profile field.

```
#
#       @(#)rules 1.12 94/07/27 SMI
#
# The rules file is a text file used to create the rules.ok file for
# a custom JumpStart installation. The rules file is a lookup table
# consisting of one or more rules that define matches between system
# attributes and profiles.
#
# This example rules file contains:
#   o syntax of a rule used in the rules file
#   o rule_keyword and rule_value descriptions
#   o rule examples
#
# See the installation manual for a complete description of the rules file.
#
#
###########################################################################
#
# RULE SYNTAX:
#
# [!]rule_keyword rule_value [&& [!]rule_keyword rule_value]... begin profile finish
#
```

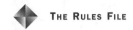

```
#     "[ ]"  indicates an optional expression or field
#     "..."  indicates the preceding expression may be repeated
#      "&&"  used to "logically AND" rule_keyword and rule_value pairs together
#       "!"  indicates negation of the following rule_keyword
#
#  rule_keyword          a predefined keyword that describes a general system
#                        attribute. It is used with the rule_value to match a
#                        system with the same attribute to a profile.
#
#  rule_value            a value that provides the specific system attribute
#                        for the corresponding rule_keyword. A rule_value can
#                        be text or a range of values (NN-MM).
#                        To match a range of values, a system's value must be
#                        greater than or equal to NN and less than or equal to MM.
#
#  begin                 a file name of an optional Bourne shell script
#                        that will be executed before the installation begins.
#                        If no begin script exists, you must enter a minus sign (-)
#                        in this field.
#
#  profile               a file name of a text file used as a template by the
#                        custom JumpStart installation software that defines how
#                        to install Solaris on a system.
#
#  finish                a file name of an optional Bourne shell script
#                        that will be executed after the installation completes.
#                        If no finish script exists, you must enter a minus sign (-)
#                        in this field.
#
# Notes:
# 1.        You can add comments after the pound sign (#) anywhere on a line.
# 2.        Rules are matched in descending order: first rule through the last rule.
# 3.        Rules can be continued to a new line by using the backslash (\) before
#           the carriage return.
# 4.        Don't use the "*" character or other shell wildcards, because the rules
#           file is interpreted by a Bourne shell script.
#
#
###############################################################################
#
# RULE_KEYWORD AND RULE_VALUE DESCRIPTIONS
#
#
#       rule_keyword   rule_value Type      rule_value Description
# ------------     --------------      ---------------------
#       any            minus sign (-)       always matches
#       arch           text                 system's architecture type
#       domainname     text                 system's domain name
#       disksize       text range           system's disk size
#                                           disk device name (text)
#                                           disk size (MBytes range)
#       hostname       text                 system's host name
```

```
#        installed      text text          system's installed version of Solaris
#                                          disk device name (text)
#                                          OS release (text)
#        karch          text               system's kernel architecture
#        memsize        range              system's memory size (MBytes range)
#        model          text               system's model number
#        network        text               system's IP address
#        totaldisk      range              system's total disk size (MBytes range)
#
#
##########################################################################
#
# RULE EXAMPLES
#
# The following rule matches only one system:
#

#hostname sample_host     -        host_class       set_root_pw

# The following rule matches any system that is on the 924.222.43.0 network
# and has the sun4c kernel architecture:
#    Note: The backslash (\) is used to continue the rule to a new line.

#network 924.222.43.0 && \
#        karch sun4c      -        net924_sun4c       -

# The following rule matches any sparc system with a c0t3d0 disk that is
# between 400 to 600 MBytes and has Solaris 2.1 installed on it:

#arch sparc && \
#               disksize c0t3d0 400-600 && \
#               installed c0t3d0s0 solaris_2.1 - upgrade   -

#
# The following rule matches all x86 systems:

#arch i386   x86-begin   x86-class   -

#
# The following rule matches any system:

#any -    -    any_machine   -
#
# END RULE EXAMPLES
#
#
hostname pyramid2         -           sparc_lx          -
```

Table 15-3 describes the syntax that the rules file must follow.

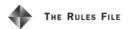

Table 15-3 Rule Syntax

Field	Description
!	Use this before a rule keyword to indicate negation.
[ ]	Use this to indicate an optional expression or field.
...	Use this to indicate that the preceding expression might be repeated.
`rule_keyword`	A predefined keyword that describes a general system attribute, such as a host-name (`hostname`) or the memory size (`memsize`). It is used with `rule_value` to match a system with the same attribute to a profile. The complete list of `rule_keywords` is described in Table 15-4.
`rule_value`	Provides the specific system attribute value for the corresponding `rule_keyword`. See Table 15-4 for the list of `rule_values`.
&&	Use this to join rule keyword and rule value pairs in the same rule (a logical AND). During a custom JumpStart installation, a system must match every pair in the rule before the rule matches.
`<begin>`	A name of an optional Bourne shell script that can be executed before the installation begins. If no begin script exists, you must enter a minus sign (-) in this field. All begin scripts must reside in the JumpStart directory. See the section "begin and finish Scripts" for more information.
`<profile>`	The name of a text file that defines how the Solaris software is installed on the system if a system matches the rule. The information in a profile consists of profile keywords and their corresponding profile values. All profiles must reside in the JumpStart directory. Profiles are described in the section "Creating Profiles."
`<finish>`	The name of an optional Bourne shell script that can be executed after the installation completes. If no finish script exists, you must enter a minus sign (-) in this field. All finish scripts must reside in the JumpStart directory. See the section "begin and finish Scripts" for more information.

The rules file must have the following:

- At least one rule
- The name "rules"
- At least a rule keyword, a rule value, and a corresponding profile
- A minus sign (-) in the `begin` and `finish` fields if there is no entry

The rules file should be saved in the JumpStart directory, should be owned by root, and should have permissions equal to 644.

The rules.ok file allows the following:

- A comment after the pound sign (#) anywhere on a line. If a line begins with a #, the entire line is a comment. If a # is specified in the middle of a line, everything after the # is considered a comment.
- Blank lines.
- Rules to span multiple lines. You can let a rule wrap to a new line, or you can continue a rule on a new line by using a backslash (\) before Enter gets pressed.

Table 15-4 describes the various `rule_keywords` and `rule_values` that were introduced earlier.

Table 15-4 Rule Keyword and Rule Value Descriptions

Rule Keyword	Rule Value	Description
`any`	Minus sign (-)	The match always succeeds.
`arch`	`processor_type`	The following table lists the valid values for `processor_type`:

`platform`
SPARC
x86
	`processor_type`
	`sparc`
	`i386`
		Matches a system's processor type. The `uname -p` command reports the system's processor type.

`domainname`	`domain_name`	Matches a system's domain name, which controls how a name service determines information. If you have a system already installed, the `domainname` command reports the system's domain name.
disksize	<disk_name> <size_range> <disk_name> A disk name in the form c?t?d?, such as c0t3d0, or the special word rootdisk. If rootdisk is used, the disk to be matched is determined in the following order: 1. The disk that contains the preinstalled boot image (a new SPARC-based system with factory JumpStart installed)	Matches a system's disk (in MB). Example: disksize c0t3d0 250-300 This example tries to match a system with a c0t3d0 disk that is between 250 and 300MB.

Table 15-4 Rule Keyword and Rule Value Descriptions (continued)

Rule Keyword	Rule Value	Description
	2. The c0t3d0s0 disk, if it exists. 3. The first available disk (searched in kernel probe order). 4. <size_range> The size of disk, which must be specified as a range of MB (xx-xx).	Note: When calculating `size_range`, remember that a megabyte equals 1,048,576 bytes. A disk might be advertised as a "535MB" disk, but it might have only 510 million bytes of disk space. The Solaris installation program views the "535MB" disk as a 510MB disk because 535,000,000 / 1,048,576 = 510. Therefore, a "535MB" disk would not match a `size_range` equal to 530 to 550MB.
`hostaddress`	<IP_address>	Matches a system's IP address.
`hostname`	<host_name>	Matches a system's host name. If you have a system already installed, the `uname -n` command reports the system's host name.
`installed`	<slice> <version> <slice> A disk slice name in the form c?t?d?s?, such as c0t3d0s5, or the special words `any` or `rootdisk`. If `any` is used, all the system's disks will try to be matched (in kernel probe order). If `rootdisk` is used, the disk to be matched is determined in the following order: 1. The disk that contains the preinstalled boot image (a new SPARC-based system with factory JumpStart installed). 2. The c0t3d0s0 disk, if it exists. 3. The first available disk (searched in kernel probe order).	Matches a disk that has a root file system corresponding to a particular version of Solaris software. Example: `installed c0t3d0s1 Solaris_2.5` This example tries to match a system that has a Solaris 2.5 root file system on 0t3d0s1.

continues

Table 15-4 Rule Keyword and Rule Value Descriptions (continued)

Rule Keyword	Rule Value	Description
	4. `<version>` A version name, Solaris_2.x, or the special words any or `upgrade`. If any is used, any Solaris or SunOS release is matched. If `upgrade` is used, any upgradable Solaris 2.1 or greater release is matched. Matches a disk that has a root file system corresponding to a particular version of Solaris software.	
`karch`	`<platform_group>` Valid values are `sun4d`, `sun4c`, `sun4m`, `sun4u`, `i86pc`, and `prep`.	Matches a system's platform group. If you have a system already installed, the `arch -k` command or the `uname -m` command reports the system's platform group.
`memsize`	`<physical_mem>` The value must be a range of MB (xx-xx) or a single MB value.	Matches a system's physical memory size (in MB). Example: `memsize 16-32` The example tries to match a system with a physical memory size between 16 and 32MB. If you have a system already installed, the output of the `prtconf` command (line 2) reports the system's physical memory size.
`model`	`<platform_name>`	Matches a system's platform name. Any valid platform name will work. To find the platform name of an installed system, use the `uname -i` command or the output of the `prtconf` command (line 5). Note: If the `<platform_name>` contains spaces, you must enclose it in single quotes (`'`). Example: `'SUNW,Sun 4_50'`

Table 15-4 Rule Keyword and Rule Value Descriptions (continued)

Rule Keyword	Rule Value	Description
`network`	`<network_num>`	Matches a system's network number, which the Solaris installation program determines by performing a logical AND between the system's IP address and the subnet mask. Example: `network 193.144.2.1` This example tries to match a system with a 193.144.2.0 IP address (if the subnet mask were 255.255.255.0).
`osname`	`<Solaris_2.x>`	Matches a version of Solaris software already installed on a system. Example: `osname Solaris_2.5` This example tries to match a system with Solaris 2.5 already installed.
`totaldisk`	`<size_range>` The value must be specified as a range of MB (xx-xx).	Matches the total disk space on a system (in MB). The total disk space includes all the operational disks attached to a system. Example: `totaldisk 300-500` This example tries to match a system with a total disk space between 300 and 500MB.

During a custom JumpStart installation, the Solaris installation program attempts to match the system being installed to the rules in the rules.ok file in order—the first rule through the last rule. A rule match occurs when the system being installed matches all the system attributes defined in the rule. As soon as a system matches a rule, the Solaris installation program stops reading the rules.ok file and begins installing the software based on the matched rule's profile.

For example, the rule `karch sun4c - basic_prof -` specifies that the Solaris installation program should automatically install any system with the sun4c platform group based on the information in the basic_prof profile.

As another example, `hostname pyramid2 - sparc_lx -` specifies that the Solaris installation program will automatically install a system named pyramid2 based on the information in the sparc_lx profile. No `begin` or finish script is specified.

Validating the Rules File

Before the rules file can be used, you must run the check script to validate that this file is set up correctly. If all the rules are valid, the rules.ok file is created. It is required by the custom JumpStart installation software to match a system to a profile.

To validate the rules file, make sure that the check script resides in the JumpStart directory. The check script is provided in the Solaris_2.7/Misc/jumpstart_sample directory on the Solaris CD.

Change the directory to the JumpStart directory and run the check script to validate the rules file:

```
./check [-p path] [-r file_name]
```

The check script options are described in Table 15-5.

Table 15-5 check Script Options

Option	Description
-p <path>	Validates the rules file by using the check script from a specified Solaris 7 CD image, instead of the check script from the system you are using. <path> is the pathname to a Solaris installation image on a local disk or a mounted Solaris CD. Use this option to run the most recent version of check if your system is running a previous version of Solaris.
-r <file_name>	Specifies a rules file other than a file named "rules." Using this option, you can test the validity of a rule before integrating it into the rules file.

When you use check to validate a rules file, the following things happen:

1. The rules file is checked for syntax. check makes sure that the rule keywords are legitimate, and the <begin>, <class>, and <finish> fields are specified for each rule.
2. If no errors are found in the rules file, each profile specified in the rules file is checked for syntax.
3. If no errors are found, check creates the rules.ok file from the rules file, removing all comments and blank lines, retaining all the rules, and adding the following comment line to the end:

   ```
   version=2 checksum=num
   ```

4. As the check script runs, it reports that it is checking the validity of the rules file and the validity of each profile. If no errors are encountered, it reports the following:

   ```
   The custom JumpStart configuration is ok.
   ```

The following is a sample session that uses check to validate a rules file. I named it rulestest temporarily, and I am using the `-r` option. With `-r`, the rules.ok file is not created, and only the rulestest file is checked.

```
# ./check /tmp/rulestest
Usage: check [-r <rules filename>] [-p <Solaris 2.x CD image path>]
# ./check -r /tmp/rules
Validating /tmp/rulestest...
Validating profile host_class...
Validating profile net924_sun4c...
Validating profile upgrade...
Validating profile x86-class...

Error in file "/tmp/rulestest", line 113
                any - - any_maine -
ERROR: Profile missing: any_maine
```

In this example, the check script found a bad option. I misspelled "any_machine" as "any_maine." The check script reported this error.

In the next example, I fixed the error, copied the file from rulestest to rules, and re-ran the check script:

```
#cp rulestest rules
# ./check
Validating /tmp/rules...
Validating profile host_class...
Validating profile net924_sun4c...
Validating profile upgrade...
Validating profile x86-class...
Validating profile any_machine...
The custom JumpStart configuration is ok.
```

As the check script runs, it reports that it is checking the validity of the rules file and the validity of each profile. If no errors are encountered, it reports `The custom JumpStart configuration is ok`. The rules file is now validated.

After the rules.ok file is created, verify that it is owned by `root` and that it has permissions equal to 644.

begin and finish Scripts

A begin script is a user-defined Bourne shell script, specified within the rules file, that performs tasks before the Solaris software is installed on the system. You can set up begin scripts to perform the following tasks:

- Backing up a file system before upgrading
- Saving files to a safe location
- Loading other applications

Output from the begin script goes to /var/sadm/begin.log.

CAUTION! *Be careful not to specify something in the script that would prevent the mounting of file systems to /a during an initial or upgrade installation. If the Solaris installation program cannot mount the file systems to /a, an error occurs, and the installation fails.*

begin scripts should be owned by root and should have permissions equal to 744.

In addition to begin scripts, you can also have finish scripts. A finish script is a user-defined Bourne shell script, specified within the rules file, that performs tasks after the Solaris software is installed on the system but before the system restarts. finish scripts can be used only with custom JumpStart installations. You can set up finish scripts to perform the following tasks:

- Move saved files back into place
- Add packages or patches
- Set the system's root password

Output from the finish script goes to /var/sadm/finish.log.

When used to add patches and software packages, begin and finish scripts can ensure that the installation is consistent between all systems.

Creating Profiles

A profile is a text file that defines how to install the Solaris software on a system. Every rule in the rules file specifies a profile that defines how a system is installed when the rule is matched. You usually create a different profile for every rule; however, the same profile can be used in more than one rule.

A profile consists of one or more profile keywords (they are described in the following sections). Each profile keyword is a command that controls one aspect of how the Solaris installation program installs the Solaris software on a system. Use the vi editor to create a profile in the JumpStart directory. You can create a new profile or edit one of the sample profiles located in /cdrom/cdrom0/s0/Solaris_2.7/Misc on the Solaris CD. The profile can be named anything, but it should reflect the way in which it installs the Solaris software on a system. Sample names are basic_install, eng_profile, and accntg_profile.

A profile must have the following:

- The `install_type` profile keyword as the first entry

- Only one profile keyword on a line
- The `root_device` keyword if the systems being upgraded by the profile have more than one root file system that can be upgraded

A profile allows the following:

- A comment after the pound sign (#) anywhere on a line. If a line begins with a #, the entire line is a comment. If a # is specified in the middle of a line, everything after the # is considered a comment.
- Blank lines

The profile is made up of profile keywords and their values. They are described in the following sections.

backup_media

`backup_media` defines the medium that is used to back up file systems if they need to be reallocated during an upgrade because of space problems. If multiple tapes or disks are required for the backup, you are prompted to insert these during the upgrade. Here is the `backup_media` syntax:

```
backup_media <type> <path>
```

`type` can be one of the keywords listed in Table 15-6.

Table 15-6 *backup_media* Keywords

Keyword	Description
`local_tape`	Specifies a local tape drive on the system being upgraded. The `<path>` must be the character (raw) device path for the tape drive, such as /dev/rmt/0.
`local_diskette`	Specifies a local diskette drive on the system being upgraded. The `<path>` is the local diskette, such as /dev/rdiskette0. The diskette must be formatted.
`local_filesystem`	Specifies a local file system on the system being upgraded. The `<path>` can be a block device path for a disk slice or the absolute `<path>` to a file system mounted by the /etc/vfstab file. Examples of `<path>` are /dev/dsk/c0t0d0s7 and /home.
`remote_filesystem`	Specifies an NFS file system on a remote system. The `<path>` must include the name or IP address of the remote system (host) and the absolute `<path>` to the NFS file system. The NFS file system must have read/write access. A sample `<path>` is sparc1:/home.

continues

Table 15-6 *backup_media* Keywords (continued)

Keyword	Description
remote_system	Specifies a directory on a remote system that can be reached by a remote shell (rsh). The system being upgraded must have access to the remote system through the remote system's .rhosts file. The <path> must include the name of the remote system and the absolute path to the directory. If a user login is not specified, the login is tried as root. A sample <path> is bcalkins@sparc1:/home.

Here are some examples:

```
backup_media local_tape /dev/rmt/0

backup_media local_diskette /dev/rdiskette0

backup_media local_filesystem /dev/dsk/c0t3d0s7

backup_media local_filesystem /export

backup_media remote_filesystem sparc1:/export/temp

backup_media remote_system bcalkins@sparc1:/export/temp
```

`backup_media` must be used with the `upgrade` option only when disk space re-allocation is necessary.

boot_device

`boot_device` designates the device where the installation program installs the root file system and consequently what the system's startup device is. The `EEPROM` value also lets you update the system's `EEPROM` if you change its current startup device so that the system can automatically start up from the new startup device.

Here's the `boot_device` syntax:

```
boot_device <device> <eeprom>
```

The `device` and `eeprom` values are described in Table 15-7.

Table 15-7 *boot_device* Keywords

Keyword	Description
<device>	Specifies the startup device by specifying a disk slice, such as c0t1d0s0. It can be the keyword `existing`, which places the root file system on the existing startup device, or the keyword any, which lets the installation program choose where to put the root file system.

Table 15-7 *boot_device* Keywords (continued)

Keyword	Description
`<eeprom>`	Specifies whether you want to update the system's EEPROM to the specified startup device. `<eeprom>` specifies the value `update`, which tells the installation program to update the system's EEPROM to the specified startup device, or `preserve`, which leaves the startup device value in the system's EEPROM unchanged. An example is `boot_device c0t1d0s0 update`.

The installation program installs the root file system on c0t1d0s0 and updates the EEPROM to start up automatically from the new startup device.

client_arch

`client_arch` indicates that the OS server supports a platform group other than its own. If you do not specify `client_arch`, any diskless client or Solstice AutoClient system that uses the OS server must have the same platform group as the server. `client_arch` can be used only when `system_type` is specified as the server. You must specify each platform group that you want the OS server to support.

Here's the `client_arch` syntax:

```
client_arch karch_value [karch_value...]
```

Values for `karch_value` include `sun4d`, `sun4c`, `sun4m`, `sun4u`, and `i86pc`.

Here's an example:

```
client_arch sun4m
```

client_root

`client_root` defines the amount of root space, in MB, to allocate for each client. If you do not specify `client_root` in a server's profile, the installation software automatically allocates 15MB of root space per client. The size of the client root area is used in combination with the `num_clients` keyword to determine how much space to reserve for the /export/root file system.

Here's the syntax:

```
client_root root_size
```

`root_size` is specified in MB.

Here's an example:

```
client_root 20
```

client_swap

`client_swap` defines the amount of swap space, in MB, to allocate for each diskless client. If you do not specify `client_swap`, 32MB of swap space is allocated. Physical memory plus swap space must be a minimum of 32MB. If a profile does not explicitly specify the size of swap, the Solaris installation program determines the maximum size that the swap file can be, based on the system's physical memory. The Solaris installation program makes the size of swap no more than 20 percent of the disk where it resides, unless there is free space left on the disk after the other file systems are laid out.

Here's the syntax:

```
client_swap swap_size
```

`swap_size` is specified in MB.

Here's an example:

```
client_swap 64
```

This example specifies that each diskless client has a swap space of 64MB.

cluster

`cluster` designates what software group to add to the system. The software groups are listed in Table 15-8.

Table 15-8 Software Groups

Software Group	*group_name*
Core	XSUNWCreq
End-user system support	SUNWCuser
Developer system support	SUNWCprog
Entire distribution	SUNWCall
Entire distribution plus OEM support	SUNWCXall (SPARC-based systems only)

You can specify only one software group in a profile, and it must be specified before other cluster and package entries. If you do not specify a software group with `cluster`, the end-user software group, SUNWCuser, is installed on the system by default.

Here is `cluster`'s syntax:

```
cluster group_name
```

Here's an example:

```
cluster SUNWCall
```

This example specifies that the Entire Distribution group should be installed.

The `cluster` keyword can also be used to designate whether a cluster should be added to or deleted from the software group that was installed on the system. `add` and `delete` indicate whether the cluster should be added or deleted. If you do not specify `add` or `delete`, `add` is set by default.

Here's the syntax:

```
cluster cluster_name [add | delete]
```

`cluster_name` must be in the form SUNWCname. To view detailed information about clusters and their names, start AdminTool on an installed system and choose Browse, Software.

dontuse

`dontuse` designates one or more disks that you don't want the Solaris installation program to use. By default, the installation program uses all the operational disks on the system. `disk_name` must be specified in the form c?t?d? or c?d?, such as c0t0d0.

Here's the syntax:

```
dontuse disk_name [disk_name...]
```

Here's an example:

```
dontuse c0t0d0 c0t1d0
```

NOTE. *You cannot specify the* `usedisk` *keyword and the* `dontuse` *keyword in the same profile.*

filesys

`filesys` sets up the installed system to mount remote file systems automatically when it starts up. You can specify `filesys` more than once. The following syntax describes using `filesys` to set up mounts to remote systems:

```
filesys <server>:<path> <server_address> <mount_pt_name> [mount_options]
```

The `filesys` keywords are described in Table 15-9.

Table 15-9 ***filesys* Keywords**

Keyword	Description
`<server>:`	The name of the server where the remote file system resides. Don't forget to include the colon (:).
`<path>`	The remote file system's mount point name.
`<server_address>`	The IP address of the server specified in `server:path`. If you don't have a name service running on the network, this value can be used to populate the /etc/hosts file with the server's IP address, but you must specify a minus sign (-).
`<mount_pt_name>`	The name of the mount point that the remote file system is mounted on.
`[mount_options]`	One or more mount options that are added to the /etc/vfstab entry for the specified `mount_pt_name`. If you need to specify more than one mount option, the mount options must be separated by commas and no spaces. An example is `ro,quota`.

Here's an example:

```
filesys zeus:/export/home/user1 192.9.200.1 /home ro,bg,intr
```

`filesys` can also be used to create local file systems during the installation by using this syntax:

```
filesys <slice> <size> [file_system] [optional_parameters]
```

The values listed in Table 15-10 can be used for `<slice>`.

Table 15-10 ***<slice>* Values**

Value	Description
`any`	This variable tells the installation program to place the file system on any disk.
`c?t?d?s?` or `c?d??z`	The disk slice where the Solaris installation program places the file system, such as c0t0d0s0.
`rootdisk.sn`	The variable that contains the value for the system's root disk, which is determined by the Solaris installation program. The `sn` suffix indicates a specific slice on the disk.

The values listed in Table 15-11 can be used for `<size>`.

Table 15-11 *<size>* Values

Value	Description
`num`	The size of the file system in MB.
`existing`	The current size of the existing file system.
`auto`	The size of the file system is determined automatically, depending on the selected software.
`all`	The specified slice uses the entire disk for the file system. When you specify this value, no other file systems can reside on the specified disk.
`free`	The remaining unused space on the disk is used for the file system.
`start:size`	The file system is explicitly partitioned. `start` is the cylinder where the slice begins, and `size` is the number of cylinders for the slice.

`file_system` is an optional field when `slice` is specified as `any` or `c?t?d?s?`. If `file_system` is not specified, `unnamed` is set by default, but you can't specify the `optional_parameters` value.

The values listed in Table 15-12 can be used for `file_system`.

Table 15-12 *file_system* Values

Value	Description
`mount_pt_name`	The file system's mount point name, such as /opt.
`swap`	The specified slice is used as swap.
`overlap`	The specified slice is defined as a representation of the whole disk. `overlap` can be specified only when `<size>` is `existing`, `all`, or `start:size`.
`unnamed`	The specified slice is defined as a raw slice, so the slice does not have a mount point name. If `file_system` is not specified, `unnamed` is set by default.
`ignore`	The specified slice is not used or recognized by the Solaris installation program. This can be used to ignore a file system on a disk during an installation so that the Solaris installation program can create a new file system on the same disk with the same name. `ignore` can be used only when existing partitioning is specified.

In the following example, the size of swap is set to 32MB, and it is installed on c0t3d0s1:

```
filesys                 c0t3d0s1 32 swap
```

In the next example, /usr is based on the selected software, and the installation program determines what disk to put it on when you specify the any value:

```
filesys                 any auto /usr
```

The optional_parameters field can be one of the options listed in Table 15-13.

Table 15-13 *optional_parameters* Options

Option	Description
preserve	The file system on the specified slice is preserved. preserve can be specified only when size is existing and slice is c?t?d?s?.
mount_options	One or more mount options that are added to the /etc/vfstab entry for the specified mount_pt_name.

install_type

install_type specifies whether to perform the initial installation option or the upgrade option on the system. install_type must be the first profile keyword in every profile.

Here's the syntax:

```
install_type [initial_install | upgrade]
```

Select either initial_install or upgrade.

Here's an example:

```
install_type initial_install
```

layout_constraint

layout_constraint designates the constraint that auto-layout has on a file system if it needs to be re-allocated during an upgrade because of space problems. layout_constraint can be used only for the upgrade option when disk space re-allocation is required.

With layout_constraint, you specify the file system and the constraint you want to put on it.

Here's the syntax:

```
layout_constraint <slice> <constraint> [minimum_size]
```

The <slice> field specifies the file system disk slice on which to specify the constraint. It must be specified in the form c?t?d?s? or c?d?s?.

Table 15-14 describes the options for layout_constraint.

Table 15-14 ***layout_constraint*** **Options**

Option	Description
changeable	Auto-layout can move the file system to another location and can change its size. You can change the file system's size by specifying the minimum_size value. When you mark a file system as changeable and minimum_size is not specified, the file system's minimum size is set to 10 percent greater than the minimum size required. For example, if the minimum size for a file system is 100MB, the changed size would be 110MB. If minimum_size is specified, any free space left over (the original size minus the minimum size) is used for other file systems.
movable	Auto-layout can move the file system to another slice on the same disk or on a different disk, and its size stays the same.
available	Auto-layout can use all the space on the file system to re-allocate space. All the data in the file system is then lost. This constraint can be specified only on file systems that are not mounted by the /etc/vfstab file.
collapse	Auto-layout moves (collapses) the specified file system into its parent file system. You can use this option to reduce the number of file systems on a system as part of the upgrade. For example, if the system has the /usr and /usr/openwin file systems, collapsing the /usr/openwin file system would move it into /usr (its parent).
minimum_size	This value lets you change the size of a file system by specifying the size you want it to be after auto-layout re-allocates. The size of the file system might end up being more if unallocated space is added to it, but the size is never less than the value you specify. You can use this optional value only if you have marked a file system as changeable. The minimum size cannot be less than the file system needs for its existing contents.

The following are some examples:

```
layout_constraint c0t3d0s1 changeable 200
```

The file system c0t3d0s1 can be moved to another location, and its size can be changed to more than 200MB but no less than 200MB.

```
layout_constraint c0t0d0s4 movable
```

The file system on slice c0t0d0s4 can move to another disk slice, but its size stays the same.

```
layout_constraint c0t2d0s1 collapse
```

c0t2d0s1 is moved into its parent directory to reduce the number of file systems.

locale

`locale` designates which language or locale packages should be installed for the specified `locale_name`. A locale determines how online information is displayed for a specific language or region, such as date, time, spelling, and monetary value. Therefore, if you want English as your language but you also want to use the monetary values for Australia, you would choose the Australia locale value (`en_AU`) instead of the English language value (`C`).

The English language packages are installed by default. You can specify a `locale` keyword for each language or locale you need to add to a system.

Here's the `locale` syntax:

```
locale locale_name
```

Here's an example:

```
locale es
```

This example specifies Spanish as the language package you want installed.

num_clients

When a server is installed, space is allocated for each diskless client's root (/) and swap file systems. `num_clients` defines the number of diskless clients that a server supports. If you do not specify `num_clients`, five diskless clients are allocated.

Here's the syntax:

```
num_clients client_num
```

Here's an example:

```
num_clients 10
```

In this example, space is allocated for 10 diskless clients.

package

`package` designates whether a package should be added to or deleted from the software group that is installed on the system. `add` or `delete` indicates the action required. If you do not specify `add` or `delete`, `add` is set by default.

Here's the syntax:

```
package package_name [add | delete]
```

`package_name` must be in the form `SUNWname`.

Here's an example:

```
package SUNWxwman delete
```

In this example, `SUNWxwman` (X Window online man pages) is not installed on the system.

partitioning

`partitioning` defines how the disks are divided into slices for file systems during the installation. If you do not specify partitioning, the default is set.

Here's the syntax:

```
partitioning default|existing|explicit
```

The partitioning options are described in Table 15-15.

Table 15-15 *partitioning* Options

Option	Description
`default`	The Solaris installation program selects the disks and creates the file systems where the specified software is installed. Except for any file systems specified by the `filesys` keyword, rootdisk is selected first. Additional disks are used if the specified software does not fit on rootdisk.
`existing`	The Solaris installation program uses the existing file systems on the system's disks. All file systems except /, /usr, /usr/openwin, /opt, and /var are preserved. The installation program uses the last mount point field from the file system superblock to determine which file system mount point the slice represents. When you specify the `filesys` profile keyword with `partitioning`, `existing` must be specified.
`explicit`	The Solaris installation program uses the disks and creates the file systems specified by the `filesys` keywords. If you specify only the root (/) file system with the `filesys` keyword, all the Solaris software is installed in the root file system. When you use the `explicit` profile value, you must use the `filesys` profile keyword to specify which disks to use and what file systems to create.

root_device

root_device designates the system's root disk.

Here's the syntax:

```
root_device slice
```

Here's an example:

```
root_device c0t3d0s2
```

system_type

system_type defines the type of system being installed. If you do not specify system_type in a profile, standalone is set by default.

Here's the syntax:

```
system_type [standalone | server]
```

Here's an example:

```
system_type server
```

usedisk

usedisk designates one or more disks that you want the Solaris installation program to use when the partitioning default is specified. By default, the installation program uses all the operational disks on the system. disk_name must be specified in the form c?t?d? or c?d?, such as c0t0d0. If you specify the usedisk profile keyword in a profile, the Solaris installation program uses only the disks that you specify.

Here's the syntax:

```
usedisk disk_name [disk_name]
```

Here's an example:

```
usedisk c0t0d0 c0t1d0
```

NOTE. *You cannot specify the* usedisk *keyword and the* dontuse *keyword in the same profile.*

Testing Profiles

After you create a profile, you can use the `pfinstall` command to test it. Testing a profile is sometimes called a "dry run" installation. By looking at the installation output generated by `pfinstall`, you can quickly determine whether a profile will do what you expect. For example, you can determine if a system has enough disk space to upgrade to a new release of Solaris before you actually perform the upgrade.

To test a profile for a particular Solaris release, you must test it within the Solaris environment of the same release. For example, if you want to test a profile for Solaris 7, you have to run the `pfinstall` command on a system running Solaris 7.

To test the profile, change to the JumpStart directory that contains the profile and type

```
/usr/sbin/install.d/pfinstall -d
```

or

```
/usr/sbin/install.d/pfinstall -D
```

CAUTION! *Without the* `-d` *or* `-D` *option,* `pfinstall` *actually installs the Solaris software on the system by using the specified profile, and the data on the system is overwritten.*

Here is the syntax for `pfinstall`:

```
/usr/sbin/install.d/pfinstall [-D | -d] disk_config [-c path] profile
```

The `pfinstall` options are described in Table 15-16.

Table 15-16 *pfinstall* Options

Option	Description
`-D`	Tells `pfinstall` to use the current system's disk configuration to test the profile against.
`-d disk_config`	Tells `pfinstall` to use a disk configuration file, `disk_config`, to test the profile against. If the `disk_config` file is not in the directory where `pfinstall` is run, you must specify the path. This option cannot be used with an upgrade profile (an install-type upgrade). You must always test an upgrade profile against a system's disk configuration using the -D option. A disk configuration file represents a disk's structure. It describes a disk's bytes per sector, flags, and slices. See the example following this table of how to create the `disk_config` file.
`-c path`	Specifies the path to the Solaris CD image. This is required if the Solaris CD is not mounted on /cdrom. For example, use this option if the system is using Volume Manager to mount the Solaris CD.
`profile`	Specifies the name of the profile to test. If `profile` is not in the directory where `pfinstall` is being run, you must specify the path.

You can create a `disk_config` file by issuing the following command:

```
prtvtoc /dev/rdsk/device_name > disk_config
```

`/dev/rdsk/device_name` is the device name of the system's disk. `device_name` must be in the form `c?t?d?s2` or `c?d?s2`. `disk_config` is the name of the disk configuration file.

NOTE. `c?t?d?s2` *designates a specific target for a SCSI disk, and* `c?d?s2` *designates a non-SCSI disk.*

Here's an example:

```
prtvtoc/dev/rdsk/c0t3d0s2 >test
```

The file named "test" created by this example would be your `disk_config` file, and it would look like this:

```
* /dev/rdsk/c0t3d0s2 partition map
*
* Dimensions:
*      512 bytes/sector
*      126 sectors/track
*        4 tracks/cylinder
*      504 sectors/cylinder
*     4106 cylinders
*     4104 accessible cylinders
*
* Flags:
*     1: unmountable
*    10: read-only
*
*                                First     Sector    Last
* Partition     Tag      Flags   Sector    Count     Sector    Mount Directory
       0         2       00      0         268632    268631    /
       1         3       01      268632    193032    461663
       2         5       00      0         2068416   2068415
       3         0       00      461664    152712    614375    /export
       4         0       00      614376    141624    755999    /export/swap
       6         4       00      756000    1312416   2068415   /usr
```

NOTE. *If you want to test installing Solaris software on multiple disks, concatenate single disk configuration files and save the output to a new file.*

The following example tests the sparc10_prof profile against the disk configuration on a Solaris 7 system on which `pfinstall` is being run. The sparc10_prof profile is located in the /jumpstart directory, and the path to the Solaris CD image is specified because Volume Management is being used.

In addition, if you want to test the profile for a system with a specific system memory size, set SYS_MEMSIZE to the specific memory size in MB as follows:

```
SYS_MEMSIZE=memory_size
export SYS_MEMSIZE
cd /jumpstart
/usr/sbin/install.d/pfinstall -D -c /cdrom/cdrom0/s0 sparc10_prof
```

The system tests the profile and displays several pages of results. Look for the following message, which indicates that the test was successful:

```
Installation complete
Test run complete. Exit status 0.
```

Setting Up Clients

Now you need to set up the clients to install over the network. After setting up the /jumpstart directory and the appropriate files, use the add_install_client command on the install server to set up remote workstations to install Solaris from the install server. Use this code:

```
cd /export/install/Solaris_2.7/Tools
./add_install_client -c <servername>:/jumpstart <clientname> sun4m
```

Here's the syntax:

```
add install client [options]
```

The add_install_client options are described in Table 15-17.

Table 15-17 *add_install_client* Options

Option	Description
<servername>	The name of the install server.
<clientname>	The hostname for each workstation.
-c	Specifies the server (<servername>) and path (/jumpstart) to the JumpStart directory.
sun4m	Specifies the platform group of the systems that use <servername> as an install server.

For additional options to the add_install_client command, see the Solaris online manual pages.

A Sample JumpStart Installation

The following example shows how you would set up a custom JumpStart installation for a fictitious site. The network consists of an Enterprise 3000 server and five Sparc10 workstations.

Setting Up the Install Server

The first step is to set up the install server. You'll choose the enterprise server. This is where the contents of the Solaris CD are located. The contents of the CD can be made available by either loading the CD in the CD-ROM drive or copying the CD to the server's local hard drive. For this example, you will copy the files to the local hard drive. Use the `setup_install_server` command to copy the contents of the Solaris CD to the server's local disk. Files are copied to the /export/install directory. Follow these steps to create the install server:

1. Insert the Solaris CD into the server's CD-ROM drive.
2. Type the following:

   ```
   cd /<CD_mount_point>/Solaris_2.7/Tools
   ./setup_install_server /export/install/sparc_2.7
   ```

   The system responds with this:

   ```
   Verifying target directory...
   Calculating space required for the installation boot image
   Copying Solaris_2.7 Tools hierarchy...
   Install Server setup complete
   ```

Creating the JumpStart Directory

After you install the install server, you need to set up a JumpStart directory on the server. This directory holds the files necessary for a custom JumpStart installation of the Solaris software. You set up this directory by copying the sample directory from one of the Solaris CD images that has been put in /export/install. Do this by typing the following:

```
mkdir /jumpstart
cp -r /export/install/sparc_2.7/Solaris_2.7/Misc/jumpstart_sample /jumpstart
```

Any directory name can be used. You'll use /jumpstart for this example.

Setting Up a Profile Server

The next step is to set up a profile server. Follow these steps:

1. Log in as root on the server where you want the JumpStart directory to reside.

2. Edit the /etc/dfs/dfstab file. Add the following entry:

   ```
   share -F nfs -o ro,anon=0 /jumpstart
   ```

3. Type `shareall` and press Enter. This makes the contents of the /jumpstart directory accessible to systems on the network.

4. Add the profile and rules files to the JumpStart directory. You can copy sample custom JumpStart files from the directory containing the Solaris CD image. These files are located in /export/install/sparc_2.7/Solaris_2.7/Misc. These are only sample files, so they must be modified for your installation. To copy them into the /jumpstart directory, type the following:

   ```
   cd /export/install/sparc_2.7/ Solaris_2.7/Misc
   cp -r jumpstart_sample/* /jumpstart
   ```

For this example, the profile is named engrg_prof. It looks like this:

```
#Specifies that the installation will be treated as an initial
#installation, as opposed to an upgrade.
install_type initial_install
#Specifies that the engineering systems are standalone systems.
system_type standalone
#Specifies that the JumpStart software uses default disk
#partitioning for installing Solaris software on the engineering
#systems.
partitioning default
#Specifies that the developer's software group will be
#installed.cluster
SUNWCprog
#Specifies that each system in the engineering group will have 50
#Mbytes of swap space.
filesys any 50 swap
```

The rules file contains the following rule:

```
network 192.9.200.0 - engrg_prof -
```

This rules file states that systems on the 192.9.200.0 network are installed using the engrg_prof profile.

Validate the rules and profile files as follows:

```
cd /jumpstart
./check
/usr/sbin/install.d/pfinstall engrg_prof
```

If check doesn't find any errors, it creates the rules.ok file. Look for the following message, which indicates that the pfinstall test was successful:

```
Installation complete
Test run complete. Exit status 0.
```

You are finished creating the profile server.

Setting Up Clients

Now, on the install server, set up each client as follows:

```
cd /export/install/sparc_2.7/Solaris_2.7/Tools
./add_install_client -c sparcserver:/jumpstart sparc1 sun4m
./add_install_client -c sparcserver:/jumpstart sparc2 sun4m
```

This example sets up two engineering workstations, sparc1 and sparc2, so that they can be installed over the network from the install server named sparcserver.

Starting Up the Clients

After the setup is complete, you can start up the engineering systems by using the following startup command at the OK (PROM) prompt of each system:

```
boot net  -  install
```

The client reads the rules.ok and profile files on the server. You are then asked to input the time zone, name service, subnet, and date and time information. The system then automatically installs the Solaris operating environment.

This completes the JumpStart configuration.

Summary

It's been my experience that JumpStart is not widely used, mainly because of its complexity. Many system administrators would rather go through an interactive installation for each system than automate the process. Many of the popular UNIX systems have installation programs similar to JumpStart, and most are underutilized. System administrators could save a great deal of time if they would only learn more about this type of installation.

The next chapter describes device configuration and naming. You'll see how the kernel communicates with the system's peripheral devices, such as disk and tape drives.

CHAPTER

16

Device Configuration and Naming

The following test objectives are covered in this chapter:

- Understanding device and driver naming and configurations
- Displaying device and driver configuration information
- Understanding a device instance
- Understanding meta devices

Device management in the Solaris 7 environment includes adding and removing peripheral devices, such as tape drives, disk drives, printers, and modems, from a system. It might also involve adding a third-party device driver to support a device. System administrators need to know how to specify device names if using commands to manage disks, file systems, and other devices.

This chapter describes disk device management in detail. It also describes disk device naming conventions as well as adding, configuring, and displaying information about disk devices that are attached to your system.

Device Drivers

A Sun computer typically uses a wide range of peripheral and mass-storage devices, such as a SCSI disk drive, a keyboard and a mouse, and some kind of magnetic backup medium. Other commonly used devices include CD-ROM drives, printers, and plotters. Solaris communicates with peripheral devices through files called device files or drivers. A *device driver* is a low-level program that allows the kernel to communicate with a specific piece of hardware. The driver serves as the operating system's "interpreter" for that piece of hardware. Before Solaris can communicate with a device, the device must have a device driver.

When a system is started for the first time, the kernel creates a device hierarchy to represent all the devices connected to the system. This is the auto-configuration process, which is described later in this chapter. If a driver is not loaded for a particular peripheral, that device is not functional. In Solaris, each disk device is described in three ways, using three distinct naming conventions:

- **Physical device name**—Represents the full device pathname in the device information hierarchy.
- **Instance name**—Represents the kernel's abbreviation name for every possible device on the system.
- **Logical device name**—Used by system administrators with most file system commands to refer to devices.

System administrators need to understand these device names when using commands to manage disks and file systems. We will discuss these device names throughout this chapter.

Physical Device Name

Before the operating system (OS) is loaded, the system locates a particular device through the full device pathname. Full device pathnames are described in Chapter 2, "OpenBoot." However, after the kernel is loaded, a device is located by its physical device pathname.

Physical device names represent the full device pathname for a device. Note that the two names have the same structure. For example, let's view the full device pathname for a SCSI disk at target 0 by typing `show-devs` at the OpenBoot prompt. The full device pathname is displayed as

```
/iommu@f,e0000000/sbus@f,e0001000/espdma@f,400000/esp@f,800000/sd
```

Now, let's look at the corresponding physical device name from the OS level. Use the `dmesg` command, described later in this section, to obtain information about devices connected to your system. By typing `dmesg` at the command prompt, you'll receive the following information about SCSI disk 0:

```
iommu0 at root: obio 0xe0000000
sbus0 at iommu0: obio 0xe0001000
espdma0 at sbus0: SBus slot f 0x400000
esp0:       esp-options=0x46
esp0 at espdma0: SBus slot f 0x800000 sparc ipl 4
sd0 at esp0: target 0 lun 0
sd0 is /iommu@f,e0000000/sbus@f,e0001000/espdma@f,400000/esp@f,800000/sd@0,0
    <SEAGATE-ST32550N-0014 cyl 3495 alt 2 hd 11 sec 109>
```

NOTE. *This same information is also available in the /var/adm/messages file.*

The physical device pathname for disk 0 is

```
/iommu@f,e0000000/sbus@f,e0001000/espdma@f,400000/esp@f,800000/sd@0,0
```

As you can see, the physical device name and the full device name are the same. The difference is that the full device pathname is simply a path to a particular device. The physical device is the actual driver used by Solaris to access that device from the OS.

Physical device files are found in the /devices directory; therefore, the physical device file for SCSI disk 0 would be

```
/devices//iommu@f,e0000000/sbus@f,e0001000/espdma@f,400000/esp@f,800000/sd@0,0:<#>
```

where <#> is a letter representing the disk slice.

The system commands used to provide information about physical devices are described in Table 16-1.

Table 16-1 Device Information Commands

Command	Description
`prtconf`	Displays system configuration information, including the total amount of memory and the device configuration, as described by the system's hierarchy. This useful tool verifies whether a device has been seen by the system.
`sysdef`	Displays device configuration information, including system hardware, pseudo devices, loadable modules, and selected kernel parameters.
`dmesg`	Displays system diagnostic messages, as well as a list of devices attached to the system since the most recent restart.

The following is an example of the output presented by the `prtconf` command:

```
#  prtconf
System Configuration:  Sun Microsystems  sun4u
Memory size: 128 Megabytes
System Peripherals (Software Nodes):

SUNW,Ultra-5_10
    packages (driver not attached)
        terminal-emulator (driver not attached)
        deblocker (driver not attached)
        obp-tftp (driver not attached)
        disk-label (driver not attached)
        SUNW,builtin-drivers (driver not attached)
        sun-keyboard (driver not attached)
        ufs-file-system (driver not attached)
    chosen (driver not attached)
    openprom (driver not attached)
        client-services (driver not attached)
    options, instance #0
    aliases (driver not attached)
    memory (driver not attached)
    virtual-memory (driver not attached)
    pci, instance #0
        pci, instance #0
            ebus, instance #0
                auxio (driver not attached)
                power, instance #0
                SUNW,pll (driver not attached)
                se, instance #0
                su, instance #0
                su, instance #1
                ecpp (driver not attached)
                fdthree, instance #0
                eeprom (driver not attached)
                flashprom (driver not attached)
                SUNW,CS4231 (driver not attached)
```

```
          network, instance #0
          SUNW,m64B, instance #0
          ide, instance #0
              disk (driver not attached)
              cdrom (driver not attached)
              dad, instance #0
              sd, instance #2
      pci, instance #1
          pci (driver not attached)
              pci108e,1000 (driver not attached)
              SUNW,qfe (driver not attached)
              pci108e,1000 (driver not attached)
              SUNW,qfe (driver not attached)
              pci108e,1000 (driver not attached)
              SUNW,qfe (driver not attached)
              pci108e,1000 (driver not attached)
              SUNW,qfe (driver not attached)
  SUNW,UltraSPARC-IIi (driver not attached)
  pseudo, instance #0
```

Next is an example of the output displayed by the `sysdef` command:

```
# sysdef
*
* Hostid
*
  80a26382
*
* sun4u Configuration
*
*
* Devices
*
packages (driver not attached)
        terminal-emulator (driver not attached)
        deblocker (driver not attached)
        obp-tftp (driver not attached)
        disk-label (driver not attached)
        SUNW,builtin-drivers (driver not attached)
        sun-keyboard (driver not attached)
        ufs-file-system (driver not attached)
chosen (driver not attached)
openprom (driver not attached)
        client-services (driver not attached)
options, instance #0
aliases (driver not attached)
memory (driver not attached)
virtual-memory (driver not attached)
pci, instance #0
        pci, instance #0
                ebus, instance #0
                        auxio (driver not attached)
```

```
                        power, instance #0
                        SUNW,pll (driver not attached)
                        se, instance #0
                        su, instance #0
                        su, instance #1
                        ecpp (driver not attached)
                        fdthree, instance #0
                        eeprom (driver not attached)
                        flashprom (driver not attached)
                        SUNW,CS4231 (driver not attached)
                network, instance #0
                SUNW,m64B, instance #0
                ide, instance #0
                        disk (driver not attached)
                        cdrom (driver not attached)
                        dad, instance #0
                        sd, instance #2
        pci, instance #1
                pci (driver not attached)
                        pci108e,1000 (driver not attached)
                        SUNW,qfe (driver not attached)
                        pci108e,1000 (driver not attached)
                        SUNW,qfe (driver not attached)
                        pci108e,1000 (driver not attached)
                        SUNW,qfe (driver not attached)
                        pci108e,1000 (driver not attached)
                        SUNW,qfe (driver not attached)
SUNW,UltraSPARC-IIi (driver not attached)
pseudo, instance #0
        clone, instance #0
        ip, instance #0
        tcp, instance #0
        udp, instance #0
        arp, instance #0
        log, instance #0
        sad, instance #0
        consms, instance #0
        conskbd, instance #0
        wc, instance #0
        mm, instance #0
        ptsl, instance #0
        tl, instance #0
        cn, instance #0
        kstat, instance #0
        sy, instance #0
        pm, instance #0
        openeepr, instance #0
        tod, instance #0
        vol, instance #0
        ptm, instance #0
        pts, instance #0
        icmp, instance #0
```

```
        logindmux, instance #0
        ksyms, instance #0
        devinfo, instance #0
*
* Loadable Objects
*
* Loadable Object Path = /platform/sun4u/kernel
*
...
...
sched/RT
sched/RT_DPTBL
*
* System Configuration
*
  swap files
swapfile              dev  swaplo blocks   free
/dev/dsk/c0t0d0s1   136,1      16  262688 262688
*
* Tunable Parameters
*
 2490368        maximum memory allowed in buffer cache (bufhwm)
    1898        maximum number of processes (v.v_proc)
      99        maximum global priority in sys class (MAXCLSYSPRI)
    1893        maximum processes per user id (v.v_maxup)
      30        auto update time limit in seconds (NAUTOUP)
      25        page stealing low water mark (GPGSLO)
       5        fsflush run rate (FSFLUSHR)
      25        minimum resident memory for avoiding deadlock (MINARMEM)
      25        minimum swapable memory for avoiding deadlock (MINASMEM)
*
* Utsname Tunables
*
     5.7  release (REL)
  ultra5  node name (NODE)
   SunOS  system name (SYS)
 Generic  version (VER)
*
* Process Resource Limit Tunables (Current:Maximum)
*
  Infinity:Infinity     cpu time
  Infinity:Infinity     file size
  Infinity:Infinity     heap size
0x00800000:Infinity     stack size
  Infinity:Infinity     core file size
0x00000040:0x00000400   file descriptors
  Infinity:Infinity     mapped memory
*
* Streams Tunables
*
     9  maximum number of pushes allowed (NSTRPUSH)
 65536  maximum stream message size (STRMSGSZ)
```

```
  1024  max size of ctl part of message (STRCTLSZ)
*
* IPC Messages
*
      0  entries in msg map (MSGMAP)
      0  max message size (MSGMAX)
      0  max bytes on queue (MSGMNB)
      0  message queue identifiers (MSGMNI)
      0  message segment size (MSGSSZ)
      0  system message headers (MSGTQL)
      0  message segments (MSGSEG)
*
* IPC Semaphores
*
     10  entries in semaphore map (SEMMAP)
     10  semaphore identifiers (SEMMNI)
     60  semaphores in system (SEMMNS)
     30  undo structures in system (SEMMNU)
     25  max semaphores per id (SEMMSL)
     10  max operations per semop call (SEMOPM)
     10  max undo entries per process (SEMUME)
  32767  semaphore maximum value (SEMVMX)
  16384  adjust on exit max value (SEMAEM)
*
* IPC Shared Memory
*
   1048576       max shared memory segment size (SHMMAX)
      1  min shared memory segment size (SHMMIN)
    100  shared memory identifiers (SHMMNI)
      6  max attached shm segments per process (SHMSEG)
*
* Time Sharing Scheduler Tunables
*
60       maximum time sharing user priority (TSMAXUPRI)
SYS      system class name (SYS_NAME)
```

Finally, here's an example of the device information for an Ultra system displayed using the `dmesg` command:

```
# dmesg

Apr 29 15:39
60 target 0 lun 0
dad0 is /pci@1f,0/pci@1,1/ide@3/dad@0,0
        <ST34321A cyl 8892 alt 2 hd 15 sec 63>
root on /pci@1f,0/pci@1,1/ide@3/disk@0,0:a fstype ufs
PCI-device: ebus@1, ebus0
su0 at ebus0: offset 14,3083f8
su0 is /pci@1f,0/pci@1,1/ebus@1/su@14,3083f8
su1 at ebus0: offset 14,3062f8
su1 is /pci@1f,0/pci@1,1/ebus@1/su@14,3062f8
keyboard is </pci@1f,0/pci@1,1/ebus@1/su@14,3083f8> major <37> minor <0>
```

```
mouse is </pci@1f,0/pci@1,1/ebus@1/su@14,3062f8> major <37> minor <1>
se0 at ebus0: offset 14,400000
se0 is /pci@1f,0/pci@1,1/ebus@1/se@14,400000
stdin is </pci@1f,0/pci@1,1/ebus@1/se@14,400000:a> major <20> minor <0>
stdout is </pci@1f,0/pci@1,1/ebus@1/se@14,400000:a> major <20> minor <0>
SUNW,hme0: CheerIO 2.0 (Rev Id = c1) Found
PCI-device: network@1,1, hme0
hme0 is /pci@1f,0/pci@1,1/network@1,1
dump on /dev/dsk/c0t0d0s1 size 128 MB
SUNW,hme0: Using Internal Transceiver
SUNW,hme0: 10 Mbps half-duplex Link Up
syncing file systems...cpu0: SUNW,UltraSPARC-IIi (upaid 0 impl 0x12 ver 0x13 clock
➥270 MHz)
SunOS Release 5.7 Version Generic 64-bit [UNIX(R) System V Release 4.0]
Copyright (c) 1983-1998, Sun Microsystems, Inc.
mem = 131072K (0x8000000)
avail mem = 122757120
Ethernet address = 8:0:20:a2:63:82
root nexus = Sun Ultra 5/10 UPA/PCI (UltraSPARC-IIi 270MHz)
pci0 at root: UPA 0x1f 0x0
pci0 is /pci@1f,0
PCI-device: pci@1,1, simba0
PCI-device: pci@1, simba1
PCI-device: ide@3, uata0
...
...
...
```

Use the output of the `prtconf` and `sysdef` commands to identify which disk, tape, and CD-ROM devices are connected to the system. As shown in the previous examples, some devices display the `driver not attached` message next to the device instance. This message does not always mean that a driver is unavailable for this device. It means that no driver is currently attached to the device instance because there is no device at this node or the device is not in use. The OS automatically loads drivers when the device is accessed, and it unloads them when it is not in use.

The system determines what devices are attached to it at startup. This is why it is important to have all peripherals powered on at startup, even if they are not currently being used. During startup, the kernel configures itself dynamically, loading needed modules into memory. Device drivers are loaded when devices, such as disk and tape devices, are accessed for the first time. This process is called auto-configuration, because all kernel modules are loaded automatically if needed. As described in Chapter 2, the system administrator can customize the way in which kernel modules are loaded by modifying the /etc/system file.

Device Auto-Configuration

Auto-configuration offers many advantages over the manual configuration method used in earlier versions of UNIX, in which device drivers were manually added to the kernel, the kernel was recompiled, and the system had to be restarted. Now, with auto-configuration, the administrator simply connects the new device to the system and performs a reconfiguration startup as follows:

1. Create the /reconfigure file with the following command:

   ```
   touch /reconfigure
   ```

   The /reconfigure file causes the Solaris software to check for the presence of any newly installed devices the next time you turn on or start up your system.

2. Shut down the system using the shutdown procedure described in Chapter 1, "System Startup."

   If you need to connect the device, turn off power to the system and all peripherals after Solaris has been properly shut down.

3. After the new device is connected, restore power to the peripherals first and then to the system. Verify that the peripheral device has been added by attempting to access it.

An optional method of performing a reconfiguration startup is to interrupt the start process and type `boot -r` at the OpenBoot prompt. I like the first method described because the system administrator can instruct the system to perform the reconfiguration startup at any time by creating the /reconfigure file. Now, at the next restart, whether the administrator is there or not, the system performs the reconfiguration startup. This could happen at 3 a.m. if you like.

During a reconfiguration restart, a device hierarchy is created in the /devices directory to represent the devices connected to the system. The kernel uses this to associate drivers with their appropriate devices. Also, any kernel parameter changes that were made to the /etc/system file are parsed by the kernel at this time.

Auto-configuration offers the following benefits:

- Main memory is used more efficiently, because modules are loaded as needed.
- There is no need to reconfigure the kernel if new devices are added to the system. When you add devices such as disks or tape drives, however, the system needs to be shut down before you connect the hardware so that no damage is done to the electrical components.
- Drivers can be loaded and tested without having to rebuild the kernel and restart the system.

Occasionally, you might install a new device for which Solaris does not have a supporting device driver. Always check with the manufacturer to make sure that any device you plan to add to your system has a supported device driver. If a driver is not included with the standard Solaris release, the manufacturer should provide the software needed for the device to be properly installed, maintained, and administered.

Third-party device drivers are installed as software packages using the `pkgadd` command. At a minimum, this software includes a device driver and its associated configuration (.conf) file. The .conf files reside in the /kernel/drv directories. Table 16-2 describes the contents of the subdirectories located in the /kernel directory.

Table 16-2 The /kernel Directory

Directory	Description
drv	Contains loadable device drivers and pseudo-device drivers.
exec	Contains modules used to run different types of executable files or shell scripts.
fs	Contains file system modules, such as ufs, nfs, proc, and so on.
misc	Contains miscellaneous system-related modules, such as swapgeneric and ipc.
sched	Contains OS schedulers.
strmod	Contains System V STREAMS loadable modules.
sys	Contains loadable system calls, such as system semaphore and system accounting operations.

Instance Name

The instance name represents the kernel's abbreviated name for every possible device on the system. For example, on an Ultra system, dad0 represents the instance name of the IDE disk drive, and hme0 is the instance name for the network interface. Instance names are mapped to a physical device name in the /etc/path_to_inst file. The following shows the contents of a path_to_inst file:

```
more /etc/path_to_inst
#
#       Caution! This file contains critical kernel state
"/pci@1f,0" 0 "pci"
"/pci@1f,0/pci@1,1" 0 "simba"
"/pci@1f,0/pci@1,1/ide@3" 0 "uata"
"/pci@1f,0/pci@1,1/ide@3/sd@2,0" 2 "sd"
"/pci@1f,0/pci@1,1/ide@3/dad@0,0" 0 "dad"
"/pci@1f,0/pci@1,1/ebus@1" 0 "ebus"
"/pci@1f,0/pci@1,1/ebus@1/fdthree@14,3023f0" 0 "fd"
```

```
"/pci@1f,0/pci@1,1/ebus@1/su@14,3062f8" 1 "su"
"/pci@1f,0/pci@1,1/ebus@1/se@14,400000" 0 "se"
"/pci@1f,0/pci@1,1/ebus@1/su@14,3083f8" 0 "su"
"/pci@1f,0/pci@1,1/ebus@1/ecpp@14,3043bc" 0 "ecpp"
"/pci@1f,0/pci@1,1/ebus@1/SUNW,CS4231@14,200000" 0 "audiocs"
"/pci@1f,0/pci@1,1/ebus@1/power@14,724000" 0 "power"
"/pci@1f,0/pci@1,1/network@1,1" 0 "hme"
"/pci@1f,0/pci@1,1/SUNW,m64B@2" 0 "m64"
"/pci@1f,0/pci@1" 1 "simba"
"/pci@1f,0/pci@1/pci@1" 0 "pci_pci"
"/pci@1f,0/pci@1/pci@1/SUNW,qfe@1,1" 1 "qfe"
"/pci@1f,0/pci@1/pci@1/SUNW,qfe@0,1" 0 "qfe"
"/pci@1f,0/pci@1/pci@1/SUNW,qfe@3,1" 3 "qfe"
"/pci@1f,0/pci@1/pci@1/SUNW,qfe@2,1" 2 "qfe"
"/options" 0 "options"
"/pseudo" 0 "pseudo"
#
```

Instance names can also be displayed by using the commands `dmesg`, `sysdef`, and `prtconf`, which were described earlier. For example, you can determine the mapping of an instance name to a physical device name by looking at the `dmesg` output, as shown in the following example from an Ultra system:

```
dad0 at pci1095,6460 target 0 lun 0
dad0 is /pci@1f,0/pci@1,1/ide@3/dad@0,0
```

If you have an older Sparcstation with an SBus and SCSI disk drives, here's similar output for a SCSI disk drive:

```
sd3 at esp0: target 3 lun 0
sd3 is /iommu@f,e0000000/sbus@f,e0001000,espdma@f,400000/esp@f,800000/sd@3,0
```

In the first example, `dad0` is the instance name and `/pci@1f,0/pci@1,1/ide@3/dad@0,0` is the physical device name. After the instance name has been assigned to a device, it remains mapped to that device. To keep instance numbers consistent across restarts, the system records them in the /etc/path_to_inst file. This file is read only at startup, and it is updated by the `add_drv` and `drvconfig` commands described later in this section.

Devices already existing on a system are not rearranged when new devices are added, even if new devices are added to sbus slots that are numerically lower than those that are occupied by existing devices. In other words, the /etc/path_to_inst file is appended to, not rewritten, when new devices are added.

CAUTION! *Do not remove the path_to_inst file; the system cannot start up without it. The system relies on information found in this file to find the root, usr, and swap device. Make changes to this file only after careful consideration.*

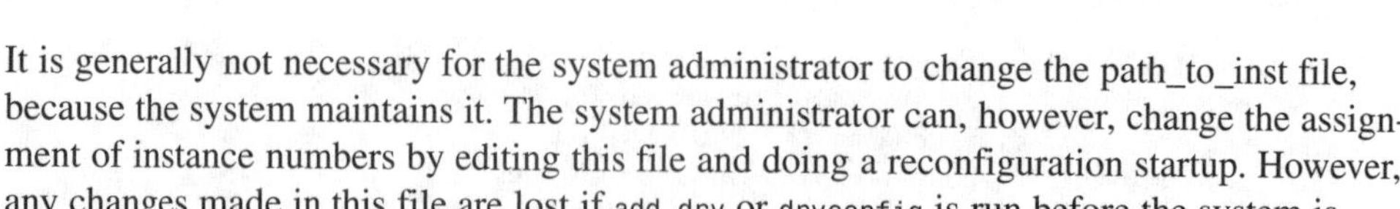

It is generally not necessary for the system administrator to change the path_to_inst file, because the system maintains it. The system administrator can, however, change the assignment of instance numbers by editing this file and doing a reconfiguration startup. However, any changes made in this file are lost if `add_drv` or `drvconfig` is run before the system is restarted.

NOTE. *If you can't start up from the startup disk because of a problem with the /etc/path_to_inst file, you should start up from the CD-ROM (*`boot -sw cdrom`*) and copy the /etc/path_to_inst file contained on the CD-ROM to the /etc/path_to_inst on the startup disk. To do this, start up from the CD-ROM using* `boot -sw cdrom` *at the OpenBoot prompt. Then mount the startup disk on /a. Copy the /etc/path_to_inst file to /a/etc/path_to_inst. If you still can't start up, the problem is deeper than just with the /etc/path_to_inst file.*

The `add_drv` command adds a new device driver to the system. The command syntax is as follows:

```
add_drv [ -b <basedir> ] [ -c <class_name> ] [ -i 'identify_name' ]
➥ [ -m 'permission','...' ] [ -n ] [ -f ] [ -v ] <device_driver>
```

Options to the `add_drv` command are described in Table 16-3.

Table 16-3 *add_drv* Options

Option	Description
`-b <basedir>`	Sets the path to the root directory of the diskless client. It is used on the server to execute add_drv for a diskless client. The client machine must be restarted to install the driver.
`-c <class_name>`	Exports the class `<class_name>` for the driver being added to the system.
`-i 'identify_name'`	Specifies a whitespace-separated list of aliases for the driver `<device_driver>`.
`-m 'permission'`	Specifies the file system permissions for device nodes created by the system on behalf of `<device_driver>`.
`-n`	Does not try to load and attach `<device_driver>`; just modifies the system configuration files for the `<device_driver>`.
`-f`	Forces `add_drv` to add the driver even if a reconfiguration startup is required. See the `-v` flag. Normally, if a reconfiguration startup is required to complete the configuration of the driver into the system, `add_drv` does not add the driver.
`-v`	Provides additional information regarding the success or failure of a driver's configuration into the system.

The following example adds the `SUNW,test` driver to the system, with an alias name of `SUNW,alias`. It assumes that the driver has already been copied to the /usr/kernel/drv directory:

```
add_drv -m '* 0666 bin bin','a 0644 root sys' -i 'SUNW,alias' SUNW,test
```

Every minor node created by the system for the `SUNW,test` driver has the permission 0666 and is owned by a user bin in the group bin, except for the minor device `a`, which is owned by root, the group sys, and has a permission of 0644.

The `add_drv` command is used to inform the system about newly installed device drivers. Specifically, it updates the files listed in Table 16-4.

Table 16-4 Device Driver-Related Files

Filename	Description
/etc/name_to_major	This file contains driver name-to-major number mapping. Every driver has a major number; the instances of the devices it manages each have their own unique minor number.
/etc/minor_perm	This file contains permission, owner, and group information used by drivers when creating new /devices entries (as when a device is accessed for the first time).
/etc/driver_aliases	This file contains alternative names for device drivers.
/etc/driver_classes	This file contains classes for device drivers (SBUS, VME, SCSI, and so on).

`add_drv` invokes the `drvconfig` command to configure the driver and then calls `devlinks` to make any device links from the /dev directory.

Syntax:

```
drvconfig [options]
```

The options for the `drvconfig` command are described in Table 16-5.

Table 16-5 *drvconfig* Options

Option	Description
-d	Prints debugging information.
-i	Configures the driver for the specified driver filename only.
-r	Builds the device tree under the specified directory instead of the /devices directory, which is the default.

The drvconfig utility is responsible for configuring the /devices directory to reflect the dev_info tree held in the kernel. This utility is run automatically by the /etc/rcS script, which executes drvconfig during a reconfiguration startup. If necessary, the command can also be run from the command line.

An example of when to use the drvconfig command would be if the system has been started but the power to the CD-ROM or tape drive was not turned on. During startup, the system did not detect the device; therefore, its drivers were not installed. This can be verified by issuing the sysdef command and examining the output for sd6, the SCSI target ID normally used for the external CD-ROM:

```
sd, instance #6 (driver not attached)
```

To gain access to the CD-ROM, you could halt the system, turn on power to the CD-ROM, and start the system back up, or you could simply turn on power to the CD-ROM and issue the following command at the command prompt:

```
drvconfig cdrom
```

Now if you issue the sysdef command, you'll see the following output for the CD-ROM:

```
sd, instance #6
```

Major and Minor Device Numbers

Each device has a major and minor device number assigned. These numbers identify the proper device location and device driver to the kernel. This number is used by the operating system to key into the proper device driver whenever a physical device file corresponding to one of the devices it manages is opened. The major device number indicates the general device class, such as disk, tape, or serial line. The minor device number indicates the specific member within that class. All devices managed by a given device driver contain a unique minor number. Some drivers of pseudo-devices (software entities set up to look like devices) create new minor devices on demand. Together, the major and minor numbers uniquely define a device and its device driver.

Physical device files have a unique output when listed with the ls -l command, as shown in the following example:

```
cd /devices/iommu@f,e0000000/sbus@f,e0001000/espdma@f,400000/esp@f,800000
ls -l sd@0
```

The system responds with this:

```
brw-r-----   1 root    sys       32,  0 Jul 21 07:44 sd@0,0:a
crw-r-----   1 root    sys       32,  0 Jul 21 07:44 sd@0,0:a,raw
brw-r-----   1 root    sys       32,  1 Jul 21 07:44 sd@0,0:b
crw-r-----   1 root    sys       32,  1 Aug 16 06:15 sd@0,0:b,raw
brw-r-----   1 root    sys       32,  2 Jul 21 07:44 sd@0,0:c
```

```
crw-r-----   1 root     sys       32,  2 Jul 21 07:44 sd@0,0:c,raw
brw-r-----   1 root     sys       32,  3 Jul 21 07:44 sd@0,0:d
crw-r-----   1 root     sys       32,  3 Jul 21 07:44 sd@0,0:d,raw
brw-r-----   1 root     sys       32,  4 Jul 21 07:44 sd@0,0:e
crw-r-----   1 root     sys       32,  4 Jul 21 07:44 sd@0,0:e,raw
brw-r-----   1 root     sys       32,  5 Jul 21 07:44 sd@0,0:f
crw-r-----   1 root     sys       32,  5 Jul 21 07:44 sd@0,0:f,raw
brw-r-----   1 root     sys       32,  6 Jul 21 07:44 sd@0,0:g
crw-r-----   1 root     sys       32,  6 Aug 16 06:13 sd@0,0:g,raw
brw-r-----   1 root     sys       32,  7 Jul 21 07:44 sd@0,0:h
crw-r-----   1 root     sys       32,  7 Jul 21 07:44 sd@0,0:h,raw
```

This long listing includes columns showing major and minor numbers for each device. All the devices listed in this example are managed by the sd driver, which is major number 32 in this example. Minor numbers are listed after the comma.

During the process of building the /devices directory, the `drvconfig` utility assigns each device a major device number by using the name-to-number mappings held in the /etc/name_to_major file. This file is maintained by the system and is undocumented. The following is a sample of the /etc/name_to_major file:

```
more /etc/name_to_major
cn 0
rootnex 1
pseudo 2
ip 3
logindmux 4
icmp 5
fas 6
hme 7
p9000 8
p9100 9
sp 10
clone 11
sad 12
mm 13
iwscn 14
wc 15
conskbd 16
consms 17
ipdcm 18
dump 19
se 20
log 21
sy 22
ptm 23
pts 24
ptc 25
ptsl 26
bwtwo 27
audio 28
```

```
zs 29
cgthree 30
cgtwo 31
sd 32
st 33
...
...

envctrl 131
cvc 132
cvcredir 133
eide 134
hd 135
tadbat 136
ts102 137
simba 138
uata 139
dad 140
atapicd 141
```

To create the minor device entries, the `drvconfig` utility uses the information placed in the dev_info node by the device driver. Permissions and ownership information are kept in the /etc/minor_perm file.

Logical Device Name

The final stage of the auto-configuration process involves the creation of the logical device name to reflect the new set of devices on the system. The logical device name is a link from the /dev directory to the physical device name located in the /devices directory. To see a list of logical device names for the disks connected to your system, execute a long listing on the /dev/dsk directory as follows:

```
ls -l /dev/dsk
total 48
lrwxrwxrwx    1 root      root              84 Jul 21 07:45 c0t0d0s0 -> ../../devices/
➥iommu@f,e0000000/sbus@f,e0001000/espdma@f,400000/esp@f,800000/sd@0,0:a
lrwxrwxrwx    1 root      root              84 Jul 21 07:45 c0t0d0s1 -> ../../devices/
➥iommu@f,e0000000/sbus@f,e0001000/espdma@f,400000/esp@f,800000/sd@0,0:b
lrwxrwxrwx    1 root      root              84 Jul 21 07:45 c0t0d0s2 -> ../../devices/
➥iommu@f,e0000000/sbus@f,e0001000/espdma@f,400000/esp@f,800000/sd@0,0:c
lrwxrwxrwx    1 root      root              84 Jul 21 07:45 c0t0d0s3 -> ../../devices/
➥iommu@f,e0000000/sbus@f,e0001000/espdma@f,400000/esp@f,800000/sd@0,0:d
lrwxrwxrwx    1 root      root              84 Jul 21 07:45 c0t0d0s4 -> ../../devices/
➥iommu@f,e0000000/sbus@f,e0001000/espdma@f,400000/esp@f,800000/sd@0,0:e
lrwxrwxrwx    1 root      root              84 Jul 21 07:45 c0t0d0s5 -> ../../devices/
➥iommu@f,e0000000/sbus@f,e0001000/espdma@f,400000/esp@f,800000/sd@0,0:f
...
...
```

On the second line of output from the `ls -l` command, notice that the logical device name c0t0d0s0 is linked to the physical device name:

```
../../devices/iommu@f,e0000000/sbus @f,e0001000/espdma@f,400000/esp@f,800000/sd@0,0:a
```

The logical device name is the name that the system administrator uses to refer to a particular device if running various Solaris file system commands. For example, if running the `mount` command, use the logical device name /dev/dsk/c0t0d0s7 to mount the file system /home:

```
mount /dev/dsk/c0t0d0s7 /home
```

Logical device files in the /dev directory are symbolically linked to physical device files in the /devices directory. Logical device names are used to access disk devices if you

- Add a new disk to the system.
- Move a disk from one system to another.
- Access (or mount) a file system residing on a local disk.
- Back up a local file system.
- Repair a file system.

Logical devices are organized in subdirectories under the /dev directory by their device types, as shown in Table 16-6.

Table 16-6 Device Directories

Directory	Description of Contents
/dev/dsk	Block interface to disk devices
/dev/rdsk	Raw or character interface to disk devices
/dev/rmt	Tape devices
/dev/term	Serial line devices
/dev/cua	Dial-out modems
/dev/pts	Pseudo terminals
/dev/fbs	Frame buffers
/dev/sad	STREAMS administrative driver

The *disks* Command

The `disks` command creates entries in the /dev directory for disk drives attached to the system. Similarly, the `tapes` command creates entries for tape drives attached to a system, the `ports` command creates entries for the serial ports, and `esp` creates entries for SCSI host adapters. All these commands create the symbolic links found in the /dev directories. In the context of this chapter, the `disks` command uses the following syntax:

```
/usr/sbin/disks [ -r rootdir ]
```

where `[-r rootdir]` is an optional parameter that looks for the /dev/dsk, /dev/rdsk, and /devices directory under rootdir, not directly under /.

The `disks` command creates symbolic links in the /dev/dsk and /dev/rdsk directories pointing to the actual physical device files found under the /devices directory tree. It performs the following steps:

1. `disks` searches the kernel device tree to see what hard drives are attached to the system. It notes the /devices pathnames for the slices on the drive and determines the physical component of the corresponding /dev/dsk or /dev/rdsk name.
2. The /dev/dsk and /dev/rdsk directories are checked for disk entries—that is, symbolic links with names of the form `cN[tN]dNsN`, where *N* represents a decimal number. `cN` is the logical controller number, an arbitrary number assigned by this program to designate a particular disk controller. The first controller found on a system is assigned number 0. `tN` is the SCSI target ID of the disk attached to the SCSI bus. If the system has IDE disk drives, the `tN` field is not used. `dN` refers to the disk number attached to the controller. This number is always 0 except on storage arrays. `sN` is the slice number on the disk. Here are a few examples of logical device filenames for disk drives:

   dev/dsk/c0t0d0s0 refers to slice 0 on a SCSI disk drive with a target ID of 0 on SCSI controller 0 buffered device.

   dev/rdsk/c0t0d0s0 refers to slice 0 on a SCSI disk drive with a target ID of 0 on SCSI controller 0 raw device.
3. If not all the disk entries are found in the /dev/dsk directory for a disk that has been found under the /devices directory tree, `disks` creates the missing symbolic links. If none of the entries for a particular disk are found in /dev/dsk, `disks` checks to see if any entries exist for other disks attached to the same controller. If they do, it creates new entries using the same controller number that is used for other disks on the same controller. If no other /dev/dsk entries are found for slices of disks belonging to the same physical controller as the current disk, `disks` assigns the lowest unused controller number and creates entries for the disk slices using this newly-assigned controller number.

Block and Raw Devices

Disk drives have an entry under both the /dev/dsk and the /dev/rdsk directories. The /dsk directory refers to the block or buffered device file, and the /rdsk directory refers to the character or raw device file. The "r" in rdsk stands for "raw." If you are not familiar with these devices, refer to Chapter 3, "Installing the Solaris 7 Software," where block and character devices are described.

The /dev/dsk directory contains the disk entries for the block device nodes in /devices, as shown in the following command:

```
ls -l /dev/dsk
total 48
lrwxrwxrwx    1 root      root            84 Jul 21 07:45 c0t0d0s0 ->
/devices/iommu@f,e0000000/sbus@f,e0001000/espdma@f,400000/esp@f,800000/sd@0,0:a
lrwxrwxrwx    1 root      root            84 Jul 21 07:45 c0t0d0s1 ->
/devices/iommu@f,e0000000/sbus@f,e0001000/espdma@f,400000/esp@f,800000/sd@0,0:b
lrwxrwxrwx    1 root      root            84 Jul 21 07:45 c0t0d0s2 ->
/devices/iommu@f,e0000000/sbus@f,e0001000/espdma@f,400000/esp@f,800000/sd@0,0:c
...
...
```

The /dev/rdsk directory contains the disk entries for the character device nodes in /devices, as shown in the following command:

```
ls -l /dev/rdsk
lrwxrwxrwx    1 root      root            88 Jul 21 07:45 c0t0d0s0 ->
/devices/iommu@f,e0000000/sbus@f,e0001000/espdma@f,400000/esp@f,800000/sd@0,0:a,raw
lrwxrwxrwx    1 root      root            88 Jul 21 07:45 c0t0d0s1 ->
/devices/iommu@f,e0000000/sbus@f,e0001000/espdma@f,400000/esp@f,800000/sd@0,0:b,raw
lrwxrwxrwx    1 root      root            88 Jul 21 07:45 c0t0d0s2 ->
/devices/iommu@f,e0000000/sbus@f,e0001000/espdma@f,400000/esp@f,800000/sd@0,0:c,raw
...
...
```

The `disks` command is run automatically each time a reconfiguration startup is performed or if `add_drv` is executed. If you're invoking `disks` manually, first run `drvconfig` to ensure that /devices is consistent with the current device configuration.

If you're executing a reconfigure startup, a number of utilities are run to build the logical device names:

1. The /devices directory is built by the `drvconfig` utility.

2. The links from the /dev directory to the /devices directory are built by a number of Solaris utilities:

`disks`	Installs /dev links for disks.
`tapes`	Installs /dev links for tapes.
`ports`	Installs /dev links for serial lines.
`devlinks`	Installs /dev links for miscellaneous and pseudo devices.

3. The `devlinks` command builds the /dev directory links according to specifications found in the /etc/devlink.tab file.

Meta Devices

With standard disk devices, each disk slice has its own physical and logical device. Remember from Chapter 4, "Introduction to File Systems," that a file system cannot span more than one disk slice. In other words, a file system is limited to the size of a single disk. On a large server with many disk drives, standard methods of disk slicing are inadequate and inefficient. Sun has addressed these issues with two unbundled Sun packages: Solstice DiskSuite and Enterprise Volume Manager. Both packages allow disk slices to be grouped to form a logical device that is referred to as a meta device (also known as a virtual device). A meta device driver is a logical device that represents several disks or disk slices. Typically, DiskSuite is used on smaller Sun systems—those using multipacks. The Enterprise Volume Manager package is much more robust. It is used on larger servers that use SparcStorage arrays.

Meta devices are the basic functional unit of the meta disk driver. After you create meta devices, you can use them like physical disk partitions. These logical devices can be made up of one of the following components:

- A single partition or disk.
- A concatenated partition called a concatenated stripe. Concatenated stripes work much the way the UNIX `cat` command is used to concatenate two or more files to create one larger file. If partitions are concatenated, the addressing of the component blocks is done on the components sequentially. The file system can use the entire concatenation.

- A stripe is similar to concatenation, except that the addressing of the component blocks is interlaced on the slices rather than sequentially. Striping is used to gain performance. When data is striped across disks, multiple controllers can access data simultaneously.
- A mirror replicates all writes to a single logical device (the mirror) and then to multiple devices (the submirrors) while distributing read operations. This provides redundancy of data in the event of a disk or hardware failure.

Meta devices can provide increased capacity, higher availability, and better performance. To gain increased capacity, the system administrator creates meta devices that are either concatenations or stripes. Mirroring and UFS logging provide higher availability, and striping can help performance. Furthermore, meta devices are transparent to applications software and to component and controller hardware.

The meta device driver is implemented as a set of loadable pseudo device drivers. It uses other physical device drivers to pass I/O requests to and from the underlying devices. The meta device driver resides between the file system interface and the device driver interface, and it interprets information between the two. After passing through the meta device driver, information is received in the expected form by both the file system and the device drivers. The meta device is a loadable device driver, and it has all the same characteristics as any other disk device driver.

The standard meta device name begins with "d" and is followed by a number. By default, there are 128 unique meta devices in the range 0 to 127. Additional meta devices can be added. The meta block device accesses the disk using the system's normal buffering mechanism. There is also a character (or raw) device that provides for direct transmission between the disk and the user's read or write buffer. The names of the block devices are found in the /dev/md/dsk directory, and the names of the raw devices are found in the /dev/md/rdsk directory.

Summary

This chapter discussed device drivers and device names. Device drivers are discussed in several chapters of this book because they are used in many aspects of the system administrator's job. Devices are referenced when we install and boot the OS (Chapters 1 and 3), when creating and mounting file systems (Chapter 4), when setting up printers (Chapter 10, "The LP Print Service"), and in general troubleshooting of system problems. It is very important that you have a good understanding of how device drivers are configured and named in the Solaris operating system.

The next chapter describes networking. As I stated earlier, Solaris was designed to operate in a networked environment. Sun sums it up in their slogan "The network is the computer." Most administrators agree that Solaris without a network is like a fish out of water.

CHAPTER

17

Networking

The following are the test objectives for this chapter:

- Defining fundamental networking terms
- Planning and configuring the network
- Understanding IP addressing
- Understanding name services
- Understanding network commands used to copy files and executing commands on remote systems
- Performing network maintenance

One chapter isn't enough to cover network administration; in fact, Sun has developed a certification exam specifically for this area. The Solaris 7 Administrator exam includes some questions on networking fundamentals, however, and this chapter provides you with that basic information. The topics include designing and planning the network, setting up the network, and maintaining the network.

Network Fundamentals

Before you start, you need to know the definitions of some terms used in networking. You'll find an alphabet soup of acronyms, which I'll try to sort out a bit here. First I'll describe the types of networks available, and then I'll describe the various network protocols. Finally, I'll identify the physical components of the network hardware, including the network interfaces and cabling.

Network Topologies

The term *network topology* refers to the overall picture of the network. The topology describes small and large networks, including LANs and WANs.

LAN

A *local area network (LAN)* is a set of hosts, usually in the same building and on the same floor, connected by a high-speed medium such as Ethernet. A LAN might be a single IP network, or it might be a collection of networks or subnets connected through high-speed routers.

The network interface and cabling or wiring used for computer networks is referred to as *network media*. A Solaris LAN is connected by some sort of thick or thin coaxial cable, twisted-pair telephone wire, or fiber-optic cable. In the Solaris LAN environment, twisted-pair wire is the most commonly used network medium, although fiber-optic is becoming a common medium as well.

WAN

A *wide area network (WAN)* is a network that covers a potentially vast geographic area. An example of a WAN is the Internet. Other examples of WANs are enterprise networks linking the separate offices of a single corporation into one network spanning an entire country or perhaps an entire continent.

Network Protocols

The network protocol is the part of the network you configure but cannot see. It's the software portion of the network that controls data transmission between systems across the network.

Packet

A *packet* is the basic unit of information to be transferred over the network. A packet is organized much like a conventional letter. Each packet has a header that corresponds to an envelope. The header contains the addresses of the recipient and the sender, plus information on how to handle the packet as it travels through each layer of the protocol suite. The message part of the packet corresponds to the letter itself. Packets can contain only a finite number of bytes of data, depending on the network medium in use. Therefore, typical communications such as email messages are sometimes split into packet *fragments*.

TCP/IP

Transmission Control Protocol/Internet Protocol (TCP/IP) is a network communications protocol consisting of a set of formal rules that describe how software and hardware should interact within a network. For the network to function properly, information must be delivered to the intended destination in an intelligible form. Because different types of networking software and hardware need to interact to perform the network function, designers developed the TCP/IP communications protocol, now recognized as a standard by major international standards organizations and used throughout the world. Because it is a set of standards, TCP/IP runs on many different types of computers, making it easy for you to set up a heterogeneous network running any operating system that supports TCP/IP. The Solaris operating system includes the networking software to implement the TCP/IP communications protocol suite.

TCP/IP offers a slew of commands and features that are supported by Solaris. They are described later in this chapter.

Ethernet

Ethernet is a standard that defines the physical components a machine uses to access the network and the speed at which the network runs. It includes specifications for cabling, connectors, and computer interface components. Ethernet is a LAN technology that transmits information between computers at speeds of up to 10 million bits per second (Mbps). A newer version of Ethernet called 100Base-T, or Fast Ethernet, pushes the speed up to 100Mbps, and Gigabit Ethernet supports data transfer rates of 1 gigabit (1,000 megabits) per second. Ethernet can be run over four types of physical media, as described in Table 17-1.

Table 17-1 Ethernet Media

Media	Name
Thick Ethernet	Type 10Base5
Thin Ethernet	Type 10Base2
Twisted-pair Ethernet	Type 10Base-T
Fiber-optic Ethernet	Types FOIRL and 10Base-F

The 10Base-T type of Ethernet has been the most popular medium but is quickly being replaced by 100Base-T.

Ethernet uses a protocol called CSMA/CD, which stands for Carrier Sense, Multiple Access, Collision Detect. The "Multiple Access" part means that every station is logically connected to a single cable. The "Carrier Sense" part means that before transmitting data, a station checks the cable to determine if any other station is already sending something. If the LAN appears to be idle, the station can begin to send data. When several computers connected to the same network need to send data, two computers might try to send at the same time, causing a collision of data. The Ethernet protocol senses this collision and notifies the computer to send the data again.

How can two computers send data at the same time? Isn't Ethernet supposed to check the network for other systems that might be transmitting before sending data across the network?

Here's what happens: An Ethernet station sends data at a rate of 10Mbps. This means it allows 100 nanoseconds per bit of information that is transmitted. The signal travels about one foot in a nanosecond. After the electrical signal for the first bit has traveled about 100 feet down the wire, the station begins sending the second bit. An Ethernet cable can run for hundreds of feet. If two stations are located 250 feet apart on the same cable and both begin transmitting at the same time, they will be in the middle of the third bit before the signal from each reaches the other station.

This explains the need for the "Collision Detect" part of CSMA/CD. If two stations begin sending data at the same time, their signals will "collide" nanoseconds later. When such a collision occurs, the two stations stop transmitting and try again later after a randomly chosen delay period.

Although an Ethernet network can be built using one common signal wire, such an arrangement is not flexible enough to wire most buildings. Unlike an ordinary telephone circuit, Ethernet wire cannot be spliced to connect one copper wire to another. Instead, Ethernet requires a *repeater,* a simple station that is connected to two wires. When the repeater receives data on one wire, it repeats the data bit-for-bit on the other wire. When collisions occur, the repeater repeats the collision as well. In buildings that have two or more types of Ethernet cable, a common practice is to use repeaters to convert the Ethernet signal from one type of wire to another.

FDDI

Fiber Distributed Data Interface (FDDI) is a standard for data transmission on fiber-optic lines in a LAN that can extend up to 200km (124 miles). The FDDI protocol is based on the token-ring protocol. In a token-ring network, all the computers are arranged schematically in a circle. A *token,* which is a special bit pattern, travels around the circle. To send a message, a computer catches the token, attaches a message to it, and then lets it continue to travel around the network to be delivered. In addition to being large geographically, an FDDI local area network can support thousands of users. FDDI also allows for larger packet sizes than lower-speed LANs using Ethernet.

An FDDI network can contain two token rings: a primary token ring and a secondary token ring for possible backup in case the primary ring fails. The primary ring offers up to 100Mbps capacity. If the secondary ring is not needed for backup, it can also carry data, doubling the capacity to 200Mbps.

Network Hardware

The *network hardware* is the physical part of the network you can actually see. The physical components connect the systems and include the NIC, host, cabling, connectors, hubs, and routers, some of which I will discuss here.

NIC

The computer hardware that lets you connect it to a network is known as a *Network Interface Card (NIC)* or network adapter. The network interface can support one or more communication protocols to specify how computers use the physical medium—the network cable—to exchange data. Many computers come with a preinstalled network interface (such as Sun workstations); others require you to purchase it separately (such as PCs).

Each LAN media type has its own associated network interface. For example, if you want to use Ethernet as your network medium, you must have an Ethernet interface installed in each host that is to be part of the network. The connectors on the board to which you attach the Ethernet cable are referred to as Ethernet ports. The same is true if you plan to use FDDI, and so on.

Host

If you are an experienced Solaris user, you are no doubt familiar with the term *host,* often used as a synonym for "computer" or "machine." From a TCP/IP perspective, only two types of entities exist on a network: routers and hosts. When a host initiates communication, it is called a sending host, or the sender. For example, a host initiates communications when the user types `ping` or sends an email message to another user. The host that is the target of the communication is called the receiving host, or recipient.

Each host has a hostname, Internet address, and hardware address that help identify it to its peers on the network. These are described in Table 17-2.

Table 17-2 Host Information

Identity	Description
Hostname	Every system on the network has a unique hostname. Hostnames let users refer to any computer on the network by using a short, easily remembered name rather than the host's network IP address.
Internet address	Each machine on a TCP/IP network has an Internet address (or IP address) that identifies the machine to its peers on the network.
Hardware address	Each host on a network has a hardware address that also identifies it to its peers. The manufacturer physically assigns this address to the machine's CPU or network interface. Each hardware address is unique.

Hub

Ethernet cabling is run to each system from a *hub*. The hub does nothing more than connect all the Ethernet cables so that the computers can connect to one another. It does not boost the signal or route packets from one network to another. When a packet arrives at one port, it is copied to the other ports so that all the computers on the LAN can see all the packets. Hubs can support from two to several hundred systems.

A passive hub serves as a conduit for the data, allowing it to go from one device, or segment, to another. Intelligent hubs include additional features that let an administrator monitor the traffic passing through the hub and to configure each port in the hub. Intelligent hubs are also called manageable hubs.

A third type of hub, called a packet-switching hub (or switch), is a special type of hub that forwards packets to the appropriate port based on the packet's address. Conventional hubs simply rebroadcast every packet to every port. Since switching hubs forward each packet only to the required port, they provide much better performance. Most switching hubs also support load balancing so that ports are dynamically reassigned to different LAN segments based on traffic patterns.

Some newer switching hubs support both traditional Ethernet (10Mbps) and Fast Ethernet (100Mbps) ports. This lets the administrator establish a dedicated Fast Ethernet channel for high-traffic devices such as servers.

Router

A *router* is a machine that forwards Ethernet packets from one network to another. In other words, the router connects LANs, and the hub connects computers. To do this, the router must have at least two network interfaces. A machine with only one network interface cannot forward packets; it is considered a host. Most of the machines you set up on a network will be hosts.

Routers use headers and a forwarding table to determine where packets go, and they use ICMP (Internet Control Message Protocol) to communicate with each other and configure the best route between any two hosts. Very little filtering of data is done through routers. Routers do not care about the type of data they handle.

Planning the Network

You need to do a great deal of planning before you set up your network. As part of the planning process, you must go through the following steps:

1. Obtain a network number and, if applicable, register your network domain with the InterNIC.
2. After you receive your IP network number, devise an IP addressing scheme for your hosts.
3. Create a list containing the IP addresses and hostnames of all machines to comprise your network. You will use this list as you build network databases.
4. Determine which name service to use on your network: NIS, NIS+, DNS, or the network databases in the local /etc directory. Name services are discussed later in this chapter.
5. Establish administrative subdivisions, if appropriate, for your network.
6. Determine if your network is large enough to require routers. If appropriate, create a network topology that supports them.
7. Set up subnets, if appropriate, for your network.

Only after carefully planning your network are you ready to start setting it up.

Setting Up the Network

During the installation of the operating system, you'll use the Solaris software installation program to configure your network. Here are the network configuration files set up by the Solaris installation program:

/etc/hostname.*interface*

/etc/nodename

/etc/defaultdomain

/etc/inet/hosts

/etc/defaultrouter

/etc/hostname.*interface*

This file defines the network interfaces on the local host. At least one /etc/hostname.*interface* file should exist on the local machine. The Solaris installation program creates this file for you. In the filename, *interface* is replaced by the device name of the primary network interface.

The file contains only one entry: the hostname or IP address associated with the network interface. For example, suppose le0 is the primary network interface for a machine called system1. The file would be called /etc/hostname.le0, and the file would contain the entry `system1`.

/etc/nodename

This file should contain one entry: the hostname of the local machine. For example, on a computer named xena, the file /etc/nodename would contain the entry `xena`.

/etc/defaultdomain

This file is present only if your network uses a name service (described later in this chapter). This file should contain one entry: the fully qualified domain name of the administrative domain to which the local host's network belongs. You can supply this name to the Solaris installation program or edit the file at a later date.

For example, if the host is part of the domain pyramid, which is classified as a .com domain, /etc/defaultdomain should contain the entry `pyramid.com`.

/etc/inet/hosts

The hosts database contains details of the machines on your network. This file contains the hostnames and IP addresses of the primary network interface and any other network addresses the machine must know about. When a user enters a command such as `ping xena`, the system needs to know how to get to the host named xena. The /etc/hosts file provides a cross-reference to look up and find xena's network IP address. For compatibility with BSD-based operating systems, the file /etc/hosts is a symbolic link to /etc/inet/hosts.

Each line in the /etc/inet/hosts file uses the following format:

```
address hostname <nickname> [#comment]
```

Each field in this syntax is described in Table 17-3.

Table 17-3 /etc/inet/hosts File Format

Field	Description
address	The IP address for each interface the local host must know about.
hostname	The hostname assigned to the machine at setup and the hostnames assigned to additional network interfaces that the local host must know about.
<nickname>	An optional field containing a nickname or alias for the host. There can be more than one nickname.
[# comment]	An optional field where you can include a comment.

When you run the Solaris installation program on a system, it sets up the initial /etc/inet/hosts file. This file contains the minimum entries the local host requires: its loopback address, its IP address, and its hostname.

For example, the Solaris installation program might create the following entries in the /etc/inet/hosts file for a system called xena:

```
127.0.0.1       localhost       loghost     #loopback address
192.9.200.3     xena                        #host name
```

In the /etc/inet/hosts file for machine xena, the IP address 127.0.0.1 is the loopback address, the reserved network interface used by the local machine to allow interprocess communication so that it sends packets to itself. The operating system, through the `ifconfig` command, uses the loopback address for configuration and testing. Every machine on a TCP/IP network must have an entry for the localhost and must use the IP address 127.0.0.1.

If you've already installed your operating system and answered no to installing a network, you can either edit the network configuration files manually or reissue the network configuration portion of the installation program.

To reissue the program portion, you must first be superuser. Then type `sys-unconfig` at the command line to restore the system's configuration to an "as-manufactured" state. After you run the command, the system starts up again and prompts you for the system information described in Table 17-4.

Table 17-4 System Information

Information	Action
Hostname	Input a unique name for the computer.
Name service	Select NIS, NIS+, DNS, or a local file you will use.
Time zone	Input your local time zone.
IP address	Input the unique IP address for this host.
IP subnet mask	If your network uses subnets, input the subnet mask.
Root password	Enter a root password.

When the system is finished prompting you for input, it continues the startup process. When the system is started, the network has been configured.

/etc/defaultrouter

This file is present only when you need to define a router for a host. The /etc/defaultrouter file should contain an entry for each router directly connected to the network. The entry should be the name for the network interface that functions as a router between networks.

Network Security Files

Chapter 6, "System Security," covered network security. If necessary, refer to that discussion of configuring the network security files /etc/hosts.equiv and /.rhosts.

IP Addressing

Each host on the TCP/IP network has a unique 32-bit network address—referred to as the *IP address*—that is unique for each host on the network. If the host will participate on the Internet, this address must also be unique to the Internet. For this reason, Internet IP addresses are controlled by an administrative agency, such as the InterNIC.

The IP address is a sequence of four bytes and is written in the form of four decimal integers separated by periods (for example, 0.0.0.0). Each integer is 8 bits long and ranges from 0 to 255. The IP address consists of two parts: a network ID assigned by the InterNIC administrative agency and the host ID assigned by the local administrator. The first integer of the address (0.0.0.0) determines the address type and is referred to as its *class*. There are five classes of IP addresses: A, B, C, D, and E. Without going into great detail, the following is a brief description of each class.

Class A Networks

Class A networks are used for very large networks with millions of hosts, such as the Internet. A class A network number uses the first 8 bits of the IP address as its network ID. The remaining 24 bits comprise the host part of the IP address. The values assigned to the first byte of class A network numbers fall within the range 0 to 127. For example, consider the IP address 75.4.10.4. The value 75 in the first byte indicates that the host is on a class A network. The remaining bytes, 4.10.4, establish the host address. The InterNIC assigns only the first byte of a class A number. Use of the remaining 3 bytes is left to the discretion of the owner of the network number. Only 127 class A networks can exist; each of these networks can accommodate up to 16,777,214 hosts.

Class B Networks

Class B networks are medium-sized networks, such as universities and large businesses with many hosts. A class B network number uses 16 bits for the network number and 16 bits for host numbers. The first byte of a class B network number is in the range 128 to 191. In the number 129.144.50.56, the first 2 bytes, 129.144, are assigned by the InterNIC and comprise the network address. The last 2 bytes, 50.56, make up the host address and are assigned at the discretion of the network's owner. A class B network can accommodate a maximum of 65,534 hosts.

Class C Networks

Class C networks are used for small networks containing fewer than 254 hosts. Class C network numbers use 24 bits for the network number and 8 bits for host numbers. A class C network number occupies the first 3 bytes of an IP address; only the fourth byte is assigned at the discretion of the network's owner. The first byte of a class C network number covers the range 192 to 223. The second and third bytes each cover the range 1 to 255. A typical class C address might be 192.5.2.5, with the first 3 bytes, 192.5.2, forming the network number. The final byte in this example, 5, is the host number. A class C network can accommodate a maximum of 254 hosts.

Class D and E Networks

Class D addresses cover the range 224 to 239 and are used for IP multicasting as defined in RFC 988. Class E addresses cover the range 240 to 255 and are reserved for experimental use.

Planning for IP Addressing

The first step in planning for IP addressing on your network is to determine which network class is appropriate for your network. After you have done this, you can obtain the network number from the InterNIC addressing authority. When you receive your network number, you can plan how you will assign the host parts of the IP address. You can reach the InterNIC Registration Services in several ways:

- Web site: `internic.net`

  Read the FAQ at this Web site to learn more about domain name registration.

- The United States mailing address is

  Network Solutions
  Attn: InterNIC Registration Services
  505 Huntmar Park Drive
  Herndon, VA 22070

- You can send email regarding network registration to `hostmaster@rs.internic.net`.
- The InterNIC phone number is 703-742-4777. Phone service is available from 7 a.m. to 7 p.m. (Eastern Standard Time).
- You can also visit the Internet Corporation for Assigned Names and Numbers (ICANN). ICANN is the new nonprofit corporation that is assuming responsibility from the U.S. Government for coordinating certain Internet technical functions, including the management of the Internet domain name system. More information about ICANN can be found at `www.icann.org`.

NOTE. *Do not arbitrarily assign network numbers to your network, even if you do not plan to attach it to other existing TCP/IP networks. As your network grows, you might decide to connect it to other networks. Changing IP addresses at that time can be a great deal of work and can cause downtime.*

Name Service

When a user enters a command such as `ping xena`, one of the first things that must happen is translation of the hostname xena to an IP address. This can happen in one of two ways.

The IP address can be determined from the /etc/hosts file, or it can be resolved through the *domain name service (DNS)*. For a small network, using just /etc/hosts is not a problem. For a larger network, trying to keep the /etc/hosts file in sync on all hosts can result in a great deal of work, because these files must be exactly the same on each host. If the same address gets used on two different systems, the network could fail.

DNS relies on the named (pronounced “name d”) server to provide hostname-to-IP address translations. The *named server* is a host that permanently stores hostname and IP address information for a specific domain. A *domain name* is the network equivalent of a hostname.

A hostname refers to a specific system on the network, and a domain name refers to a specific network. Sites and institutions are assigned a domain name for their network. In turn, they assign hostnames to systems within their domain. The Internet domain name system provides a scheme by which every site in the world has a unique name.

Name services are discussed again in more detail in Chapter 19, "Name Services."

TCP/IP Commands

TCP/IP offers several commands and features that are supported on the Solaris operating environment. These commands are part of the TCP/IP networking package and are available on most UNIX systems.

telnet

`telnet` is used to log into another system on the network. The following is a sample session:

```
# telnet pyramid1
Trying 192.9.200.4...
Connected to pyramid1.
Escape character is '^]'.

SunOS 5.6
login: bill
Password:
Last login: Sat Jan 16 07:55:03 from 192.9.200.1
Sun Microsystems Inc.   SunOS 5.6       Generic August 1997
pyramid1%
```

rlogin

`rlogin` is also a command for logging into another system on the network. Unlike `telnet`, `rlogin` has a mechanism whereby you don't have to enter a login name and password if the /.rhosts and /etc/hosts.equiv files are in place. These files are discussed in Chapter 6.

ftp

The *File Transfer Protocol (FTP)* is used to transfer one or more files between two systems on the network. Here is a sample `ftp` session:

```
pyramid1% ftp pyramid1
Connected to pyramid1.
220 pyramid1 FTP server (SunOS 5.6) ready.
Name (pyramid1:bill): <cr>
331 Password required for bill.
```

```
Password: <enter password>
230 User bill logged in.
ftp> pwd
257 "/users/bill" is current directory.
ftp> ls
200 PORT command successful.
150 ASCII data connection for /bin/ls (192.9.200.4,47131) (0 bytes).
admin
file1
data
226 ASCII Transfer complete.
19 bytes received in 0.049 seconds (0.38 Kbytes/s)
ftp> get file1 /tmp/file1
200 PORT command successful.
150 ASCII data connection for file1 (192.9.200.4,47132) (31311 bytes).
226 ASCII Transfer complete.
local: /tmp/file1 remote: file1
31441 bytes received in 0.12 seconds (266.82 Kbytes/s)
ftp> bye
221 Goodbye.
pyramid1%
```

rcp

You can also use the `rcp` (remote copy) command to transfer one or more files between two hosts on a network. The other system must trust your ID on the current host. This trust relationship was discussed in Chapter 6.

The `rcp` command is more convenient than `ftp`. First, `rcp` does not require a login or password if the proper trust relationship exists between the systems, which makes it suitable for scripts. Second, `rcp` allows complete directory trees to be copied from one system to another. However, `ftp` has more options and is considered more secure. Here is a sample use of `rcp`:

```
rcp /etc/hosts systemB:/etc/hosts
```

This example uses `rcp` to copy the file /etc/hosts from the local system to systemB.

rsh

You use the `rsh` (remote shell) command to execute a shell on another system on the network. The other system must trust your ID on the current system. The following example uses `rsh` to get a long listing of the directory /etc on systemB:

```
rsh systemB ls -la /etc
```

rexec

The rexec command is also used to execute a shell on a remote system. This command differs from rsh in that you must enter a password. At many sites, rsh is disabled for security reasons and rexec is used as a replacement.

rwho

The rwho command produces output similar to the who command, which was described in Chapter 6, but for all systems on the network.

finger

The finger command displays information about users logged on to the local system or other systems. If finger is used without an argument, it gives information concerning users currently logged in. If finger is used with an argument (for example, the user name glenda), it displays information about all users matching the argument. You can also use the finger command to look up users on a remote system by specifying the user as *username@host*. To protect user privacy, many remote systems do not allow remote fingering of their systems.

rup

The rup command shows the host status of remote systems, similar to the uptime command. For example, to get uptime information about the remote host named sparc14, type

```
rup sparc14
```

The system responds with this:

```
sparc14    up  2 days, 41 mins,  load average: 0.00, 0.00, 0.01
```

ping

Use the ping command to test network connectivity to a particular host. The syntax for the ping command is

```
/usr/sbin/ping <options> <host> [timeout]
```

<host> is the hostname of the machine in question, and [timeout] is an optional argument to specify the time in seconds for ping to keep trying to reach the machine. 20 seconds is the default.

Some of the more common options to the ping command are described in Table 17-5.

Table 17-5 *ping* Options

Option	Description
-v	Verbose output. Lists any ICMP packets, other than ECHO_RESPONSE, that are received.
-I <interval>	Specifies the interval between successive transmissions. The default is 1 second.
-s	When the -s flag is specified, ping sends one datagram per second (adjustable with -I) and prints one line of output for every ECHO_RESPONSE it receives.

When you run `ping`, the ICMP protocol sends a datagram to the host you specify, asking for a response. ICMP is the protocol responsible for error handling on a TCP/IP network.

To test network connectivity between ultra5 and sparc14, type the following:

```
ping sparc14
```

If host sparc14 is up, this message is displayed:

```
sparc14 is alive
```

It indicates that sparc14 responded to the ICMP request. However, if sparc14 is down or cannot receive the ICMP packets, you receive the following response:

```
no answer from sparc14
```

If you suspect that a machine might be losing packets even though it is up, you can use the `-s` option of `ping` to try to detect the problem. For example, type

```
ping -s sparc14
```

`ping` continually sends packets to sparc14 until you send an interrupt character or a timeout occurs. The responses on your screen will resemble this:

```
PING sparc14: 56 data bytes
64 bytes from sparc14 (192.9.200.14): icmp_seq=0. time=1. ms
64 bytes from sparc14 (192.9.200.14): icmp_seq=1. time=0. ms
64 bytes from sparc14 (192.9.200.14): icmp_seq=2. time=0. ms
64 bytes from sparc14 (192.9.200.14): icmp_seq=3. time=0. ms
64 bytes from sparc14 (192.9.200.14): icmp_seq=4. time=0. ms
...
...
----sparc14 PING Statistics----
8 packets transmitted, 8 packets received, 0% packet loss
round-trip (ms)  min/avg/max = 0/0/1
```

The packet loss statistic at the end of the output indicates whether the host has dropped packets, which could indicate a network problem.

spray

The `spray` command tests the reliability of your network. It can tell you whether packets are being delayed or dropped. `spray` sends a one-way stream of packets to a host using a Remote Procedure Call (RPC). It reports how many were received, as well as the transfer rate.

The syntax is

```
spray  [ -c <count> -d <interval> -l <packet_size>] <hostname>
```

Each option in this syntax is described in Table 17-6.

Table 17-6 *spray* Options

Field	Description
`-c <count>`	Specifies the number of packets to send.
`-d <interval>`	Specifies the number of microseconds to pause between sending packets. If you don't use a delay, you might run out of buffers.
`-l <packet_size>`	Specifies the packet size.
`<hostname>`	Specifies the system to send packets to. The `hostname` argument can be either a name or an Internet address.

`spray` is not useful as a networking benchmark, because it uses unreliable connectionless transports such as the User Datagram Protocol (UDP). `spray` can report a large number of packets dropped when the drops were caused by `spray`'s sending packets faster than they could be buffered locally (before the packets got to the network medium). `spray` is used, however, to verify connectivity between two hosts and to test the operation of the network.

The following example illustrates the use of `spray` to send 100 packets to sparc14 (`-c 100`). Each packet has a size of 2048 bytes (`-l 2048`). The packets are sent with a delay time of 20 microseconds between each burst (`-d 20`):

```
spray -c100 -d20 -l2048 sparc14
```

The system responds with this:

```
sending 100 packets of length 2048 to sparc14 ...
2 packets (2.000%) dropped by sparc14
567 packets/sec, 1161394 bytes/sec
```

Network Maintenance

In addition to the TCP/IP set of commands, Solaris provides several network commands that the system administrator can use to check and troubleshoot the network. To verify that the network is operational, follow these steps:

1. Check the network connection to another system by typing

   ```
   ping <options> <ip address>
   ```

   For example, to check the network between systemA and systemB, type `ping systemB` from systemA. If the check is successful, the remote system replies with this:

   ```
   systemB is alive
   ```

   If the network is not active, you get this message:

   ```
   no answer from systemB
   ```

   If this is the response, check your cabling and make sure the remote system is configured properly.

2. Check for network traffic by typing

   ```
   netstat -i 5
   ```

   The system responds with this:

   ```
     input    le0     output             input(Total)    output
   packets  errs    packets  errs  colls packets  errs   packets  errs  colls
   95218    49983   189      1     0     218706   49983  123677   1     0
   0        0       0        0     0     3        0      3        0     0
   0        0       0        0     0     4        0      4        0     0
   1        1       0        0     0     144      1      143      0     0
   0        0       0        0     0     256      0      256      0     0
   0        0       0        0     0     95       0      95       0     0
   0        0       0        0     0     1171     0      1171     0     0
   ```

   The `netstat` command is used to monitor the system's TCP/IP network activity. `netstat` can provide some basic data about how much and what kind of network activity is happening. The `-i` option shows the state of the network interface used for TCP/IP traffic. The last option, `5`, reissues the `netstat` command every 5 seconds to get a good sampling of network activity. Press Ctrl+C to break out of the `netstat` command.

3. Look in the `colls` column for a high number of collisions. To calculate the network collision rate, divide the number of output collisions (output colls) by the number of output packets. A network-wide collision rate of greater than 10 percent can indicate an overloaded network, a poorly configured network, or hardware problems.

4. Examine the `errs` column for a high number of errors. To calculate the input packet error rate, divide the number of input errors by the total number of input packets. If the input error rate is high—more than 25 percent—the host might be dropping packets due to transmission problems. Transmission problems can be caused by other hardware on the network, as well as heavy traffic and low-level hardware problems. Routers can drop packets, forcing retransmissions and causing degraded performance.

5. Type `ping -sRv <hostname>` from the client to determine how long it takes a packet to make a round trip on the network. If the round trip takes more than a few milliseconds, there are slow routers on the network, or the network is very busy. Issue the `ping` command twice and ignore the first set of results. The `ping -sRv` command also displays packet losses. If you suspect a physical problem, use `ping -sRv` to find the response time of several hosts on the network. If the response time (in milliseconds) from one host is not what you expect, investigate that host.

Summary

In a networked environment, system performance depends on how well you've maintained your network. An overloaded network will disguise itself as a slow system and can even cause downtime. Monitor your network continuously. You need to know how the network looks when things are running well so that you know what to look for when the network is performing poorly. The network commands described in this chapter only report numbers. You're the one who decides if these numbers are acceptable for your environment. As stated earlier, when it comes to system administration, practice and experience will help you excel as a system administrator. The same holds true for administering a network.

In the next chapter, I'll describe how to access remote file systems across the network using NFS.

CHAPTER

18

The NFS Environment

The following test objectives are covered in this chapter:

- Understanding the relationship between Network File System (NFS) servers and NFS clients
- Understanding NFS on Solaris
- Mounting remote file systems using NFS
- Understanding WebNFS
- Sharing and accessing remote resources
- Configuring and using a CacheFS
- Configuring and using Autofs

The NFS service lets computers of different architectures, running different operating systems (OSs), share file systems across a network. Just as the `mount` command lets you mount a file system on a local disk, NFS lets you mount a file system that is located on another system anywhere on the network. Furthermore, NFS support has been implemented on many platforms, ranging from MS-DOS on personal computers to mainframe OSs, such as MVS. Each OS applies the NFS model to its file system semantics. For example, a Sun system can mount the file system from a Windows NT or Linux system located miles away. File system operations, such as reading and writing, function as though they were accessing a local file. Response time might be slower because of network traffic, but the connection is transparent to the user regardless of the hardware or OS.

The NFS service provides the following benefits:

- Lets multiple computers use the same files so that everyone on the network can access the same data. This eliminates the need to have redundant data on several systems.
- Reduces storage costs by having computers share applications and data.
- Provides data consistency and reliability, because all users can read the same set of files.
- Makes mounting of file systems transparent to users.
- Makes accessing remote files transparent to users.
- Supports heterogeneous environments.
- Reduces system administration overhead.

The NFS service makes the physical location of the file system irrelevant to the user. You can use NFS to allow users to see all the data, regardless of location. Instead of placing copies of commonly used files on every system, NFS lets the system administrator place one copy on one computer's disk and have all other systems access it across the network. Under NFS operation, remote file systems are almost indistinguishable from local ones.

Servers and Clients

With NFS, systems have a client-server relationship. The NFS server is where the file system resides. Any system with a local file system can be an NFS server. As I will describe later in this chapter, the system administrator configures the NFS server to make file systems available to other systems and users. The system administrator has complete control over which file systems can be mounted and who can mount them.

An NFS client is a system that mounts a remote file system from an NFS server. I'll describe later in this chapter how the system administrator creates a local directory and mounts the file system. As you will see, a system can be both an NFS server and an NFS client.

NFS on Solaris

NFS was developed by Sun Microsystems, and it has been ported to most popular OSs. The implementation of NFS is large, and it varies from system to system. As the NFS service evolved, it went through a few different versions. Therefore, if you are using NFS to connect to another system, you need to be aware of the different versions of NFS.

NFS version 2 was the first version of the NFS protocol in wide use. It continues to be available on a large variety of platforms. SunOS releases prior to Solaris 2.5 support version 2 of the NFS protocol. It should be noted that NFS 2.0 suffers many shortcomings. For example, UNIX-based servers are now moving to faster 64-bit implementations, and the 8KB data packet size used by NFS version 2 is a bottleneck for transferring data. Sun, Digital, IBM, Hewlett-Packard, and Data General toiled with these and other problems. Together, they released NFS 3.0 in 1995 as RFC 1813. The only time you should have to deal with version 2.0 is if you are dealing with an older version of an operating system such as Solaris 2.4 or HP-UX version 10.

NFS 3.0 was introduced with Solaris 2.5. Several changes have been made to improve interoperability and performance, including the following enhancements over version 2:

- Enables safe asynchronous writes onto the server, which improves performance by allowing the server to cache client write requests in memory. The client does not need to wait for the server to commit the changes to disk; therefore, the response time is faster.
- The server can batch requests, which improves the response time on the server.
- All NFS operations return the file attributes, which are stored in the local cache. Because the cache is updated more often, the need to do a separate operation to update this data arises less often. Therefore, the number of remote procedure calls to the server is reduced, improving performance.
- The process for verifying file access permissions has been improved. In particular, version 2 would generate a message reporting a "write error" or a "read error" if users tried to copy a remote file to which they did not have permission. In version 3, the permissions are checked before the file is opened, so the error is reported as an "open error."
- Version 3 removes the 8KB transfer size limit and lets the client and server negotiate a maximum transfer size.

- Access control list (ACL) support was added to the version 3 release. ACLs, described in Chapter 6, "System Security," provide a finer-grained mechanism to set file access permissions than is available through standard UNIX file permissions.
- The default transport protocol for the NFS protocol was changed from User Datagram Protocol (UDP) to Transport Control Protocol (TCP), which helps performance on slow networks and wide-area networks (WANs). UDP was preferred initially because it performed well on local-area networks (LANs) and was faster than TCP. Although UDP benefited from the high bandwidth and low latency typical of LANs, it performed poorly when subjected to the low bandwidth and high latency of WANs, such as the Internet. In recent years, improvements in hardware and TCP implementations have narrowed this advantage enough that TCP implementations can now outperform UDP. A growing number of NFS implementations now support TCP. TCP provides congestion control and error recovery.
- Version 3 improved the network lock manager, which provides UNIX record locking and PC file sharing for NFS files. The locking mechanism is now more reliable for NFS files; therefore, commands such as `ksh` and `mail`, which use locking, are less likely to hang.

It should be noted that to take advantage of these improvements, the version 3 protocol must be running on both the NFS server and the NFS clients.

With Solaris 2.6, the NFS 3.0 protocol went through still more enhancements:

- Correct manipulation of files larger than 2GB, which was not formerly possible.
- Defaults to a 32KB transfer size. The effect of larger transfer sizes is to reduce the number of NFS requests required to move a given quantity of data, providing a better use of network bandwidth and I/O resources on clients and servers. If the server supports it, a client can issue a read request that downloads a file in a single operation.
- Supports dynamic failover of read-only file systems. This provides a high level of availability. With failover, multiple replicas are specified in case an NFS server goes down, and another mount point on an alternative server can be specified.
- Gives WebNFS the ability to make a file system on the Internet accessible through firewalls using an extension to the NFS protocol. WebNFS provides greater throughput, under a heavy load, than Hypertext Transfer Protocol (HTTP) access to a Web server. In addition, it provides the ability to share files over the Internet without the administrative overhead of an anonymous File Transfer Protocol (FTP) site. WebNFS is described later in this chapter.

NOTE. *When using NFS, make sure that the systems you'll be connecting to are all at the same version of NFS. You might experience problems if your system is at NFS version 2 and the system to which you are trying to connect is at NFS 3.0.*

NFS Daemons

NFS uses a number of daemons to handle its services. These services are initialized at startup from the /etc/init.d/nfs.server and /etc/init.d/nfs.clients startup scripts. The most important NFS daemons are outlined in Table 18-1.

Table 18-1 NFS Daemons

Daemon	Description
`nfsd`	Handles file system exporting and file access requests from remote systems. An NFS server runs multiple instances of this daemon. This daemon is usually invoked at run level 3 and is started by the /etc/init.d/nfs.server startup script.
`mountd`	Handles mount requests from NFS clients. This daemon also provides information about which file systems are mounted by which clients. Use the `showmount` command, described later in this chapter, to view this information.
`lockd`	Manages file locking on both the NFS server and the NFS client systems.
`statd`	Interacts with `lockd` to provide the crash and recovery functions for the locking services on NFS.
`rpcbind`	Facilitates the initial connection between the client and the server.

Setting Up NFS

Servers let other systems access their file systems by sharing them over the NFS environment. A shared file system is referred to as a shared resource. You specify which file systems are to be shared by entering the information in a file called /etc/dfs/dfstab. Entries in this file are shared automatically whenever you start the NFS server operation. You should set up automatic sharing if you need to share the same set of file systems on a regular basis. Most file system sharing should be done automatically; the only time manual sharing should occur is during testing or troubleshooting.

The /etc/dfs/dfstab file lists all the file systems your NFS server shares with its NFS clients. It also controls which clients can mount a file system. If you want to modify /etc/dfs/dfstab to add or delete a file system or to modify the way sharing is done, edit the file with a text editor, such as vi or textedit. The next time the computer enters run level 3, the system reads the updated /etc/dfs/dfstab to determine which file systems should be shared automatically.

Each line in the dfstab file consists of a `share` command, as shown in the following example:

```
more /etc/dfs/dfstab
```

The system displays the contents of /etc/dfs/dfstab:

```
#       Place share(1M) commands here for automatic execution
#       on entering init state 3.
#
#       Issue the command '/etc/init.d/nfs.server start' to run the NFS
#       daemon processes and the share commands, after adding the very
#       first entry to this file.
#
#       share [-F fstype] [ -o options] [-d "<text>"] <pathname> [resource]
#       .e.g,
#       share  -F nfs  -o rw=engineering  -d "home dirs"  /export/home2
share -F nfs /export
share -F nfs /cdrom/solaris_srvr_intranet_ext_1_0
```

The `/usr/sbin/share` command exports a resource or makes a resource available for mounting. If invoked with no arguments, `share` displays all shared file systems. The `share` command, described in Table 18-2, can be run at the command line to achieve the same results as the /etc/dfs/dfstab file, but use this method only when testing.

The syntax for the `share` command is

```
share -F <FSType> -o <options> -d <description> <pathname>
```

where `<pathname>` is the name of the file system to be shared.

Table 18-2 The *share* Command

Option	Description	
`-F <FSType>`	Specify the file system type, such as NFS. If the `-F` option is omitted, the first file system type listed in /etc/dfs/fstypes is used as the default.	
`-o <options>`	Select from the following options:	
	`rw`	`pathname` is shared read/write to all clients. This is also the default behavior.
	`rw=client[:client]...`	`pathname` is shared read/write but only to the listed clients. No other systems can access `pathname`.
	`ro`	`pathname` is shared read-only to all clients.
	`ro=client[:client]...`	`pathname` is shared read-only, but only to the listed clients. No other systems can access `pathname`.

continues

Table 18-2 The *share* Command (continued)

Option	Description	
	aclok	Allows the NFS server to do access control for NFS version 2 clients (running SunOS 2.4 or earlier). When aclok is set on the server, maximum access is given to all clients. For example, with aclok set, if anyone has read permissions, everyone does. If aclok is not set, minimal access is given to all clients.
	anon=<uid>	Sets uid to be the effective user ID of unknown users. By default, unknown users are given the effective uid nobody. If uid is set to -1, access is denied.
	index=<file>	Loads a file rather than a listing of the directory containing this specific file when the directory is referenced by an NFS Uniform Resource Locator (URL). See the section "WebNFS" later in this chapter.
	nosub	Prevents clients from mounting subdirectories of shared directories.
	nosuid	The server file system silently ignores any attempt to enable the setuid or setgid mode bits. By default, clients can create files on the shared file system if the setuid or setgid mode is enabled. See Chapter 6 for a description of setuid and setgid.
	public	Enables NFS browsing of the file system by a WebNFS-enabled browser. Only one file system per server can use this option. The -ro=list and -rw=list options can be included with this option.
	root=host[: host]...	Only root users from the specified hosts have root access. By default, no host has root access, so root users are mapped to an anonymous user ID (see the previous description of the anon=<uid> option).
	sec=<mode>	Uses one or more of the security modes specified by <mode> to authenticate clients.
-d <description>	Provides a description of the resource being shared.	

To share a file system as read-only every time the system is started up, add this line to the /etc/dfs/dfstab file:

```
share -F nfs -o ro /data
```

After editing the /etc/dfs/dfstab file, restart the NFS server by either restarting it or by typing this:

```
/etc/init.d/nfs.server start
```

You only need to start the nfs.server script after you make the first entry in the /etc/dfs/dfstab file. This is because at startup, when the system enters run level 3, `mountd` and `nfsd` are not started if the /etc/dfs/dfstab file is empty. After you have made an initial entry and have executed the nfs.server script, you can modify /etc/dfs/dfstab without restarting the daemons. You simply execute the `shareall` command, and any new entries in the /etc/dfs/dfstab file are shared.

NOTE. *Even if you share a file system from the command line by typing the* `share` *command,* `mountd` *and* `nfsd` *still won't run until you make an entry into /etc/dfs/dfstab and run the nfs.server script.*

After you have at least one entry in the /etc/dfs/dfstab file and after both `mountd` and `nfsd` are running, you can share additional file systems by typing the `share` command directly from the command line. Be aware, however, that if you don't add the entry to the /etc/dfs/dfstab file, the file system is not automatically shared the next time the system is restarted.

The `dfshares` command displays information about the shared resources available to the host from an NFS server. Here is the syntax for `dfshares`:

```
dfshares <servername>
```

You can view the shared file systems on a remote NFS server by using the `dfshares` command as follows:

```
dfshares apollo
```

If no `servername` is specified, all resources currently being shared on the local host are displayed. Another place to find information on shared resources is in the server's /etc/dfs/sharetab file. This file contains a list of the resources currently being shared.

NFS Security

With NFS, you need to be concerned about security. When you issue the `share` command, any system can access the file system through your network. It's a good idea to be more specific about who can mount the file system. The following examples illustrate how to set up a share with restrictions as to which hosts can mount the shared resource:

```
share -F nfs -o ro=apollo:neptune:zeus /data
```

The file system named /data is shared read-only to the listed clients only. No other systems can access /data. Another method is to share a file system read-only to some hosts and read-write to others. Use the following command to accomplish this:

```
share -F nfs -o ro=apollo rw=neptune:zeus /data
```

In this example, apollo has read-only access, and neptune and zeus have read-write access.

The next example specifies that root access be granted to the client named zeus. A root user coming from any other system is recognized only as nobody and has limited access rights:

```
share -F nfs -o root=zeus /data
```

CAUTION! *Root permissions should not be enabled on an NFS file system. Administrators might find this annoying if they're trying to modify a file through an NFS mount, but disastrous mistakes can be eliminated. For example, if a root user wants to purge a file system called /data on one host, an* `rm -rf *` *would be disastrous if there is an NFS mounted file system with root permission mounted under /data. If /data/thor is a mounted file system under /data, the files located on the NFS server would be wiped out.*

To remove a shared file system, issue the `unshare` command on the server as follows:

```
unshare /data
```

The /data file system is no longer shared. You can verify this by issuing the `share` command with no options:

```
share
```

The system responds with this:

```
-              /home    ro,anon=0     ""
```

Only the file system named /home is returned as shared.

NOTE. *If* `share` *commands are invoked multiple times on the same file system, the last* `share` *invocation supersedes the previous ones. The options set by the last* `share` *command replace the old options.*

Mounting a Remote File System

Chapter 4, "Introduction to File Systems," described how to mount a local file system using the `mount` command. We'll use the same `mount` command to mount a shared file system on a remote host using NFS. Here is the syntax for mounting NFS file systems:

```
mount -F nfs <options> <-o specific_options > <-O> <server>:<filesystem> <mount_point>
```

In this example, `server` is the name of the NFS server in which the file system is located, `filesystem` is the name of the shared file system on the NFS server, and `mount_point` is the name of the local directory that serves as the mount point.

As you can see, this is similar to mounting a local file system. The options are described in Table 18-3.

Table 18-3 NFS *mount* Command

Option	Description	
-F <Fstype>	Used to specify the FSType on which to operate. The FSType must be specified in /etc/vfstab, or by consulting /etc/default/fs or /etc/dfs/fstypes.	
-r	Mounts the specified file system as read-only.	
-m	Does not append an entry to the /etc/mnttab table of mounted file systems.	
-o <specific_options>	`specific_options` is any of the following options separated by a comma:	
	rw | ro	The resource is mounted read-write or read-only. The default is rw.
	suid | nosuid	setuid execution is enabled or disabled. The default is suid.
	remount	If a file system is mounted as read-only, this option remounts it as read-write.
	bg | fg	If the first attempt to mount the remote file system fails, retry in the background (bg) or in the foreground (fg). The default is fg.
	quota	Lets quota check whether the user is over the quota on this file system. If the file system has quotas enabled on the server, quotas will still be checked for operations on this file system.
	noquota	Prevents quota from checking whether the user exceeded the quota on this file system. If the file system has quotas enabled on the server, quotas will still be checked for operations on this file system.
	retry=n	The number of times to retry the mount operation. The default is 10000.
	vers=<NFS version number>	By default, the version of NFS protocol used between the client and the server is the highest one available on both systems. If the NFS server does not support NFS 3.0 protocol, the NFS mount uses version 2.

continues

Table 18-3 NFS *mount* Command (continued)

<table>
<tr><th>Option</th><th>Description</th><th></th></tr>
<tr><td></td><td>port=n</td><td>The server IP port number. The default is NFS_PORT.</td></tr>
<tr><td></td><td>rsize=<n></td><td>Sets the read buffer size to <n> bytes. The default value is 32768 if you're using version 3 of the NFS protocol. The default can be negotiated down if the server prefers a smaller transfer size. If you're using NFS version 2, the default value is 8192.</td></tr>
<tr><td></td><td>wsize=<n></td><td>Sets the write buffer size to <n> bytes. The default value is 32768 if you're using version 3 of the NFS protocol. The default can be negotiated down if the server prefers a smaller transfer size. If you're using version 2, the default value is 8192.</td></tr>
<tr><td></td><td>timeo=<n></td><td>Sets the NFS timeout to <n> tenths of a second. The default value is 11 tenths of a second for connectionless transports and 600 tenths of a second for connection-oriented transports.</td></tr>
<tr><td></td><td>retrans=<n></td><td>Sets the number of NFS retransmissions to <n>; the default value is 5. For connection-oriented transports, this option has no effect, because it is assumed that the transport will perform retransmissions on behalf of NFS.</td></tr>
<tr><td></td><td>soft | hard</td><td>Returns an error if the server does not respond (soft), or continues the retry request until the server responds (hard). If you're using hard, the system appears to hang until the NFS server responds. The default value is hard.</td></tr>
<tr><td></td><td>intr | nointr</td><td>Enables or does not enable keyboard interrupts to kill a process that hangs while waiting for a response on a hard-mounted file system. The default is intr, which makes it possible for clients to interrupt applications that might be waiting for an NFS server to respond.</td></tr>
<tr><td></td><td>-O</td><td>The overlay mount lets the file system be mounted over an existing mount point, making the underlying file system inaccessible. If a mount is attempted on a preexisting mount point without this flag's being set, the mount fails, producing the error "device busy."</td></tr>
</table>

Here's a note regarding foreground (fg) and background (bg) mounts: File systems mounted with the bg option indicate that mount is to retry in the background if the server's mount daemon (mountd) does not respond when, for example, the NFS server is restarted. From the NFS client, mount retries the request up to the count specified in the retry=<n> option. After the file system is mounted, each NFS request made in the kernel waits a specified number of seconds for a response (specified with the timeo=<n> option). If no response arrives, the time-out is multiplied by 2, and the request is retransmitted. If the number of retransmissions has reached the number specified in the retrans=<n> option, a file system mounted with the soft option returns an error, and the file system mounted with the hard option prints a warning message and continues to retry the request. Sun recommends that file systems mounted as read-write, or containing executable files, should always be mounted with the hard option. If you use soft mounted file systems, unexpected I/O errors can occur. For example, consider a write request. If the NFS server goes down, the pending write request simply gives up, resulting in a corrupted file on the remote file system. A read-write file system should always be mounted with the specified hard and intr options. This lets users make their own decisions about killing hung processes. Use the following to mount a file system named /data located on a host named thor with the hard and intr options:

```
mount -F nfs -o hard,intr thor:/data /data
```

If a file system is mounted hard and the intr option is not specified, the process hangs until the remote file system reappears if the NFS server goes down. For a terminal process, this can be annoying. If intr is specified, sending an interrupt signal to the process kills it. For a terminal process, this can be done by pressing Ctrl+C. For a background process, sending an INT or QUIT signal as follows usually works:

```
kill -QUIT 3421
```

NOTE. *Sending a KILL signal (-9) does not kill a hung NFS process.*

To mount a file system called /data, which is located on an NFS server called thor, issue the following command, as root, from the NFS client:

```
mount -F nfs -o ro thor:/data /thor_data
```

In this case, the /data file system from the server thor is mounted read-only on /thor_data on the local system. Mounting from the command line enables temporary viewing of the file system. If the umount command is issued or the system is restarted, the mount is lost. If you would like this file system to be mounted automatically at every startup, add the following line to the /etc/vfstab file:

```
thor:/data - /thor_data nfs - yes ro
```

NOTE. *The* `mount` *and* `umount` *commands require root access. The* `umount` *command and /etc/vfstab file are described in Chapter 4.*

To view resources that can be mounted on the local or remote system, use the `dfmounts` command as follows:

```
dfmounts sparcserver
```

The system responds with a list of file systems currently mounted on sparcserver:

```
RESOURCE    SERVER       PATHNAME                                         CLIENTS
   -        sparcserver  /cdrom/sol_2_6_hw2_sparc_smcc_dt/s0              pyramid2
   -        sparcserver  /cdrom/solaris_srvr_intranet_ext_1_0 (anon)      ntserver
   -        sparcserver  /jumpstart                                       pyramid2
   -        sparcserver  /usr/local/boot/Solaris_2.6/Tools/Boot           pyramid2
```

Sometimes you rely on NFS mount points for critical information. If the NFS server were to go down unexpectedly, you would lose the information contained at that mount point. You can address this issue by using client-side failover. With client-side failover, you specify an alternative file system to use in case the primary file system fails. These file systems should contain equivalent directory structures and identical files. This option is available only on read-only file systems. To set up client-side failover, follow this procedure:

On the NFS client, mount the file system using the `-ro` option. You can do this from the command line or by adding an entry to the /etc/vfstab file that looks like the following:

```
zeus,thor:/data   -   /remote_data   nfs   -   no   -o ro
```

If multiple file systems are named and the first server in the list is down, failover uses the next alternative server to access files. To mount a replicated set of NFS file systems, which might have different paths to the file system, use the following `mount` command:

```
mount -F nfs -o ro zeus:/usr/local/data,thor:/home/data /usr/local/data
```

Replication is discussed again in the section that describes Autofs.

WebNFS

WebNFS is a product and proposed standard protocol from Sun Microsystems that extends its NFS to the Internet. Sun believes WebNFS offers considerable performance advantages over the current Internet protocols, HTTP and FTP. Netscape, Oracle, IBM, Apple, and Novell have announced support for WebNFS.

The World Wide Web has become the people's choice for information distribution and sharing across the Internet. The Web's ease of use and widespread availability have helped it outshine similar technologies. Unfortunately, the protocol for the Web, HTTP, leaves much to be desired in terms of performance. HTTP is a one-way protocol that transfers multiple data formats inefficiently. Entire pages and all their contents must be transferred at the same time to the requesting browser. On the other hand, NFS works with only portions of files at a time, usually only the sections that are in use. It is possible to update sections of a file with NFS, a task that is virtually impossible with HTTP. The following are the benefits of WebNFS over HTTP and FTP:

- **Connection management**—A WebNFS client can download multiple files over a single persistent TCP connection.
- **Concurrency**—WebNFS clients can issue multiple concurrent requests to an NFS server. The effect is a better use of server and network resources and better performance for the end user.
- **Fault tolerance**—WebNFS is well-known for its fault tolerance in the face of network and server failures. If interrupted, other FTPs require the download to be restarted from the beginning, causing users to retrace steps and waste time in duplicating efforts. However, if a WebNFS client faces an interruption, it can resume a download from where it left off.
- **Performance and scalability**—NFS servers currently handle over 21,000 operations per second. They are highly integrated with the OS, tuned for maximum system performance, and easy to administer.

WebNFS makes remote file access simple and safe. In addition, it can work with and through firewalls, meaning that system administrators can now specify which directories or files they want to "export," or make available over the Internet. After these files are exported and an application requests them, WebNFS can automatically locate them, negotiate file access privileges, and transparently "mount" the files from anywhere on the Internet. Users can then access that data as if it were local to their machine.

Unlike current file access protocols, such as FTP and HTTP, WebNFS is a complete file system that supports in-place editing of a file, eliminating the need to download, edit, and upload the file. Instead, users can edit the original file right from their desktops. This saves time and preserves the integrity of shared files.

WebNFS can mount an entire file system at a time, or it can communicate with individual files on the server. This feature is known as multi-component lookup (MCL), and it lets the client look up a document based on a full given path to a file rather than having to look up individual components of that path until deriving the actual file location. For example, to look up a file such as /books/solaris/test.txt in NFS, you have to look up the individual components (books and solaris) before you can find test.txt. With WebNFS, you simply pass the entire path to the server itself and have the server return the file handle directly. This improves performance by saving several steps of data transfers.

WebNFS also follows the improvements in NFS 3.0 by including larger data transfers than the 8KB limit imposed in NFS 2.0, a 64-bit data word size for files, and file systems larger than 4GB.

To use WebNFS, your Web browser needs a client, and the Web or FTP server needs to have a WebNFS server. If you request a file with WebNFS, your Internet address or URL would look something like one of the following:

```
nfs://computer.site.com/filedirectory/file

nfs://<server>:<port>/<path>

nfs://mymachine.javaworld.com:2049/home/rawn/webnfs.txt

nfs://mymachine.javaworld.com/pub/edit.doc
```

NOTE. *Note that a pathname for an NFS URL should not begin with a slash. A path that begins with a slash is evaluated relative to the server's root rather than the public file handle directory.*

NFS replaces the HTTP or FTP schema and needs to be implemented directly into the browser. The default port number is 2049; if the port is omitted, it defaults to 2049. This is the NFS port for TCP connections. The directory structure just shown is actually a relative path from a base that the NFS server understands.

Sun Microsystems suggests that WebNFS might be a technology proposal to replace, or be part of, the next generation of HTTP, currently being worked on by members of the World Wide Web Consortium (W3C).

How to Enable WebNFS Access

Starting with Solaris 2.6, all file systems available for NFS mounting are automatically available for WebNFS access. To manually configure a file system for WebNFS access, follow these steps:

1. Edit the /etc/dfs/dfstab file. Add one entry to the /etc/dfs/dfstab file for the file system you want shared automatically. The `index` tag is optional, but the `public` option enables NFS browsing of the file system by a WebNFS-enabled browser (see Table 18-2):

   ```
   share -F nfs -o ro,public,index=index.html /export/ftp
   ```

2. Check that the NFS service is running on the server. If this is the first `share` command (or set of `share` commands) that you have initiated, it is likely that the NFS daemons are not running. The following commands kill and restart the daemons:

   ```
   /etc/init.d/nfs.server stop
   /etc/init.d/nfs.server start
   ```

3. Share the file system. After the entry is in /etc/dfs/dfstab, the file system can be shared either by restarting the system or by using the `shareall` command. If the NFS daemons were restarted in step 2, this command does not need to be run, because the init.d script runs the command.

   ```
   shareall
   ```

4. Verify that the information is correct. Execute the `share` command to check that the correct options are listed:

   ```
   share
   ```

   The system should respond with output that looks something like this:

   ```
   -        /export/share/man    ro    ""
   -        /usr/src      rw=eng    ""
   -        /export/ftp     ro,public,index=index.html   ""
   ```

Using a Browser to Access an NFS URL

Browsers that can support WebNFS access should provide access using an NFS URL that looks something like this:

```
nfs://<server>:<port>/<path>
```

`server` is the name of the file server, `port` is the port number to use (the default value is 2049), and `path` is the path to the file or file system. The path can be either relative to the public file handle or relative to the root file system on the server.

NOTE. *Make sure your browser supports WebNFS. If it doesn't, you'll get an error similar to the following: "NFS URLs are not supported." Currently, Sun's HotJava browser supports WebNFS, and Netscape says that it will provide support in a future release. Microsoft's Internet Explorer does not support WebNFS.*

You can enable WebNFS access for clients that are not part of the local subnet by configuring the firewall to enable a TCP connection on port 2049. Just allowing access for httpd does not allow NFS URLs to be used.

CacheFS

A fundamental factor in computer performance is file access time. In a networked environment using NFS, every file access request across the network affects performance. The Cache File System (CacheFS) can be used to improve performance of NFS mounted file systems or slow devices such as a CD-ROM. When a file system is cached, the data read from the remote file system or CD-ROM is stored in a cache on the local system's disk. First, let's introduce some terms:

- **Back file system**—The file system on the remote host, or CD-ROM, that is being cached. Typically this is an NFS or HSFS file system. Files in the back file system are called back files.
- **Front file system**—The file system that contains the cached data, typically a UFS file system. Files in the front file system are called front files.
- **Cached file system**—The file system that resides on the local disk. Files in it are cached files.
- **Cache directory**—The directory on the local disk where the data for the cached file system is stored.
- **Cold cache**—A cache that does not yet have any data in its front file system. To create a cache, requested data must be copied from the back file system to the front file system. This is referred to as populating the cache. An attempt to reference data that is not yet cached is referred to as a cache miss.
- **Warm cache**—A cache that contains the desired data in its front file system. Requested data is available to the user without requiring any action from the back file system. An attempt to reference data that is already cached is referred to as a cache hit.

Creating the Cache

A cache must exist before a CacheFS mount can be performed. No special disk partitioning is required for cache creation. A cache file system may be created in a subdirectory of an existing file system, or you can dedicate an entire file system to caching. The only requirement is that you create the cache in mounted local file systems. The `cfsadmin` command creates the local cache.

NOTE. *Do not make the front file system read-only, and do not set quotas on it. A read-only front file system prevents caching, and file system quotas interfere with control mechanisms built into CacheFS.*

There are two steps to setting up a cached file system:

1. Create the cache with the `cfsadmin` command. `cfsadmin` administers disk space used for caching file systems with CacheFS. The syntax for creating the cache with the `cfsadmin` command is

   ```
   cfsadmin -c <cache-directory>
   ```

   `<cache-directory>` indicates the name of the directory where the cache resides.

NOTE. *After you have created the cache, do not perform any operations in the cache directory itself. This causes conflicts within the CacheFS software.*

The following example creates a cache:

```
mkdir /local
cfsadmin -c  /local/cache1
```

The `cfsadmin` command creates a subdirectory called cache1 that contains the CacheFS data structures necessary to allow a CacheFS mount.

2. Mount the file system you want cached using the `-F cachefs` option to the `mount` command. Here is the syntax to mount a file system in a cache with the `mount` command:

```
mount -F cachefs -o backfstype=<fstype>,cachedir=<cache-directory>[, options]
➥<back-filesystem mount-point>
```

`backfstype=<fstype>` indicates the file system type of the back file system. (`fstype` can be either `nfs` or `hsfs`.)

`cachedir=<cache-directory>` indicates the name of the directory where the cache resides. This is the same name you specified when you created the cache in step 1.

`[options]` specifies other mount options that you can include when mounting a file system in a cache. These options, listed in Table 18-4, are preceded with `-o` and can be grouped in a comma-separated list with no spaces.

`<back-filesystem>` is the mount point of the back file system to cache. If the back file system is an NFS file system, you must specify the host name of the server from which you are mounting the file system and the name of the file system to cache (separated by a colon), such as `sparc21:/data`.

`<mount-point>` indicates the directory where the file system is mounted.

Table 18-4 *mount* Options

Option	Description
acdirmax=n	Specifies that cached attributes are held for no more than *n* seconds after a directory update. After *n* seconds, all directory information is purged from the cache. The default value is 30 seconds.
acdirmin=n	Specifies that cached attributes are held for at least *n* seconds after directory update. After *n* seconds, CacheFS checks to see if the directory modification time on the back file system has changed. If it has, all information about the directory is purged from the cache, and new data is retrieved from the back file system. The default value is 30 seconds.

continues

Table 18-4 *mount* Options (continued)

Option	Description
acregmax=n	Specifies that cached attributes are held for no more than *n* seconds after file modification. After *n* seconds, all file information is purged from the cache. The default value is 30 seconds.
acregmin=n	Specifies that cached attributes are held for at least *n* seconds after file modification. After *n* seconds, CacheFS checks to see if the file modification time on the back file system has changed. If it has, all information about the file is purged from the cache, and new data is retrieved from the back file system. The default value is 30 seconds.
actimeo=n	Sets acregmin, acregmax, acdirmin, and acdirmax to n.
cacheid=<ID>	ID is a string specifying a particular instance of a cache. If you do not specify a cache ID, CacheFS will construct one.
demandconst	Verifies cache consistency only when explicitly requested, rather than the periodic checking that is done by default. You can request a consistency check by using the -s option of the cfsadmin command. This option is useful for back file systems that change infrequently, such as /usr/openwin. demandconst and noconst are mutually exclusive.
local-access	Causes the front file system to interpret the mode bits used for access checking instead of having the back file system verify access permissions. Do not use this argument with secure NFS.
noconst	Disables cache consistency checking. By default, periodic consistency checking is enabled. Specify noconst only when you know that the back file system will not be modified. Trying to perform a cache consistency check using cfsadmin -s will result in an error. demandconst and noconst are mutually exclusive.
purge	Purges any cached information for the specified file system.
ro | rw	Is read-only or read-write (the default).
suid | nosuid	Allows (the default) or disallows setuid execution.
write-around | non-shared	Write modes for CacheFS. The write-around mode (the default) handles writes the same as NFS does. In other words, writes are made to the back file system, and the affected file is purged from the cache. You can use non-shared mode when you are sure that no one else will be writing to the cached file system. In this mode, all writes are made to both the front and the back file system, and the file remains in the cache.
-O	Overlays mount. Allows the file system to be mounted over an existing mount point, making the underlying file system inaccessible. If you attempt a mount on a preexisting mount point without setting this flag, mount will fail with this error: mount -F cachefs: mount failed Device busy.

The following example creates the mount point /sparc21data and mounts the NFS file system sparc21:/data as a cached file system named /sparc21data in the cache named /local/cache1:

```
mkdir /sparc21data
mount -F cachefs -o backfstype=nfs,cachedir=/local/cache1 sparc21:/data /sparc21data
```

Now the CacheFS mount point, /sparc21data, can be accessed just like any other mounted file system.

To make the mount point permanent, add the following line to your /etc/vfstab file as follows:

```
sparc21:/data  /local/cache1  /sparc21data  cachefs  3  yes  backfstype=nfs,
➥cachedir=/local/cache1
```

Verify that the cache you created was actually mounted by using the `cachefsstat` command as follows:

```
cachefsstat /sparc21data
      /sparc21data
          cache hit rate:       0% (0 hits, 8 misses)
      consistency checks:       7  (5 pass, 2 fail)
                modifies:       0
      garbage collection:       0
```

If the file system was not mounted in the cache, you will receive an error message similar to the following:

```
cachefsstat /sparc21data
cachefsstat: /sparc21data: not a cachefs mountpoint
```

There is some overhead when data is initially referenced from the CacheFS file system associated with the cache population, but subsequent references to the same data can be satisfied without access to the back file system. A warm cache provides performance close to that of a local file system, without the administration and overhead associated with local file systems. The performance of the CacheFS file system over traditional NFS mounts is much faster for clients accessing slow network links or heavily loaded servers.

You can also cache more than one file system in the same cache. There is no need to create a separate cache for each CacheFS mount. In other words, you should need to run `cfsadmin -c` only once to create a single cache for all your CacheFS mounts.

Many types of back file systems can potentially be cached. For example, there are performance benefits to caching slow media such as a CD-ROM on a faster hard drive using CacheFS. However, local file systems (UFS) are usually not cached.

Any file system that is "read mostly" is a likely candidate for caching. An example of an excellent candidate for caching is /usr/share/man. File systems that are usually read one time only, such as /var/mail, are not good candidates for caching because data is typically read once and then discarded. In this case, you pay the cost of cache population without gaining any of the benefits of subsequent cache accesses.

CacheFS provides no benefit for write operations. This is because CacheFS is strictly a "write-through" cache. CacheFS write performance will never be any better than that of the back file system.

CacheFS is not an NFS performance accelerator. It's possible that a single client will not see much of a performance boost from caching, particularly on a lightly loaded fast LAN where the server is a powerful machine with fast disks without much load. The benefits of caching show up on busy networks with heavily loaded servers.

Monitoring the Cache

You can use CacheFS statistics to monitor the performance of your cache to determine the appropriate cache size. The three commands listed in Table 18-5 help you determine the trade-off between your cache size and the desired performance of the cache.

Table 18-5 CacheFS Statistics Commands

Command	Description
`cachefslog`	Specifies the location of the log file. This command also displays where the statistics are currently being logged and lets you halt logging.
`cachefswssize`	Interprets the log file to give a recommended cache size.
`cachefsstat`	Displays statistical information about a specific file system or all cached file systems. The information provided in the output of this command is taken directly from the cache.

The default values for the cache parameters used by `cfsadmin` are for a cache to use the entire front file system for caching. The parameter values should be changed if the cache is limited to only a portion of the front file system. The `cfsadmin` command allows you to specify the options listed in Table 18-6.

Table 18-6 *cfsadmin* Options

Options	Description
`maxblocks`	Sets the maximum number of blocks that CacheFS is allowed to claim within the front file system. It does not guarantee that the resources are available for CacheFS. The default is 90%. Note: Performance decreases significantly if a UFS file system exceeds 90% capacity.

Table 18-6 *cfsadmin* Options (continued)

Options	Description
minblocks	Works together with threshblocks. It does not guarantee the availability of a minimum level of resources. The default is 0%.
threshblocks	Works together with minblocks. This value is ignored until the minblocks value is reached. CacheFS can claim more than minblocks only if the percentage of available blocks in the front file system is greater than threshblocks. This value applies to the entire front file system, not only the cached portion. The default is 85%.
maxfiles	Sets the maximum number of files (inodes) that CacheFS can claim. It does not guarantee that the resources are available for CacheFS. The default is 90%.
minfiles/threshfiles	Work together in the same fashion as minblocks and threshblocks. The minfiles default is 0% and the threshfiles default is 85%.

You should not need to change any of these parameter values. They are set to default values to achieve optimal cache behavior. However, as shown in the next example, you might want to modify the `maxblocks` and `maxfiles` settings if you have some room in the front file system that is not used by the cache and you want to use it for some other file system. The following example creates a cache named /local/cache1 that can use up to 80 percent of the disk blocks in the front file system. It can grow to use 55 percent of the front file system blocks without restriction unless 60 percent (or more) of the front file system blocks are already used:

```
cfsadmin -c -o maxblocks=80,minblocks=55,threshblocks=60 /local/cache1
```

To modify a CacheFS parameter, first unmount the file system. The following example unmounts /local/cache1 and changes the `threshfiles` parameter to 65 percent:

```
umount /sparc21data
cfsadmin -u -o threshfiles=65 /local/cache1
mount /sparc21data
```

NOTE. *The size of a cache, either by number of blocks or number of inodes, can only be increased. In the case of decreasing, the cache must be removed and re-created with a new value.*

To display information about all file systems cached under the specified cache directory, type

```
cfsadmin -l <directory_name>
```

and press Enter.

The following example illustrates how to display cache information:

```
cfsadmin -l /local/cache1
```

The system responds with this:

```
cfsadmin: list cache FS information
    maxblocks       90%
    minblocks        0%
    threshblocks    85%
    maxfiles        90%
    minfiles         0%
    threshfiles     85%
    maxfilesize     3MB
  sparc21:_data:_mnt
  sparc21:_data:_sparc21data
```

Deleting a Cache

Before you delete a cached file system, you must unmount all the cached file systems for that cache directory.

To delete a file system in a cache, type

```
cfsadmin -d <cache_id> <cache_directory>
```

and press Enter.

`<cache_id>` is part of the information returned by `cfsadmin -l`.

After one or more file systems are deleted, you must run the `fsck_cachefs` command to correct resource counts for the cache. The next example unmounts a cached file system, deletes it from the cache, and runs `fsck_cachefs`:

```
umount /sparc21data
cfsadmin -d sparc21:_data:_sparc21data  /local/cache1
fsck -F cachefs /local/cache1
```

You can delete all file systems in a particular cache by using `all` as an argument to the `-d` option, as shown in the following example. This example deletes all file systems cached under /local/cache1 and the specified cache directory:

```
cfsadmin -d all /local/cache1
```

Checking Consistency

To ensure that the cached directories and files are kept up to date, CacheFS periodically checks the consistency of files stored in the cache with files on the back file system. To check consistency, CacheFS compares the current modification time to the previous modification time. If the modification times are different, all data and attributes for the directory or file are purged from the cache, and new data and attributes are retrieved from the back file system.

When a user requests an operation on a directory or file, CacheFS checks to see if it is time to verify consistency. If it is, CacheFS obtains the modification time from the back file system and performs the comparison.

By default, CacheFS does always perform cache consistency checking. When the `noconst` keyword is specified with the `mount` command, consistency checking is disabled. In this mode, no attempt is made to see that the cache remains consistent with the back file system. In the case of a read-only back file system, consistency checking is completely unnecessary. Use the `noconst` keyword when the back file system is a read-only file system.

By specifying the `demandconst` option of the `mount` command, you can perform consistency checks only when you explicitly request them for file systems mounted with this option. After specifying the `demandconst` option when you mount a file system in a cache, you use the `cfsadmin` command with the `-s` option to request a consistency check. By default, consistency checking is performed file by file as they are accessed. If no files are accessed, no checks are performed. Use of the `demandconst` option avoids a situation in which the network is flooded with consistency checks.

The following example uses the `demandconst` option to specify consistency checking on demand for the NFS cached file system /sparc21data, whose back file system is sparc21:/data:

```
mount -F cachefs -o backfstype=nfs,cachedir=/local/cache1,demandconst sparc21:/data
➥ /sparc21data
```

Autofs

When a network contains even a moderate number of systems, all trying to mount file systems from each other, managing NFS can quickly become a nightmare. The Autofs facility, also called the automounter, is designed to handle such situations by providing a method in which remote directories are mounted only when they are being used.

When a user or application accesses an NFS mount point, the mount is established. When the file system is no longer needed, or it has not been accessed for a certain period, the file system is automatically unmounted. As a result, network overhead is lower, the system boots faster because NFS mounts are done later, and systems can be shut down with fewer ill effects and hung processes.

File systems shared through the NFS service can be mounted using Autofs. Autofs, a client-side service, is a file system structure that provides automatic mounting. The Autofs file system is initialized by automount, which is run automatically when a system is started. The `automount` daemon, named `automountd`, runs continuously, mounting and unmounting remote directories on an as-needed basis.

Mounting does not need to be done at system startup, and the user no longer needs to know the superuser password to mount a directory. With Autofs, users do not use the `mount` and `umount` commands. The Autofs service mounts file systems as the user accesses them and unmounts file systems when they are no longer required, without any intervention on the part of the user.

However, some file systems still need to be mounted using the `mount` command with root privileges. For example, a diskless computer must mount / (root), /usr, and /usr/kvm using the `mount` command and cannot take advantage of Autofs.

Two programs support the Autofs service: `automount` and `automountd`. Both are run when a system is started by the /etc/init.d/autofs script.

The `automount` service sets up the Autofs mount points and associates the information in the auto_master files with each mount point. The `automount` command, called at system startup time, reads the master map file named auto_master to create the initial set of Autofs mounts. These mounts are not automatically mounted at startup time. They are trigger points, also called trigger nodes, under which file systems are mounted in the future. The syntax for `automount` is

```
automount -t <duration> -v
```

`-t <duration>`	Sets the time, in seconds, that a file system is to remain mounted if it is not being used.
`-v`	Selects verbose mode. Running this command in verbose mode allows easier troubleshooting.

If not specifically set, the value for `duration` of an unused mount is set to 5 minutes. In most circumstances, this value is good; however, on systems that have many automounted file systems, you might need to increase the `duration` value. In particular, if a server has many users, active checking of the automounted file systems every 5 minutes can be inefficient. By unmounting the file systems every five minutes, it is possible that /etc/mnttab, which is checked by `df`, can get large. Checking the Autofs file systems every 1800 seconds (30 minutes) could be more optimal. Edit the /etc/init.d/autofs script to change the default values.

If Autofs receives a request to access a file system that is not currently mounted, Autofs calls `automountd`, which actually mounts the requested file system under the trigger node.

The `automountd` daemon handles the mount and unmount requests from the Autofs service. The syntax of the command is

```
automountd < -Tnv > < -D name=value >
```

`-T`	Displays each Remote Procedure Call (RPC) to standard output. Use this option for troubleshooting.
`-n`	Disables browsing on all Autofs nodes.
`-v`	Logs all status messages to the console.

`-D name=value` Substitutes `value` for the `automount` map variable indicated by `name`. The default value for the `automount` map is /etc/auto_master.

The `automountd` daemon is completely independent from the `automount` command. Because of this separation, it is possible to add, delete, or change map information without first having to stop and start the `automountd` daemon process.

To illustrate Autofs in action, here is what happens:

`automount` and `automountd` initiate at startup time from the /etc/init.d/autofs script. If a request is made to access a file system at an Autofs mount point, the system goes through the following steps:

1. Autofs intercepts the request.
2. Autofs sends a message to the `automountd` daemon for the requested file system to be mounted.
3. `automountd` locates the file system information in a map and performs the mount.
4. Autofs allows the intercepted request to proceed.
5. Autofs unmounts the file system after a period of inactivity.

NOTE. *Mounts managed through the Autofs service should not be manually mounted or unmounted. Even if the operation is successful, the Autofs service does not check that the object has been unmounted, resulting in possible inconsistency. A restart clears all Autofs mount points.*

To see who might be using a particular NFS mount, use the `showmount` command, described in Table 18-7. The syntax for `showmount` is

```
showmount <options>
```

Table 18-7 The *showmount* Command

Option	Description
-a	Prints all the remote mounts in the format `hostname : directory`. `hostname` is the name of the client, and `directory` is the root of the file system that has been mounted.
-d	Lists directories that have been remotely mounted by clients.
-e	Prints the list of shared file systems.

The following example illustrates the use of showmount to display file systems currently mounted from remote systems. On the NFS server named neptune, type the following command:

```
showmount -a
```

The system displays the following information:

```
apollo:/export/home/neil
```

showmount tells you that the remote host, apollo, is currently mounting /export/home/neil on this server.

Autofs Maps

The behavior of the automounter is governed by its configuration files, called maps. Autofs searches through these maps to navigate its way through the network. Map files contain information, such as the password entries of all users on a network or the names of all host computers on a network.

Master Map

To start the navigation process, the automount command reads the master map at system startup. This map is what tells the automounter about map files and mount points. The master map lists all direct and indirect maps and their associated directories.

The master map, which is in the /etc/auto_master file, associates a directory with a map. The master map is a list that specifies all the maps that Autofs should check. The following example shows what an auto_master file could contain:

```
# Master map for automounter
#
 +auto_master
 /net   -hosts      -nosuid,nobrowse
 /home  auto_home   -nobrowse
 /xfn   -xfn
```

This example shows the default auto_master file. The lines beginning with # are comments. The line that contains +auto_master specifies the Autofs NIS table map, which is explained in Chapter 19, "Name Services." Each line thereafter in the master map, /etc/auto_master, has the following syntax:

```
<mount-point> <map-name> <mount-options>
```

Each field is described in Table 18-8.

Table 18-8 /etc/auto_master Fields

Field	Description
`mount-point`	This is the full (absolute) pathname of a directory that is used as the mount point. If the directory does not exist, Autofs creates it if possible. If the directory does exist and is not empty, mounting on it hides its contents. In this case, Autofs issues a warning. Using the notation /- as a mount point indicates that a direct map with no particular mount point is associated with the map.
`map-name`	This is the map that Autofs uses to find directions to locations or mount information. If the name is preceded by a slash (/), Autofs interprets the name as a local file. Otherwise, it searches for the mount information using the search specified in the name-service switch configuration file (/etc/nsswitch.conf). Name service switches are described in Chapter 19.
`mount-options`	This is an optional comma-separated list of options that apply to the mounting of the entries specified in map-name, unless the entries list other options. Options for each specific type of file system are listed in Table 18-3 under the `mount` command syntax. For NFS-specific mount points, the `bg` (background) and `fg` (foreground) options do not apply.

NOTE. *A line beginning with a number sign (#) is a comment, and everything that follows it until the end of the line is ignored. To split long lines into shorter ones, put a backslash (\) at the end of the line. The maximum number of characters in an entry is 1024.*

Every Solaris installation comes with a master map, called /etc/auto_master, that has the default entries just shown. Without any changes to the generic system setup, clients should be able to access remote file systems through the /net mount point. The following entry in /etc/auto_master allows this to happen:

```
/net    -hosts    -nosuid,nobrowse
```

For example, let's say you have an NFS server named apollo that has the /export file system exported. Another system exists on the network named zeus. This system has the default /etc/auto_master file, and by default, it has a directory named /net. If you type

```
ls /net
```

the command comes back showing that the directory is empty—nothing is in it. Now type

```
ls /net/apollo
```

The system responds with this:

```
export
```

Why was it empty the first time I issued the `ls` command? When I issued `ls /net/apollo`, why did it find a subdirectory? This is the automounter in action. When I specified /net with a host name, `automountd` looked at the map file—in this case, /etc/hosts—and found apollo and its IP address. It then went to apollo, found the exported file system, and created a local mount point for /net/apollo/export. It also added this entry to the /etc/mnttab file:

```
-hosts   /net/sparc48/export     autofs  nosuid,nobrowse,ignore,nest,dev=2b80005\
➥ 941812769
```

This entry in the /etc/mnttab file is referred to as a trigger node.

If I type `mount`, I don't see anything mounted at this point:

```
mount
/ on /dev/dsk/c0t3d0s0 read/write/setuid/largefiles on Mon Nov  1 06:05:46 1999
/usr on /dev/dsk/c0t3d0s6 read/write/setuid/largefiles on Mon Nov  1 06:05:46 1999
/proc on /proc read/write/setuid on Mon Nov  1 06:05:46 1999
/dev/fd on fd read/write/setuid on Mon Nov  1 06:05:46 1999
/export on /dev/dsk/c0t3d0s3 setuid/read/write/largefiles on Mon Nov  1 06:05:49 1999
/export/swap on /dev/dsk/c0t3d0s4 setuid/read/write/largefiles on Mon Nov  1 06:5:49
➥ 1999
/tmp on swap read/write on Mon Nov  1 06:05:49 1999
```

Now type this:

```
ls /net/apollo/export
```

You'll notice a bit of a delay while `automountd` mounts the file system; the system then responds with this:

```
files   lost+found
```

The files listed are files located on apollo in the /export directory. If I type `mount`, I'll see a file system mounted on apollo that wasn't listed before:

```
mount
/ on /dev/dsk/c0t3d0s0 read/write/setuid/largefiles on Mon Nov  1 06:05:46 1999
/usr on /dev/dsk/c0t3d0s6 read/write/setuid/largefiles on Mon Nov  1 06:05:46 1999
/proc on /proc read/write/setuid on Mon Nov  1 06:05:46 1999
/dev/fd on fd read/write/setuid on Mon Nov  1 06:05:46 1999
/export on /dev/dsk/c0t3d0s3 setuid/read/write/largefiles on Mon Nov  1 06:05:49 1999
/export/swap on /dev/dsk/c0t3d0s4 setuid/read/write/largefiles on Mon Nov  1 06:05:49
➥ 1999
/tmp on swap read/write on Mon Nov  1 06:05:49 1999
/net/apollo/export on apollo:/export nosuid/remote on Fri Nov  5 09:48:03 1999
```

The automounter automatically mounted the /export file system that was located on apollo. Now look at the /etc/mnttab file again, and you see additional entries:

```
more /etc/mnttab
/dev/dsk/c0t3d0s0        /        ufs     rw,suid,dev=800018,largefiles    941454346
/dev/dsk/c0t3d0s6        /usr     ufs     rw,suid,dev=80001e,largefiles    941454346
/proc    /proc    proc    rw,suid,dev=2940000       941454346
fd       /dev/fd fd       rw,suid,dev=2a00000       941454346
/dev/dsk/c0t3d0s3        /export ufs      suid,rw,largefiles,dev=80001b    941454349
/dev/dsk/c0t3d0s4        /export/swap     ufs     suid,rw,largefiles,dev=80001c
➥ 941454349
swap     /tmp     tmpfs   dev=1    941454349
-hosts   /net     autofs  ignore,indirect,nosuid,nobrowse,dev=2b80001      941454394
auto_home        /home    autofs  ignore,indirect,nobrowse,dev=2b80002     941454394
-xfn     /xfn     autofs  ignore,indirect,dev=2b80003      941454394
sparcserver:vold(pid246)         /vol     nfs     ignore,noquota,dev=2b40001 941454409
-hosts   /net/apollo/export      autofs  nosuid,nobrowse,ignore,nest,dev=2b80005
➥ 941812769
apollo:/export /net/apollo/export     nfs     nosuid,dev=2b40003 941813283
```

If the /net/apollo/export directory is accessed, the Autofs service completes the process with these steps:

1. It pings the server's mount service to see if it's alive.
2. It mounts the requested file system under /net/apollo/export. Now /etc/mnttab file contains the following entries:

```
-hosts   /net/apollo/export      autofs  nosuid,nobrowse,ignore,nest,dev=2b80005
➥ 941812769
apollo:/export /net/apollo/export     nfs     nosuid,dev=2b40003 941813283
```

Because the automounter lets all users mount file systems, root access is not required. It also provides for automatic unmounting of file systems, so there is no need to unmount them when you are done.

Direct Map

A direct map lists a set of unrelated mount points, which might be spread out across the file system. A complete path (that is, /usr/local/bin or /usr/man) is listed in the map as a mount point. The best example of where to use a direct mount point is for /usr/man. The /usr directory contains many other directories, such as /usr/bin and /usr/local; therefore, it cannot be an indirect mount point. If you were to use an indirect map for /usr/man, the local /usr file system would be the mount point, and you would cover up the local /usr/bin and /usr/etc directories when you established the mount. A direct map lets automounter complete mounts on a single directory entry such as /usr/man, appearing as a link with the name of the direct mount point.

A direct map is specified in a configuration file called /etc/auto_direct. With a direct map, there is a direct association between a mount point on the client and a directory on the server. Direct maps have a full pathname and indicate the relationship explicitly. This is a typical /etc/auto_direct map:

```
/usr/local                -ro
/bin                      ivy:/export/local/sun4
/share                    ivy:/export/local/share
/src                      ivy:/export/local/src
/usr/man                  -ro         oak:/usr/man \
                          rose:/usr/man \
                          willow:/usr/man
/usr/games                -ro         peach:/usr/games
/usr/spool/news           -ro         pine:/usr/spool/news \
                          willow:/var/spool/news
```

NOTE. *A backslash at the end of a line splits it into two shorter lines. The operating system sees it as one line.*

Lines in direct maps have the following syntax:

```
<key> <mount-options> <location>
```

The fields are described in Table 18-9.

Table 18-9 Direct Map Fields

Field	Description
key	This field indicates the pathname of the mount point in a direct map. This pathname specifies the local directory on which to mount the NFS file system.
mount-options	This field indicates the options you want to apply to this particular mount. They are required only if they differ from the map default options specified in the /etc/auto_master file. Options are listed in Table 18-3 under the mount command syntax. There is no concatenation of options between the automounter maps. Any options added to an automounter map override all the options listed in previously searched maps. For instance, options included in the auto_master map would be overwritten by corresponding entries in any other map.
location	This field indicates the remote location of the file system specified as server:pathname. More than one location can be specified. The pathname should not include an automounted mount point; it should be the actual absolute path to the file system. For instance, the location of a home directory should be listed as server:/export/home/username, not as server:/home/username.

In the previous example of the /etc/auto_direct map file, the mount points, /usr/man and /usr/spool/news, list more than one location:

```
/usr/man                -ro       apollo:/usr/man \
                                  zeus:/usr/man \
                                  neptune:/usr/man
/usr/spool/news         -ro       jupiter:/usr/spool/news \
                                  saturn:/var/spool/news
```

Multiple locations, such as those shown here, are used for replication, or failover. For the purposes of failover, a file system can be called a replica if each file is the same size and is the same type of file system. Permissions, creation dates, and other file attributes are not a consideration. If the file size or the file system types are different, the remap fails, and the process hangs until the old server becomes available.

Replication makes sense only if you mount a file system that is read-only, because you must have some control over the locations of files you write or modify. You don't want to modify one server's files on one occasion and, minutes later, modify the "same" file on another server. The benefit of replication is that the best available server is used automatically without any effort required by the user.

If the file systems are configured as replicas, the clients have the advantage of using failover. Not only is the best server automatically determined, but, if that server becomes unavailable, the client automatically uses the next-best server.

An example of a good file system to configure as a replica is the manual (man) pages. In a large network, more than one server can export the current set of manual pages. Which server you mount them from doesn't matter, as long as the server is running and exporting its file systems. In the previous example, multiple mount locations are expressed as a list of mount locations in the map entry. With multiple mount locations specified, you can mount the man pages from the apollo, zeus, or neptune servers. The best server depends on a number of factors, including the number of servers supporting a particular NFS protocol level, the proximity of the server, and weighting. The process of selecting a server goes like this:

- During the sorting process, a count of the number of servers supporting the NFS version 2 and 3.0 protocols is made. The protocol supported on the most servers is the protocol supported by default. This provides the client with the maximum number of servers to depend on. If version 3 servers are more abundant, the sorting process becomes more complex. Normally servers on the local subnet are given preference over servers on a remote subnet. A version 2 server can complicate matters, because it could be closer than the nearest version 3 server. If there is a version 2 server on the local subnet and the closest version 3 server is on a remote subnet, the version 2 server is given preference. This is checked only if there are more version 3 servers than version 2 servers. If there are more version 2 servers, only a version 2 server is selected.

- After the largest subset of servers that have the same protocol version is found, that server list is sorted by proximity. Servers on the local subnet are given preference over servers on a remote subnet. The closest server is given preference, which reduces latency and network traffic. If several servers are supporting the same protocol on the local subnet, the time to connect to each server is determined, and the fastest is used.
- You can also influence the selection of servers at the same proximity level by adding a numeric weighting value in parentheses after the server name in the Autofs map. For example:

  ```
  /usr/man -ro apollo,zeus(1),neptune(2):/usr/man
  ```

  Servers without a weighting have a value of 0, which makes it the most likely server to be selected. The higher the weighting value, the less chance the server has of being selected. All other server selection factors are more important than weighting. Weighting is considered only when selecting between servers with the same network proximity.

With failover, the sorting is checked once at mount time, to select one server from which to mount, and again if the mounted server becomes unavailable. Failover is particularly useful in a large network with many subnets. Autofs chooses the nearest server and therefore confines NFS network traffic to a local network segment. In servers with multiple network interfaces, Autofs lists the host name associated with each network interface as if it were a separate server. It then selects the nearest interface to the client.

In this example, I will set up a direct map for /usr/local on zeus. Currently, zeus has a directory called /usr/local with the following directories:

```
ls /usr/local
```

The following local directories are displayed:

```
bin   etc   files   programs
```

If you set up the automount direct map, you'll see how the /usr/local directory is overwritten by the NFS mount.

First, I need to add the following entry in the master map file called /etc/auto_master:

```
/-    /etc/auto_direct
```

Next, I'll create the direct map file called /etc/auto_direct with the following entry:

```
/usr/local    zeus:/usr/local
```

Because I'm modifying a direct map, I need to stop and restart automount as follows:

```
/etc/init.d/autofs stop
/etc/init.d/autofs start
```

Now, if you have access to the /usr/local directory, the NFS mount point is established using the direct map you have set up. The contents of /usr/local have changed because the direct map has covered up the local copy of /usr/local:

```
ls /usr/local
```

You'll see the following directories listed:

```
fasttrack    answerbook
```

NOTE. *The local contents of /usr/local have not been overwritten. After the NFS mount point is unmounted, the original contents of /usr/local are redisplayed.*

By typing the `mount` command, you see that /usr/local is now mounted remotely from zeus:

```
mount
/ on /dev/dsk/c0t3d0s0 read/write/setuid/largefiles on Mon Nov 1 06:05:46 1999
/usr on /dev/dsk/c0t3d0s6 read/write/setuid/largefiles on Mon Nov 1 06:05:46 1999
/proc on /proc read/write/setuid on Mon Nov 1 06:05:46 1999
/dev/fd on fd read/write/setuid on Mon Nov 1 06:05:46 1999
/export on /dev/dsk/c0t3d0s3 setuid/read/write/largefiles on Mon Nov 1 06:05:49 1999
/export/swap on /dev/dsk/c0t3d0s4 setuid/read/write/largefiles on Mon Nov 1 06:05:49
➥ 1999
/tmp on swap read/write on Mon Nov 1 06:05:49 1999
/usr/local on zeus:/usr/local read/write/remote on Sat Nov 6 08:06:40 1999
```

Indirect Map

Indirect maps are the simplest and most useful automounter conventions. An indirect map uses a key's substitution value to establish the association between a mount point on the client and a directory on the server. Indirect maps are useful for accessing specific file systems, such as home directories, from anywhere on the network. The following entry in the /etc/auto_master file is an example of an indirect map:

```
/share       /etc/auto_share
```

With this entry in the /etc/auto_master file, /etc/auto_share is the name of the indirect map file for the mount point /share. For this entry, you also need to create an indirect map file named /etc/auto_share, which would look like this:

```
# share directory map for automounter
 #
 ws           neptune:/export/share/ws
```

If the /share directory is accessed, the Autofs service creates a trigger node for /share/ws, and the following entry is made in the /etc/mnttab file:

```
-hosts  /share/ws      autofs  nosuid,nobrowse,ignore,nest,dev=###
```

If the /share/ws directory is accessed, the Autofs service completes the process with these steps:

1. It pings the server's mount service to see if it's alive.
2. It mounts the requested file system under /share. Now /etc/mnttab file contains the following entries:

```
-hosts  /share/ws      autofs  nosuid,nobrowse,ignore,nest,dev=###
neptune:/export/share/ws /share/ws   nfs   nosuid,dev=####    #####
```

Lines in indirect maps have the following general syntax:

```
<key>  <mount-options>  <location>
```

The fields in this line are described in Table 18-10.

Table 18-10 Indirect Map Fields

Field	Description
key	key is a simple name (no slashes) in an indirect map.
mount-options	The mount-options are the options you want to apply to this particular mount. They are described in Table 18-4. They are required only if they differ from the map default options specified in the /etc/auto_master file.
location	location is the remote location of the file system specified as server:pathname. More than one location can be specified. The pathname should not include an automounted mount point; it should be the actual absolute path to the file system. For instance, the location of a directory should be listed as server:/usr/local, not as server:/net/server/usr/local.

An example of an indirect map would be for user home directories. As users log into several different systems, their home directory is not always local to the system. It's convenient to use automounter to access their home directory regardless of the system to which they log in. To accomplish this, the default /etc/auto_master map file needs to contain the following entry:

```
/home      /etc/auto_home        -nobrowse
```

/etc/auto_home is the name of the indirect map file that contains the entries to be mounted under /home. A typical /etc/auto_home map file might look like this:

```
more /etc/auto_home
 dean                        willow:/export/home/dean
 william                     cypress:/export/home/william
 nicole                      poplar:/export/home/nicole
 glenda                      pine:/export/home/glenda
 steve                       apple:/export/home/steve
 burk                        ivy:/export/home/burk
 neil      -rw,nosuid        peach:/export/home/neil
```

Now let's assume that the /etc/auto_home map is on the host oak. If user neil has an entry in the password database specifying his home directory as /home/neil, whenever he logs in to computer oak, Autofs mounts the directory /export/home/neil residing on the computer peach. His home directory is mounted read-write, nosuid. Anyone, including Neil, has access to this path from any computer set up with the master map referring to the /etc/auto_home map in this example.

Under these conditions, user neil can run `login`, or `rlogin`, on any computer that has the /etc/auto_home map setup, and his home directory is mounted in place for him.

Another example of when to use an indirect map is if you want to make all project-related files available under a directory called /data. This directory is to be common across all workstations at the site. Follow these steps to set up the indirect map:

1. Add an entry for the /data directory to the /etc/auto_master map file:

   ```
   /data       /etc/auto_data      -nosuid
   ```

   The auto_data map file, named /etc/auto_data, determines the contents of the /data directory.

2. Add the `-nosuid` option as a precaution.

   The `-nosuid` option prevents users from creating files with the setuid or setgid bit set. Refer to Chapter 6 if you're unfamiliar with setuid/setgid.

3. Create the /etc/auto_data file and add entries to the auto_data map.

   The auto_data map is organized so that each entry describes a subproject. Edit /etc/auto_data to create a map that looks like the following:

   ```
   compiler                 apollo:/export/data/&
   windows                  apollo:/export/data/&
   files                    zeus:/export/data/&
   drivers                  apollo:/export/data/&
   man                      zeus:/export/data/&
   tools                    zeus:/export/data/&
   ```

NOTE. *The ampersand (&) at the end of each entry is an abbreviation for the entry key. For instance, the first entry is equivalent to* `compiler apollo:/export/data/compiler`.

Because the servers apollo and zeus view similar Autofs maps locally, any users who log in to these computers find the /data file system as expected. These users are provided direct access to local files through loopback mounts instead of NFS mounts.

4. Because you changed the /etc/auto_master map, the final step is to stop Autofs and restart it as follows:

```
/etc/init.d/autofs stop
/etc/init.d/autofs start
```

Now, if a user changes to the /data/compiler directory, the mount point to apollo:/export/data/compiler is created:

```
cd /data/compiler
```

5. Type `mount` to see the mount point that was established:

```
mount
```

The system shows that /data/compiler is mapped to apollo:/export/data/compiler as follows:

```
/data/compiler on apollo:/export/data/compiler read/write/remote on
➥ Fri Nov  5 17:17:02 1999
```

If the user changes to /data/tools, the mount point to zeus:/export/data/tools is created under the mount point /data/tools.

NOTE. *There is no need to create the directory /data/compiler to be used as the mount point. Automounter creates all the necessary directories before establishing the mount.*

The system administrator can modify, delete, or add entries to maps to meet the needs of the environment. As applications (and other file systems that users require) change their location, the maps must reflect those changes. You can modify Autofs maps at any time. However, changes do not take place until the file system is unmounted and remounted. If a change is made to the auto_master map, or to a direct map, those changes do not take place until the automounter is restarted as follows:

```
/etc/init.d/autofs stop
/etc/init.d/autofs start
```

Another method is to force auto_master and direct map changes to be recognized immediately by running `automount` from the command line as follows:

```
automount -v
```

When to Use Automount

The most common and most advantageous use of automount is for mounting infrequently used file systems on an NFS client, such as online reference manual pages. Another common use is accessing user home directories anywhere on the network. This use works well for users who do not have a dedicated system and who tend to log in from different locations. In the past, to permit access, the system administrator had to create home directories on every system into which the user logged in. Data had to be duplicated everywhere, and it was always out of sync. You certainly don't want to create permanent NFS mounts for all user home directories on each system, so this is an excellent use for automount.

Automount is also used if a read-only file system exists on more than one server. By using automount instead of conventional NFS mounting, you can configure the NFS client to query all the servers on which the file system exists and mount from the server that responds first.

Avoid using automount to mount frequently used file systems, such as those containing user commands or frequently-used applications; conventional NFS mounting is more efficient in this situation. It is quite practical and typical to combine the use of automount with conventional NFS mounting on the same NFS client.

Summary

When managing NFS, and especially automounter, a system administrator can quickly become overwhelmed with all the configuration files that must be kept consistent across the many different systems. For example, the /etc/auto_master and the related direct and indirect map files must be updated whenever the name of a host or file system changes. This can be nearly impossible on a large network. Chapter 19 describes how NIS can be used to help manage all these configuration files, including/etc/passwd and /etc/hosts, from a single location.

CHAPTER

19

Name Services

The following test objectives are covered in this chapter:

- Understanding the Solaris naming services
- Configuring and managing local files, NIS, NIS+, and DNS
- Understanding NIS+ security
- Understanding DNS

This chapter explains how to configure and administer the servers and clients in a NIS (Network Information Service) domain. NIS is a huge topic that could potentially span several volumes. The purpose of this chapter is to prepare you for questions regarding NIS that might appear on the exam. I also want to provide an overview of NIS, complete enough so that you are equipped to set up a basic NIS network and understand its use.

Name Services Overview

Name services store information in a central location that users, systems, and applications must have to communicate across the network. Information is stored in files, maps, or database tables. Without a central name service, each system would have to maintain its own copy of this information. Therefore, centrally locating this data makes it easier to administer large networks. The information handled by a name service includes

- System (host) names and addresses
- User names
- Passwords
- Access permissions

The Solaris 7 release provides the name services listed in Table 19-1.

Table 19-1 Name Services

Name Service	Description
/etc files	The original UNIX naming system
NIS	The Network Information Service
NIS+	The Network Information Service Plus (NIS+ is described in greater detail later in this chapter)
DNS	The Domain Name System (DNS is described in greater detail later in this chapter)

A name service enables centralized management of host files so that systems can be identified by common names instead of by numerical addresses. This simplifies communication, because users do not have to remember and try to enter cumbersome numerical addresses such as 129.44.3.1.

Addresses are not the only network information that systems need to store. They also need to store security information, email addresses, information about their Ethernet interfaces, network services, groups of users allowed to use the network, services offered on the network, and so on. As networks offer more services, the list grows. As a result, each system might need to keep an entire set of files similar to /etc/hosts.

As this information changes, without a name service, administrators must keep it current on every system in the network. In a small network, this is simply tedious, but on a medium or large network, the job becomes not only time-consuming but also nearly unmanageable.

A name service solves this problem. It stores network information on servers and provides the information to any workstation that asks for it.

/etc Files

/etc files are the traditional UNIX way of maintaining information about hosts, users, passwords, groups, and automount maps, to name just a few. These files are text files located on each individual system that can be edited using the vi editor or Solstice AdminSuite. They are described in Chapters 7, 17, 18, and 20.

NIS

The NIS, formerly called the Yellow Pages (YP), is a distributed database system that lets the system administrator administer the configuration of many hosts from a central location. Common configuration information, which would have to be maintained separately on each host in a network without NIS, can be stored and maintained in a central location and then propagated to all the nodes in the network. NIS stores information about workstation names and addresses, users, the network itself, and network services. This collection of network information is referred to as the NIS *namespace*.

NOTE. *As stated, the NIS was formerly known as the Sun Yellow Pages (YP). The functionality of the two remains the same; only the name has changed. The name "Yellow Pages" is a registered trademark in the United Kingdom of British Telecommunications PLC, and it may not be used without permission.*

Before I begin a discussion of the structure of NIS, you need to be aware that the NIS administration databases are called *maps*. A domain is a collection of systems that share a common set of NIS maps.

Structure of the NIS Network

The systems within a NIS network are configured in the following ways:

- Master server
- Slave servers
- Clients of NIS servers

The center of the NIS network is the NIS *master server*. The system designated as master server contains the set of maps that you, the NIS administrator, create and update as necessary. After the NIS network is set up, any changes to the maps must be made on the master server. Each NIS domain must have one, and only one, master server. The master server should be a system that can propagate NIS updates with minimal performance degradation.

In addition to the master server, you can create backup servers, called NIS *slave servers,* to take some of the load off the master server and to substitute for the master server if it goes down. If you create a NIS slave server, the maps on the master server are transferred to the slave server. A slave server has a complete copy of the master set of NIS maps. If a change is made to a map on the master server, the updates are propagated among the slave servers. The existence of slave servers lets the system administrator evenly distribute the load that results from answering NIS requests. It also minimizes the impact of a server's becoming unavailable.

Typically, all the hosts in the network, including the master and slave servers, are *NIS clients*. If a process on a NIS client requests configuration information, it calls NIS instead of looking in its local configuration files. For group and password information and mail aliases, the /etc/files might be consulted first, and then NIS might be consulted if the requested information is not found in the /etc/files.

Any system can be a NIS client, but only systems with disks should be NIS servers, whether master or slave. Servers are also clients of themselves.

As mentioned earlier, the set of maps shared by the servers and clients is called the NIS domain. The master copies of the maps are located on the NIS master server, in the directory /var/yp/<domainname>, in which domainname is the chosen name for your own domain. Under the domainname directory, each map is stored as two files: mapname.dir and mapname.pag. Each slave server has an identical directory containing the same set of maps.

When a client starts up, it broadcasts a request for a server that serves its domain. Any server that has the set of maps for the client's domain, whether it's a master or a slave server, can answer the request. The client "binds" to the first server that answers its request, and that server then answers all its NIS queries.

A host cannot be the master server for more than one NIS domain. However, a master server for one domain might be a slave server for another domain. A host can be a slave server for multiple domains. A client belongs to only one domain.

Determining How Many NIS Servers You Need

The following guidelines can be used to determine how many NIS servers you need in your domain:

- You should put a server on each subnetwork in your domain. When a client starts up, it broadcasts a message to find the nearest server. Solaris 7 does not require the server to be on the same subnet; however, earlier implementations of NIS historically required that a server exist on every subnet using NIS.
- In general, a server can serve about 30 NIS clients if the clients and servers run at the same speed. If the clients are faster than the servers, you need more servers. If the clients are slower than the servers, each server can serve 50 or more clients.

Determining Which Hosts Will Be NIS Servers

Determine which systems on your network will be NIS servers as follows:

- Choose servers that are reliable and highly available.
- Choose fast servers that are not used for CPU-intensive applications. Do not use gateways or terminal servers as NIS servers.
- Although it isn't a requirement, it's a good idea to distribute servers appropriately among client networks. In other words, each subnet should have enough servers to accommodate the clients on that subnet.

Information Managed by NIS

As discussed, NIS stores information in a set of files called maps. Maps were designed to replace UNIX /etc files, as well as other configuration files.

NIS maps are two-column tables. One column is the key, and the other column is the information value related to the key. NIS finds information for a client by searching through the keys. Some information is stored in several maps because each map uses a different key. For example, the names and addresses of systems are stored in two maps: hosts.byname and hosts.byaddr. If a server has a system's name and needs to find its address, it looks in the hosts.byname map. If it has the address and needs to find the name, it looks in the hosts.byaddr map.

Maps for a domain are located in each server's /var/yp/<domainname> directory. For example, the maps that belong to the domain pyramid.com are located in each server's /var/yp/pyramid.com directory.

A NIS makefile is stored in the /var/yp directory of the NIS server at installation time. If you run the `/usr/ccs/bin/make` command in that directory, `makedbm` creates or modifies the default NIS maps from the input files. For example, an input file might be /etc/hosts. By now, you should be familiar with the content of this file. Issue the following command to create the NIS map files:

```
cd /var/yp
/usr/ccs/bin/make
```

NOTE. *Never* `make` *the maps on a slave server. Always run the* `make` *command on the master server.*

Creating NIS maps is described in more detail in the later section "Configuring a NIS Master Server."

Solaris provides a default set of NIS maps. They are described in Table 19-2. You might want to use all or only some of these maps. NIS can also use whatever maps you create or add if you install other software products.

Table 19-2 Default NIS Maps

Map Name	Corresponding NIS Admin File	Description
`bootparams`	bootparams	This map contains the pathnames that clients need during startup: root, swap, and possibly others.
`ethers.byaddr`	ethers	This map contains system names and Ethernet addresses. The Ethernet address is the key in the map.
`ethers.byname`	ethers	This map contains system names and Ethernet addresses. The system name is the key.
`group.bygid`	group	This map contains group security information. The GID (group ID) is the key.
`group.byname`	group	This map contains group security information. The group name is the key.
`hosts.byaddr`	hosts	This map contains the system name and IP address. The IP address is the key.
`hosts.byname`	hosts	This map contains the system name and IP address. The system (host) name is the key.
`mail.aliases`	aliases	This map contains aliases and mail addresses. The aliases are the key.
`mail.byaddr`	aliases	This map contains mail addresses and aliases. The mail addresses are the key.

continues

Table 19-2 Default NIS Maps (continued)

Map Name	Corresponding NIS Admin File	Description
netgroup	netgroup	This map contains the group name, user name, and system name. The group name is the key.
netgroup.byhost	netgroup	This map contains the group name, user name, and system name. The system name is the key.
netgroup.byuser	netgroup	This map contains the group name, user name, and system name. The user name is the key.
netid.byname	passwd	This map is used for UNIX-style hosts and group authentication. It contains the system name and mail address (including domain name). If a netid file is available, it is consulted, in addition to the data available through the other files.
netmasks.byaddr	netmasks	This map contains the network masks to be used with IP subnetting. The address is the key.
networks.byaddr	networks	This map contains names of networks known to your system and their IP addresses. The address is the key.
networks.byname	networks	This map contains names of networks known to your system and their IP addresses. The name of the network is the key.
passwd.adjunct.byname	passwd and shadow	This map contains auditing shadow information and the hidden password information for C2 clients.
passwd.byname	passwd and shadow	This map contains password shadow information. The user name is the key.
passwd.byuid	passwd and shadow	This map contains password shadow information. The user ID is the key.
protocols.byname	protocols	This map contains the network protocols known to your network. The protocol is the key.
protocols.bynumber	protocols	This map contains the network protocols known to your network. The protocol number is the key.

Table 19-2 Default NIS Maps (continued)

Map Name	Corresponding NIS Admin File	Description
rpc.bynumber	rpc	This map contains the program number and the name of Remote Procedure Calls (RPCs) known to your system. The program number is the key.
services.byname	services	This map lists Internet services known to your network. The key port or protocol is the key.
services.byservice	services	This map lists Internet services known to your network. The service name is the key.
ypservers	N/A	This map lists the NIS servers known to your network.

The information in these files is put into NIS databases automatically when you create a NIS master server. Other system files can also be managed by NIS if you want to customize your configuration.

NIS makes updating network databases much simpler than with the /etc file system. You no longer have to change the administrative /etc files on every system each time you modify the network environment. For example, if you add a new system to a network running NIS, you only have to update the input file in the master server and run `/usr/ccs/bin/make`. This process automatically updates the hosts.byname and hosts.byaddr maps. These maps are then transferred to any slave servers and made available to all the domain's client systems and their programs.

Just as you use the `cat` command to display the contents of a text file, you can use the `ypcat` command to display the values in a map. Here is the basic `ypcat` syntax:

```
ypcat <mapname>
```

In this case, `mapname` is the name of the map you want to examine.

You can use the `ypwhich` command to determine which server is the master of a particular map:

```
ypwhich -m <mapname>
```

In this case, `mapname` is the name of the map whose master you want to find. `ypwhich` responds by displaying the name of the master server.

These and other NIS commands are covered in the following sections.

Planning Your NIS Domain

Before you configure systems as NIS servers or clients, you must plan the NIS domain. Each domain has a domain name, and each system sharing the common set of maps belongs to that domain. Follow these steps to plan your domain:

1. Decide which systems will be in your NIS domain.
2. Choose a NIS domain name. A NIS domain name can be up to 256 characters long, although much shorter names are more practical. A good practice is to limit domain names to no more than 32 characters. Domain names are case-sensitive. For convenience, you can use your Internet domain name as the basis for your NIS domain name. For example, if your Internet domain name is pdesigninc.com, you can name your NIS domain pdesigninc.com.
3. Before a system can use NIS services, the correct NIS domain name and system name must be set. A system's name is set by the system's /etc/nodename file, and the system's domain name is set by the system's /etc/defaultdomain file. These files are read at startup, and the contents are used by the `uname -s` and `domainname` commands, respectively. A sample /etc/nodename file would look like this:

   ```
   more /etc/nodename
   ```

   The system responds with this:

   ```
   sparcserver
   ```

   A sample /etc/defaultdomain file would look like this:

   ```
   more /etc/defaultdomain
   ```

   The system responds with this:

   ```
   pdesigninc.com
   ```

You are now ready to configure your NIS master server.

Configuring a NIS Master Server

Before configuring a NIS master server, make sure the NIS package is installed. The package names are SUNWypu and SUNWypr. Use the `pkginfo` command to check for these packages. Both packages are part of the standard Solaris 7 release. The daemons that support the NIS service are described in Table 19-3.

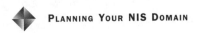

Table 19-3 NIS Daemons

Daemon	Function
`ypserv`	This daemon is the NIS database lookup server. The `ypserv` daemon's primary function is to look up information in its local database of NIS maps. If the /var/yp/ypserv.log file exists when ypserv starts up, log information is written to it if error conditions arise. At least one `ypserv` daemon must be present on the network for the NIS service to function.
`ypbind`	This daemon is the NIS binding process that runs on all client systems that are set up to use NIS. The function of `ypbind` is to remember information that lets all NIS client processes on a node communicate with some NIS server process.
`ypxfr`	This daemon is the high-speed map transfer. `ypxfr` moves a NIS map in the default domain to the local host. It creates a temporary map in the directory /var/yp/ypdomain.
`rpc.yppasswdd`	This daemon handles password change requests from the `yppasswd` command. It changes a password entry in the passwd, shadow, and security/passwd.adjunct files.
`rpc.ypupdated`	This daemon updates NIS information. `ypupdated` consults the updaters file in the /var/yp directory to determine which NIS maps should be updated and how to change them.

The commands that you use to manage the NIS service are shown in Table 19-4. I'll describe some of these commands in more detail later as I show examples of setting up NIS.

Table 19-4 NIS Commands

Utility	Function
`make`	This command updates NIS maps by reading the makefile (if run in the /var/yp directory). You can use `make` to update all maps based on the input files or to update individual maps.
`makedbm`	This command creates a dbm file for a NIS map. The `makedbm` command takes the infile and converts it to a pair of files in ndbm format. When you run `make` in the /var/yp directory, `makedbm` creates or modifies the default NIS maps from the input files.
`ypcat`	This command lists data in a NIS map.
`ypinit`	This command builds and installs a NIS database and initializes the NIS client's (and server's) ypservers list. `ypinit` is used to set up a NIS client system. You must be the superuser to run this command.
`yppoll`	This command gets a map order number from a server. The `yppoll` command asks a ypserv process what the order number is and which host is the master NIS server for the named map.

continues

Table 19-4 NIS Commands (continued)

Utility	Function
yppush	This command propagates a new version of a NIS map from the NIS master server to NIS slave servers.
ypset	This command sets binding to a particular server. ypset is useful for binding a client node that is on a different broadcast network.
ypstart	This command is used to start NIS. After the host has been configured using the ypinit command, ypstart automatically determines the machine's NIS status and starts the appropriate daemons.
ypstop	This command is used to stop the NIS.
ypwhich	This command returns the name of the NIS server that supplies the NIS name services to a NIS client, or it returns the name of the master for a map.

A NIS master server holds the source files for all the NIS maps in the domain. Any changes to the NIS maps must be made on the NIS master server. The NIS master server delivers information to NIS clients and supplies the NIS slave servers with up-to-date maps. Before the NIS master server is started, some of the NIS source files need to be created.

One of the primary uses of NIS is to manage user logins and host files in a large networked environment. In a large network of systems, with several hundred users, imagine trying to keep the /etc/hosts, /etc/passwd, and /etc/group files up to date. Without NIS, every time a new system is added or removed, the /etc/hosts file must be updated. It's important to keep your /etc/hosts files in sync on every system on the network. Furthermore, without NIS, if a user changes a password, that user must notify the system administrator that his or her password has changed. The system administrator must then make sure that all the /etc/shadow files are updated across the network. If they aren't, the user can't log in to another system using the new password.

The system administrator can manage the system configuration files, such as /etc/hosts and /etc/passwd, using NIS. With NIS, the system administrator sets up the /etc/hosts, /etc/passwd, and /etc/group files on one server. Rather than keeping a copy of the configuration file on each system, all systems look to this server for configuration information.

Creating the Master passwd File

The first task in setting up a NIS master server is to prepare the source file for the passwd map. However, be careful with this source file. The source files can be located either in the /etc directory on the master server or in some other directory. Locating the source files in /etc is undesirable because the contents of the maps are then the same as the contents of the local files on the master server. This is a special problem for passwd and shadow files, because all users would have access to the master server maps and because the root password would be passed to all YP clients through the passwd map.

Sun recommends that for security reasons, and to prevent unauthorized root access, the files used to build the NIS password maps should not contain an entry for root. Therefore, the password maps should not be built from the files located in the master server's /etc directory. The password files used to build the passwd maps should have the root entry removed from them, and they should be located in a directory that can be protected from unauthorized access.

For this exercise, copy all the source files from the /etc directory into the /var/yp directory. Because the source files are located in a directory other than /etc, modify the makefile in /var/yp by changing the `DIR=/etc` line to `DIR=/var/yp`. Also, modify the PWDIR password macro in the makefile to refer to the directory in which the passwd and shadow files reside by changing the line `PWDIR=/etc` to `PWDIR=/var/yp`.

Now, to create the passwd source file, use a copy of the /etc/passwd file on the system that becomes the master NIS server. Create a passwd file that has all the logins in it. This file is used to create the NIS map. You can do this by following these steps:

1. Copy the /etc/passwd file from each host in your network to the /var/yp directory on the host that will be the master server. Name each copy /var/yp/passwd.<hostname>, in which <hostname> is the name of the host it came from.
2. Concatenate all the passwd files into a temporary passwd file, as follows:

```
cd /var/yp
cat passwd passwd.hostname1 passwd.hostname2 ... > passwd.temp
```

3. Issue the `sort` command to sort the temporary passwd file by user name, and then pipe it to the `uniq` command to remove duplicate entries:

```
sort -t : -k 1,1 /var/yp/passwd.temp | uniq > /var/yp/passwd.temp
```

NOTE. *NIS does not require that the passwd file be sorted in any particular way. Sorting the passwd file simply makes it easier to find duplicate entries.*

4. Examine /var/yp/passwd.temp for duplicate user names that were not caught by the previous `uniq` command. This could happen if a user login occurs twice but the lines are not exactly the same. If you find multiple entries for the same user, edit the file to remove redundant ones. Make sure each user in your network has a unique user name and UID (user ID).
5. Issue the following command to sort the temporary passwd file by UID:

```
sort -o /var/yp/passwd.temp -t: -k 3n,3 /var/yp/passwd.temp
```

6. Examine /var/yp/passwd.temp for duplicate UIDs once more. If you find multiple entries with the same UID, edit the file to change the UIDs so that no two users have the same UID.
7. Remove the root login from the /var/yp/passwd.temp file. If you notice that the root login occurs more than once, remove all entries.
8. After you have a complete passwd file with no duplicates, move /var/yp/passwd.temp (the sorted, edited file) to /var/yp/passwd. This file is used to generate the passwd map for your NIS domain. Remove all the /var/yp/passwd.<hostname> files from the master server.

Creating the Master group File

Just like creating a master /var/yp/passwd file, the next task is to prepare one master /var/yp/group file to be used to create a NIS map:

1. Copy the /etc/group file from each host in your NIS domain to the /var/yp directory on the host that will be the master server. Name each copy /var/yp/group.<hostname>, in which <hostname> is the name of the host it came from.
2. Concatenate all the group files, including the master server's group file, into a temporary group file:

```
cd /var/yp
cat group group.hostname1 group.hostname2 ... > group.temp
```

3. Issue the following command to sort the temporary group file by group name:

```
sort -o /var/yp/group.temp -t: -k1,1 /var/yp/group.temp
```

   NIS does not require that the group file be sorted in any particular way. Sorting the group file simply makes it easier to find duplicate entries.

4. Examine /var/yp/group.temp for duplicate group names. If a group name appears more than once, merge the groups that have the same name into one group and remove the duplicate entries.
5. Issue the following command to sort the temporary group file by GID:

```
sort -o /var/yp/group.temp -t: -k 3n,3 /var/yp/group.temp
```

6. Examine /var/yp/group.temp for duplicate GIDs. If you find multiple entries with the same GID, edit the file to change the GIDs so that no two groups have the same GID.
7. Move /var/yp/group.temp (the sorted, edited file) to /var/yp/group. This file is used to generate the group map for your NIS domain.
8. Remove the /var/yp/group.<hostname> files from the master server.

Creating the Master hosts File

Now create the master /etc/hosts file the same way you created the master /var/yp/passwd and /var/yp/group files by following these steps:

1. Copy the /etc/hosts file from each host in your NIS domain to the /var/yp directory on the host that will be the master server. Name each copy /var/yp/hosts.<hostname>, in which <hostname> is the name of the host from which it came.

2. Concatenate all the hosts files, including the master server's host file, into a temporary hosts file, as follows:

```
cd /var/yp
cat hosts hosts.hostname1 hosts.hostname2 ... > hosts.temp
```

3. Issue the following command to sort the temporary hosts file so that duplicate IP addresses are on adjacent lines:

```
sort -o /var/yp/hosts.temp /var/yp/hosts.temp
```

4. Examine /var/yp/hosts.temp for duplicate IP addresses. If you need to map an IP address to multiple host names, include them as aliases in a single entry.

5. Issue the following command to sort the temporary hosts file by host name:

```
sort -o /var/yp/hosts.temp -b -k 2,2 /var/yp/hosts.temp
```

6. Examine /var/yp/hosts.temp for duplicate host names. A host name can be mapped to multiple IP addresses only if the IP addresses belong to different LAN cards on the same host. If a host name appears in multiple entries that are mapped to IP addresses on different hosts, remove all the entries but one.

7. Examine the /var/yp/hosts.temp file for duplicate aliases. No alias should appear in more than one entry.

8. Move /var/yp/hosts.temp (the sorted, edited file) to /var/yp/hosts. This file is used to generate the host's map for your NIS domain.

9. Remove the /var/yp/hosts.<hostname> files from the master server.

Other Source Files

The following files can also be copied to the /var/yp directory to be used as source files for NIS maps, but first make sure that they reflect an up-to-date picture of your system environment:

- auto.home or auto_home
- auto.master or auto_master
- bootparams

- ethers
- netgroup
- netmasks
- networks
- protocols
- rpc
- services
- shadow

Unlike other source files, the /etc/mail/aliases file cannot be moved to another directory. This file must reside in the /etc/mail directory. Make sure that the /etc/mail/aliases source file is complete by verifying that it contains all the mail aliases that you want to have available throughout the domain.

Preparing the Makefile

After checking the source files and copying them into the source file directory, you need to convert those source files into the ndbm format maps that the NIS service uses. This is done automatically for you by ypinit. I describe how to set up ypinit in the next section.

The ypinit script calls the program `make`, which uses the makefile located in the /var/yp directory. A default makefile is provided for you in this directory. It contains the commands needed to transform the source files into the desired ndbm format maps.

The function of the makefile is to create the appropriate NIS maps for each of the databases listed under "all." After passing through `makedbm`, the data is collected in two files, mapname.dir and mapname.pag. Both files are located in the /var/yp/<domainname> directory on the master server.

The makefile builds passwd maps from the /PWDIR/passwd, /PWDIR/shadow, and /PWDIR/security/passwd.adjunct files, as appropriate.

Setting Up the Master Server with ypinit

The /usr/sbin/ypinit shell script sets up master and slave servers and clients to use NIS. It also initially runs `make` to create the maps on the master server. To use ypinit to build a fresh set of NIS maps on the master server, follow these steps:

1. Become root on the master server and ensure that the name service receives its information from the /etc files, not from NIS, by typing the following:

   ```
   cp /etc/nsswitch.files /etc/nsswitch.conf
   ```

2. Edit the /etc/hosts file to add the name and IP address of each of the NIS servers.
3. To build new maps on the master server, type

   ```
   /usr/sbin/ypinit -m
   ```

   ypinit prompts you for a list of other systems to become NIS slave servers. Type the name of the server you are working on, along with the names of your NIS slave servers. Enter the server name, and then press Enter. Do this for each server. Enter each server on a separate line. Press Ctrl+D when you're finished.
4. ypinit asks whether you want the procedure to terminate at the first nonfatal error or to continue despite nonfatal errors. Type `y`.

   If you choose `y`, ypinit exits upon encountering the first problem; you can then fix it and restart ypinit. This procedure is recommended if you are running ypinit for the first time. If you prefer to continue, you can manually try to fix all the problems that might occur and then restart ypinit.

NOTE. *A nonfatal error might be displayed if some of the map files are not present. These errors do not affect the functionality of NIS.*

5. ypinit asks whether the existing files in the /var/yp/<domainname> directory can be destroyed.

   This message is displayed only if NIS was previously installed. You must answer Yes to install the new version of NIS.
6. After ypinit has constructed the list of servers, it invokes `make`.

   The `make` command uses the instructions contained in the makefile located in /var/yp. It cleans any remaining comment lines from the files you designated and then runs `makedbm` on them, creating the appropriate maps and establishing the name of the master server for each map.
7. To enable NIS as the naming service, type

   ```
   cp /etc/nsswitch.nis /etc/nsswitch.conf
   ```

   This command replaces the current switch file with the default NIS-oriented one. You can edit this file as necessary. See the section "Name Service Switch" for information on the contents of this file.

Now that the master maps are created, you can start the NIS daemons on the master server.

Starting and Stopping NIS on the Master Server

To start up the NIS service on the master server, you need to start ypserv on the server and run ypbind. The daemon ypserv answers information requests from clients after looking them up in the NIS maps. You can start up the NIS service on the server by running the /usr/lib/netsvc/yp/ypstart script from the command line. After you configure the NIS master server by running ypinit, ypstart is automatically invoked to start up ypserv whenever the system is started up.

To stop the NIS service, run the ypstop command on the server as follows:

```
usr/lib/netsvc/yp/ypstop
```

Name Service Switch

The next step in setting up the NIS service is to set up the name service switch, which involves editing the /etc/nsswitch.conf file. The name service switch controls how a client workstation or application obtains network information. The name service switch is often simply referred to as the switch. The switch determines which naming services an application uses to obtain naming information, and in what order. It is a file called nsswitch.conf, which is stored in each system's /etc directory.

Each workstation has a nsswitch.conf file in its /etc directory. In every system's /etc directory, you find a template file called /etc/nsswitch.nis that was installed when you loaded Solaris 7. This template file contains the default switch configurations used by the NIS service and local files. When the Solaris 7 release software is first installed, if you designate NIS as the default name service, the template file is copied to /etc/nsswitch.conf. If during software installation you select "files" as the default name service, /etc/nsswitch.conf is created from nsswitch.files, which looks like this:

```
#
# /etc/nsswitch.files:
#
# An example file that could be copied over to /etc/nsswitch.conf; it
# does not use any naming service.
#
# "hosts:" and "services:" in this file are used only if the
# /etc/netconfig file has a "-" for nametoaddr_libs of "inet" transports.

passwd:    files
group:    files
hosts:    files
networks:  files
protocols: files
rpc:     files
ethers:    files
netmasks:  files
bootparams: files
publickey: files
```

```
# At present there isn't a 'files' backend for netgroup; the system will
#  figure it out pretty quickly, and won't use netgroups at all.
netgroup:  files
automount: files
aliases:  files
services:  files
sendmailvars:  files
```

If you did not select NIS as your name service during software installation, you can move this file into place manually as follows:

```
cp /etc/nsswitch.nis /etc/nsswitch.conf
```

The default /etc/nsswitch.nis file looks like this:

```
#
# /etc/nsswitch.nis:
#
# An example file that could be copied over to /etc/nsswitch.conf; it
# uses NIS (YP) in conjunction with files.
#
# "hosts:" and "services:" in this file are used only if the
# /etc/netconfig file has a "-" for nametoaddr_libs of "inet" transports.

# the following two lines obviate the "+" entry in /etc/passwd and /etc/group.
passwd:   files nis
group:   files nis

# consult /etc "files" only if nis is down.
hosts:   xfn nis [NOTFOUND=return] files
networks:  nis [NOTFOUND=return] files
protocols: nis [NOTFOUND=return] files
rpc:    nis [NOTFOUND=return] files
ethers:   nis [NOTFOUND=return] files
netmasks:  nis [NOTFOUND=return] files
bootparams: nis [NOTFOUND=return] files
publickey: nis [NOTFOUND=return] files

netgroup:  nis

automount: files nis
aliases:  files nis

# for efficient getservbyname() avoid nis
services:  files nis
sendmailvars:  files
```

Each line of the /etc/nsswitch.nis file identifies a particular type of network information, such as host, password, and group, followed by one or more sources, such as NIS+ tables, NIS maps, the DNS hosts table, or the local /etc. The source is where the client looks for the network information. For example, the system should first look for the passwd information in the /etc/passwd file. Then, if it does not find the login name there, it needs to query the NIS server.

Setting Up NIS Clients

You must perform two tasks to set up a system as a NIS client:

- Set up the nsswitch.conf file as described in the preceding section.
- Configure the system to use NIS, as explained next.

After setting up the nsswitch.conf file, you configure each client system to use NIS by logging in as root and running the `ypinit` command as follows:

```
ypinit -c
```

You will be asked to identify the NIS servers from which the client can obtain name service information. Enter each server name, followed by a carriage return. You can list as many master or slave servers as you want. The servers that you list can be located anywhere in the domain. It is a good practice to first list the servers closest (in network terms) to the system, followed by the more distant servers on the net.

Finally, on the NIS client, remove from the /etc/passwd file all the entries that are managed by the NIS server. Don't forget to update the /etc/shadow file. Also, remove entries from /etc/group, the /etc/hosts file, and any other network files that are now managed by NIS.

Test the NIS client by logging out and logging back in using a login name that is no longer in the /etc/passwd file and is managed by NIS. Test the host's map by pinging a system that is not identified in the local /etc/hosts file.

Setting Up NIS Slave Servers

Before setting up the NIS slave server, you must first set it up as a NIS client. After you've verified that the NIS master server is functioning properly by testing the NIS service on this system, you can set up the system as a slave server. Your network can have one or more slave servers. Having slave servers ensures the continuity of NIS services if the master server is unavailable. Before actually running `ypinit` to create the slave servers, you should run the `domainname` command on each NIS slave to make sure the domain name is consistent with the master server. Remember, the domain name is set by adding the domain name to the /etc/defaultdomain file.

Follow these steps to set up the NIS slave server:

1. As root, edit the /etc/hosts file on the slave server to add the name and IP addresses of all the other NIS servers. This step is optional and for convenience only. At this point, I'm assuming you're not using DNS to manage hostnames (as will be explained later in this chapter). Step 3 prompts you for the hostname of the NIS server. You need an entry for this hostname in the local /etc/hosts file; otherwise, you need to specify the IP address of the NIS server.
2. Change directories to /var/yp on the slave server.
3. To initialize the slave server as a client, type the following:

   ```
   /usr/sbin/ypinit -c
   ```

   The `ypinit` command prompts you for a list of NIS servers. Enter the name of the local slave you are working on first, then the master server, followed by the other NIS slave servers in your domain, in order, from the physically closest to the furthest (in network terms).

NOTE. *You must first configure the new slave server as a NIS client so that it can receive the NIS maps from the master for the first time.*

4. Next, you need to determine if `ypbind` is already running. If it is running, you need to stop and restart it. Check to see if `ypbind` is running by typing this:

   ```
   ps -ef | grep ypbind
   ```

   If a listing is displayed, `ypbind` is running. If `ypbind` is running, stop it by typing this:

   ```
   /usr/lib/netsvc/yp/ypstop
   ```

   Type the following to restart `ypbind`:

   ```
   /usr/lib/netsvc/yp/ypstart
   ```

5. To initialize this system as a slave, type the following:

   ```
   /usr/sbin/ypinit -s master
   ```

   In this example, master is the system name of the existing NIS master server.

   Repeat the procedures described in this list for each system you want configured as a NIS slave server.

6. Now you can start daemons on the slave server and begin the NIS service. First, you must stop all existing yp processes by typing

   ```
   /usr/lib/netsvc/yp/ypstop
   ```

7. To start `ypserv` on the slave server and run `ypbind`, you can either restart the server or type the following:

```
/usr/lib/netsvc/yp/ypstart
```

NIS+

NIS+ is similar to NIS, but with more features. NIS+ is not an extension of NIS, but a new software program. It was designed to replace NIS.

NIS addresses the administrative requirements of small-to-medium client/server computing networks—those with less than a few hundred clients. Some sites with thousands of users find NIS adequate as well. NIS+ is designed for the now-prevalent larger networks in which systems are spread across remote sites in various time zones and in which clients number in the thousands. In addition, the information stored in networks today changes much more frequently, and NIS had to be updated to handle this environment. Last, systems today require a high level of security, and NIS+ addresses many security issues that NIS did not.

NOTE. *NIS+ is not covered in depth on the System Administrator Certification exam, Part II. You are asked a few general overview questions regarding NIS+ that are covered in this book, but a working knowledge of NIS+ is not required until you take the Sun Certified Network Administrator examination.*

Hierarchical Namespace

NIS+ lets you store information about workstation addresses, security, mail, Ethernet interfaces, and network services in central locations where all workstations on a network can access it. This configuration of network information is referred to as the NIS+ namespace.

The NIS+ namespace is the arrangement of information stored by NIS+. The namespace can be arranged in a variety of ways to fit an organization's needs. NIS+ can be arranged to manage large networks with more than one domain. Although the arrangement of a NIS+ namespace can vary from site to site, all sites use the same structural components: directories, tables, and groups. These components are called objects, and they can be arranged into a hierarchy that resembles a UNIX file system.

Directory objects form the skeleton of the namespace. When arranged in a treelike structure, they divide the namespace into separate parts, much like UNIX directories and sub-directories. The topmost directory in a namespace is the root directory. If a namespace is flat, it has only one directory—the root directory. The directory objects beneath the root directory are called directories.

A namespace can have several levels of directories. When identifying the relation of one directory to another, the directory beneath is called the child directory, and the directory above is the parent.

Although UNIX directories are designed to hold UNIX files, NIS+ directories are designed to hold NIS+ objects: other directories, tables, and groups. Any NIS+ directory that stores NIS+ groups is named groups_dir, and any directory that stores NIS+ system tables is named org_dir.

NIS+ Tables

In a NIS+ environment, most namespace information is stored in NIS+ tables; think of them as being similar to NIS maps, which were described earlier. All NIS+ tables are stored in the domain's org_dir NIS+ directory object except the admin and groups tables, which are stored in the groups_dir directory object. The tables that come as default with the standard distribution of NIS+ are described in Table 19-5. Users and application developers frequently create NIS+-compatible tables for their own purposes.

Table 19-5 Standard NIS+ Tables

NIS+ Table	Description
auto_home	This table is an indirect automounter map that allows a NIS+ client to mount the home directory of any user in the domain.
auto_master	This table lists all the automounter maps in a domain. For direct maps, the auto_master table provides a map name. For indirect maps, it provides both a map name and the top directory of its mount point.
bootparams	This table stores configuration information about every diskless workstation in a domain. A diskless workstation is a workstation that is connected to a network but has no hard disk.
client_info	This optional internal NIS+ table is used to store server preferences for the domain in which it resides.
cred	This table stores credential information about NIS+ principals. Each domain has one cred table, which stores the credential information of client workstations that belong to that domain and the client users who can log into them.
ethers	This table stores information about the 48-bit Ethernet addresses of workstations in the domain.
group	This table stores information about UNIX user groups.
hosts	This table associates the names of all the workstations in a domain with their IP addresses. The workstations are usually NIS+ clients, but they don't have to be.
mail_aliases	This table lists the domain's mail aliases recognized by sendmail.

continues

Table 19-5 Standard NIS+ Tables (continued)

NIS+ Table	Description
netgroup	This table defines network-wide groups used to check permissions for remote mounts, logins, and shells. The members of net groups used for remote mounts are workstations; for remote logins and shells, the members are users.
netmasks	This table contains the network masks used to implement standard internetwork subnetting.
networks	This table lists the networks of the Internet. It is normally created from the official network table maintained at the Network Information Control Center (NIC), although you might need to add your local networks to it.
passwd	This table contains information about the accounts of users in a domain. These users generally are NIS+ principals, but they don't have to be. However, remember that if they are NIS+ principals, their credentials are not stored here but in the domain's cred table. The passwd table usually grants read permission to the world (or to nobody). This table contains all logins except root, which is stored in the local /etc/passwd file.
protocols	This table lists the protocols used by the internetwork.
rpc	This table lists the names of RPC programs.
services	This table stores information about the services available on the internetwork.
timezone	This table lists the default time zone of every workstation in the domain.

NIS+ tables can be manipulated with AdminTool. The NIS+ master server updates its objects immediately; however, it tries to batch several updates before it propagates them to its replicas (slaves).

NIS+ Security

NIS+ security is enhanced in two ways. First, it can authenticate access to the service, so it can discriminate between access that is enabled to members of the community and other network entities. Second, it includes an authorization model that allows specific rights to be granted or denied based on this authentication.

Authentication

Authentication is used to identify NIS+ principals. A NIS+ principal might be someone who is logged in to a client system as a regular user, someone who is logged in as superuser, or any process that runs with superuser permission on a NIS+ client system. Thus, a NIS+ principal can be a client user or a client workstation. Every time a principal (user or system) tries to access a NIS+ object, the user's identity and secure RPC password are confirmed and validated.

Authorization

Authorization is used to specify access rights. Every time NIS+ principals try to access NIS+ objects, they are placed in one of four authorization classes, or categories:

- Owner: A single NIS+ principal
- Group: A collection of NIS+ principals
- World: All principals authenticated by NIS+
- Nobody: Unauthenticated principals

The NIS+ server finds out what access rights are assigned to that principal by that particular object. If the access rights match, the server answers the request. If they do not match, the server denies the request and returns an error message.

NIS+ authorization is the process of granting NIS+ principals access rights to a NIS+ object. Access rights are similar to file permissions. There are four types of access rights:

- Read: The principal can read the contents of the object.
- Modify: The principal can modify the contents of the object.
- Create: The principal can create new objects in a table or directory.
- Destroy: The principal can destroy objects in a table or directory.

Access rights are displayed as 16 characters. They can be displayed with the command `nisls -l` and changed with the command `nischmod`.

The NIS+ security system lets NIS+ administrators specify different read, modify, create, and destroy rights to NIS+ objects for each class. For example, a given class could be permitted to modify a particular column in the passwd table but not read that column, or a different class could be allowed to read some entries of a table but not others.

The implementation of the authorization scheme I just described is determined by the domain's level of security. A NIS+ server can operate at one of three security levels. They are summarized in Table 19-6.

Table 19-6 NIS+ Security Levels

Security Level	Description
0	Security level 0 is designed for testing and setting up the initial NIS+ namespace. A NIS+ server running at security level 0 grants any NIS+ principal full access rights to all NIS+ objects in the domain. Level 0 is for setup purposes only, and it should only be used by administrators for that purpose. Level 0 should not be used on networks in normal operation by regular users.

continues

Table 19-6 NIS+ Security Levels (continued)

Security Level	Description
1	Security level 1 uses AUTH_SYS security. This level is not supported by NIS+, and it should not be used.
2	Security level 2 is the default. It is the highest level of security currently provided by NIS+ and is the default level assigned to a NIS server. It authenticates only requests that use Data Encryption Standard (DES) credentials (DES is described in the next section). Requests with no credentials are assigned to the nobody class and have whatever access rights have been granted to that class. Requests that use invalid DES credentials are retried. After repeated failures to obtain a valid DES credential, requests with invalid credentials fail with an authentication error. (A credential might be invalid for a variety of reasons, such as the principal making the request is not keylogged in on that system, the clocks are out of sync, there is a key mismatch, and so forth.)

DES Authentication

DES (Data Encryption Standard) authentication uses the DES and public key cryptography to authenticate both users and systems in the network. DES is a standard encryption mechanism; public key cryptography is a cipher system that involves two keys: one public and one private.

The security of DES authentication is based on a sender's ability to encrypt the current time, which the receiver can then decrypt and check against its own clock. The timestamp is encrypted with DES. Two things are necessary for this scheme to work: The two agents must agree on the current time, and the sender and receiver must be using the same encryption key.

If a network runs a time synchronization program, the time on the client and the server is synchronized automatically. If a time synchronization program is not available, timestamps can be computed using the server's time instead of the network time. The client asks the server for the time before starting the RPC session, and then it computes the time difference between its own clock and the server's. This difference is used to offset the client's clock when computing timestamps. If the client and server clocks become out of sync to the point where the server begins to reject the client's requests, the DES authentication system resynchronizes with the server.

The client and server arrive at the same encryption key by generating a random conversation key and then using public key cryptography (an encryption scheme involving public and secret keys) to deduce a common key. The common key is a key that only the client and server are capable of deducing. The conversation key is used to encrypt and decrypt the client's timestamp; the common key is used to encrypt and decrypt the conversation key.

DNS

DNS is the name service provided by the Internet for Transmission Control Protocol/Internet Protocol (TCP/IP) networks. It was developed so that workstations on the network could be identified by common names instead of Internet addresses. DNS is a program that converts domain names to their IP addresses. Without it, users would have to remember numbers instead of words to get around the Internet. The process of finding a computer's IP address by using its host name as an index is referred to as *name-to-address resolution*, or *mapping*.

The collection of networked systems that use DNS are referred to as the *DNS namespace*. The DNS namespace can be divided into a hierarchy of domains. A *DNS domain* is simply a group of systems. Each domain is supported by two or more name servers: the primary, secondary, or cache-only server. Each domain must have one primary server and should have at least one secondary server to provide backup.

Each server implements DNS by running a daemon called `in.named`. On the client side, DNS is implemented through the *resolver*. The resolver's function is to resolve users' queries. The resolver is neither a daemon nor a single program; rather, it is a set of dynamic library routines used by applications that need to know system names. After the resolver is configured, a system can request DNS service from a name server. If a system's /etc/nsswitch.conf file specifies `hosts: dns`, the resolver libraries are automatically used. If the nsswitch.conf file specifies some other name service before DNS, such as NIS, that name service is consulted first for host information. Only if that name service does not find the host in question are the resolver libraries used.

For example, if the hosts line in the nsswitch.conf file specifies `hosts: nis dns`, the NIS name service is first searched for host information. If the information is not found in NIS, the DNS resolver is used. Because name services, such as NIS and NIS+, contain only information about hosts in their own network, the effect of a `hosts:nis dns` line in a switch file is to specify the use of NIS for local host information and DNS for information on remote hosts on the Internet. If the resolver queries a name server, the server returns either the requested information or a referral to another server.

Name-to-address mapping occurs if a program running on your local system needs to contact a remote computer. The program most likely knows the host name of the remote computer but might not know how to locate it, particularly if the remote system is in another company, miles from your site. To obtain the remote system's address, the program requests assistance from the DNS software running on your local system, which is considered a DNS client.

Your system sends a request to a DNS name server, which maintains the distributed DNS database. The files in the DNS database bear little resemblance to the NIS+ host table or even to the local /etc/hosts file, although they maintain similar information: the host names,

IP addresses, and other information about a particular group of computers. The name server uses the host name your system sent as part of its request to find or "resolve" the IP address of the remote system. It then returns this IP address to your local system if the host name is in its DNS database.

If the host name is not in that name server's DNS database, this indicates that the system is outside its authority, or, to use DNS terminology, outside the local administrative domain.

Because maintaining a central list of domain name/IP address correspondences would be impractical, the lists of domain names and IP addresses are distributed throughout the Internet in a hierarchy of authority. A DNS server that maps the domain names in your Internet requests or forwards them to other servers in the Internet is probably within close geographic proximity to your Internet access provider.

NOTE. *DNS is not covered in depth on the System Administrator Certification exam, Part II. You need to know the definition of DNS, but a working knowledge of it is not required until you take the Sun Certified Network Administrator examination.*

Summary

This chapter covered all the name service topics that appear on the Certified Solaris Administrator examination for Solaris 7, Part II. Of course, better understanding of the topics will come as you use the products described and become experienced over time. Many large networks that use a name service are heterogeneous, meaning that they have more than just Solaris systems connected to the network. You need to refer to the vendor's documentation for each particular system type to understand how each different operating system implements name services. You will see that most are similar in their implementation, with only subtle differences. As you gain experience and complete the Solaris Administrator Certification exams, your next goal should be to become certified as a Sun Network Administrator for Solaris. Certification in both fields is valuable for any UNIX system administrator.

The next chapter describes the Solstice AdminSuite product and how it can help you manage your network.

CHAPTER

20

Solstice AdminSuite

The following test objectives are covered in this chapter:

- Understanding Solstice AdminSuite GUI tools and the command-line equivalents
- Starting the Solstice AdminSuite Tools
- Customizing the Launcher window
- Using the AdminSuite tools

I introduced Solstice AdminSuite in Chapter 14, "Installing a Server," when we installed the operating system (OS) on the server and used Host Manager to set up the AutoClients and OS server. This chapter describes the entire AdminSuite Graphical User Interface (GUI).

Solstice AdminSuite is a collection of GUI tools and commands used to perform administrative tasks, such as managing users, groups, hosts, system files, printers, disks, file systems, terminals, and modems. It's similar to AdminTool in that it helps the system administrator with tasks such as setting up printers, serial ports, file systems, and user accounts. The main difference is that Solstice AdminSuite lets you perform these tasks either locally or over the network from one system. It also provides additional functionality not found in AdminTool, such as setting up AutoClients and JavaStations.

Solstice AdminSuite and the Command-Line Equivalents

Just like AdminTool, Solstice AdminSuite provides tools that execute numerous commands in a single menu pick. However, you must run AdminSuite from a bitmapped screen that supports the X Window System. It's important for the system administrator to understand the command-line equivalent of each task performed by AdminSuite just in case a graphics terminal is not available. Table 20-1 describes the tools available in Solstice AdminSuite. It also lists the command-line equivalent of each tool provided in the AdminSuite GUI.

Table 20-1 Solstice AdminSuite Tools and Their Command-Line Equivalents

AdminSuite Tool	Command-Line Equivalent	Description of Task Performed

Host Manager	`admhostadd`
	`admhostdel`
	`dmhostmod`
	`admhostls`
		Configures system information and server support for AutoClient and stand-alone systems, diskless clients, and JavaStations.

Group Manager	`admgroupadd`
	`admgroupdel`
	`admgroupmod`
	`admgroupls`
		Maintains UNIX group information.

User Manager	`admuseradd`
	`admuserdel`
	`admusermod`
	`admuserls`
		Maintains user account information.

continues

Table 20-1 Solstice AdminSuite Tools and Their Command-Line Equivalents (continued)

AdminSuite Tool	Command-Line Equivalent	Description of Task Performed
Serial Port Manager	admserialdel admserialmod admserialls	Configures serial port software for terminals and modems.
Printer Manager	None	Configures print servers and clients.
Database Manager	None	Maintains network-related system files, such as aliases and hosts.
Storage Manager	None	Configures disk slices on a single disk or a group of disks. It is also used to set up file systems for a server or group of clients on a server.

Each AdminSuite tool is described in its entirety in this chapter.

Starting the Solstice AdminSuite Tools

To get to the AdminSuite tools, you must first install the Solstice AdminSuite product; it is not automatically installed with the OS. (The process of installing the product was described in Chapter 14, "Installing a Server.") Verify that AdminSuite is installed on your system by typing the following command:

```
pkginfo | grep AdminSuite
```

If the following is displayed, the Solstice AdminSuite packages are installed:

```
system      SUNWadmsm     Solstice AdminSuite Storage Manager Application
system      SUNWsadma     Solstice AdminSuite Applications
system      SUNWsadmb     Solstice AdminSuite CLI
system      SUNWsadmc     Solstice AdminSuite Core Methods
system      SUNWsadmm     Solstice AdminSuite man pages
system      SUNWsadmo     Solstice AdminSuite Object Libraries
system      SUNWsadmp     Solstice AdminSuite Data Files
system      SUNWspapp     Solstice AdminSuite print application
```

To actually use the AdminSuite tools, start the Solstice Launcher by entering the following command:

```
solstice &
```

The Solstice Launcher window opens, as shown in Figure 20-1.

Figure 20-1
The Solstice Launcher window.

In the Solstice Launcher window, click an icon to start a tool. Alternatively, you can use the Tab key or the mouse to move from icon to icon, and press the spacebar to open a tool.

Choose the Launcher menu on the toolbar. You see the three menu options shown in Figure 20-2.

Figure 20-2
The Launcher pull-down menu.

The following is a description of the three options found on the Launcher menu:

- **Add Application**—Use this option to add and register applications with the Launcher. It's possible to add your own tools to the Solstice Launcher.
- **Properties**—Use this option to customize the launcher by showing, hiding, or removing applications; reordering the icons; changing the Launcher window width; modifying application properties; and adding applications.
- **Exit**—Use this option to stop running the Solstice Launcher. This does not affect open Solstice applications.

Applications that are displayed in the Solstice Launcher are registered. This means that you can add custom applications, such as a third-party backup application, to the Launcher main window. Applications are registered in three ways:

- **Private registry**—Registered applications are private to the user. Applications are registered privately using the Add Application option on the Launcher menu. Privately registered applications can be added or removed, and their properties can be modified from the Solstice Launcher.

- **Local registry**—Registered applications are local to the system. Applications registered locally are available to all local users of the system. Applications can only be registered locally with the `/usr/snadm/bin/soladdapp` command and can only be removed using the `soldelapp` command. Their properties cannot be modified from the Solstice Launcher.
- **Global registry**—Registered applications are shared by all local and remote users using the Solstice Launcher in a particular /opt directory. Applications can only be registered globally with the `soladdapp` command and can only be removed using the `soldelapp` command. Their properties cannot be modified from the Solstice Launcher.

Customizing the Launcher Window

You might want to customize the applications that appear in the Launcher window. The following example describes how to modify your Private Registry to customize the Launcher window for your login only:

1. Choose the Launcher menu in the main Launcher window and select Properties. The Launcher: Properties window opens, as shown in Figure 20-3.

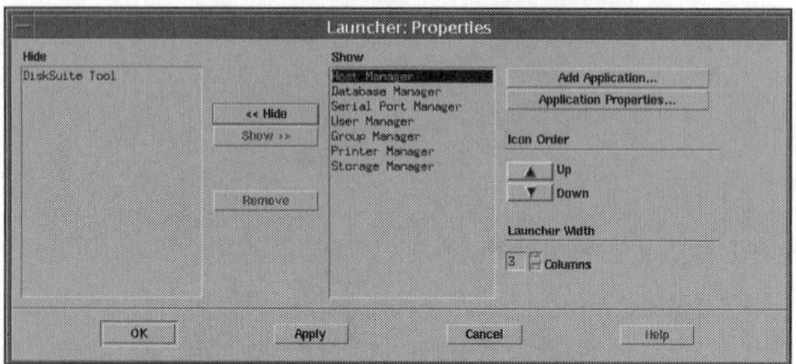

Figure 20-3
The Launcher: Properties window.

2. In the Launcher: Properties window, highlight the application you want to hide, and then click Hide. Figure 20-3 shows the Launcher: Properties window with the DiskSuite Tool on the Hide list. Repeat this process until you're finished with your selections. After you've hidden the applications, click OK. You'll return to the Solstice Launcher window, which now contains your customizations, as shown in Figure 20-4.

Figure 20-4
The customized Launcher window.

Using the Solstice AdminSuite Tools

When you select a tool icon in the Launcher, the tool's main window opens. The main window contains two areas: a menu bar and a display area. The menu bar usually contains four menus: File, Edit, View, and Help. Each of these menus is described in this chapter.

You can set up a log file to record each major operation completed with the Solstice AdminSuite tools. After you enable logging, the date, time, server, user ID (UID), and description of every operation are written to the specified log file. To enable logging, log in as root and follow these steps:

1. Edit the /etc/syslog.conf file and add an entry at the bottom of the file that follows this format:

   ```
   user.info filename
   ```

   The filename must be the absolute pathname of the file, such as /var/log/adminsuite.log.

2. Create the log file if it does not already exist using the `touch` command as follows:

   ```
   touch /var/log/filename
   ```

3. To make the changes in /etc/syslog.conf take effect, stop and start the syslog service as follows:

   ```
   /etc/init.d/syslog stop
   /etc/init.d/syslog start
   ```

   Solstice AdminSuite operations will now be logged to the file you specified.

Now we'll look at each individual tool in AdminSuite.

Host Manager

We took a detailed look at Host Manager in Chapters 14 and 15, when I described how to set up and maintain server and client support. Refer to those chapters for information on the Host Manager tool.

User Manager

User Manager is a GUI that lets you manage user accounts in a NIS or NIS+ domain or in a local system. Use the User Manager to perform the following tasks:

- Add, modify, or delete a user account
- Display and sort user-account information

Start User Manager by clicking the User Manager icon in the Solstice Launcher window. The User Manager window opens, with the User Manager: Load window on top of it (see Figure 20-5).

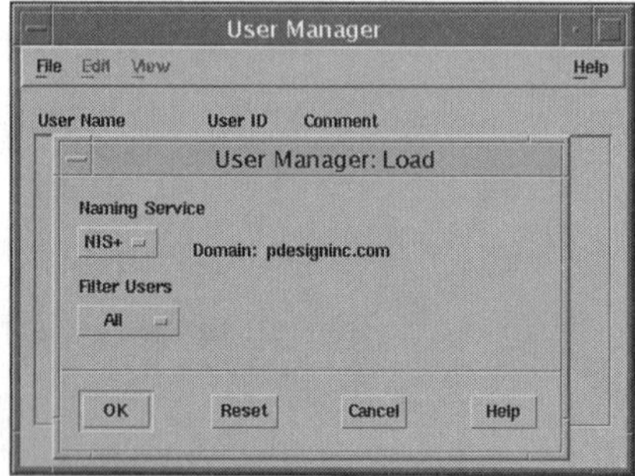

Figure 20-5
The User Manager: Load window.

Select your naming service, check that the domain or host name is correct, and click OK. The User Manager main window displays the list of users for the context you chose, as shown in Figure 20-6.

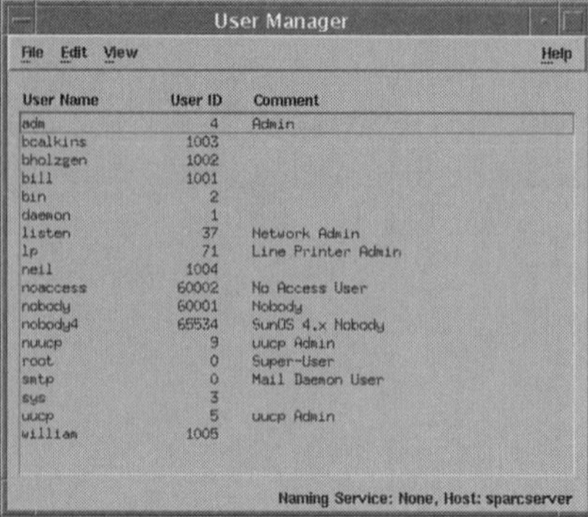

Figure 20-6
The User Manager main window.

Setting Up User Account Defaults

If you'll be adding several new user accounts, you might want to create a set of defaults that each user will share. If you have a standard value that you employ repeatedly for users, you can set that value as a default so that you do not have to enter it each time you add a user. The defaults you select will be the initial default values assigned to the new account whenever you add a new user. To access the Set Add Defaults window, select Edit, Set Defaults. The Set Add Defaults window opens, as shown in Figure 20-7.

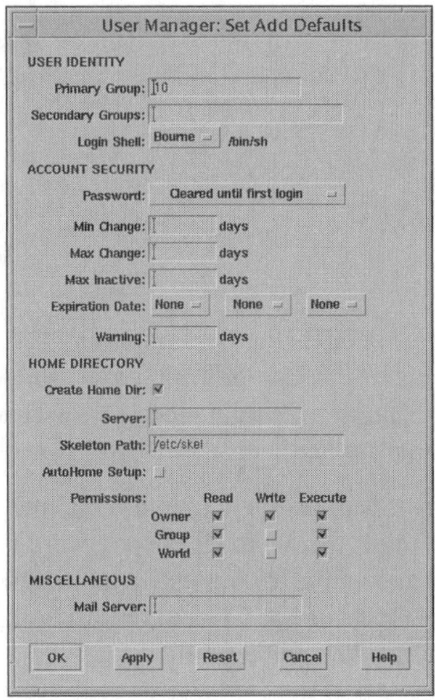

Figure 20-7
The Set Add Defaults window.

You can set the following defaults:

- **Primary Group**—Specifies a group ID number or group name that the OS will assign to files created by the user. Users in the same group can then access these files, assuming that they have the correct permissions set.

NOTE. *Group 10 (staff) is the default primary group that is appropriate for most users.*

- **Secondary Groups** (Optional)—Specifies one or more additional groups that the user can also belong to. You can specify either a group ID number or group name. If you specify more than one group, separate them with commas.
- **Login Shell**—Specifies a login shell (Bourne, Korn, or C shell) for the user. You can also select Other to specify a shell not in the list.

- **Password**—Specifies a password scheme for the user. The password options are as follows:

Cleared until first login	The account will not have a password. The user will be prompted for a new password at the first login. The user must set a password after first logging in.
Account is locked	The account is locked. The user will not be able to log in until the administrator assigns a password.
No password—setuid only	The account cannot be logged in to, but account programs are allowed to run.

- **Min Change** (Optional)—Specifies the minimum number of days allowed between password changes. This can be used to prevent a user from changing a password and immediately changing it back to the original password. This option is not available if you are using the NIS name service.
- **Max Change** (Optional)—Specifies the maximum number of days the user can go without having to set up a new password. If the password is not changed within this number of days, the user account is locked until you modify the user account's Password field to Normal Password or Cleared until first login. This option is not available if you are using the NIS name service.
- **Max Inactive** (Optional)—Specifies the maximum number of days the user account can be inactive before the user account is locked. The user account remains locked until you modify the user account's Password field to Normal Password or Cleared until first login. This option is not available if you are using the NIS name service.
- **Expiration Date** (Optional)—Specifies the day, month, and year when the user account expires and is locked. The user account remains locked until you modify the user account's Password field to Normal Password or Cleared until first login.
- **Warning** (Optional)—Specifies when the user will start receiving a warning message about his password's expiration.
- **Create Home Dir**—Specifies whether to automatically create the user's home directory.
- **Server**—Specifies the name of the system that contains the home directory.

- **Skeleton Path**—Specifies the path that contains the user initialization files that you have created for the user. The files are copied into the user's home directory. The default directory is /etc/skel.
- **AutoHome Setup**—Specifies whether to create an Autofs entry for the user's home directory. If you create an Autofs entry, the user's home directory will be mounted automatically.
- **Permissions**—Specifies the permissions to set on the user's home directory.
- **Mail Server**—Specifies the name of the system that contains the user's mailbox.

Adding a New User Account

To add a new user account, select Edit, Add in the User Manager main window. The User Manager: Add window opens, as shown in Figure 20-8.

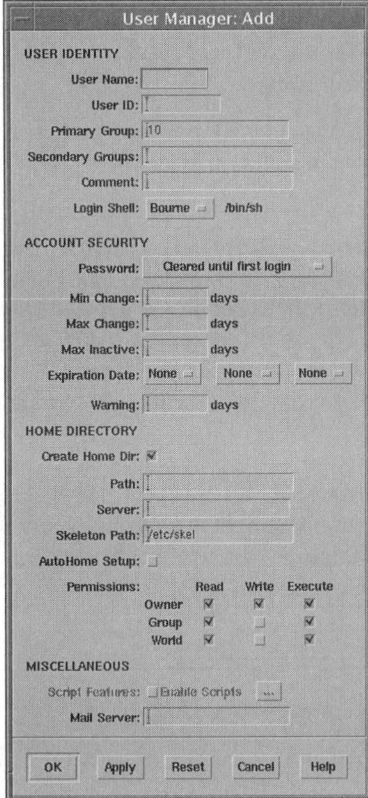

Figure 20-8
The User Manager: Add window.

Fill in the appropriate boxes. When they are complete, click OK. Refer to the preceding section for information on each field. In addition to the fields described in that section, you will also see the following fields in the User Manager: Add window:

- **User Name**—Specifies a login name to identify an individual user. A username must be a unique name composed of uppercase or lowercase alphabetic characters (A through Z, a through z) or digits (0 through 9). A username must be one to eight characters long and must include at least one lowercase letter. In addition, the first character of a user's name must be a letter.
- **User ID**—Specifies a unique number by which the OS can identify a user. In Solaris 7, the maximum value is 2147483647. The UIDs 60001 (nobody) and 65534 (nobody4) are reserved and are not to be used.

NOTE. *It is strongly recommended that UIDs be kept under 60000 to minimize software incompatibilities. Some software packages, such as third-party PC-NFS packages, can't handle UIDs over 60000.*

- **Comment** (Optional)—Specifies notes about this user account, such as a user's full name, phone number, or department.
- **Normal Password**—Displays the Set Password window, which allows you to assign a password to the account when adding the user.
- **Path**—Specifies the path for the user's home directory. By convention, this is /export/home/<user-name>.

Another option on the Edit menu is the capability to copy an existing account. Simply highlight an existing account in the User Manager main window and select Edit, Copy. The User Manager: Copy window opens with blank User Name and User ID fields. The rest of the fields are filled in with the settings from the user you chose to copy.

Modifying a User Account

To make changes to a user account, highlight the account you want to modify by clicking the account name in the User Manager main window. Select Edit, Modify. The User Manager: Modify window opens, as shown in Figure 20-9.

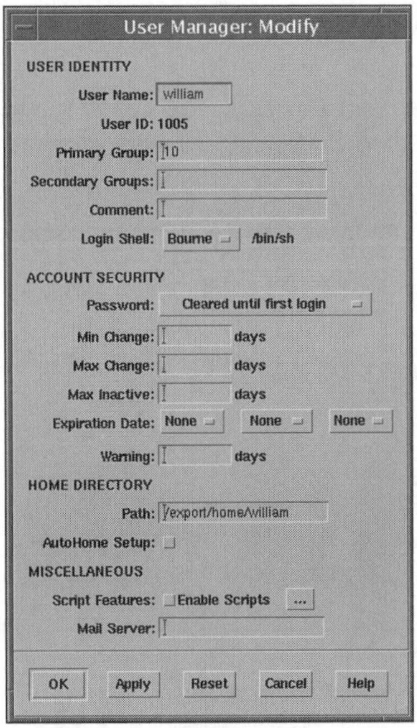

Figure 20-9
The User Manager: Modify window.

Change the appropriate boxes and click OK after it's complete. Refer to the previous section, "Setting Up User Account Defaults," for information on each field.

Deleting a User Account

To delete a user account, highlight the account you want to delete by clicking the account name in the User Manager main window. Then select Edit, Delete.

The User Manager: Delete window opens to confirm the removal of the user account, as shown in Figure 20-10.

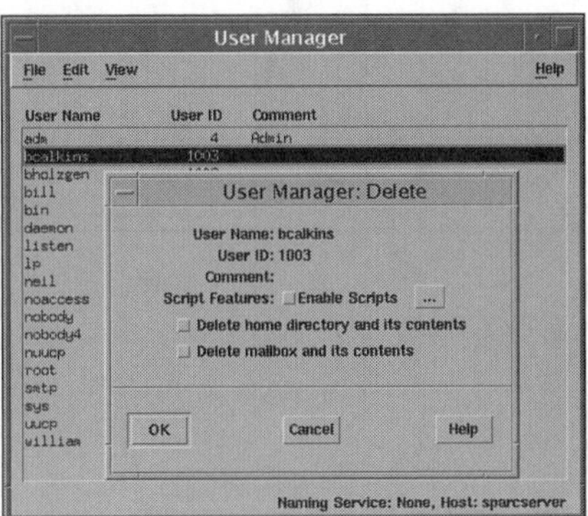

Figure 20-10
The User Manager: Delete window.

In the User Manager: Delete window, you are presented with a few options before you delete the account.

- Click the Script Features box to specify scripts to be run before or after the account is deleted from the system. You can specify whether to run the scripts before or after the account is deleted.
- Click the first check box to delete the user's home directory and its contents.
- Click the second check box to delete the user's mailbox and its contents.

Click OK when you are ready to delete the user account. The user account entry is deleted from the User Manager main window.

Group Manager

To add, modify, or delete groups, click the Group Manager Icon in the Solstice Launcher main window. The Group Account Manager window opens, with the Load window on top of it (see Figure 20-11).

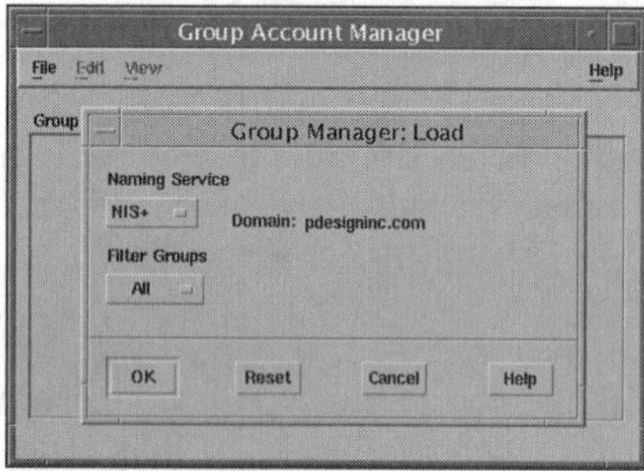

Figure 20-11
The Group Manager: Load window.

Select the name service and click OK. The Group Manager main window opens, as shown in Figure 20-12.

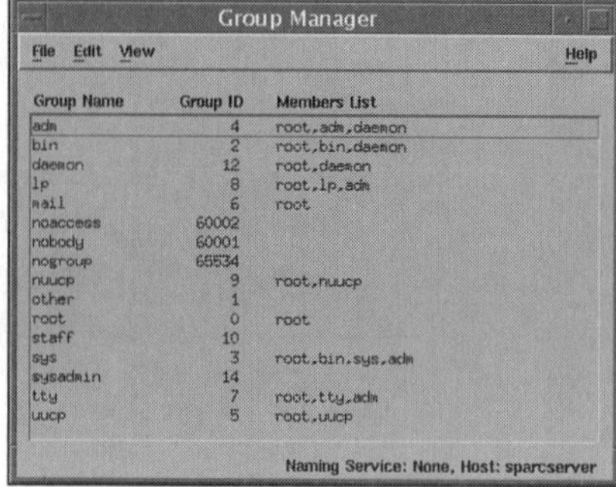

Figure 20-12
The Group Manager main window.

To add a group, from the Group Manager main window select Edit, Add. The Group Manager: Add window opens, as shown in Figure 20-13.

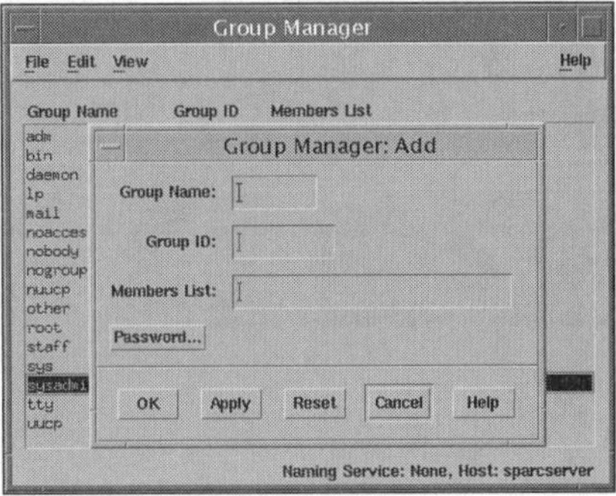

Figure 20-13
The Group Manager: Add window.

In the Group Manager: Add window, you are presented with four items, two of which are mandatory and two of which are optional:

- **Group Name**—Type the name of the new group in the Group Name text box. A group name contains lowercase alphabetic characters (a through z) and digits (0 through 9). A group name can be from 1 to 9 characters long.
- **Group ID**—Specify the group ID (GID) for the new group. This GID must be a non-negative decimal integer between 100 and 2147483647. GIDs from 0 to 99 are reserved by SunOS for future applications. GIDs 60002 (noaccess) and 65534 (nogroup) are also reserved.

NOTE. *It is strongly recommended that GIDs be kept below 60000 to minimize software incompatibilities. Some software packages, such as third-party PC-NFS packages, can't handle GIDs over 60000.*

- **Members List** (Optional)—Specify the users (either by their login name or UID) or groups who belong to this group. If there is to be more than one member in the list, separate the names with a comma. Spaces are not allowed.

  Example: neil,glenda,nicole
- **Password** (Optional)—Displays the password window, which lets you enter the group password.

To modify a group, highlight the group name in the Group Manager main window, and then select Edit, Modify. The Group Manager: Modify window opens. It contains the selected group entry, as shown in Figure 20-14.

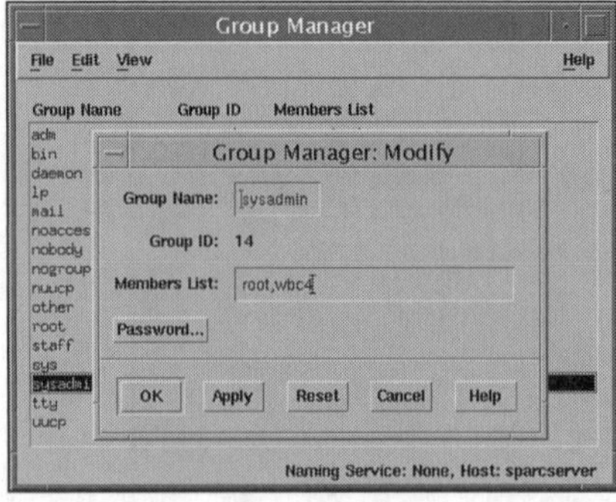

Figure 20-14
The Group Manager: Modify window.

You can modify either the group's name or the users in the group. Usernames must be separated by commas.

Modify the group's password by clicking the Password button. Enter the group password, and then verify it in the fields provided in the Password dialog box.

Click OK when the modifications are complete.

Serial Port Manager

The Serial Port Manager configures the serial port software to work with terminals and modems by calling the `pmadm` command and supplying the appropriate information. Serial Port Manager allows you to do the following:

- Display serial port information
- Use templates for common terminal and modem configurations
- Configure, modify, or delete multiple ports at the same time

The Serial Port Manager consists primarily of two windows: the Serial Port Manager main window, shown in Figure 20-15, and the Serial Port Manager: Modify window, shown in Figure 20-16. To access the Serial Port Manager main window, click the Serial Port Manager icon in the Launcher window.

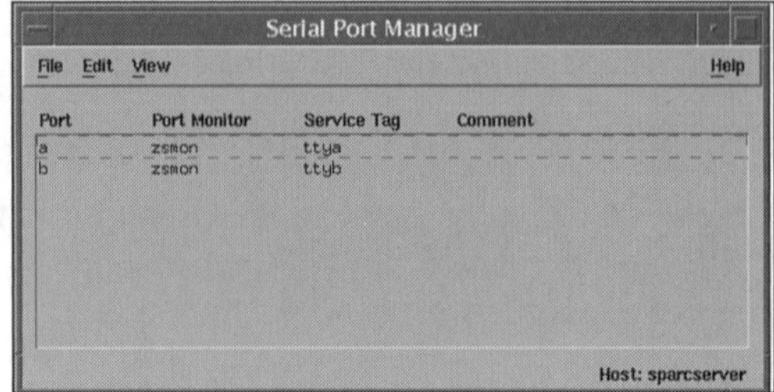

Figure 20-15
The Serial Port Manager main window.

In this window, three pull-down menus let you do the following:

- Select the port you want to modify
- Delete modems and terminals
- View serial ports for different hosts
- Exit the Serial Port Manager

The three pull-down menus are described in Table 20-2.

Table 20-2 Pull-Down Menus

Pull-Down Menu	Options	Description
File	Exit	Closes the Serial Port Manager tool.
Edit	Modify	Opens the Serial Port Manager: Modify window.
	Delete	Removes the port monitor and service tag configuration for the selected port.
View	Host	Brings up the Host window, from which you can select from a list of available hosts.

The most commonly used option is Edit, Modify. To modify a port, highlight the port you want to modify, and then select Edit, Modify. (To configure multiple ports at the same time using Serial Port Manager, highlight more than one port.) The Serial Port Manager: Modify window opens, as shown in Figure 20-16.

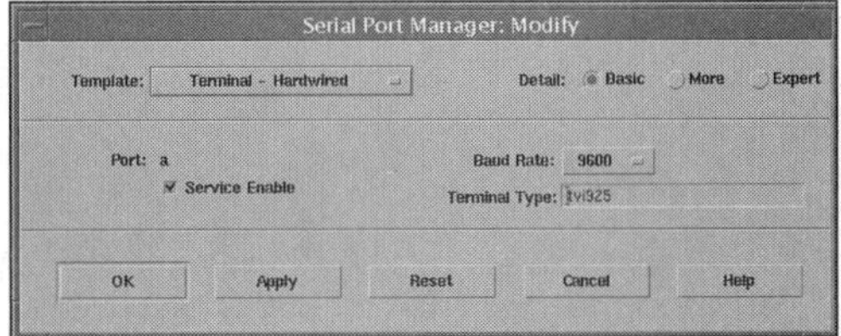

Figure 20-16
The Serial Port Manager: Modify window.

In this window, you have many options to choose from, including templates for commonly used terminal and modem configurations. You can view the templates by clicking the Template button. This allows you to choose one of the template options shown in Figure 20-17.

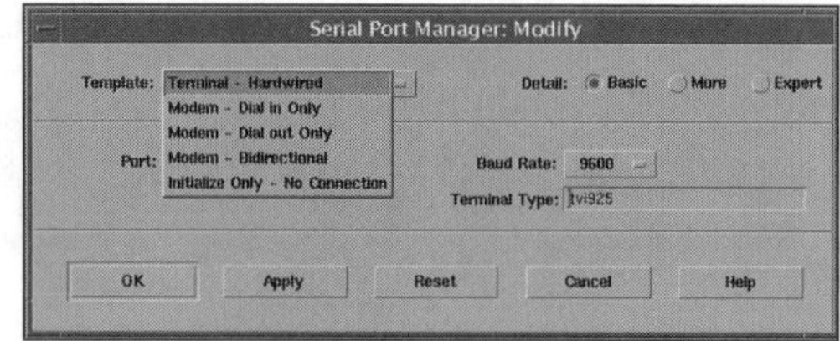

Figure 20-17
The Serial Port templates.

The template selections are described in Table 20-3.

Table 20-3 Serial Port Templates

Option	Description
Terminal – Hardwired	Users can log in via a terminal that is directly connected to the system.
Modem – Dial in only	Users can dial into the modem, but they can't dial out.
Modem – Dial out Only	Users can dial out from the modem, but they can't dial in.
Modem – Bidirectional	Users can dial in or out from the modem.
Initialize Only – No Connection	The port service is initialized but not configured. Use this to initialize the port connection without actually connecting a device to the port.

The Serial Port Manager: Modify window has three levels of detail that can be displayed: Basic, More, and Expert. Figure 20-18 shows the Expert level of detail.

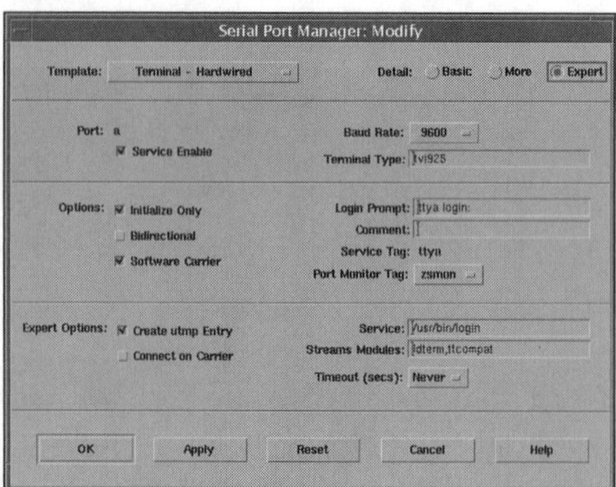

Figure 20-18
The Serial Port Manager: Modify window—Expert-level detail.

Each option in the window is described in Table 20-4. Chapter 13, "Device Administration," provides details on setting up serial ports for modems and terminals.

Table 20-4 Serial Port Manager Options

Option	Description
Port	Lists the port or ports you selected from the Serial Port main window.
Service Enable	Select this box to enable the serial port service on the specific serial port.
Baud Rate	Specifies the line speed used to communicate with the terminal. The line speed represents an entry in the /etc/ttydefs file.
Terminal Type	Shows the abbreviation for the type of terminal, such as ansi or vt100. Similar abbreviations are found in /etc/termcap. This value is set in the $TERM environment variable.
Option: Initialize Only	Specifies that the port software is initialized but not configured.
Option: Bidirectional	Specifies that the port line is used in both directions.
Option: Software Carrier	Specifies that the software-carrier detection feature is used. If this option is not checked, the hardware-carrier detection signal is used.
Login Prompt	Shows the prompt displayed to a user after a connection is made.
Comment	Shows the comment field for the service.
Service Tag	Lists the service tag associated with this port, which is typically an entry in the /dev/term directory.
Port Monitor Tag	Specifies the name of the port monitor to be used for this port. The default monitor is typically correct.
Create utmp Entry	Specifies that a utmp entry is created in the accounting files upon login.
Connect on Carrier	Specifies that a port's associated service is invoked immediately after a connect indication is received.
Service	Shows the program that is run upon connection.
Streams Modules	Shows the STREAMS modules that are pushed before the service is invoked.
Timeout (secs)	Specifies the number of seconds before a port is closed if the open process on the port succeeds and no input data is received.

Print Client Software

Before we discuss how to use Printer Manager to set up printers, it's important to take a look at the SunSoft Print Client software and how it compares with the LP print service described in Chapter 10, "The LP Print Service." Let me begin by describing a print server and a print client, and then I'll describe the SunSoft print process by illustrating the path of a typical print request.

The Print Server

The print server is a system that has a local printer connected to it and makes the printer available to other systems on the network. The SunSoft print client commands use the BSD (Berkley Standard Distribution) printing protocol. The main advantage of this protocol is that it can communicate with a variety of print servers:

- SunOS 4.x BSD (lpd) print servers
- SunOS 5.x SVR4 (LP) print servers
- Any other print server or printer that accepts the BSD printing protocol

The BSD printing protocol is an industry standard. It is widely used, and it provides compatibility between different types of systems from various manufacturers. Sun has chosen to support the BSD printing protocol to provide interoperability in the future. The System V protocol, on the other hand, is not as widely used and does not provide compatibility with BSD print servers.

The print server is set up using the Solstice AdminSuite Printer Manager tool described later in this chapter.

The Print Client

The print client is a system that sends print requests to a print server. A system becomes a SunSoft print client when you install the SunSoft print client software and enable access to remote printers on the system. After you install the Print Client software on a system, some of the print commands in Solaris are replaced by SunSoft print client commands. These commands have the same names, accept the same command-line options, generate the same output, and work with the same tools as the standard Solaris print commands. The difference, however, is that the SunSoft commands perform their tasks using a method that improves printing performance by providing more options to locate printer configuration information. The print configuration resources are a key component of the SunSoft Print Client software. They increase printing efficiency because of the method they use to locate printer information.

The SunSoft print client commands check the following resources to locate printers and printer configuration information:

- The command-line interface
- A printer alias file in the user's home directory
- Local (print client) configuration files
- A network (shared) configuration file if you use a name service

In contrast, the standard print commands in Solaris use fewer options to locate printer information. In addition, the standard Solaris print commands do not check information on the network, and they do not support a name service.

The SunSoft print client commands let clients submit requests directly to the print server.

The SunSoft print client sends its requests to the print server's queue; the client does not have a local queue. The client writes the print request to a temporary spooling area only if the print server is unavailable or an error occurs. This streamlined path to the server decreases the print client's use of resources, reduces the chances of printing problems, and improves performance.

In contrast, the standard Solaris print commands depend on a local print daemon to communicate with the print server. The print commands write every print request to a local spooling area on the print client and then tell another set of processes to transfer the request, even if the print server is available and there are no error conditions.

Processing a Print Request

The following steps outline how the SunSoft Print Client software processes a print request:

1. A user submits a print request from a SunSoft print client by using a SunSoft print client command.
2. The print client command checks a hierarchy of print configuration resources to determine where to send the print request.
3. The print client command sends the print request directly to the appropriate print server. A SunSoft print server can be any server that accepts the BSD printing protocol, including SVR4 (LP) print servers and BSD print servers (such as the SunOS 4.x BSD print server).
4. The print server sends the print request to the appropriate printer.
5. The print request is printed.

Printer Manager

Use the Printer Manager to set up and manage the SunSoft print client software. The following tasks can be performed using Printer Manager:

- **Install a printer on a print server**—Installs a printer on the system to which it is attached. This procedure tells the system about the printer so that it can act as a print server. If you use a name service, this task also makes the printer available to all SunSoft print clients.
- **Install a network printer**—Installs a printer on your network that provides access to all network users.

- **Give print clients access**—Gives SunSoft print clients access to a printer that is installed on a print server.
- **Modify printer information**—Modifies the current configuration information for a printer.

To start Printer Manager, click the Printer Manager icon in the Launcher window. The Printer Manager window opens, with the Printer Manager: Load window on top of it (see Figure 20-19).

Figure 20-19
The Printer Manager: Load window.

Select the correct naming service from the pull-down menu, and then click OK. The Printer Manager main window opens, as shown in Figure 20-20.

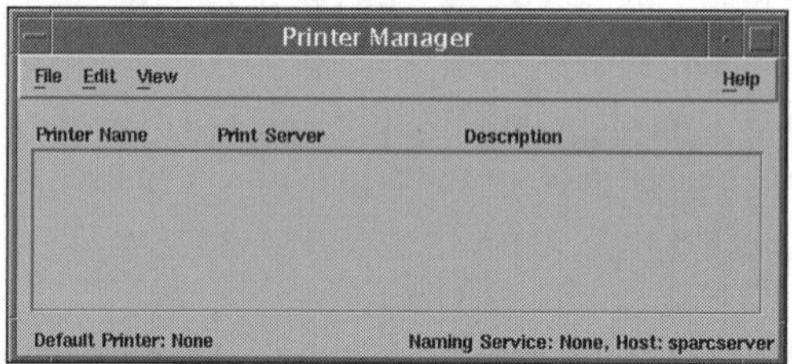

Figure 20-20
The Printer Manager main window.

Installing a Printer

If you use Printer Manager to install a printer on a system, you define the characteristics of the printer and identify the users who are permitted to access it. The system on which you install the printer becomes the print server.

Installing a printer means something different depending on whether or not you use a name service. If you are using a name service, Printer Manager adds the printer in the NIS or NIS+ master file, and the printer is then available to all SunSoft print clients. If you aren't using a name service, Printer Manager adds the printer in the print server's configuration files only, and the print clients do not know about the printer.

To install a new printer, connect it to the system and turn on the power to the printer. Start the Printer Manager as described earlier, and select either Edit, Install Local Printer or Edit, Install Network Printer. In this example, I will install a local printer.

The Install Local Printer window opens, as shown in Figure 20-21.

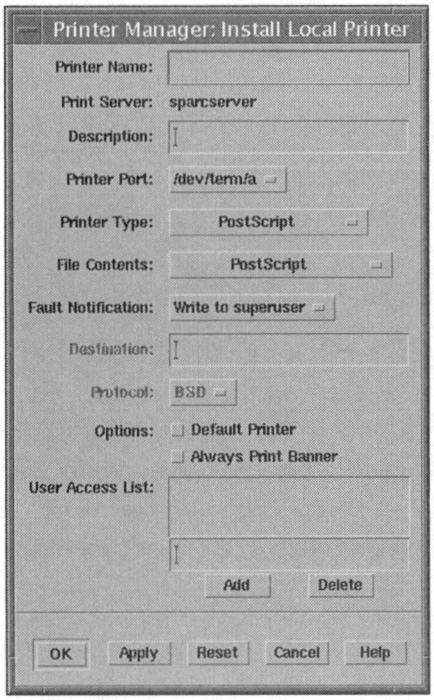

Figure 20-21
The Install Local Printer window.

Fill in the fields, and click Apply when you're finished.

NOTE. *Clicking Apply allows you to save your changes and stay in the same window to add more printers. Clicking OK saves your changes and takes you out of the window and back to the Printer Manager main window.*

Here are descriptions of the different fields:

- **Printer Name**—Specifies a name for the printer. It can include uppercase or lowercase alphabetic characters (A through Z), digits (0 through 9), minus signs, and underscores. A printer name can have a maximum of 14 characters, and the name must be unique within the network. It must start with an alphabetic character (A through Z, a through z).
- **Print Server**—Specifies the name of the system to which the printer is physically connected. The system manages local and remote print requests for the printer.
- **Description** (Optional)—Specifies a description for the printer that helps identify it. The description you assign to a printer should contain information that will help users identify the printer. You might include the department where the printer is located, the type of printer, or the manufacturer.

Example: Printer in Computer Room

The description must start with an alphabetic character (A through Z, a through z) and cannot contain a colon (:), a semicolon (;), an ampersand (&), or a double quote (").

- **Printer Port**—Specifies the port to which the printer is connected (printer device name). If you select Other, you need to enter a port name that the print server recognizes.
- **Printer Type**—Specifies a generic name for the type of printer. The printer type identifies the terminfo database entry that contains various control sequences for the printer. Supported printer types correspond to printers listed in the /usr/share/lib/terminfo directory.
- **File Contents**—The File Contents entry tells the LP print service the type of file contents that can be printed directly, without filtering. To print without filtering, the necessary fonts must be available in the printer. PostScript is the default. In Printer Manager, you can select a specific type of file contents from the pull-down menu. Not all available types of file contents are listed on the menu. You must use the `lpadmin` command to specify file content types that are not included on the Printer Manager pull-down menu.
- **Fault Notification**—Specifies how the superuser (root) is to be notified in case of a printer error. "Write to superuser" displays a message in the print server's root console window, and "Mail to superuser" sends email to root.
- **Option: Default Printer**—Specifies whether to set the printer as the default printer, which is where print requests are sent if you do not specify a printer. If you are using NIS or NIS+, this option sets the default printer for all the SunSoft print clients in the name service.

  If an application doesn't provide a specific printer destination, or if you don't provide a printer name when using a print command, `lp` searches for the default printer in a specific order:

  1. The `LPDEST` variable
  2. The `PRINTER` variable
  3. _default in the .printers file
  4. _default in the /etc/printers.conf file
- **Option: Always Print Banner**—A banner page identifies who submitted the print request, the print request ID, and when the request was printed. A banner page can also have an optional title that the requester can use to better identify a printout. This option specifies whether or not to give users control over printing a banner page. If it is disabled, users can use a command option (`-o nobanner`) to prevent a banner page from printing. If it's enabled, a banner page always prints.

- **User Access List** (Optional)—Lists the users who are allowed access to the printer. If you leave this box blank, all users can submit print requests to the printer. If you add one or more usernames, only those users can access the printer.

You might want to control which users can access some or all of the available printers. For example, you might want to prevent some users from printing on a high-quality color printer to minimize expense.

If you select Install Network Printer from the Print Manager main window, you see the Install Network Printer window, shown in Figure 20-22.

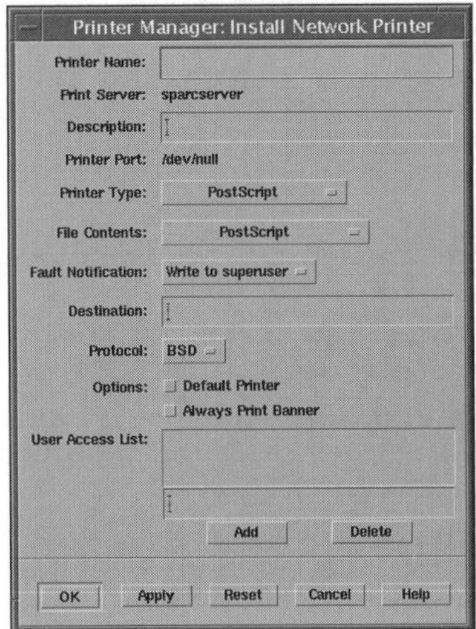

Figure 20-22
The Install Network Printer window.

Here are some of the additional options you can select:

- **Destination**—The name of the system to which the printer is connected.
- **Protocol**—This option sets the over-the-wire protocol to the printer. You can select BSD or TCP. The default is BSD. It should always be selected unless you're told otherwise by the manufacturer. You select the TCP option for printers that don't support BSD.

NOTE. *If you're setting up network printers, it's always best to use the printer manufacturer's spooling software to set up and maintain network printers that have their own IP address. Often, free software is available from the manufacturer of the printer's network card. If the software is available in both System V and BSD, obtain the BSD version.*

When you're finished filling in the fields, click OK. You return to the Print Manager main window, where you should see the printer listed that you just added.

Modifying a Printer

To modify a printer, highlight the printer in the Print Manager main window, and then select Edit Modify. If you're modifying a network printer, the Modify Network Printer window opens. If you're modifying a local printer, the Modify Local Printer window opens, as shown in Figure 20-23.

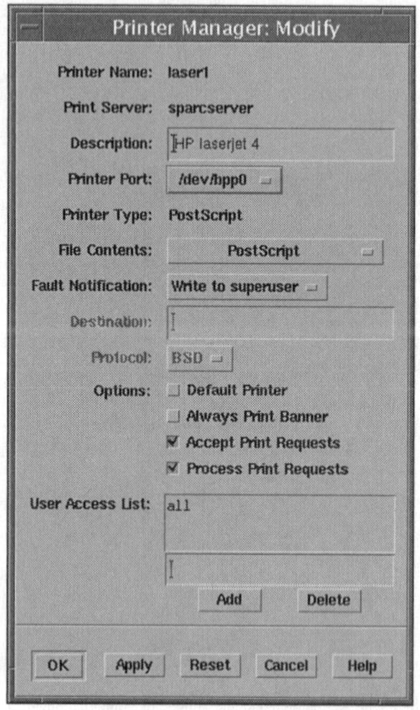

Figure 20-23
The Printer Manager: Modify window.

Make your changes in this window and click OK when you're finished. You'll return to the Print Manager main window.

Deleting a Printer

To delete a printer, highlight the printer you want to delete in the Print Manager main window, and then select Edit, Delete. You'll receive a warning message, asking if you really want to delete the printer. Click OK. You return to the Print Manager main window. The printer will no longer appear in the list of printers.

Database Manager

Database Manager is used to manage the network-related system files. With Database Manager, you can edit system files in a system's /etc directory, NIS name service, or NIS+ name service. Using Database Manager to add an entry to a system file usually managed by another tool can save time. For example, Host Manager requires you to enter the Ethernet address in the /etc/ethers file when adding a standalone system, although you might just want to use this system for remote login only. An entry in the /etc/hosts file is all that is required for remote logins. If you use Database Manager to add the entry to the /etc/hosts file, you won't be prompted for additional information, and the process will go much quicker.

The network-related system files that can be modified with Database Manager are described in Table 20-5.

Table 20-5 System Files

File	Description
aliases	Aliases in ASCII format for the local host. Or, for a NIS+ or NIS file, aliases available for use across the network.
auto.home	Entries for client systems to mount their auto_home (NIS+) home directories automatically. An indirect or /etc automounter map.
bootparams	Entries that client systems need to start from the network.
ethers	Ethernet addresses of network client systems.
group	Entries that define group access.
hosts	Entries for systems on the network and their associated IP addresses.
locale	The default locales used by network clients.
netgroup	Entries for netgroups: a group of systems granted identical access to network resources for security and organizational reasons.
netmasks	Network mask values used to implement IP subnetting.
networks	Information about available networks.
passwd	User account and password entries.
protocols	Information about Internet protocols used in your network.
rpc	Entries for available RPC services (by name) and their associated program numbers and aliases.
services	Information about network services and their port numbers.
timezone	Entries for systems and their geographic region and time zone used at installation.

The following steps describe how to use Database Manager to manage network services files.

1. Click the Database Manager icon located in the Solstice Launcher window. The Database Manager: Load window opens, as shown in Figure 20-24.

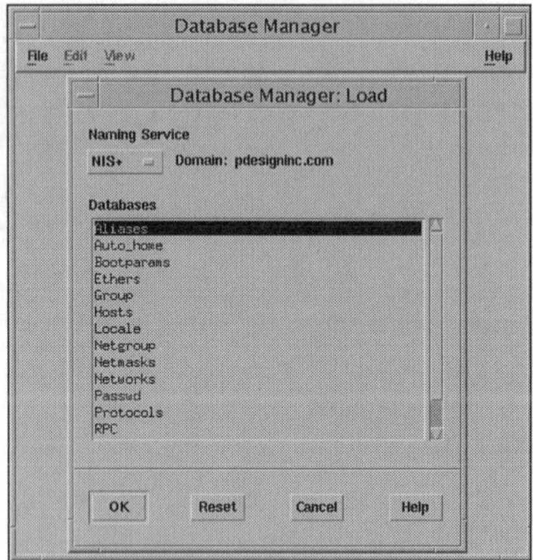

Figure 20-24
The Database Manager: Load window.

2. Select the file you want to modify from the Databases box, select your naming service from the pull-down menu, and then click OK. A window opens with the contents of that database for you to modify.

   In the following example, I entered the wrong Ethernet address when adding an AutoClient system, so I will quickly change the entry in the /etc/ethers file. For some people, this might be much quicker and easier than deleting the entry and reentering all the client information in the Host Manager tool. I'll simply modify an entry in the Ethers database.

3. I'll start by clicking Database Manager in the Launcher window. After the Database Manager: Load window appears, I select None as my naming service and highlight the Ethers database, as shown in Figure 20-25.

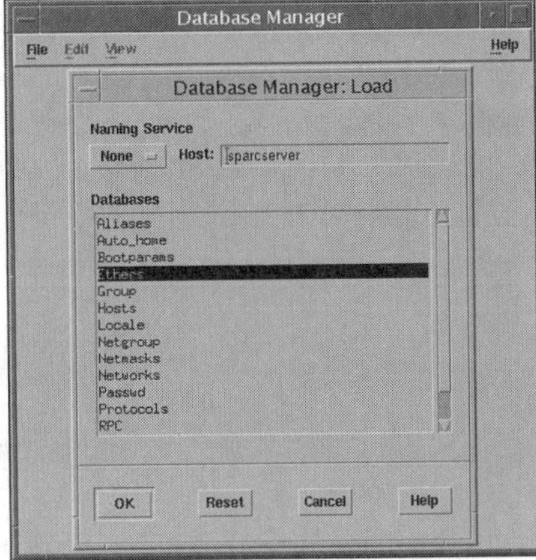

Figure 20-25
Modifying the Ethers database.

4. Click OK when you are finished making your selection. The Ethers Database window opens, as shown in Figure 20-26.

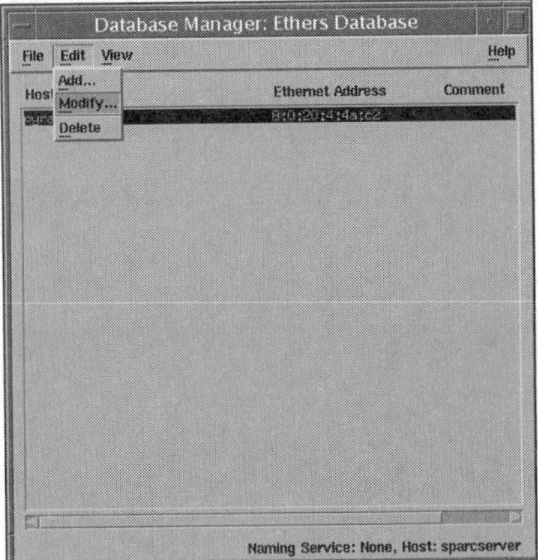

Figure 20-26
The Ethers Database window.

5. Highlight the entry you want to modify, and then select Edit, Modify.
6. The Database Manager: Modify window opens, as shown in Figure 20-27. Modify the entry in the Ethernet Address box, and click OK.

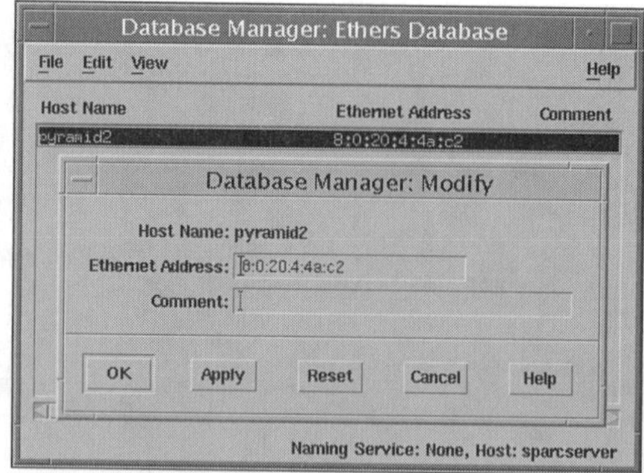

Figure 20-27
The Database Manager: Modify window.

7. You return to the Database Manager: Ethers Database window. The entry reflects the new Ethernet address. Select File, Exit to return to the Solstice Launcher window.

Storage Manager

The Storage Manager application contains two tools, File System Manager and Disk Manager. These tools let you manage disk configurations and file systems on servers that are on your network. Because setting up file systems and disk drives was covered in more depth in earlier chapters, I'll briefly describe the function of Storage Manager here.

You access Storage Manager, shown in Figure 20-28, by clicking the Storage Manager icon in the Launcher window.

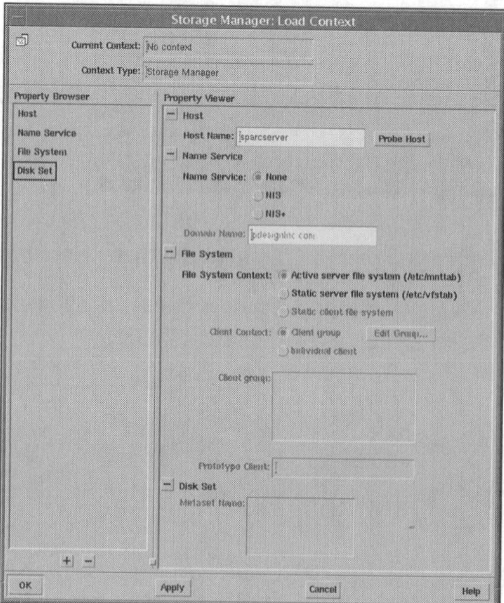

Figure 20-28
The Storage Manager: Load Context window.

The Load Context window opens when you start Storage Manager. You must select a host in the Host chapter before you can use File System Manager or Disk Manager. Sun uses several terms throughout the Storage Manager that might seem confusing, so Table 20-6 defines some of these terms.

Table 20-6 Storage Manager Terms

Term	Definition
Context	Describes the environment or components of the object whose properties you will view and edit. For the File System Manager, the context includes what name service to modify and how to view and modify the file systems on a server.
Current Context	The server you will manage and how you will view the server's file systems.
Context Type	Indicates the name of the tool with which the current context is associated.
Chapter	Represents an object's properties. You can view and change the properties in a chapter by opening it.
Host Chapter	Use this chapter to specify a different system on which to manage file systems or disks. Specify a remote host to manage disks or file systems on a remote system.
Property Viewer	Displays the object or context properties you can view and/or modify.
Property Book	The mechanism by which you identify, view, and modify the properties of editable objects.

You begin by entering a host in the Host Name box and clicking Apply at the bottom of the window. The File System Manager window opens for the host specified, as shown in Figure 20-29.

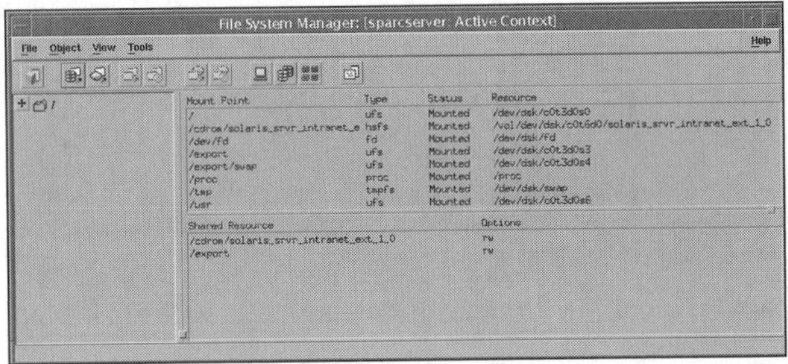

Figure 20-29
The File System Manager window.

File System Manager is a tool that lets you create and modify file systems, mount points, and directories using two types of windows—the main window and a Property Book. The main window displays a hierarchical view of directories and file systems, as well as the mount points and shared resources for the current context. The Property Book displays the chapters and their properties for a selected directory or file system that you can view or modify.

Specifically, File System Manager lets you perform the following tasks:

- Create new file systems
- Modify file system options in the /etc/vfstab file
- Manage /etc/vfstab files on one or more diskless clients or AutoClient systems
- Mount or unmount file systems
- Share or unshare file systems
- Include a file system in existing automounter maps
- Convert a directory into a mount point

Also in Storage Manager is Disk Manager, a tool that lets you view and edit disk partitions and slices. In the File System Manager window, select Tools, Disk Manager. The Disk Manager window opens, as shown in Figure 20-30.

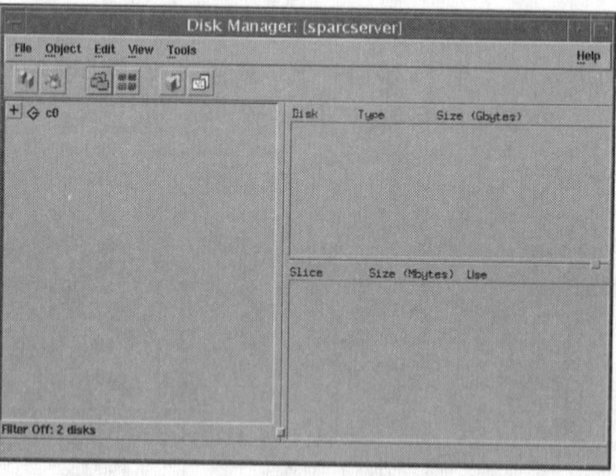

Figure 20-30
The Disk Manager window.

Specifically, you can perform the following tasks with Disk Manager:

- Assign a volume name to a disk
- View and modify fdisk partitions on x86 platforms

- Show and set the active fdisk partition on x86 platforms
- View and modify slice geometry on SPARC and x86 platforms
- Copy a disk's characteristics to one or more disks of the same type

Summary

Solstice AdminSuite provides an easy-to-use graphical interface for managing your systems from anywhere on the network. The tools and commands in the GUI are much faster than using numerous Solaris commands to perform the same tasks. Spend some time getting familiar with the AdminSuite tools. Whenever you're in the GUI, you can click the Help button to obtain more information on using AdminSuite.

To use AdminSuite, you need a graphical interface such as the Common Desktop Environment (CDE). The administration and configuration of CDE are described in the next chapter.

CHAPTER

21

Administration and Configuration of the CDE

The following are the test objectives for this chapter:

- Understanding and configuring the Login Manager, Session Manager, and Front Panel
- Customizing the Common Desktop Environment
- Understanding actions and data types
- Adding and administering applications with Application Manager

The Solaris Common Desktop Environment (CDE) is an easy-to-use graphical interface that provides a consistent look and feel across UNIX environments and even some non-UNIX environments such as OpenVMS. SunSoft, Inc., Hewlett-Packard, IBM, and Novell, Inc. each contributed "best-of-breed" technologies to establish the new standard for user and application interfaces based on the X Window System and MOTIF. While maintaining compliance with the CDE standards, Solaris CDE offers additional benefits to its users and developers. For example, you can use an image viewer to display, rotate, zoom, and convert images and PostScript files.

If you have used Sun's older windowing environment, OpenWindows, you have seen the familiar backdrops, color palettes, and pop-up Workspace menu. In CDE, a user can also run OpenWindows applications without modification. For instance, CDE supports drag-and-drop interaction between OpenWindows applications and CDE applications.

The key features available to you within CDE are the CDE environment, desktop tools, and the CDE development environment. This chapter discusses customization and administration of the CDE environment, which consists of the following:

- **Login Manager**—A graphical login window that comes up after the system is booted.
- **Session Manager**—A service that starts users' applications on the desktop at login and "remembers" the desktop state the next time they log in.
- **Front Panel**—The set of pop-ups and icons that appear at the bottom of the CDE screen and set the CDE back to its default environment.
- **Actions and data types**—Associate commands with icons.
- **Application Manager**—The desktop container that displays applications available to the user.
- **`dtksh` shell**—kshell scripting within the desktop.

The Login Manager

The *Login Manager* is a server responsible for displaying a login screen, authenticating users, and starting a user's session. Displays managed by the login server can be directly attached to the login server or to an X terminal or workstation on the network.

The login screen, displayed by the login server, is an attractive alternative to the traditional character-mode login screen. It provides capabilities beyond those provided by a character-mode login. As with a character-mode login, the user enters a username, followed by a password. If the user is authenticated, the login server starts a desktop session for the user. When the user exits the desktop session, the login server displays a new login screen, and the process begins again.

You can customize the login screen in the following ways:

- Change the login screen appearance
- Configure X server authority
- Change the default language
- Issue commands prior to displaying the login screen
- Change the contents of the login screen Language menu
- Specify the command to start the user's session
- Issue commands prior to the start of the user's desktop session
- Issue commands after the user's session ends

Each of these customizations can be done for all displays or on a per-display basis. Because these customizations are not on the exam, I do not cover them in this chapter. If you're interested in learning more about customizing CDE, I recommend that you refer to the *Solaris CDE Advanced User's and System Administrator's Guide*.

Starting the Login Server

The login server usually starts up the CDE environment when the system is booted. It can also be started from the command line. For example, to start the login server from the command line, type the following:

```
/usr/dt/bin/dtlogin -daemon; exit
```

NOTE. *Although you can start the login server from the command line for temporary configuration testing, you normally set it up to start when the system is booted.*

To set the login server to start CDE the next time the system is booted, type the following:

```
/usr/dt/bin/dtconfig -e
```

The login server will then start automatically after the user reboots the system.

Stopping the Login Server

To disable the login server CDE startup the next time the system is booted, type the following:

```
/usr/dt/bin/dtconfig -d
```

This command tells the system not to start the login server on the next reboot.

You can stop the login server immediately by killing its process ID. Type the following:

```
/usr/dt/bin/dtconfig -kill
```

This issues the command `kill login_server_process_ID`.

CAUTION! *If the user is logged in to the desktop at the time you kill the login server, the desktop session immediately terminates.*

Displaying a Login Screen on a Local Display

On startup, the login server checks the Xservers file to determine whether an Xserver needs to be started and to determine whether, and how, login screens should be displayed on local or network displays. Here is the format of a line in the Xservers file:

```
display_name display_class display_type X_server_command
```

Each field in the Xservers file is described in Table 21-1.

Table 21-1 Fields in the Xservers File

Field	Description
display_name	Tells the login server what name to use when connecting to the Xserver (:0 in the following example). A value of * (asterisk) is expanded to hostname:0. The number specified must match the number specified in the X_server_command connection number.
display_class	Identifies resources specific to this display (Local in the following example).
display_type	Tells the login server whether the display is local or network and how to manage the Command Line Login option on the login screen (local@console in the following example).
X_server_command	Identifies the command line, connection number, and other options that the login server will use to start the Xserver (/usr/bin/X11/X:0 in the following example). The connection number specified must match the number specified in the display_name field.

The default line in the Xservers file is similar to this:

```
:0 Local local@console /usr/bin/X11/X:0
```

To modify the Xservers file, copy it from /usr/dt/config to /etc/dt/config. The /etc/dt directory contains customized workstation-specific configuration files. If /etc/dt does not exist, you might need to create it. The system administrator can modify the system default resources by creating the /etc/dt/config/ directory. In this directory, you can create configuration files to override default resources or to specify additional resources for all desktop users. This file is merged into the desktop default resources during session startup. Resources specified in this file take precedence over those specified in the desktop default resource file. After modifying /etc/dt/config/Xservers, tell the login server to reread Xservers by typing this:

```
/usr/dt/bin/dtconfig -reset
```

`dtconfig -reset` issues the command `kill -HUP login_server_process_ID`.

If your login server system has a character display instead of a bitmap display, you need to set `display_terminal_device` to `none` in the Xservers file to disable the login screen and enable the character-mode login screen.

The Session Manager

A *session* is the collection of applications, settings, and resources present on the user's desktop. Session management is a set of conventions and protocols that let the Session Manager save and restore a user's session. When users log in to the desktop for the first time, a default initial session is loaded. Afterward, users can log in to the system and see the same set of running applications, settings, and resources that were present when they last logged out.

Session Manager is responsible for starting the desktop and automatically saving and restoring running applications, colors, fonts, mouse behavior, audio volume, and keyboard click. Using Session Manager, you can do the following:

- Customize the initial session for all desktop users
- Customize the environment and resources for all desktop users
- Change the session startup message
- Change parameters for session startup tools and daemons
- Customize desktop color usage for all users

Session Manager is started through /usr/dt/bin/Xsession. When the user logs in using Login Manager, Xsession is started by default. When Session Manager is started, it goes through the following steps to start the user's session:

1. Sources the .dtprofile script.
2. Sources the Xsession.d scripts.
3. Displays a welcome message.
4. Sets up desktop search paths.
5. Gathers available applications.
6. Optionally sources $HOME/.profile or $HOME/.login.
7. Starts the ToolTalk messaging daemon.
8. Loads session resources.
9. Starts the color server.
10. Starts Workspace Manager.
11. Starts the session applications.

Sourcing the $HOME/.dtprofile Script

At session startup, the Xsession script sources the user's $HOME/.dtprofile script—a /bin/sh or /bin/ksh script that lets users set up environment variables for their sessions. .dtprofile accepts only sh or ksh syntax. The desktop default is /usr/dt/config/sys.dtprofile. If the $HOME/.dtprofile script does not exist (for example, when a user is logging in for the first time), Xsession copies the desktop default sys.dtprofile to $HOME/.dtprofile.

You can customize the sys.dtprofile script by copying it from /usr/dt/config to /etc/dt/config and editing the new file. You can also set up personal environment variables in $HOME/.dtprofile. For example, `export MYVARIABLE="value"` sets the variable `MYVARIABLE` in the user's environment at the next login.

To set system-wide environment variables, create a file in the /etc/dt/config/Xsession.d directory that sets and exports the variable. For example, if you create an executable ksh script, /etc/dt/config/Xsession.d/sitevars, that contains `export SITEVARIABLE="value"`, the variable `SITEVARIABLE` will be set in each user's environment at the next login.

NOTE. *Although Session Manager does not automatically read the .profile or .login files, it can be configured to use these files. To tell Xsession to source the .profile or .login scripts, set the variable* `DTSOURCEPROFILE` *to* `true` *in $HOME/.dtprofile.*

Sourcing the Xsession.d Scripts

After sourcing the $HOME/.dtprofile script, the Xsession script sources the Xsession.d scripts. These scripts set up additional environment variables and start optional daemons for the user's session.

CAUTION! *Errors in any of the session startup files could prevent a user from logging in. To troubleshoot session startup problems, check the file $HOME/.dt/startlog. Session Manager logs each user's session startup progress in this file.*

Customizing the Welcome Message

After sourcing /etc/dt/config/sys.dtprofile (if it exists), $HOME/.dtprofile, and the Xsession.d scripts, Xsession displays a welcome message that covers the screen. You can customize the welcome message or turn it off entirely.

The `dthello` client is used to display the welcome message. To alter the message text, change the `dthello` options by modifying the `dtstart_hello[0]` variable. To change `dtstart_hello[0]`, create a /usr/dt/config/Xsession.d script that sets the new value. For example, to display the message of the day for all users, create an executable sh or ksh script called usr/dt/config/Xsession.d/myvars and set `dtstart_hello[0]` as follows:

```
dtstart_hello[0]="/usr/dt/bin/dthello -file /etc/motd &"
```

Users can also change the welcome message for their sessions by setting `dtstart_hello[0]` in $HOME/.dtprofile.

To turn off the welcome message, set `dtstart_hello[0]=" "`.

Setting Desktop Search Paths

The desktop uses search paths, created at login, to locate applications and their associated desktop files. The desktop provides four search paths, described in Table 21-2.

Table 21-2 Desktop Search Paths

Search Path	Description
Applications	Used to locate applications. Application Manager uses the application search path to dynamically populate its top level when a user logs in.
Database	Used to specify additional locations for action- and data-type definition files (*.dt files) and Front Panel files (*.fp files).

Table 21-2 Desktop Search Paths (continued)

Search Path	Description
Icons	Used to specify additional locations for icons.
Help data	Used to specify additional locations for desktop help data.

Modifying a Search Path

To modify the search path for a particular user, follow these steps:

1. Open $HOME/.dtprofile for editing.
2. Add or edit a line that defines and exports the personal input variable.

   For example, the following line adds a location to the user's personal application search path:

   ```
   export DTSPUSERAPPHOSTS=/projects1/editors
   ```

3. To make the change take effect, log out and then log back in.

Gathering Available Applications

After you set up the desktop search paths, the next step is to gather available applications by using `dtappgather`. These are the applications that will be displayed in the Application Manager window. The `dtappgather` utility gathers application files for presentation by the Application Manager and is responsible for creating and refreshing the user's Application Manager subdirectory.

To alter `dtappgather`'s command-line options, modify the `dtstart_appgather` variable either in the /etc/dt/config/Xsession.d/sitevars file for all users or in $HOME/.dtprofile for individual users. Set `dtstart_appgather` as follows:

```
dtstart_appgather="/usr/dt/bin/dtappgather &"
```

Sourcing a User *.profile* or *.login* File

Xsession can source a user's traditional $HOME/.profile or $HOME/.login scripts, but by default this capability is disabled. To instruct Xsession to source the .profile or .login script, set `DTSOURCEPROFILE` to `true` in $HOME/.dtprofile as follows:

```
DTSOURCEPROFILE=true
```

Starting the ToolTalk Messaging Daemon

The next task for Xsession is to start the ToolTalk messaging daemon. The ToolTalk service lets independent applications communicate without having direct knowledge of each other. Applications create and send ToolTalk messages to communicate with each other. The ToolTalk service receives these messages, determines the recipients, and then delivers the messages to the appropriate applications. Users can change the `ttsession` options for their own sessions by setting the `dtstart_ttsession` variable in $HOME/.dtprofile as follows:

```
dtstart_ttsession="/usr/dt/bin/ttsession -s"
```

Loading Session Resources

Resources are used by applications to set certain aspects of appearance and behavior. For example, Style Manager (`dtstyle`) provides resources that let you specify where the system looks for files containing information about color palettes by entering the following line of information in the sys.resources file located in the /etc/dt/config/<language> directory:

```
dtstyle*paletteDirectories: /usr/dt/palettes/C \/$HOME/.dt/palettes
```

NOTE. *If the sys.resources file does not exist, it might need to be created using the instructions in the next paragraph.*

Resources are loaded at session startup by Session Manager. The desktop default resources can be found in /usr/dt/config/<language>/sys.resources. These resources are made available to each user's session via the `RESOURCE_MANAGER` property. This file should not be edited, because it is overwritten on subsequent desktop installations. The system administrator can modify the system default resources by creating /etc/dt/config/<language>/sys.resources. In this file, you can override default resources or specify additional resources for all desktop users. To set personal resources, make the entries in the $HOME/.Xdefaults file.

Users can modify the desktop default and system-wide resources through their $HOME/.Xdefaults file. Resources specified in this file take precedence over those specified in the desktop default or system administrator resource files.

Starting the Color Server

You can choose a wide range of colors for your display either by using Style Manager (as shown in Figure 21-1) or by customizing color resources used by Style Manager to control desktop color usage.

Figure 21-1
The Style Manager.

Set color server resources for all users by creating /etc/dt/config/<language>/sys.resources and specifying the color server resources in that file. Users can similarly set these for their own sessions by specifying them in $HOME/.Xdefaults.

Starting the Workspace Manager

Session Manager is responsible for starting the Workspace Manager. By default, /usr/dt/bin/dtwm is started. The Workspace Manager is the window manager provided by the desktop. It controls the following:

- The appearance of window frame components
- The behavior of windows, including their stacking order and focus behavior
- Key bindings and button bindings
- The appearance of minimized windows
- Workspace and window menus

In addition, the Workspace Manager controls the desktop components outlined in Table 21-3.

Table 21-3 Desktop Components

Component	Description
Workspaces	The Workspace Manager controls the number of workspaces and keeps track of which windows are open in each workspace.
Workspace backdrops	The user can change the backdrop image by using Style Manager. Backdrop management, however, is a function of the Workspace Manager.
The Front Panel	Although the Front Panel uses its own configuration files, it is created and managed by the Workspace Manager.

Additional modifications that can be made to the Workspace Manager include changing the number of workspaces and providing system-wide workspace names.

Changing the Number of Workspaces on a System-Wide Basis

The default desktop configuration provides four workspaces. The user can add, delete, and rename workspaces by using the pop-up menu associated with the workspace switch.

In the /usr/dt/app-defaults/C/Dtwm file, the `workspaceCount` resource is set to the following default number of workspaces:

```
Dtwm*0*workspaceCount: 4
Dtwm*workspaceCount:   1
```

Multiple workspaces are specified on screen 0; a single workspace is specified on any other screen. You can create the /etc/dt/config/C/sys.resources file (or modify it if it exists) to change the default number of workspaces for all new users on a workstation.

Use the `0*workspaceCount` resource to set the system-wide default on the primary screen:

```
Dtwm*0*workspaceCount: number
```

For example, the following resource sets the number of workspaces system-wide on the primary screen to six:

```
Dtwm*0*workspaceCount: 6
```

Providing System-Wide Workspace Names

Internally, the workspaces are numbered by the numbering convention ws*n,* where *n* is 0, 1, 2, and so on. For example, the default four workspaces are numbered internally ws0 through ws3.

Use the `title` resource to change the name of a specified workspace in the sys.resources file described earlier:

```
Dtwm*wsn*title: name
```

For example, the following resources set the default four workspaces to the specified names:

```
Dtwm*ws0*title:  Glenda
Dtwm*ws1*title:  Neil
Dtwm*ws2*title:  Nicole
Dtwm*ws3*title:  William
```

Starting the Session Applications

At session startup, Session Manager restarts any applications saved in the previous session. The system default set of applications to be restored as part of the user's initial session can be found in /usr/dt/config/<language>/sys.session. Do not edit this file.

A system administrator can replace the set of applications started as part of the user's initial session by copying /usr/dt/config/<language>/sys.session to /etc/dt/config/<language>/ sys.session and modifying the latter file. Unlike the resource files, this file is used as a complete replacement for the desktop default file.

The Front Panel

The Front Panel contains a set of icons and pop-up menus (more like roll-up menus) that appear at the bottom of the screen. The two main elements of the Front Panel are the Main Panel and the subpanels. The Main Panel includes the workspace switch, shown in Figure 21-2, which contains the buttons you use to change from one workspace to another.

Figure 21-2
The Front Panel workspace switch.

If a control in the Main Panel has an arrow button on top of it, that control has a subpanel, as shown in Figure 21-3.

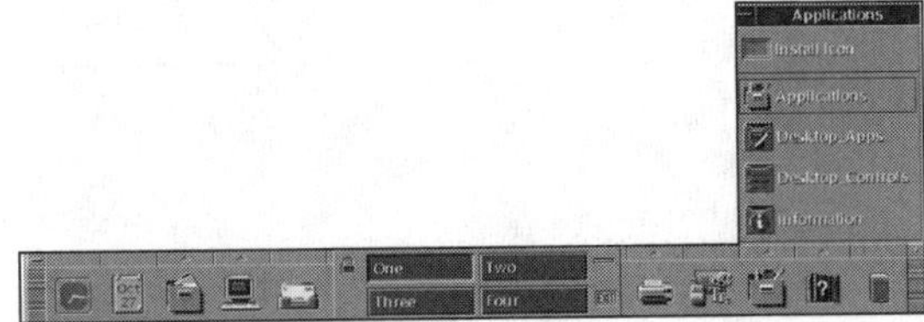

Figure 21-3
A subpanel.

Users can drag and drop icons from the File Manager or Application Manager to add them to the subpanels. Up to 12 additional workspaces can be configured, each with different backgrounds and colors. Each workspace can have any number of applications running in it, and an application can be set to appear in one, more than one, or all workspaces simultaneously. In some instances, the system administrator might find it necessary to lock the Front Panel so that users can't change it.

Using the desktop's interface, the Front Panel can easily be modified in the following ways:

- Customizing a workspace
- Adding and deleting a workspace
- Renaming a workspace
- Adding and deleting controls to subpanels

The System Administrator can also do more advanced customization outside the CDE environment by editing CDE configuration files directly from the UNIX command line. However, advanced customization is not covered on the exam. Therefore, for more information on advanced Front Panel customization, see the *CDE Advanced User's and System Administrator's Guide.*

Customizing Workspaces

Users can use the Front Panel workspace switch to rename or change the number of workspaces. Click on the workspace buttons to change workspaces. When the cursor is positioned on a workspace button, clicking the third mouse button displays its pop-up menu, as shown in Figure 21-4.

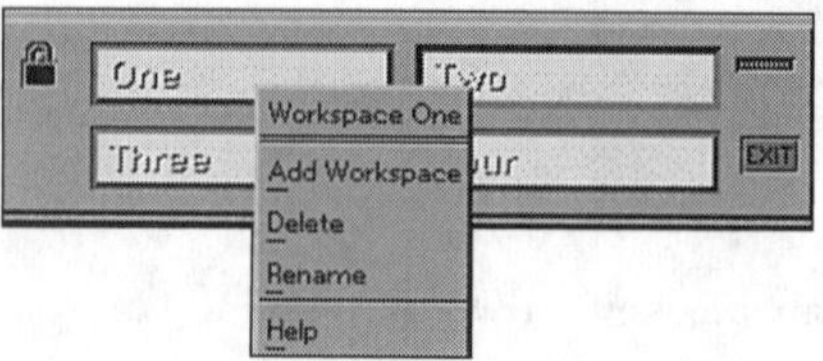

Figure 21-4
The workspace button pop-up menu.

The workspace button pop-up menu includes the items described in Table 21-4.

Table 21-4 Pop-Up Menu Options

Option	Description
Add Workspace	Adds a workspace to the list of workspaces.
Delete	Deletes the workspace.
Rename	Changes the button into a text field for editing the name.
Help	Displays help for the workspace switch.

Use the pop-up menu to modify workspace button parameters. For example, to rename a workspace, follow these steps:

1. Point to the button of the workspace you want to rename.
2. Choose Rename from the button's pop-up menu (displayed when you click the third mouse button). The workspace button turns into a text field.
3. Edit the text field.
4. Press Enter.

To add a workspace, follow these steps:

1. Point to any area in the workspace switch and click the third mouse button to display the pop-up menu.

2. Choose Add Workspace from the pop-up menu. The new workspace, named New, is placed at the end of the set of workspaces. (If more than one new workspace is created, the workspaces are named New_1, New_2, and so on.)
3. Rename the workspace as described earlier.

To remove a workspace, follow these steps:

1. Point to the workspace button of the workspace you want to remove.
2. Choose Delete from the button's pop-up menu (displayed when you press the third mouse button).

Customizing Workspace Controls

Customizing the controls in the workspace switch is an advanced task that requires the system administrator to create a Front Panel configuration file. This section describes some easy customizations that can be performed from the desktop. Advanced customization is covered in the *CDE Advanced User's and System Administrator's Guide.*

Customizing the Front Panel Switch Area

The switch area shown in Figure 21-5 is the portion of the workspace switch that is not occupied by other controls or workspace buttons.

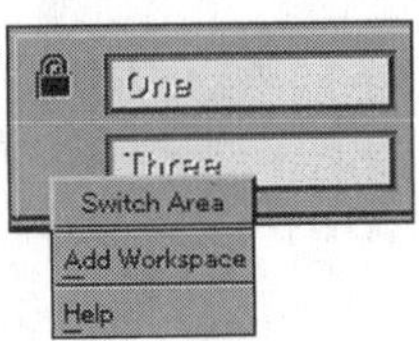

Figure 21-5
The switch area.

The switch area has a pop-up menu containing these items:

Add Workspace	Adds a workspace and creates a workspace button in the workspace switch.
Help	Displays help for the workspace switch.

Adding an Application or Other Icon to a Subpanel

The user can add any type of File Manager or Application Manager icon to the Front Panel. The most convenient use of this feature is to add application icons. To add an application icon to a subpanel, follow these steps:

1. Display the object's icon in File Manager or Application Manager.
2. Display the subpanel to which the object is to be added.
3. Drag the object to the Install Icon control, using the first mouse button, and drop it on the control.

The behavior of controls added to the Front Panel by using the Install Icon control depends on the type of icon dropped. Table 21-5 describes the control behavior for each type of icon.

Table 21-5 Icon Control Behavior

Type of Icon	Behavior
File	The same behavior as the file's icon in File Manager. When the user clicks the file icon, the Text Editor displays the contents of the file, ready to be edited.
Folder	Opens a File Manager view of the folder.
Application group	Opens an Application Manager view of the application group.
Application icon	The same behavior as an application's icon in File Manager or Application Manager. When the user clicks the icon, the application is automatically launched.

Resetting All User Customizations

To reset the Front Panel and remove all user customizations, follow these steps:

1. Open Application Manager and double-click the Desktop_Tools application group icon.
2. Double-click Restore Front Panel.

The screen goes blank for several seconds while the Workspace Manager is restarted. The Restore Front Panel action removes all customizations made by using the Install Icon control or the Front Panel's pop-up menus.

NOTE. *This procedure does not affect advanced customizations made by manually editing Front Panel configuration files.*

Actions and Data Types

Actions are instructions that automate desktop tasks such as running applications and opening data files. Actions work much the same as application macros or programming functions. They can be assigned to icons so that associated commands are invoked when an icon is clicked.

An action can be created by using the Create Action menu, as described in the following steps:

1. Bring up the Applications pop-up menu, shown in Figure 21-6.

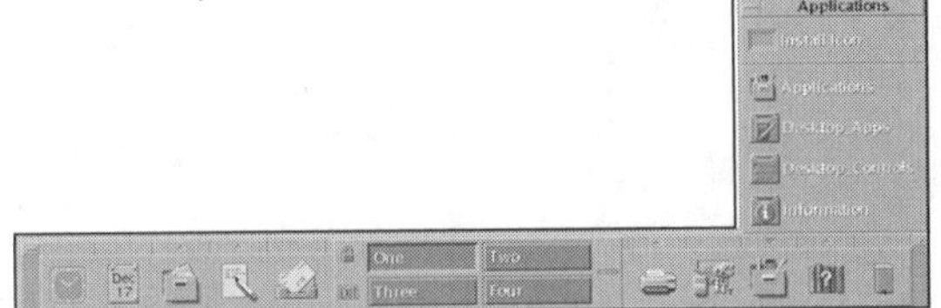

Figure 21-6
The Applications pop-up menu.

2. Select Desktop_Apps from the pop-up menu. The Desktop_Apps window appears, as shown in Figure 21-7.

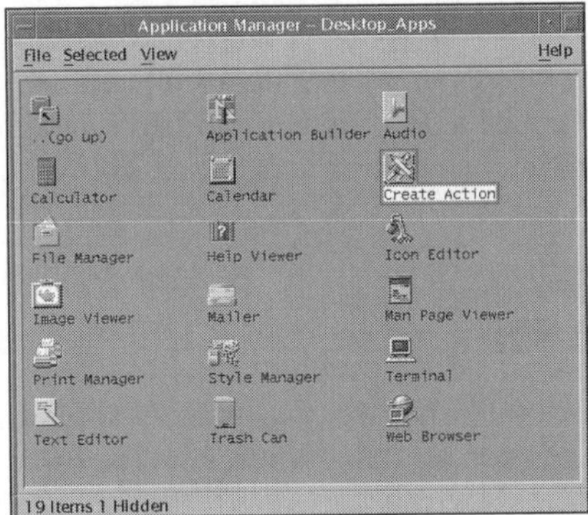

Figure 21-7
The Desktop_Apps window.

3. In the Desktop_Apps window, click the Create Action icon. The Create Action window appears, as shown in Figure 21-8.

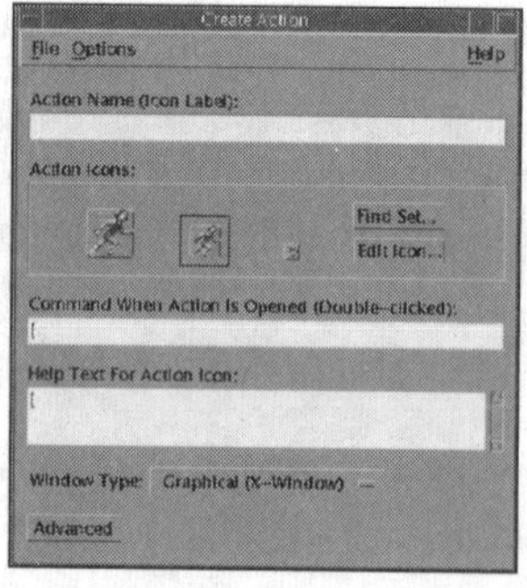

Figure 21-8
The Create Action window.

NOTE. *For information on filling in the appropriate fields and creating an action, click Help, located at the top of the Create Action window.*

After you define an action, you can use that action in the desktop user interface to simplify tasks. The desktop provides the ability to attach user interface components such as icons, Front Panel controls, and menu items to actions. Each of these icons performs an action when the icon is double-clicked.

Another common use of actions is in menus. Data files usually have actions in their selected menu in File Manager. For example, XWD files (files with names ending in .xwd or .wd) have an Open action that displays the screen image when you run the Xwud action.

Actions and data types are powerful components for integrating applications into the desktop. They provide a way to create a user interface for starting applications and manipulating data files. For more information on creating actions, see the *Solaris CDE Advanced User's and System Administrator's Guide.*

The Application Manager

Application Manager is the desktop container displaying applications available to users. It is selected from the Applications pop-up menu located on the Front Panel, shown earlier in Figure 21-6.

When initially opened, the window displays the top-level directory of the Application Manager. User interaction with the Application Manager is similar to the use of the File Manager, except that the Application Manager contains executable modules. The user launches the Application Manager from an icon on the Front Panel, opening the window shown in Figure 21-9.

Figure 21-9
The Application Manager window.

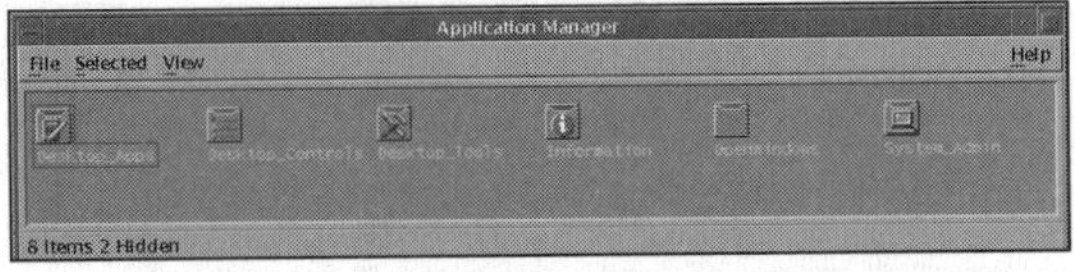

Programs and icons can be installed in the Application Manager by the system administrator and can be pushed out to other workstations as part of the installation process. By default, the Application Manager comes preconfigured to include several utilities and programs (see Figure 21-9). Each of these utilities is located in a directory, which—with its contents—is called an application group. Application groups provided with the default desktop are described in Table 21-6.

Table 21-6 Application Groups

Group	Description
Desktop_Apps	Desktop applications such as File Manager, Style Manager, and Calculator.
Desktop_Tools	Desktop administration and operating system tools such as User Registration, Reload Application, vi text editor, and Check Spelling.
Information	Icons representing frequently used help topics.
System_Admin	Tools used by system administrators.
Desktop Controls	Tools to set your CDE environment, such as mouse behavior, desktop fonts, screen saver, and window behavior.
OpenWindows	Contains several OpenWindows-style actions, such as the mail tool and File Manager.

The top-level directory for the Application Manager is the directory /var/dt/appconfig/appmanager/login-hostname-display, created dynamically each time the user logs in. For example, if user bcalkins logs in from display sparc1:0, the following Application Manager directory is created:

```
/var/dt/appconfig/appmanager/bcalkins-sparc1:0
```

The Application Manager is built by gathering application groups from directories located along the application search path. The default path consists of the locations listed in Table 21-7.

Table 21-7 Default Application Search Path Locations

Scope	Location
Built-in	/usr/dt/appconfig/appmanager/<language>
System-wide	/etc/dt/appconfig/appmanager/<language>
Personal	$HOME/.dt/appmanager

To create the top-level directory of the Application Manager, links are created at login time from the application group directories to the Application Manager directory, which is /var/dt/appconfig/appmanager/<login-hostname-display>. The gathering operation is done by the desktop utility `dtappgather`, which is automatically run by Login Manager after the user has successfully logged in.

For example, the desktop provides the built-in application group /usr/dt/appconfig/appmanager/<language>/Desktop_Tools. At login time, a symbolic link is created to /var/dt/appconfig/appmanager/<login-hostname-display>/Desktop_Tools.

Applications can be added to the Application Manager by copying icons from other application groups to the personal application group. To create a personal application group, follow these steps:

1. From your home folder, change to the .dt/appmanager subfolder.
2. Create a new folder. The folder name will become the name of the new application group.
3. Double-click Reload Applications in the Desktop_Apps application group.
4. Your new application group becomes registered at the top level of Application Manager.

A personal application group is an application group that users can alter because they have write permission to it. For example, users can copy (by pressing the Ctrl key and dragging) the Calculator icon from the Desktop_Tools application group to a new personal application group. Another method is to create an action for an application and then place an application (action) icon in the personal application group.

The *dtksh* Shell

Available in CDE is the Desktop KornShell (`dtksh`), which gives kshell scripting the ability to easily access most of the existing Xt and MOTIF functions. The Desktop KornShell is based on ksh-93, which provides a powerful set of tools and commands for the shell programmer and supports the standard set of `kshell` programming commands. `dtksh` is used by developers and programmers to create MOTIF applications for the CDE environment.

Summary

This question always arises: Should users be allowed to customize the CDE environment themselves? Most large institutions frown on letting users customize their own environments. Usually, the system administrator provides a default setup that is applied to all users. This default setup promotes consistency and prevents the "self-inflicted" problems that can occur when users incorrectly modify system files. The answer also depends on how much pain you're willing to endure for the good of your user community. Users love an administrator who gives them the flexibility to arrange their own desktops. However, you can quickly have plenty of problems if users are not properly trained in the use of customization utilities.

The graphical user interface available in CDE is a welcome enhancement to UNIX. With CDE, users no longer need to be exposed to the cryptic UNIX shell. Most of the routine tasks performed by users can now be done by using the menus and icons provided through CDE. As a system administrator, your job is to customize and manage CDE, using the tools provided, to facilitate tasks and maintain productivity in your specific environment.

Customizing the CDE environment is a weighty topic. Although this chapter introduced you to some basic customization topics, additional information can be found in publications focusing on the subject.

This concludes the study material for the second exam. I encourage you to use the test exams on the enclosed CD-ROM to test your knowledge of the chapters you've read. You might find it necessary to go back and review some of the chapters. When you're confident that you understand all the material in this section, you are ready to take the real exam. Good luck!

SECTION III

Appendixes

This section covers the following Solaris-related information:

- The history of the UNIX operating system
- The fundamentals of client/server computing
- A brief overview of SCSI devices
- Helpful Web resources
- The Web Start program

APPENDIX

A

The History of UNIX

UNIX is plural. It is not one operating system but many implementations of an idea that originated in 1965. As a system administrator, you'll want to understand the history of the UNIX operating system—where it came from, how it was built, and where it is now. Understanding the various versions of UNIX and its origins makes it clear why UNIX became known as a somewhat hostile operating system. For example, UNIX was not developed by a single company with a large marketing organization driving the user interface. (In other words, it did not follow the development path of, say, Microsoft Windows.) On the other hand, UNIX was not invented by hackers who were fooling around; it grew out of strong academic roots. The primary contributors to UNIX were highly educated mathematicians and computer scientists employed by what many people feel is the world's premier industrial research center, Bell Laboratories. Although knowledgeable and experienced in their own right, these developers maintained professional contacts with researchers in academia, leading to an exchange of ideas that proved beneficial for both sides. Understanding the symbiotic relationship between UNIX and the academic community means understanding the background of the system's inventors and the history of interactions between universities and Bell Laboratories.

How It All Began

It all began at Bell Labs, the research lab of AT&T, one of the largest and most powerful companies of our time. Ironically, AT&T was not interested in developing and selling computers or operating systems. In fact, the U.S. Department of Justice did not allow AT&T to sell software. However, AT&T's existing systems, made up of people and paper, were in danger of being overwhelmed in the boom of the 1960s. By the 1970s, the phone business was in jeopardy. Out of desperation and need, Ken Thompson of AT&T set out to develop what no computer company was ready to provide—a multiuser, multiprocessing operating system to be used in-house for its own information processing department. Specifically, the goal was an operating system to support several programmers simultaneously in a more hospitable environment.

What follows is an account of major dates and events in the development cycle of the UNIX operating system.

1965–1969

In 1965, Bell Labs joins with MIT and General Electric in a cooperative development of Multics, a multiuser interactive operating system running on a GE 645 mainframe computer. However, unhappy with the progress in the development of a system that is experiencing many delays and high costs, Bell Labs drops out of the development of Multics in 1969.

In 1969, Ken Thompson, exposed to Multics at Bell Labs, meets up with Dennis Ritchie, who provides a Digital Equipment Corporation PDP-7 minicomputer to continue the development of an operating system capable of supporting a team of programmers in a research environment. After they create a prototype, Thompson returns to Bell Labs to propose the use of this new operating system as a document preparation tool in the Bell Labs patent department. The new operating system is named UNIX to distinguish it from the complexity of Multics. Efforts to develop UNIX continue, and UNIX becomes operational at Bell Labs in 1971.

The first version of UNIX is written in assembly language on a PDP-11/20. It includes the file system, `fork`, `roff`, and `ed`. It is used as a text-processing tool for the preparation of patents.

1970–1972

During the early 1970s, UNIX begins to gain popularity throughout Bell Labs, and as word of the new operating system spreads, universities embrace it. However, although it is viewed favorably by the academic and high-tech sectors, it is met with skepticism by the business community. In a move to heighten the popularity of UNIX, AT&T begins to license the UNIX source code to universities at a minimal cost. AT&T gives many licensees the software code and manuals but doesn't provide technical support. By the late 1970s, 70 percent of all colleges and universities have UNIX. Computer science graduates are using it, even modifying the code to make it more robust. UNIX is written in assembly language and runs primarily on DEC hardware—first on the PDP-7, and then the PDP-11/40, the 11/45, and finally the 11/70, on which it gains wide popularity.

1973–1979

This period will become the most significant in the development of UNIX. Ritchie and Thompson had developed the C programming language between 1969 and 1973 and now rewrite the UNIX kernel in the high-level C language. Now the OS can be compiled to run on different computers. Within months, UNIX can be ported to new hardware. Modifications to the OS are easy. Again, Thompson resonates with members of the academic community who are already using UNIX in many of their system design courses. UNIX, now written in a general-purpose language featuring modern commands, begins to take off in the areas of word processing and programming.

By now, UNIX is at version 6. This is the first release of UNIX to be picked up by a commercial firm, Whitesmiths, Inc., which creates a commercial copy of version 6 called Idris.

In 1975, Thompson visits Berkeley while on sabbatical and installs version 6 on a PDP-11/70. It is at this time that two graduate students, Bill Joy and Chuck Haley, get involved with version 6 and later play an important role in the development of the UNIX system at Berkeley. The first project they work on is the development of the UNIX ex editor.

Joy and Haley begin to take interest in the internal operations of UNIX—specifically, the kernel. Joy puts together a distribution of UNIX called the Berkeley Software Distribution (BSD). He includes enhancements such as the C shell (a C-like interface to UNIX) and the vi editor. 1BSd is released in 1975. By the second release of BSD in 1978, Joy has added virtual memory support, which allows programs to run even if they require more physical memory than is available at the time. This second edition of BSD has a strong influence on the release of Bell Labs' version 7 of UNIX, which is released in 1979 and is the last of the "clean" versions of UNIX (produced solely by Bell Labs). Version 7 gave rise to a number of UNIX ports to other platforms, and for the first time, both industry and academia supplied enhancements, which were incorporated into future releases.

In the late 1970s, the United States Department of Defense's Advanced Research Projects Agency (DARPA) decides to base its universal computing environment on Berkeley's version of UNIX. In the 4.1 release of BSD, DARPA provides some important performance tune-ups. The `fast` file system, which provides a way to improve the file system's performance and prevent file fragmentation, is added in release 4.2.

1982–1983

AT&T formally releases a beta version of UNIX to the commercial sector in 1982. In 1983, AT&T releases the first true production version of UNIX, naming it System III (Systems I and II never existed). Although it's based on version 7 of UNIX, and thus includes some BSD utilities, the release of System III does not include the vi editor or the C shell. Instead, AT&T includes the programmer's workbench.

With the release of System III, AT&T sees a future in UNIX and soon releases System V. (System IV is never seen outside of AT&T.) System V includes the editor, `curses` (the screen-oriented software libraries), and the `init` program, which is used to start up processes at UNIX boot-up.

In the early 1980s, Joy leaves Berkeley with a master's degree in electrical engineering and becomes cofounder of Sun Microsystems (Sun stands for Stanford University Network). Sun's implementation of BSD is called SunOS. Sun extends the networking tools of the operating system to include the Networked File System (NFS), which is to become an industry standard. Sun also does some of the early work in developing windowing software for UNIX. SunOS first gets released in 1983.

With workstation products now being offered by Sun, UNIX begins to gain acceptance in the high-tech arena, especially in computer-aided design and computer-aided engineering (CAD/CAE) environments. The early 1980s see CAD/CAE become popular. Additional workstation vendors such as HP and Apollo begin to exploit CAD/CAE capabilities and performance gains over the popular personal computers of the time. These UNIX workstations can out-perform PCs and, with UNIX as an operating system, can provide a multiuser environment.

In other business computing environments, however, UNIX is still considered a hostile environment and does not pose a threat to the mainframes of the time. UNIX has yet to define itself as a user-friendly, tried-and-tested operating system. However, it is gaining ground in the areas of multitasking and networking. More important, UNIX is being touted as the operating system that provides portability between different hardware architectures, and as a consequence, software developers are getting excited about UNIX. In theory, a program written in C for UNIX would be portable to any hardware platform running the UNIX operating system.

1984–1987

In 1984, AT&T releases System V, release 2, and in 1987, release 3. Release 2 introduces the terminal capability database `termcap` file, named `terminfo`, which provides support for various CRT terminals connected to the UNIX system. Other changes include the addition of `Streams` and Remote File Systems.

1988–1992

In 1988, AT&T shocks the UNIX community by purchasing a percentage of Sun Microsystems, already a leader in the industry. Other hardware vendors see this as an unfair advantage for Sun, so they quickly form a consortium group called the Open Software Foundation (OSF). Together they raise millions of dollars to develop a new UNIX standard to compete against Sun's.

In a counterstrike, AT&T, Sun, Data General, and Unisys join forces to start their own organization to fight OSF. This consortium of companies, called UNIX International (UI), is formed to oversee the development of System V standards. OSF and UI will turn out to be the two major competing commercial standards for UNIX.

By the late 1980s, AT&T concludes that UNIX is a distraction from the company's focus on producing hardware. As a result, AT&T forms the UNIX Software LAB (USL), ultimately purchased by Novell in 1992.

In 1992, at the summer UseNIX conference, Berkeley announces it will conclude its development activities at version 4.4 of BSD. Several people who were involved with BSD form smaller companies to try to continue the development of BSD, but without Berkeley and ARPA, it is not the same.

In the 1990s, BSD and System V dominate the industry, with several vendors providing their versions of one of the two operating systems. Soon UNIX, an operating system meant to provide portability of applications between multiple hardware platforms, is getting out of control. Applications are not portable between UNIX System V, release 3, and BSD. To create even more confusion, hardware vendors are enhancing their versions of BSD and System V.

1993

Sun announces that SunOS, release 4.1.4, will be its last release of an operating system based on BSD. Sun sees the writing on the wall and moves to System V, release 4, which they name Solaris. System V, release 4 (SRV4) is a merger of System V and BSD, incorporating the important features found in SunOS.

As more hardware vendors, such as Sun, begin to enter the picture, a proliferation of UNIX versions emerges. Although these hardware vendors have to purchase the source code from AT&T and port UNIX to their hardware platforms, AT&T's policy toward licensing the UNIX brand name allows nearly any hardware vendor willing to pay for a license to pick up UNIX. Because UNIX is a trademark, hardware vendors have to give their operating systems a unique name. Here are a few of the more popular versions of UNIX that have survived over the years:

- **SCO UNIX**—SCO Open Desktop and SCO Open Server from the Santa Cruz Operation for the Intel platform. Based on System V.
- **SunOS**—Sun's early OS and the best-known BSD operating system.
- **Solaris**—Sun's SRV4 implementation, also referred to as SunOS 5.x.
- **HP-UX**—Hewlett-Packard's version of UNIX. HP-UX 9.x was System V, release 3, and HP-UX 10 is based on the System V, release 4 OS.
- **Digital UNIX**—Digital Equipment's version of OSF/1.
- **IRIX**—The Silicon Graphics version of UNIX. Early versions were BSD-based; version 6 is System V, release 4.
- **AIX**—IBM's System V-based UNIX.
- **Linux**—A free UNIX operating system for the INTEL platform.

With the uncontrolled proliferation of UNIX versions, standards become a major issue. In 1993, Sun announces that it is moving to System V in an effort to promote standards in the UNIX community. With two major flavors of UNIX, standards cannot become a reality. Without standards, UNIX will never be taken seriously as a business computing system. Thus, Sun develops BSD but provides its users with System V, release 4, shrink-wrapped directly from AT&T. In addition, any applications developed by Sun to be added onto UNIX are to be SRV4-compliant. Sun challenges its competitors to provide true portability for the user community.

The Graphical User Interface (GUI) is the next wave in the development of the UNIX operating system. As each hardware vendor tries to outdo the others, ease of use becomes an issue. Again, in this area especially, standards are important. Applications that are to be portable need a GUI standard. Therefore, Sun and AT&T start promoting OPEN LOOK, which they jointly developed. Their goal is to create a consistent look and feel for all flavors of UNIX, but unfortunately, OSF has its own GUI called OSF/MOTIF. Thus, round two of the fight for standards begins, with MOTIF beating out OPEN LOOK.

MOTIF is based on a GUI developed at MIT named the X Window System, which lets a user sitting at one machine run programs on a remote machine while still interacting with the program locally. X is, in effect, one way for different systems to interface with each other. X lets a program run on one computer and display its output on another computer, even when the other computer is of a different operating system and hardware architecture. The program displays its output on the local machine and accepts keyboard and mouse input from the local machine but executes on the CPU of the remote machine.

The local machine is typically a workstation or terminal called a dedicated X terminal and built specifically to run the X Window System. The remote machine may be a minicomputer or server, a mainframe, or even a supercomputer. In some cases, the local machine and the remote machine might, in fact, be the same. In summary, X is a distributed, intelligent, device-independent, operating-system-independent windowing system.

As stated earlier, MOTIF beat OPEN LOOK in the standards war. Sun concedes and starts to provide a package that contains both OPEN LOOK and MOTIF—called the Common Desktop Environment (CDE)—as standard equipment beginning with Solaris 2.5.1.

Into 2000

Today, many hardware vendors have buried the hatchet and, for the sake of users, are moving their implementations of UNIX to be SRV4-compliant. SVR4 will clearly be the dominant flavor of UNIX across most major platforms. As all vendors begin to implement SVR4 along with the CDE, users will begin to see a more consistent implementation of UNIX. In addition, software providers can be assured that applications written to be SVR4-compliant will be portable across many hardware platforms.

Solaris

No other flavor of UNIX is more popular or has enjoyed a wider user base and cultural following than Sun Microsystems' Solaris. Since it was founded in 1982, Sun Microsystems' focus has been on UNIX, and it appears to have no intention of moving away from the UNIX operating system. Sun's user base has strong loyalty to the company as well as to the operating system. Sun's most recent version is Solaris 8, based on System V, release 4. The Solaris operating system is available for the SPARC architecture, Sun's own processor, and the Intel platform.

Milestones in the Development of UNIX

1965	Bell Laboratories joins with MIT and General Electric to develop Multics.
1970	Ken Thompson and Dennis Ritchie develop UNIX.
1971	The B-language version of the OS runs on a PDP-11.
1973	UNIX is rewritten in the C language.
1974	Thompson and Ritchie publish a paper and generate enthusiasm in the academic community. Berkeley starts the BSD program.
1975	The first licensed version of BSD UNIX is released.
1979	Bill Joy introduces "Berkeley Enhancements" as BSD 4.1.
1982	AT&T first markets UNIX. Sun Microsystems is founded.
1983	Sun Microsystems introduces SunOS.
1984	About 100,000 UNIX sites exist worldwide.
1988	AT&T and Sun start work on SVR4, a unified version of UNIX.
1988	OSF and UI are formed.
1989	AT&T releases System V, release 4.
1990	OSF releases OSF/1.
1992	Sun introduces Solaris, which is based on System V, release 4. SunOS, which is based on BSDF UNIX, will be phased out.
1993	Novell buys UNIX from AT&T.
1994	Solaris 2.4 is available.
1995	Santa Cruz Operation buys UNIXware from Novell. SCO and HP announce a relationship to develop a 64-bit version of UNIX. Solaris 2.5 is available.
1997	Solaris 2.6 is available.
1998	Solaris 7 is available.
2000	Solaris 8 is available.

APPENDIX

B

The Fundamentals of Client/Server Computing

hen speaking of client/server, open systems, and distributed computing environments, UNIX comes up in the same conversation. UNIX provides the foundation required to support these environments. This section describes the role of UNIX in the world of client/server computing.

The First UNIX Server

Before 1990, UNIX was used exclusively by scientists, mathematicians, engineers, and graduate students. During this period, UNIX ran only on minicomputers, smaller than a mainframe but larger than a PC. A typical mini was equipped with 300MB of disk space and 2 to 4MB of RAM. A minicomputer usually supported one to 12 users and was accessed via dumb alphanumeric terminals.

An OS Designed for Speed

Disks operate in milliseconds, and RAM operates in nanoseconds. UNIX was designed to take advantage of RAM; thus, the more RAM, the better the performance. When RAM was limited, disk space was substituted for physical RAM. As the number of users on a server grew, performance degraded, and another server was added. As users were moved to the new server, data was shared via the network. Soon, graphical terminals became available and replaced the character-based terminals; before long, these graphical terminals had their own CPUs and RAM. Because they had no disk drive and relied on the minicomputer or "server" for storage, the terminals were termed "diskless clients." With their own processing capability, the terminals could off-load the task of processing from the server, which, by this time, was simply used for storing applications and data. At power-on, the client downloaded UNIX into its local memory and—except for retrieving data—operated in a stand-alone mode.

The Birth of the Workstation

As disk drives became less expensive, disks were added to the client, and UNIX could be loaded locally. The term "diskful" client was coined, but these were soon referred to as "workstations" to differentiate them from the less-expensive personal computers. Workstations operating with the UNIX OS were multitasking multiuser systems, but the PC was still a single-tasking single-user environment.

Workstations were fueled by cheaper memory and faster CPUs. Servers and workstations were equipped with 16 to 32MB of RAM, and applications could be loaded directly on the workstations to further improve performance. Workstations could access data across several servers and share processing tasks with other workstations, allowing the processing load to be distributed across a network of computers.

In the early 1980s, workstation costs averaged between $35,000 and $55,000, with servers in the $100,000 range. Use of these systems was mainly in high-tech and engineering environments. The systems were stand-alone units, and system management was not a big issue for this group of users; however, workstation vendors looking for new opportunities knew they had to break out of the technical arena. They looked toward general business applications such as accounting, finance, and business information systems—environments that required larger systems, supporting hundreds of users and large data pools. Uptime was required 24 hours a day, seven days a week, and system failures and data loss were disastrous to these environments.

Distributed Computing

In the late 1980s, something else was happening in the computer world that changed the course of UNIX: Mainframes were running out of power because of the large numbers of users and the more complex applications they were supporting. With more users came more data and the need to access this data in a more timely fashion. To further complicate matters, businesses were no longer centralized, and many users needed to connect to the mainframe over telephone lines. When the mainframe failed, all users were affected.

UNIX fit perfectly into this environment. It already had the network functionality for computers to communicate, and it acted as a single system while providing a distributed computing environment. Local systems could run processes on other, less-loaded systems, and data access was transparent across multiple networks. As performance degraded, another server could be added to lighten the load. The UNIX system now had a chance to infiltrate the mainframe world. A typical scenario placed multiple UNIX servers on a network. Workstations, called clients, were placed at the users' desks. Applications ran on the users' desktops, accessing data on the servers. In a nutshell, this was client/server computing and was the advantage UNIX used to gain new markets.

Since they were introduced in the early 1980s, PCs and workstations have grown more powerful and less expensive. At first, cost and performance constituted the difference between a workstation and a personal computer. Today, the distinction between a workstation and a PC is less obvious. Whatever we call the desktop system, users no longer need to rely on the mainframe when they have high performance and adequate storage on their desktop computers. Application developers are porting their applications to these high-performance desktops, using the mainframe for storage and large database transactions. By moving the application to the local desktop, the load of users and their applications is distributed over the network and off the mainframe. Unfortunately, this means the network takes a beating and soon becomes the performance bottleneck.

Many advances in network technology are addressing this network bottleneck. Ethernet switches and network interfaces that support 100 megabit to 1 gigabit transfer rates are being implemented, adding complexity to the system administrator's job. Network management is as important as managing the UNIX system. The system administrator not only needs to understand the UNIX operating system and hardware, but also must be knowledgeable in network design and management as well.

UNIX Administration in a Mainframe Environment

Since the early 1990s, many businesses have replaced mainframes with several less expensive, more powerful UNIX servers. The mainframe world, however, requires consistency and robust system management utilities. With more than 25 years of development under its belt, UNIX provides much of the functionality a user would expect. In fact, the last few releases of SVR4 have not seen much more development in this area, other than the development of GUIs and the windowing system. User enhancements that provide general functionality within the OS have been developed and tested and are as solid as any OS in existence. Development now lies in the area of performance, high availability, and system administration. Hardware vendors competing against mainframes are rapidly developing applications and utilities to compete in this arena. To appear open and SVR4-compliant, vendors usually refer to features as extensions or enhancements. In addition, third-party software developers create new applications daily as additional "extensions" to UNIX to meet the demands of the server community. This area is rapidly changing for the UNIX system administrator.

Unfortunately, even when a system is SVR4-compliant, system administration is not consistent between hardware vendors. As standards are developed for the UNIX operating system, the area of system administration is often overlooked. Although everyone is moving toward SVR4, and to the general user, UNIX is UNIX. Be aware that system administration on HP, IBM, DEC, and such is very different and will probably always remain that way.

APPENDIX

C

Overview of SCSI Devices

SCSI (pronounced "scuzzy") is an acronym for the Small Computer Systems Interface. This interface is an American National Standards Institute (ANSI) standard for high-speed parallel data communication between computers and their peripheral devices. The SCSI standard can be divided into SCSI-1, SCSI-2, and SCSI-3. SCSI-3 is the most recent version of the SCSI command specification and is also called Fast/Wide SCSI. SCSI-2 and SCSI-3 allow scanners, hard disk drives, CD-ROM players, tapes, and many other devices to connect to a computer.

You might be familiar with IDE disk drives but not SCSI drives. IDE drives are much more prevalent on PCs. IDE/ATAPI is also a data interface that is often provided by PC manufacturers and is generally included when you purchase a new personal computer. Usually, the computer motherboard comes with a primary and secondary IDE bus. Up to two IDE/ATAPI devices, a master and slave, can be connected to each bus. Because this interface is less sophisticated than the SCSI one, ATAPI devices are usually more affordable. Note, however, that IDE/ATAPI devices are often slower and—particularly in the case of CD-readers—less accurate. The benefits of SCSI are probably best explained by listing the reasons why someone would use SCSI:

- SCSI makes it easy to add new peripheral devices to a computer system.
- Because the development cycle for SCSI devices is very short, the latest generation of SCSI peripherals keeps pace with the latest generation of computer systems. SCSI disk drives usually out-perform IDE disk drives.
- SCSI maintains high performance standards, which is why SCSI is still the dominant interface for medium and large systems.
- SCSI is a smarter bus than IDE. On operating systems that allow multitasking, the SCSI drive is a better choice because the extra intelligence on the SCSI bus is used. IDE also uses controllers on each device, but they cannot operate at the same time, and they do not support command queuing. The performance overhead of SCSI over IDE comes from the structure of the bus, not the drive. The nature of the SCSI bus provides much better performance when you're doing data-hungry tasks such as multitasking. The SCSI bus controller can control the drives without any work by the processor. Also, all drives on a SCSI chain can operate at the same time. With IDE, you're limited to two drives in a chain, and these drives cannot work at the same time (in essence, they must "take turns").
- SCSI is an intelligent interface, which means that the intelligence about I/O operations is moved from the host CPU to the peripheral device. Data can then be transferred at high speeds between the devices without taking any CPU power. Also, computer systems can use a standard set of commands to accomplish the moving of data between the host and device. Adding to the simplicity of the SCSI interface, you can connect a new peripheral device to an existing system with no hardware changes or additional hardware parts.

- SCSI has a demonstrated track record of keeping pace with the growing and evolving requirements of desktop and server systems.
- Using SCSI both preserves the investment of installed-base environments and maintains a platform for future enhancements of SCSI systems.

Here are the definitions of a few SCSI terms you'll come across:

- **Host adapter**—The host adapter, or SCSI controller, is the card that connects your computer to the SCSI bus.
- **SCSI device**—Any device that attaches to the SCSI host adapter, such as a tape drive or disk drive.
- **SCSI ID**—Also referred to as the target ID, this is a unique ID assigned to each SCSI device. It usually can be selected on the rear of the device. No two devices on the same SCSI chain can share the same ID.
- **SCSI chain**—Devices such as disk drives and tape drives are daisy-chained from the host adapter. This chain of devices is referred to as a SCSI chain.
- **SCSI terminator**—The last device on the SCSI chain must be terminated. Termination must be present at only two positions on the SCSI bus—the beginning and the end. Termination at the beginning of the SCSI bus is done on the motherboard automatically. The system administrator usually has to install a terminator on the last SCSI device. There must be two terminators on the bus—no more, no less. The terminator is either passive or active and is usually labeled as such; some active terminators have a small LED as well. A passive terminator is a group of resistors on the physical end of a single-ended SCSI bus that dampens reflected signals from the ends of the bus. Passive terminators do not use a voltage regulator and might not be exactly +5 volts. Active terminators use a voltage regulator to make sure the voltage is exactly +5 volts. You need to determine what type of termination to use, so follow the instructions in the hardware installation guide that comes with the equipment. Some peripherals are auto-terminating; terminating these devices twice can cause undesirable results.
- **Single-ended SCSI**—An early type of SCSI-1 device. The maximum length of a SCSI-1 chain is 6 meters, and the maximum number of devices is eight.
- **Differential SCSI**—The next-generation SCSI type. Allows a maximum cable length of 25 meters and is electrically incompatible with single-ended devices. Differential SCSI supports a maximum of 16 devices.

- **Asynchronous SCSI**—A way of sending data over the SCSI bus. The initiator sends a command or data over the bus and then waits until it receives a reply.
- **Synchronous SCSI**—Rather than waiting for a reply, two connected devices that both support synchronous SCSI can send multiple bytes over the bus. This improves throughput, especially if you use long cables.
- **Fast SCSI (SCSI-2)**—Fast SCSI allows faster timing on the bus—10MHz instead of 5MHz. On an 8-bit SCSI bus, this increases the maximum speed from 5MBps to 10MBps.
- **Ultra SCSI**—Allows up to 20MHz signals on the bus to achieve speeds of up to 20MBps.
- **Ultra-2 Wide SCSI**—Allows up to 40MHz signals on the bus to achieve speeds of up to 40MBps.
- **Wide SCSI (SCSI-3)**—Uses an extra cable (or 68-pin P cable) to send the data 16 or 32 bits wide. This allows for double or quadruple speed over the SCSI-1 bus. Currently, no single drive reaches these speeds, but groups of several drives can.

The following is a visual guide for SCSI connectors.

Most SCSI Slow (5MBps) computers and host adapters use the Centronics-type 50-pin connector shown in Figure C-1.

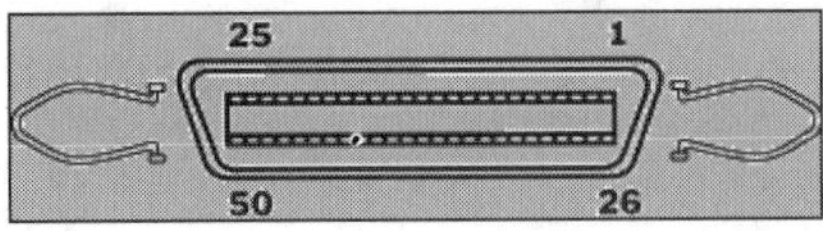

Figure C-1
50-pin Centronics SCSI connector.

Many 8-bit SCSI Fast (up to 10MBps) computers and host adapters use the 50-pin high-density connector shown in Figure C-2.

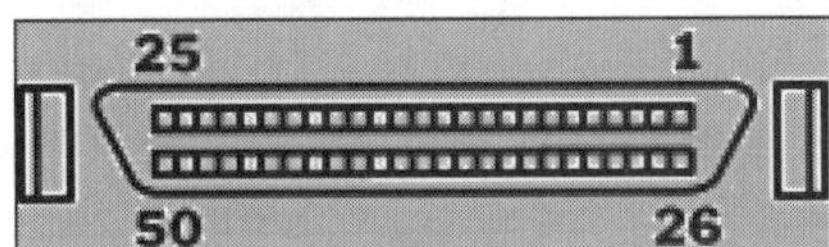

Figure C-2
50-pin high-density SCSI connector.

All Fast or Wide (16-bit) SCSI-3 computers and host adapters, as well as old DEC single-ended SCSIs, use the 68-pin high-density connector shown in Figure C-3.

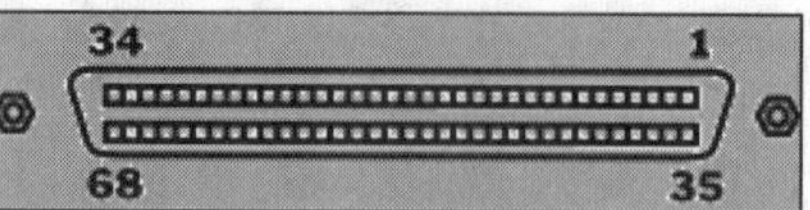

Figure C-3
68-pin high-density SCSI connector.

A less-common Ultra-SCSI connector, the New SCA 80-pin connector, is shown in Figure C-4.

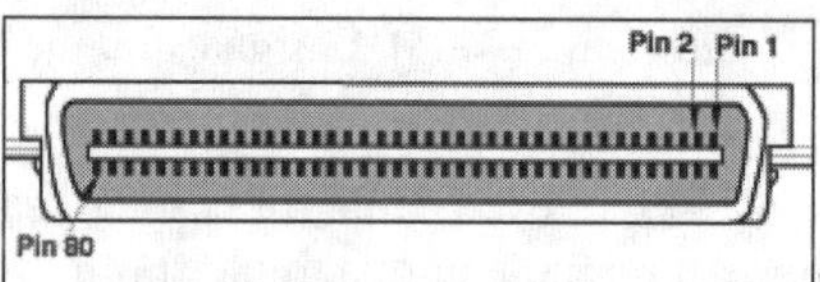

Figure C-4
SCA 80-pin SCSI connector.

As when adding any other peripheral or equipment to your system, consult with the manufacturer first. When adding equipment to your Sun system, first call Sun and make sure the equipment is supported under Solaris and that you can obtain instructions for connecting the equipment. Again, a few minutes of planning will save you hours of grief and downtime. Most system administrators are more comfortable having their hardware maintenance person install the equipment.

APPENDIX D

On the Web

The Internet is a great source of information, especially for system administrators. You might be interested in the following newsgroups and Web sites to further your knowledge of UNIX. These sites are valuable as you search for information regarding Solaris and Sun Microsystems. All these links are also available on my Web site at `www.pdesigninc.com`. These Web sites change frequently, so visit my Web site for the links. I'll do my best to keep them up-to-date.

Newsgroups

`comp.sys.sun.admin`

A newsgroup for Sun system administration issues and questions.

`comp.sys.sun.announce`

A newsgroup used for Sun announcements and Sunergy mailings.

`comp.sys.sun.apps`

A newsgroup covering software applications for Sun computer systems.

`comp.sys.sun.hardware`

A newsgroup for Sun Microsystems hardware. A good place to buy used equipment. Also check out `sun.forsale`.

`comp.sys.sun.misc`

A newsgroup of miscellaneous discussions about Sun products.

`comp.sys.sun.wanted`

A newsgroup for people looking for Sun products and support.

`comp.unix.admin`

A general UNIX system administration newsgroup.

`comp.unix.solaris`

Discussions about the Solaris operating system. This is the most active newsgroup for Solaris system administrators.

Web Sites

`www.pdesigninc.com`

My Web page. This site provides links to all the sites mentioned in this book, as well as other sites as I find them and they become available.

`www.sun.com`

Sun's official Web site.

`www.netline.com/sunex`

Server/Workstation Expert. A free magazine with UNIX tips and news and technology from the world of Sun.

`www.sunworld.com`

SunWorld. Sun's own online magazine for the Sun community.

`sunsolve.sun.com`

A source of free and recommended security support information. This Web site contains collections of informational documents, patch descriptions, a symptom/resolution database, and download access to the latest system patches. If you are a Sun contract customer, you can log in here and submit incident reports and read FAQs and Info Docs.

`http://docs.sun.com`

This Web site contains all the Sun product documentation, including manuals, guides, and AnswerBooks. Everything on the exam is here—you just need to dig for it.

`http://mysun.sun.com`

Sun's one-stop site for Solaris system administrators. Lots of good links to popular Solaris Web sites.

`http://sun.icsnet.com`

A site providing links to Solaris FAQs, software, and manual pages.

`www.latech.edu/sunman.html`

An archive of summaries of questions posted to the Sun managers' mailing list.

`www.sunfreeware.com`

Lots of freeware, precompiled in package format for Solaris running on SPARCs and x86.

`http://www.net-kitchen.com/~sah/`

Suns-at-Home is a mailing list devoted to folks who have Sun workstations at home.

UNIX-Related Publications Available on the Web

Visit my Web site for a list of all Solaris- and UNIX-related magazines.

APPENDIX

E

Web Start

Web Start is Sun's Java-based installation program that simplifies and accelerates the installation of Solaris Software. Web Start uses technology from InstallShield, which is widely recognized as the provider of de facto installation technology for Microsoft Windows applications. This tool lets network administrators use a familiar Web browser utilizing a point-and-click interface to install all the software bundled with Solaris. Through Solaris Web Start, you select and install all the software your machine requires, including the Solaris software group and Solstice utilities. In addition, Web Start is the only installation utility that also installs the other software provided on the additional CDs. It's much like the Solaris interactive installation program described in Chapter 14, "Installing a Server," but with a much more user-friendly interface. Solaris Web Start uses the JumpStart utility to read the configuration profile automatically, thus installing the Solaris software and other selected products with minimal intervention.

If you're setting up a machine that includes a frame buffer, keyboard, and monitor, you can run Web Start directly from that machine. If you only have a character-based terminal connected via the serial port, you can still start up to the CD-ROM and enter the system identification information.

After the system identification is complete, you have two choices of how you want to continue the installation:

- You can continue using the character-based interactive installation, as explained in Chapter 14.
- You can use Web Start, with its graphical user interface, by utilizing a bitmapped terminal connected to a system (or PC) over the network. This process is explained later in this chapter.

Minimum System Requirements for Solaris Web Start

If you want to run Solaris Web Start, your computer must have the following:

- At least 48MB of RAM
- A 1.05GB startup disk just to run Solaris Web Start, after which the program determines whether your system has enough disk space to install the products you selected. 2GB of disk space is recommended for installing server software.

Modes of Operation

There are two ways to use Web Start: in local mode or in client/server mode.

Local Mode

If you run Web Start locally on the machine you're setting up, it writes the profile to disk and uses that profile information when you select and confirm the Install Now option. Your computer system must include a CD-ROM drive, frame buffer, keyboard, and monitor if you are to use this mode.

To start up Web Start in local mode, simply start up from the Solaris 7 software CD using the following command at the startup PROM:

```
ok boot cdrom - browser
```

NOTE. *Be sure to include a space before and after the hyphen.*

After the system starts up from the CD, follow the instructions on the screen.

Client/Server Mode

Use client/server mode if the system does not have a bitmapped graphics display. In this mode, Web Start runs on the machine being configured, but Java applets in Web Start interact with you on your desktop Web browser. You can run Web Start from any system connected to the network that has a Web browser, such as Netscape Navigator or Microsoft Internet Explorer. Client/server mode is useful for installing software on a "headless server," which does not include a frame buffer for bitmapped graphics.

Solaris Web Start's client/server mode lets you take advantage of the ease and convenience of a browser-based installation, even if the machine on which you're loading the software doesn't support a graphical user interface.

If the system has no monitor, connect a PC or dumb terminal, such as a VT-100, to the system's serial port. Use a null modem cable to connect the terminal to the serial port on the Sun system. I use a laptop with a communications package, such as ProComm or HyperTerminal in Windows 98. Configure the PC for a direct connection from Com1 to serial port A on the back of your Sun system. When the system is powered on, it detects that the keyboard and monitor are missing and defaults to using serial port A. You'll get the familiar `ok` prompt on your PC. To get into client/server mode, start up from the CD the same way you would get into local mode:

```
ok boot cdrom - browser
```

A system identification tool asks you to supply system and network information about the machine you're adding to the network. This is a standard part of Sun's installation process and was described in Chapter 14.

After you've finished entering the system identification information, the following message appears:

```
System identification is completed.
Starting Solaris installation program...
Initializing, please wait...

Solaris software has been detected on disk -'c0t0d0s0'

Solaris Web Start is not intended to support software upgrade.
If you choose to run Solaris Web Start on a machine which already has system software
loaded on it, everything on your computer's system disk will be wiped out, and you risk
losing data on other disks.
----------------------

What do you want to do?
----------------------

[1] Reinstall everything using Solaris Web Start.
[2] Upgrade software using Solaris interactive installation.
Type 1 or 2, then press the Return key=>
```

Select option 1.

Solaris Web Start then figures out that your machine lacks graphical support and displays the following message:

```
You cannot run Solaris Web Start on this system - it requires a bitmapped graphics
display.
----------------------

You have two options:
----------------------

[1] Continue running Solaris Web Start using a web-browser window on another machine
connected over the network.
[2] Run the Solaris interactive installation.

Options other than Solaris Web Start only install Solaris software on your computer.
Solaris Web Start installs both Solaris software and co-packaged products.

Solaris Web Start provides a suite of online information to guide you through product
selection and installation. If you change your mind, you can exit from Solaris Web
Start at any time and return to the Solaris interactive installation.

Type 1 or 2 then press the Return key=>1
```

To switch to the Interactive Installation program and continue using this terminal, select option 2.

If you choose to proceed using Web Start by selecting option 1, you'll be instructed to provide a password. This authentication password is distinct from any others you might have. The password restricts who can use Web Start to install software over the network on your machine.

```
Before Solaris Web Start can begin, you must choose a special
Solaris Web Start authentication password for user 'webstart'.

Adding password for webstart
Enter password:
Re-enter password:
```

Web Start next explains how you can run your installation over the network by going to another machine and pointing your Web browser program to a special Uniform Resource Locator (URL).

The URL is different for each system you set up, because it contains the hostname that has been assigned to the new system—in this case, sparc1.

```
------------------------------------
To continue with Solaris Web Start
------------------------------------

Step 1. Go to another machine connected to this network.

Step 2. On the other machine, start the HotJava(TM) or another supported web-browser
program.

Step 3. Point the browser at this URL: http://ultra5/start.html

Step 4. When you are prompted to enter a user name and password, respond by typing:
'webstart' for the user name and the authentication password you chose earlier.

The next line that appears on this console is a status message. Ignore it and proceed
with the browser install.

May 12 20:55:47 sws[2021]: SWS-1.0 server started.
```

If you follow these steps on a remote system, after you enter the URL, you'll be prompted to enter a username and password, as shown in Figure E-1.

Figure E-1
The Login window.

After you enter the correct username and password, you see the Solaris Web Start welcome page in your Web browser, as shown in Figure E-2.

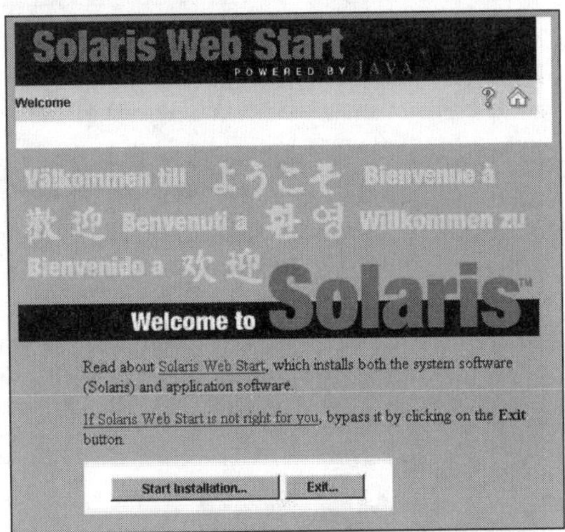

Figure E-2
The Web Start Welcome page.

Click the Start Installation button. Web Start begins the installation process by opening a window that asks you to select the product you purchased. In Figure E-3, I selected Solaris 7 Desktop and then clicked the Next button.

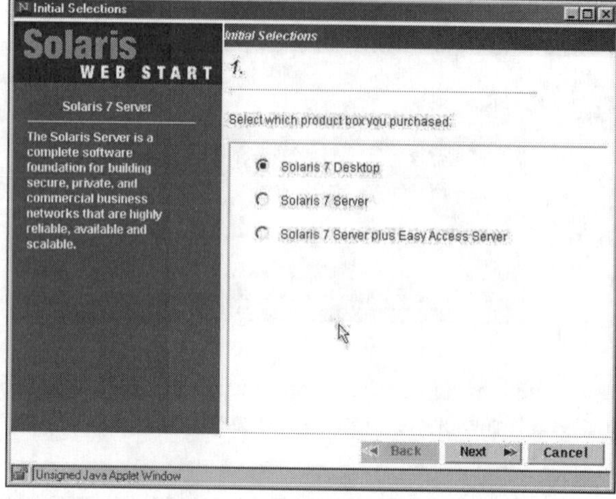

Figure E-3
The Product Selection window.

The next window that appears asks you to set the root password, as shown in Figure E-4.

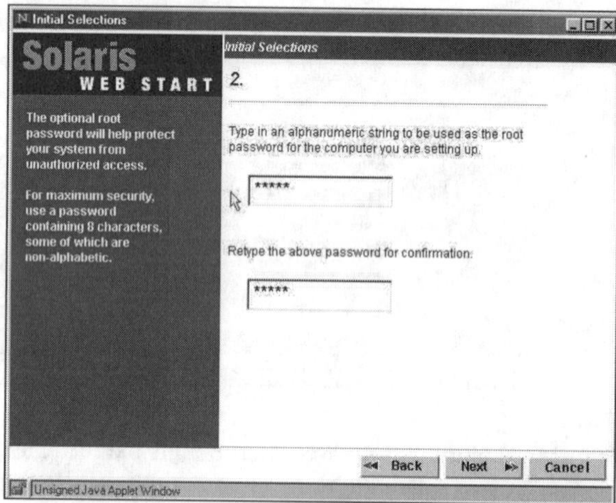

Figure E-4
The Password Setup window.

Enter the password twice and click Next. The next window that appears asks you if you want to turn power management on or off, as shown in Figure E-5. Select your preference and click Next.

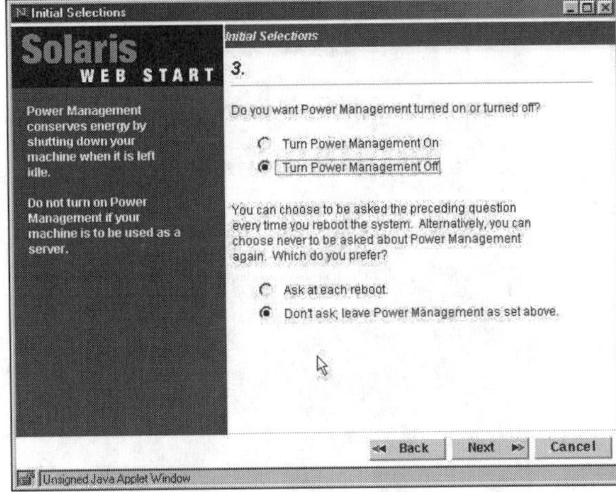

Figure E-5
The Power Management window.

A confirmation window appears, as shown in Figure E-6.

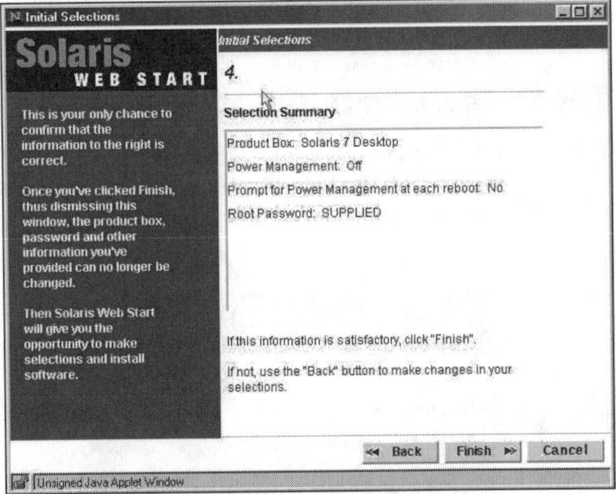

Figure E-6
The Confirmation window.

Click the Finish button. Web Start begins the installation process by opening the Selection window, shown in Figure E-7.

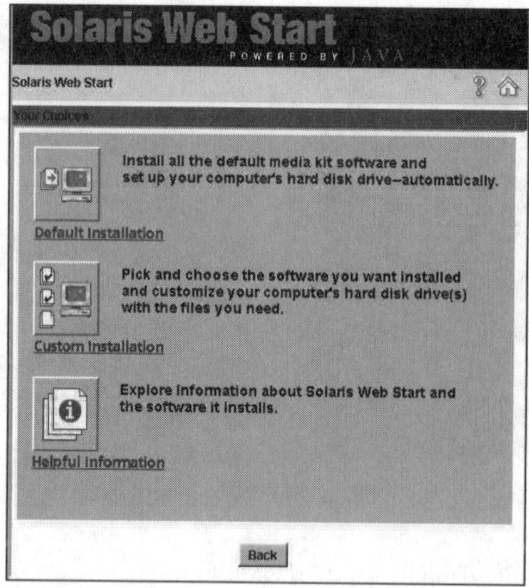

Figure E-7
The Web Start Selection window.

The following sections describe the options that are presented in the selection window.

Web Start Default Installation Selection

The Default Installation option in Web Start is the easiest way to install system and copackaged additional software on your computer. Just click the Default Installation button shown in Figure E-7. The Default Installation Configuration window opens, as shown in Figure E-8.

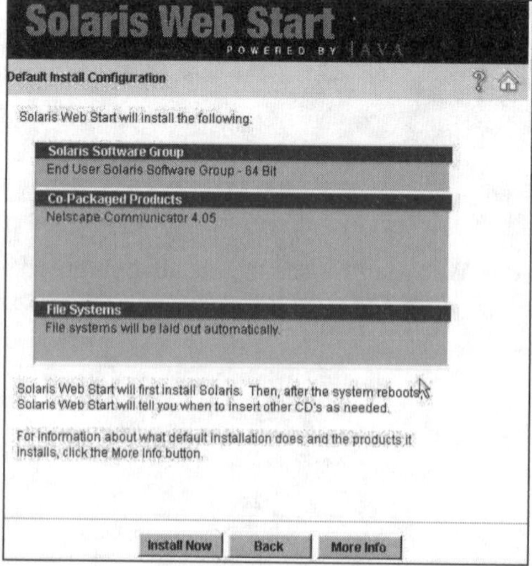

Figure E-8
The Default Installation Configuration window.

Click the Install Now button. Web Start does the following:

- Automatically calculates and creates root and swap partitions on the system disk.
- Automatically calculates and creates an /opt partition for the copackaged software utilities.
- Installs the entire Solaris Software cluster on server systems and the End User Software Group on desktop systems.
- Installs all the software that comes with the Solaris Server plus Intranet Extension product boxes. The software that is packaged in other product boxes varies, and the copackaged software automatically installed also varies. Check the products listed in the Web Start interface for details.
- Installs AnswerBook2 documentation on server systems. On desktops, the documentation that is installed varies. Check the products listed in the Web Start interface for details.

Limitations of the Default Installation

If you are installing software on a system that has multiple disks, the Default Installation option sets up only the system disk. Other disks are not recognized by the operating system unless you manually set up and mount file systems on them and create entries for them in /etc/vfstab after the Web Start installation.

If you want Web Start to set up all the disks in your system, use the Custom Installation option described next and then choose to lay out the file systems manually.

Web Start Custom Installation

Use this option to customize the software installation. Unlike the default installation, in which software selections and file systems are already defined, this option lets you select the installation of software and the creation of file systems. The customized installation is similar to the Interactive Software Installation described in Chapter 14, with the following exceptions:

- Solaris Web Start does not perform software upgrades. It is designed to install software on a new computer.
- Solaris Web Start installs entire software clusters and does not provide the flexibility of selecting and deselecting particular packages within a cluster.
- Solaris Web Start installs Solstice utilities and other software in the /opt directory and does not allow you to choose an alternative location.

- Solaris Web Start installs the full versions of all software packages. It does not install "light" or "nil" versions of any software.
- Solaris Web Start lets you choose a system disk, but it does not let you move the root partition off the system disk afterward.

If you need to do any of these things, use the Solaris Interactive Installation program instead of Solaris Web Start.

After you've decided to proceed with the custom installation, click the Custom Installation button in the Web Start Selection window (see Figure E-7). The Customize window opens. You are presented with three options, as shown in Figure E-9.

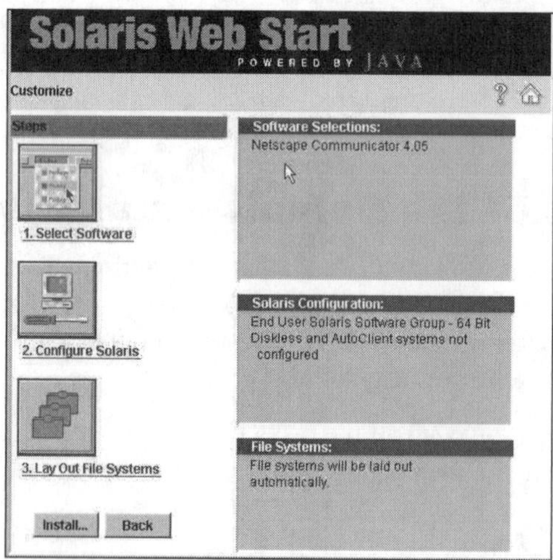

Figure E-9
The Customize window.

The options are as follows:

1. Select Software

   If you click this button, you see the Software Selection window, as shown in Figure E-10.

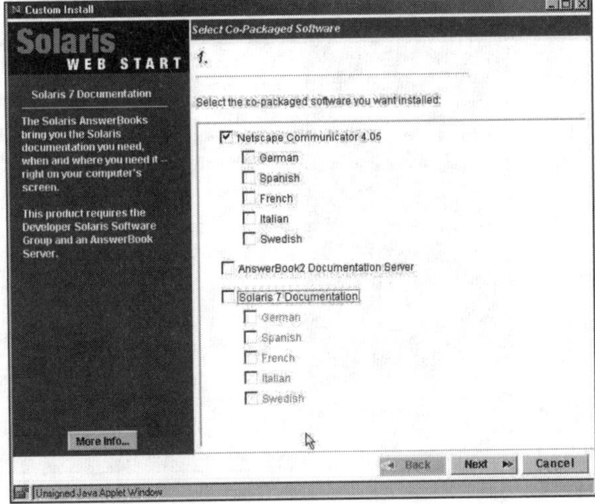

Figure E-10
The Software Selection window.

Use this option to select the copackaged software you want to install. The software includes such packages as Netscape Communicator and Answerbook2. When you position the cursor over each option, a brief description of that product appears in the frame on the left side of the window. If you click the More Info button, another window opens, describing the software package in more detail, as well as the system requirements needed to run it.

When you are finished, click Next. A window displaying the selected options opens. Click Finish, and you return to the Customize window.

2. Configure Solaris

   Use this option to select the software group you want installed, such as the End User Software Group or the Developer Software Group. After you've made your selection, the Solaris 7 Configuration window opens, as shown in Figure E-11.

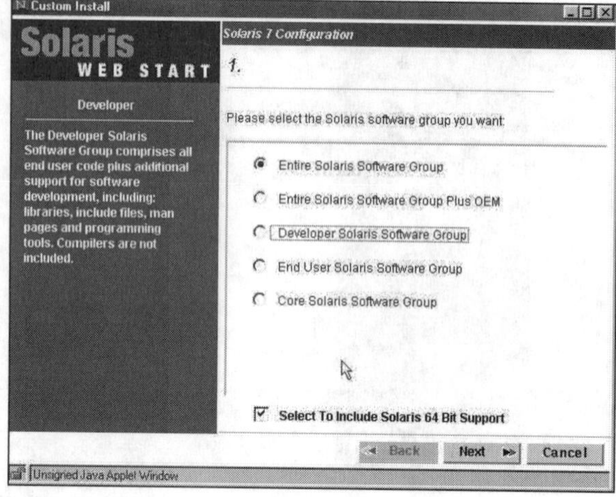

Figure E-11
The Solaris 7 Configuration window.

Select the software group and click Next. Verify your selections in the confirmation message box that appears, and then click the Finish button to return to the Customize window.

3. Lay Out File Systems

   After selecting this option, you see the Lay Out File Systems window, as shown in Figure E-12.

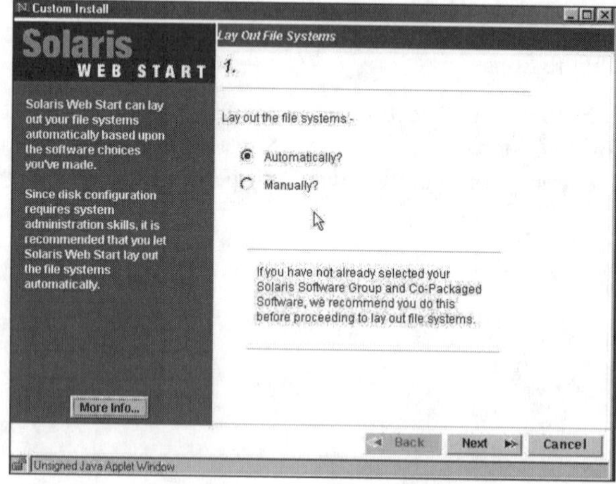

Figure E-12
The Lay Out File Systems window.

To have the installation program lay out the file systems automatically, select the Automatically? option. The file systems are laid out automatically based on the software selections you made; therefore, this step should be performed last. Click Next to continue. The File System Layout Summary window opens, as shown in Figure E-13.

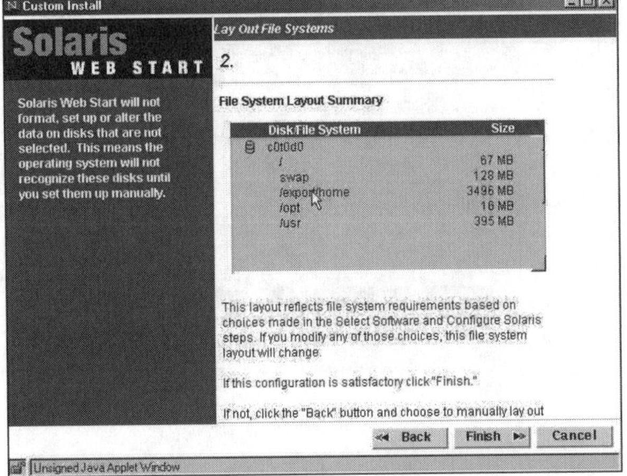

Figure E-13
The File System Layout Summary window.

However, if you want to manually configure the disks and file systems, click Back to return to the Lay Out File Systems Window (see Figure E-12), and select the Manually? option. After you click Next, the prompts displayed in the subsequent windows allow you to select the disks and create the file systems.

When to Lay Out File Systems Manually

If you do not have experience in laying out file systems, let Web Start lay out the file systems for you automatically. Web Start does this in a way that mirrors the Interactive Installation. The major difference between Web Start and the Interactive Installation is that Web Start lays out enough space (in /opt) for all the selected copackaged software products—not just Solaris.

The file system configuration automatically provided by Web Start is adequate for most situations. However, you might consider laying out file systems manually if either of the following is true:

- Other products that are not included in your Solaris product box need to be installed. These products must share the same file systems (root, /usr, and /swap) used by the copackaged software in the product box.
- It has been your experience that the file systems provided by the Interactive Installation program do not work for your situation.

After you are finished selecting software, configuring Solaris, and laying out the file systems, click the Install button. You see one more window, which summarizes the current installation configuration, as shown in Figure E-14.

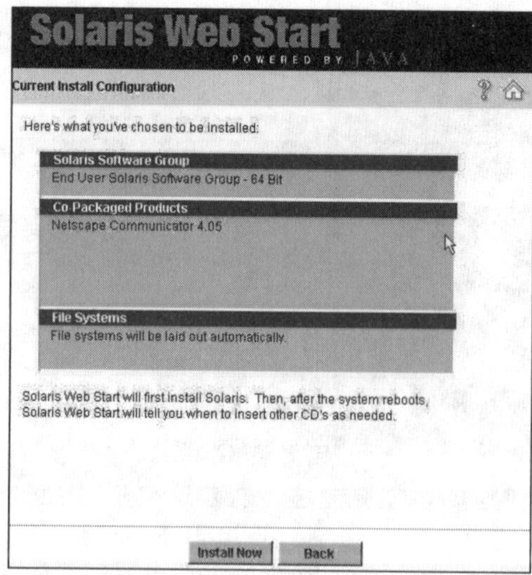

Figure E-14
The Install Summary window.

Confirm your selections, and then start the installation by clicking the Install Now button. Web Start first installs Solaris, and then, after the system restarts, it tells you when to load the other CDs as needed.

Helpful Web Start Information

The Helpful Information and More Info buttons in the Web Start windows are your sources of information about the Web Start program, as well as the software products it installs.

This completes the discussion of the Web Start installation utility. Look for further developments in this package—specifically, in the area of wizards. Solaris Web Start wizards enhance application software written for the Solaris platform. Application vendors are already starting to use Web Start wizards, which allow their applications to be installed from a Java desktop environment, or remotely from a Java-enabled Web browser, to any Solaris server or desktop on the network.

INDEX

Symbols

A

B

C

D

E–F

G

H

I

J–K

N

Q–R

S

T

U

V

W

X–Z

Other Books from New Riders

UNIX/Linux Titles

Solaris Essential Reference

By John P. Mulligan
1st Edition
350 pages, $24.95
ISBN: 0-7357-0023-0

Looking for the fastest, easiest way to find the Solaris command you need? Need a few pointers on shell scripting? How about advanced administration tips and sound, practical expertise on security issues? Are you looking for trustworthy information about available third-party software packages that will enhance your operating system? Author John Mulligan—creator of the popular Unofficial Guide to Solaris Web site (`sun.icsnet.com`)—delivers all that and more in one attractive, easy-to-use reference book. With clear and concise instructions on how to perform important administration and management tasks and key information on powerful commands and advanced topics, *Solaris Essential Reference* is the reference you need when you know what you want to do and you just need to know how.

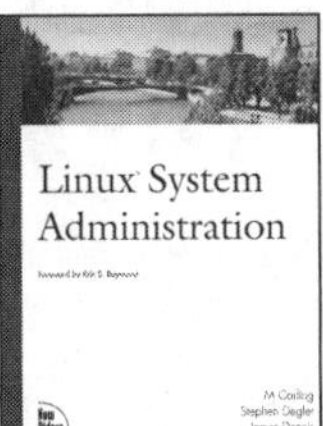

Linux System Administration

By M Carling and James T. Dennis
1st Edition
450 pages, $29.99
ISBN: 1-56205-934-3

As an administrator, you probably feel that most of your time and energy is spent in endless firefighting. If your network has become a fragile quilt of temporary patches and workarounds, then this book is for you. For example, have you had trouble sending or receiving your email lately? Are you looking for a way to keep your network running smoothly with enhanced performance? Are your users always hankering for more storage, more services, and more speed? *Linux System Administration* advises you on the many intricacies of maintaining a secure, stable system. In this definitive work, the author addresses all the issues related to system administration, from adding users and managing file permissions to Internet services and Web hosting to recovery planning and security. This book fulfills the need for expert advice that will ensure a trouble-free Linux environment.

Developing Linux Applications

By Eric Harlow
1st Edition
400 pages, $34.99
ISBN: 0-7357-0021-4

We all know that Linux is one of the most powerful and solid operating systems in existence. And as the success of Linux grows, there is an increasing interest in developing applications with graphical user interfaces that really take advantage of the power of Linux. In this book, software developer Eric Harlow gives you an indispensable development handbook focusing on the GTK+ toolkit. More than an overview on the elements of application or GUI design, this is a hands-on book that delves deeply into the technology. With in-depth material on the various GUI programming tools and loads of examples, this book's unique focus will give you the information you need to design and launch professional-quality applications.

Linux Firewalls

By Robert Ziegler
1st Edition
400 pages, $39.99
ISBN: 0-7357-0900-9

New Riders is proud to offer the first book aimed specifically at Linux security issues. While there are a host of general UNIX security books, we think it is time to address the practical needs of the Linux network. Author Robert Ziegler takes a balanced approach to system security, discussing topics like planning a secure environment, firewalls, and utilizing security scripts. With comprehensive information on specific system compromises, and advice on how to prevent and repair them, this is one book that Linux administrators should have on their shelves.

GIMP Essential Reference

by Alex Harford
1st Edition
400 pages, $24.95
ISBN: 0-7357-0911-4

GIMP Essential Reference is designed to fulfill a need for the computer expert. It is made to bring someone experienced in computers up to speed with the GNU Image Manipulation Program. It provides essential information on using this program effectively. This book is targeted at you if you want to efficiently use the GIMP. *GIMP Essential Reference* will show you how to quickly become familiar with the advanced user interface using a table-heavy format that will allow users to find what they're looking for quickly.

GIMP Essential Reference is for users working with GIMP who know what they want to accomplish, but don't know exactly how to do it.

KDE Application Development

by Uwe Thiem
1st Edition
216 pages, $39.99
ISBN: 1-57870-201-1

KDE Application Development offers a head start into KDE and Qt. The book will cover the essential widgets available in KDE and Qt, and it offers a strong start without the "first try" annoyances that sometimes make strong developers and programmers give up. This book explains KDE and Qt by writing a real application from the very beginning stages, where it can't do anything but display itself and offer a button to quit. Then it will finally bring the user to a full-featured application. The process of developing such an application takes the potential KDE developer through all stages of excitement.

Grokking the GIMP

by Carey Bunks
1st Edition, Winter 2000
352 pages, $45.00
ISBN: 0-7357-0924-6

This titles is a technical and inspirational reference covering the intricacies of the GIMP's feature set. Even if you have little background in image manipulation, you can succeed at using the GIMP to achieve your goals, using this book as a guide. Keeping in mind that all tools are not created equal, author Carey Bunks provides an in-depth look at the GIMP's most useful tools. The content focuses on the intermediate to advanced topics of interest to most users, like photo touchup and enhancement, compositing, and animations. Invaluable is the conceptual approach of the author, in which he avoids the cookbook approach to learning image manipulation and helps you become self-sufficient.

Inside Linux

by Michael Tobler
1st Edition, Fall 2000
800 pages, $39.99
ISBN: 0-7357-0940-8

With in-depth complete coverage on the installation process, editing and typesetting, graphical user interfaces, programming, system administration, and managing Internet sites, *Inside Linux* is the only book "smart" users new to Linux will need. If you have an understanding of computer technology and are looking for just the right reference to fit your sophisticated needs, this book guides you to a high level of proficiency with all the flavors of Linux, and helps you with crucial system administration chores. *Inside Linux* is different than other books available because it's a unique blend of a how-to and a reference guide.

Development Titles

GTK+/Gnome Application Development

By Havoc Pennington
1st Edition
400 pages, $39.99
ISBN: 0-7357-0078-8

GTK+/Gnome Application Development provides the experienced programmer the knowledge to develop X Window applications with the powerful GTK+ toolkit. The author provides the reader with a checklist of features every application should have, advanced GUI techniques, and the ability to create custom widgets. The title also contains reference information for more experienced users already familiar with usage, but requires knowledge of function prototypes and detailed descriptions. These tools let the reader write powerful applications in record time.

Python Essential Reference

By David Beazley
1st Edition
300 pages, $34.95
ISBN: 0-7357-0901-7

This book describes the Python programming language and its library of standard modules. Python is an informal language that has become a highly valuable software development tool for many computing professionals. This language reference covers Python's lexical conventions, built-in datatypes, control flow, functions, statements, classes, and execution model. This book also covers the contents of the Python library as bundled in the standard Python distribution.

Lotus Notes and Domino Titles

Domino System Administration

By Rob Kirkland
1st Edition
880 pages, $49.99
ISBN: 1-56205-948-3

Your boss has just announced that you will be upgrading to the newest version of Lotus Notes and Domino when it ships. As a Premium Lotus Business Partner, Lotus has offered a substantial price break to keep your company away from Microsoft's Exchange Server. How are you supposed to get this new system installed, configured, and rolled out to all of your endusers? You understand how Lotus Notes works—you've been administering it for years. What you need is a concise, practical explanation about the new features, and how to make some of the advanced stuff really work. You need answers and solutions from someone like you, who has worked with the product for years, and understands what it is you need to know. *Domino System Administration* is the answer—the first book on Domino that attacks the technology at the professional level, with practical, hands-on assistance to get Domino running in your organization.

Lotus Notes & Domino Essential Reference

By Dave Hatter and
Tim Bankes
1st Edition
700 pages, $45.00
ISBN: 0-7357-0007-9

You're in a bind because you've been asked to design and program a new database in Notes that will keep track of and itemize a myriad of inventory and shipping data for an important client. The client wants a user-friendly interface, without sacrificing speed or functionality. You are experienced (and could develop this app in your sleep), but feel that you need to take your talents to the next level. You need something to facilitate your creative and technical abilities, something to perfect your programming skills. Your answer is waiting for you: *Lotus Notes & Domino Essential Reference.* It's compact and simply designed. It's loaded with information. All of the objects, classes, functions, and methods are listed. It shows you the object hierarchy and the overlaying relationship between each one. It's perfect for you. Problem solved.

Networking Titles

Cisco Router Configuration & Troubleshooting, 2E

By Mark Tripod
2nd Edition
450 pages, $39.99
ISBN: 0-7357-0999-8

Want the real story on making your Cisco routers run like a dream? Why not pick up a copy of *Cisco Router Configuration & Troubleshooting* and see what Mark Tripod has to say? His company is the one responsible for making some of the largest sites on the Net scream, like Amazon.com, Hotmail, USAToday, Geocities, and Sony. In this book, he provides advanced configuration issues, sprinkled with advice and preferred practices. You won't see a general overview on TCP/IP—he talks about more meaty issues like security, monitoring, traffic management, and more. In the troubleshooting section, Mark provides a unique methodology and lots of sample problems to illustrate. By providing real-world insight and examples instead of rehashing Cisco's documentation, Mark gives network administrators information they can start using today.

Understanding Data Communications

By Gilbert Held
6th Edition
550 pages, $39.99
ISBN: 0-7357-0036-2

Updated from the highly successful fifth edition, this book explains how data communications systems and their various hardware and software components work. Not an entry-level book, it approaches the material in a textbook format, addressing the complex issues involved in internetworking today. A great reference book for the experienced networking professional, written by noted networking authority, Gilbert Held.

DCE/RPC over SMB

by Luke Leighton
1st Edition
280 pages, $45.00
ISBN: 1-57870-150-3

When Microsoft's systems were locked into offices and chained to small LANs, they were relatively safe. Now, as they've been unleashed onto the Internet, they are more and more vulnerable to attack. Security people, system and network administrators, and the folks writing tools for them all need to be familiar with the packets flowing across their networks. It's the only way to really know how much trouble a system is in. This book describes how Microsoft has taken DCE/RPC (Distributed Computing Environment / Remote Procedure Calls) and implemented it over SMB (Server Message Block) and TCP/IP. SMB itself runs over three transports: TCP/IP, IPX/SPX, and NETBEUI.

Luke Leighton presents Microsoft Developer NT system calls (including what some such calls would be, if they were documented) and shows what they look like over-the-wire by providing example C code to compile and use. This gives administrators and developers insights into how information flows through their network, so that they can improve efficiency, security, and heterogeneous transfers.

Network Intrusion Detection: An Analyst's Handbook

by Stephen Northcutt

2nd Edition

500 pages, $45.00

ISBN: 0-7357-1008-2

Get answers and solutions from someone who has been in the trenches with *Network Intrusion Detection: An Analyst's Handbook*. Author Stephen Northcutt, original developer of the Shadow intrusion detection system and former Director of the United States Navy's Information System Security Office at the Naval Security Warfare Center, lends his expertise to intrusion detection specialists, security analysts, and consultants responsible for setting up and maintaining an effective defense against network security.

Other Books By New Riders

Microsoft Technologies

ADMINISTRATION

Inside Windows 2000 Server
1-56205-929-7 • $49.99 US / $74.95 CAN
Windows 2000 Essential Reference
0-7357-0869-X • $35.00 US / $52.95 CAN
Windows 2000 Active Directory
0-7357-0870-3 • $29.99 US / $44.95 CAN
Windows 2000 Routing and Remote Access Service
0-7357-0951-3 • $34.99 US / $52.95 CAN
Windows 2000 Deployment & Desktop Management
0-7357-0975-0 • $34.99 US / $52.95 CAN
Windows 2000 DNS
0-7357-0973-4 • $39.99 US / $59.95 CAN
Windows 2000 User Management
1-56205-886-X • $34.99 US / $52.95 CAN
Windows 2000 Professional
0-7357-0950-5 • $34.99 US / $52.95 CAN
Planning for Windows 2000
0-7357-0048-6 • $29.99 US / $44.95 CAN
Windows 2000 Server Professional Reference
0-7357-0952-1 • $75.00 US / $111.95 CAN
Windows 2000 Security
0-7357-0991-2 • $39.99 US / $59.95 CAN
Available October 2000
Windows 2000 TCP/IP
0-7357-0992-0 • $39.99 US / $59.95 CAN
Windows 2000 Registry
0-7357-0944-0 • $34.99 US / $52.95 CAN
Available December 2000
Windows 2000 Terminal Services and Citrix MetaFrame
0-7357-1005-8 • $39.99 US / $59.95 CAN
Available December 2000
Windows NT/2000 Network Security
1-57870-253-4 • $45.00 US / $67.95 CAN
Windows NT/2000 Thin Client Solutions
1-57870-239-9 • $45.00 US / $67.95 CAN
Windows 2000 Virtual Private Networking
1-57870-246-1 • $45.00 US / $67.95 CAN
Available December 2000
Windows 2000 Active Directory Design & Deployment
1-57870-242-9 • $45.00 US / $67.95 CAN
Windows 2000 and Mainframe Integration
1-57870-200-3 • $40.00 US / $59.95 CAN
Windows 2000 Server: Planning and Migration
1-57870-023-X • $40.00 US / $59.95 CAN
Windows 2000 Quality of Service
1-57870-115-5 • $45.00 US / $67.95 CAN
Windows NT Power Toolkit
0-7357-0922-X • $49.99 US / $74.95 CAN
Windows NT Terminal Server and Citrix MetaFrame
1-56205-944-0 • $29.99 US / $44.95 CAN
Windows NT Performance: Monitoring, Benchmarking, and Tuning
1-56205-942-4 • $29.99 US / $44.95 CAN
Windows NT Registry: A Settings Reference
1-56205-941-6 • $29.99 US / $44.95 CAN
Windows NT Domain Architecture
1-57870-112-0 • $38.00 US / $56.95 CAN

SYSTEMS PROGRAMMING

Windows NT/2000 Native API Reference
1-57870-199-6 • $50.00 US / $74.95 CAN
Windows NT Device Driver Development
1-57870-058-2 • $50.00 US / $74.95 CAN
DCE/RPC over SMB: Samba and Windows NT Domain Internals
1-57870-150-3 • $45.00 US / $67.95 CAN

APPLICATION PROGRAMMING

Delphi COM Programming
1-57870-221-6 • $45.00 US / $67.95 CAN
Windows NT Applications: Measuring and Optimizing Performance
1-57870-176-7 • $40.00 US / $59.95 CAN
Applying COM+
ISBN 0-7357-0978-5 • $49.99 US / $74.95 CAN
Available October 2000

WEB PROGRAMMING

Exchange & Outlook: Constructing Collaborative Solutions
ISBN 1-57870-252-6 • $40.00 US / $59.95 CAN

SCRIPTING

Windows Script Host
1-57870-139-2 • $35.00 US / $52.95 CAN
Windows NT Shell Scripting
1-57870-047-7 • $32.00 US / $45.95 CAN
Windows NT Win32 Perl Programming: The Standard Extensions
1-57870-067-1 • $40.00 US / $59.95 CAN
Windows NT/2000 ADSI Scripting for System Administration
1-57870-219-4 • $45.00 US / $67.95 CAN
Windows NT Automated Deployment and Customization
1-57870-045-0 • $32.00 US / $45.95 CAN

BACK OFFICE

SMS 2 Administration
0-7357-0082-6 • $39.99 US / $59.95 CAN
Internet Information Services Administration
0-7357-0022-2 • $29.99 US / $44.95 CAN
SQL Server System Administration
1-56205-955-6 • $29.99 US / $44.95 CAN
SQL Server 7 Essential Reference
0-7357-0864-9 • $35.00 US / $52.95 CAN

Open Source

MySQL
0-7357-0921-1 • $49.99 US / $74.95 CAN
Web Application Development with PHP 4.0
0-7357-0997-1 • $39.99 US / $59.95 CAN
PHP Functions Essential Reference
0-7357-0970-X • $35.00 US / $52.95 CAN
Available December 2000
Python Essential Reference
0-7357-0901-7 • $34.95 US / $52.95 CAN
Autoconf, Automake, and Libtool
1-57870-190-2 • $40.00 US / $59.95 CAN
Available December 2000

Linux/UNIX

ADMINISTRATION

Linux System Administration
1-56205-934-3 • $29.99 US / $44.95 CAN
Linux Firewalls
0-7357-0900-9 • $39.99 US / $59.95 CAN
Linux Essential Reference
0-7357-0852-5 • $24.95 US / $37.95 CAN
UnixWare 7 System Administration
1-57870-080-9 • $40.00 US / $59.99 CAN

DEVELOPMENT

Developing Linux Applications with GTK+ and GDK
0-7357-0021-4 • $34.99 US / $52.95 CAN
GTK+/Gnome Application Development
0-7357-0078-8 • $39.99 US / $59.95 CAN
KDE Application Development
1-57870-201-1 • $39.99 US / $59.95 CAN

GIMP

Grokking the GIMP
0-7357-0924-6 • $39.99 US / $59.95 CAN
GIMP Essential Reference
0-7357-0911-4 • $24.95 US / $37.95 CAN

SOLARIS

Solaris Advanced System Administrator's Guide, Second Edition
1-57870-039-6 • $39.99 US / $59.95 CAN
Solaris System Administrator's Guide, Second Edition
1-57870-040-X • $34.99 US / $52.95 CAN
Solaris Essential Reference
0-7357-0023-0 • $24.95 US / $37.95 CAN

Networking

STANDARDS & PROTOCOLS

Cisco Router Configuration & Troubleshooting, Second Edition
0-7357-0999-8 • $34.99 US / $52.95 CAN
Understanding Directory Services
0-7357-0910-6 • $39.99 US / $59.95 CAN
Understanding the Network: A Practical Guide to Internetworking
0-7357-0977-7 • $39.99 US / $59.95 CAN
Understanding Data Communications, Sixth Edition
0-7357-0036-2 • $39.99 US / $59.95 CAN
LDAP: Programming Directory Enabled Applications
1-57870-000-0 • $44.99 US / $67.95 CAN
Gigabit Ethernet Networking
1-57870-062-0 • $50.00 US / $74.95 CAN
Supporting Service Level Agreements on IP Networks
1-57870-146-5 • $50.00 US / $74.95 CAN
Directory Enabled Networks
1-57870-140-6 • $50.00 US / $74.95 CAN
Differentiated Services for the Internet
1-57870-132-5 • $50.00 US / $74.95 CAN
Quality of Service on IP Networks
1-57870-189-9 • $50.00 US / $74.95 CAN

Designing Addressing Architectures for Routing and Switching
1-57870-059-0 • $45.00 US / $69.95 CAN
Understanding & Deploying LDAP Directory Services
1-57870-070-1 • $50.00 US / $74.95 CAN
Switched, Fast and Gigabit Ethernet, Third Edition
1-57870-073-6 • $50.00 US / $74.95 CAN
Wireless LANs: Implementing Interoperable Networks
1-57870-081-7 • $40.00 US / $59.95 CAN
Wide Area High Speed Networks
1-57870-114-7 • $50.00 US / $74.95 CAN
The DHCP Handbook
1-57870-137-6 • $55.00 US / $81.95 CAN
Designing Routing and Switching Architectures for Enterprise Networks
1-57870-060-4 • $55.00 US / $81.95 CAN
Local Area High Speed Networks
1-57870-113-9 • $50.00 US / $74.95 CAN
Network Performance Baselining
1-57870-240-2 • $50.00 US / $74.95 CAN
Economics of Electronic Commerce
1-57870-014-0 • $49.99 US / $74.95 CAN

SECURITY

Intrusion Detection
1-57870-185-6 • $50.00 US / $74.95 CAN
Understanding Public-Key Infrastructure
1-57870-166-X • $50.00 US / $74.95 CAN
Network Intrusion Detection: An Analyst's Handbook
0-7357-0868-1 • $39.99 US / $59.95 CAN
Linux Firewalls
0-7357-0900-9 • $39.99 US / $59.95 CAN
Windows NT/2000 Network Security
1-57870-254-3 • $45.00 US / $67.95 CAN

LOTUS NOTES/DOMINO

Domino System Administration
1-56205-948-3 • $49.99 US / $74.95 CAN
Lotus Notes & Domino Essential Reference
0-7357-0007-9 • $45.00 US / $67.95 CAN

Software Architecture & Engineering

Designing for the User with OVID
1-57870-101-5 • $40.00 US / $59.95 CAN
Designing Flexible Object-Oriented Systems with UML
1-57870-098-1 • $40.00 US / $59.95 CAN
Constructing Superior Software
1-57870-147-3 • $40.00 US / $59.95 CAN
A UML Pattern Language
1-57870-118-X • $45.00 US / $67.95 CAN

Professional Certification

TRAINING GUIDES

MCSE Training Guide: Networking Essentials, 2nd Ed.
156205919X • $49.99 US / $74.95 CAN
MCSE Training Guide: Windows NT Server 4, 2nd Ed.
1562059165 • $49.99 US / $74.95 CAN
MCSE Training Guide: Windows NT Workstation 4, 2nd Ed.
1562059181 • $49.99 US / $74.95 CAN
MCSE Training Guide: Windows NT Server 4 Enterprise, 2nd Ed.
1562059173 • $49.99 US / $74.95 CAN
MCSE Training Guide: Core Exams Bundle, 2nd Ed.
1562059262 • $149.99 US / $223.95 CAN
MCSE Training Guide: TCP/IP, 2nd Ed.
1562059203 • $49.99 US / $74.95 CAN
MCSE Training Guide: IIS 4, 2nd Ed.
0735708657 • $49.99 US / $74.95 CAN
MCSE Training Guide: SQL Server 7 Administration
0735700036 • $49.99 US / $74.95 CAN
MCSE Training Guide: SQL Server 7 Database Design
0735700044 • $49.99 US / $74.95 CAN
CLP Training Guide: Lotus Notes 4
0789715058 • $59.99 US / $84.95 CAN
MCSD Training Guide: Visual Basic 6 Exams
0735700028 • $69.99 US / $104.95 CAN
MCSD Training Guide: Solution Architectures
0735700265 • $49.99 US / $74.95 CAN
MCSD Training Guide: 4-in-1 Bundle
0735709122 • $149.99 US / $223.95 CAN
CCNA Training Guide
0735700516 • $49.99 US / $74.95 CAN
A+ Certification Training Guide, 2nd Ed.
0735709076 • $49.99 US / $74.95 CAN
Network+ Certification Guide
073570077X • $49.99 US / $74.95 CAN
Solaris 2.6 Administrator Certification Training Guide, Part I
157870085X • $40.00 US / $59.95 CAN
Solaris 2.6 Administrator Certification Training Guide, Part II
1578700868 • $40.00 US / $59.95 CAN
MCSE Training Guide: Windows 2000 Professional
0735709653 • $49.99 US / $74.95 CAN •
MCSE Training Guide: Windows 2000 Server
0735709688 • $49.99 US / $74.95 CAN •
MCSE Training Guide: Windows 2000 Network Infrastructure
0735709661 • $49.99 US / $74.95 CAN
MCSE Training Guide: Windows 2000 Network Security Design
073570984X • $49.99 US / $74.95 CAN
MCSE Training Guide: Windows 2000 Network Infrastructure Design
0735709823 • $49.99 US / $74.95 CAN
MCSE Training Guide: Windows 2000 Directory Svcs. Infrastructure
0735709769 • $49.99 US / $74.95 CAN
MCSE Training Guide: Windows 2000 Directory Services Design
0735709831 • $49.99 US / $74.95 CAN
MCSE Training Guide: Windows 2000 Accelerated Exam
0735709793 • $69.99 US / $104.95 CAN
MCSE Training Guide: Windows 2000 Core Exams Bundle
0735709882 • $149.99 US / $223.95 CAN

How to Contact Us

IF YOU NEED THE LATEST UPDATES ON A TITLE THAT YOU'VE PURCHASED:

1) Visit our Web site at www.newriders.com.

2) Enter the book ISBN number, which is located on the back cover in the bottom right-hand corner, in the site search box on the left navigation bar.

3) Select your book title from the list of search results. On the book page you'll find available updates and downlods for your title.

IF YOU ARE HAVING TECHNICAL PROBLEMS WITH THE BOOK OR THE CD THAT IS INCLUDED:

1) Check the book's information page on our Web site according to the instructions listed above, or

2) Email us at nrfeedback@newriders.com, or

3) Fax us at 317-581-4663 ATTN: Tech Support.

IF YOU HAVE COMMENTS ABOUT ANY OF OUR CERTIFICATION PRODUCTS THAT ARE NON-SUPPORT RELATED:

1) Email us at nrfeedback@newriders.com, or

2) Write to us at New Riders, 201 W. 103rd St., Indianapolis, IN 46290-1097, or

3) Fax us at 317-581-4663.

IF YOU ARE OUTSIDE THE UNITED STATES AND NEED TO FIND A DISTRIBUTOR IN YOUR AREA:

Please contact our international department at international@mcp.com.

IF YOU ARE INTERESTED IN BEING AN AUTHOR OR TECHNICAL REVIEWER:

Email us at opportunities@newriders.com. Include your name, email address, phone number, and area of technical expertise.

IF YOU WISH TO PREVIEW ANY OF OUR CERTIFICATION BOOKS FOR CLASSROOM USE:

Email us at nrmedia@newriders.com. Your message should include your name, title, training company or school, department, address, phone number, office days/hours, text in use, and enrollment. Send these details along with your request for desk/examination copies and/or additional information.

IF YOU ARE A MEMBER OF THE PRESS AND WOULD LIKE TO REVIEW ONE OF OUR BOOKS:

Email us at nrmedia@newriders.com. Your message should include your name, title, publication or website you work for, mailing address and email address.

We Want to Know What You Think

To better serve you, we would like your opinion on the content and quality of this book. Please complete this
and mail it to us or fax it to 317-581-4663.

Name ____________________

Address ____________________

City ____________ State ______ Zip ____________

Phone ____________ Email Address ____________

Occupation ____________________

Which certification exams have you already passed? ____________

Which certification exams do you plan to take? ____________

What influenced your purchase of this book?

- ❑ Recommendation
- ❑ Cover Design
- ❑ Table of Contents
- ❑ Index
- ❑ Magazine Review
- ❑ Advertisement
- ❑ Reputation of New Riders
- ❑ Author Name

How would you rate the contents of this book?

- ❑ Excellent
- ❑ Very Good
- ❑ Good
- ❑ Fair
- ❑ Below Average
- ❑ Poor

What other types of certification products will you buy/hav
you bought to help you prepare for the exam?

- ❑ Quick reference books
- ❑ Testing software
- ❑ Study guides
- ❑ Other

What do you like most about this book? Check all that app

- ❑ Content
- ❑ Writing Style
- ❑ Accuracy
- ❑ Examples
- ❑ Listings
- ❑ Design
- ❑ Index
- ❑ Page Count
- ❑ Price
- ❑ Illustrations

What do you like least about this book? Check all that apply.

- ❑ Content
- ❑ Writing Style
- ❑ Accuracy
- ❑ Examples
- ❑ Listings
- ❑ Design
- ❑ Index
- ❑ Page Count
- ❑ Price
- ❑ Illustrations

What would be a useful follow-up book to this one for you? ____________

Where did you purchase this book? ____________

Can you name a similar book that you like better than this one, or one that is as good? Why? ____________

How many New Riders books do you own? ____________

What are your favorite certification or general computer book titles? ____________

What other titles would you like to see us develop? ____________

Any comments for us? ____________

Fold here and tape to mail

Place
Stamp
Here

New Riders
201 W. 103rd St.
Indianapolis, IN 46290

By opening this package, you are bound by the following agreement:

Some of the software included with this product may be copyrighted, in which case all rights are reserved by the respective copyright holder. You are licensed to use software copyrighted by the publisher and its licensors on a single computer. You may copy and/or modify the software as needed to facilitate your use of it on a single computer Making copies of the software for any other purpose is a violation of the United States copyright laws.

This software is sold "as is" without warranty of any kind, either expressed or implied, including, but not limited to the implied warranties of merchantability and fitness for a particular purpose. Neither the publisher nor its dealers or distributors assume any liability for any alleged or actual damages arising from the use of this program. (Some states do not allow for the exclusion of implied warranties, so the exclusion may not apply to you.)